S0-AED-406

you're only human

you're only human

How Your Limits Reflect God's Design
and Why That's Good News

KELLY M. KAPIC

a division of Baker Publishing Group
Grand Rapids, Michigan

Published by Brazos Press
a division of Baker Publishing Group
PO Box 6287, Grand Rapids, MI 49516-6287
www.brazospress.com

Printed in the United States of America

Library of Congress Cataloging-in-Publication Data
Names: Kapic, Kelly M., 1972– author.
Title: You're only human : how your limits reflect God's design and why that's good news / Kelly M. Kapic.
Description: Grand Rapids, Michigan : Brazos Press, a division of Baker Publishing Group, [2022] | Includes index.
Identifiers: LCCN 2021020366 | ISBN 9781587435102 (cloth) | ISBN 9781493435258 (ebook)
Subjects: LCSH: Theological anthropology—Christianity. | Image of God. | Christian life. | Finite, The.
Classification: LCC BT702 .K37 2022 | DDC 233/.5—dc23
LC record available at https://lccn.loc.gov/2021020366

Baker Publishing Group publications use paper produced from sustainable forestry practices and post-consumer waste whenever possible.

22 23 24 25 26 27 28 7 6 5 4 3 2 1

Jonathan, my beloved son,
you have taught me so much
about courage and determination
in the face of finitude
while also being a compassionate defender
of the vulnerable.
I'm so grateful for you.

contents

PART 1

particularity and limits

1

have i done enough?

facing our finitude

> The result of busyness is that an individual is very seldom permitted to form a heart.
>
> Søren Kierkegaard, journal entry

Many of us fail to understand that our limitations are a gift from God, and therefore good. This produces in us the burden of trying to be something we are not and cannot be.

Not in Control

Creaturely finitude is less an idea we discover than a reality we run into.

Todd and Liz had been married and childless for many years, so Liz's sudden pregnancy filled them with joy and expectation. They were going to have a baby but hadn't found out yet if it was a boy or girl, let alone picked the baby's name. Without warning, however, events spiraled out of control. The baby was born prematurely, at just twenty-five weeks, three days after Christmas. Their joy had turned to alarm. Unsure of how long he would live, they immediately named him Findley Fuller after their mothers' maiden names; Liz and Todd told me that in the uncertainty of whether he would live or die they chose a name for their son that reflected his place in a larger family and a larger story. He was not alone; to the God of the living they entrusted their son and his story.

In previous centuries, or even previous decades, medical practice would not have been able to save Finn's life. He needed twenty-four-hour care, and even with medical advances the prognosis didn't look great. Would he make it through the night, through the week? His system was very fragile: he struggled with everything from breathing to seizures, from infections to dangers to his young eyes. Each day brought not only fresh hope but also new obstacles. Finn was a strong little guy and a fighter, but the odds didn't look good.

Finitude, *n.* The condition or state of being finite; the condition of being subject to limitations; = FINITENESS *n.*

Finiteness, *n.* The quality or condition of being finite; the condition of being limited in space, time, capacity, etc.

Oxford English Dictionary

A few weeks into his son's fight for life, despite his exhaustion, Todd found the strength to send out a CarePage update on their son's condition, commenting, "All of this brings loads of new fears and anxieties to Liz and me. But we trust in God's faithfulness, mercy, and love. And we have confidence in the NICU medical staff. We acknowledge fear, but we cling to hope." Todd then reminded us that he was writing on Martin Luther King Jr. Day and quoted from this American minister and civil rights advocate, who once said, "We must accept finite disappointment, but we must never lose infinite hope."[1] And then Todd signed off, "God is able." He didn't mention our limits as an excuse for the doctors to give up but rather as the context for their best efforts. Only God was and is infinite.

The vulnerability of their son's life reminded Todd and Liz of their own tiny and comparatively weak place in an incomprehensibly huge and threatening cosmos. Standing in the hospital beside Findley, they were freshly aware that, from the odd asteroid to everyday germs, the parts of the world that can hurt us often operate beyond our control or even prediction. They had given their newborn son into the care of doctors, but even more so into the care of God. Still, even with this, how does one "accept finite disappointment" while maintaining "infinite hope"? Excellent nurses and doctors were working as hard as they could to preserve little Finn's life, and Todd and Liz knew that the infinite God of grace and love cares more about them and their child than they ever could, so they took some comfort there. But when the brokenness of the world hits our human limitations, it strains our emotions, will, and understanding past their abilities.

All of us bounce between the illusion that we are in control and the world's demonstration that we are not. Thank God Finn has both survived and flourished as the months and now years have passed: as you can imagine, his baptism and first birthday were great celebrations! But the memories of this frightening and humbling season of life remind Todd and Liz and their friends that the boundaries of our abilities to handle life are closer than we would like.

Whether through tragedy or simply as the result of aging, we all are repeatedly reminded that we are fragile and dependent creatures.[2] But it is not just our bodies that face us with these upsetting limits—we also see them in a coworker with greater intellectual gifts than ours, or a fellow athlete who is so much faster, or an aging parent whose waning emotional and psychological stability has threatened the health of our relationship with them. We have far less control of the world and even of ourselves than we would like to imagine. Some people respond by living as passive victims, while others aggressively seize as much control as possible.

We know our actions matter, and matter a lot. A doctor who studied hard is usually better than one who simply wanted to pass exams. Parents who want to be thoughtful about rearing their children, seeking to avoid mistakes they inherited from their own parents, are better than negligent guardians. Unfortunately, patients still die in surgery under the care of excellent physicians, and earnest parents mistakenly assume they can get it perfectly "right," ignorant of their own blind spots, larger cultural factors, and personality differences. What we *do* matters. We can and do change things. But when we suppose that we can control all our circumstances, we soon find that we can't. We don't say the words, but we live as though the weight of the world were on our own shoulders. And it exhausts us. Behind the patient grin on our faces we hide a lingering rage about the endless demands that must be met, unrealized dreams, and relational disappointments.

The odd thing is that, even when we run into our inevitable limits, we often hang on to the delusion that if we just work harder, if we simply squeeze tighter, if we become more efficient, we can eventually regain control. We imagine we can keep our children safe, our incomes secure, and our bodies whole. When I complain about getting older, my wife sometimes laughs and says to me, "You have two options: either you are getting older or you are dead." Denying our finitude cripples us in ways we don't realize. It also distorts our view of God and what Christian spirituality should look like.

• ● •

Finitude is an unavoidable aspect of our creaturely existence. We run into it constantly and in different ways. If we are paying attention, we can see it. It doesn't take a car accident or an unexpected hospital visit for us to discover our limits and dependency. But are we listening? Do we recognize the signs? They're all around us. Far too often our lives testify to the fact that we believe we really can and should do everything. Thomas Merton, drawing on an observation by Douglas Steere, once observed,

> There is a pervasive form of contemporary violence to which the idealist most easily succumbs: activism and overwork. The rush and pressure of modern life are a form, perhaps the most common form, of its innate violence. To allow oneself to be carried away by a multitude of conflicting concerns, to surrender to too many demands, to commit oneself to too many projects, to want to help everyone in everything, is to succumb to violence. The frenzy of our activism neutralizes our work for peace. It destroys our own inner capacity for peace. It destroys the fruitfulness of our own work, because it kills the root of inner wisdom which makes work fruitful.[3]

Merton wrote this over fifty years ago, but his concern is even more relevant now than it was then.

The Crushing Weight of Expectation

Are you exhausted? Do you experience a consistent background feeling of guilt about how little you accomplish each day? Are you weighed down by a sense of how much there is to do and how little progress you are making? How are your plans, hopes, and dreams doing?

One of the areas I had not planned to investigate while doing research for this book, but which proved truly significant, was the American educational system. I paid most attention to high schools and colleges. What I noticed was how the educational patterns we learned there often foster unhealthy expectations of how much one should "get done" in a day. Now, before I say more on this, let me clarify that this appears to affect middle- and upper-income public and private schools more than it does schools in low-income areas. That said, here is an average day for many high school students:

- Leave home for school around 7:30 a.m. or earlier.
- Attend classes until 3:30 p.m.
- Immediately go to extracurricular activity (sport, theater, etc.) until 6:00–7:00 p.m.
- Rush home; quick dinner and shower.
- Then, for the rest of the evening, work almost nonstop on homework, only finishing and heading to bed at 10:30 p.m. or later.

This basic schedule sounds painfully familiar to my own students, but they are hesitant to admit the toll it has taken on them. They have absorbed the view that this pattern is morally "right" and "expected": pack your day from morning to bedtime with as many things as possible. Consequently, many students who have been rushing around like this and can't keep up have come to believe they are disappointments, weak, or worse. They can't keep up and they equate this inability with a moral shortcoming on their part. Add to that the challenges of getting into college, and they reach the unquestioned view that getting certain grades is not just valuable; it defines your worth. It's easy for adults to say "Grades aren't everything," but all our other actions and words teach the students not to believe the intended comfort. So getting a B−, let alone a C, isn't just taken to reflect one's struggles in a class; it is often subconsciously used as a moral assessment of them.

I am a college professor who regularly deals with students. Anyone willing to listen will discover that they often live with at least a low-level sense of guilt over how much they are not getting done. So many pages they didn't read, endless assignments they rushed, activities they missed, and friendships they have neglected or never formed. Sure, it is easy to say they are not using their time well, that they fool around too much (which is sometimes true!), but that line usually functions as an easy excuse to avoid honestly considering whether there are any problems with how we have set things up in formal education. Funnily enough, some students also tell me they don't feel so guilty about not getting all the assigned work done because they believe their professors (including me) have such unrealistic expectations—they believe there is no way they could possibly do all of what is expected in any given week. In other words, not only students but professors, too, struggle to have realistic expectations or understand how much time and work assignments really take. So some students detach while others frantically try to keep up even as they feel like they are slowly drowning. However, this is not just a challenge for students and faculty.

At my work there are always people and projects that need more attention than I can give them. Others face similar frustrations: the warehouse operator could always become more efficient at dealing with inventory; the realtor has never sold enough houses; the stay-at-home parent never seems to get to that neglected mess in the corner of the house. Counselors might have asked better questions; teachers could be better prepared each day for classes; and students wish they could focus their attention longer. Receptionists could be more organized and efficient, while managers dream of being proactive rather than reactive. We all constantly collide with our limits. Your work circumstances probably differ from mine, but we both wonder if we have done "enough." Maybe we are being driven by the wrong impulses and have the wrong goals in mind?

> How I spend this ordinary day in Christ is how I will spend my Christian life.
>
> Tish Harrison Warren, *Liturgy of the Ordinary*

What about church and missional concerns? We should offer prayers, write encouraging notes, and provide meals to those in need. Countless excellent organizations desperately require time and resources so someone can care for the poor, adopt the orphan, and come alongside the prisoner; yet how rarely do I participate? And when I do, it almost always feels like a tiny drop in a massive, empty bucket of need. Shouldn't I do more? Then, when I sense my limits, I am tempted to pretend that these problems are not that bad or that Jesus didn't really say that they require his people's attention. Maybe helping the poor and orphan is optional rather than essential. Maybe prayer is a great idea, but not genuinely needed. But such denial isn't healthy either, since it distorts our view of Jesus and warps our understanding of God himself. What should we do, then? How should we respond to these gospel needs and our own limited ability to answer them?

Then there is my body. With every passing year the metabolism slows down, the aches increase, and there is the undeniable sense that it needs greater attention, from the food I eat to the exercise that I need to counter my sedentary work patterns. To neglect caring for our bodies has greater consequences than we want to admit: the problems are not just related to our waistlines, but to our relationships and countless other areas of life. Proverbs long ago warned us how misusing our bodies or never restricting our appetites can produce negative consequences (e.g., Prov. 20:1; 23:1–3, 20–21; 25:16, 27).

What about my mind? I'm an academic, paid to spend my hours studying, teaching, and writing. Guess what: I simply can't keep up—not even close! Please don't tell anyone. Fresh books and articles appear every week. Not only that, I meet more people every year, including fresh crops of students and new people at church—it is painful how many names I forget. Or, more accurately, it is painful how few names I remember. My mind simply cannot keep up with the endless demands . . . and I feel guilty about it. When Paul calls us to the renewal of our minds (Rom. 12:2), what does that require of us? And why do we always approach these questions by assuming that an idealized genius is the goal or model, rather than looking to people with severely limited IQs who yet profoundly love God and neighbor? Maybe we have inappropriately valued our brains in a way that distorts our view of *being* human.[4]

What about family? I'm a parent of two amazing children—this should be easy since I know folks with four or more kids. Yet I could always spend more time with my two—more time playing cards, laughing, talking, and just hanging out. Similarly, I'm married, and any self-reflective spouse easily recognizes his or her shortcomings. I want to be more thoughtful, more attentive; there is always more that can be given. We could all do more to encourage, empower, and care for our spouses. And how well am I keeping up relationships with extended family who live all around the country? Shouldn't I check in more? Wouldn't it be good to gather together more often?

The list could go on to touch other spheres of life, from home maintenance to education, from community involvement to recreation. In area after area we sense our shortcomings, our longings to be more, to do more, and yet we run smack dab into our limits. So how should we respond to this guilt and the endless needs and demands?

A Time-Management Problem?

Here we face a crucial question: Does this dissatisfaction always mean that we have sinned, or is something else going on? Are we *required* to overcome these perceived shortcomings? Some treat these limitations as indicating a moral deficiency or as an obstacle in a competition that can and should be conquered.

One common response in the West is to seek self-improvement through greater organization in our lives. We skim the internet for short articles on time management, since we long ago gave up on reading whole books. Sometimes we decide to get up earlier or stay up later, hoping to add another hour or two of productivity to our lives. Since we can't put more hours into the day, we try to change ourselves. We try to do more, be more.

Normally at this point in the story we draw attention to how much TV the average American watches, how much time is lost consuming mindless digital content and games. But what if our problem is not time management? *What if rather than serving as the cause of our problems, the draw of mind-numbing screen time was a sign of a deeper malady?* Maybe such escapism reveals a sickness in our souls that we have been neglecting. And rather than just being a problem for the "world" out there, these are signs to which Christians should also pay attention.

I think we have a massive problem, but it is not a time-management issue. It is a *theological* and *pastoral* problem.

• ● •

A few years ago I had a podcast interview with a woman who had read my book *A Little Book for New Theologians* and wanted to talk about it.[5] Part of what made this interview stimulating was that most of her audience were mothers who primarily spent their time caring for their young children. She wanted her listeners to discover how relevant theology was to their lives.

Near the end of the interview she asked, "Any other big theological concepts that we moms should major in?" She apparently thought I would use the softball question to talk about divine sovereignty or some other high-octane doctrine, but instead my answer was, "Human finitude." She was fairly surprised. My response grew out of my concern that many of us North American Christians have a very weak and underdeveloped doctrine of creation. This problem is something I can only hint at here, though in a later chapter I will revisit this point.

What I mean is that we must rediscover that being *dependent* creatures is a constructive gift, not a deficiency. Clever readers might even notice that using "dependent" as an adjective for "creature" is basically redundant—there are no creatures who are not, by their very nature, dependent beings. Our dependency does not merely point to abstract ideas of divine providence, but takes concrete form when we rely on others, on the earth, on institutions and traditions. We must learn the value and truthfulness of our finitude, eventually getting to the point where *we might even praise God for our limits*. I didn't say praise him for *evil*: we need to see the difference between the gift of finitude (i.e., human limits) and the lamentable reality of sin and misery.[6]

> As deficient beings, humans are in danger of working themselves up into a frenzy of activity and thus destroying themselves.
>
> Ingolf U. Dalferth, *Creatures of Possibility*

Returning to the interview, the connection between finitude and child-rearing was not difficult to make. Our kids don't need to be good at everything. In fact, they are *not* supposed to be good at everything! And once we finally believe and embrace this, it liberates our children (and us!). We can now start delighting in other people rather than viewing them as challengers to be overcome.

Almost immediately the host responded in a most delightful way. Although she said this "came out of left field," she started making all kinds of wonderful connections, from parents' inclination to overschedule their children's lives, to how they imagine their kids should be stars in everything. Such homes are consumed with activity and have little space for rest and reflection. Relationships remain superficial when everyone—from the children to the parents—is constantly trying to be the best, to win. That distorting expectation—whether or not one realizes it—necessarily makes all of us come out as losers rather than winners. Thus, we sign up the kids for more activities, hoping they will eventually succeed. And until they do succeed, we lie to them and tell them they are amazing at everything, hoping one day it will be true. Kids start to believe the problem lies not with their own shortcomings, but with the judges, with the teachers, with their peers—with anyone and everyone but themselves. Although meant to encourage self-esteem and success, this strategy eventually undermines our children's long-term self-esteem and view of self because the myth of their "excellence" at everything cannot be sustained.

At some point the course of life will expose what we then receive as painful truths: we are not the best, the brightest, the most able. There are always stronger, more beautiful, more brilliant people. At some point the illusion comes crashing down, and when it does, it can have devastating consequences. As a college professor, I frequently see young adults coming to terms with these very difficult facts that had been, in various ways, hidden from them. But no "helicopter" or even "bulldozing" parents can protect the child forever. Each of us must face our limits and weaknesses at some point, whether we want to or not.

Finitude Is *Not* Sin

We live in a fallen world. Sin has affected everything from our heads to our hearts, from our body chemistry to sociopolitical dynamics. Because of this we sometimes wrongly attribute all our problems to sin, when in fact they are often a matter of running up against the limits inherent in being finite creatures instead of being God.

We are, by God's good design, finite. For the purposes of this book, when I say "finite," I will normally be focusing on *good, created human limits*: all creatures are limited by space, time, and power, and our knowledge, energy, and perspective also have always been limited. In other words, please do not necessarily read "death" into the word "finitude" as used here, since that raises a whole set of different questions and is not, for the most part, what I am focused on in these pages. This book focuses on the limits that are part of God's original act of making us, which he called "good."

Often when we rush to meet all the expectations that surround us and look at our bottomless to-do lists, we desire to become infinite in capacity. We think, "If only I had more time, energy, and ability, then I could get everything done, which would make me and everyone else happy." But meeting endless expectations would require that we possess God's infinite attributes and prerogatives as our own. Sometimes lurking under our desires to expand our abilities is the unspoken temptation: "If only I were the infinite Creator, not a finite creature . . ."

Indeed, this impulse to reject our creaturely limits is as old as sin itself. Genesis shows us that God made all that is not God, and everything he made was "good" (Gen. 1). But we quickly meet a serpent who seems to appear out of nowhere and raises an unsettling question: "Did God actually say . . . ?" (3:1). Using his words to warp his hearer's imagination, the snake declares, "God knows that when you eat of [the fruit] your eyes will be opened, and you will be like God" (3:5). Subtly insinuating doubt and uncertainty, the serpent introduces distrust into the divine-human relationship.

With these indirect tactics the serpent encourages his hearers to imagine they can and should *know more*. They should *be more*. He implies that divinely given limits are a fault to be overcome rather than a beneficial gift to be honored. This knowledge is not just about information, nor merely about morality, but as Old Testament scholar Gerhard von Rad observes, it is about "mastery" of "all things." Von Rad further explains, "By endeavouring to enlarge his being on the godward side, seeking a godlike intensification of his life beyond his creaturely limitations, that is, by wanting to be like God, man stepped out from the simplicity of obedience to God."[7] The man and woman disdained their creaturely limits as faults instead of gifts, barriers that kept them from obtaining divine qualities. Taking a bite of the fruit was only the outward sign of the terrible lie the serpent got them to believe.

> The human being's limit is at the center of human existence, not on the margin. . . . There where the boundary—the tree of knowledge—stands, there stands also the tree of life, that is, the very God who gives life. God is at once the boundary and the center of our existence.
>
> Dietrich Bonhoeffer, *Creation and Fall*

Though they were the pinnacle of God's creation in the Genesis narrative, they became dissatisfied, rejecting love to gain power. Being finite creatures, even made in the divine image, was simply not enough. God had given Adam and Eve the fullness of the garden and many other rich gifts; accordingly, the original sin has the shape of *taking the one thing that was not given to them*.[8] Rather than perceiving this limitation also as a good gift, they viewed it naively and greedily as an opportunity, like children doubting their parents when they tell them not to stick their finger into an electrical outlet. Parents do not set such limits because they disrespect or hate their children, but because they so love them and recognize the danger of ignoring their natural limits. The shock could kill them!

Thus from chapter 3 onward, Genesis tells of our discomfort with any divine restrictions, moving from obedience to disobedience. As von Rad claims, "A movement began in which man pictures himself as growing more and more powerful, more and more titanic."[9] In fact, the Genesis narrative appears to represent a turning from the original good ordering of creation to a disordering: shalom is disrupted. And now we all live in this disordered relationship to our limits.

So what does it mean that we are creatures and not God? What does it mean that we have *these* talents and resources and not *all* talents and resources? What does it mean that we are finite, particular, and rooted, and not infinite, universal, or standing above all local circumstances? Answering these questions honestly will change how we imagine the world, ourselves, and our relationship to God and others.

Recognizing and rejoicing in our particular kind of finitude is a massive challenge, especially in the affluent, driven West. This shows up not just in our unrealistic expectations about how much we can accomplish in a day but also in our failure to value rest and slow-growing relationships. This problem takes many forms, from inappropriate expectations placed on our children to dehumanizing practices in the workforce. Christians often burn out from overcommitment to church activities or ministries; or they go to the opposite extreme, never volunteering for anything because they fear the unending demands that will come once they have committed. Too often the options are either try to do everything or simply to do nothing.

So how can we proceed? I want us to take time to carefully think about our creatureliness. This will reveal limits, dependence, love, reliance on the grace of God, and worship. We will examine the joy of being a creature and the freedom of resting on the promises of the Creator. We will question harmful and unrealistic ideals and begin to appreciate the messiness of our complex lives.

As we do this, the following central concepts will guide my reflections:

1. We are not under any requirement to be infinite—infinity is reserved for God alone. Rather, *in and through* our creaturely limits we are called to love God with our whole heart, soul, mind, and strength and to love our neighbor as ourselves.

   In other words, loving both God and neighbor falls completely within the range of creaturely finitude. This takes us to my second guiding observation.
2. We need to stop asking (or feeling that we should ask) for God's forgiveness when we can't do everything, and we need to ask forgiveness for ever imagining we could!

These and other reflections throughout the book are built on some basic theological assertions:

- God is the good Creator who designed us as good creatures.
- Part of the good of being a creature is having limits.
- The incarnation is God's great yes to his creation, including human limits.
- God designed the person for the community and the community for the person.
- The Creator is also the Sustainer and Redeemer.
- We are never asked to relate to God in any way other than as human creatures.
- God's goal for humanity is for us to become lovers of God, neighbor, and the rest of creation.

Once we see ourselves within this framework, where our creaturely finitude plays a good and essential part, the pressures to fulfill endless expectations take on a different appearance. We begin to relate to God and others in a more fruitful way: no longer do we aspire to have infinite capacity—that is God's job! We worship him as he made us: dignified, purposeful, vulnerable, finite creatures. We do not apologize for our creaturely needs and dependence on others, for we discover this is how God made us, and it is good.

• • •

This book aims to help us discover the theological and pastoral significance of embracing the gift of being limited: it is just part of being human. Each chapter will explore a different question that allows us to look at our creaturely limits from a slightly different perspective. We have already observed that we often feel we have not done enough, which raises a nagging concern: *Am I enough*? If we are ever to answer that well, we must ask the central question (which we will look at in chap. 2): *What does God think of me?* Not generic humanity, but me, in my singularity, my particularity, my smallness? How do I relate to Christ without ceasing to be me? We then consider the particular humanity of Mary's son, including his physicality: this gives us a deeper and more realistic appreciation of our own humanity (chap. 3). From there we explore why our bodies are necessarily tied to our self-perception, relationships, and even worship: one aspect of our original makeup is that we worship in and through our bodies, so ignoring or abusing a person's body has significant consequences (chap. 4). God made each of us with distinct particularity, with different bodies and personalities, but not to be isolated individuals who generate our identities on our own: our identity is necessarily linked to our families, cultures, and historical contexts (chap. 5). Since sin has also affected every aspect of our lives, including our limited self-understanding, we must carefully navigate the daily challenge of being a saint who sins.

Having laid the groundwork for the value of our particularity and limits, we spend the rest of the book exploring what healthy interdependence looks like. We examine humility: concerned about the problematic results that come from too often grounding it in sin, we show humility's true basis in the good of our creaturely limits (chap. 6). Next we explore some of the problematic ways we relate to time. Cultivating awareness of God's presence can liberate us from the despotism of the clock and recenter us in truly human pursuits (chap. 7). On a related theme, our sense that we lack time often leads us to want immediate and radical improvement in ourselves. We discover, to the contrary, that God has purposes in taking his time and that, since process itself is also a good aspect of the created world, we should learn to honor rather than belittle it (chap. 8). We also look at the apparently endless legitimate demands we face in the church, from proclaiming the gospel to caring for the materially poor. Our finitude drives us back together, to depend on each other in the church and on our God. What is impossible for the particular Christian becomes possible for the church as Christ's body (chap. 9). Finally, I offer practical reflections on four patterns of life that can help us have a healthier experience of our human limits: rhythm, vulnerability, gratitude, and rest (chap. 10).

> We have no other experience of God but human experience. When I experience God, what sustains me is, at least first of all, God made human.
>
> Emmanuel Falque, *The Metamorphosis of Finitude*

Examining some of our false assumptions (outside and inside the church) will show us why we struggle with our human limits and how to celebrate the goodness of being a creature of the God who loves what he made. God delights in our finitude: he is not embarrassed or shocked by our creatureliness. Since he is not apologetic about it, we should stop apologizing for it ourselves. But if we are ever going to appreciate how this is good, we need to start by asking: How does God view me?

2

does God love . . . me?

crucified . . . but i still live

The indwelling Christ enables each person to be more himself than he was ever able to be before.

Frederica Mathewes-Green, *Praying the Jesus Prayer*

God loves his children; therefore, by his Son and Spirit he is liberating us from the entanglements of sin that distort our true selves, which were made for communion with the Creator and our fellow creatures.

A FAIR PLACE TO BEGIN thinking about the good of human finitude is by understanding the importance of our particularity. We are often far more uncomfortable with who we are than we might at first realize. Understanding what God thinks of you is, therefore, a great place to start.

What Does God Think of *You*?

If you ask most Christians if God loves them, they don't normally hesitate to answer yes, maybe even enthusiastically. Having listened to plenty of young people and adults, not to mention my own heart, I have come to suspect that we are not as sure of this as we seem. Are we simply repeating an automatic "right answer" that doesn't truly reflect our internal world? Often lurking under such quick responses are deep and abiding insecurities about God's attitude toward us. Consequently, asking a different question has often yielded a more revealing answer that can open up a more compelling conversation. So now I ask you . . .

Does God *like* you?[1]

Alicia Zanoni wrote a children's book titled *I Like You, Samantha Sarah Marie*, based on the experience of her family when her adopted sister joined them.[2] Samantha Sarah Marie was "as little as a fiddle" when she came to live in the "Zs" house. Everything was new: new adults, new kids, new place. As she entered this new home, she wondered if she would like them, but, more significant, she wondered if they would like her. Zanoni describes the mishaps and misdeeds in the family, from wild dances that resulted in broken vases, to endless loud singing in the car, to coloring on the walls with crayons. In each case Mrs. Z responded with care and grace, never a pushover, but also very warm and never flinching from fundamental acceptance and embrace. Cuddling one evening on the rocking chair, Mrs. Z told Samantha Sarah Marie just how grateful she was to have her in the family. Based on previous experience, the boundary-bursting spunky girl wondered aloud if that was true even when she got in trouble. "Well," sighed Mrs. Z, "I don't like it when you break my things or color on my walls. And it makes me very sad when you disobey and yell and I have to discipline you. But that doesn't change the fact that you are so very special to our family. There is no other girl like you who has your spunk, or your smile, or your imagination, or your laugh."[3] Part of what is so insightful about Zanoni's book is that she pushes us to think afresh about belonging. She invites us to admit our own lingering fears about being liked, especially when our foibles and failures are exposed. We wonder this not just about parents and classmates, but even about our heavenly Father.

Distinguishing *Love* and *Like*

Love is a beautiful word. Said in the right context and by the right person, it can still bring goosebumps to the most hardened person, enliven the saddest soul, and calm the angriest heart. Love draws together, unites, and heals. God's love animates the entire gospel story, making it good news for us sinners. Love, true and real love, is cool water for a parched soul, food for the hungry, and welcome for the stranger. God's love makes the world go 'round and sustains it despite human sin and cosmic brokenness.[4] However, we have so often heard of God's love that the word often bounces off us like a marshmallow being thrown around in a game of tag. When it hits us, it feels so light we are not sure if it actually touched us or not. "Sure, I'm it," we confess, but not really convinced we were tagged in the first place. We know we are supposed to believe and affirm that God loves us, but if you probe deep enough, you see that the doubts persist.

What about the word *like*? I like cheesecake. I like a cool spring morning. I like leaning back at the table after a meal with my wife and kids, listening to their adventures as well as their painfully accurate teasing of me. I like sitting around a campfire with Jay and Jeffrey, eating, drinking, and filling the evening with ridiculous laughter, philosophical reflections, and tear-inducing stories. I like my coffee black and my office desk clean. *Like* often carries with it a sense of preference, inclination, and delight, as when a woodworker looks at the gorgeous table they built and says, "Oh, I like that, that is really good. I want that in my house."

Have you ever felt that your parents, or spouse, or your God loved you, and yet wondered if they actually *liked* you? *Love* is so loaded with obligations and duty that it often loses all emotive force, all sense of pleasure and satisfaction. *Like* can remind us of an aspect of God's love that we far too easily forget. Forgetting God's delight and joy in us stunts our ability to enjoy God's love. Forgiveness—as beautiful and crucial as it is—is not enough. Unless it is understood to come from love and to lead back to love, unless we understand the gospel in terms of God's fierce delight in us and not merely a wiping away of prior offenses, unless we understand God's battle for us as a dramatic personal rescue and not merely a cold forensic process, we have ignored most of the Scriptures as well as the needs of the human condition.

The story of Samantha Sarah Marie describes a little girl who surely was told her new parents loved her. Of course they did. She knew they "had to" since she was now their daughter. Whether adopted or natural-born, most of us know our parents have to "love" us. But life is more complicated than that, isn't it? In our struggle to make everyday life function, kids inevitably get inundated with corrections, advice, and demands; they also pile up sins and shortcomings. The conflict involved here can create subtle instability and foster insecurities. Further, parents easily project onto their children what they want to see rather than what stands right there in front of them. Some long for football players while others for math geniuses; some want their children to be popular while others push them to be radically independent because the parents are too busy to be present. All the while, the kids wonder to themselves, "Does my dad actually like me, even when I am not good?"

A long-experienced youth minister recently told me that the current pressure on high school kids is intense, but especially for young women. He explained that the "guys need to at least be excellent at one thing, whether that be baseball, chemistry, or computers. As long as you are really good at one thing you can be okay, but you better be really good at something." Then he went on: "The young women, they are expected to be great at *everything*. They should get straight As, look gorgeous, be athletic, funny, and socially plugged in." Plus, they should be able to do all of this without appearing flustered or out of control. Having to be great at just one thing is a high enough standard to make most guys insecure and always on edge; having to be perfect at everything is enough to make the young women feel that they can barely breathe. It's no wonder that self-harm is a growing phenomenon among our young people.[5] Reading Shauna Niequist's *New York Times* bestselling memoir *Present over Perfect* has recently shown me that this is not simply a challenge for high school women.[6] I believe it is a challenge for most of us, although women seem targeted even more than men. Impulses toward contemporary forms of "perfectionism" are not a joke, but have proven to be mentally, physically, and relationally crippling.[7]

Our culture in the West, even as it glorifies radical individualism, fosters far more of a herd mentality than most realize.[8] What an irony that our modern age on the one hand exhausts us by its calls for complete self-expression and, on the other hand, suffocates us by its pressures to conform. We must constantly adopt ever-changing fashions, humor, and music, and yet keep up the appearance that we are independently minded. This tension fuels our economy—and our insecurities![9]

With pressures from home, the classroom, and peers, young people often feel isolated and unsure if anyone likes them. Even with friends, many people sense that these are more like tribal packs that hold together only to the extent that each member keeps up their contribution. Failure to do so produces a fear of rejection. Your hobbies, your fashion, your athletic abilities all need to be in line with your group; the threat of exile consistently hovers over youth. That can sound silly to us adults, but it is the common experience of many kids and teenagers.[10] If we were more self-aware, we would likely see how common it is among adults as well. We walk on the knife's edge between the demand to "be yourself" and the unspoken requirement to conform to current social trends that often masquerade as self-expression. School and social pressures are not new, since they go back millennia, but social media and other cultural changes have clearly intensified them.[11]

> Whoever has any knowledge of people will certainly admit that just as he has often wished to be able to move them to relinquish self-love, he has also had to wish that it were possible to teach them to love themselves.
>
> Søren Kierkegaard, *Works of Love*

Even when these young people have been told, just like Samantha Sarah Marie, that they are loved, they still wonder whether anyone actually likes them. Do their parents like them? Similar questions worry them as they consider their teachers and school friends. There is a reason so many kids (not to mention adults) find animals such a relief. When my kids burst through the door at home, Ruby can barely contain herself, wagging her tail so hard it seems her body is being bent in half. Cotton the cat jumps onto the lonely lap, waiting to exchange comforting purrs for kind caresses. No judgment arises from these furry friends, just acceptance and affection. Welcoming Suzie or Sam, the pet enjoys this time with the young person, with its mutual acceptance and kindness. As gratifying and therapeutic as an animal's presence can be, it doesn't resolve the questions about our other relationships. And behind them all is the lingering concern about what *God* thinks of you.

• ● •

So I ask again, does God *like* you?

I have addressed that question not just to teenagers, but to adults of all ages. When I ask it, I try to keep eye contact, but it is amazing how quickly people drop their eyes to the ground. It is painfully clear this is an uncomfortable question. Rather than interrupting the uneasy silence that often follows such a question, I sometimes notice eyes starting to moisten. Why? What is behind this visceral reaction to a simple question? Let's step back and consider potential roots to this problem.

Does God See *Me*?

Have you ever heard a gospel presentation that starts out something like the following?

- God is holy and loving.
- You are a sinner.
- God hates sin and can't be in sin's presence.
- Don't worry. The cross brings good news because now the Father no longer sees you but instead looks at Christ and his cross.

How many believers have heard some version of this proclaimed by well-meaning ministers and Christian counselors? Sitting there in the unforgiving wooden pews or across the room in a tired leather chair is a tender conscience feeling the weight of sin and failure. The speaker intends to proclaim the good news of Christ's death and to comfort the believer with this presentation. Yes, one's first response to this message can be a sense of promise and profound relief (after all, it is pointing us to Christ and him crucified!). Hearers may be grateful to discover the good news of Christ's death for us and God's complete forgiveness, deeply moved to hear of God's love. But for all that is good and right in this outline, it contains threads of misunderstanding that consequently can distort the hearers' views of God, themselves, and the Christian life.

Some traditions, like my own, place so much emphasis on our identity as "sinners" that we leave no room for our deeper identity as the ones whom God designed in his own image to experience life in fellowship, or to experience his original delight in us ourselves, with our particular spunk, our personality, our difference. Since a presentation like the previous one often works solely in terms of obligations and our failure to meet them, we absorb the idea that God thinks and acts only in terms of obligations too. Thus, we can misperceive God's love, as we misperceive that of our parents, as consisting largely of self-imposed obligations. Things like joy or delight or approval are just too good to be true. God, like our parents, *has* to love us (or so we have been told). That's just part of the deal. He is God after all, and there's no way we can ever meet his standards. We are repeatedly told so. Why should we think that God likes us? Nothing in the sermon outlined above indicates that there is anything especially likable about us—far from it! We are told that there is nothing good in us, aren't we?[12] Maybe the best we can hope for is that God will put up with us if we keep our heads down and hang around with Jesus. We imagine God's acceptance of us like we're attending a party with our older brother, Jesus. Our presence is tolerable to the host because we tagged along with someone that he actually likes, Jesus. In truth, that is how many of us experience "God's love": mere divine toleration toward us. Some versions attempt to offer comfort to the believer by telling them that since they are covered in Christ's blood, God "doesn't see" them (since they are sinners) but only sees Christ (since he alone is free from sin).[13] In this version, God really doesn't want to look at you. Or maybe he just can't.

It's entirely understandable (and a symptom of growth) if the listener who has heard versions of this message for years—maybe even decades—at some point gets the courage to ask, "If God only sees me in Christ, does he even see *me*? Does he know *me*? How can you say God loves me? Maybe he just loves his Son?"

> The unholy is the absurd affair in which the creature seeks to be creature in a way other than that which is purposed by God.
>
> John Webster, *Holiness*

Sometimes it is the non-Christian who is first to raise these awkward questions. Looking at the Christian faith, they ask, "Do I have to stop being *me* in order to become a Christian?" Answering this question may be trickier than most people realize. Dismissing such questions as self-absorbed or individualistic is often just a way of avoiding them. Rugged individualism may be the particular temptation of Western culture, but that isn't the same as asking what place particular persons have in the kingdom of God. Jesus, after all, spent quite a lot of time doing just this.

What Does the Father Think of Me?

Difficult questions like these, honestly asked, are immensely helpful. They can slow us down enough to see if we have wandered away from the biblical presentation of the good news. That wandering takes the forms both of misstating God's role as Redeemer and forgetting his role as Creator: the two should not be separated.

Too often in some offerings of the gospel, for example, we are presented with a wrathful Father and a loving Christ. In this way, the Father appears as an easily offended, furious perfectionist, who is only persuaded to forgive us by a more compassionate Son. The Father is now willing to put up with us, but only because Jesus loves us. The obvious tension between the Father and the Son in such a story clearly violates the oneness of God and the many passages in the Bible that highlight God's love for us flowing out of the Father himself (e.g., John 3:16; Rom. 5:8; 2 Cor. 13:14; Eph. 2:4; 1 John 4:8). When we get this wrong regarding the triune God, we feel that God is like a father who is irritated by his kid's friends but nevertheless lets them play at his house because their presence makes his kid happy. Oh how I wish such a rendering were a figment of my imagination, but I have dealt with far too many people from across the country and beyond who have received such an impression: crudely put, the Father is associated with anger (or irritable toleration) and the Son with love. This is deeply antithetical to the gospel. Try this test: Do you tend to avoid prayer because you feel like a stranger in the Father's presence rather than a safe and welcomed daughter or son?

While I understand where they come from, claims that God can't stand to be in the presence of sin are fundamentally opposed to the gospel and the nature of God. This claim and its many variants are backward: it's sin that can't stand the presence of God. To say that God can't stand the presence of sin makes him out to be like the person I heard of who couldn't stand the presence of a spider and would demand that someone else deal with it. It gives sin leverage over God. It makes God out to be either finicky and weak or a kind of irritable, narcissistic fusspot who is more concerned that things go smoothly than that his beloved is safe and whole. It makes God out to be the kind of being who doesn't have a beloved at all, except perhaps himself. It undercuts and denies the divinity of Christ, who, as God incarnate, was present with and to sinners his whole life. It misunderstands the Holy Spirit, who comes to dwell *in* sinners in order that they might be saints.[14] It can develop from the kind of theology that sees justice only in terms of retribution with little concern for restoration.

When our pulpits and our psychologies link the Father with wrath and the Son with love, we end up with a deeply distorted conception of the triune God. John Owen (1616–83) dealt with a similar misconception among seventeenth-century Christians, recognizing that worship, delight, rest, and love all shrivel up rather than grow when this view takes root.[15] To combat these views, he preached the New Testament, emphatically proclaiming, "God [the Father] so loved the world that he sent his only Son" (John 3:16). Divine persons are not pitted against one another; there is no friction or tension between the Father, Son, and Spirit, for God is One. There is no friction or tension between his holiness and his love, for God is One. Furthermore, the Son is not passive, but, as Morna D. Hooker observes, he freely and actively "gives himself up" for us, not reluctantly, but for the joy set before him.[16] And the Spirit freely unites us to the Son so that he might liberally distribute God's gifts as he draws us into the life and love of God. United to the Son by the Spirit, our hearts cry out "Abba, Father." God is holy. God is love. And this holy God genuinely loves you and does what is necessary to reconcile you to himself.

The gifts of the Son and Spirit are not what secure the Father's love for us but are the fruit of his love for us. Rather than solving an abstract accounting problem, God's *love* for his world, his people, and you shapes the meaning of the cross for us. God does not hate you; rather, he manifests his love in his delight to be about the work of redemption. Believers are those who have experienced the love of the Father, the grace of the Son, and the fellowship of the Spirit (2 Cor. 13:14). Redemption is not just for some generic humanity but for particular people: the Shepherd knows his sheep, he lays down his life for them, and he calls them by name (John 10:3, 11, 14). As we will see later, we need to emphasize community far more strongly than is common in the Western church today, but that should not undercut the complementary biblical truth that God calls not just generic humanity or the world, but particular people (cf. Exod. 33:12, 17; Isa. 40:6; John 6:37; 10:3). He knows your name. He sees you. He loves *you*.

If we interpret redemption as merely a form of problem solving, where we are the problem, then we are also apt to forget that the good Creator created us good. We forget God's delight, pleasure, and satisfaction. God likes what he made, and he apparently really likes human creatures. After all, he made us in his own image and likeness—not just generic humanity, but particular people, young and old, male and female, quick-witted and slow, you and me. This does not mean God is blind to our rebellion and sin, just as Samantha Sarah Marie's mother did not ignore her child's occasional ill behavior. God doesn't like hard hearts, greedy hands, and violent responses. God is not and cannot be indifferent to sin *precisely because it perverts his good creation*. In the end God will deal with it by straightening it out and making it right. But whenever fallen humanity's sinfulness becomes not just *a* theme but the *chief* theme in our assessment of humanity, then it prevents us from appreciating the particularity of God's work in individual humans.

We begin to interpret healthy aspects of creaturely life as expressions of sin. Because bad preaching and bad theology also typically present the preacher's specific view of how to live as the only right pattern (e.g., Christians should be highly educated, or work for particular causes), listeners are left to believe that every deviation from this particular pattern is sin.

To disconnect redemption from creation encourages a form of self-loathing and shame among God's people. As we will explore more fully in chapters five and six, right repentance and humility are never about self-hatred, but a recognition that we are not living as God created us; our sin damages and distorts us, it warps our understanding, and it hurts the way we relate to our God and his world. Repentance is always unto life, not death.[17] It is a turning around (Greek: *metanoia*), away from self-harm and toward our healing God. That is why it is linked to resurrection, which, according to Paul, points to the dawning of a new creation (2 Cor. 5:17). But we will need to ask, "What does *new* mean here?" As a redeemed and forgiven people—as *new* creatures—we can and need to respond in gratitude, grounded in the dignity that we have in Christ: the triune Creator is making all things new through "the grace of the Lord Jesus Christ, and the love of God, and the fellowship of the Holy Spirit" (13:14), and we praise him for his work of renewal.

> You would not see yourself so clearly if you did not already know the love of the Savior.
>
> Fleming Rutledge, *The Undoing of Death*

To start affirming our creaturely finitude as a good quality rather than an evil to be overcome, we must confess that God loves me and not just Christ instead of me. His love is not driven by ignorance (e.g., "He doesn't see you"), but by delight and purpose (seeing you as his own lost sheep in need of a Shepherd): he likes how he made you, and his overflowing love now pours out toward you, his particular creature; he is about rescuing and renewing *you*.

Holding together creation and redemption allows you to make sense of this dynamic, a dynamic employed by the apostle Paul.

Revisiting Galatians 2:20

Near the beginning of Paul's Letter to the Galatians, he repeats the account of his calling from God (Gal. 1:12–17), mentioning his retreat into Arabia and return to Syria and Cilicia, where he "preached the faith he once tried to destroy" (1:23). Next we hear of his trip to Jerusalem with Barnabas some fourteen years later (2:1). Paul then recounts the painful story of confronting Peter, who started to distance himself from the gentiles, not eating with them, and holding aloof from them as if they were *unclean* rather than *cleansed* by Christ (2:11–14). Paul would have none of this, for such an attitude betrays the gospel. God shows no partiality (1:6). No one stands justified before God or others because of birth or based on "the works of the law" (2:16); no, our righteousness and our life come through Christ, who lives in us (2:20). And he comes to each where we are, calling us as individuals and communities to believe. Christ alone is the Savior of the world, and so we must view our salvation, our life, our death, and everything else in terms of Jesus's life, death, and resurrection. This takes us to Paul's paradigm-shifting claim:

> I have been crucified with Christ. It is no longer I who live, but Christ who lives in me. And the life I now live in the flesh I live by faith in the Son of God, who loved me and gave himself for me. (Gal. 2:20)

While this is one of the most memorized New Testament texts, it is still possible to misunderstand and misapply it. Have we only listened to part of the verse? What is Paul arguing here, and what is he not advocating? I want to highlight three aspects of this text: union with Christ, "I live," and the call to believe. These three points help us hold together redemption and creation, and in so doing, they can help us avoid confusing creaturely finitude with sinfulness. They are not the same thing!

To Be United . . .

Has it ever occurred to you how strange it can sound to people when Christians talk about Jesus? We don't merely talk about him as a great teacher of wisdom, or simply as an edgy sage or prophet, but as the very Son of God who became man, becoming like us in all ways, except that he never sinned (John 1:1, 14; Heb. 4:15). It is one thing to talk about Jesus as a historical figure, as someone who started movements, offered insightful counsel, and was courageous enough to stand up to the power structures of his day. While he did all of that, those actions are not primarily why he has followers to this day. Christian worship around the globe centers on understanding him as the Messiah, and we make claims far more world-shaking than that he was merely a teacher of wisdom or powerful prophet. Believers claim that we somehow personally (and corporately) continue to have fellowship with this man and benefit from his life, death, resurrection, ascension, and ongoing intercession in heaven. What does all of that mean?

Central to our Christian identity is the union of believers with Christ by the Spirit. Paul refers to this in Galatians 2:20 when he says, "I have been crucified with Christ. . . . Christ . . . lives in me." Wait, Paul wasn't crucified, was he? What is going on here? This is going to take a bit of work, so be patient, but what we learn here will have crucial implications for our lives.

Although you don't find the phrase "union with Christ" in the New Testament, this idea is essential to Paul's view of Christian existence. Woven throughout Paul's letters are phrases that denote such union: saints are "in Christ" (e.g., 1 Cor. 1:2; Eph. 1:1; Phil. 1:1; etc.), and Christ is "in" those who believe (e.g., Rom. 8:10; Col. 1:27; etc.). Believers are members of the body of Christ (Rom. 12:4–5; 1 Cor. 6:15; 12:12–27; Eph. 4:11–13; 5:30). The church is the bride of Christ, united to her groom (1 Cor. 6:15–17; 2 Cor. 11:2–3; Eph. 5:25–32), and thus we are united to one another (Rom. 7:4). We are those who "put on" or are clothed in Christ (Rom. 13:12–14; 1 Cor. 15:53–54; 2 Cor. 5:3; Gal. 3:26–27). Whereas we were once linked simply to the first Adam, now we are to find our identity in the final Adam (Greek: *eschatos Adam*) (Rom. 5:12–21; 1 Cor. 15:22, 45). Believers are those who are now "in the Lord" and found "in him" (e.g., Rom. 16:2, 8, 11, 13; Eph. 1:4; 2:21; 5:8; Phil. 3:8–9).

Constantine R. Campbell nicely surveys the variety of Paul's imagery and his interpretation of what we call union with Christ: "A believer is united to Christ at the moment of coming to faith; their union is established by the indwelling of the Spirit. The person united to Christ therefore entered into participation with Christ in his death, resurrection, ascension, and glorification. As a participant in Christ's death and resurrection, the believer dies to the world and is identified with the realm of Christ. As a member of the realm of Christ, the believer is incorporated into his body, since union with Christ entails union with his members."[18] These comments reflect the various ways Paul brings together themes of identification, participation, and incorporation within the larger idea of union with Christ.

Similar imagery and assumptions are found throughout the New Testament, not just in Paul.[19] For example, believers are the Israel of God, adopted into his family, so that those connected to Christ—who "is the new covenant"—live "in the covenant through his representative headship."[20] Because the Suffering Servant (whom Isaiah portrays both as singular and corporate)[21] entered into solidarity with us, we are able to participate in the benefits of his suffering—specifically, to be healed.[22] He has absorbed and dealt with our sin because it has been laid on him (Isa. 52:13–53:12; Matt. 8:14–17); thus, we who had been contaminated with sin have become clean in our union with Israel's Suffering Servant—we have been crucified with Christ.

John's writings likewise capture this idea, using such agricultural imagery as the vine and the branches (e.g., John 15:4–20; 1 John 2:24–27). How do we benefit from what Christ has done for us? Like branches on a vine, we are united to the Son of God and draw all our life from him. How? John answers this explicitly: "By this we know that we abide in him and he in us, because he has given us his Spirit" (1 John 4:13). His Spirit brings together what was apart. Again, the triune God acts on our behalf—there is no division within God.

The sacraments similarly highlight the beauty and centrality of this union with Christ and serve as an instrument of it. Baptized into the name of Christ, we are declared united with him (Rom. 6). Having these sacred waters fall over our body links us to his death, and in this we experience newness of life (e.g., 1 Cor. 6:11; Gal. 3:27–28). Gathered around the Lord's Table we give thanks as we drink the wine and eat the bread. Here we encounter the Christ who is present with us, and here we praise him for rescuing us by his death and resurrection and for dwelling in and among us by his life-giving Spirit (1 Cor. 10:16–17). By our participation in baptism and the Eucharist, we are likewise united to fellow believers, whether to celebrate or to bear one another's burdens (12:13, 26). Union with Christ does not dissolve our particularity, but rather establishes it. In Christ we are reborn into a new family, a new life, a new world. Sharing in this feast reconnects us with God's original desires for human creatures.

United to the Son by the Spirit, our hearts cry out "Abba, Father." As sons and daughters (via that union), we now moan from a position of hope and trust, rather than despair and apathy.[23] John Calvin understood this when he claimed, "As long as Christ remains outside of us, and we are separated from him, all that he has suffered and done for the salvation of the human race remains useless and of no value for us."[24] In Christ we are renewed or "new" creatures, freed to worship and enjoy our Lord. When Paul says that we have been crucified with Christ, he reminds us that all of our sin and shame were also crucified. In light of the cross we happily see that Christ, not our sin, defines us! Paul's declaration in Galatians 2:20 means that he "sees his own life as now constituted by the presence of Christ within him."[25] Similarly, in Colossians 3:3 he declares: "For you have died, and your life is hidden with Christ in God." The result of this union and burial with Christ is that your "life"—your value, dignity, and future—are secure in Christ. They do not depend on your performance or your perceived acceptability before others and God. Instead, they depend on the steadfastness of the risen Christ. This equips us with the confidence to encounter our limits without fear.

This Christ to whom we are united is risen! Therefore, the last word is not death; it is not sin; it is not terror or fear. No, the last words are the first words: "He has risen." And so we rise. We worship on Sunday, the first day of the week, because in the dawning of a new creation he has come as the King bringing us into his kingdom—yes, us. We who believe are in Christ, and Christ is in us. This union is our comfort, hope, and life. There is no salvation apart from this union to Christ. The Creator acts also as the Redeemer.

I Live

We are not accustomed (at least, outside the church) to concepts like being executed with someone else (Gal. 2:20) or being buried with someone else (Col. 2:11–12) or having died with someone else (2:20), especially when those events happened about two thousand years before we were born. Consequently, we find them awkward to handle. How literally should we take them? If they are metaphors, what are they pointing to?

If you look at what Paul is talking about here and in similar passages (see also 2 Cor. 5:14–17; Col. 3:1–5; 2 Tim. 2:11), Paul seems to affirm two realities we must keep in mind: he tells us how to approach our day-to-day existence (as in Rom. 12:1–2), and yet he also says that our lives—the center of our being—are already elsewhere, "hidden with Christ in God" (Col. 3:3). Something is *already* true even as we are also in *process*.

If we only look at Galatians 2:20, it's easy to get the impression that we have been removed and only Christ is left. "I no longer live." Asking, "Where is the 'me' in all this?" is a fair question. The more we look at the related passages, however, the more it becomes clear that Paul is not saying you no longer have existence or meaning or value. As Susan Eastman notes, despite being crucified with Christ, "Paul certainly has a strong sense of himself as a thinking, intending, emoting, and acting self with a distinctive history and vocation."[26] Paul is showing us where and what the real "me" is so that we might see ourselves more clearly. He shows us that all of God's action in creation and redemption embraces me, the real me that is free from the distortion of sin. Recognizing that me amid the ongoing struggles with sin can be a real challenge. But the "I," the "ego," does still matter to the Creator.

On November 17, 1867, Charles Spurgeon preached a sermon entitled "Christus et Ego," based on Galatians 2:20. Right at the beginning Spurgeon observes that the first-person singular pronouns ("I" and "me") are "swarming" everywhere in this passage, whereas the plural is absent. Elsewhere—and even normally—the apostle Paul will stress the communal, the plural, the whole, but here he speaks in terms of the singular individual. The Creator Lord does not merely love his creation as a system, or some generic humanity; rather, he "loved *me* and gave himself for *me*." Doesn't it sound a bit selfish or self-absorbed of the apostle Paul to speak this way? Spurgeon doesn't think so, because he sees it as a mark of true Christian religion. Again, while the biblical faith commonly will press us to elevate the whole over the part, the community over the solitary figure, it never loses sight of the importance of the single, the particular. God's love through Christ by his Spirit moves all the way to the individual.

According to Spurgeon's reading, one "distinguishing mark of the Christian religion" is that, rather than treating humans as cookie-cutter creatures, it brings out a person's individuality. He clarifies, "It does not make us selfish. On the contrary it cures us of that evil, but it still does manifest in us a selfhood by which we become conscious of our personal individuality in an eminent degree."[27] He then provides a helpful analogy: "In the nocturnal heavens there had long been observed bright masses of light—the astronomers called them 'nebulae'—they supposed them to be stores of shapeless chaotic matter until the telescope of Herschell resolved them into distinct stars. What the telescope did for stars the religion of Christ, when received into the heart, does for men!"[28]

Let's look again at Galatians 2:20. Paul's statement that we have been crucified with Christ provokes a question: "*What* or *who* was crucified?"

I am still here, standing before you. My biology hasn't changed. My personal upbringing and history did not evaporate. The fact that I prefer coffee over tea didn't change. So, what died?

Martin Luther, the great Reformer, observed that "Christ abiding in me drives out every evil. This union with Christ . . . separates me from my sinful self."[29] *Sin* functioned to separate rebellious creatures from the Creator, but Christ has overcome it, bringing the human creature back into fellowship with the Maker of Heaven and Earth. The distorted sinful self, according to Luther, stands under the law and judgment. That is any "I" apart from Christ. We were originally made as worshiping creatures who are appropriately dependent on their Creator and freely responsive to him. Sin disrupted our relationship to the rest of creation and its Creator; but we have been rescued by Christ and given life by his Spirit, so that the true ego—rather than the sinful self—may live. In redemption, "I" will always and only be free through union with Christ. Again, Luther: "Christ clings and dwells in us as closely and intimately as light or whiteness clings to a wall. . . . Christ himself is the life that I now live."[30] The apostle says not only that we were crucified with Christ but also that "Christ lives in me. And the life *I* now live in the flesh *I* live . . ."

The warnings in the earlier parts of Galatians (especially 1:6–9) are not merely about heretics but also about a far more common problem that we might call "projection." We tend to portray the Christian life in ways that reflect our own personalities and proclivities. Passionate Christian leaders and spiritual gurus commonly fall into this error. While we do not have space to fully deal with personality differences here, an example may prove helpful.

It has been argued that large swaths of the American church have received a spirituality framed in strongly extroverted terms.[31] Serious Christians, says this view, need to love being with a lot of people, doing very expressive things, while constantly sharing their feelings and failures with everyone. But what if you are more introverted? Do you have to become extroverted to show signs of sanctification?

Is one personality godlier than another? When Paul tells us that we have been crucified with Christ and "it is no longer I who live," he doesn't mean you actually need to cease being you. Each of us is different. Some are more extroverted, some more introverted. Some of us are publicly animated, others more reserved. Some seek adventure, others enjoy quiet. Some prefer action, others prefer reflection. Some find energy from being with a crowd, others from being alone. Some deal with stress through humor, others through increased focus. Each can express a faithful identity in Christ.

Does the call to be a faithful Christian mean that "you" actually have to stop being you? Listen to me carefully. You cannot escape you! Stop running from yourself. The you that Christ lives in is still *you*. He does not obliterate, deform, or deaden you. Who made you? When God made you, did he make a mistake? The Father of life created each of us in our particularity, and he delights in his creation.

When unpacking the doctrine of union with Christ, John Owen anticipated various misunderstandings, including the temptation to think our individuality is absorbed and lost. When the Son of God comes to inhabit a person, Owen reminds us, "he doth not assume our [individual] nature, and so prevent our personality, which would make us one person with him." No, instead, by the Spirit he "dwells in our persons, keeping his own and leaving us our personality infinitely distinct."[32] From time to time through the history of the church, some have pretended that our union with Christ "destroyed the person of believers, affirming that in their union with Christ they lose their own personality,—that is, cease to be men, or at least these or those individual men."[33] That misunderstands the whole point of our union altogether and distorts our view of God and ourselves. What secures this union is not the loss of personality or particularity, but rather that "the one and self-same Spirit dwells in him and us."[34] We have received his Spirit, and so his Spirit now produces fruit in us (Gal. 5:22–23; see also John 10). Love, joy, peace, patience, kindness, goodness, faithfulness, gentleness, and self-control are all the Spirit's fruit, but they often look and taste a bit different among the variety of particular trees that inhabit the Lord's land. Each tree produces fruit, nourishes others, and grows strong; but that is far from saying each tree is the same as the next. We see evidence of such misunderstandings when Christian artists don't feel welcomed in the church, when evangelism is always required to have a particular style to it, and when spirituality is always presented in either introverted or extroverted terms (depending on the leader). Sameness is not the goal. The life and fruit of the Spirit are. Similarly, when two people are united in marriage, they do not cease to be a distinctive woman and man, but in their differences they nevertheless become one. When the church is the one body of Christ, this

> For where not I, there more happily I.
>
> Augustine, *On Continence*

does not eliminate our differences of personality, backgrounds, hobbies, or delights, but it does show our shared union with Christ amid our diversity.

We are not trying to run from ourselves; rather, Christ has freed us from the entanglements of sin, which deface and deform his image in us. The Redeemer has freed us in order that we may be our true selves. Run from your sin? Yes! But don't imagine that to be a serious Christian you need to have a different temperament or personality. God's goal is not for all of us to end up looking, sounding, and being the same. That confuses sameness with godliness. Not everyone needs to wear khakis, nor do they all need tattoos. But everyone needs to be united to the Son by the Spirit that they might fully enjoy the love of the Father: because of this union we actively participate in communion with the triune God.

To Believe

Why is "living by faith" so hard? We are called to live by faith, a faith that we are found in Christ and that his life, death, and resurrection are now determinative for our lives. His story must be believed above our own story. Let me explain.

Union with Christ is not, at least biblically speaking, a universal or generic phenomenon. As Grant Macaskill's Oxford University Press volume on this theme makes clear, even among New Testament authors who "offer the strongest statements of God's universal love, such as John, union with Christ is limited to those who are acting subjects of faith."[35] This is because *faith* is the biblical term for the sinner's renewed relation with God; it is a term that includes personal trust, eyes that have been opened to reality, a life enabled by God himself, and a delight in him. The reason it is impossible to please God apart from faith (Heb. 11:6) is that being apart from faith means standing essentially in opposition to God. Faith is the relational dynamic in which we see God and our neighbor as who they really are, and then respond accordingly.

I think the difficulties of living by faith in the Son are related to two specific things Paul calls us to believe in Galatians 2:20. First, that Jesus "loved me," and second, that he "gave himself for me." Yes, this includes each "me" along with our particularities, our differences (Jew, gentile, male, female, young, old), our creatureliness, even our sin.

Many of us don't have a hard time with the idea that there is a God and he loves the world. But even mature Christians, who have spent their whole life in the church, get very uncomfortable when told individually, "Christ came for you. He gave himself for *you*." Years ago I had a pleasant and engaging conversation with someone after church. But as I later walked to the car, my then nine-year-old son Jonathan said to me, "That man must have never learned to look at people in the eye, or he was really nervous." Jonathan had picked up on the situation. Here was a grown man who had done nothing wrong, and yet it was almost impossible for him to look me in the eye as we talked. If we struggle to look one another in the eye (which we do!), how can we ever imagine being secure in the Father's presence? I think that we all struggle to believe God likes us. So our problem becomes learning how, given our sin, struggles, and inadequacies, we can really receive words of personal grace in a way that reaches the depths of our hearts as well as our rational understanding.

> The presence of evil separates us not only from God, but also from our true selves.
> John Swinton, *Raging with Compassion*

We might believe Christ could die for someone awesome like Mother Teresa, Billy Graham, or an abandoned orphan. But what about me? No one even knows my name. What if I don't like to lead Bible studies, or I don't go on mission trips, or I have hardly any money to give to the poor? Your Christian identity needs to be shaped by the fact that God in Christ loved "you," and gave himself for you—*you*!

The sixteenth-century Heidelberg Catechism beautifully captures the message that the gospel applies to each of us in particular. It proclaims not just that God is good, or that God is love, but that he has been good to me, that he loves me, that he has provided for me. Consequently, when it describes the "holy supper" that God's people eat, it tells the reader just how personal this sacrifice, this meal, this good news is when the feast is eaten: "As surely as I see with my eyes the bread of the Lord broken *for me* and the cup shared with *me*, so surely his body was offered and broken *for me* and his blood poured out *for me* on the cross."[36] Similarly, that same catechism tells us that true faith is not mere knowledge, not a general acceptance of God's kindness, but that what "God has freely granted" is "not only to others but to me also."[37] God doesn't just forgive generic sins: he forgives *my* sin. He doesn't just save the cosmos; he saves *me*. Why? Because he loves you and me as particular people.

Who are you?

As a believer, you are in Christ, and Christ is in you. You are secure by the power of the Spirit, who applies the finished work of Christ to your life. He enables you to grow and blossom as the real you, which involves communion with God and with your neighbor. If you were no more than a copy of a single pattern, just like everyone else, we would not have a communion but an echo chamber. You are connected but distinctive, adding your unique voice and actions to the universe. God delights in you as you use the particular gifts he has given. You are a child of the King. You are an irreplaceable member of the body of Christ. God wants you to flourish as the particular *you* that you are, to enjoy his creation and to enjoy him. That is your calling and privilege as a particular human creature he made and delights in. This is crucial for recapturing a healthy embrace of our creaturely limits. He doesn't just love a generic world or amorphous humanity; he loves you, and he even likes you.

Fundamental to what God loves and likes about you is your body, which he joyfully created. Too often we treat our bodies as insignificant or even bad, but when we do that we risk undervaluing what is central to the good news: in Christ "the whole fullness of deity dwells bodily" (Col. 2:9). Part of being human is being limited by having a body. The incarnation—the Son of God taking on human flesh—is God's great yes to his creation in general, and to finite human creatures in particular. Only when we fully appreciate this reality can we learn to live more comfortably in our own skin. To this story we now turn.

3

are the limits of my body bad?

praise God for Mary

> That unreachable power came down and put on limbs that could be touched so that the needy could approach Him and, embracing His humanity, become aware of His divinity.
>
> St. Ephrem the Syrian, *Homily on our Lord*

The Creator God is not embarrassed by the limitations of our bodies and his material world but fully approves of them in and through the Son's incarnation. Only when we appreciate this can we clearly see how human limits should not be confused with sin but, rather, seen as a positive aspect of our humanity.

The Same Story?

Imagine sitting beside a campfire warming yourself; you are excited by what is about to happen. It's the early part of what will eventually be known as the second century.[1] You have grown up in a devout Jewish home where one of the great comforts you have always enjoyed is spending evenings at a fire listening to the elders quote vast passages of the Torah.

Sometimes one man would begin and speak a few lines and then the next person would recite as soon as the first one decided to pause. It was like a game: each person needed to follow along carefully and see if they could—from memory—immediately start up where the last one left off. Some of the most respected leaders have memorized huge portions of the Hebrew Scriptures. As an ambitious child you listened carefully, hoping one day you would be leading the group through these pious acts of memory and faith.

Recently your parents have been spending a lot of time with another Jewish family that made unsettling yet exciting claims about the promised Messiah. They have not denied their faith in Yahweh, but they speak of a divine visitation, saying that Yahweh has broken his silence. Tonight they are going to join the campfire: your parents have promised that these friends can speak tonight about this visitation. Supposedly their teaching will build on the Hebrew Scriptures and more fully point to the God of Abraham, Isaac, and Jacob. Yet the teaching that the friends are bringing comes not from Moses or Isaiah, but apparently from a man named John. While the fire supplies the expected warmth, curiosity mixed with suspicion fills your breast. What will they say? Why does their message seem to stir your Aba (father) and Eema (mother) so powerfully? Expectation is in the air.

Gently coughing to clear his throat, the man motions for silence, and then begins: "In the beginning . . ." What is this? You know these words, and you know them well. This will be nothing new! Here are the very first words of the Hebrew Scriptures. Rather than becoming unnerved, you instantly start to recite the text in your own mind: "In the beginning . . . God created the heavens and the earth. . . ."

But "God" is not the next word the man says. Rather, what began as familiar turns strange and unexpected: "In the beginning . . . was the Word, and the Word was with God, and the Word was God." This Word (*Logos*) was uniquely identified with God: "The Word was with God, and the Word *was* God." Has blasphemy just been uttered?

"All things were made through him," the man continues. This Word was none other than the Creator himself, somehow fitting within the one divine identity. Your head spins, moving from Genesis back to John, wondering how these two stories might fit together. Through your distraction you hear the man continue speaking. Then, when you can focus again you hear what you had never even dared to imagine: "And the Word *became flesh* and dwelt among us, and we have seen his glory, glory as of the only Son from the

Father, full of grace and truth." Wait, how could this be? How could the Word, who was with God and is God, "become flesh"? That is scandalous. God is the Creator. He can't also be created, can he? This Word of God was even given a historical name, identified as a particular person: Jesus of Nazareth, the Messiah.

Amid all these unfamiliar ideas, you start to make connections that are deeply uncomfortable, maybe even offensive, but also possibly the most beautiful claim about the transcendent and holy God that could be made: the eternal *I Am* has become one with us, distinctly entering into solidarity with his human creatures. Somehow God "became" man in Jesus. What could this possibly mean? This oral recitation was sure to be followed by a long evening of lively discussion and debate.

• • •

Christians are familiar with the creation narrative and the Gospel story about Jesus. Unfortunately, it is far too common that we don't connect these two pivotal parts of the Bible. Once we begin to connect them, we see how deeply they inform and explain one another. These ideas, that Jesus the Redeemer is also the Word of the creation; that the Word through whom all creation came into being has taken on human flesh and walked among us; that, from the beginning, God in Christ has always looked out for us, made a place for us, pursued and caught us: all these explosive ideas show that we cannot truly understand either Genesis 1 or John 1 if we separate them. Separating these passages undervalues both creation and redemption by blinding us to what the Bible tells us about the Christ.

Jesus the Messiah is both Creator and Redeemer. Only by seeing the links between creation and *re*-creation, between Genesis 1 and John 1, can we understand how the lordship of Jesus liberates us. Only in that way can we see and appreciate God's love for us *in* our creatureliness rather than in spite of it. In his incarnation, the Creator Lord did not come to destroy his creation but to enter it, to love and heal it.

> In his humiliation, God had to breathe, eat, drink, and sleep. When cut he bled.
>
> Elyse M. Fitzpatrick, *Found in Him*

The doctrine of the incarnation of God, that the Father sends the Son in the Spirit to become human, includes the teaching that God puts a high value on the particular humanity and finitude of each of us. That being the case, our failure to put a similarly high value there means a rejection of God's own judgment. Once we examine God's endorsement of our humanity, we can then ask what our relation is to our Creator-Redeemer and what it means for living faithfully with him.

Is the Material World Evil?

Two outspoken leaders from the second and third centuries represent for us a problem that has repeatedly arisen within the church, a problem that comes from the tension hinted at in the story above. Let's begin with Marcion (died ca. 160), a theologian who later was declared a heretic. Marcion, like many before and after him, understood the world in terms of opposing the material to the spiritual, seeing the physical aspects of life as crass and corrupt distractions from a spirituality that seeks a pure and moral life that leads one away from embodiment: at least that is how the early fathers often represent him.[2] He viewed the Hebrew creator god of the Old Testament as too entangled with this world and too belligerent to be worthy of worship, and he pitted that god against the more spiritual, gracious, loving god of the New Testament; thus he associated the first with materiality and evil, and the second with pure spirituality and freedom.[3] Physical creatureliness was a burden of disgrace and evil, while the nonmaterial world of spirits and ideas was a goal worth seeking.

Marcion's thinking becomes most problematic for Christians in his view of Jesus. Given his negative judgment of the physical world and his positive attitude about Jesus, Marcion seems to have concluded that the Christ could *not* have experienced a real birth, nor could he have known childhood and growth.[4] For example, his body must have been a convincing *phantasm*, more an impression than a genuine physical substance.[5] This is an example of what became known as "docetism" (Greek: *dokein*, "to seem"): Jesus *seemed* to have a body and to be human, but he really wasn't.[6] If Jesus were a human being, with real bones and blood, then he would be considered *necessarily* evil or sinful by Marcionites. Bodies bring limits and shame, and the good God would never condescend to become genuinely united with such restrictions and creatureliness. Salvation, according to Marcion, was about souls, certainly not the flesh! This is why orthodox opponents of Marcion emphasized two key teachings from the Gospels: Jesus's birth and his bodily resurrection.[7]

Then as now, it was appealing to pursue spirituality by pitting the physical creation against a nonphysical spirit world: body against soul, spirit against flesh, heaven against earth, God against creation. Marcion's distinctive views became accepted by a growing number of people, eventually creating not just theological but also pastoral problems within the church.

Leaders influenced by the Marcionite and Gnostic traditions sometimes differed in how they talked about Jesus's relationship to Mary. These problematic teachers were creative with their reasoning, some of them asserting "that Jesus . . . passed through Mary as water through a tube."[8] According to the early church father Irenaeus's report, these "heretics" all agreed on one thing: they denied that "the Word of God [had] become flesh."[9] Some embraced the phantasm explanation, that he only appeared to take the "form of a man" but his body was more like a ghost, "while others assert[ed] that he did not even take the form of man, but descended as a dove upon Jesus who was born of Mary."[10]

No matter the explanation, their common foundation was the claim that God cannot become united with the material, limiting, earthy world because the good God is fundamentally transcendent. The physical is at best a distraction and at worst an evil cloak covering everything. For them, the flesh—the earthly—was that from which people needed to be freed.

Marcion's god obviously cannot become genuinely united with the messiness of this world. To do so would be, according to Marcion, "unbecoming" and "unworthy" of God; it is simply unthinkable. Consequently, if Jesus is truly divine, he most certainly cannot have had real skin, bones, and nose hairs. That is just ridiculous. The good God, even this God's Son, could not be so closely linked with the material world. Or could he?

Taking On Flesh

In Africa there emerged one of the great gifts to the ancient church: Tertullian of Carthage (ca. 155–220). A brilliant thinker, witty communicator, and passionate though flawed leader, Tertullian fiercely opposed Marcionite ideas that had lingered well after Marcion's death. Like Irenaeus[11] (130–202), one of the early leaders who had opposed the teachings of Marcion and the Gnostics, Tertullian wrote a response that nicely captures the heart of the issue for us.

On the Flesh of Christ (*De carne Christi*) is Tertullian's sharp-witted reply to Marcionite distortions. The opening paragraph gets right to the point of the main dispute: "Let us examine our Lord's bodily substance, for *about His spiritual nature all are agreed.*"[12] Tertullian dismisses the topic of Christ's spiritual nature because the issue that concerns him here is the *humanity* rather than the divinity of Jesus. This priority interestingly contrasts with twentieth- and twenty-first-century controversies, for which the main flashpoint has more often been the Messiah's divine nature.

One can argue that over the past 150 years evangelicals in the West have spent a great deal more of their energy defending the deity of Jesus the Messiah than examining the equally important confession of his full human nature.[13] If you ask many Christians today, "Do you believe that Jesus was really a human?" they normally nod their heads without hesitation: but experience makes me wonder if we understand that doctrine and its implications. Scratch below the surface and ask a few uncomfortable questions (e.g., did Jesus go through puberty?), and many believers will become squeamish about affirming fairly normal aspects of the full earthiness of the incarnate Son. I believe this nervousness partly grows out of a lopsided apologetic focus. If we spend all our energy concentrating on the divine nature of Jesus, we can easily get lost in idealized abstractions that look nothing like the messiness of true and full humanity. We begin to attribute our own embarrassment at our bodily functions to the God who gave them to us.

Affirming the full humanity of the "Word become flesh" genuinely shocked people when John did it in the first century and when Tertullian did it in the third century, and it does so in the twenty-first century. This doctrine is still a serious obstacle for many non-Christians and an unsettling creedal affirmation for some pious congregants. I believe that many evangelicals, for example, have not fully embraced or worked out the implications of believing that their Savior, the Son of God, is also the son of Mary.

> . . . this flesh, in fact, suffused with blood, scaffolded of bones, threaded through with sinews, intertwined with veins, competent to be born and to die, human unquestionably, as born of a human mother.
>
> Tertullian, *On the Flesh of Christ*

This takes us back to Tertullian, who used Jesus's birth to unflinchingly affirm the Savior's full humanity, his fleshiness. And although some scholars have argued that Tertullian was a misogynist—some of his statements clearly appear indefensible and offensive—Donna-Marie Cooper recently offered significant evidence that his rhetorical methodology and the emphases found in his full corpus call into question purely critical modern readings; she even worries that many thus miss some of the potentially positive contributions Tertullian may make to ancient understandings of women.[14] Our interests, however, simply require that we examine Tertullian's references to Mary as his way of affirming the full humanity of the Messiah.

I am convinced that only when we have grasped the implications of the humanity of Jesus will we be able to properly assess our own humanity. The doctrine that the Word became flesh means that God himself affirms our flesh as good, and that affirmation liberates us from apologizing for our creaturely limitations. If we believe that Jesus, who was free from all sin, was fully human, then this means that he considered creaturely restrictions to be part of his good creation and not evil at all. It means that we must not apologize for what the Son of God freely embraces.

Thank God for Mary

Modern doubts about the eternal Son of God becoming incarnate have put us into the habit of thinking of the virgin birth primarily as a statement of Jesus's divinity. But for many early orthodox church leaders, the virgin birth highlighted the truth of Jesus's complete *humanity*. Tertullian wrote of the womb of Mary and the physical details of her pregnancy, with all of the accompanying bodily functions and fluids. He writes of Mary's real, actual pregnancy, of how she was "expanding daily, heavy, troubled, uneasy even in sleep, torn between the impulses of fastidious distaste and those of excessive hunger" because Jesus was growing in her womb.[15]

We tend to focus on the *virgin* part, but Tertullian brings us back to what is so obvious we risk missing it—namely, that Jesus was *born* just like everyone else, the only difference being that this pregnancy was not initiated by sex with a man (Matt. 1:18–20; Luke 1:34). That is a *big* difference, and it matters.[16] But we must not lose sight of the fact that Jesus and Mary—in their respective ways—experienced all the other normal parts of fetal development (cf. Luke 2:5).

Although I've never been pregnant, my wife has, twice. And when the children were young, she liked to remind them of the debt they owed her. If they hesitated to do a job, she would joke: "Hey, how about you take out the trash and I give you life?" Mary was Jesus's mother as much as Tabitha is the mother of Jonathan and Margot. Mary's was a real pregnancy; baby Jesus's life was dependent on hers. She gave birth to him in Bethlehem—at a real place in real time. When others encountered Jesus and praised him, they didn't doubt his human mother but blessed her "womb" that brought forth the child and "breasts" that sustained him: these very physical symbols remind us of the intimate bond between mother and child (Luke 11:27), an intimacy that was *more* but *never less than bodily*. Jesus would look to her as his cherished mother throughout his whole life (John 19:26). There is no aspect of the New Testament that does not presuppose this. When Mary asked her young son Jesus to take out the trash, he would. He was a faithful son who loved and honored his mother.[17]

While the Son of God is eternal, there is no embodied human being called Jesus of Nazareth *apart from Mary*. Let me be clear—Jesus gets his full humanity through his *mother*. Forgive the pun, but it is a great loss when we Protestants throw the baby out with the bathwater, when we fail to speak of Mary with deep appreciation, simply from fear that people might misunderstand and treat her as a "coredeemer." As a Protestant, I don't believe that the Scriptures present Mary in that way, but this is not to say she isn't essential to the biblical story of salvation. She is not the Messiah. But we must also confess, as the biblical revelation requires that we confess (cf. Matt. 1:16; Mark 6:3): *there is no historical human named Jesus apart from Mary, who gave birth to him!*

> What makes Christianity is not solely the *extra*ordinary in Christ's revelation of his glory. . . . It is also and indeed primarily the sharing by the Word incarnate of our most ordinary human condition independently of sin (that is, human finitude and the humanization of the divine).
>
> Emmanuel Falque, *The Metamorphosis of Finitude*

In the sixteenth century John Calvin joined in spirited debates about this very point in response to his contemporary Menno Simons.[18] Calvin, who affirmed the full divinity of Jesus as the Son of God, also refused to back away from affirming that Mary was genuinely his mother. Jesus did not have "heavenly flesh," as Simons and some others seem to claim.[19] Mary, Calvin emphasized, was no mere "vessel" for the baby in her womb. Simons and others, as it appeared to Calvin, made the same mistake some Marcionites made, treating Jesus like an alien pod deposited in Mary, but always foreign rather than native to her—such doctrine undermines the real connection, dependence, and humanity of the Savior. Calvin would have none of it. Mary really was his mother; they were most intimately connected like any mother and child.

After Eve was created from the first Adam in Genesis 2, the creation narrative declares, "The man said, 'This is now bone of my bones and flesh of my flesh.'" The second or final Adam, however, comes not from a man, but from a woman, *this* woman! A profound reversal takes place. Jesus is fully human, deriving his full humanity through Mary. Imagine Mary looking down at her precious child, holding him close and whispering to him, "You are 'bone of my bones and flesh of my flesh.'"

This is partly why many in the ancient church saw a clear link not only between Jesus and Adam but also between Mary and Eve.[20] That link, however, contained the contrast that whereas Eve was disobedient, Mary trusted in God.[21] Eve was tempted to think of her limitations as chains that should be thrown off, whereas Mary believed that within her smallness God would delight to accomplish his grandness. As Richard Bauckham rightly observes, "Mary is most fully herself, the active and responsible subject of her own story, when she acts as the Lord's servant (Luke 1:38, 48), taking God at his word and taking responsibility for acting with trust in that word (1:38, 45)."[22] When the Creator revealed his intentions, Mary trusted him, whereas Eve and Adam did not.

Eve sought to escape her finitude, whereas Mary embraced it, opening herself up in utter dependence to the Creator Lord. When the Spirit hovered over Mary, just as the Spirit of creation (Latin: *Creator Spiritus*) hovered over the newly created waters (Luke 1:35; Gen. 1:2), God did not negate her humanity but *affirmed* it. These are not different spirits, but the same Spirit of God. In both narratives God affirms and commits himself to the goodness of his creation. Only now, the promise cannot be understood apart from this woman's willingness to obey her God even amid her questions and fears. Praise God for Mary!

Let us not miss the immensity of the claim here. The God of creation has done the work of *re*-creation by entering it, by becoming one with us. The Creator somehow "becomes" a creature. How? The way all humans come to be: born of a woman! The infinite is united with the finite in Mary's womb.[23] For the holy Son of God, "becoming" finite is not sinful but an appropriate aspect of creaturely existence and something he freely assumes in the incarnation.

The Beautiful Earthiness of Jesus's Birth

Tertullian describes the normalcy of Jesus's birth: Mary's son was brought into this world together with the "afterbirth."[24] His vivid language may sound coarse to some, inappropriate, or maybe even impious. Why would an early church pastor speak so crassly about Jesus? Tertullian was convinced, however, that if we distance ourselves from the earthiness of Jesus's birth, then we also distance ourselves from his concrete humanity and therefore diminish the good news of Yahweh's coming in the Son. Tertullian dwells on the messiness of Jesus's birth to challenge his Marcionite opponents: Why should we be embarrassed about the material world if Jesus wasn't?

Some people object to this kind of elaboration. Scripture doesn't mention Mary's afterbirth, does it? No, it doesn't. And that is the point: it doesn't! It is all taken for granted. Do you know why the Scriptures do not talk about this stuff? For the same reason the newspapers don't dwell on the normal, the everyday: "The grass is green today, Joe went to the bathroom, and Sally laughed heartily at a friend's joke." Newspapers draw our attention to what is different, unexpected, and newsworthy. If we miss this, we will not appreciate the profundity of Tertullian's observation. He comments, "It was actually the ordinary condition of his terrene [i.e., earthy] flesh which made all things else about Him wonderful."[25] Here is a fully human person, he says, who would hunger, thirst, weep, tremble with strong emotion, and pour out his very blood—real, iron-filled blood. Here is one who also will rise from the grave with a genuine bodily resurrection. Why does this matter?

The God we worship is not embarrassed by his creation; rather, he loves it, and he acts from that love. Tertullian rebukes those who are uncomfortable with God's commitment to his human creation and his willingness to unite himself with it. Some want the benefits of the cross without the earthiness of the Son's birth, but you can't have one without the other: "What is more demeaning to God, what is more shameful—getting born or dying? To carry flesh or to carry a cross? To be circumcised or to be hanged? To be fed at the breast or to be buried? . . . But you will not be wise unless, by believing God's 'foolish things,' you have been foolish in this age."[26] Jesus was born dependent on his mother, just like the rest of us.[27]

Our ideas about our own bodies interact with ideas we have about Jesus's body. We must grow comfortable with our creaturely existence, delimited by embodied living. God fully demonstrates his delight in our humanity, demonstrates that creation is lovely and lovable, in the event of Jesus's very physical, very human birth. Tertullian doesn't want us to miss the wonder of divine humiliation, for this points not only to the path of spiritual salvation but also to God's affirmation of our created materiality. To miss this is to miss God's plan for human flourishing.

Love, Flesh, and God's Yes

Tertullian shows that the way we think about Jesus's "flesh" reveals a great deal about our understanding of love and life. He challenged Marcionites: Since you "detest a human being at his birth, then after what fashion do you love anybody?"[28] Although we think we don't have a problem with the birth of Jesus, Tertullian's comment shows that this may not be the case.

We all claim to love, but when the romanticized idea of love fails us and we are faced with *embodied* love, filled with earthiness, contingency, and conflict, our love falters. To love our neighbors means we must affirm both their and our creaturely existence. Truly loving Neal requires that we get close enough to see his pimples, smell his sweat, and become familiar with his strengths and weaknesses. "Nothing can be loved apart from that by which it is what it is."[29] Love requires affirming Neal in his particularity and limits, not a sanitized version of him.

> I am human, I consider nothing human alien to me.
>
> Publius Terentius Afer [Terence] (died 159 BC), *Hauton Timorumenos* (The self-tormentor)

If we are ever going to move from a time-management view of our limitations to a theological one, we need to reconnect creation with re-creation, Genesis 1 with John 1. Imagine a baby not more than twenty pounds and crawling around on the floor. A real baby. Not the sentimentalized babe in a manger that has no more substance than the Easter bunny. A real peeing, pooping, nursing, squalling, melt-your-heart baby boy. And then try to imagine that this little one is also none other than the Word who is God. How is that possible? And why would God do that? Become that? The answer is simple.

Love.

God loves his world. In Jesus, God incarnate (*en*-fleshed), we encounter God's resounding *Yes!* to his creation. Taking on physicality as a genuine baby, the Word of God takes us back to Genesis and forward to the new creation. The fact that the Son became incarnate in Mary's womb and grew to a man reminds us that our bodies and this world were made for good. Sarcastically Tertullian cries out, "Remove the flesh and bring forward the one whom God redeemed," knowing that you cannot so separate these things. "Will you render what he redeemed shameful to him?"[30] If we are ashamed of our bodies, of our physicality and finitude, we are in danger of being ashamed of our Creator. But God is not ashamed of our physicality. Why are we ashamed of what he freely loves?

To confuse finitude with sinfulness by rejecting our physicality is a denial that to be a creature is a good thing. If we seek to be freed from the mundane and ordinary in order to focus on the spiritual, we are refusing the concrete path of obedience that God has set before us.

I think that behind some of our misconceptions of godliness and Christian living there lurks a deep uneasiness with the fact that we are creatures. To refute Marcion and others who imagined the material world as embarrassing to God, Tertullian takes us back to Jesus's birth, to the necessary fleshiness of our creaturely humanity. "If Christ belongs to the Creator, then it was his own creation he loved—rightly."[31] Here is God's great *Yes!* to his creation, even his fallen creation. Rather than turn from it, rather than reject its existence, the Son of God is sent by the Father and empowered in the Spirit to enter into it, becoming human, with full physicality and creaturely need. Tertullian picks up the argument: "He restores our flesh so that it is free from trouble; he cleanses it when leprous, gives sight to it when blind, heals it when paralyzed, purifies it when it is demon-possessed, raises it when it has died. Does he then blush to be born in it?"[32]

God's concern is not to erase or destroy our humanity, but to renew it. Human flourishing comes not in the absence of our creaturely limits but in the healthy wholeness of them.

The Beginning, Jesus, and Embracing Finitude

We began this chapter with a story of a campfire recitation, where a young Jewish boy listened carefully, comparing Genesis with the beginning of John's Gospel. It is time to close the loop.

In Matthew's Gospel we hear another apostle open his narrative by harking back to the beginning. Whereas John used the word *archē* for "beginning" (John 1:1; cf. Gen. 1:1 in the Septuagint, the Greek translation of the Old Testament), Matthew employs another word to convey a similar idea, but this one will be immediately familiar to most contemporary

Bible readers. Matthew picks the Greek word *genesis*—meaning "source" or "origin"—in his opening sentence. Notice the movement:

- In the beginning [*archē*] God (Gen. 1:1 Septuagint)
- In the beginning [*archē*] the Word (John 1:1)
- An account of the beginning/genealogy [i.e., *geneseōs*; this is a form of the word *genesis*] of Jesus the Messiah (Matt. 1:1)
- Now the beginning/birth [i.e., *geneseōs*] of Jesus the Messiah (Matt. 1:18)

What is Matthew doing? We may find genealogies to be boring, but this one reveals the author's purpose. Matthew here alludes to the Septuagint translation of Genesis 5:1—specifically, the "book of the generations [*hē biblos geneseōs*] of Adam," which in turn echoes "the generations of the heavens and the earth when they were created" (Gen. 2:4). Matthew presents Jesus as the fulfillment of God's promises to and presence with his people, from Abraham to the exile, from the post-Babylonian period to the early first century. After mapping out a genealogy claiming that Jesus is the culmination of promises and time, the mystery that was previously hidden, Matthew then continues with his particular version of the story.[33]

God is the Creator. Everything that is not God falls into the category "creation." This includes plants and spiders, Neptune and Saturn, oxygen and humans. All that is not God, however, points to God as the Creator and Sustainer of all things. God alone has no origin, no beginning. He is the eternal One: all things are from him, through him, and to him (Rom. 11:36).

It is true that this created world has been compromised, causing rupture, disorder, and disharmony. This disruption affects all our relationships, from communion with God to fellowship with others, from our cancer-infected bodies to our distorted connection to the earth. Because of that disruption, we also misunderstand the creation by confusing created limits with sinfulness. This can lead us, like Marcion, to pit the Creator against the Redeemer, furthering our misunderstanding of God and his purposes for his creation and for us in it.

Part of the remedy for that mistake is to renew our grasp of the connections between the original "beginning" in creation and the "new beginning" in redemption. God in Christ demonstrates his love for his world. He loves it so much that through a particular and unique act of the triune God, the eternal Son of God "became flesh and dwelt among us" (John 1:14). God, who has no DNA, no genetic parentage, humbled himself through the Son, who considered equality with God not a thing to be grasped, but instead became human (Phil. 2). Basil of Caesarea put it this way: the Son became genuinely human, just as Adam was originally created; otherwise, "we who died in Adam would not have been made alive in Christ. . . . And what need was there of the Holy Virgin, if the God-bearing flesh was not to be assumed from the material from which Adam was molded?"[34]

By this you know the Spirit of God: every spirit that confesses that Jesus Christ has come in the flesh is from God.

1 John 4:2

Strangely, without ceasing to be divine, the Son assumes a genuine human nature. He doesn't pick between the divine and human. Wrapped in finitude—within the limits of the creaturely experience—the Son paradoxically comes as the divine embrace of the creation. He comes to draw near and renew. In this coming we discover the heart of God. And his coming links human flourishing to our creaturely limits.

Although our culture still has traces of Gnosticism in it, for the most part it accepts and celebrates our physicality—indeed, to the point of ignoring spiritual matters. We complain less often about having a body generally than we do about having *this* particular body. The next chapter looks at this issue, calling us to honor each human body by rejecting abuses on the one hand and encouraging physical engagement in worship on the other.

4

why does physical touch matter?

images, trauma, and embodied worship

I am not here, touch me . . . that I may be here.

Samuel Taylor Coleridge

We are human creatures made to relate to God, our neighbors, and even the earth in and through our physicality. This is not a consequence of sin but God's good design for us. Space and time are the arena of our physicality, especially enabling us to be present to each other. Consequently, we need to be touched, both physically and spiritually, and this need goes well beyond sexuality to an expression of trust and affirmation.

Pretending the Body Doesn't Matter

How we view ourselves and others is inseparable from how we perceive our bodies. Our flesh is not an insignificant, disposable container carrying an internal spirit, although we are sometimes tempted to see the body as unimportant and only the soul as valuable. All of us, from athletes to quadriplegics, are embodied creatures located in real time and space: we are here and not there, this body and not that one. Computer technology, because it tends to engage the mind rather than the whole body, may allow us to hide behind avatars, but in real life we cannot escape our actual sweat glands, digestive tract, or nervous system.

You may have heard about video game centers in Korea that never close. Apparently, some young people come and stay for days until the business is eventually forced to kick them out because they smell so bad. Lost in their digital worlds, they still inhabit the chair they are sitting in, producing odors and body waste, whether they want to acknowledge it or not. Ignoring your body and pretending it is "not you" normally has detrimental effects on both you and others.

Occasionally one hears the saying, "You don't have a soul. You are a soul. You have a body." Although it is sometimes attributed to C. S. Lewis, he never said it. The idea behind it, as the Lutheran writer Mathew Block argues, often supports a "Spiritualist" rather than "Christian Framework,"[1] and, as we saw in the previous chapter, it's just another reappearance of the Marcionite/Gnostic heresy. We can't separate ourselves from our bodies because we do not exist as bodiless selves but as both body and soul.[2]

The recent comedy *The Upside* features a brilliant and wealthy quadriplegic, Philip (played by Bryan Cranston), who misses his deceased wife and is racked with loneliness and guilt. He develops a correspondence with Lily, who lives in another part of the country, exchanging letters, poems, and kindnesses. Philip has never heard Lily's voice, let alone seen her—they merely share exchanges of beautiful words on the page. Eventually, Philip works up the courage to meet her at a restaurant. Aware of his condition, she researches it and feels prepared for the encounter. But by the end of the meal with this man who cannot move his arms and needs constant help, she hesitates. This personal encounter with his many disabilities overwhelms her, and she simply cannot—or will not—accept it, thus realizing all his fears: the relationship was better in writing because he could abstract it from his body, his vulnerability, and his dependence on others. Her hesitation to accept his physical condition is, despite her protests, a rejection of *him*, filling him with a mixture of anger, confusion, and despair.

We all want to be loved. Not the *idea* of us, not simply words about or by us, but we, in our totality, need to be welcomed, known, and loved. Under normal conditions, we experience this holistic love through touch and communication, both of which are vital to our humanity.

Admittedly, Philip's paralysis points to a fundamental brokenness in the world (this is *not* how it is supposed to be), but everyday human vulnerability and dependence do not (this *is* how it is supposed to be). The countless needs of all human bodies are intentional design elements to the way we were made—not to be independent loners, but connected to each other in a web of interdependence and relationships; not ghostly, disembodied souls, but dust-derived, spirit-breathed creatures. And this is good! Our physicality opens us up to interactions with each other and with the world around us. And even the limitations of that physicality become elements of our creativity. Being human has always been an embodied state, and that has always been a good, not a bad, thing.

Even dependence, contrary to the individualist philosophy of our culture, is part of the blessing of human existence. The first creation account (Gen. 1) describes the entire material world as "good," but the second account (Gen. 2) examines the creation of humanity in two parts. When it considers Adam as a creature to himself, "alone," the text declares this "*not* good" (2:18). Adam's body is not bad; his aloneness is the problem. So God responds by bringing Adam another like him, another who bears a body like his, but different—not the *idea* of another, but the bodily presence of Eve. Adam experiences the goodness of creation when he connects his dependence with this other. We are designed for communion with each other, and our physicality supplies a medium for that communion. This communion itself exemplifies a kind of need: for God, our neighbors, and the earth. Genesis shows that physicality and its corresponding needs are not a flaw but a good element of God's original design. The sin and brokenness in the world, however, have twisted and undermined that goodness and made us vulnerable to the manipulation of others.

Consequently, we live in an insecure space between needing others and fearing that they won't accept us. This drives us to pretend we don't need them, but our attempts at self-sufficiency deny the relational nature of our core being. As we will see, even our purchasing habits and body issues support this.

So in order to understand our fundamental bodily need for one another, we must explore the question "Who are we?"

Suggested answers to this question that ignore our bodies are neither realistic nor Christian. Lilian Calles Barger reflects on our quickness to believe that we are *not* our bodies: we look into the mirror and think to ourselves,

"This isn't who I am."[3] A truly Christian spirituality must always also be a *body-affirming* spirituality. As Barger explains, Christian spirituality "must provide freedom—not from the body, but to imagine what is possible even within the body's limitations." Whether one believes or rejects Christian faith, spiritual practices always involve bodily practices. "My actions and work in the world are done through and in my body; the truest test of what I profess to be. What we need is a spirituality that honors the body we have and comprehends its social meaning but does not reduce us to it."[4] And yet we are not always comfortable with our physicality, are we?

> Though touch should be important for everyone, its importance should be especially clear for believers because our God made a touchable, material world. And he made humans within that world with five senses to purposefully engage it.
>
> Lore Ferguson Wilbert, *Handle with Care*

Christians, especially conservative Christians, are often accused of hating their bodies.[5] Such accusations are often made in the context of discussions about sexuality.[6] But let's not kid ourselves: in contemporary America there is plenty of reason to recognize that we *all* are tempted to have unhealthy views of our bodily existence. Bodies are treated as merely instrumental, which breeds a fair number of conflicting approaches to human physicality. We must examine this phenomenon more closely, for what we think about our bodies shapes our view of spirituality, including our discomfort with our creaturely limits. This can distort our internal views of ourselves, thus allowing our external relationships to be manipulated harmfully. Add to this the abundance of marketing that plays on our latent insecurities with our bodies, and the destruction multiplies.

Ideal Images or Real Bodies?

In the early 1970s the average American saw about five hundred advertising images a day; now we encounter about five thousand a day (although few of us believe it).[7] We are inundated with commercials intended to stir desires and provoke us to buy cosmetics and clothing, burgers and beer, all to keep our economy going. The product is often tied to a particular body image, almost always young and seductive; rarely—despite occasional efforts by some companies—does it foster healthy views of the self or others. Whether an advertisement is aspirational (e.g., gym membership) or blandly practical (vacuum cleaners), some form of judgment is almost always implied: "You could do more"; "You ought to be better." Whatever the current version, each judgment has the shared implication: "You are not enough." The product or program offers at least part of the solution: "This will help you become whole." These implicit messages occupy so much of the air we breathe that we rarely notice how we are manipulated and affected by our immersion in it. How we view our bodies—*ourselves!*—becomes deeply affected, distorted, and hurt.

These efforts at grabbing our attention tempt us to imagine that the normal rules of life don't apply to us: "Sure, I can eat this two-thousand-calorie dinner and it won't be a problem," or, "With this product I can instantly have ripped abs and tight muscle tone." We don't want to be told that our bodies can digest only so much food without uncomfortable consequences. When ice cream is available, it doesn't matter how much I have already eaten, I'm taking it! And, (*not!*) surprisingly, the pounds don't just melt away, so I loosen the belt instead. But my body, mind, affections, and will are all wrapped up together in these motions and movements. A healthy diet says, "This much and no more," but I don't always listen. Proverbs warns that too much of a *good* thing causes our bodies to react: "If you find honey, eat just enough—too much of it, and you will vomit" (Prov. 25:16 NIV).

We live within a strange incongruity: On the one hand, we hear strident voices saying that human bodies matter, maybe they are *all* that matter. Yet the bodies on our screens and billboards are usually well under thirty, tight skinned, and with a perfect complexion—even when they are presented as grungy. They rarely look like most of "us"—the viewers who are absorbing the images. Add to that the fact that the image (whether of a man or a woman) is almost always sexualized, whether the model has juice from a burger running down her lips or he is in the middle of a tire commercial flirting with the viewer. In our cultural moment in the West, bodies are almost always reduced to sexuality. Is this how I am supposed to see myself, how I am to relate to others? But many of us sense a huge problem with this reductionist view. We are sexual creatures, no doubt about it! But are our sexual urges the full story of our body's importance? To raise such a question doesn't require us to hate our bodies, does it?

Given our shared obsession with culturally defined beautiful bodies in advertisements and entertainment, there's no way a critic can accuse American culture of being squeamish about the human body, right? Aren't the people who raise such questions simply to be dismissed as "puritanical"? And yet, even among the irreligious and those who have never heard of the Puritans, there is plenty of evidence of widespread embarrassment and unease with our own bodies. I'm too tall or short, too round or skinny, too dark or pale, too . . .

I remember talking to Tabitha (my wife) after walking through an airport lined with massive, sexualized ads for everything from vodka to watches. She told me how sorry she felt for the models plastered on the walls and on the front of the magazines. *What?* I didn't get it at first. Her point: none of us, including the models, are safe from the insidious self-condemnation such imagery tends to foster. As we walk through the airport (or mall, or flip through the latest ads on Facebook) we are shown uncountable images of stunningly beautiful people, which doesn't tend to make any of us feel better about our actual bodies . . . *about ourselves*. Tabitha's keen observation, however, was about a cruel unspoken reality: What happens when you are the model in those ads, walking through the same airport, and you see images of "yourself"? Sure, in many ways it is flattering and makes you feel fantastic; but even the model who sees herself there knows she doesn't actually look like the picture in front of her—it isn't even *her*! Advertisers employ airbrushes and digital manipulation, erasing small bruises on the skin, narrowing thighs, enhancing chests, elongating necks, thickening hair, and . . . Even the laughing model in the blown-up picture experiences the judgment of the image. Recently, Dove Soap produced four short videos that soberly show just how much manipulation occurs in the images we see, creating unhealthy expectations that help cultivate deep dissatisfaction with our bodies.[8]

Should we really be surprised that some actresses and models have started to raise objections about how unrealistic the alterations have become?[9] They can see and feel the damage this myth building does. Subtly but powerfully it depreciates their real physical bodies and seduces the watching public into greater discomfort with their own bodies. Is it any surprise that we have an epidemic of people dealing with body-image issues? Do you and I have a healthy view of our bodies?

Bodies, we are tempted to believe, must constantly be manipulated and always ready for the judgment of public viewing. The natural process of bodily change in the experience of aging is something we are now constantly told we must fight and overcome. One article confidently proclaims, "Fifty is the new thirty."[10] Postpartum women face endless ads to get their pre-pregnancy bodies back, often through surgery, so they will show no signs of change. Might this not underestimate the power and significance of giving birth and creating new flesh out of your very own body? We want to erase the marks of real humanity and change from our bodies to fit a societal image of perfection and flawlessness—again, almost always idealizing youth. Continued unrealistic expectations often breed toxic comparative impulses and insecurities that tend to pit us against one another, rather than uniting us. This is, as we will see, a sign of discomfort with our human particularity, which always implies having these lips and not those, this shape and not that one. As a result, our own self-image and our relationships suffer.[11]

Not Just a Female Struggle

It usually doesn't take much to convince people that women are often viewed merely as sexualized objects and that this produces huge personal and social problems for them, depersonalizing and overwhelming them with unrealistic expectations. But recent research shows that men are increasingly presented as sexualized objects and are beginning to feel the pressures that have historically been the burden of women.[12] Historian Lynne Luciano, for example, describes the evolution over the last seventy years of American perceptions of the male body. From the "organizational man" in the 1950s to the quest for self-discovery in the '60s, giving way to the narcissism of the '70s and the "bingeing and buffing" movements of the '80s, each period changed what we expect of the male body. Luciano writes that, by the 1990s, men began to sense their new predicament: "Baby boomers were discovering unexpected—and unpleasant—limitations to the benefits of working out. No amount of jogging could indefinitely fend off the effects of aging; getting lean and muscular became harder with each passing year. Even exercise had a negative aspect: as flabby businessmen shed excess pounds sweating in health clubs, sudden weight loss left lean bodies festooned with loose, sagging skin and toned torsos at odds with tired, aging faces."[13] In other words, it was not just the slothful who were tempted to dislike their bodies, but even the most physically active.

So, what are we to do? Cultural shifts have prompted an explosion of male cosmetic surgery and "improvements," with everything from liposuction to hair transplants, from penis enlargement devices to Viagra. Medical promises of renewed youth held out new hope and became hugely popular.[14] Ample evidence has shown that, contrary to popular imagination, such optional cosmetic interventions are of interest not only to women. While the stereotype is that men are more comfortable with their bodies than women, there is growing evidence that negative body-image issues affect them, too. Ironically, it appears some have started to believe that public objectification of the male figure is a sign of progress.[15] Instead of liberation, however, we find that "male body dissatisfaction" is spiking among those who internalize sociocultural ideals of the male body, giving this group a rough equivalent to female dissatisfaction with their bodies.[16] Rather than correcting the degrading objectification of women, which seems to be a never-ending battle, we have apparently decided we should just give men the same treatment. This way we can all grow in our insecurity together! Luciano affirms that the tensions have only intensified in more recent years.

As a result, we now reduce *both* men and women to objects of desire or repulsion, rather than treating them as whole human beings who have dignity and worth. At the risk of sounding like a grumpy old man (which I am not, at least I'm not *that* old!), I find it strange—but no longer surprising—that, while prominent voices in the entertainment industry and others bemoan rampant sexism (a *very* legitimate concern!), this same business as a whole continues to promote unrealistic physical stereotypes and an objectification that feeds the problem rather than fights it. Instead of honoring the whole human person, it exalts artificial and digitally manufactured images. They produce and promote an artificial and distorted cultural ideal rather than a realistic and healthy view of actual earthly flesh and blood.

Affirming the Person in Front of You

So who am I? How should I relate to you?

We must resist the temptation either to disparage people's bodies or to idealize them: the former action undermines the goodness of our creatureliness, while the latter increases our distance from the real people in front of us.[17] Similarly, we must reject the trendy narrative that tells us that our sexual desires are the most important thing about us, just as we should reject the claim that our sexuality is inherently evil. Obviously, the land mines are everywhere in this area, but my main goal is simply to help us recognize our discomfort with our physicality: we need to affirm what God has called good. Our bodies and their inherent limits are a good gift from a good Creator.

We can always improve, always look better, can't we? And that's not all bad. Faithfully caring for our bodies is good. But we need to ask what underlies many of these desires. Except when speaking to tweens and teenagers, we tend not to use the language of "acceptance," but all of us, regardless of age, struggle to feel comfortable in our literal skin. We want to belong, to be welcomed, to be accepted, to be smiled at. Does our instinct to suck in our guts and avoid shirts with horizontal stripes point to insecurities we have with our bodies? Our problem is not just what others think of us but what we think of ourselves. We must come to terms with our physicality and with our particular, respective versions of it. Maybe this will provoke some of us to eat less, some of us to eat more. But all bodies need food and friends, for without the acceptance of others, both body and soul begin to wither.

A healthy view of our bodies appreciates the real, the particular, and the commonplace. We are called to affirm our creaturely existence in its distinctiveness, seeing it as a blessing rather than a curse. As we will explore more in later chapters, our bodies both unite us to the whole of humanity and are crucial to our particularity. They are not meant for shame but for freedom, health, and faithfulness.

> For though we aren't our bodies, yet of nothing on earth do we have more intimate possession than these. Only through these do we dwell here.
>
> Nicholas Wolterstorff, *Lament for a Son*

Again, who am I? Who are you? To know me is to know the physical person standing in front of you; it is to listen to the sound of my voice as it moves the tiny bones in your ear canal so you hear and recognize my tone. Our bodies both distinguish us and allow us to come together.

At the core of this Christian vision is a particular human being, a first-century Jewish man, the son of Mary. The final Adam. Here was a man who knew the realities of time and space pushing against his body. Here was a vulnerable baby, a prepubescent adolescent, a developing teenager, a hammer-holding young adult, and eventually an animated teacher. Here was a sinless one, Jesus of Nazareth, born and dwelling in real time and space, with fingers, knees, and taste buds. Here was a man with a real body, real restrictions, real curves, and real birthmarks. He knew and related to other humans through the physical space-time medium of their bodily presence.

In this way, he didn't negate their humanity but instead affirmed their physicality, healed them, and in the process restored relationships.

We will return to our consideration of Christ's earthly ministry, but let's talk first about contemporary worship gatherings and some basic ways that the church can address our physicality.

Embodied Worship?

Standing next to the soccer field with little kids jumping around—it would be a stretch to say "running"—I had a great conversation with a friend who is an accomplished physician. She had grown up in the church and continued there as an adult believer, and so she is deeply aware of both the strengths of church culture and its weaknesses. This has given her insightful questions and some sense of uneasiness. In our conversation she decided to be open with me about her experience: "To be honest, in recent years, I have often felt like my time in a yoga class has been more meaningful to me than going to church. I don't know, the bodily experiences there often just resonate with me in a way I rarely experience at church." As the sun was shining on this cool, crisp morning, her comments prompted my curiosity. I kept asking questions and listening: under the particulars of her story was an observation that I have discovered is a fairly common challenge for folks, including myself.

Put succinctly, at church she felt as if she was reduced to a brain on a stick, simply there to receive information. Sit, listen, take notes, and then go home ready to try harder for another week. She felt that her yoga class treated her as a whole person, engaging her body, mind, and will. Often, she found quiet and reflection more valued in her stretching sessions than they were in the sacred space of the holy church. Conversations like this made me wonder how we have lost sight of the importance of our physical presence in worship.

When a church service feels more like attending a lecture than being physically present in worship before the triune God, should it really surprise us that we feel somehow disconnected? I'm a Presbyterian, and we love lectures; we tend to attract ministers and members who place great emphasis on the intellect—it is one of the great gifts of the tradition. We are—or so we suppose—a *reasonable* people. Yet this inclination is also one of the great dangers in our history. In our appreciation of the mind, we often can end up (unintentionally?) acting as if our minds are *all* that matter. This partiality distorts our view of God, ourselves, and life in this world.

Take corporate worship for example. Have you ever noticed how much of the biblical material that is associated with the gathering of God's people and worship emphasizes our physicality: eat the bread (1 Cor. 11:23–24), drink the wine (11:25–26), clap your hands (Ps. 47:1), lift them in prayer (1 Tim. 2:8), fill your lungs and cry out to God (Ps. 95:1–2), bow down and kneel (95:6), anoint with oil (James 5:14), and baptize with water (e.g., Matt. 3:11)? Worship in the Bible engages all five senses: see, touch, smell, taste, and hear. This cannot be fully experienced by sitting on the couch in front of a TV or listening to a podcast. Sure, in some cases, especially among the sick and homebound, television and podcasts are a genuine gift. But whether we think of the 1970s trend of "drive-in church services" or claims that one can worship God just as well alone on a ski slope, these play into the individualistic errors of our culture and deny the vision of worship presented in the Old and New Testaments.

When COVID-19 spread throughout the world, including in America, Christian congregations were not allowed to physically gather together. All of a sudden the embodiment that serves to ground our worship services was missing, and we could feel it. Streaming services or video small groups were better than nothing, but they were a far cry from hugging, singing, shaking hands, and sitting close to one another. Persecuted sisters and brothers around the world have long known the less-than-ideal nature of such gatherings, since they have often been dependent on digital resources that allow fellowship even when they cannot physically be together. In Saudi Arabia, for example, believers have long praised God for broadcast services on the radio and now the internet making connections even more possible, but their deeper hope and yearning has always been for a time when they can, without fear or hesitation, warmly embrace other believers *in the flesh*.[18] Let us not naively romanticize a believer sitting alone in their bedroom quietly listening to a worship service on the radio. Praise God they are receiving some nourishment, but their body and soul rightly long for more! Physical encounters are powerful for all humanity, and the Christian life gives those bodily connections even deeper significance. Those of us who live in lands that honor religious liberty too easily forget the value of connecting our bodies and worship.

When we gather for worship, we—our physical selves—engage each other to receive strength, to meet each other, to meet Jesus, and to be sent out into the world renewed in God's presence, love, and healing grace. But notice, God's love is framed in terms of gathering many people, not just an individual. As Paul declares, "So in Christ we, though many, form one body, and each member belongs to all the others" (Rom. 12:5 NIV). Our bodies come together to make one body, and here, in response to the forgiveness and enlivening grace of God, we are given acceptance, courage, and hope. We feast on the bread and wine, the body and blood of Christ: these embodied realities affect us to our gut. Jesus as the bread of life and the living water reminds us of our absolute dependence on him and our continuing reliance on the body of Christ. We were created with dependency in mind, but we think maturity looks like independence. Dependent on his body and blood, all believers are united in Christ: not just spiritually, but physically. Our corporate worship time together changes us, and part of the way we are changed is through the way the church treats our physicality.

The Holy Kiss

Greeting one another with a "holy kiss" or a "kiss of love" appears as a command surprisingly often in the New Testament (Rom. 16:16; 1 Cor. 16:20; 2 Cor. 13:12; 1 Thess. 5:26; 1 Pet. 5:14). Uninformed outsiders who heard this kind of language emerging from the ancient church accused believers of orgies and sexual misconduct.[19] Rather than yield to this kind of misrepresentation, believers kept this affectionate gesture—beyond the immediate family—as a strong (physical!) mark of Christian unity and love. Former strangers now treated one another as brothers and sisters.

What God joins together let no sociocultural pressures divide: rich and poor, Greek and non-Greek, male and female, young and old, slave and free—all assembled together as the new family of God (Rom. 3:29; Col. 3:11). Hugs and kisses are welcomed and expected in a healthy family. Just as family members embrace one another while saying goodbye to departing relatives after a holiday feast, so the ancient church believed that corporate prayers should sometimes end with a kiss that "sealed the prayer" in Christian unity.[20] Tertullian, for example, warns of those who have started to "withhold the kiss of peace (which is the seal of [corporate] prayer). . . . What prayer is complete if separated from the holy kiss?"[21] Worship and prayers were not simply the exercises of isolated individuals but the acts of physical human creatures who came together to worship. Similarly, by the eighth century when the divine liturgy was celebrated in Constantinople in the great Hagia Sophia, "the holy kiss was initiated immediately before reciting the creed," when congregants were called to a shared belief and to love each other, sealed by this kiss of peace.[22] Faith and practice, spirit and body, all affirmed and united before Lord and neighbor.

Given the possibility of abuse, however, the church also issued warnings about not exploiting or misapplying this intimate gesture.[23] So, for example, even when it was still largely considered important, the *Apostolic Constitutions* (ca. AD 390) called for "the Lord's kiss" to be divided by the sexes (women to women, men to men), as a way of protecting against any inappropriate misuse of this custom.[24] Although aware of the dangers and seeking to address them, the ancient church still sought to affirm physical embrace and warm hospitality, all with integrity and dignity. In reaction against the widespread physical exploitation of underclasses by the powerful, the early church stood out as a refuge for women and the poor: they knew the church to be a place where they were welcomed and treated on equal level with all the other believers instead of being exploited (cf. James 2:1–9). This precaution did not ignore their bodies, their particularity, but instead affirmed their physical nature and needs. Believing the church to be a space where they could experience the mutual dependence and love in moments of shalom characteristic of the original Eden, believers expectantly gathered together for worship. Historians observe how the unifying expression of embrace and shared dignity was a crucial part of the church's explosive growth in its early centuries.[25]

> But to love oneself in the divine sense is to love God, and truly to love another person is to help that person to love God or in loving God.
>
> Søren Kierkegaard, *Works of Love*

For me and others like me, one of the least enjoyable parts of our Sunday morning service is the time for greeting one another. Most introverts feel like crawling under the nearest pew during this awkward exchange. And yet, as uncomfortable as it often makes me feel, physical interactions like this are necessary for grounding our worship: we touch hands, give hugs, pat kids on the head, kiss babies, look each other in the eye, and exchange the "peace of the Lord." This is as close as we often get to the "kiss of peace." The church is not a gathering of spirits, but the congregation of humans with bodies. These gestures can seem silly or unnecessary, but I can assure you, they are most definitely not silly. Whether we realize it or not, they connect our embodiment, and therefore our full selves, to this context of worship. They help integrate our lives and protect us from unhealthy divisions between body and soul, between the physical and spiritual, between creation and redemption. Short and tall, slender and robust, old and young, clever and simple, all are brought together and treated as one body in Christ through embrace, acceptance, and dignified love. This action tells us, at a visceral level, that our bodies are important and loved, that we are important and loved, that neither our bodies nor our whole selves can be reduced to sexuality or any other single appetite; rather, our whole selves are welcomed, loved, and then sent out renewed in the peace of the Lord.

Longing for Embrace

Do you know one of the main things my students will miss most when they graduate from college? It's not the cafeteria food or endless homework. It is something they probably don't even know they currently enjoy every day: physical touch!

It is fairly common to see college students happily squish tightly next to a friend on a sofa, lay their heads on one another, fall laughingly into each other's arms, or playfully wrestle on the grass. Physical touch is expected and normal. Every day! Girls and guys—this is not divided by sex. I clearly don't want to universalize, since divergent personalities even on college campuses handle these situations differently. Yet, whether introverts or extroverts, whether they have one or ten good friends, these physical expressions are regularly witnessed and experienced almost daily, especially when the community resists sexualizing any and all touch (which, admittedly, is getting rarer and rarer, not only on Western college campuses).

But more often than not, when students leave college, the daily physical contact dries up. They didn't even realize how often they enjoyed an embrace, a subtle affirming touch, the physical presence of another. Hearing a roommate's loud breathing while they sleep was sometimes annoying at the time, but now the silence creates an unexpected yearning when one sits alone in an empty apartment. It is *not* good for us to be alone. This problem is made worse in our culture when it tells people they are not really "grown-ups" until they live *alone*—a perspective Christians should at least raise questions about. Graduates sometimes tell me that the year or so between graduation and establishing a new community can be an unexpectedly isolating and painful season. And it has really struck me how often their narratives express the loss and longing for physical touch. More than once I have heard a single person describe the awful realization that it had been days, or weeks, and sometimes even months since they had any healthy physical touch. It unnerves them, especially those who didn't even realize they needed such physical affirmation.

Appropriate (!) physical touch is crucial to human wholeness. Our bodies are meant to establish, sustain, and encourage mutual relationships. Pope John Paul II has argued that the Genesis account of creation presents our bodies as both a gift and a calling: humans are made from the dust and connected to the rest of creation, but the human person is also distinguished from other living beings (Latin: *animalia*). Although Adam could have been led to see the many commonalities between himself and other animals, which could have fostered some sense of belonging, instead, he "reached the conviction that he was 'alone.'"[26] Strange, isn't it? *Alone?* He is not alone; he has the animals with him, the trees and fruit; he even has God. Yet he comes to see himself as *alone*.[27] John Paul II argued that this "original solitude with the awareness of the body" distinguishes the human creature from other creatures, that it is essential to one's self-understanding as a person.[28]

Each of us was made for communion with others like us, and without it we experience the isolation and solitude that easily breed loneliness and despair. "It is not good for the Adam to be alone" (Gen. 2:18 [my translation], where "Adam" is used not simply as a name but also to denote a member of the human race—almost like "earthling"). So, God moved "the Adam" from solitude and isolation into companionship, from one to two: Adam and Eve. Even more fundamental than sexual differentiation is the human need for other humans, which is never less than the physical presence of other people. There is a reason that many consider solitary confinement as a form of torture, while others now engage in "cuddle parties" in order to address this unmet need.[29]

Trauma and Touch

Expressions of love invariably include physical presence, touch, and care. When people have gone through traumatic experiences, renowned psychologist Bessel van der Kolk explains, "the most natural way that we humans calm down our distress is by being touched, hugged, and rocked."[30] This points to something primal in us—not to a flaw, but to the good work of our Creator Lord. We were made for mutual embrace. Sadly, in our fallen world, which is afflicted with the twisting effects of sin, these creaturely needs can be co-opted and betrayed. For example, when clergy act in evil ways and abuse the bodies of their congregants, it is devastating on multiple levels. The consequences are catastrophic for how the wounded then relate to God and to other humans. But when we don't appreciate the importance of our physicality, we underestimate just how significant these betrayals can be.

John Howard Yoder, for example, was a brilliant Mennonite theologian and widely published ethicist, most known for his book *The Politics of Jesus*. In his writings, filled with insightful cultural criticism and biblical application, he called the church to live in a way that reflected their belief that Jesus, not Caesar, is really the King. And yet, despite his learning and apparent wisdom, he had a frightening dark side. Because it was so hard to believe, many appeared to ignore the signs and eventual accusations that surfaced against him. Yoder, who focused on a "theology of peace," understood the human condition, which he knew meant that we must take our physicality seriously. Despite this, we now have a fair amount of evidence that he appears to have abused that insight with vulnerable sisters in Christ. Before Yoder died, he was accused by at least eight different women of pressuring them to engage in inappropriate intimate contact and even groping. There is some evidence that the numbers are much larger than that.[31] If the testimonies are true (which is not widely doubted now), he was abusing what he knew to be true: relationships are inseparable from our bodies, and physical touch can be an important part of our healing and flourishing. That makes it all the more wicked when someone like this takes such an observation and uses it for evil manipulation and sexual self-gratification.

Even more recently new investigations have sadly raised serious questions along similar lines about the founder of L'Arche, Jean Vanier. Again, significant evidence has emerged that he manipulated his position to sexually abuse at least six women.[32] And even as I am making final revisions to this manuscript as we prepare it for publication, it has become abundantly clear that the famed Christian apologist Ravi Zacharias had long been mistreating women and abusing his powerful position.[33]

Part of the painful recognition here is how the inherent spiritual-physical connection of worship can be co-opted for evil; when those in positions of power use God's design of human creatures for their own self-satisfaction, the church must unequivocally and clearly condemn the abuse and protect the victims. But we must resist the temptation to imagine all touch is bad. God has made us for physical touch. Physicality isn't the problem; the perversion and inappropriateness of abuse is the problem. Quality child protection policies and thoughtful community accountability can and must help protect the community so that healthy and God-honoring practices can occur among the people of God.

Recent decades have revealed painful abuse throughout our ecclesial communities, from the Roman Catholic Church to every denomination in the Protestant world. It is devastating how our churches are littered with a history of physical and nonphysical abuse, sexual and otherwise. These instances of abuse are not only deviations from God's good gift of physical touch and care but a rejection of God-given limits on us and of the dignity of the victim, who was never made to be abused in these ways. Whether by cruel punches, violent words, or unwanted touches, the abuser is functionally assuming a power and control over another person that was never meant for them. By wickedly rejecting the divinely given good restraints of our holy Creator, abusers are not only hurting others; they are also deforming themselves.

But the answer is not to rule out all physical contact, any more than our history of verbal abuse should push us to complete silence.[34] The only thoroughly realistic response here is to look to the one perfect man, not only for answers, but for life.

The Touch of Jesus

Jesus was so different. He did not hesitate to welcome, to touch, to greet others as if he belonged to them. Having been given all authority in heaven and earth, he knew that true authority is always tied to service and not domination, so he never used his authority, his power, or his presence to dominate but instead to serve the needy. In a historical context in which women and children had few protections and were systematically treated as lesser—not even among those who are "counted" (e.g., Matt. 14:21; 15:38)—their consistent presence during Jesus's ministry speaks volumes.

There is good reason for the Gospels to highlight that not just men but women followed Jesus in the worst of times (e.g., Luke 23:27, 49). Cultural barriers and negative expectations commonly circulated about women in first-century Israel, but the Gospels reflect Jesus's affirmative perspective toward his female contemporaries, which ended up being crucial for the early church.[35] Rather than just meeting generic "women," in the Gospels we encounter specific names: Mary, Joanna, and Susanna, for example, proved vital to Jesus's ministry (8:1–3). Women were the ones who watched his body laid in the tomb (23:55) and then prepared to return with burial spices to honor his dead body (23:56–24:1). *He honored their bodies, and they wanted to honor his.* Even though the testimony of women was not considered legitimate in the law courts of first-century Israel, the first Gospel accounts of Jesus's bodily resurrection were given by women, not men (24:2–11).[36]

Jesus does not belittle or ignore women and children (Mark 9:33–37), nor does he dominate, manipulate, or abuse them. Instead, he loves them. His presence—his *body*—was never a threat to them, but instead a comfort. "He took [the children] in his arms and blessed them, laying his hands on them" (10:16). Augustine picks up on this story in Luke's Gospel (Luke 18:15–17), noticing that Jesus's reaction to the children is told immediately after Jesus warns of the arrogant Pharisee and praises a needy tax collector (18:9–14): one thought he was complete and righteous before God (Pharisee), while the other recognized his sin and need before the Holy One (tax collector). But what is the connection to the children? Augustine writes, "Here are the babies coming along, or rather being brought and held up to be touched."[37] Touched by whom? The "doctor" and the "savior." "Let the Lord bless the little ones together with the great, let the doctor touch both the little ones and the great."[38] The children make no pretense about being complete and needing nothing from God or others. Instead, they embody need and interdependence in all its forms. No one sees infants as independent: we and they know they need others. But somehow as we grow older we are tempted to deny this interdependence—and this denial contributes to the making of a Pharisee. Augustine presents the touch of Jesus as an affirmation, a blessing, a sign

> Jesus' healings are not supernatural miracles in a natural world. They are the only truly "natural" thing in a world that is unnatural, demonized, and wounded.
>
> Jürgen Moltmann, *The Way of Jesus Christ*

of grace extended to the *dependent* rather than those who live within the myth of self-sufficiency.

Jesus welcomes those on the margins, often subtly and not so subtly affirming the physicality of their being. Yet he never sexualizes the people in these exchanges. For example, rather than worry about his reputation when he sits alone with a Samaritan woman at a well, Jesus looks at her and begins a conversation. He asks for a drink. We don't think twice about such a request, but that is because we don't see how contrary to the culture of the times such a request is. In contrast, she immediately shows that she gets the difference: "How is it that you, a Jew, ask for a drink from me, a woman of Samaria?" John provides editorial comment: "For Jews have no dealings with Samaritans" (John 4:9). She was considered "unclean," so Jesus's request that she provide him a drink of water is stunning.[39] His lips would touch what she touched, so he risked contamination (i.e., becoming socially and ritually unclean). Yet he recognizes her physical needs (she needs water every day) and employs that to point to deeper needs (4:7–24). She is out of sorts with God and with others. He can help her. When the disciples arrive and react, we are reminded, as Craig Keener notes, not only of the "social scandal of Jesus's activity" but also of the level of trust the disciples have in him (4:27).[40] What would people think? Whereas such an action would not be surprising in a twenty-first-century Western context, a religious leader doing this in first-century Israel was taking a serious risk. Jesus, however, appears not to feel threatened by her—by *her body*—but instead treats her with dignity and care. Nor does she respond to his presence as a threat; she responds instead with hospitality and dignity.

Similarly, when Martha's sister, Mary, takes about a pound of pure nard—an extremely expensive ointment—to anoint Jesus's feet, she takes the posture of a servant, using her hair as a towel (John 12:1–3). The perfume, which may have links to the scent associated with prostitution, is not received by Jesus in any sexual way, but rather as preparation for his approaching death: this physical exchange engages touch, smell, and sight in a holy manner, affirming their physicality in a healthy and healing way.

How fitting, then, that Jesus displays his lordship when he bends the knee as a servant and takes a towel and a basin with cool water to clean the feet of his disciples, one at a time (John 13:4–5). We wear sneakers and boots, but the disciples' feet would have been exposed to the muck of the roads even if they were wearing the usual sandals. The roads, especially those of a city, were often a mixture of dust and excrement (both animal and human). This is not like kissing the toes of a freshly washed infant; instead, Jesus's fingers went over heavily worn heels and misshapen toes, with bony knobs and abundant calluses. "When he had washed their feet and put on his outer garments and resumed his place, he said to them, 'Do you understand what I have done to you? You called me Teacher and Lord, and you are right, for so I am. If I then, your Lord and Teacher, have washed your feet, you also ought to wash one another's feet. For I have given you an example, that you should also do just as I have done to you'" (13:12). Decades later, this foot washing became a mark of a godly saint, modeled by faithful widows (1 Tim. 5:9–10). I suspect we would do well to recapture this ancient public practice in our churches with more regular consistency: it is meant to foster humility, grace, physicality, and service, all realities that we urgently need in our individual and corporate lives.

Jesus expresses his lordship not only in words of grace but in a posture of service and healing touch. His act of washing his disciples' feet reaffirms God's good work of creating human bodies and the mutual relationships that are meant to occur between people. There is nothing sexual going on here; rather, by this very bodily activity Jesus affirms both the spiritual and physical aspects of his disciples' being.

We must apply all our wisdom and courage to protect people from sexual and physical misconduct of any kind. But let us not make the mistake of imagining that we can adequately express the gospel merely with words that don't require embodied actions. Jesus reminds us (Matt. 25:31–46) that we are called to feed and clothe those in need, acting out our faith in embodied deeds of mercy and generosity: the needs of the body matter. In her wonderful book *Handle with Care: How Jesus Redeems the Power of Touch in Life and Ministry*, Lore Ferguson Wilbert makes the necessary connections: "God made us with bodies and came in a body and died in a body and rose again in a body, and one day all His people will dwell with him forever—every one of us in our own glorified body. Each of those realities matter to the entire gospel narrative and so they should each inform the way we interact with the world around us, our fellow humans on earth."[41] The good news is good news because the Messiah has restored belonging, reconnecting us sinful human creatures with our Creator and *also* with one another. Our bodies need other bodies, and the body of Christ is meant to be a sacred space for holy healing to happen with dignity, honor, and love.

Conclusion

How many of us like standing in front of a mirror when we are naked? Not many! Many of us who have delivered multiple babies or find our youthful metabolism a distant memory might struggle with this more. When we feel ugly or awkward, we are tempted to distance ourselves from our bodies. But this produces a debilitating mix of self-consciousness and self-condemnation. We cannot disentangle our flesh from our souls, or our mind from our body, and attempting to separate them denies the reality of our wholeness as God created us. It denies our finitude.

Our bodies, with all their needs and dependencies, were made good. And part of the intrinsic good of our bodies is that they are an ever-present reminder of our creaturely needs: to be human is to be *dependent* on the Creator Lord, *dependent* on other human creatures who provide their presence and love, and *dependent* on the earth, which provides for our physical needs, from oxygen to lettuce, from shade to springs of water. This dependence, when recognized and remembered, raises serious questions about the emphasis on self-generated identity that is so often assumed and encouraged in our modern world. As embodied finite creatures, do we have a purely self-generated identity? How do I value my particularity without ignoring the countless ways my identity is given as much as it is self-created? To appreciate the good of our limits, these are questions that definitely deserve our attention.

5

is identity purely self-generated?

understanding the self in context

> Discovering my own identity doesn't mean I work it out in isolation, but that I negotiate it through dialogue, partly overt, partly internal, with others. . . . My own identity crucially depends on my dialogical relations with others.
>
> Charles Taylor, *Multiculturalism: Examining the Politics of Recognition*

Western culture tends to define personal identity by isolating the person from all context. The Christian faith always understands the person as finite and necessarily in connection: with God, with other persons, with the creation at large, and within the person. Because sin distorts both our internal world and external relations, restoration requires that we understand our connectivity and view ourselves as objects of God's love and delight.

DESPITE OUR CULTURE'S CALLS to "be true to yourself" and "just be you," that same culture often interferes with our attempts to know who we are. Although these calls are worded in terms of liberation, they often produce far more restlessness and self-doubt than clarity. In addition to offering platitudes as substitutes for wisdom, Western culture has acquired several mistaken assumptions about personal identity that we need to examine and correct.

Simplistic assumptions in our Christian culture also get in the way: for example, calls to find one's "identity in Christ" apart from a robust doctrine of creation can produce problems. When we spiritualize in a non-creation-affirming way, we often universalize and abstract, failing to appreciate how human creatures are shaped in real time and space. The fact that my identity must be in Christ doesn't change the fact that I am *this* person and not that one, that I am from here and not there, and that I have this history and these relationships and not those. We also tend to mistake our natural human limits as faults we must overcome. But when our search for identity in Christ includes a healthy view of creaturely finitude and particularity, then we see something truly beautiful and unique take shape. The church starts to look like it was meant to look: diverse, united, gracious, and most of all, loving. All in and around Christ!

One sign that we neglect the biblical picture of human finitude as part of our identity is when we suppose that diversity is purely about political correctness rather than a theological value. But a healthy Christian view of human limits and differences encourages mutual delight, an awareness of our dependence on others, the integrity of relationships, and contentment. Christian conceptions of creation allow us to value our particularity without failing to appreciate what people from different cultures and experiences bring; it allows us to recognize our common humanity without assuming that solidarity requires sameness. As we will see, we can and should value our particularity while seeing this as related to our communities, culture, and history, rather than simply my own self-choosing.

So, how do we go about knowing ourselves? That is a question worth asking yet again, but it is going to take some time to provide more than a cliché for an answer. We will need to think seriously about connections, dependence, and responsibility. Let's begin with what is undeniable but far too often ignored . . . *you have a belly button.*

Sartre and Belly Buttons

Just days away from leaving for Christmas break, I look out at the exhausted faces of my students. Many of them will soon head home. They can't wait to sleep! But experience tells me that going home is not necessarily a blessing for each of them. Often such trips mean returning to dysfunctional relationships, or at least complicated family dynamics. They may love their parents, but that doesn't mean it is always easy, and sometimes it is painfully difficult. Others head home with joy and expectation: since absence often does makes the heart grow fonder (or at least forgetful!), and they have fairly healthy relationships with their folks, warm feelings of anticipation fill them. And yet . . .

It doesn't take more than a few days, no matter the background, for the average young adult to become irritated with Dad—the way he breathes so loud, is always late, or is incredibly awkward in public. Or maybe Mom, whose questions were welcomed at first but now feel intrusive and tiresome . . . plus her fashion is embarrassing. Whatever the reason, within a few days the college student has often returned to the struggle of relating to their parents. Inhabiting the same shared space together can quickly become surprisingly difficult, and it can frustrate and unnerve all involved. Mom and Dad's presence has jeopardized the student's sense of independence and identity, and it tempts them to either bolt or just shut down.

Drawing from former Duke professors Stanley Hauerwas and William H. Willimon, I give my students a homework assignment for over the break. It is a dangerous one. If you don't listen to the whole thing, it can just sound creepy! After being home for a bit, as the frustrations emerge and the distance between student and parent threatens to grow, I encourage them to *take a shower*. And while they are in the shower, they need to look down at their . . . belly button! Why? Because during these times of growing pains with one's parents, it is all too easy in today's Western culture for us to imagine that we are self-made people. Hauerwas and Willimon, when exploring the biblical commandment to honor your parents, explain: "Nothing is quite as ontologically revealing as our belly button. . . . By noting that we are creatures, creations of mothers and fathers, the Decalogue tells us that we have life as a gift. We are begotten, not manufactured. Someone even changed our diapers, our first hint of what grace must be like. No wonder some of us despise our parents, for they are a visible, ever-present reminder that we were created, that the significance of our lives is not exclusively self-derived."[1]

This view differs profoundly from what Western society currently believes. Whether or not the average person knows the names of philosophers like Martin Heidegger (1889–1976) and Jean-Paul Sartre (1929–80), our culture has absorbed their axiom, "Existence precedes essence."[2] That is, we *make* our meaning; we don't receive it. This gives great dignity to our choices, but it can foster the illusion that we are born as blank slates, devaluing the immense significance that our biological and social backgrounds have in shaping who we are.

As Sartre concludes: "*Man is nothing other than what he makes of himself.* That is the first principle of existentialism."[3] Existentialism may not remain popular as a formal philosophy, but in our psychological and cultural assumptions, its power still lingers and continues to influence us. We love the idea that you make yourself: Be whoever you want to be. Don't let any person, culture, or religion tell you who you are. No, you simply exist. You are thrown into a raging and tumultuous ocean, and it is now all up to you to make something of it and of yourself.

Isn't this honest, courageous, and impressively bold? Isn't this Frenchman just having the guts to tell us what is really the case, avoiding the fairy tale of a deity that breeds passivity and instead calling us to the audacious action of self-determination?

As appealing as Sartre was to me as a teenager (and I still think there is much to learn from him), I now find him far less heroic than I originally did. This is partly because I see the consequences for those who grow up thinking they have to *create* their own meaning, their own value. I've personally felt it. This vision can be so enormous and exhausting. Sartre can be hurtful because he speaks a grain of truth while embedding that grain within a matrix of error.

Yes, as we live we shape our lives. We change. To that extent, our actions bring about a new form of being, and in that way *existence precedes essence.* But that does not happen in a vacuum or apart from a larger context. Maybe putting this in terms of two contrasting options can prove helpful. Are we (a) individual isolated units in a godless world, or are we (b) somehow vitally connected to God and each other, and is this connection the very foundation of our identity? Sartre picks the first option and undervalues how dependent on others we really are. As becomes clear throughout this book, I think that this view naively contradicts reality and that following it actually hurts us, given how God designed human creatures.

Back to the belly button and parents. In the shower, each of us is reminded of something that is as obvious as it is profound: *we owe our very existence to others*. We all have biological parents: we are part of a genealogy and have received a particular DNA. The belly button, as Hauerwas and Willimon argue, has profound theological importance. It is our body's way of reminding us that we are not self-made people, we are not separate islands, we are not merely rugged individuals. Instead, we are inevitably and necessarily bound together with others: it has been so from the beginning and will always be. Each of us is someone's child, whether we know their names or not. All of us owe our existence not simply to God but to other human creatures.

> But God did not create man a solitary being. From the beginning "male and female he created them" (Gen. 1:27). This partnership of man and woman constitutes the first form of communion between persons. For by his innermost nature man is a social being; and if he does not enter into relations with others he can neither live nor develop his gifts.
>
> Pope Paul VI, *Gaudium et Spes*

Once we start to ponder it, we realize that our whole lives, from our food to our shelter, from our health to our incomes—all of it involves the interdependence of human beings. Why? Because we are finite creatures. And the gift of these relationships with God, others, and even the earth, is meant to provide the matrix for self-understanding, giving our lives meaning and purpose no matter what our socioeconomic status. Ironically, only when I stop thinking of myself as chiefly an isolated center of consciousness and begin to consider my identity in terms of my relationships to others can I start to see clearly who I am.

The Self in Social Context

Historically—and it is still true today in much of the non-Western world—the default way people viewed themselves (the "self") was through their social relations. Who am I? I am a daughter or son from this family that does this trade and lives in this land.[4] Identity was essentially found through social and physical location and networks rather than through introspection. Questions of identity were less about solitary figures and far more about communities and connections. *Who* you were was all about *whose* you were (your parents, clan, land, etc.). There were some good results in that (e.g., relationships connected people) and some bad (e.g., sinful power structures often distorted and abused those relationships).[5] Negatively, this could mean an individual was lost in the crowd, not able to develop any distinctive gifts but always forced into a mold of sameness. Positively, when functioning well, social identity meant a person was never alone or carried the burden of self-actualization, but instead could find contentment in belonging and contribution to the common good. Samuel Waje Kunhiyop reflects on such cultural instincts: "The strong concept of community means that the common good takes precedence over the individual good."[6] By contrast, our strong tendency in the West to focus on our internal world alone can prevent us from realizing just how much we are shaped by the social webs around us.

Matthew Vos, a sociologist and good friend of mine, has developed a basic exercise to help freshmen college students think about their connections to others. On the first day of class, right after the new students have found their seats, he asks for a couple of volunteers—one female, the other male—to publicly introduce themselves. Seems simple. The catch is that their introductions must avoid making any reference to groups in which they hold membership. The first student typically begins by stating her name. Immediately Vos stops her, interjecting that her name, of all things, ties her to a family—one of the most important groups to which she belongs. He also remarks that her choice to speak in English represents close ties to a group, and her clunky narrative uses conceptual categories of Western thought, also a group product. Not so easy, is it? Though the student valiantly attempts to complete the task, it rarely amounts to much more than "I like pizza." Of course, here too, her professor points out that pizza is not universally loved, but is something that American college students experience and come to enjoy as a by-product of group membership. The second student, believing he can do better, suffers the same fate. About all he can offer are a handful of idiosyncratic preferences that his professor easily links to various group memberships and the people who structure his life, give it meaning, and sustain his identity.

But there's more to the exercise. After both students "crash and burn" at introducing themselves, Vos asks them to try again, this time referring to any groups they like. This changes things considerably. Now they can talk freely about their families, a soccer team they played on in high school, someone they're in love with, the way a mission trip changed their life, or anticipated good times in college with new roommates. The point? We are more a product of things outside us than things inside us, and we cannot talk about what we love without referring to other people. In fact, most of what we experience "inside" ourselves—things deeply personal and private, both pleasurable and painful—is inseparable from relationships with others. Even "personal" emotions like anger, sadness, or joy result from our connections to others and do not exist in some private, inner space untouched by the people around us. Worry, for example, often arises from fear of not measuring up to perceived expectations of others important to us. Our worry about grades and academic achievement, which may feel self-imposed, frequently links back to childhood experiences that led us to believe our acceptance by others depended on our effort and performance. Does something like anxiety exist in any important way apart from pressures generated in "the social"? Not really.

Humans are necessarily social creatures with histories.[7] Trying to deny this is a rejection of what constitutes our humanity. "Culture" is not just something "out there"; we breathe it like air: it includes the artifacts we use (whether a shovel or an iPhone), the songs we sing, the language we employ, and the people we know. There is no escaping culture, nor should we wish to escape it. Should we reject sinful perversions of people and culture? Yes, absolutely. But let us be careful not to confuse *difference* with sin. Our particularity is not in the absence of context, but embedded in it.

Sometimes I hear well-meaning Christians say things like, "Your identity is in Christ, not in being an Asian American," or some other group. This has an element of truth: union with Christ subverts all the categories (like family, nationality, or social class) we normally use to pigeonhole people: Saint Paul writes, "There is neither Jew nor Greek, there is neither slave nor free, there is no male and female, for you are all one in Christ Jesus" (Gal. 3:28).

But calls to find one's "identity in Christ" can sound shallow when someone who is part of a majority culture speaks to someone who isn't. It is easy for any of us to unintentionally smuggle unexamined cultural assumptions into our understanding of identity. What may look to me like "politicizing the gospel" may in fact be no more than resistance to this kind of smuggling. Throughout history, Christians have often made the connections between the gospel and seeking changes in their homes, villages, or even societies. If we fail to appreciate the social dynamics of our identity, we will make this mistake and hurt one another. This happens when I *assume* my culture rather than relativizing it, such as when I confuse my subculture's etiquette with binding biblical commands, asking others to conform to practices that may make me comfortable but that really are not required for Christian faithfulness. We have examples of nineteenth-century missionaries to Japan believing sitting on raised-up chairs rather than on the floor was a sign of Christian growth, rather than merely one culture's preferences. It is always dangerous to baptize certain practices. Or, this challenge arises when I take a positive assessment of police or government for granted—because I have personally been treated well and fairly—and negatively judge those who raise concerns because they have witnessed police brutality or governmental bias. All of us speak and act from our social locations and history. No one escapes this challenge, but most of us who are part of majority culture find it much harder to recognize this social force.

While it is true that our identity is in Christ, that doesn't mean that our family, our culture, or other aspects of our particular experience are irrelevant. Our identity in Christ isn't something apart from our cultures and backgrounds but rather his transformation of them as he brings us to himself. Yes, we must reject sinful behaviors and impulses, but we must also recognize the parts that others play in shaping both who we are and our understanding of ourselves. Sometimes our cultural assumptions make it hard to tell the difference between sinful patterns and godly ones: for example, when does self-reliance move from a positive virtue to arrogant isolation? This is part of why a healthy church, family, and friendships are vital to healthy spirituality. I need others if I am to be the most faithful version of "me." We expose one another's blind spots and help one another imagine a more beautiful, flourishing life. The Christian insight is that "I" flourish not so much by exalting myself as by learning to love and sacrifice for others as well as learning to accept such love and sacrifice from others.

Dietrich Bonhoeffer: Connecting the Self to Others

Addressing a small church of eighty people in Madrid, Spain, on October 21, 1928, a twenty-two-year-old German pastor named Dietrich Bonhoeffer preached a short sermon. On his mind were the struggles of the youth who were present; their wrestling with identity questions provided an opportunity for him to help the whole congregation think about a question that had particular force in modernity: "Who am I?" His text was Luke 17:33: "Whosoever shall seek to preserve his soul shall lose it; and whosoever shall lose his life shall preserve it."[8]

Challenges to Self-Understanding

Among the congregation were many teens who were not much younger than the preacher, so he appears to have shared an existential solidarity with them, believing that "only one question" really animated their lives.[9] What is the one thing? Sex or gender? Maybe sports or fashion? No, he was looking for the deeper question that was the "center of all their thinking and action." In their transition from children to young adults, a strange and disquieting change happens: "Their souls are divided." What does he mean?

Bonhoeffer had a complicated relationship to the discipline of psychology in his day, but he was interested in the complexity of people's self-understanding,[10] approaching these questions from a sociological perspective.[11] As exemplified in his earliest theological work, *Communion of Saints* (*Sanctorum Communio*, 1923), he tended to view the individual in communal terms.[12]

Bonhoeffer addressed the psychological mysteries people face when they begin to "become the object of their own observation."[13] As they start to ask about the *I* (the "ego"), they start to recognize that they are a "separate self."[14] Rather than comforting, this can be painful, turbulent, revealing an internal "seething and surging and raging." A chasm can develop between how others perceive the young person and how that person feels, and so the questions of the ego—of the self—can gain unsettling power. Teachers or parents may think I am confident and able, while internally I feel like a fraud and see all my blemishes. With the growing awareness of that chasm, one begins to see this internal world as different and often divided from the external world.

Living in an age of social media, we take for granted that people "brand" themselves to construct a public image—not just famous actors, but your high school classmates, your coworkers, or even celebrity pastors. As is well known, social media can produce an unhealthy chasm between external perception and internal realities. Bonhoeffer's reflections on the "separate self" start to resonate with people who feel a growing divide between internal thoughts and external perceptions. Despite romantic ideals of self-discovery, the internal "self" is not normally calm and attractive but unsettling, accusatory, and wild. People bounce around in their heads, as Bonhoeffer testifies, unable to decide who they are: "That's me? No, that's not me. . . . It *is* me, for in me, too, things are seething and surging like that."[15] Out of that turbulent sea a person is occasionally thrust up to the top for a gulp of air, and in those moments the questions come out as quickly as the oxygen goes in: "Who am I? Why am I here? Where did I come from? What am I to do?" The transition from child to adult involves this turmoil, as does midlife crisis or end-of-life self-reflection: one can never escape questions about personal identity.

Bonhoeffer preached this sermon five years before Hitler came to power, so Nazism did not yet have a presence in his imagination. What frightened him here was not an external evil force, as would happen later, but an awareness of the "misery of human existence [that] seizes our heart for the first time and we ourselves seize up in our distress in our unredeemed state." From that position one main thing occupies our heart's cry, and that is "release from the demon I, for control over it, for redemption. How do I save my ego? How do I become free?"[16] The sermons of this period exhibit a restless spirit akin to that in Augustine's fourth-century *Confessions*.[17] When people of any age, but especially those between the ages of fifteen and thirty, find themselves struggling with these kinds of questions, we commonly provide them a few typical suggestions. Bonhoeffer is aware of these and mentions two of them, recognizing the shortcomings of each.

First, we tell people to heed the ancient Greek admonition: "Know thyself." While this historical inscription in the temple of Apollo at Delphi has been repeated through the ages by philosophers and teachers, a nagging problem is inescapable: *Who really ever knows oneself?* This takes us back to the fundamental challenge of human finitude—our limited abilities include a necessary humility about our chances at self-understanding. Might there be ways in which other people know us better than we know ourselves? While a spouse, parent, or friend could easily abuse this claim, those who live, work, and inhabit the world with us can sometimes see parts of us that we fail to appreciate or purposely ignore. We change over time, we surprise ourselves by our thoughts or actions, and we occasionally even lie to ourselves. Slow down and think about that for a second: How and why would we lie to *ourselves*? This points to a great mystery. According to Bonhoeffer's sober conclusion, "we are and remain unknown to ourselves—known only by God," which helps explain times of brooding and despair. No matter how excited you are about the Enneagram, admitting the genuine limits of self-understanding is necessary if we are ever going to take our creaturely finitude seriously.

Second, when self-knowledge has proven insufficient, we are sometimes pointed toward "self-control" or "self-formation." We need to try harder.

We just need greater willpower so that we can mold ourselves into what we want to be: this reminds one of Sartre's existential imperative. In Christian circles, as Bonhoeffer observes, this often sounds like a call to focus on the "soul," giving all one's attention to the internal world. Almost a century after Bonhoeffer preached this sermon, I do believe there is a strange parallel between a culture that tells everyone they can and should be whatever they want to be and Christians who understand the gospel in almost exclusively internal categories (e.g., understanding peace and grace only as feelings without any social or relational aspects). Both the church and the world—each in its own ways—thus reduce the self to psychological states of mind. If we are uncritical of the social trends around us, we easily accept an individualistic view of the self, with psychotherapy as the main tool for forming the self.[18] Even the most spiritual sounding of these models tend to breed an "egotism in its purest state . . . and thus all the more dangerous."[19] They reduce sin to feelings and motivations, downplay concern for and connection with the external world, and undermine the value and function of relationships.

Losing the Self to Gain Life

Scripture does not call us to the "moral polishing" of our own souls, but to something entirely different. Bonhoeffer challenges his anxious audience with a promise: let your passion be for an*other*; submerge yourself in service and sacrifice for the beloved, and you will "in some incomprehensible way [know] that we have been created anew as another, new, better self."[20] You must be willing to lose your life to gain it. This new self is not discovered by fostering a pattern of isolation, but in a new connection to others that is fostered through sacrifice, service, and love.

Both in our own experience and in the biblical accounts, people who act as if they were isolated units or at the center of the world exhibit a distorted sense of self.[21] Bonhoeffer, in contrast, claims that we can find ourselves by self-surrender, subordinating ourselves to others: "Being able to surrender oneself, to forget and lose oneself, being able to bow beneath the claim of one's neighbor in the spirit of passionate sacrifice—and being able to find oneself again here on the altar of the most extreme surrender, that is our blessing, that is God's grace."[22] But if I give myself up for others, doesn't that mean "I" will cease to be me? Will I remain "unformed" and insignificant? Will my soul be lost rather than saved?

Luke 17:33 oddly claims that seeking to preserve your soul will actually mean you lose it. Why? There is a strangeness to the "redemption of the ego" that Scripture and Bonhoeffer speak about. Focusing on one's soul—on one*self*—means you lose yourself. It reminds me of the hedonic paradox: *if you focus on gaining your happiness, it will constantly elude you.* Only by *not* focusing on your own happiness can you experience the true depths of actual happiness. Similarly, the soul is lost and saved not by denying one's particularity but by laying oneself before the living God, letting his will be more important than my will, thus submitting myself to his purposes and plans. To our surprise, when this happens, we discover true life.

Redemption of the self, as Bonhoeffer puts it, comes not through efforts of self-improvement nor ever greater explorations into self-knowledge, "but through beholding God's singular goodness."[23] And yet, this "redemption" always takes place "in the world," not in some platonic sphere. Why? Because this world is where our neighbors are, and *we need our neighbors to even know ourselves in relation to God.* "You who give yourself completely to your neighbor are giving yourself to God; through your neighbor, you will be redeemed by God."[24] While this will sound difficult to many, Bonhoeffer is pushing us to see the intrinsic link between the biblical commandments of loving God and loving neighbor. Remember, we are necessarily social creatures—that is how God created us.

We don't have a complete manuscript of the sermon, but the final recorded words that we have are, "You have liberated yourself—no, God has bound you, bound . . ." One can imagine that, as a good Lutheran pastor, Bonhoeffer would complete this thought: liberated from the slavery to sin, one discovers that one is bound to God and his righteousness.[25] As the apostle Paul repeatedly claims, we move out of slavery to sin into being slaves of righteousness (Rom. 6:16, 18–19, 20). Yet this is not slavery, but true freedom. Luther's axiom captures this dynamic:

> A Christian is a perfectly free lord of all, subject to none.
> A Christian is a perfectly dutiful servant of all, subject to all.[26]

Jesus embodies this paradox. How we relate to God changes how we relate to others. This is freedom in the Creator and Redeemer who tells us who we are and who sets us free to live and love. The liberated self is always necessarily a *self-in-relation.*

What does all of this mean? Bonhoeffer knows that when we focus on ourselves, when we try to center our lives on our isolated egos, the result is not calm but chaotic, not clear but confused, not generous but selfish. Why? Because, as with Matt Vos's students who try to describe themselves apart from their relationships, any attempt to live as my own center shows that I need others to understand myself, and I need them even more to be a healthy and thriving human creature. This is how God made us.

Because we have our being *in relation* and not apart from it, knowing one's self rightly can only occur in the context of being known, of being in relationships, of being loved. The self alone—the isolated ego—is a contradiction in terms: pursuing that contradiction leads not to life-giving knowledge but to suffocating loneliness and unending self-doubt. Such a wrongheaded pursuit is fostered by the brokenness of the world outside us and the disordered world within us.

Augustine: The Problem of Disordered Loves

It is not our creaturely limits that make us sinful, but rather the absence or deformation of love. We arrive at this idea from Augustine's treatment of a fundamental question, "What is sin?" which he answers, "To act against Christ's commandment."[27] What is his commandment? The apostle John records it as "to love one another" (John 13:34; 15:12, 17). The commandment to love God and neighbor expresses the relational nature of human creatures as God made us (see, e.g., Lev. 19:18; Deut. 6:5; 10:12–13; 30:6; Matt. 19:19; 22:37–40; Mark 12:29–31; Luke 10:27; cf. Rom. 12:10; 13:9; Gal. 5:13; 1 Thess. 4:9; 1 John 3:11, 23; 4:7, 11; 2 John 5). "Sin," Augustine says, "refers to the willful misdirection of the love that is fundamental to the life of the soul."[28] We were made to love (i.e., to be in positive relation to the other); sin is a form of rebellion because it rejects these good designs of our good Creator.[29]

Sin is a problem; being human is not! *Love*, not escaping or overcoming one's creaturely limits, is the goal of life. Sin undermines our true humanity, our true selves, because it distorts all of our relationships by disordering our loves. We were not created intrinsically evil by design, but created intrinsically good—we were made by a good God for good purposes and pleasures. Sin, by deforming our loves and life, takes us away from our God and neighbor. God's law does not make us sinners, but simply declares what is now sadly the case.[30] Looking to the law now as a kind of map or GPS system shows how far off track we have gone. Sin has turned royal daughters and sons of the Creator Lord into thieves and prisoners, beggars and bastards; rather than delighting in others, we treat them like instruments for our self-serving impulses. We no longer hear God's benediction, so our original security has been replaced by endless longings and unease. We try to create our own meaning and give our lives significance, but instead we live in a tiresome world of self-accusation and self-justification.

> To go against self is the beginning of salvation.
> Evagrius Ponticus

Augustine is helpful because he never forgets the centrality of love. But we no longer understand love as Augustine did. In the twenty-first century we have inherited the modern heresy that imagines love to be *self*-generated. The individual is everything. Love comes from within us, for it seems that we are isolated units of willing. Love is something that we create, that we maintain, that we let die. Love and its proper destination is—we tend to believe—up to us: no one can make us love another. And the idea of being *commanded* to love strikes us as downright offensive. Why? Because we imagine we are the originators of love, and so no external authority or person can or should require it of us. For example, the modern romantic view of marriage as created and maintained only by self-generated emotion, instead of by covenant and the community, produces a multitude of problems because our loves are so often unstable.

Conversely, according to Augustine and the classic orthodox tradition, love is not something creatures generate, but rather it is a divine reality we participate in. Creation flows out of the preexistent triune love of God; we love because we live in the flow of God's love. Sin so distorts our experience that we now imagine ourselves, rather than God, to be central. Having rejected God as our center and anchor point, we cannot help but see ourselves as the center of the world. Reduced to relying on our individual perceptions, we can only see what is around us and ourselves at the middle. Our interests follow our perceptions, so we also treat all our relationships in a self-centered way. Only by reckoning with God can we navigate the mysterious complexities of knowing ourselves and every other person as part of a community, as part of all of humanity.

Divine love alone is able to secure the one and the many, the whole and the part. Divine love holds us all together even when we fail to recognize it.[31]

One's failure to know the name or even the concept of gravity doesn't reduce its presence and power. Similarly, ignoring or denying the presence and power of divine love does not make it disappear. Yet, in rebellion against this holy Lover, we have distorted the world, and most especially ourselves. A right view of the self then always takes us into this web of relations with God, neighbor, and the rest of creation. But sin has left us in confusion, insecurity, and self-condemnation. Only God himself can restore us to ourselves and to our right relations; and only by resting secure in the divine benediction can a person courageously ask and answer the question: *Who am I?*

What Is Most True about Me?

Given that we are not merely finite human creatures but also sinful ones, the difficulties of self-understanding are exponentially multiplied. I conclude this chapter with two significant challenges that grow out of this situation: each can only be answered by both accepting our finitude and leaning on the promises of the God who is present and is not silent.

First, what do we do when the view that others have of us conflicts with the way we see ourselves? *Who am I? The person others say I am or who I say I am?* Second, what do we do with our internal conflicts, especially in our experience of a divided self that struggles between sinful actions and godly desires? *Who am I? Are my failures or my successes more revealing of who I am?* Though the two questions are different, each will find its answer only in God's presence and declaration.

Public Perception and Internal Insecurities

On November 30, 1943, Eberhard Bethge, who was serving in the military, wrote a letter to his imprisoned best friend, Dietrich Bonhoeffer. They were now in very different contexts, but each "shared the loss of self-determination."[32] Neither was where he wanted to be or doing what he wanted to do. Yet, when Bethge had a chance to visit Bonhoeffer, he was astonished to see not a distraught man but a cheerful one.[33] This image of Bonhoeffer as a noble martyr was just starting to grow, but is that really who the imprisoned man was?[34]

In one of his later letters to Bethge, Bonhoeffer addressed this conversation and admitted that he yearned for better times and that despite the impression he sometimes gave in person or in letters, "it is horrible here" and he was struggling.[35] Physical deprivations and discomforts were things he could get used to in prison, but the psychological pressures were what really got to him. Hearing the cries and seeing the injustices made him feel like he was aging way too fast, filling him with a "nauseating burden." His deeper challenge had less to do with the wearisome environment and more to do with his unsettling internal world: "I often wonder who I really am: the one always cringing in disgust, going to pieces at these hideous experiences here, or the one who whips himself into shape, who on the outside (and even to himself) appears calm, cheerful, serene, superior, and lets himself be applauded for this charade—or is it real?" About fifteen years after his sermon in Spain, Bonhoeffer revealed his lingering questions about the psychological imperative to "know yourself": at any given moment he might be different. This is less about an internal conflict between sinful and righteous desires and more a question about his continuity of self—was he really this person or that one? In Bonhoeffer's case what others think of him tended to be positive, yet his internal struggles pointed toward more negative feelings. Conversely, one can also imagine a similar dynamic that moves in the opposite direction, like having a parent who only speaks negatively of you while you have reasons to believe you are not so bad as all that. Sadly, this kind of situation occurs in dysfunctional homes where children consistently hear they are "worth nothing" or "won't amount to anything." Whether one receives external praise or accusations, the common element is that we can experience a disconnect between what others say about us and what we believe about ourselves. So what should we believe? We need others, but basing our concept of ourselves completely on them produces as many problems as relying only on ourselves.

Many months later, while Bonhoeffer was reflecting from his prison cell in Tegel in the summer of 1944, less than one year before his execution, he revisited this theme. From the confines of his room he wrote a poem entitled "Who Am I?"[36] Structurally his poem is driven by repeating this question and providing different answers. The first set of answers is what others say of him.

> Who am I? They say to me often,
> I step out of my cell

calm and serene and strong,
like a lord from his castle.

Who am I? They say to me often,
I speak with my guards
freely and cordially and clearly,
as if I were giving orders.

Who am I? They say to me also,
I bear the days of misfortune
temperately, smiling, and proud,
like one for whom victory is customary.

And yet Bonhoeffer felt a disconnect between the perceptions of others and his own internal doubt and worry. So he continues:

Am I really what others say of me?
Or am I only what I myself know of me?
Restless, yearning, sick, like a bird in a cage,
struggling for life-breath, as if one were choking me by the throat,
starving for colors, for flowers, for bird-songs,
thirsting for good words, for human companionship,
trembling with rage over capriciousness and the smallest slight,
plagued by waiting on great things,
helplessly worried about friends at endless distance,
too exhausted and empty to pray, to think, to work,
faint and ready to bid everything farewell?

What was true? Who was Bonhoeffer? Was he the composed, wise, and capable leader others encountered, or was he the exhausted, frightened, self-absorbed person that was constantly taunted with doubts, fears, and pettiness? Which "self" was the real one? He felt the weight of the unanswerable question:

Who am I? This one or that one?
Am I then this one today and tomorrow another?
Am I both at the same time? To people a hypocrite
And to myself a contemptuous, sniveling weakling?
Or is what remains in me akin to the defeated army,
that yields in disarray to a victory already won?

The poem concludes:

> Who am I? The solitary query mocks me.
> Whoever I am, You know me. I am *Yours*, O God!

Bonhoeffer came to believe that "more important matters are at stake than self-knowledge."[37] What matters most is what *God* thinks of us. Bonhoeffer's trust in God relieved him from having to resolve conflicts between the way others perceived him and his self-perception. By saying to God, "You know me," he was not simply including himself within God's knowledge of everything: this is personal more than technical knowledge, because we *belong* to God. He claims us. That relationship with this God of heaven and earth means that some things are God's task and not ours, and perfect knowledge of anything, including knowledge of ourselves, is his business and not ours. In this fellowship we can rely on God to bring to our attention whatever knowledge that we need for the task at hand. As a result of this confidence, we know ourselves more truly than endless self-examination could ever accomplish.

Sinner or Saint: Our Daily Inner Conflict

When we are talking to the person in front of us, whom are we dealing with? They may have a nicely shaven face rather than an unkempt beard, they may be rich rather than poor, and physically strong rather than weak, but *who are they*? And who should they be? Looks can be deceiving. We look at the financially successful investment banker or the Christmas-card family, and we assume everything is fine, until . . . until we scratch below the surface, until we discover the insecurities, the anger, the frustrations and fears. It is not just those with a messy appearance whom we misjudge, but also those who appear jovial and content. Counselors and pastors, schoolteachers and police officers can look at a crowd of faces and see what the uninitiated do not. The naive often interpret a sea of happy expressions and carefree people by surface appearances, but those who daily have to look behind the curtain know better.

Part of the difficult but penetrating insight of Christianity is that it holds tensions where we might prefer simpler answers. Christian anthropology—our conception of being human—puts us right in the middle of such tensions. For example, on the one hand, we are sinners![38] This doesn't mean merely that we transgress God's law from time to time, but that from the bottom up we are infected with a bias against God, against love, even against our own best interests. And yet . . . And yet, we also insist that humans are glorious creatures distinctly made in the very *image* of the invisible God. Humans are *like* God! We don't have to get into detailed debates about what that means to let the fundamental truth of it floor us. We are made in the image and likeness of God. We are glorious humans made by God.[39] And yet . . . And yet, we are people who, as the old Book of Common Prayer reminds us, "have left undone those things which we ought to have done; And we have done those things which we ought not to have done."[40]

Who are we? Glorious creatures! Who are we? Self-absorbed sinners! Who are we? Creatures who, as Søren Kierkegaard demonstrated, are living with a "sickness unto death."[41] We have to affirm both. Some want to affirm "life" and our agency but ignore personal sin and guilt; others are so emphatic about the depth of human sin that they fail to remember humanity's dignity and true glory. Jesus himself reminds us of the danger of human sin even as he goes about the work of new creation.

The Creator has come among us as our Redeemer. God has made us "new" or "born again": we are a new creation (2 Cor. 5:14–21)! Christ has reconciled us with God and with each other. This is true not merely of my psychology but also of my being and therefore my relationships. The incarnate, crucified, and risen Lord therefore provides not just forgiveness but a new being, a new creation. Because I am in Christ, this new being-in-relation means that I am also necessarily called to a ministry of reconciliation with others (2 Cor. 5:17–18).

• ● •

Because of some relationships that God brought my way, I have had occasion to visit prisoners. Before I spent time with prisoners serving long sentences, I did not realize how nightmarish this inner conflict could be. Some prisoners in their cots at night are often taunted by self-accusations. They know what they have done (even if they do not admit it to others), and the damning arrows fly at their hearts—day after day, year after year. The devil is no fool, so he doesn't have to invent anything new, repeating instead our own thoughts about our lives to crush us, even if he exaggerates and distorts the facts.

A prisoner named Miguel,[42] reflecting on suffering and related challenges, once said to me, "It is easy to make sense of lamenting to God when we are talking about people who haven't really done anything. We can understand their grief, their complaints and confusion before God amid their suffering and aches. But what about those who have done things, terrible things. Can they lament? And how should we view ourselves? My mom and my children are kept at arm's length even by the church because of what I did. So how am I to think about myself now?" He had already been locked up for about fifteen years, the first ten in a very dangerous prison that was like hell. But even in a somewhat safer place, prison was still awful. He is someone's son and another's father; a military veteran and former community member; a gentle, soft-spoken man; a murderer. So, what is true about him? Who is he? Is he a man who wickedly killed another person? Yes. Is he a child of God who throws his entire hope on divine love and forgiveness? Yes. But what is *most* true about him? This isn't a debate about whether or not he should be in prison; it is a question about his identity. He now spends his time studying the Scriptures, in prayer, unevenly loving his neighbors within a rough context. Who is Miguel?

In the seventh chapter of his letter to some Roman Christians, the apostle Paul wrote of his own internal conflict and confusion. "For I [*egō*] do not understand my own actions. For I do not do what I want, but I do the very thing I hate" (Rom. 7:15). Although there are debates about how best to interpret this section of Paul's letter, there are good reasons to think that when Paul speaks of this inner conflict, he isn't just talking about people in general, but Christians in particular.[43] Although everyone experiences a similar psychological conflict, Christians have the benefit of scriptural insights into it and the Spirit's sanctifying presence. In addition, we experience the conflict within a distinctive eschatological tension, living between the "now" and "not yet." We can have noble and right desires that we fail to act on, or sometimes we act in ways that go against our deeper desires. In contrast with Socrates, who stated that people do bad things only because they are ignorant of what is truly good, Paul said that even when we know better, we often act in ways that are hurtful, discordant, and destructive. Such behaviors affect our relationships with God, neighbors, and even the earth, and they exhibit our internal conflict. As New Testament scholar Susan Eastman writes of this Pauline dynamic: "This self watches its own actions with horror and ascribes them to sin, with an 'I, yet not I' agency."[44] To understand this conflict we need to think less in terms of isolated individualism and more in terms of "self-in-relationship, corporately constituted yet still a distinct self."[45] In Christ we have our being in a new relationship to God and neighbor, so our sin creates even greater disturbance than for those outside of faith.

Despite having received the gift of the Spirit, who secures us in God's promises (Eph. 1:13–14), believers still wrestle with what the Puritans used to call "indwelling sin."[46] Paul often discusses such inner conflicts, as in Romans 7:15.[47] While this can get a little complicated, it is important to follow Paul's logic. Here he points to a "distinction between the true self—'I'—and the sin-dominated flesh."[48] Despite the tendency to think Paul is pitting a "good" I against a "bad" I, he doesn't actually do that, since he "nowhere ascribes corrupt desires to the 'I.'"[49]

> As a gift of the new covenant, the Spirit makes real to (and in) believers "the truth as it is in Jesus." . . . What this means is that our selves are defined by and, indeed, *in* another. This is not simply formal but real, because of the Spirit's presence.
>
> Grant Macaskill, *Union with Christ in the New Testament*

For Saint Paul, sinful actions arise not from his true "I" but instead from "sin," this corrupt "flesh" that distorts the good creation. Sin is a disordering of our passions, our minds, and our actions, and therefore a disordering of our being itself. It is parasitic, as in Augustine's view that evil has no being of its own but only as a negation or corruption of the good. The believer is a new creature, liberated from the domination of sin, death, and the devil. Our new being is a being-in-communion with God, each other, the created world, and ourselves. Sin consists in the attempted negation of our own being and existence. It is no wonder that Christians experience sin as being torn apart, as the destruction of self and of communion.

Because we experience that disruption of life in cycles of moving into and then out of sin into repentance, it is sometimes compared to the pilgrim life of tent dwellers who long for a more stable home (2 Cor. 5:1–10). We are new, but we do not yet experience the fullness of our (re)new(ed) life. Why? Not because we are finite creatures, but because this side of glory all of our relations remain distorted by sin and disordered loves. So even now we still long for what is to come.

Because our identity is found in Christ, the problem with our sin is less that we have broken a rule and more that we are not acting according to who we are. We properly respond to sin not by hating ourselves but by turning to Christ and trusting him, leaning on his Spirit to resist sin and cultivate the fruit of love, joy, peace, patience, kindness, gentleness, goodness, and truth.[50]

Eastman furnishes a parable for understanding the relation of identity to daily actions, a parable we can apply to the eschatological tension of the now and not yet. Employing what therapists have learned in caring for those dealing with anorexia/bulimia, she sees a strong parallel to what we find in Paul. Earlier treatments used to apply labels (e.g., "anorexic") to people, thus blurring distinctions between a hurtful behavior and a person's fundamental identity. When this happens, one can easily suppose that the person is the problem: this way of using language feeds shame and judgment, because the patients cannot escape themselves! They can seek to shed a behavior or resist an impulse, but they can't stop *being* who they are. If I *am* a bulimic, I have lost my agency and must act according to this identity: the best I can hope for is learning to be a better bulimic. Therapists have more recently applied narrative language to distinguish the person from these behaviors, which are a "hostile and alien enemy of the person, which lodges within and uses its victim's own desire to do the right thing to deceive and literally kill her."[51]

Distinguishing the person from the addictive behavior helps the patient identify, fight, and resist the self-harming actions: similarly, those tempting voices are sin, not the true and good ego God created. By God's grace, I am most free when I resist sin and instead love what, and as, God loves. The goal of these distinctions between identity and behavior, whether in therapy or in preaching, is not to undermine human agency but to encourage freedom and action. We call Christians to act according to who we are (i.e., saint), and not according to these destructive sinful desires (sinner). You are free from shame, for you are a saint. Live out of that freedom.

Furthermore, Paul calls us to fight sin not merely as an internal battle but as part of the living community, the body of Christ. The *I* set free from sin is one of a multitude of *I*'s connected to each other in Christ. Therefore, just as those fighting anorexia are best served through supportive relationships, each Christian is most free, most true, and most empowered to fight sin when living in that fellowship, when surrounded and strengthened by God's people.

Conclusion

Susan Eastman convincingly argues that Paul writes of Christian experience as a "double participation." Two things are true for believers living in this world: (1) Christ is victorious and we are secure in his finished work; and (2) since we still live vulnerably "in the flesh" this side of the eschaton, we do not escape ongoing challenges from within and from without.[52]

Although sin has disrupted all our relationships, God's in-breaking into time and space has accomplished what we could not do ourselves: he has brought grace, forgiveness, and reconciliation. Given the conflicting narratives around and within us, God alone can tell us what is most true about us. Miguel committed murder, but that is not what is most true about him. Actually, he is a saint, loved by God, forgiven, and now set free to love his (imprisoned) neighbors and called to be an ambassador of reconciliation. This is why Paul declares, "What we proclaim is *not ourselves*, but Jesus Christ as Lord, with *ourselves as your servants* for Jesus' sake" (2 Cor. 4:5; emphasis added).

We turn away from sin because it is unfaithfulness to God and it destroys fellowship with him, his people, and even ourselves.[53] As a Christian, I am a holy one (saint) whom God has claimed for himself, to rest in his grace and to be an ambassador of his reconciliation. This is the meaning and purpose of life he has given his people. Each Christian's calling will look different in the expression of this purpose, just as different parts of the body express a common purpose (supporting the life of the body) in different ways. My belly button does not merely remind me of Mom and Dad, but of my Creator and Redeemer, from whom I have life, meaning, and purpose.

So who am I? I am a Christian. I am a saint. I am a child of God whom he has called to good and meaningful work. As a finite creature, I am from a particular place and people; I don't ignore my ethnicity, native language, socioeconomic setting, or the relationships that surround me. As God's child, I am called not to deny my context or past but to see all of these relationships changed in and through God's holy love. Here my identity is shaped and reshaped. Secure in Christ and aware of my dependence on others, I know that the Spirit works in me against the distorting effects of sin that harm the relationships God created us for. With gratitude I have been set free to engage in acts of love and reconciliation that now foster mutual life-giving communion. In this way, my identity can be properly found in Christ, in the community, and in relationship to God's whole creation. This, as we will now see, is the path of humility, which is the path of being a truly human creature.

PART 2

healthy dependence

6

have we misunderstood humility?

joyful realism

> Ah, but what a joy it is when the Spirit of God teaches us and gives us understanding. . . . I don't intend to bury my talent, if the Lord gives me grace.
>
> Argula von Grumbach, letter dated September 20, 1523

Within a Christian view of the world, humility consists in recognizing that our limitations do not threaten us but liberate us both to worship God and to cherish others. It gratefully participates in communal life, exalting the needs of others over one's own while still honoring one's own finitude.

Noticing Others

As I was sitting with a Christian businessman, I started discussing with him some implications of the doctrine of finitude, wondering how he might find it relevant to his own life. It didn't take him long at all. He is a retired southern gentleman in his late seventies with a master's degree from Harvard, and he responded, "Oh yes, leaders in business have been talking about this for a long time. You hear again and again how important it is to surround yourself with other people who are different from you. They need different skills from you, different perspectives, different strengths and weaknesses. Oh yes, this is really crucial if you are ever going to have a successful business in the long run."

I loved a lot of things about that conversation, but I was most moved by his passion. You could tell he absolutely delighted in what other people brought to the table. He was well aware of his own limits, but when he talked of others he focused on their strengths and not on their weaknesses. He once had an employee who was a bit of a curmudgeon, but she had put in a lot of years for the company long before he led it. Her life had, as he explained, probably not turned out as she would have liked, and she had a bit of an edge. But he saw what she uniquely brought to the organization, even in her somewhat "low" position, and that without her behind-the-scenes work, the organization would not function nearly as well. So he would occasionally go to her and say, "You know what, without you we would be so much poorer. I think of you often and I just want you to know how thankful I am to have you as part of this community." Well, she may have been a curmudgeon to some people, but not to him. He actually "saw" her, *really* saw her and valued her, not just as a worker, but as a human. And his positive response to her made a difference in her life—I later discovered this firsthand. Could she have sometimes been friendlier to others and more productive? Absolutely, and that would have helped. Yet this corporate president was able to see past her challenges because he saw in her a value that could not be reduced to dollar amounts. She embodied institutional memory and long-term commitment, but he also took into account her difficult situation. Despite her struggles and shortcomings, he chose to accept her and build her up by highlighting her value rather than tearing her down because of her failings. This man was humble.

If you don't see your own finitude as a gift and a way of appreciating the gifts of others, then all you see in others will be their problems and the ways they could be better. Of course, all people—all employees included—can "get better" at things. We can grow in our skill levels, develop stronger interpersonal abilities, or even improve our skill at organizing and carrying out tasks. There is nothing wrong with that, and such faithfulness and good stewardship should be encouraged. But it is the fool who looks at others as isolated individuals and then wonders why they fall so short. This one is too detail-focused and not relational enough, while that one is too relational and appears unable to accomplish goals. She loves vision but struggles with implementation; he loves the daily grind but seems unable to keep in mind the larger goals and priorities. It's like the person who endlessly dated different women, and because he liked aspects of each of them (one was funny while another was stunningly beautiful, one financially successful while the other loved working with children, etc.), he kept breaking up with people because he imagined he could find a single woman who had all of those characteristics at the same time. Looking at the problem like that, we see how ridiculous it can be in business or marriage, because we realize we are asking a single individual to have all the skills, all the experience, all the power and ability. We, not they, are the problem here, for we are trying to live a myth rather than a reality. Each person we meet is gifted, valuable, and beloved by God—and we are embedded in community with them.

True Christian humility does not simply bow down and worship our triune God; it also elevates others and gives us an appropriate assessment of ourselves.

Who Believes in Humility?

Ethicist Alasdair MacIntyre once observed, "Aristotle would certainly not have admired Jesus Christ and he would have been horrified by St. Paul."[1] Why? Because of their view of humility. To praise humility as a goal and a mode of living does not make sense in the conceptual world of this Greek philosopher.[2] Aristotle encouraged his readers, for example, to avoid the two different extremes of vanity and undue humility: properly placed pride was the center of a balanced life.[3] Although there is much to admire and learn from Aristotle's virtue theory, his view of humility rests on a set of assumptions that we do not hold. Given his view of the world, this is understandable—he knew nothing of a Creator-Redeemer.

> The tree of life is high, and humility climbs it.
>
> Hyperichius

Since Christian conceptions of humility ultimately rest on corresponding views of reality (i.e., God, ourselves, others, the earth), let's dig into that reality a bit, beginning with honest evaluations of individual achievements.

Everything Points Back to Gift

We enter society by moving through the birth canal right into a large web of mutual relations—moms and dads, doctors and nurses, teachers and farmers, sisters and brothers. We don't cause ourselves to have a brain, or a will, or affections, or a body—everything about our existence points back to *gift*. Yes, our existence results from the sexual union of a man and a woman, but even that physical union is part of a larger network of connections, with DNA and life stories, languages and traditions. As we said before, your belly button is your personal token of connection to your parents and the whole history of the human race.

And yet we occasionally hear it said, "He is a self-made man,"[4] or, "No one helped me or gave me anything; I am an independent person, not needing anyone." *Self-made*. Really? No belly button? The people who use these expressions will obviously deny intending any such implication, but we experience a cultural pressure to be, if not exactly "self-made," then at least self-sufficient. We tend to admire the driven individual who seeks personal triumph more than we do the relational person who is embedded within a community. Both people clearly depend on others, but one ignores that fact (whether he buys eggs, puts on clothes, or appreciates his former teachers), while the other expresses gratitude and gives credit to those who are essential to his flourishing. But the story of the isolated hero is much easier to tell than the complicated narrative of community and mutual relations, so we focus on the superheroes.

False narratives distort our imaginations. Did the great mathematicians, artists, and philosophers truly work alone, needing no one and nothing besides their own genius to achieve greatness? Stories that describe them that way are more myth than history. Randall Collins has written a massive study on the "sociology of philosophies," which investigates the less obvious and easy-to-forget networks and relationships behind these "individual" contributions.[5] He discusses Plato (429?–347 BC), Descartes (AD 1596–1650), Ibn Sina (980–1037: aka Abu Ali Sina), Al-Ghazali (1058–1111), and many others, all of whom drew heavily not just from past sources but from their contemporary networks and relationships. It's just easier to single out a brilliant and articulate individual than to trace the contributing influences and support. "Individuals do not stand apart from society, as if they are what they are without ever having interacted with anyone else. . . . The particularity of the individual is the particularity of the social path."[6] In Protestant circles, we often tell the story of Martin Luther as if he were a lone figure who came up with the idea of "justification by faith alone" by himself, and yet the evidence shows that the Reformation was "initiated by the Wittenberg theological faculty as a whole," with Luther serving as the brilliant and distinctly gifted figurehead.[7] Moving from theology to pop music, let's just pick one easy illustration: Elvis was often credited with utter originality in his dance and sound; yet his work drew heavily on many others, including black R&B singers and performers like Jackie Wilson (1934–84) and Chuck Berry (1926–2017).[8] Even if we don't realize it, we all constantly depend on others, whether in developing our talents or filling our stomachs. From our laughter to the reproduction of the species, from learning accounting to acquiring skill in carpentry, all of it points to reciprocity and interdependence.

> Humility is the self turned outward. . . . Humility is not thinking you are small. It is thinking that other people have greatness within them.
>
> Rabbi Jonathan Sacks, "The Greatness of Humility (Shoftim 5776)"

Mutual relations and obligations are part of the good of creaturely existence. From the start of human existence, we have been distinctly related to the earth. This included a vocation of protecting and cultivating the land, helping the world yield and sustain flourishing life for all. The original vision for humanity was one of love and harmony, where shalom reigned in our communion with God, one another, and even the earth. Humans received and participated in the reality of the gift of life. This then frames human existence. When the sense of gift and interdependence is lost, however, then we get arrogance, discord, and eventually oppression.

We extol this virtue of celebrating the abilities of others and seeing our life as a gift because we have derived it from a Judeo-Christian concept of the human person. Not everyone, however, holds to such a concept. In our culture we confront competing views that derive from pagan philosophies like those of Aristotle or the modern existentialists. Thus, we live in a tension between the current Western (largely pagan) focus on self-actualization and ancient Christian values and vision. This tension prompts us to examine with some care what Christian humility actually is, what its foundations are, and how it functions in our life with each other.

Rethinking Humility

The Old and New Testaments understand and evaluate humility differently from the pagan world. Unfortunately, many Christians have, through the ages, misunderstood why and how to be humble. This is not just an ancient problem; I am convinced it is also a contemporary challenge in the church. So here is the question: *On what foundation should you build a Christian approach to humility?* I will first discuss what I think has been the common answer, and then I will turn to what I think is a more promising starting point.

Christians have often grounded the need for humility in our *sin*. Bernard of Clairvaux (1090–1153), who has some profoundly helpful things to say about humility, nevertheless defines it thus: "the virtue which enables a man to see himself in his true colors and thereby to discover his *worthlessness*."[9] Some translate it as "vileness." John Calvin didn't live until several centuries after this comment was made, so we can't just blame the "Calvinists" for grounding humility in sin, although versions of this tendency are commonly assumed in Reformed teaching. Though in the same treatise Bernard will point to Christ as a model of humility, his first step at defining it raises puzzling questions. Is Jesus humble because he is vile or worthless? Is the taking on of human flesh necessarily "vile"? That doesn't seem to fit the descriptions in the New Testament, and Bernard never adequately addresses the problem. I chose Bernard not because there is nothing to learn from him, but to demonstrate that using sin as a foundation for understanding humility has happened for centuries.[10]

We can go back even further for examples. Theophilus, the early church bishop of Alexandria (serving as patriarch, 385–412), went to Mount Nitria to meet a hermit there and glean from his wisdom. Upon arriving, he asked the hermit: "What have you discovered in your life, abba?" The ascetic declared, "To blame myself unceasingly."[11] A generous interpretation of this statement can prove helpful (i.e., stop being defensive, take critique, don't assume it's the fault of others, etc.). Yet, as someone who is prone to "blame myself unceasingly," I have to say, it seems more like a corrupted version of humility. Ironically, it tends to make the practitioner too important: You really are not at fault for every difficulty that happens around you.

It is very tempting to tell people that the reason they should be humble is that they are sinners. The logic of this is straightforward: If we think of humility as the opposite of self-assertion, then the obvious course of action is to make people think that the self isn't worth asserting. Get them to believe that their actions are immoral, their motivations are twisted, and they themselves are just plain bad. Once people feel shame and guilt, they will live more humbly, if we define "humbly" as thinking only bad about yourself and never asserting yourself. This mistake confuses humility with self-loathing. A relatively recent work on Christian humility tries to persuade its readers of humility's importance by making the main opening chapters about (1) God's wrath, (2) the final judgment, (3) the sinfulness of sin.[12] Yes, sin and judgment are serious facts that really do matter, and the author, thankfully, responds to them by citing the grace and forgiveness of God. But grounding humility simply in our horror of sin or fear of divine punishment cannot help but seriously distort how we view human existence.

If there had been no sin and no fall, would we have needed humility? Is humility, as discussed in the Old and New Testaments, precisely a rejection of sin and no more? As serious as sin is, to treat it as the most important aspect of our existence and then to use it as the starting point for understanding what it means to be human is to build on a foundation that opposes God and all goodness in creation. Any building on such a foundation is compromised. Eventually walls will crack, windows will no longer open and close with ease, and the entire structure is surely at risk of crumbling in on itself. The results are often ugly, destructive, and unstable. Ugly versions of humility have popped up through the ages (e.g., self-harming, or constant belittling of oneself), built on a foundation that could never inform us truly about God's good creation. In short, taking sin as our starting point for a doctrine of humility twists our understanding and hurts us. Foundations matter.

Instead of starting with sin, we must ground our theology of humility in the goodness of *creation*. Humility is a distinctly biblical virtue *because it begins with the knowledge that there is a good Creator Lord and we are the finite creatures he made to live in fellowship with him*. Everything from the air we breathe to the water we drink, from our eyes to our taste buds—everything goes back to this gift of blessed existence. Our being itself comes out of the overflow of divine love and creativity.

Humility consists in a recognition of (and a rejoicing in) the good limitations that God has given us; it is not a regrettable necessity, nor simply a later addition responding to sinful disorders. Even if there had never been a fall into sin, humility would still have the essential character of gratitude for our dependence on God and for his faithful supply of our need. Humility is built on the Creator/creature distinction; its response to sin emphasizes our further need for God to restore us to the fellowship that he always intended us to inhabit.

What difference does this make? Building on creation rather than sin avoids distortions like un-Christian self-hatred (I'm so terrible I am not worth anything) and self-absorption (look, Mom, I'm humble!). While our struggles with sin and the ways sin distorts our lives can, of course, reinforce the need for taking a posture of humility before God, his actions of creation and redemption alone (not our sin) are the solid foundation on which we can build our doctrine.

Thomas Aquinas: Humility, Magnanimity, and Needing Others

Thomas Aquinas (1225–74) discusses humility with some care and therefore deserves our attention. He advocates humility as "a praiseworthy self-abasement to the lowest place."[13] Self-abasement could indicate a belittling of oneself or even a movement toward self-hatred, but a fuller reading of Aquinas will interpret this word choice as focusing on the good of others rather than on one's own needs. "Self-abasement" is linked to being a dependent creature, and the "Angelic Doctor" later notes that the language of humility comes from *humo acclinis*, which literally means "bent toward the ground": this points to an awareness of and connection with the "dust and ashes" motif of Scripture (e.g., Gen. 18:27). We are made from the dust and will return to the dust. But he also warns that we may fail to appreciate our "honor" by comparing ourselves to animals, becoming merely like them rather than recognizing the unique image of God we were created to reflect. So humans are from the dust, but they are not merely dust; they are creatures like the animals, but they alone reflect God's image. Here we will discover the beautiful blend of humility and honor, significance and service, the individual and interconnections. To see this more fully, however, we must do some careful thinking.

In order to be humble, Aquinas argues, a person must come to recognize "his disproportion to that which surpasses his capacity."[14] Humility means happily admitting that we lack what we need and that others can supply that need. "Deficiencies" and dependence may result from evil and sin; however, they may result simply from our condition of being finite creatures; one creature can depend on other creatures apart from sin. Dependence is simply a recognition of scarcity and creaturely need.

An accurate assessment of one's place in the world as a particular human creature yields these two insights: (1) your very life is a gift from the Creator and Sustainer, and (2) you are a fellow creature who recognizes both your contributions and your dependencies on others. Elsewhere in the *Summa Theologica*, when he examines the virtue of magnanimity (i.e., "greatness of soul"), Aquinas sees similar connections: "There is in man something great which he possesses through the gift of God; and something defective [*defectus*] which accrues to him through the weakness of nature."[15] The former is linked with magnanimity, the latter with humility. There will be some dispute about this, but one could argue that human *defectus* need not point to sin, but can point to the reality of creaturely finitude.[16]

Aquinas does not oppose striving to accomplish difficult and significant things. For him, magnanimity can be the virtue of having a "great" mind or heart, but he inserts a crucial qualification. Unlike Aristotle, Aquinas distinguishes magnanimity from pride, which aims "at greater things through confiding in one's own powers," rather than "through confidence in God's help, which is not contrary to humility."[17]

> Between the being of God and that of man remains the gulf of creaturehood, and creaturehood means precisely this: the being of each human person is *given* to him.
>
> John Zizioulas, *Being as Communion*

Simply put, pride ignores God as the giver of one's mind and skills, while humility gratefully employs these gifts as an expression of worship and as a way to help others. G. K. Chesterton compares Aristotle's magnanimous man "who is great and knows that he is great" with Aquinas's view of the "miracle of the more magnanimous man, who is great and knows that he is small."[18] Humility and magnanimity are, as Mary Keys explains, the twin virtues (*duplex virtus*) that belong together when we are considering "greatness" and the use of one's gifts.[19] No matter how "great" one is, all one's actions ought to be (and, apart from the fall, could be and would have been) expressions of worship of God and in generous service of neighbor. Jesus kneeling down and washing the dusty feet of his disciples is, for Aquinas, the model that captures the heart of the humility we ought to imitate.[20]

For Aquinas, pride is not the only problem: faintheartedness (i.e., pusillanimity) is simply the other extreme.[21] Rather than arrogance, faintheartedness points to "smallness of spirit," which can come across as timidity, a lack of courage, or what Aquinas might call a defective ambition. Aristotle comments that certain versions of humility will keep people from doing hard things and making worthwhile contributions.[22] For Aquinas, both presumption and faintheartedness are sinful—the first because it arrogantly acts as if one has far more power and ability than one in fact has, and the second because it fails to recognize and act according to the power and ability clearly at hand.[23] Drawing on Jesus's parable about the servant who received gifts from his master but was afraid to use them (Matt. 25; Luke 19), Aquinas observes that "fainthearted fear" can be just as wrong as its haughty opposite. In fact, Aquinas believes that faintheartedness can, just like arrogance, grow out of pride: "A man clings too much to his own opinion, whereby he thinks himself incompetent for those things for which he is competent" (cf. Prov. 26:16).[24] Sometimes we need to listen to others and believe them when they tell us we can and should do certain things. Other people not only are good at helping us discover our faults but also help us discover our gifts.

Aristotle's view of the magnanimous person is, in the end, fundamentally egocentric, while Aquinas's approach to magnanimity is centered on *others*: God, neighbor, and earth. Drawing on Benedict's sixth-century *Rule* with some alteration, Aquinas carefully emphasizes a division between that which is given by God (i.e., gifts, abilities, etc.) and that which comes from humanity's rebellion (i.e., sin).[25] Aquinas uses this distinction between divinely given gifts and distorting sin to show us how to relate to others: we should exercise what God has given while rejecting our sinful impulses, which tempt us to distort and abuse those gifts.[26] Humility, concludes Aquinas, comes primarily as "a gift of grace," and only secondarily "by human effort."[27] That grace reconnects us with our Creator and puts us in proper relationship to the rest of creation: this is the context of true humility.

Each of us has gifts from God. We should value and honor these gifts and not use them as weapons against others who do not have them. Teachers should not belittle students, but educate them, musicians ought to avoid elitism and employ their skills so others enjoy their beauty, and so on. In this way, humility allows us both to employ our gifts and to happily benefit from our neighbor, who also has gifts from God that we lack in ourselves.[28] A small section from one of Aquinas's prayers on acquiring the virtues lays out this dynamic:

> Grant that
>   whatever good things I have,
>   I may share generously
>   with those who have not

and that
whatever good things I do not have,
I may request humbly
from those who do.[29]

I can't sing well and my ability with math is dismal, but as others exercise these gifts, I and the church and the world around us enjoy the benefits. "Humility makes us honor others and esteem them better than ourselves, in so far as we see some of God's gifts in them."[30] Since it would be foolish to imagine any of us has all possible gifts, it would be equally arrogant to neglect celebrating the good gifts God has given to others.

When ranking the virtues, Aquinas puts "charity"—*love!*—at the top of the list, not humility.[31] This recognition helps further orient the goal and purpose of humility in the first place, since it points to something greater, something more fundamental, something true, right, and beautiful. Out of the love of the Father for the Son in the Spirit, God creates a good world filled with good creatures, a world created out of love and for love. Humility allows us to participate in that multidimensioned power that was meant to animate the world from the very beginning: love! Our discussion thus far makes it apparent that humility itself *is* an expression of love. We love God by using our gifts in his service; and we love our neighbors by using our gifts for their benefit and by gratefully receiving the benefit of their gifts.

With Aquinas's insights on humility and magnanimity in mind, let us consider the contributions of another helpful thinker.

John Calvin on Sinful Distortions

Sin has clearly distorted and disordered not only our individual lives but also our ability to live in community with each other. Sixteenth-century Reformer John Calvin addresses this problem in his comments on the Christian life and on the way we relate to others. Emphasizing again and again that we "are not our own" but belong to God, Calvin encourages us as believers to "forget ourselves."[32] That is, instead of ordering my life merely around what is beneficial to me, I can make serving God to be my first priority, and serving my neighbor fits in the same pattern. Calvin's language of "self-forgetfulness" is his way of warning us against the habits of greed, power, self-aggrandizement, and inappropriate ambition; although we adopt these to protect ourselves, they will actually destroy our lives rather than keep us safe.

In Calvin's view, we all must ultimately "do business with God" (Latin: *negotium cum Deo*).[33] Like Luther's phrase *coram Deo* (before God), Calvin's view of doing business with God puts before us a mode of living that takes God into account in everything, not just in religious services.[34] Calvin emphasizes that "the Christian must surely be so disposed and minded that he feels within himself it is with God he has to deal throughout his life."[35] We are moral creatures, accountable to God not simply for our responses to him but for how we treat our neighbors. When we forget this, our lives become self-centered and destructive. Frequently mentioning the destructive perversions of "self-love," Calvin offers self-denial as the antidote. The clearest way of cultivating self-denial is by replacing sinful self-centeredness with the practice of treating the needs of others as more important than our own. Devoting ourselves to the needs and concerns of others causes our self-centeredness to recede (i.e., leads to self-forgetfulness). It crowds out pride, arrogance, and greed even as it produces humility.[36]

Calvin discusses self-denial as practiced both toward our neighbor and toward God. Let's begin with how we view and treat our neighbor. Infected with the blinding and disordering effects of sin, "we all rush into self-love" with an overly inflated view of our own importance, even while it also makes us "despise all others in comparison."[37] Theodore Roosevelt is commonly credited with the saying that "comparison is the thief of joy," but Calvin was hinting at the same thing centuries earlier. In our sinful world, argues Calvin, we tend to underestimate and hide our own vices, sometimes even pretending they are virtues. Yet thinking of others produces a very different emotional response: "If others manifest the same [good] endowments we admire in ourselves, or even superior ones, we spitefully belittle and revile these gifts in order to avoid yielding place to such persons."[38] We downplay their strengths and "hatefully exaggerate" their shortcomings. This shortsighted strategy of self-preservation distorts our view of ourselves and others. Sadly, we use it to separate ourselves from "the common lot" so that we might view others as "inferior." In his own premodern society, for example, even though the uneducated tended to yield to the learned and the poor to the rich, Calvin thinks no group of people escape the impulse to belittle others and exalt themselves. Each person "bears a kind of kingdom in his breast."[39]

Calvin observes that most of us have a "sweet" disposition as long as nothing disturbs or offends us. But when something provokes conflict between people, it can shock us how much "venom bursts forth."[40] Racism is an example of just this phenomenon. Gentle ladies suddenly spew shocking racial slurs, while jealousy or bitterness turns people into bigoted bullies; we wonder where it came from. We all wear a veneer of politeness, but truly frightening hate can poke through it when we feel our own preeminence threatened. We want to be on top, to be the best, to be superior, but our insecurities and vulnerabilities can quickly turn manners into mayhem. Perhaps ironically, the root of this behavior is not self-love but self-hatred! Too often we tear down others when we sense our own vulnerability and sin.

Honoring Others' Gifts—Calvin Completes the Circle

To know what you really think of God and your relationship to him, watch how you respond to your neighbor. If we don't love our neighbor, then chances are pretty good that there's a problem with our love for God, too (1 John 4:21). Few of us think of ourselves as "haters," however, so let's ask the following two questions.

1. Do you recognize that all your talents are gifts from God?

Most Christians quickly respond, "Of, course, only thanks to God can I do this or have such an ability." We don't struggle with that idea so much. Or do we? When people offer us compliments, how often do we respond with dismissive retorts like, "It wasn't that great," or, "Well, I know I messed up this part of it," or the like. Some Christians have been trained to respond in ways that belittle themselves rather than delight in their gifts. Years ago, after an evening show in which students performed an amazing dance at the college, one of my colleagues stayed afterward to encourage one of the performers: "That was fantastic! Just so incredible to see how good you guys were . . ." To which the student responded, "Oh, it wasn't that good. I messed up a few moves . . ." Now there may be lots of reasons for the student's discomfort, since we are all a bundle of conflicting perceptions and feelings. For some, praise feels like unwelcomed examination, or it does make them feel guilty because even though they know they have gifts, they feel like they could have developed them more by that point. Receiving praise can make us uncomfortable.

But if our abilities are truly gifts from God (Deut. 8:17–18),[41] they are meant to be used and enjoyed. As Calvin comments, "Those talents which God has bestowed upon us are not our own goods but the free gifts of God."[42] Since all the goods we possess come from God's grace and he happily allows us to participate in them (even imperfectly), we are able to reply, simply, "Thank you." It may on occasion be appropriate to respond, "Praise God," but in many contexts that sounds bizarre or falsely spiritual rather than authentic. In any case, you can happily receive compliments because you see yourself in light of God's presence and grace, rather than as a self-made solitary figure. Without God's gifts you would not be able to dance; without others you would not be able to dance. Paul links our gifts with the creation when he asks a series of rhetorical questions: "For who makes you different from anyone else? What do you have that you did not receive? And if you did receive it, why do you boast as though you did not?" (1 Cor. 4:7 NIV). We are all gifted. All of us. Humility in this case is the happy exercise of those gifts, which is also a way of giving them to others around us and to God.

2. How do you react to the talents you see in others?

We know that the right answer is to recognize that those are also gifts from God, but how do we actually respond to other people's talents?

For question 1 above, we tend to be more open to seeing our abilities as gifts rather than self-generated, but it is often harder to praise God for the abilities we witness in others. Calvin presses us here: "We are bidden so to esteem and regard whatever gifts of God we see in other [people] that we may honor those [people] in whom they reside."[43] Notice that he doesn't just say we should praise God for their gifts; he says we should *honor them*. The objection "I don't want that person to become proud or self-absorbed" is as rude and ungracious as refusing to thank someone for giving you a birthday present. Calvin writes, "It would be great depravity on our part to deprive [those who bear these gifts] of that honor which the Lord has bestowed upon them."[44] This gracious response to God's gifts to others grows out of a positive view of creation and out of humility.

If all good points back to the good God (James 1:17), then God is rightly praised for any goods we recognize and enjoy. We can happily praise people, because such praise recognizes God's own work. We can freely praise a creative thinker for a brilliant insight even as we recognize she knows but an infinitesimal amount compared to God. Rightly framed, she is participating in divine creativity. Her offerings rightly reflect God when she utilizes them for good, and that is praiseworthy action. We not only praise God; we praise her for rightly employing what has been entrusted to her.

We are always to use these gifts for the purpose of love, for the "common good" rather than selfishly; or, as Calvin might put it, we are to use them to "get out of ourselves" and move in love toward our neighbor. "Whatever benefits we obtain from the Lord have been entrusted to us on this condition: that they be applied to the common good of the church."[45] And then he makes the final connection: "All the gifts we possess have been bestowed by God and entrusted to us on condition that they be distributed for our neighbors' benefit [cf. 1 Peter 4:10]."[46] His remarks about honoring people who use their gifts echo something Aquinas argued for earlier: "We must not only revere God in Himself, but also that which is His in each one, although not with the same measure of reverence as we revere God."[47]

> There is at once something very humbling and yet infinitely elevating for the individual in the fact that God concerns himself just as much, absolutely just as much, with the least as with the greatest.
>
> Søren Kierkegaard, journal entry

Calvin, like those before him, draws on the biblical imagery of a body with its different members, each "endowed" with distinctive powers (1 Cor. 12:12–31). Although Calvin here is focusing on the church rather than on the world at large, the basic principle still applies. As stewards of all God has given, we must seek to "help our neighbor" and not merely use our gifts for personal benefit.[48] Only the "rule of love" can therefore help us determine if we are employing our gifts for the good of the whole, rather than selfishly. It is not that we can't benefit from our talents and developed skills, but we should subordinate our personal benefits to the interests of others.[49]

Some Biblical Reflections

The last section of this chapter examines a small sample of how the New Testament addresses humility. We will look at three aspects of Christian humility, then briefly explore a scene from the Gospels, and finally examine the Epistle of James. Let's begin with a worked-out description of the virtue.

Christian humility

1. recognizes God as our Creator and Sustainer,
2. delights in the gifts of others, and
3. gratefully participates in communal life, exalting the needs of others over one's own.

These dynamics appear again and again in the biblical witness. Notice that sin has nothing to do with the basis of humility as defined above, so that this three-part attitude would describe finite creaturely life even if there were no problem of sin. It is also clear that such an attitude is completely contrary to sin, which shows us two things.

First, sin perverts our perception of humility and opposes our efforts to live humbly. God's invasion of our world and our lives, however, corrects our vision and enables us to live for others and not only for ourselves. God unambiguously opposes the proud and gives grace to the humble (James 4:6b; 1 Pet. 5:5; cf. Prov. 3:34 in the Septuagint).

Second, humility opposes sin just as sin opposes humility. Humility becomes a tool for us to fight and avoid sin, a pattern of life and love with God and neighbor. God calls us to humility not so that he might feel better about himself but in order that the goodness of God might again be made manifest in worship, neighborly love, and stewardship of the earth. Humility both rests on and points back to the goodness of creation, and it points forward to the promise of new creation.

Becoming like Children

Let's begin with a simple but profound illustration from Jesus: he says we must "become like little children" (Matt. 18:3) in order to see the kingdom of God. Why? What aspect of children is Jesus highlighting here? Not an imagined innocence nor some assumed childish diligence, but their fundamental position of dependence and faith. Children are needy. Only with age do we start masking (to ourselves and others) our dependence on others. Children are aware of their neediness, and so they look not only to parents but even to God to feed them and keep them safe. Recent psychological studies by scholars like Justin Barrett have shown, for example, that children are much more intuitively able to understand and receive grace than adults are; with age we become jaded, and our openness and receptivity appear to diminish.[50] To humble yourself like a child, as Jesus demands of us, is not to become mindful of your sin, but to be fundamentally aware of your need. As Hans-Helmut Esser comments, this passage "does not mean that one should make oneself lower than one actually is. Rather, one should know, like the child, how lowly one really is."[51] Here we perceive our place before the majestic God and before the vastness of his world.

Children don't hide awe; they express it. Whether they see a giant rock, a majestic lion, or even a juggler who keeps ten things in the air at once, children don't hesitate to praise. "Wow, that's amazing." They are open to their smallness and to the vastness of God and his world. Sometimes adults reenter that awareness by receiving the generosity of others and seeing in it the reflection of God's own love. Vulnerability is not to be mocked or abused, but honored and emulated. The humble are those who discover how vulnerable they are before God and others, and this vulnerability opens them up to faith, hope, and love. Consequently, Jesus sternly warns against causing these children to stumble (Matt. 18:6). Yes, temptations will come, but if your hand or foot causes you to sin, cut it off, and if your eye causes you to sin, pull it out (18:8–9). Why? Because with our eyes we tend to covet what we see, wanting what has not been given, and with our hands we grab and take what is not ours, and with our feet we put ourselves in places where we do not belong. Limits can be good, and sin often grows where faith is belittled and where limits are ignored, and thus, relationships are disrupted.

James on Cultivating Humility

The Epistle of James in the New Testament is especially interesting here because it seems to address people who have not yet translated their understanding of God's care for them into daily habits of caring for other people. The book calls its readers and hearers to change their behavior because of the good news they have received concerning their life in Christ. The author points out current behaviors that are inconsistent with the gospel, and he calls the people to reverse worldly habits that are still distorting their lives. This new life, he tells them, will bring trials, but they will be able to endure them because of the gifts they have received from the Father of lights (James 1:17). So those with meager means can rejoice: even as the world ignores them, God exalts them! On the other hand, the one with the security of wealth must learn to "boast . . . in his humiliation," for the illusions of self-made security will pass away as easily as dandelion fluff flies off in the slightest breeze (1:9–11). In God's economy, the mountains are brought low and the valleys made high.

Their general prosperity tempts James's readers to indulge their old habits, and this threatens their community life. In particular, they have reverted to favoring the rich over the poor, a complete contradiction of the grace that all of them received from God (2:1–7). What is the root of this temptation? It is that the wealthy are more able to ignore their need for God and their neighbors because they can use their wealth to manipulate the world. But *all* people have been made in the image of God, each different and with particular gifts, and all of them deserve to be treated as valuable whether or not they have wealth or power (2:9). Contrary to the world's values, God honors the poor because, though they have so little in terms of worldly riches, God has chosen them to be "rich in faith" and to inherit his kingdom (2:5). Showing favoritism to the wealthy because of their riches is a rejection of God's kingdom and its values. James calls his readers to act out their faith by loving and taking care of one another (2:14–26). They must also reform their manner of speaking, taming their tongues to speak gentleness and truth; and he calls them to exhibit "the gentleness of wisdom" (3:13 NRSV), seeking the common good instead of selfish ambition (3:1–18).

James then asks his readers a series of questions that have everything to do with our description of humility.

> Those conflicts and disputes among you, where do they come from? Do they not come from your cravings that are at war within you? You want something and do not have it; so you commit murder. And you covet something and cannot obtain it; so you engage in disputes and conflicts. You do not have, because you do not ask. You ask and do not receive, because you ask wrongly, in order to spend what you get on your pleasures. Adulterers! Do you not know that friendship with the world is enmity with God? (4:1–4 NRSV)

They want the wrong things, they don't get what they want, and their lives are a mixture of violent disputes and conflict. The underlying problem is not that a person wants this or that, but that their desires come only from selfish considerations rather than from love of the community. We, too, are tempted to ask for gifts from God in order to "spend" them on our own isolated pleasures; but his gifts are intended for life with each other in his church and world. The humble receive God's gifts for that life in community. They are friends of God (cf. Isa. 41:8; James 2:23; 4:4). Those who are proud (i.e., enemies of God) never see this, and so God resists them but gives grace (including gifts) to the humble (4:6).

How do we begin to live this way? First by recognizing that God already has hold of you and that you are safe. Your ambitions and desires don't need to be selfish ones. Spend some time comparing the two patterns that we see in James: the one stuck in the selfish old habits of life before Jesus, and the community-oriented one that James recommends. Compare them to the lives you see around you and to your own life. The life of humility puts everything into God's hands, only to realize that it was already there, so you may as well trust him for it.

Sounding like he is echoing the prophets, James seems to say the way to draw near to God is *by identifying with the vulnerable and helping the needy*.

For example, in Isaiah 1 God voices profound frustration with his people—you might even say, they are acting like enemies of God, rather than his friends (cf. James 4:4). Although they are keeping the Sabbath, offering prayers and incense (Isa. 1:11–15), and performing all the rituals, their hearts—their values and loves—seem far from Yahweh. So, what advice does God give them?

> *Wash* yourselves; make yourselves *clean*;
> *remove* the evil of your deeds from before my eyes;
> cease to do evil,
> learn to do good; [How . . . ?]
> seek justice,
> correct oppression;
> bring justice to the fatherless,
> plead the widow's cause. (Isa. 1:16–17; emphasis added)

This prophetic admonition echoes the kind of material James has in mind here. He already declared that the heart of true religion is care for the orphan and the widow (cf. James 1:27). So now he tells his readers to submit to God, drawing near to him. Doesn't James's answer sound similar to the kind of thing we find in Isaiah? "Come near to God and he will come near to you. *Wash* your hands, you sinners, and *purify* your hearts, you double-minded. Grieve, mourn and wail. Change your laughter to mourning and your joy to gloom. Humble yourselves before the Lord, and he will lift you up"[52] (James 4:8–10 NIV; emphasis added). When James tells us to grieve, mourn, and wail, he isn't telling us to make ourselves miserable by just thinking negative thoughts about ourselves. He is telling us to be aware of the misery of others in the world, the poor, those with no family or social resources, those who are on the run, those who, for whatever reason, are in pain—even if, as some people say, they brought it on themselves.

The Son of God did not consider equality with God a thing to be grasped, but made himself nothing, taking the form of a servant (Phil. 2:6–7). We identify with those in misery for at least three reasons: First, that's exactly what God in Christ has done and continues to do. Second, the only life we have now is life in Christ. To participate in his life requires us to participate in his work, and that means ministering to the weak, the vulnerable, the hurting, and the sinner. Third, when we do so, we will find ourselves at home.

You want to know where God's heart goes? Follow the weakness, follow the need, follow the cries. How do you wash your hands and purify your hearts? Become friends with the wounded and needy (cf. Rom. 12:16). James doesn't call you to solve all their problems, but to be with them (grieve, mourn, wail). Their tears become your tears; their fears and pain cause you to wail; their hurt is your hurt. We stand not as outsiders but as their friends. In this way we will find ourselves concerned about injustice, drawn to the orphan and widow, and sensitive to the marginalized. James is unflinching when he calls us to stop flirting with the adulterous powers and dominions of the world and to start reflecting the humility of God's Son. Christ, the embodiment of humility, lifts others up that they might see God.

> For, what pride can be cured, if it is not cured by the humility of the Son of God?
>
> Augustine, *The Christian Combat*

Finally, James turns to a test for genuine biblical humility. Our goal is not to emphasize our failures and how bad we are, let alone to condemn anyone else: one of the main results of genuine humility is that we cease to condemn or have contempt for others. Right after calling us to humility, James warns us about speaking evil against one another (4:11). He warns us against judging one another, acting as if we were the lawgiver rather than recognizing that we ourselves are under the law (4:12).

Imagine a field trip of seven-year-olds to an airplane engine factory. As the kids watch the workers on the assembly line make jet engines, they eventually get to the end, where there is a final inspection. The job of the inspector is to give the thumbs-up or thumbs-down on the finished engine before it is installed on the airplane. All of a sudden, one of them, with the unique confidence and pride of a seven-year-old, pushes the inspector aside and takes his place, saying, "I can do this myself." As the line of engines continues to pass by, the *kid* is now inspecting them, deciding if they are good and safe. Watching the child usurp the inspector's place, you immediately think a couple of things. First, this is ridiculous and foolish. Second, it could only lead to destruction. The kid is not looking for the right things, and, in his ignorance, he is unable to judge correctly. Because he fails to see his own weaknesses and doesn't depend on others, lives are now in danger.

What James is telling us is that when we pass judgment on others, we look like that seven-year-old to God. We appear foolish and ill-informed, which is why our judgments are ultimately so often hurtful. We have forgotten who we are. It is for God to judge. We are not qualified. Still, do you notice how easy it is for us to judge others in areas where we are strong, conveniently ignoring areas where we are weak? How easy it is for us to look at others and judge their parenting skills. Someone struggles to keep a job or excel in school, and we sit in silent judgment. The rich judge the poor and the poor judge the rich. Some struggle with controlling their appetites while others try to be in control of everything—and so we judge each other. We find it is easy to be judgmental when either of two things happens: when we are ignorant of the details and complexity of a situation, or when we are ignorant of our own shortcomings and sin. We are all in need of grace and forgiveness. God opposes the proud but gives grace to the humble.

One of the remarkable parts of real friendship is the gift of forgiveness and a willingness to be slow to judge one another. Why is this possible? Because friends know and love one another. It is not that we are blind to one another's limitations and even sins, nor do we make excuses for each other, but we understand one another, and the friendship is more important than temporary irritations. We forgive and we help. This reflects the attitude of our God: he is quick to forgive, slow to anger, full of compassion. Think of Jesus, hanging on the cross, suffering under the scorn and judgment of human beings. What is his response? "Father, forgive them, for they know not what they do" (Luke 23:34). The only one who has the right to judge is the truly humble one, proclaiming grace on those that judged him. We who have experienced God's forgiveness, grace, and aid are called to similarly extend compassion, patience, and help to those in need. Rather than judge one another, we mourn with those who struggle, we weep with those battling, we enter into their fight for faithfulness. For we have our own weaknesses and sins, our own heartbreaks. God values humility and neighbor love. Christian humility lifts others up that they might see God, rest in his compassion, and flourish in his friendship. As we practice such humility, we experience and participate in the motions and movements of divine grace that reconnect us with our Creator and Redeemer.

Conclusion

Humility does not simply say, "I'm sorry," or, "Please forgive me." Humility also says, "I don't know," "Can you help me?" and "How should I do this?" It begins by saying, "God favors me, so I don't have to be self-absorbed," "Loving people is the most sensible way to live," and "I can't do everything, but God reigns and cares for me and others, so that's okay." Humility is not chiefly a response to sinful behaviors, because it has taken to heart our situation as finite creatures and appreciates the goodness of mutual dependence and love. It opposes the pride and hubris of sin, but it also opposes the fear and desperation of sin. Consequently, the humble not only recognize their limits before God and neighbor; they also ask for forgiveness when they have wronged others.

Our limits are no longer seen as a threat. We do not have to grab every commodity we can store, nor must we figure everything out. Yes, we should work, learn, and most importantly love, but this will all be done from within the peace of humility rather than frantic self-centeredness. We are not self-made, nor self-kept, nor self-saved. Unfortunately, we are not merely finite creatures, but rebellious sinners. Humility equips us to repent of rebelling against the triune God and harming our neighbors and the earth. Humility is our stance of openness toward our Creator and Redeemer, our preparation for worship, delight, and love. Humility equips us to better understand our place in the world, allowing us to become more patient and less anxious, ongoing challenges to which we now turn.

7

do i have enough time?

clocks, anxiety, and presence

> Stress is a perverted relationship to time.
>
> John O'Donohue, *To Bless the Space between Us*

Appreciating our finitude as a good requires a harmonious relationship to time and an awareness of God's presence. Recognizing how technological advancements have affected the human relationship to time, we must rediscover the importance of presence: sensitive to the triune God's presence, we are liberated to be fully present with others.

Overwhelmed

How are you doing? *Really?* You've been asked that countless times, usually deflecting it with, "Fine! How are you?" or the like. More open responses, like "I'm stressed," "I'm just so busy," "I'm worn out," are rarer, but even so, we've said and heard them so often they don't even sound strange to us anymore. Sometimes we subtly change the words: we are being *buried*, *overwhelmed*, *crushed*, or *stretched*, because we feel that something is being done *to* us.

Stress and anxiety can teem above our heads like mosquitoes on a humid evening in Louisiana: you want to be free of them, but no matter how much you swat, there always seem to be more. And not only do they endlessly annoy; they seem to get their life by draining yours. When will all the mosquitoes just die so I can finally sit back, relax, and enjoy my beverage, my friend, and the music I like best? The insectoid stress and anxiety keep me from hearing the tune, feeling the comfort of the chair, tasting the flavor of the cool drink, or listening attentively to my friend. The distraction interferes with my ability to be present, to see, hear, and feel as I should. We keep waiting for our stress and anxiety to disappear, but it seems as unlikely as being free from all those irritating mosquitoes.

Expectations

I have been thinking with some care over the past twenty-plus years about the doctrine of our creaturely existence, giving particular thought to finitude. I think it has held my attention for so long because I find it so difficult to accept, so difficult to live.

Sitting at the dinner table with my wife and kids, when they ask me how my day was, I instantly think about "how little I got done." As with other Americans, productivity easily becomes my sole measure. But it is tricky, because that measure so often allows a few dissatisfactions to become the barometer for the whole. And the activities that tend to register as productive or significant are those that are most easily quantifiable. How many classes did I teach, or what did I read, or how many words did I write? For you, the measurables will be different. How many sales calls completed? How many widgets made? How many lawns mowed? How much code written? What projects have I moved forward?

Now here is the key: while none of those questions are bad (in fact, they're all very good), that way of thinking risks narrowing our evaluation of work (and life) to a very mechanistic measure of productivity. When our evaluations of work and life become mechanistic, then we begin to see ourselves and others as mechanisms. When that happens, people and relationships suffer. The materialistic leanings of our culture are not obscure: we exalt the accumulation of material goods, self-gratification, and power, treating relative goods as ultimate goods.[1] When productivity alone reigns, we cultivate idolatry rather than worship, isolation rather than community, and selfishness rather than love. It pushes away our awareness that God is with us and inviting us into his fellowship, even if, in my mind, I still affirm God's existence. Despite knowing better, how often do I use productivity as my chief measure of value? Until we admit and reject that habit, there is no healthy way to address stress and anxiety. Our current harried state obscures the Spirit's presence and deafens us to the divine benediction whispered to us throughout the day.

Tabitha, Jonathan, and Margot have tried patiently and faithfully to help me reorder my thinking and how I experience my days. Where I am inclined to beat myself up about what I have not completed, they help me see what God has given me, how he was present and working, and how to look at the whole and not merely a part. I recently heard someone say, "Expectations are planned disappointments." That was uncomfortably funny to me. So what are your expectations each day? Are these fostering your communion with God, or hindering it?

> God never changes.
> Patience attains
> All that it strives for.
> He who has God
> Finds he lacks nothing:
> God alone suffices.
>
> Teresa of Ávila, "Poem IX"

Rethinking my expectations for my average day—and, beyond that, for my life—has made it clear that I need to wrestle with experience and theology, with subjective and objective realities. In order to address our common experience of feeling stressed, exhausted, anxious, and disappointed with our day, we need to go on a bit of a journey. Along the way we will talk about time and technology, but also about cultivating a renewed sense of divine presence.

The Tyranny of Time?

So why do we feel so busy, stressed out, and anxious? In order to dive into this question, we need to consider our relationship to time. In order to get our bearings, I want us to consider how technological advancements affect our experience each day. We don't even tend to think about what is arguably the most significant invention that influences this experience: the clock. A little history is necessary to open up some practical insights into the effects that clocks have on us.

Measuring Time: From Sundials to Clocks

"What then is time? Provided that no one asks me, I know."[2] Looking at my watch, I tell you "the time," but really what have I done? I consulted the dial on a timepiece strapped to my wrist, and, without even realizing it, I implied that "time" can be measured, divided up, managed, and mastered. But people have not always viewed "time" this way.

When Scripture speaks of the "beginning," it is not referring to the start of the Creator, but to the start of the created world, to all that is *not* God.[3] By his inconceivable power, and overflowing with love and delight, the Lord not only makes stuff; he also by his Spirit orders and organizes it. He makes finite creatures to participate in the movement of time. Following Augustine's example, many Christians speak of time itself as part of God's good creation;[4] but the question for us is how we do or can or *should* relate to time. Knowing a bit of the history of timekeeping will help us find an answer.

In a sense, "telling time" is no new thing. Drawing from the sun, stars, and moon, for millennia people have employed temporal scales, although different cultures in various regions of the world created somewhat distinctive patterns or ways of organizing time.[5] Geography, religion, and history have all helped shape the differences among these methods. Genesis represents an ancient ordering around the sun and the moon, which "separate[d] the day from the night" (Gen. 1:14). Israel counted from morning to morning as "a day" and followed natural patterns to subdivide the day, such as the breeze before sunrise, dawn, morning, midday, the hottest time of the day, the setting of the sun, and the evening breeze.[6]

Embodiment in the material world molded our relation to time: what we saw, experienced, and felt governed this sense of moving through each day. In this way all time was what is called "contextual": time was always understood in reference to the material world. Consequently, some days are "longer" than others; some seasons are more appropriate for harvest, or festivals and feasts; and some hours are more fitting for napping than labor. Childbirth brings a period of expectations that differ from those associated with a time of war. Time was not an abstract idea or detached aspect of the world: it *necessarily* related to one's physical environment and community dynamics. Not all seasons, days, or hours, therefore, are the same: these rhythms of the created world shaped how humans understood and responded to time. As we will see, the arrival of mechanized clocks and then electricity moved us from contextual to noncontextual time, which deeply reshapes our expectations and experiences of time. But that took many thousands of years.

Throughout history, people developed technologies—from the sundials to early water clocks—for measuring time. Each brought its own challenges: the sundial, for example, only worked during the hours of light, and the water clock could freeze in cooler climates. But under appropriate conditions they provided a fairly reliable and predictable measurement for the day. Aristotle reflected and strengthened the tradition that thought of time as movement and measurement.[7] Augustine later asked questions about God's relationship to time, trying to figure out how the Divine might be over or outside of time and yet still be able to distinguish between the past, present, and future for a particular creature living within time.[8] But one's daily experience of time was primarily shaped by events in one's environment.

Although mechanical public clocks began to show up in the West around the thirteenth century, only the largest cities had them; for most people, "hours and minutes were irrelevant."[9] What did guide people was not so much the sight of time, but its sound: the monastery or parish church bells would ring, tolling the appropriate hours of the Divine Office or summoning people to services. While sovereign kings were masters of land and politics, the church in this period was seen as the sovereign over time. Others generally shared an "indifference to time," but the church "kept time" as a way to foster a recognition of God's concern and providential care.[10] Assigning saints to the various days and setting apart periods of times for praise and lament, the church celebrated a year that walked through the Christian story: Advent, Christmas, Epiphany, Lent, Easter, and Ordinary Time.[11] Nevertheless, in this medieval context it was still nature, from the cockcrow to dusk, that set the dominant patterns: different seasons brought different patterns to the day, depending on daylight, temperature, and so on. While common people had no need to measure time by seconds, minutes, or even hours, they would occasionally refer to the duration of an activity with sayings such as "the time it takes to walk a mile" or "the time it takes to recite ten Pater-Nosters."[12] Furthermore, local time was what mattered to most people, since the "time" in each place was relevant to the people who lived there, and the "time" in some other place was irrelevant.

> So teach us to number our days that we may get a heart of wisdom.
> Psalm 90:12

It was within the confines of Christian monasteries that significant developments in relating to time occurred in the West. Max Weber and Lewis Mumford used to depict medieval monasteries as protocapitalist institutions driven by clocks and "iron discipline" under strict factory-like patterns. More recent compelling arguments, however, have shown this to be a misconception and failure to appreciate how those monasteries related to time.[13] Following

Benedict's *Rule*, worship—not efficiency or productivity—governed these monasteries. Clocks served to foster worship, not distract from it. The bells rang to announce the hours of the Divine Office, but liturgy itself, rather than some abstract sense of time limits, drove their patterns—the liturgy was done when it was done, not controlled by any absolute sense or signal of time.[14] In order to help the community, early mechanical clocks (without hands) were invented to help keep a rhythmic schedule that consistently moved back and forth between prayer and work throughout the day.[15]

But clocks did not stay in the monasteries nor even in the town square. As they spread and became more common, they began to change the human experience of time.

George Woodcock, in his memorable 1944 essay "The Tyranny of the Clock," argued that "in no characteristic is existing society in the West more sharply distinguished from earlier societies, whether of Europe or the East, than in its conception of time."[16] Although astronomers and others had previously observed hours and even minutes, there was no reliable mechanism to standardize the measurement of time across locations, nor did everyday people have any desire or need for precise time telling. Minutes and seconds had been mathematically worked out centuries earlier, but only with the pendulum of 1657 did clocks attain a sufficient level of accuracy to allow the addition of a reliable minute hand, and in the eighteenth century the second hand begins to appear.[17] We don't really find a widespread standardization of time until the nineteenth century: as traffic moved from horseback and slow water traffic to train travel, some consistency in time telling became a more pressing issue.[18] Railway companies drew up timetables and standardized clocks at all the different stations, eventually tying them all back to Greenwich Mean Time. In 1883 the US and Canadian railroads adopted a five-zone "standard time," and in 1918 the US government passed the Standard Time Act, which further reinforced this abstract concept of time. Today, when someone says it is "seven o'clock," what they are actually saying is shorthand for "the time of the clock is 7:00." *Clock* time has become the main way we now experience time. And this shift to the dominance of clock time has affected us in important ways.

Clocks and Efficiency

People now inhabit a relationship to time that differs from that of previous eras. In his book *The Age of Distraction*, Robert Hassan observes that today each person experiences "clock time as habit and as institution," which "means that for the first time in human history, the world becomes plannable, schedulable, and organizable."[19] This is a wonderful blessing in countless ways, helping coordinate commerce, travel, and family activities. We reap benefits from the standardizing of time, and it is certainly not my goal to sound like a Luddite who romanticizes the past and demonizes the present. But since we do inhabit this present age, it can be hard for us to see how driven we are by the clock. And not all the effects are positive.

The past is not the only place one can look to imagine a different relationship to time. For example, Nwaka Chris Egbulem helpfully articulates eight key "traditional African values" that need to be understood and appreciated by those who serve on that continent. One of those values shared across the countries of Africa is the importance of "ritual time," which is different from "clock time."[20] In a way far more reminiscent of ancient Israel than New York City, *events* rather than *timepieces* still often regulate an African account of time. According to Egbulem, people of a village gather for a meeting and remain as long as the discussion needs attention; dance exhibitions last as long as they still entertain, continuing if exceptional but ending sooner if not. Event and ritual (i.e., *context*) take precedence over the clock. "Time, in essence, is life celebrated."[21] This can drive Westerners crazy, tempting us to assign moral judgment against this different relationship to time. By default, we tend to be accusatory toward those driven more by ritual or event time than clock time; but might it be that each culture can learn from the other? For example, we in the West can relearn the importance of being mentally and emotionally, as well as physically, present. This has become increasingly difficult for us: when the clock keeps pressing us forward, being in the moment eludes us all the more.

It has been argued that, as Western countries have become more and more shaped by clock time in recent centuries, we have also more strongly connected time with money. Early in American history Ben Franklin quipped, "Time *is* money," arguing for the importance of efficiency. While that may not be a biblical value, it certainly is an American one. Don't "waste time" but "use time" and "spend your time" well. Speed and production were rewarded, while being slow and inefficient was penalized. It doesn't take a lot of imagination to see how this creates deep problems for those with disabilities.[22] When efficiency and productivity are always treated as having dominant moral value, then those who are "slow" will be left behind.

For good and ill, we now live with the consequences of this new clock-oriented consciousness of time and efficiency. Acclaimed British sociologist of time Barbara Adam followed this connection between time, money, and speed, noting how it has profoundly affected production patterns.[23] We strive to make things in an ever-shorter period of time, reducing the price and increasing competitive strength. Whether talking about posting news stories, getting drugs to the marketplace, making "fast food," or any other invention, to be first or quickest is a relentless factor in our economic values. Any delay costs money, creates frustration, and should be militantly avoided. However, "when speed is equated with efficiency, then time and compression and intensification of processes seem inevitable."[24]

In the West we enjoy the material benefits of this intensification, but we don't always appreciate the corresponding burden. I grew up being told that "nothing is free," and I have discovered this does not only apply to the offer of a "free" car wash. Our model of profitability and consumption—which I very much benefit from—means that we want *more* value created in *less* time by *fewer* people, so we replace laborers with machines that don't complain or grow tired or distracted. Machines are more efficient and frequently cheaper. Does that mean they are better than humans? Only if efficiency and production are your highest goods.

Now that our concepts of life have been reshaped by clock time and then linked to money and the expectation of increased production, humans find themselves in a bit of a paradox. *We have often tried to make machines that are like humans, but now we often expect humans to be like machines.* The one just needs a power source and occasional servicing, while the other requires not simply nutrients, but also sleep, laughter, and love. The differences are profound and undeniable, but under the ever-present gaze of the ticking clock and the blurring of expectations between humans and machines, this harried life has become far more common now than it was in previous centuries.

Time and Technology

Judy Wajcman, in her book *Pressed for Time: The Acceleration of Life in Digital Capitalism*, reminds us that "qualities such as speed and efficiency are not produced by technologies alone but are related to social norms that evolve as devices are integrated into daily life."[25] For example, smartphones and laptops contribute to positive life outcomes in the form of greater flexibility for employees and better long-distance communication.[26] But they have also eroded the boundaries between employment and leisure, between school and home, between day and night. Being "on the clock" has been replaced by never leaving it! As we flip on the kitchen lights and awaken the computer, it doesn't matter if it is dark outside, if our bodies feel exhausted, if our neighbor is sick, or if our blood sugar is low; all that matters is that there is work to be done and "time" to do it. An hour is an hour, whether it starts at 11:00 a.m. or 11:00 p.m. Modern technology—including everything from electricity to home Wi-Fi—has now totally *decontextualized* time, detaching it from our bodies and our environment. Can you feel it?

You are never more than a digital ping away from being summoned. Warm glowing screens greet us in the morning and put us to bed at night, all the while intensifying and extending the dominance of work. Receiving an unsettling email right before bed robs the night of rest, and starting the day with a fresh list of emails or work texts quickly disrupts any possibility of quietly gathering oneself. Devices that can deliver demands to us at all hours cultivate in us a feeling that we have "no time." The smiling faces and exciting posts on social media heighten our sense of bearing a crushing load by showing us alternatives we can never live out, the adventures we are not having, the countless ways our lives might be better. When you are on "alert" all the time, you never really rest, you are never fully present to what is right in front of you, whether that is a book or a child. "Time" hasn't changed. We have.

It is common to complain that we don't have time, but that really isn't true. Clock time has not changed the number of hours in a day, the amount of time between sunsets. There have never been more or less than 168 hours in a week. Yet we generally believe we are much busier and much more exhausted than people in the past. I know I do. But we have good reason to raise some basic questions about these perceptions.[27] For example, despite our intuitions to the contrary, "in both the United States and Europe, there has been no straightforward increase in working hours over the last fifty years."[28] Yes, segments of the population have been disproportionately affected by cultural changes that have created what some call "time poverty" (e.g., women and single parents);[29] and I also believe most of us are overcommitted and too busy. Generally speaking, however, the problem is that we have changed our expectations and how we relate to time, with the result that we try to do more than we ever used to: that "more" includes not only work but all the other areas of life. This makes us feel perpetually hurried, disappointed, and in a state of longing. And, as we shall see, it makes being present in the moment almost impossible.

From the automobile to the airplane, from the vacuum cleaner to the dishwasher, from the pencil to the keyboard, we have created countless time-saving devices. Each comes with the promise that it will "save us time." Numerous historical and sociological studies, however, have demonstrated that rather than giving users new pockets of "free time," these devices simply cause the users' expectations to evolve.[30] New levels of cleanliness and productivity replace previously acceptable standards; ironically, the new time-saving devices don't make us feel more free, but more burdened. I love my washer and dryer, and I am thankful it doesn't take me an entire day to clean a basket or two of clothing. But now we expect that clothes will be laundered after a single wearing and that people should have enough clothing that in any given week they don't wear anything twice. This increases how often we must wash garments, it increases our need for storage and resources, increasing our need for greater income . . . and so forth. Rather than having more freedom to invest in others, to rest, to daydream or pray, we instead have simply increased our expectation of how much we should be able to get done. Can you feel it?

Surveys asking Americans if they feel that they are working "too much" get an emphatic yes in response. But many studies that require people to use time logs—the most accurate way to show how people actually use their day (as opposed to their general perception)—demonstrate that on average people are not working longer hours today than they were fifty years ago. But the more interconnected we are between our jobs, homes, and leisure, the more *accelerated* our lives feel.[31] When we feel that increase of demand, when we struggle to have time for concentration, calm, laughter, and listening, then we—that is, our bodies—start to panic.

Since we feel that we are never off the clock, we compensate by inserting breaks into the day, little bits of distraction that help us feel less stressed out and less anxious. The internet has both fostered this problem and presented itself as the antidote. Whether in the office or at the kid's soccer game, playing a few games on my phone or flipping through Facebook and checking the scores have become ways to quiet the anxious feeling of endless demands. We also avoid moments of silence or "not doing anything," most often by picking up our phones.

And so, even if we don't "work" more actual hours than we used to, we still don't feel that we ever rest, because work never begins or ends, and because digital technology allows us to fill every open moment with a quick diversion. Clock time and modern technology foster in us the belief that we can and should be doing something every moment we are awake. Productivity and diversion now rule us, leaving no quiet empty spaces for the mind and body. Can you feel it?

We often live with a "chronic distraction of everyday life," which grows as we become more and more "digital."[32] As Nicholas Carr and others have argued at length, whether or not you believe Google is "making us stupid," our heavy dependence on the internet and search engines is literally changing our brains.[33] Instantly feeding our curiosities and immediately removing boredom, the internet makes it more and more difficult for us to do what some call "deep work" or "deep thinking."[34] I think it also makes what we might call "deep relationships" increasingly difficult to maintain. People now take seminars and listen to podcasts trying to figure out how to concentrate on a task, a book, or a person for more than three minutes at a time.

Let's be honest: How often during a normal conversation do we check our phones? How difficult is it to keep a person's attention? In the past we often thought that the amount of technology a person employed was a sign of success or power, whereas now the opposite is quickly becoming the case: it is the truly powerful who are not slaves to email, tethered to their laptops and phones. Only the highest tier have the luxury of requiring others to be patient and work around their pace, whereas most employees feel compelled to answer emails, texts, and calls constantly: we become passive rather than active agents navigating our time. Amid the onslaught of expectations, we have often elevated multitasking into a virtue, but multitasking is a myth: you can only do one thing at a time, and "multitasking" is simply the rapid switching among multiple small tasks. Plenty of studies have demonstrated that this behavior fosters distraction, the loss of learning, and a reduction of quality.[35] Yet we all do it. This adds to our feelings of stress and anxiety.

While it is tempting to embrace Luddite attitudes, that is probably not a productive path. Thinking that technology is always "either inherently liberating or enslaving" is a false dichotomy.[36] We know Gutenberg's printing press was a great blessing to the world, making the Bible, news, and important literature more widely available; but that technological advance has also been used to produce hateful, hurtful, and destructive literature.

Similarly, our use of clock time and technological advances have brought us both positive and negative effects, an ability to do more than we did, and also the feeling that we should do more than we can.

How can we sort all this out?

Stress and Anxiety: Related, but Not the Same

What we really want is to live in harmony with time, rather than to be driven by it. Irish poet and priest John O'Donohue once wrote that "stress is a perverted relationship to time."[37] He explains that when we are stressed, we no longer participate in time, but instead we are driven and pushed and eventually emptied by it. O'Donohue's comment about stress and his poem on this theme motivated me to write this chapter on time, but I would like to offer a small modification. I believe he is right as long as we substitute the word *anxiety* for *stress*. Let me explain.

Not long ago, on the way home from school, I asked Margot the difference between stress and anxiety: I noticed that she seemed to maintain a distinction between them. Why ask Webster's dictionary when you have Margot? She's funny, because if you ask her a question, she will always answer, even if she doesn't have an answer clearly in mind when she first starts talking. I can't imagine where she gets that. I found her perspective helpful.

As a teenager, she explained to me that she feels stressed when she is confronted with how much needs to be done, all the assignments, the demands of school, friendships, events, and so forth. Thinking about all these demands can create stress. But for her (unlike for me), she didn't treat stress and anxiety as the same thing. No. Anxiety occurred when she was in the middle of the stress and became overwhelmed by it all, normally generating the sense of being paralyzed or being out of control. Anxiety tends to produce panic or despair, sometimes both. It is the sense that the challenges and problems feel not just difficult but impossible. That is when she wants to collapse. This is when she is tempted to feel "anxious."

Though we might want to make careful psychological distinctions here, it is worth noting that those struggling with depression similarly report experiencing time differently during their dark periods: time does not simply slow down for them, but feels like it is ending, and often at the same time they feel a loss of significance, drive, and hope.[38] But that is not simply stress; it points to something deeper. It fits what we have historically called *anxiety*.

Although *stress* is such a negative buzzword in our day, stress is not intrinsically bad. Girders on a bridge undergo stress in such forms as tension, pressure, and torsion (twisting). Stress is also a positive factor in human growth and development: bodies need appropriate levels of physical stress in order to grow properly; minds need to conquer new problems in order to learn. Looking at it in this way, we can view stress as an objective situation and view anxiety as one possible subjective response to it. High stress can break a girder or a body or a mind, but only the mind can be anxious about it. In brief, the word *stress* is broadly used to describe a multitude of conditions, some of them helpful and some of them destructive. It is useful to apply the word *anxiety* more narrowly to states of mind that are especially painful or debilitating, and anxiety can certainly yield physical manifestations.

In addition to provoking physical or mental growth, stress experienced as a psychological reaction to our circumstances can tell us there are things we need to do and when it's time to do them. No more putting them off. In this way, stress can be a genuinely good thing. It is noteworthy that the Bible never commands us, "Do not stress."

Your ability to react to stress is a gift from God. Your body senses a problem and decides to respond, sometimes with fight or flight, either avoiding or confronting the threat. This can be helpful not just in war, or when walking alone at night along a dark street where you feel uncomfortable, but when you're a student or a parent with lots to do. Stress can make you run faster and work harder. God made us as psychosomatic creatures who can appropriately respond to stress and thus save lives, get great things done, and react appropriately to serious needs.

The problem we have today is that we have taken a good gift and made it a terrible master. We have accumulated stresses beyond our ability to bear them, plunging ourselves into constant anxiety. Rather than making it an occasional help, we have made stress a way of life. And we were never designed for that. We were never made to live on high alert *all* the time. An extreme example of this is post-traumatic stress disorder (PTSD), which often occurs in those who have witnessed or experienced terrifying events involving serious physical harm, for example, as a result of childhood abuse, war, or natural disasters.[39] At a lesser level, it does seem that we now commonly live with constant low-level stress from a mix of unrelenting demands, expectations, and endless distractions. A tweet from the president raises our blood pressure; a work email at 10 p.m. stirs the acids in our stomachs; pushing ourselves all weekend for kid travel teams increases anxiety about heading back to work on Monday. The pressures may be different for all of us, but common to them all is an unhealthy relationship to time and technology.

Stress can be helpful as long as it is realistic, episodic, and addressed. Stress produces anxiety when we allow it to overload our capacity to handle it. Anxiety changes us mentally, physically, and emotionally, reducing our ability to handle stress, thus making itself into a bigger and bigger problem. And anxiety typically crowds out the possibility of recognizing and responding to God's presence with us.

The Crippling Effects of Anxiety

Anxiety, as our negative inner response to the fact of stress, does not address what needs to be done so much as our inadequacies in trying to do it. Certain technologies (e.g., social media) and clock time heighten our sense of the crushing weight of demands, possibilities, and problems. Anxiety is the emotional response that tells us that *we are not enough*. If God comes to mind, anxiety tells us either that God is not enough or that he doesn't care.

Rather than allowing you to be honest about your finitude, your anxiety tells you that not only should you be able to do everything you imagine needs to be done, but you should do it perfectly. Anxiety whispers in your ear not that you are a good creature made by God but that you are insignificant, a disappointment, even a failure. Anxiety confuses limitation with sin, thus convincing us that we are letting God down. It pushes us into self-accusations and unrealistic views of ourselves (e.g., a strange mix of overconfidence and insecurity) and into bitterness and anger.

This turmoil also reveals false beliefs and attitudes about ourselves and God that have crept into our thoughts from the surrounding culture. American culture says that we should be able to do everything we set our minds to, so we believe it. The inflated expectations at work imply that we are able to and therefore should fill all the demands. We absorb that attitude, and then we add bad theology to it: we depend on God, so we are disappointed when his blessings don't include meeting the demands we have put on ourselves or have allowed others to put on us. While our doctrine denies that we can or should do all we want, and while we reject the prosperity gospel, we still have prosperity-gospel attitudes, likely without recognizing it. We reduce prayer to wish lists, asking God to top up our abilities so we can meet the endless demands, to improve us so we can overcome our limits.

But how might my relationship to God, others, and time be different if I started to look for ways to praise God for my limits rather than always trying to conquer them? Might I become a bit less anxious? Might my relationship to time and technology be reshaped?

Life does involve hard work, both in our jobs and in our families, and sometimes that means long hours and being stretched. Our goal is not to pretend life never has legitimate stress that makes special demands of us. As we said earlier, some seasons and days require the long hours for harvest or newborns, but we cannot sustain constantly being on high alert. Between the crunch times and the periods when we fear the stillness, we need to learn how to resist being anxious; that, it seems to me, can only be answered by learning the importance of being present.

The Challenge of Being Present

Amid the growing sense of feeling incessantly busy, always flirting with distraction, and rarely honoring the rhythms of the earth, our bodies, and our relationships, I would identify the underlying challenge with one word: *presence*. Being present, in the sense of being fully engaged with God and others in our immediate circumstances, does not fit our world of hurry and its demands to do more, better, constantly. We struggle to be present, and I think this makes us all the more susceptible to anxiety. Whether we are at work in a factory, eating dinner with family, praying in church, or talking to our neighbor, being truly present, living in just this moment, requires a huge shift from our current habits. We constantly think about the next thing; we worry about unfinished projects; we wonder what is happening in the news, or on social media, or at someone else's house. To attend to the here and now with your whole heart and mind, right where you are inhabiting time and space, goes against most of our training. It may become easier with practice, but at first it is extremely difficult.

Robert Erle Barham, a gifted writer and friend, recently gave a talk entitled "Seeing the World through Poetry." Near the beginning of his reflections he offered an observation connecting time and presence.

> Feeling especially scattered one day, a friend joked that she should have a baby since it meant "singularity of focus." It was a great remark—*Oh really: just*

> *have a baby?*—but I immediately knew kind of what she meant. When my children were born, time seemed to operate differently. Rather than the usual, diffused, task-oriented time, which is punctuated by things that I'm looking forward to, or not, each moment was deeply inhabited. I was rooted in the present based on necessity and joy—anticipating and meeting my children's needs, absorbed in their activity. There were stretches of sleep-deprived haze, but the experience seemed so extraordinary. As a result, I had a "singularity of focus." I was paying attention, paying it eagerly. And I was attuned to the world in a way that I usually am not. I felt like a poet in my careful attention to things.[40]

Do you ever long for a "singularity of focus"? Years ago, Tabitha and I recognized the strange delight in driving across the country. Even with all of its difficulties it provides a rare opportunity to know there is absolutely nothing else you should be doing. Just sit, talk, eat, and drive, hour after hour. It is a planned singularity of focus. We could be fully present. The fact that endless driving can be a refuge alerts us to just how crazy our lives can become.

To be truly present has perhaps never been easy, but in our day that difficulty seems only to have intensified. To be here doing *this* and not somewhere else doing *that* is surprisingly tough. To give full attention to the student, to be wholly present during the family meal, to allow yourself to enjoy rubbing your hands across the fur of your labradoodle as you snuggle on the sofa: this is being genuinely present in the moment, in real time and space.

> We come into the presence of Christ to offer him our time, we extend our arms to receive him. And he fills this time with *himself*, he heals it and makes it—again and again—the time of salvation.
>
> Alexander Schmemann, *For the Life of the World*

In our context of clock time and technological advances, learning to be fully present takes practice. We need to make it a habit, a way of life. To borrow from Chuck DeGroat's helpful book, this means learning to live with "wholeheartedness."[41] Doing so gives us an opportunity to reconnect with our humanity, with the goodness of being a finite creature in a specific location, to attend to the present even if one is mindful of the future and shaped by the past.

I am not the only person encouraging us to value "being present." There are countless self-help books and "spiritual" guides that encourage people to be present. Mindfulness techniques enable practitioners to give full attentiveness to each moment. In other words, Christians are not the only ones to observe this phenomenon: modern humanity is suffering from an inability to be present. And it moves us from mere episodes of stress to lives of chronic anxiety.

While psychologists and life coaches recognize the problem and offer techniques to improve attentiveness, many of which can be helpful, I believe we also need a theological foundation to show how being present involves our connection with God.

Divine Presence

If we are ever going to have a healthy Christian response to the challenge of time, stress, and anxiety, we don't just need better time management; we need to rediscover the fear of the Lord: that is, we need to become attentive to divine presence. We will explore this idea for the rest of this chapter, and then later in the final chapter we will look at a set of practices or habits that I believe can help us relate more strongly to our loving Lord as his finite creatures.

But we must first mention one significant qualification: *anxiety* is a complex and loaded word in our day, and I in no way intend to undervalue the various shades of it which people experience, nor do I want to pretend that what I address here covers everything that falls under the label *anxiety*. Some forms of anxiety can and should be treated medically, and often seeing a Christian therapist can prove profoundly helpful. I've always found it very off-putting when people who are dealing with significant trauma or pain are simply given a Bible verse and sent home, with the well-wisher assuming everything will now be okay. Sometimes there are physiological and psychological challenges that require special attention and care. All of this is good and right since we are embodied souls, psychosomatic creatures who should be treated in a holistic manner. Therefore, please do not hear any of what I am about to say as a rejection of counseling, of appropriate medications, of employing breathing techniques, and the like. Any and all of those could be a real gift from God and can accompany our concern here. But having said that, we do ourselves no favors by treating these challenges *only* medically and never asking theological questions—and since those are really the only ones I am qualified to address as a theologian, they are the ones I take up here.

Secularism and Worship

What if I told you that the struggle with feeling endlessly exhausted and anxious could all be greatly helped by learning to *fear the Lord*? Sounds strange, doesn't it? But just as we should not discount medical attention, neither should we undervalue divinely given instruction and practices. This archaic phrase ("the fear of the Lord") reflects ancient wisdom that can transform how we live even in a clock-driven technological age that pushes our frenetic lives. I'm convinced that it can. Let me explain.

Orthodox priest Alexander Schmemann, writing in the 1960s, understood what discussions of modern secularism easily miss. A complex web of philosophy, technology, art, geopolitics, and other social changes has contributed to the rise of secularism—first in the West, but now well beyond. Without diving into all of those disciplines, however, we can benefit from Schmemann's remark that secularism is "a *negation of worship*." He does not claim that everyone denies God's existence or rejects any use for religion. One can, in a strange way, be both religious and secular. Secularism indicates a change in our view of what it means to be human. "It is the negation of man as a worshiping being, as *homo adorans*: the one for whom worship is the essential act which both 'posits' his humanity and fulfills it."[42] Put differently, his point is that human beings were made to live in communion with the triune God. The *secular* age posits the opposite, not so much by denying God's existence as by denying his presence, not denying the possibility of worship, but its centrality.

This definition of secularism shows how we can even secularize our practice of Christianity. Christians have often, without realizing it, fallen into secularism, not so much because they use electricity or buy iPhones but because they have confined "worship" to a single experience. Worship points to an hour or two a week, and even that is probably too generous. Often when you ask evangelicals about church, they might say, "I enjoyed the worship, but the preaching was bad and the offering made me uncomfortable." *Worship* here doesn't even represent the whole formal Christian service, but now is reduced to the times of *singing* during that service. Only singing is worship? Maybe this is partly because singing engages us in more holistic ways (i.e., mind, affections, body), that it can finally help us—even if only for a few moments—to focus more fully on God's reality. On his presence. But after the few minutes of singing are over, we go back to the rest of our secular lives even as we still sit in the pews. As this pattern and habit have set in, the problem is that our world has become disenchanted to us. We no longer see and recognize God all around us. We live the majority of time assuming God's absence rather than his particular presence—not because he isn't there, but because we are not attuned to his presence. We have "disenchanted" the world by emptying God out of it, as it were, making it flattened and depersonalized. Even as Christians we often live secular lives.

So how do we resist secularism suffocating our lives? Worship! "Thus the very notion of worship is based on an intuition and experience of the world as an 'epiphany' of God, thus the world—in worship—is revealed in its true nature and vocation as 'sacrament.'"[43] While I don't think one necessarily needs to affirm Schmemann's full "sacramental" view of the world, I do believe he points us in the right direction. Corporate worship gatherings can—in their entirety, from invocation to benediction (or from welcome to sending)—provide the clearest unveiling of God's presence and action in the world; but this is meant to illuminate the rest of our lives, not to contradict them. For our purposes, then, rather than focus on Schmemann's sacramentality, we will concentrate on the biblical phrase "the fear of the Lord." This can help us reconnect divine presence and worship that should permeate our whole lives.

Recognizing God's Presence: The Fear of the Lord

The wisdom literature of Israel repeatedly links the "fear of the Lord" with the "beginning of wisdom" (e.g., Ps. 111:10; Prov. 9:10; cf. Job 28:28). In fact, this literature often contrasts two ways of life: the way of the wise and the way of the fool (Prov. 1:7; cf. Ps. 1). What is the difference? It is not how well you do on a math quiz or how high your IQ is. No, what fundamentally distinguishes the wise from the foolish is that the latter go through life either denying or ignoring God (Pss. 14:1; 92:5–6), while the former live with an active sense of God's holy presence, good power, and wise provision, aware of God's love, forgiveness, and faithfulness: "The fear of the Lord is a fountain of life" (Prov. 14:27).

Living in the fear of the Lord is not so much about being scared (although sometimes that is an appropriate response! e.g., Ps. 76:7–12), but about recognizing God's real presence all about us: from our rising to our lying down, from our food to our sexual encounters, from our laughter to our intellectual burdens. As Bruce Waltke has argued, biblical "fear of the Lord" moves at both the rational and nonrational levels, holding together both otherness and intimacy, both awe and love, both reverence and trust.[44] Whereas pagan gods could be unpredictable, ambiguous, and manipulated, Yahweh was never unconcerned or exploited, but reliably good and holy, loving and wise: in a word, he was *present*![45]

The fear of the Lord requires our full and authentic presence, which is why the Bible gives God's people a variety of ways to approach him according to their circumstances. From the praise that arises out of joy and delight to the laments we cry in our times of pain, these are how God has taught his people to give voice to their lives before him, confident that he is listening and aware. He creates space not only for positive expressions of thanks but also for arguments, questions, frustrations, and distress (e.g., Exod. 32:1–14; Josh. 7:7; Ruth 1:21). All of these can be expressions of worship. If God is ever present, then he sees and he knows everything, so we go to him not with clichés or prepackaged answers, but to wrestle and rest, to cry and laugh, to lay out our concerns even as we discover hope. And we do this not merely at a moment in the day, but throughout the whole. Those who experience the fear of the Lord discover that praying without ceasing does not require that we enter a monastery, but it does require a mindfulness of God's presence. This fosters the fear of the Lord. Writing in the twelfth century, Peter Lombard reflected the tradition of linking this particular "fear" with being loved as part of God's family: "Filial fear now makes us fear *lest we offend the one whom we love* and lest we become separated from him."[46] This is not so much a fear of punishment, but a fear of ignoring or insulting one we love and who loves us.

Seek the Lord and his strength;
seek his presence continually!
Psalm 105:4 (emphasis added)

Those who "fear the Lord" are not those who are most frightened of God, but rather those who trust him; they have eyes to see and ears to hear his presence and work all about them. That presence and work are there for all to see and hear, but only those who have the fear of the Lord will recognize his presence. Sometimes this means being overwhelmed with reverence and awe (e.g., Ps. 33:8; Jon. 1:16), but at other times it means savoring Yahweh's fatherly compassion (Ps. 103:13) and living out friendship with him (25:14). Moses captures the tension when he implores the people: "Do not fear" *so that* the "fear of [God] may be before you, that you may not sin" (Exod. 20:20; cf.

Prov. 16:6). We *don't* need to fear, precisely because we *do* fear God! He is present; he is powerful; he is wise, holy, and trustworthy. But we must anchor those beliefs not in vague images of an abstract divine force but most clearly in the person and work of Jesus!

Isaiah described his messianic expectations in terms of the fear of the Lord. From the shoot of Jesse, the Messiah would be the one on whom the Spirit uniquely rested (Isa. 11:1):

> And the Spirit of the LORD shall rest upon him,
> the Spirit of wisdom and understanding,
> the Spirit of counsel and might,
> the Spirit of knowledge and the fear of the LORD.
> And his delight shall be in the fear of the LORD. (Isa. 11:2b–3a; cf. 2 Sam. 23:1–3)

Twice repeated, this fear of the Lord indicated the Messiah's complete recognition of God's presence and power with him. In the Gospels, Christ embodies this fear of the Lord. The incarnate Son is God among us, Immanuel: he alone fully trusted in his Father's love and provision in and through the power of the Spirit. Jesus perfectly lived in the fear of the Lord because by the Spirit he saw everything in light of the presence and activity of his Father.

An irony emerges here: Jesus entered into our God-forsakenness and feelings of divine absence for the very purpose of bringing divine presence even into the darkness, into the grave, into hell itself. As the Son of David, he trusted God's presence enough not merely to sympathize with Israel but to take Israel's cause as his own and face the darkness of sin, death, and the devil. His going to the grave is not some momentary collapse of the Trinity but the transcendent God's way of appropriating our sin, fear, and rebellion to himself. Jesus hangs on the cross and is buried in the grave not as one abandoned by God—Jesus *never* ceases to be the eternal Son of God—but as the one loved by the Father and empowered by the Spirit. Jesus as the God-man, God's presence embodied with us, faces the darkness and death that we could not. The grave cannot contain God. And so, Jesus rises!

Jesus's life, as recorded in the Gospels, reminds us that the fear of the Lord does not mean escaping pain and difficulty, but it does promise God's presence and provision. In and through Jesus's life, death, and resurrection, we enter the kingdom of God so that our vision of the fear of the Lord now centers on the King himself: Jesus. His people now, as they spread the good news, are "walking in the fear of the Lord and in the comfort of the Holy Spirit" (Acts 9:31). Fear and comfort, awe and love, presence and care all belong together. For Christians, this alone is the way to encourage a "reenchantment" of this world—that is, to see it as inhabited by God.

By fearing the Lord, we can resist fearing our situations and circumstances. His presence reforms and informs our stories and our understanding of them. Strangely, when we lose our "fear of the Lord," we also lose some perception of his comfort, love, and compassion, for in downplaying the otherness and nearness of God, we replace him—his *presence*—with ideas about him or with things that are clearly not God.

We seek distractions to avoid our weariness, to numb our sense of meaninglessness, or to fill the silence that haunts us. We try to derive self-understanding, values, and a sense of worth and direction from the creation instead of looking to the Creator, who alone can show us these things.

In this situation there are at least two dangers, one for the materialist and one for the spiritualist. The materialist seeks to ease the hectic pace and anxiety of life by distracting himself with stuff and pleasure, but this doesn't work. The spiritualist seeks to ease the pain and problems of life by disconnecting from the earth and relationships, imagining that to experience God's presence we need an absence of materiality, but that doesn't work either.

In contrast with these two mistakes, the fear of the Lord allows us to see God in and through everything without trying to make "everything" God. Rather than acting like the fool who thinks that God is absent or ignorant (Pss. 14:1; 53:1; cf. Prov. 14:7–9), the wise are led by the fear of God to recognize his presence and care. This fear shows divine mercies to the believer in unexpected places, supplies courage to do difficult things, reveals the beauty around us to be from the Lord, and strengthens us to fight against evil for justice and love. The fear of the Lord is not an escape from this world, but the only way of fully living in it *coram Deo*, before the face of God.

Contentment: Life in the Fear of the Lord

Ecclesiastes is a brutally honest book that explores and then explodes our temptations toward delusional patterns of human existence. It treats time contextually (Eccles. 3:1–8) and recognizes our temptation to find satisfaction in the creation apart from the Creator. Life is vanity not because creation is bad or toil is wrong or pleasure is always evil, but because trying to live without the fear of the Lord completely disorients us and empties life of satisfaction (1:1–11; 2:24–26). Apart from seeking God, neither working harder nor becoming wealthier will satisfy us (2:18–23; 5:8–6:12). Current research affirms this.[47] We flirt with the idea that we would be satisfied if we were just more intellectually accomplished, or if we had more political influence, but this isn't so (1:12–18; 2:12–17; 4:1–16). As an academic, I can honestly tell you some of the most miserable human beings I have ever known are also some of the greatest geniuses I have ever met. But then, Ecclesiastes made this point long ago (e.g., 1:18). Just read the newspaper to see the same about so many politicians and social influencers. We are tempted to imagine that if the restrictions on pleasure were lifted and we could satisfy all our desires, then we would finally enjoy life fully; but, in fact, we discover it just isn't so (2:1–18).

Money, power, sex, brilliance, or influence won't give our lives genuine meaning and purpose. Only when we honestly believe this, only when we return to our true center, can we find the resources to resist the tyranny of being driven by clock time and endless distractions and vain attempts to give our lives meaning. So what is the final word? What is the way of wisdom, the way to our true center? Ecclesiastes closes with these words, words that at first may seem surprisingly sober: "The end of the matter; all has been heard. Fear God, and keep his commandments; for that is the whole duty of everyone. For God will bring every deed into judgment, including every secret thing, whether good or evil" (12:13–14 NRSV; cf. 8:10–13). Isn't that talk about judgment just the pessimism of someone who has given up? Well, it depends. One can read it very differently. Qoheleth ("Preacher"—the speaker in Ecclesiastes) seems to have thought this actually to be a very *positive* assessment and hope, because to live in the fear of God is to live in the real world. It takes realistic stock of human finitude, need, and temptation, and it puts them into the context of God's love and provision for us. It recognizes the world we actually live in, waking us up from a dream. It liberates us to live *coram Deo*, happily animated by the fear of the Lord, which enables us to love his creation without becoming anxious about it.

> God's time is created, gifted, slow, generous, gentle, and designed to enhance the purposes of love.
>
> John Swinton, *Becoming Friends of Time*

That is the path of life and wisdom. The fear of the Lord is the recognition of God's presence, holiness, wisdom, and love. The fear of the Lord is a way of life, living in awareness of the sovereign King who is ever present, ever wise, ever concerned. The fear of the Lord allows us to face stress and the uncertainties of life with confidence, not because everything will turn out as we wanted, but because it puts everything in perspective. In the fear of the Lord we now see everything in light of God, rather than trying to make space for God within everything.

But to maintain this vision, this fear of the Lord, (1) we need to have a vision for how God works in our lives over time, (2) we need to more fully appreciate our interdependence as the corporate church, and (3) we need a set of practices or habits to help us live in light of God's presence and action. These are the topics for our final three chapters of the book.

8

why doesn't God just instantly change me?

process, humanity, and the Spirit's work

> The new creature's response to the Spirit's work in and through him or her may be portrayed as a joyful yielding to the hands of the sculpting Spirit.
>
> Leopoldo A. Sánchez M., *Sculptor Spirit*

Time and process are aspects of the creation that God made and called "very good." When we are frustrated by the process that we call "growth," we can learn about our relationship with God by examining the frustration, the nature of the process as good, and the goal toward which we are working—namely, deeper communion with God.

Process Matters

Standing waist deep in dense kudzu on Signal Mountain in Tennessee, Jeffrey pulls out his notebook and pencil, having returned after previous visits when he had snapped photographs. Trying not to think about what insects and animals might be slithering by his legs, he now spends hours absorbing what he calls the "uncanny signs and textures of this strange place." When he eventually returns to his studio, he will spend weeks and even months slowly coating a canvas with paint, basing his work on those sketches, building one layer on another by adding colors, contrasts, and thick texture. He spends countless hours on painted details that end up covered by another layer, yet those underlying patterns, the intricate detail, and the patient care all subtly, but truly, shape and inform the final creation. Even when the viewers do not "see" most of the work, it is fair to say that they can sense it. Eventually his completed art is displayed in homes, museums, hospitals, and airports for observers to experience and enjoy.

If you ask my dear friend Jeffrey what he thinks matters most about his work, he immediately responds, "Process." As a professor he wants his students to learn that the process is at least as important as the finished product and that wonder and joy are to be discovered in the slow craft of producing a work of art. They want finished products right away, but he mentors them in the promise and delight of development. Engaging in this slow, purposeful work, he offers an echo of the Creator's own careful craftsmanship.

Many of us have difficulty valuing process. Tedious practices, the significance of slow growth, and the beauty of development are easily rejected in our culture of rapid download speeds and instant gratification.

With similar impatience we often wonder why God doesn't just instantly change us: I yell at my kids when I shouldn't; I am trapped in self-absorption that never seems to end; my endless disordered desires feed my greed and lust. Sin is not a past issue but a present struggle for believers. It takes great effort and perseverance not to give up. So we ask: When God extends his grace to our broken and needy lives, why doesn't he just immediately free us from our faults? Why are my bad habits not erased and positive virtues not instantaneously produced? If God doesn't like certain sinful attitudes and behaviors, why does it sometimes seem like he stops with forgiving us? Why doesn't the Almighty also instantly transform us so we could never fall short again?

Christians often deal with a lot of guilt and shame in their lives because of their continued struggle with disobedience and sin. They also struggle with guilt and shame over their creaturely limits, which can manifest in everything from failing to remember Scripture to falling asleep while praying. They feel that they should know more, do more, be more. We see how far short we fall from a finished product, and it weighs on us. In response, we need to ask whether God is in fact constantly frustrated or angry with us. Is he persistently irritated with his children, or is something else going on? Might it be true that, although he clearly does not enjoy our sin, God values the process of our growth and the work involved in it, and not just the final product?

When Jonathan and Margot were learning to walk, I would stand them up so they could hold the side of the couch with one hand. Backing about eight feet away, I would then call them, grinning widely while making little hand gestures to encourage them in my direction. Eventually their courage stirred them to take that first step, removing their hands from what they previously rested on for support. Inevitably, they wouldn't make it very far. Maybe a foot or two. Then they would fall. Sometimes they would cry; other times they might just hit the ground and look up, wondering how I would respond. Do you think that, when they fell, I immediately shouted at them, "You idiots, what are you doing? I clearly told you to walk!" Of course I didn't say that. What loving parent would? But did you just feel a physical reaction to reading those incendiary words? How cruel they were. How irrational. No, when my children fell I would immediately rush over to them, lift them up, offer fresh assurances and love, and then set them up to try again. I was kind and compassionate to them, not because I was indifferent to their learning to walk, but because I understood their situation. I knew where they were and where they needed to be, but I was also fully aware of the genuine challenge. Why do we pit compassion against success, grace against growth, and tenderness against effort? Without question I wanted them to walk, but I knew it was going to take time and work. They needed me to give them the gift of courage (encourage-ment) so they could keep trying and not overly worry. I delighted to see my children grow, to develop new skills and competencies even when doing so often meant a lot of crashing onto the floor. Learning to walk requires growth in balance, muscle, and confidence. It is necessarily a process, and one that requires repeated effort.

> The artist is nothing without the gift, but the gift is nothing without work.
>
> Émile Zola

Yet, when it comes to our Father in heaven, while we would never want to admit it, we often think very poorly of him. We seem to believe he expects us to be instantly flawless, to never make a mistake, to never fall back or hit the ground. When we do fall, we imagine he is surprised and frustrated—as if the holy, omniscient God were naive or ignorant about the ways sin has so deeply affected us or the ways that we were created with good limitations. Subconsciously we imagine that as Christians we should have thoughts, words, and actions that are instantly free from ever again lapsing into sin and failure. When we envision God as a temperamental Father, the Christian life seems heavy and burdensome, rather than hopeful and promising. It is endured rather than enjoyed. But if we better understood our God, who abounds with compassion and grace, we might more freely grow in our Christian lives without being crushed by our weaknesses and limits. For that to happen, however, we need to move our focus of attention from our struggles to the faithfulness of the Creator, Redeemer, and Sustainer.

God designed and made us to be finite. Understanding the Christian life, especially in our struggle with sin and affliction, requires that we connect creation with re-creation. Far too often we have tried to make sense of Christian spirituality and sanctification without being mindful that our limitations are included in God's original blueprint for us, that his tenderness toward us is only increased by our deep need for him, and that sin hasn't removed any of that. Forgetting that background distorts our view of Christian life, producing timidity instead of confidence, fear instead of hope, a sense of exhaustion and exile instead of welcome. But the Spirit of creation is the same as the Spirit of sanctification, and therefore God is working in us over the whole of our lives, not just at the moment of our conversion. To explore this vision, we need to think afresh about creation and re-creation, about communion with God, and about the growth Jesus experienced in his own earthly life. Finally, we will show that the process of sanctification in our lives both depends on God's grace and affirms human agency.

God Takes His Time

God isn't in a rush. He doesn't need to be—he is God, after all. For some reason, we tend to associate God's good work with finished projects. But that is not what we actually find in Scripture.

How fast can God do something? Because I believe God is the Sovereign Lord and Creator of all things, I have no problem believing God could have created everything in a millisecond. Or even faster! Quicker than a genie can snap his fingers, Yahweh could have instantaneously made everything. Everything! But he didn't, did he?

For almost two centuries Christians have debated *how* and *when* God created the world. Some still roughly follow the calculation Archbishop James Ussher provided in 1650, stating that the world was created on October 22, 4004 BC; other Christians believe the earth is probably about 4.5 billion years old. However, as different as these results are, they both recognize something wondrous about God. Even the most conservative view, which affirms that God created the world in six literal days, about six thousand years ago, still recognizes that *he took his time*! Since he could have made it instantly and didn't, whether it was six days or six trillion, it means *process matters to God.*

God doesn't fret about process, but seems to enjoy and value it. In fact, although God clearly can do whatever he wants and as quickly as he wants, he doesn't tend to do things instantaneously. With Creation, God takes "days": whether that be six sunsets and sunrises or six billion years is irrelevant to the point. The fact that God could have made everything at once but didn't, that he worked slowly, moving from one thing to the next in the Genesis account, reveals that the Creator enjoys creating, shaping, and sustaining what he has made. The biblical narrative clearly presents God working through time and not flouting it, day after day, building, growing his creation, interconnecting the various parts.

Not simply delighting in the finished product but also in the glorious process, God pauses after each day and recognizes his ongoing work as "good!" Humanity itself is not made out of nothing; rather, as Genesis says, Adam was shaped "of dust from the ground" (Gen. 2:7). Even a young-earth, literal, seven-day account of Genesis 1–2 must confess that the God who could make humans ex nihilo (out of nothing) instead employs this dust and his divine breath to produce human life. God is clearly building his creation with purpose and care.

This has everything to do with our own lives. From the beginning, even before sin was an issue, God affirmed and utilized the movement of time, including the value of development and growth. Part of the goodness of his finite creation is that the infinite God doesn't rush when he works; he has always valued process.

Is God Efficient?

Church buildings can be designed in different styles. A community expresses its values in its architecture. With that in mind, some ask, "Shouldn't a church be as basic as possible, with the cheapest construction allowable so that all the extra money can go to missions and helping the poor? Why would you ever pay to have higher ceilings than necessary? Why spend energy and resources on landscaping—won't asphalt and concrete cover the ground as well? Wouldn't nonessential architectural 'extras' be a form of self-indulgence?" Maybe. The definition of *indulgent* is "having or indicating a tendency to be overly generous to or lenient with someone." Is God too generous with the design of his creation? With us? Must we understand *indulgent* in a negative way? My concern is not so much about the vocabulary of indulgence, which I can happily leave behind. My concern is to get at the underlying truth.

Historians of architecture and social critics have long observed that taking efficiency to be the only criterion in the construction of buildings, especially housing, often has significant unintended consequences. Community housing with no positive aesthetic can actually suck the life out of those who inhabit that space.[1] Beige wall after beige wall, prickly indoor/outdoor carpeting, narrow hallways, low ceilings, few windows, and cold, concrete-covered outsides act like a lead blanket laid over the spirits of the inhabitants: just as beauty feeds the souls of people who see it, the lack of beauty starves us of something that we have difficulty describing, but keenly feel. Where is the life? The beauty? The loving process?

God's highest value is not efficiency, especially considered in any simple or mechanistic sense—it is *love*. He is more interested in beauty than speed of process; he is more concerned to lift our gaze, to provoke song, to stimulate our imaginations than he is to just get things done. God is not wasteful or negligent, but purposeful and wise, patient and intentional as he works. Wouldn't it have been much more efficient for God to create the entire world in a single color? What if everything God made was gray? Or shades of black and white? Someone shaped by the modern industrial mindset might negatively assess God as indulgent, wasteful, and excessive. Why the extravagance of a peacock's feathers, the careful complexity of the orchid, the multilayered nature of the human voice, or the transcendence of an orgasm? Sure, we can offer explanations for each of these, but was it really necessary to have so many colors, so much diversity, so much depth, so much wonder? Why? Because God is not driven by efficiency alone.

Love, beauty, wonder, and worship are God's main goals. Sometimes he is astonishingly efficient in his work. He can quickly turn water to wine. He can make a dead person rise. But often, because he is compelled by love rather than mere production, he takes slower routes. Exodus normally takes time, calling for faith and growth. Process has always been his normal pattern. Rather than snapping his fingers, the Father, through his Word, sends the Spirit over the darkness, hovering above turbulent waters while beginning to bring order out of the emptiness and void (Gen. 1:2).

Those of us in the West especially struggle with this because, immersed in our materialistic habits, we disproportionately value efficiency and productivity. Gary S. Selby, for example, tells the story of taking a group of American students overseas to East Africa.[2] While there they noticed that several people were performing a task together, but the students felt confident that only one person was required to get the job done. And it would be quicker. They were tempted to make a moral judgment against what appeared to them to be inefficient and even "backward" behavior, but Selby challenged them to see that, while efficiency was valued in East Africa, it wasn't the highest value. Other priorities, such as friendship and community, were more cherished. What students were witnessing was not laziness or moral failure, but a different value structure; whereas in the States people normally value efficiency over community, in East Africa the values are reversed. Similar values are found elsewhere outside the West, such as in Asia, with Indonesia as an example.[3] I know my own assumption about the good of efficiency and productivity has required serious examination, not because these traits are bad (they are genuine goods, after all), but because they do not seem to be God's highest good; thus they shouldn't be our highest good, either.

> Experience is the food of all grace, which it grows and thrives upon.
>
> John Owen, *Pnuematologia*

Love, community, and growth of character are often—though not always—at odds with efficiency. This is something God has always known and been comfortable with. One of the most *in*efficient things you can ever do is love another person. Or even a puppy. Loving another creature requires engagement, response, and patience. Loads of patience. Similarly, the artist or author knows all too well that efficiency is often the enemy rather than the friend of creativity and progress. The almighty Creator, however, has always been comfortable prioritizing love and growth over efficiency and checkmarks. I want to be more like that!

Divine Hospitality and Human Growth

In the ancient church, centuries before Charles Darwin or debates about evolution, there was a general appreciation that the Genesis narrative affirmed God's deliberate patience and purposes with humanity. Genesis did not give exact scientific descriptions of when and how God created, and the church did not view God's original creation as the end, but rather as the beginning.

Irenaeus (130–202), for example, employed images of infancy and childhood to make sense of Adam and Eve's original state. This was not because he thought they were literal children in the narrative, nor was he trying to belittle their dignity or value. Rather, he used these metaphors to show that the first chapters of Genesis lead us somewhere else; they press us forward. Adam and Eve were designed for growth.[4] In this way, "being made in God's image and likeness" was "a primordial gift as well as a calling to be realized."[5] Creation has a trajectory, a movement, a process. And this includes Adam and Eve, who were responsible agents and called to engage the rest of creation as part of their growth. The adolescent imagery Irenaeus associated with Adam and Eve stressed the responsibility and dignity they were given as being called to live with God and to grow by responding to his presence and kindness with worship. Irenaeus laid out the sequence: "It was necessary for man to be first created; and having been created, to grow; and having grown, to become mature; and having become mature, to multiply; and having multiplied, to grow strong; and having grown strong, to be glorified; and having been glorified, to see his Lord."[6] Eden was not a static condition like a still photograph: it was the setting for a developing story with promises, but also warning. Like the flowers, trees, and animals, humans lived in movement, meant to grow and fill the earth. Therefore, precisely as they were finite creatures, they were put into the process of increasing in their knowledge and love of God, their neighbor, and the rest of creation. According to Irenaeus, Genesis revealed that when God created human beings good, there was still abundant space for them to flourish, to become—in a sense—even more "perfect." This is an idea we will return to later when we consider the life of Jesus.

Gregory of Nyssa (335–95) also gives us an inviting way to make sense of how God was relating to humanity at creation's start. His volume *On the Making of Man* highlights both God's preparations and his end purposes.[7] They go together. First, God appears like a cosmic host who arranges a great meal and prepares "a royal dwelling place" so that then when the invited guests arrive, they can enjoy the feast that will culminate with the coming of a king. This dwelling place is the whole world, from the heavens to the deep waters, filled with the wealth of the entire creation. Then God brings "man into the world to behold its wonders. . . . As he enjoys these things he acquires knowledge of the one who gave them, and by the beauty and majesty of things he sees he finds traces of the power of the maker who is beyond speech and thought."[8] It would take time and growth, but humanity was meant to enjoy the fullness of God's world, since in doing so they would also increase their knowledge and love of the Creator. Gregory purposely draws on biblical imagery to connect the enjoyment of God with the enjoyment of his good earth (e.g., 1 Tim. 6:17).[9] Guests who enjoy a feast and the warmth of hospitality are, at their best, delighting not merely in the gifts but in the giver as well.

Second, Gregory connects this enjoyment with the fact that humans are uniquely made to reflect God. Whereas the rest of creation seems to come into being by simple divine command, the human is created when God ruminates, "Let us . . ." (Gen. 1:26), as "the maker of all approaches the task circumspectly, preparing materials beforehand for the business of making, and likens his form to an archetypal beauty."[10] While humanity is in some ways like the animals, that is not what appears most interesting to Gregory. Rather, human creatures alone reflected God's image and likeness—talk about dignity! So, to know what it means to be human, we should look not to an ape or an angel, but "at the face of God." Here one sees his love. As Robert Louis Wilken further summarizes Gregory's point: "We know ourselves as we transcend ourselves, and we find ourselves as we find fellowship with God."[11] Communion with God points not simply toward human origins but toward human ends, to the culmination and purpose of human creation. We were always meant to grow in our love for God and his creation. In other words, God has consistently been concerned with process and not merely with a finished product.

Divine image and likeness do not consist only in possessing a psychological capacity (e.g., reason), but also in a loving response to God and his work. When we rebel against the Creator, hurt our neighbors, and show disregard for the rest of the created world, we disturb and distort love. This is sin. In this rebellion humans fail to mirror the face of God. In his obedience Christ alone as the true and full image of God restores human nature, pointing both back to the original creation and forward toward a final consummation: as Gregory says, "The end is given in the beginning." Wilken adds, "Creation is promise as well as gift, and it is only in seeing Christ that we know what was made in the first creation."[12]

The Future Shapes the Present

Creation is not described to us as a static picture, but as a living story. God designed us to live and to grow in love and wonder. Sin didn't just distort our past or jeopardize our future; it disorders our present. Salvation in Christ by the Spirit does not undermine God's original creation but puts us back onto the trajectory of life and love, within the warmth of the divine embrace; it untwists us so that we might reach the designed culmination. Biblical scholar Richard Gaffin once cryptically wrote, "Eschatology is a postulate of protology."[13] What he means is that the *beginning* always assumed a future direction: we were meant to not merely be pushed from the past but pulled into the future. Thus, the beginning (*proto*) was always only a beginning, which means that the story doesn't stay there but moves on toward the *telos*, a purpose, an end (*eschatos*) that was built into the design of the beginning. Gaffin thus echoes what Irenaeus and Gregory wrote many centuries earlier.

Eschatology—concern with the *last* things—is not found only in the book of Revelation but is also implicit in the opening pages of Genesis. Even before sin's entrance into the human experience (Gen. 3), there was an eschatological pull on humankind.[14] As the early-twentieth-century Princeton theologian Geerhardus Vos argued, "Eschatology aims at consummation rather than restoration."[15] Purpose, development, and growth were always aspects of God's intention, and therefore good. Sin does not determine the end for which humanity was created, but it does introduce the need for a redemptive aspect to the story. Salvation, therefore, "must be restorative and consummative," not merely taking us back to an original garden filled with possibilities, but forward to the wonder of life-giving communion with God.[16] The sweep of Scripture gives us both a portrait of the formation of human creatures and a vision of their final perfective purpose. There is a *telos* not merely for humanity in general but for each human life—we are each distinctly designed for communion with God, neighbor, and the earth. Both the universal and the particular must always be kept in mind when considering "man," or humanity.

Yahweh's intentions and purposes for human creatures are consistent, from Adam to Abraham, from Israel to the church. Throughout the Scriptures, Israel regularly hears this defining claim: "You shall love the Lord your God with all your heart and with all your soul and with all your might" (Deut. 6:5; cf. 11:1, 13; 13:3; 30:6; Josh. 22:5; Ps. 31:23). They were beckoned to a love and communion with God for which they were originally created, a call that was not meant to take them beyond being fully human, but rather to the heart of it. Growth and development were not a way to cease nor surpass finite creaturely existence, but to accomplish God's perfectly humane expectation. It is wrong to understand this future-oriented call as something extra or "spiritual," added to a nonspiritual human way of life. This call to "love God" is a call to be truly and freely a human creature, created "very good" so as to enjoy ever-growing harmonious relations with the Creator and the rest of his creation.

Communion as the Goal of Being Human

If we affirm that the image of God consists in our communion with him, with each other, and with the created world, then we are driven to affirm the goodness of growth over time. Communion itself is a process, it takes time, and it results in growth. It could also be described as an embodied love, engaging the whole of our being. Traditional descriptions of the image of God have often been articulated in terms of our psychological faculties (i.e., mind, will, affections). Rather than simply dismissing this older psychological method, we can examine it from the perspective of love and communion to discover an ongoing relevance in it. We do not merely *have* bodies or faculties, but rather, as embodied psychosomatic creatures, we occupy relationships that define us through our bodies and faculties. To put it differently, if no more than the capacity to reason were the key attribute that makes one human, then one's humanity would be reduced to an Intelligence Quotient (IQ). The higher your IQ, the more human you would be. However, if we treat the faculties not in terms of measurements that can be ranked but in terms of love and communion, then the criteria are all changed.

What makes us human is our distinctive ability to love and commune with God, other humans, and the earth. Such love and communion normally take place in a body and through one's faculties (like intelligence), no matter the level of their function. Someone with an IQ that barely registers may nevertheless profoundly experience God's love, sensing his presence and responding to his kindness, even if that response is unrecognizable to the rest of us. Salvation and even communion should not be reduced to high intellectual ability. Those who cannot verbally communicate, or who have other disabilities, may nonetheless have deep communion with other people.[17] The ministry of places like L'Arche provides a place and encouragement for this communion to happen. We also see beautiful and telling connections between animals and those with disabilities all the time. There is much for us to learn from those we tend to undervalue or ignore. Communion might look different from what we sometimes imagine.

John Swinton has written a lovely volume entitled *Becoming Friends of Time: Disability, Timefullness, and Gentle Discipleship*.[18] As a Christian ethicist, Swinton has frequently taken on difficult topics and provided fresh ways to handle them. In this book he explores the power of time in our lives. We tend to value only the quick, failing to appreciate that those who force us to slow down present us with the important and rich gift of awareness, of learning to be fully present with the person in front of us. It is not difficult to see how easily we have imposed a scale of "being efficient" onto our perception of "being human," consequently valuing people in terms of productivity and speed. *Good* and *bad* are ideas we often unconsciously link with models of industry, sometimes causing us to apply mechanistic notions to people without ever realizing that this causes us to treat people as if they were machines. We try to be human *doings* instead of human *beings*. The dehumanizing effects of this quickly become apparent.

We sometimes give greater dignity to high cognitive functioning over low cognitive abilities. We value speed over plodding, we honor individual glory over communal unity, and we prize industrial productivity over relational fidelity. Swinton recognizes that the presence of those with profound intellectual disabilities often causes our communities to display what we really believe but seldom admit: your worth is tied to your productivity, or your value is linked to your IQ. Seeing this isn't pretty. These are not just problems out there in the "world": the church has not fully resisted the temptation to adopt efficiency-driven systems of value that distort our vision and experience of communion. This then disfigures our understanding of growth in the Christian life. It destroys how we imagine God sees us! Let's consider how this can happen and how it can be addressed.

Affirming finitude as a part of the creaturely domain, Swinton challenges us to realize that "love has a speed" and we should discover the beauty of "slow and gentle disciples" who are easily missed and ignored but are actually vital to the kingdom of God. We sense that we need to slow down and listen to Christ, to see him in the vulnerable and needy, and to confess our own neediness in the process. But will we slow down? When I engage those who have Down syndrome, for example, do I imagine I am the only one bringing something of value to the relationship, or can I learn from them? Might they help me better recognize God's character, purposes, and kingdom? Only the unhurried tend to value process, including God's faithful work over the long seasons of our lives. Swinton and others remind us that we can learn a great deal along these lines from those with disabilities who move at a different pace.

Chuck Colson was famous not simply as President Nixon's "hatchet man" who served prison time for his involvement in the Watergate scandal but also for his radical conversion, which resulted in an international prison ministry. Awarded the Templeton Prize and at least fifteen honorary doctorates, he was a high-powered and energetic person in all his pursuits, and it should be unsurprising that his daughter Emily called him a strong type A personality. This was part of how God made him, but if he never slowed down, he risked not growing as God intended. Only one person, the family would joke, could make him slow down: his grandson Max, Emily's son with autism. When Max was really young, Colson did not know how to relate to Max: Colson kept trying to impart his great wisdom to this little kid, but Max would just cry and avoid him. Emily remembers that when Max was six years old and they were visiting Florida to stay with the grandparents, Colson had a serious case of flu and was sapped of energy, stuck powerless on the couch.[19] All he could do was lie there and observe, day after day, how the single mom Emily and her son Max would interact. He finally saw Max for Max, and it began to transform Colson. Max would draw him into life and a fresh form of communion, but not an efficient one. As Emily explained, Max didn't care about people's agendas or schedules. "If he goes shopping with Grandpa there is no hope for a quick, in-and-out visit to the store to buy a couple of items. Max wants his grandfather to share in his enjoyment of the experience of being in a shop. This is a process which can take an hour or two. It also requires the accompanying adult to enter the autistic boy's world . . . [going] at his own slow pace."[20] Max was inviting Colson into deeply humane ways of life, pointing back to the original experience of wonder over creation and forward to a fuller, unhurried life with God and others.

Here we encounter a great mystery, part of which is that love and communion reorient how we understand and evaluate our bodies and faculties: we see them *relationally* rather than mechanistically. You don't become more human by having a higher IQ, but you do more truly reflect God as you grow in your experience of divine love and communion.

These considerations matter because Christians often feel guilty or ashamed about their limited intellectual abilities, or physical weaknesses, or how their willpower fluctuates in correspondence with their blood sugar levels. Are you an unfaithful Christian if you fall short of Michael Jordon's fanatical drivenness, which shaped his competitive "willpower" on the court? Or should we be reminded that mere exercises of determination were never the heart of the Christian concern about self-control? Christianity's goal has never been mere inner peace, nor endless programs of self-improvement, strength training, or better education. Christianity's goal or *telos* has always been to grow in love and communion with God, our neighbors, and the rest of his creation.

The classical representation of the whole person involved seeing it as a combination of the faculties of mind, will, affections, and body, and these were the means by which one related to God and the rest of creation as a finite creature. These faculties are rightly judged not by mechanistic efficiency but by how they are used—to foster or hinder loving communion. This can help explain our horror toward murder (Gen. 9:6; Exod. 20:13; Deut. 5:17): intentionally killing a fellow creature made in God's image is an attack against the very possibility of love, and thus, an attack against God and all fellow humans. For example, when people describe someone like Stalin or Hitler, they often resort to language like "beast" or "animal." Does this mean that they started to function intellectually more like a donkey than a human? Not at all. Such comments refer to their complete lack of concern for love and communion, and it dehumanized them.

Even if we reject classical "faculty psychology" for more contemporary psychological models or language, we can still find real insight in those traditions. What makes us distinctively human is not these faculties as such, but our loving response to God with whatever abilities we do have and can develop. The usefulness of looking at these faculties lies not in examining anyone's native emotional or mental brilliance, nor unbendable willpower—that would isolate the faculties from interaction with others and thus from their very purpose. No, looking at these faculties is useful when they are understood within God's purposes for their function as furthering communion between the Creator and his creation in particularly human terms. Specific instances of communion may look very different because humans are particular and unique creatures, and these differences all contribute to the richness and life of that communion. To understand what this means, we will now consider Jesus and his growth.

Christ and the In-Breaking of Divine Love

What if, rather than having an abstract ideal "man" or "woman" in mind as the model for humanity, we instead realized that the goal God has for us is to make us more like Christ, the perfect image? The historical Jesus who walked the roads of Galilee perfectly loved the Father, depended on the Spirit, loved his neighbors, and brought a foretaste of healing to the earth. Jesus may have had the highest IQ ever, but actually that would not be theologically necessary for him to be the Messiah. Others could have been better at geometry or even woodworking than he. I would have no problem admitting such a thing. If Einstein scored higher than Jesus on an IQ test, that would not in any way jeopardize our faith. Jesus's IQ is not what qualified him to be our Savior. Instead, the eternal Son entered finite human existence, really becoming one with us, which included taking on real creaturely limits. Others were inevitably taller or stronger or more handsome than Jesus. None of this made him a sinner or somehow unacceptable to the Father. By virtue of his human nature, he could even confess not knowing the answer to every question and to being so tired that he required real rest (Matt. 24:36; John 21:17; and Matt. 8:23–27; Luke 5:16; John 4:6). Jesus of Nazareth was truly like us in every way, yet without sin (Heb. 4:15).

It was because he entered our finite human existence, and not in spite of it, that he was able to secure our forgiveness and freedom and bring us back into life-giving communion with the Creator Lord. We are like Christ, therefore, not by having bigger brains but by being born again with a renewed heart now directed toward God and neighbor. Such love is both an expression of and a conduit for worship.

Even Jesus Grew

At Christmas we sing songs to celebrate the birth of our Savior, Jesus the Messiah. Stars and shepherds, donkeys and a manger—we know the basic elements of the carols. A few months later our focus turns to Good Friday and Easter Sunday. These are key Christian celebrations. Reflecting the proportions of the Gospels, we spend a bit of time on his birth and then concentrate on his teaching ministry and ultimately his death, resurrection, and ascension. Yet have you ever asked, *Why doesn't the Bible tell us more about Jesus's life?* There must have been some great stories, key insights, and helpful examples we could learn from this information. Yet we have little more than the birth narratives (Matt. 1:18–25; Luke 2:1–21) and a brief description of his stay in the temple when he was twelve years old (Luke 2:41–52) before we are taken to the final few years of his earthly life and ministry. Why is so much left out from those three decades?

Christians have always wanted to know more about the life of Jesus than the New Testament tells us, so there has always been a market for stories that fill in the details of Jesus's early years. The Infancy Gospel of Thomas (second century) offers such stories. One of its tales describes the boy Jesus creating living birds out of mere clay—a pretty cool magic trick for any kid trying to impress his friends. Although they are charming stories, they are only made up! The early church historian Eusebius (260–339), for example, judged this work fictional and even heretical.[21] Even though stories like this (if true) might make it easier to argue for Jesus's full divinity, Eusebius and other orthodox teachers resisted the temptation to use them that way. These imagined stories of Jesus's childhood fit more with fanciful imagination than with anything we actually find in Scripture, which is relatively silent about Jesus's early years.

So why doesn't Scripture give us more information about the time between Jesus's birth and his teaching ministry? We don't really know, since the New Testament also doesn't state the reason for its silence on the topic. The one passage that comments on his boyhood (Luke 2:41–52) could also be taken to indicate that he lived a relatively normal life. It is the same reason Scripture doesn't tell you every time Jesus breaks out in belly laughter or record his need to urinate: these are normal aspects of human existence, neither shameful nor worth highlighting. As we observed concerning Jesus's birth in an earlier chapter, one remarks on what is strange or different or wonderful. What would be worth recording is if he *never* needed to relieve himself or *never* laughed at a good joke; that would appear unusual enough to record for posterity. But the New Testament doesn't record any such thing. So, we should assume he was like us in all these ways. A virgin birth, a young boy with profoundly surprising insights, and a uniquely gifted rabbi who could heal bodies and hearts—these were noteworthy. His life as a seventeen-year-old was not noteworthy, at least not in terms of the purposes of the Gospels. They assume rather than detail most of his physical, psychological, and relational developments over those three decades.

Jesus doesn't just drop out of heaven as a developed adult, ready to jump up onto a cross. Apparently it was significant that, as the mediator between God and humanity, the incarnate Son experienced the fullness of human life. As Irenaeus argued, by going through—what he called recapitulating—the normal seasons of human life, the Messiah was in some mysterious way going about the work of renewing creation itself.[22] The fact that we are not taken through the details of Jesus's development—from infancy to childhood, from adolescence to early adulthood—should actually prove a comfort to us. We have no details of his learning to talk or going through puberty, so we can assume he basically went through the awkwardness of these stages just like the rest of us. Here is genuine solidarity and shared identity. In fact, we can assume that his life, from his birth through his death, was mostly filled with normal physical, mental, and emotional growth. And although Jesus always remained without sin, he inhabited a broken and sinful world: he knew not just the positives of human existence but also heartbreak and cruelty. He knew what it was to be let down, how it felt to be misunderstood by your family or to have lies told about you. He grew and developed through all of this, although he never succumbed to the temptations that inevitably arose.

Luke, for example, highlights this observation: "And the child [Jesus] grew and became strong, filled with wisdom. And the favor of God was upon him" (Luke 2:40). And then after relaying the story of Jesus as a preteen in the temple, Luke summarizes Jesus's life from twelve to the time he is baptized by John in the River Jordan many years later: "And Jesus increased in wisdom and in stature and in favor with God and man" (2:52). Growth, increase, and development. These texts assert that Jesus became stronger and wiser, which enabled him—as incarnate—to experience a deeper human communion with the Father and his fellow humanity. We must be very careful here. Jesus is definitely not moving from sin to nonsin, nor from noncommunion to communion: he was always perfectly holy and free of sinful motives and actions and was never apart from or antagonistic to the Spirit or the Father. But as Jesus grows physically, mentally, and emotionally, there appears to be a corresponding growth of what wisdom and love look like for him.

Expressions of human wisdom and grace in Jesus as a thirty-year-old are necessarily deeper and more complex than what one would find when holding Jesus as a seven-month-old baby. If Jesus fluently spoke fourteen languages before his first birthday, we would wonder if he was genuinely human like the rest of us. His bona fide creaturely limits and abilities, therefore, inform and shape his growing experience of love and communion. Luke's description appears to intentionally parallel the narrative of young Samuel's growth and development on his way to becoming a prophet (1 Sam. 2:26; 3:19); but Jesus is being prepared for more, not simply to speak prophetic words to Israel, nor to offer normal priestly sacrifices. As the one filled with the Spirit beyond measure (John 3:34), Jesus eventually is able to teach with unique power and authority during his years of ministry (Matt. 7:2; 9:6–8; 28:18; John 12:49; 14:10), and the culmination of his growth "as a man" will be that he is uniquely able to offer *himself* as the full and final sacrifice, once for all (Heb. 9:26; 10:12; cf. Eph. 5:2; Heb. 4:14–5:10). Thus Jesus's earthly life of normal development and growth also shows us God's original creation design for humans. God delighted in process, just as he does in his restorative work of new creation. Jesus's limits as a human creature should not scare Christians but instead light up the profound beauty and extent of God's love: that the eternal majestic Son of God, "though he was in the form of God, did not count equality with God a thing to be grasped, but emptied himself, taking the form of a servant, being born in the likeness of men" (Phil. 2:6–7).

We need to be careful here because we tend to think that "perfection" simply equals sinlessness, but the biblical and historical understanding of "perfect" often has more to do with being "blameless," especially in the sense of being "whole" or "complete."[23] Animal sacrifices were "perfect" not because the lamb avoided hate or resisted greed but because it was complete and unblemished (e.g., Lev. 3:1–6). This is why the author of Hebrews can say that Jesus was "being made perfect" (Heb. 2:10; 5:9; 7:28):[24] It doesn't mean that Jesus had previously been sinful and now he was holy (cf. 7:26). Instead, it points to Jesus's human life of growth, to his accumulation of experiences, and to him achieving his purposes as Savior of the world, consecrated now to serve as the unique and final High Priest.[25] He was always blameless, and yet his life was a life of growth, becoming fully equipped to complete his work. Jesus offered his life as an adult rather than as a baby. Like the original creation, the human nature assumed by the eternal Son is meant to grow and be "perfected." Similarly, if you hold a beautiful, good, "perfect" baby in your hands, as lovely as it is, you would not want that child to remain a baby. Babies are meant to grow, to mature, to have their lives expanded in good and honorable ways. Jesus's full earthly life shows that, even with him, process and development were necessary and good.

We are not Jesus, for he alone is both truly human and truly God. He is uniquely the eternal Son become incarnate (*in-the-flesh*).

But this uniqueness does not distance Jesus from us, because God the Holy Spirit connects us with him. The Gospels tell us that, from conception, Mary's son Jesus "will be great and will be called the Son of the Most High" (Luke 1:32). It is by the Holy Spirit's sanctifying presence and power that the Virgin Mary conceives (Matt. 1:18, 20; Luke 1:34–35); furthermore, Jesus lives his whole life in and with the Spirit (e.g., Luke 4:1, 14, 18; John 1:23–33; 3:34); by the Spirit's power he casts out demons, heals the hurting, and proclaims good news to the needy (e.g., Matt. 12:18, 28; Luke 4:18, 33–42; Acts 10:38); and finally, even the Messiah's death is offered up "through the eternal Spirit" (Heb. 9:14), and this same Spirit of God also raises Jesus from the dead (Rom. 8:11; cf. 1:4; 1 Pet. 3:18). Ascending into the heavens, Christ pours out his Spirit into his people, bringing faith, hope, and love where there was rebellion, sin, and death. God saves, and the God who saves is the Father who works through the Son and by the Spirit. As his people, we are empowered by the same Spirit who unites us to Christ so that we might live freely in the Father's love and grow in grace and truth.

But if we are united with Christ, how is it possible that we still sin? In what way is God working in and through us?

We Are Renewed by the Spirit

Protestant theologians have sometimes observed a distinction between justification and sanctification in how they deal with the problem of sin. As

Anthony A. Hoekema distinguishes, sin not only makes us (1) guilty before God, but it also (2) pollutes us and drives us away from communion with him. Accordingly, justification has been traditionally viewed as dealing primarily with our guilt, which comes from sin: we who were deserving condemnation no longer bear that guilt because of the finished work of Christ. Sanctification, however, was thought to deal also with the activity and influence of sin in our lives. In sanctification, "the pollution of sin is in the process of being removed (though it will not be totally removed until the life to come)."[26] Put differently, the children of God are not just relieved of the legal accusations of sin (justification), but we are being made more and more like his incarnate Son (sanctification). Sanctification is less about helping Christians avoid mistakes or miscalculations and more about fostering their love and communion with the Divine and with one's neighbor. In other words, God really doesn't just absolve us of sin; he is also committed to carrying out the transformative work he begins in us (Phil. 1:6). Certainly, this side of glory, such work will always remain incomplete in us, though we are indeed saints (i.e., God's holy ones) even now: but to imagine we can never grow would contradict many biblical injunctions. It is good and right to remind ourselves that we are forgiven and loved, dependent always on the grace of God. But this does not mean that our decisions and actions are irrelevant. No, God's people can grow, and that growth normally looks more like love and communion than like mere data accumulation or self-improvement. We grow in these ways because God loves us.

Justin Borger, a pastor and friend of mine, loves to ask people what Romans 3:23 says. From memory, people often paraphrase it by saying something like this: "For all have sinned and fallen short." But that isn't all that it says. We rarely include the key word framing this sobering text: "glory." We have sinned and "fall short of the glory of God." This statement about our condition is so sad because of how magnificent humans were made to be: reflecting God's glory! Humans are not scum. We are not vile. We are fallen glorious creatures who have allowed sin to distort and destroy, affecting both our internal and external worlds. Sin muddies our unique, glorious reflection of God.

Working in our lives, the Spirit does the immediate work of our new birth (John 3:3, 7; 1 Pet. 1:3, 23), securing our status as saints, who no longer bow to sin as our master (e.g., Rom. 6:1–2; 1 Cor. 6:11). But the same Spirit, the Spirit of creation, also transforms over time our loves and opportunities for communion. Ralph Martin explains that the believer's growth is "gradual and progressive, from one stage of glory to yet a higher stage [2 Bar. 51:3, 7, 10], climaxing in the goal reached" in our glorification with Christ (Rom. 8:17, 29, 30).[27] Paul encourages his listeners with his expectation of seeing that "Christ is formed in you" (Gal. 4:19; cf. Phil. 3:21; 1 John 3:2).

Now let's be clear, this growth does not occur with unwavering increase in godly motives, behavior, and purposes. We don't just go up, up, up. Like the child learning to walk, we inevitably fall, sometimes painfully crashing toward the ground and getting hurt in the process. No, although God has made us his saints and has promised to work in us by his Spirit, we are not always the best judges of growth. Growth is often imperceptible to us, either because it is slow, or because it isn't the kind of growth that we can see, or because we don't understand it as growth, or for other reasons. There is almost a strange paradox in this growth in many saints. Many of the godliest saints have been profoundly aware of their sin—they grew more rather than less aware of its distorting presence as the years passed. Yet those who know them sometimes find it hard to believe they really struggle with sin like the rest of us. Why? Because when we try to judge growth, we often apply categories of moralism rather than the biblical categories of the Spirit's fruit: love, joy, peace, patience, kindness, gentleness, and truth. We live in a world that works for outward and obvious triumph, so it doesn't value slow-growing character traits like gentleness and joy. But in God's kingdom these traits are the places of real growth and development.

> Christian virtue, including the ninefold fruit of the Spirit, is *both* the gift of God *and* the result of the person of faith making conscious decisions to cultivate this way of life and these habits of heart and mind.
>
> N. T. Wright, *After You Believe*

John Owen and the Spirit's Normal Work in Us

To my knowledge, the most extensive discussion on the person and work of the Holy Spirit up through the seventeenth century is found in the voluminous writings of John Owen. In particular, his massive work called *Pneumatologia* traces the Spirit's work from creation through consummation. He gives a fresh and lively treatment of the Spirit in the life of Jesus and a careful, pastoral unpacking of the Spirit's work in the life of believers. Because he so strongly connects the Spirit's presence and work at creation to his presence and work in the incarnation, he is also able to provide insightful reflections on sanctification. For our limited purposes, I will only highlight one relevant idea here.

Let's start with a brief definition of *sanctification* by Owen: "It is the universal renovation of our natures by the Holy Spirit into the image of God, through Jesus Christ."[28] The ongoing work and goal of sanctification, according to Owen, is the renewing of Christians in their whole (i.e., universal) being—mind, heart, will (and thus our embodied actions and relationships)—into the image of Christ. As we have observed, when this renewal is understood in terms of love and communion, such a holistic study makes more sense than looking at our faculties individually. God is renewing our minds, reordering our loves, and empowering our wills. This process takes place both behind the scenes, where the Holy Spirit renews our being apart from our conscious knowledge, and also in our conscious and repeated turning toward Christ, who is the perfect image of God. Only the Spirit can change our disposition and empower us for growth in grace.[29] Put differently, God's Spirit does not merely convey to us a sense of God's forgiveness; he also gives us power and purpose. He promises to transform us, although, as with most of his work, it may be slow and steady rather than instantaneous and dramatic.

God's Spirit continually moves and stirs us to faithfulness in communion with God, with each other, and with the world around us. So how do we know if God's Spirit is working in us? Should we primarily look for signs or extraordinary powers? No, we should primarily look for love (e.g., Rom. 5:5; Gal. 5:6, 22; 1 John 4:11–21).

In Owen's day there were movements of folks who claimed extraordinary experiences of the Spirit. Those experiences produced names that were originally derogatory, although the names lingered while the derogatory intent is now forgotten: Shakers, Quakers, and Enthusiasts. Such labels were given to these groups because their experiences of the Spirit seemed to produce behaviors like the loss of physical composure, mental command, and emotional balance in their worship services. They seem to "lose themselves" during these experiences. Some accounts spoke of people being cast about without control, even violently, having no sense of what they were saying or doing.[30] While such descriptions seem so far from how we think of Quakers and Shakers of the twenty-first century, these were the early reports (often circulated by their critics, but also by many participants themselves). For our purposes I will leave aside whether these reports were fair or not to these groups, since I am mostly interested in Owen's proposal rather than the accuracy of his understanding of the situation.

While reflecting on the work of the Spirit, Owen resisted what he saw as the two extremes. On the one side were the rationalists (e.g., Socinians), who appeared to deny the person and work of the Spirit altogether. For them, the "spirit" was nothing more than an element of creation itself, certainly not a distinctive divine person. On the other side were the "Enthusiasts," whom we just described. Owen feared that this second group also misunderstood the normal work of the Spirit and that their practices would undermine believers' expectations of the Christian life. He feared this vision of the Spirit's work was dehumanizing rather than (re)affirming of the dignity and purposes of human creatures. Expectations of such extreme experiences, he worried, often cultivated attitudes that belittle the way God made us—with finite minds, limited emotional capacity, and the necessity for deliberately cultivating our conscious involvement in the Spirit's work in us. The question for him, in other words, was, *Were they seeking a Spirit that undermined our humanity, or one that reaffirmed and strengthened it?* Since the Spirit of creation is the same as the Spirit of re-creation, the work of sanctification and transformation should make us more—not less—human. It reminds me of John Stott's response when he was asked about the "barking" phenomena happening in some churches in the 1990s. Being as diplomatic as he could manage, and not wanting to completely rule out that God's Spirit might be working, Stott nonetheless admitted some concern that these reported experiences tended to make people appear more like animals than like God, and that their anti-intellectual instincts seemed to undermine human dignity rather than affirm it.[31]

Owen also worried that the "spirit" people claimed to have experienced often didn't point to Christ, but instead to itself, sometimes even appearing to encourage people to downplay or ignore the person and work of Christ. But in Scripture, the Holy Spirit always points people to Christ, since the Holy Spirit is the very Spirit of the Son (e.g., Rom. 8:9; Gal. 4:6; Phil. 1:19). God's Spirit is never put in competition with Christ, because we love the Father through the Son by the Spirit (cf. Eph. 2:18). A true sign of the Holy Spirit's work, therefore, is the exaltation of Christ.

Since the Spirit of sanctification is the same as the Spirit of creation, we should expect that God's Spirit will not typically give us extraordinary powers, but rather will redirect us toward our original end—namely, fuller communion with God. For this purpose, the Spirit gives us new hearts, provokes in us a love for God and neighbor, and strengthens us in the good deeds of love and grace. Again, marks of growing in the Spirit do not include how many miracles one can do or how many astonishing experiences one has, but whether one is growing in love for God and neighbor.

We maintain, therefore, that sanctification, which yields transformation, operates with a dual character: it is all dependent on and responsive to God's work, and it never undermines the dignity of our agency or engagement. As N. T. Wright ably summarizes: "Christian virtue, including the ninefold fruit of the Spirit, is *both* the gift of God *and* the result of the person of faith making conscious decisions to cultivate this way of life and these habits of heart and mind."[32] The work of God's Spirit follows the pattern shown at creation: although sometimes his work is immediate and dramatic, more often it is slow and progressive, calling for and encouraging our agency rather than undermining it.

Do Not Lose Heart

It is easy for us to grow discouraged when we look at our lives and see how far short we fall of what we would desire. We see both our sin and our finite limits. We wish our ongoing struggles with troublesome attitudes, addictions, and actions would all immediately end. Yet God does not normally change our attitudes, free us from our addictions, and reform our actions instantaneously—although sometimes he does it that quickly. Ordinarily, God changes our lives by persistently picking us up when we fall and slowly but consistently drawing us to the love of the Father, the grace of the Son, and the fellowship of the Spirit. In this process he reconnects us with others, replacing our callousness with compassion, our hatred with love, and our fears with hope.

Do not lose heart: he who began a good work in you will see it to completion. Don't forget that God most often chooses to do this by slow but consistent work in our lives through his church, his people. So now let us turn to the question of living as the people of God, for when we are together, our personal limitations start to look different. With a more communal vision, our individual lives take on much greater significance—though with less pressure—than we may have ever imagined.

9

do i need to be part of the church?

loving the whole body

> The "isolated individual" is the product of man's fallen imagination. It is a product of sin. It does not exist. It has no reality at all. What does exist are persons in community.
>
> Thomas Hopko, *All the Fulness of God*

It takes the whole church to be the one body of Christ. Serving and depending on others constitutes a twofold dynamic that builds up the community in faith, hope, and love. The diversity within the church's unity displays God's presence and action in this world.

So Many Needs

Sitting in Sunday school listening to a visitor explain a vibrant ministry in our county's prisons, I am deeply moved. Our time together ends with his description of opportunities to support this effort through finances, by becoming a mentor and regularly meeting with an inmate, or by starting correspondence with an incarcerated person who would benefit from encouragement, shared wisdom, and the gift of friendship. A brown clipboard with a ruled, white sheet of paper for sign-ups gets passed around. Guilt, and maybe even Spirit-led conviction, begin to pierce my soul: *I really should sign up*.

A few weeks later, different visitors working in local housing projects tell the stories of what God is doing in another part of town. Within a setting of intense crime, chronic poverty, and widespread fear, God is doing beautiful and significant things. Pockets of shalom and hope are popping up in the community. Christians living there are receiving much-needed encouragement, while others are newly experiencing the love of Christ through deed and word. Yet the needs far outweigh the abilities of those currently living there and serving in the ministry. Explaining some of the opportunities, the leaders hand around the same clipboard, but now with a different set of sign-up sheets. Pierced again, I can see just how vital this powerful ministry is, and how I should unreservedly support it. Here comes the sign-up sheet . . . *What to do?*

Not too long after that we hold our annual missions conference. Here we learn not just about the work of those we already support but also about fresh challenges and opportunities. This year we concentrate on India, where gospel ministry is happening among the materially poor in some areas and the privileged elites in others. Prayers, people, and finances are always encouraged, needed, and welcomed. Last year we focused on neglected parts of the Muslim world, and next year we will consider needs in Europe. *How am I to respond?*

And then, a few weeks later, an excellent ministry to those struggling with unplanned pregnancies . . . Some months later another important need is presented . . .

You see where this is going. "Compassion fatigue" describes the reaction of our limited capacity and the unlimited need. People are always needed to serve inside and outside the church. Are the legitimate needs in God's church and world ever fully met? When was the last time you heard of a vital ministry that had too many volunteers or too much money? Should we just feel guilty all the time about how much we are not able to do, or should we overcommit and burn out?

In response to the endless requests to fill these needs, some will understandably reply that we should narrow our focus and "only do what the Bible requires," or "simplify and be like the early church."

While I am strongly sympathetic toward attempts to help overextended Christians, and I don't think the church is supposed to do *everything*, I also worry that unbiblical impulses too often lie behind our calls to narrow the church's focus, or at least Christian obligations. Yes, "simplifying" might happily mean ending some unneeded or distracting programs, but in practice it too often means downplaying concerns that are time-consuming but nonetheless very near the heart of God (the poor, widows, orphans, the lost, etc.). None of us approach Scripture without presuppositions and blind spots, and so we all tend to highlight what we are most comfortable with, while downplaying areas that make us uncomfortable. Affluent and busy parishioners like me are tempted to harden our hearts to those in material need, but that doesn't mean God does or that his church should.

One sign that something has gone wrong in efforts to focus only on the "gospel" is that a church's pastor and staff are endlessly *active* in proclaiming and doing the spiritual work, while the congregation remains *passive*. When we imagine love as directed toward us and yet hold back from loving others, we have failed to dwell in love. We become observers rather than participants, entertained rather than engaged, critics rather than contributors—we make for ourselves a comfortable place outside of love. That is not a description of the ancient church nor of God's own action. Our responses expose our lopsided thinking. For example, when the congregation is asked to do something that may threaten our standard of living, do we dismiss it as promoting "works righteousness"? Do we act as if effort and self-denial are antithetical to the grace of Christ and the Christian life? Or, in our highly charged partisan environment, do we label ministries that call us to care for the marginalized and needy as "political" or engaging in the "social gospel," as if the gospel could be separated from sociological concerns? Such a treatment of the New Testament often grows from a reductionist psychological reading of the text—ignoring the real challenges the early church was facing (e.g., overcoming divisions between Jew and gentile, rich and poor, male and female)—and from a willingness to put our cultural standards ahead of scriptural ones. The earliest church desired to live by kingdom values, thus upending the cultural values of its age. Sociological and theological concerns are not so easily untangled.

From the beginning, the early church did not just preach and pray (although those were central); they also shared their goods, cared for widows, comforted the grieving, strengthened the poor, testified to the good news with their neighbors, and modeled a different way of existing in the world (cf. Acts 2:42–47). With the bread and wine, the church uniquely offered a taste of shalom that could break into the chaos and sin of a hungry and hurting world. It displayed hope, not by avoiding the darkness and sadness of life, but by bringing the light and peace of Christ to bear on the real pain and need that we encounter. Here, in the church, sin and dysfunction could be honestly addressed, confessed, and healed. They found and experienced shalom as the Spirit of God brought fresh waves of grace, unity, and love. Such transforming love from God moves from heart to home, from the corporate worshiping experience to concrete and particular actions on behalf of broken bodies and suffocating souls. God consistently moves in and among his people, moving them to love and service to be a blessing to the world.

> Authentic community-in-Christ, in its global and local visible presence in the world, is a political community embodying, demonstrating, and proclaiming the politics of the good news of the reign of God.
>
> D. Zac Niringiye, "Churches and the Politics of the Sacraments"

It shouldn't surprise us, therefore, that those who are filled with the Spirit of God are inclined to help a hurting world in all kinds of creative ways, including words and deeds. The spiritually poor *and* materially poor *and* relationally poor are all a legitimate concern for those who worship the Creator and Redeemer.[1] Bearing witness to this God, we do not pit the material against the spiritual, but recognize him as the Lord of it all. This influences our affections and our actions. The world may tempt us to ignore vulnerable babies in the womb, but the church cannot. Our culture may tempt us to forget about the elderly who lack productivity and income, but the church must refuse to do so. Our subcultures tempt us to pick our friends according to our economic or educational background, but the church requires more from us. Oppression and division between people of different ethnic backgrounds or contrasting skin colors may sound like issues that are too "political" and secular for our churches in this polarizing age, but the church must resist such dismissals and instead engage in love.

Should the Church Care about More Than Souls?

Because we worship a King who has brought us into his kingdom, the gospel is inherently "political" and "social." We are part of a kingdom in which people from all tribes, tongues, skin colors, and cultures come together to worship the living God. Prejudices and blind spots about race, class, or ability hinder our unity and are occasions for the children of God to repent and actively seek to make things right—like Zacchaeus, who makes right his relations with his neighbors by returning to them the money he gained from a system that oppresses the powerless (Luke 19:1–10). As Proverbs clearly states, "Speak up and judge fairly; defend the rights of the poor and needy" (31:9 NIV). In other words, those who have experienced the love of the Father, the grace of the Son, and the fellowship of the Holy Spirit are called to a broad range of concerns and actions. There are corporate and individual sides to this call, but it is undeniably a call to engage in the good work God has prepared for us to do (Eph. 2:10), including the call to let him who is "our peace" overcome our hostilities and bring together "strangers and aliens" as one in him (2:13–22). This is not merely about affirming theological statements, but about reforming how we order our lives, friendships, and pocketbooks.

To be concerned that God's will be carried out on earth as it is in heaven is a gospel issue, central to the Christian mission and, thus, to the church. When we ignore the difficulty that some people have in getting their daily bread, or we think that accumulated debt has no spiritual import, or we believe we can hold grudges against individuals or groups without consequence, then we distance ourselves from God and from many for whom he deeply cares (cf. Matt. 6:9–15).

At the core of the church's being and nature is love for God and one's neighbor. Our allegiance as the church is always to the King and his kingdom, not to any earthly political party. To the extent that our life together as the church reflects this, we can show the rest of the world the goodness of our Lord and give them an appetite for the future feast and shalom that we will one day fully enjoy with him. In other words, the good news that Jesus is Lord has ramifications for all areas of life, but faithfulness in hearing and responding to that good news takes the whole church, and not just an individual.

Yes, there are all kinds of good and important works to be done. Preaching (Matt. 24:14; Rom. 10:14; 1 Tim. 4:13; 2 Tim. 3:16; 4:2), prayer (2 Chron. 7:14; Matt. 18:19–20; Acts 2:42; 2 Cor. 1:11; James 5:16), and sacraments (Matt. 26:26–28; 28:19; 1 Cor. 10:16–17; 11:23–25) are like the body's skeleton, supporting and uniting all efforts that flow from God through his church to the world. That skeleton, however, is *not* all that the church and Christians are called to: the body is much more than its bones. From sermon preparation to evangelism, from shared meals to preparing the elements for the Eucharist, from cleaning the church to accounting for the offerings, there is more work (most of it behind the scenes) than we can name that helps a healthy believing community gather and flourish together (cf. Rom. 12:11–13; Heb. 10:25). Many legitimate concerns remain to be addressed besides preaching, sacraments, and prayers.

As the church expresses God's love and concern, many needs and priorities surface. For example, shouldn't children's ministry have a high priority? Jesus himself tells us to let the little children come to him (Matt 19:14 // Mark 10:14 // Luke 18:16). Helping the local elderly widow with her crumbling home should not be overlooked—the ancient Scriptures and early apostles are clear: don't neglect the widows (e.g., Exod. 22:22; Deut. 10:18; Ps. 147:3; 1 Tim. 5:3). Prisoners need to be visited with good news (e.g., Isa. 61:1–3; Heb. 13:1–3), orphans require attention (e.g., Deut. 26:12; Job 29:12–16; Ps. 82:3; James 1:27), and the materially poor warrant our kindness and provision (e.g., Deut. 15:7–8; Prov. 14:21; 22:9; 28:27; 1 John 3:17); foreigners should receive welcome and protection among God's people (e.g., Exod. 23:9; Lev. 19:34; 23:22; 25:35; Deut. 14:28–29; 24:13–17; Ps. 146:5–9), the lonely and brokenhearted benefit from friendships in the Lord (e.g., Pss. 34:18; 147:3; Isa. 61:1–3), the downtrodden find rest and encouragement from God by being with his people (e.g., Matt. 11:28; Mark 2:17), and justice should be sought as the oppressed are defended (e.g., Ps. 72:12–14; Isa. 1:17; 10:1–3).

What Is the Church's Mission?

The central mission of the church is to point people continually to the Messiah: he alone fully reveals the love of the Father and pours out his Spirit on us. The goal of all our good efforts is to draw people to the embrace of the triune God, not to serve as a replacement for him. All the gifts we exercise must ultimately point back to the true Giver. So how can all of this happen?

The church is central to Christian existence. The church is also God's normal means of expressing his presence, love, and grace in his world. Because God acts in every corner of the world, the church faces countless needs in following its Lord; indeed, although American evangelical churches may be tempted to think the list of needs includes too many social concerns, the global and historical church has long recognized that the Bible generally and Jesus specifically promote these concerns.[2] Word and deed, love and justice, forgiveness and reconciliation, spiritual growth and material needs, future hope and present relief—these all go together and reinforce rather than oppose each other. Neglect of the poor is as unfaithful to the gospel as is failure to expound the text of the New Testament—in fact, neglect of the poor *is* a failure to expound the text of the New Testament.

> Man appears to exist in his ecclesial identity not as that which he is but as that which he will be.
>
> John Zizioulas, *Being as Communion*

God extends his love, provision, and values through the people who make up his church. His offer to be a refuge and strength frequently comes through the church. When he wants to bring a word of grace, a safe hug, and a warm meal, it often comes through his church. Even when the church cannot do everything itself, it keeps seeking to promote the common good.[3]

Given all the legitimate needs and the call on God's people, we are again faced with the question: What am *I* to do? When the sign-up sheet is passed around or when meaningful opportunities arise, what should our response be?

To intensify the problem (as if we needed that), the people presenting the needs are often directly involved in the ministries that try to meet those needs, and they are passionate—appropriately so!—about both the needs and the value of the work. They want us to share their godly zeal and conviction: Who wouldn't care about widows? Don't you think evangelism is vital? Shouldn't you want to support small group Bible studies? Do you think prayer meetings are unnecessary? Don't you want to help the struggling addicts, the exhausted caregivers, those recovering from divorce, and others weighed down by grief? There are endless legitimate ministries that echo God's heart, and those most active in them often reflect God's passionate concerns in those areas. So must I feel exactly as they do, and be as involved as they are in that ministry?

Amid this cascade of appeals, I often see two kinds of response. On the one hand, some with tender hearts and active consciences try to figure out how much they can do, signing up for everything that is presented to them. As a consequence, they are racing down the road toward burnout. On the other hand, those who have experienced or witnessed burnout, or who are already consumed by their personal lives, go to the other extreme: they shut their ears to the requests, sometimes claiming that the church is trying to do too much. Compassion fatigue has set in, so they don't end up helping with anything. They come to listen and leave immediately afterward—or they might even just stop coming.

Surely there are more than these two options: "do everything" or "do *nothing*"!

To discover that third way, we need to recall that we are, by God's good design, finite creatures who must always depend on him and on each other. We never graduate from such healthy dependence. These aspects of our being indicate another path in which, rather than pursuing the exhausting race of personal accomplishment or the deadening act of shutting down, we instead encourage a community of belonging. To get a healthier blueprint for life together, we need to think afresh about the Messiah and his body.

Can We Ignore God's Commandments?

A friend of mine called me from California wanting to talk through what he saw as biblical requirements he could neither dismiss nor fulfill: he was worn down and exhausted by his tender conscience and lively intelligence as he read about the judgment of the sheep and the goats in Matthew 25. The summary given by the band Cake in 1998 in their catchy and subversive chorus, "Sheep go to heaven, goats go to hell,"[4] probably didn't help matters. But Jesus isn't talking about sheep who blindly follow the crowds, as Cake's interpretation would have it. The sheep in the parable are those who follow the example of their loving Shepherd. Jesus offers unquestionably clear criteria for determining which is which: those who feed the hungry, shelter the stranger, clothe the naked, and visit the prisoner are the "righteous" or "sheep" on the right side of the King, who promises that they will "inherit the kingdom" and enter "into eternal life" (Matt. 25:31–40, 46). On the left side of the King are the "goats," who "will go away into eternal punishment" (25:46). What is the difference, according to this passage, between the sheep and the goats? Simple. How they treat the vulnerable, the weak, and the needy.

This passage haunted my friend Matt. Even though he had a seminary degree and knew Jesus was his only hope, he also knew passages like this could not simply be swept aside. He lived his ministry, pouring his life into other people's lives, but he had limited financial resources and he certainly didn't have any spare time and energy to visit prisons or regularly volunteer at homeless shelters. His honesty stoked his fear: Was he really a goat? Maybe somehow he could squeeze out a few more hours of ministry and work every week.

Before dismissing my friend as overly anxious and talking about the assurance of salvation, which he has ably studied, I think we need to consider Matt's hesitations carefully. He doesn't ignore the passages of Scripture that are painfully uncomfortable for many of us. He takes Jesus and his words seriously, aware that Jesus isn't messing around here. And that is what worries Matt. So is he really a goat? Am I? Are you?

If we don't feel Matt's discomfort, it usually isn't because our theology is better than his. We mostly just ignore the Scriptures that seem too demanding or uncomfortable for us. We don't really believe we need to visit prisoners. We don't really need to feed the hungry—"That's just a social justice issue, not a gospel issue." We don't take greed and lust seriously, even when Jesus starts talking about cutting off body parts (e.g., Matt. 5:29–30; 18:7–9). No, we make it tolerable by ignoring places in the Bible that ask too much. Unlike Matt, most of us don't struggle with this—*not* because we take the Bible too seriously, but because we readily ignore demands that don't fit current expressions of the American dream.

Too Many Messiahs?

One of the recurring mistakes throughout the history of the church is that individual Christians sometimes imagine that they must personally reflect the fullness of Jesus the Messiah. From certain third-century hermits to some zealous pastors and social justice activists, they imagine—often without realizing it—that they must personally embody messianic expectations. This has become even more intense in the modern Western world with our stress on individual faith and responsibility. While there is much truth in those instincts that highlight individual accountability and belief, without adjustment they lead to destructive results. We see this in the story of Charles Taylor Studd (1862–1931), who served as an English evangelical missionary.[5] He wanted to give his whole life to Christ and the spread of the gospel, serving in China, India, and eventually Africa. Giving up financial and educational privilege, he poured himself out in his work. His belief that

Christ gave up everything for him spurred him to practice what he called "reckless Christianity," which brought not only heroic stories but also some destructive consequences. His untiring devotion to the work became somewhat fanatical (at least as others experienced it): for example, by the end of his life he was working eighteen hours a day and addicted to morphine. During the last thirteen years of their marriage, he only saw his wife for two weeks despite her struggling health, and he even dismissed his daughter and son-in-law from the mission because they did not show the same level of commitment that he did. He admitted that this period of intense struggle was his "Gethsemane," which seems revealing, for it showed that he sensed that he was required to follow the exact path of Christ and to do all that was required of Jesus. At one point he admitted, "My heart seems worn out and bruised beyond repair, and in my deep loneliness I often wish to be gone." So, is such "reckless Christianity" required of us? If we don't follow such a radical life, whether in missions or in social justice, is it because we don't take the demands of God seriously enough?

Such well-meaning inclinations often demonstrate (1) how we underestimate the uniqueness of Christ and his work, (2) how we overestimate God's expectations for each individual (finite!) human being, and (3) how we underestimate the work of Christ in his body, the church. In this case the problem is that we focus on the idea of *redemption* while neglecting the truths of *creation* and *ecclesiology*. While it is vital for us to remember that Jesus did die for us (redemption), we must also remember that God originally made us good, even with our limits (creation), and that he draws us to mutual dependence on one another for spiritual health (ecclesiology). We don't take this into account nearly as much as we ought.

Jesus gave the blind sight, helped the lame to walk, healed the leper, opened the ears of the deaf, raised the dead, and preached good news to the poor (Luke 7:22; cf. Matt. 11:5). He was fulfilling the messianic expectations as God visited his people uniquely through this anointed One (cf. Isa. 29:18; 35:5; 42:6–7; 61:1–3). Jesus has ushered in the kingdom of God and taught his followers how to live there. Life in his kingdom depends on God's grace toward us, which liberates us from concern only for ourselves into service for others, opening us to patience, love, and concern for the whole world (e.g., John 13:15; 1 Tim. 1:16; 1 Pet. 2:21). Sometimes this will mean laying down our lives for others, but it doesn't mean that we can do everything that Jesus did. Without question Jesus was truly and fully human, but he also had a unique calling as the one filled with the Spirit beyond measure: Jesus, as the embodiment of Israel, faithfully loved God and neighbor with a depth and consequence beyond measure.

So where does this leave us? Are we back to the binary option: Do *everything* in an effort to be like Jesus, or do *nothing* because Jesus's blood has covered my sins and shortcomings? How are we to take seriously the story of the sheep and goats without either dismissing it or being crushed by it? Earlier we stated that the doctrine of creation indicates another path for us. Combining that with a fuller christological focus on the nature of the church will make this possibility clearer. Let me explain.

It Takes an Entire Community to Reflect the One Messiah

The *whole* church is called the body of Christ (e.g., 1 Cor. 12:12–27), not as isolated people, but as a united organism: "So we, though many, are one body in Christ, and individually members one of another" (Rom. 12:5). The *one* body of Christ consists of the *whole* church, and that body is composed of great diversity and difference, each member being dependent not only on Christ but also on the others in this union. This understanding of the church is easily lost in our individualistic culture, so those believers who pay attention to the divine commands are easily crushed when they try to fulfill all these biblical expectations alone. However, when we recognize the Spirit's life-giving power in the church as a *community*, as a united body, we are liberated to act more faithfully and effectively. Or, to use Irwyn Ince's apt description, we become the "beautiful community," thus reflecting our beautiful God.[6]

> Human beings exist in duality, and it is in this dependence on the other that their creatureliness consists.
>
> Dietrich Bonhoeffer, *Creation and Fall*

God created us for mutual dependence and delight within a life-giving community: that isn't merely a goal; it's how we are built. Part of the mission of the church is to serve as such a community, thus providing an Edenic oasis amid this fractured world, pointing toward a time when shalom will again reign unhindered. No one person can be or do everything. But together, as the whole body of Christ, even in this broken world we can recall each other and our neighbors to patterns of life that harmonize rather than conflict with the way God made us. We start to understand how to be faithful sheep, even if we can't do everything. Put differently, you can be a "sheep" even if you have not visited a prisoner—just *don't* imagine that means visiting prisoners is unnecessary.

Returning to Matt, I encouraged him the same way I encourage myself. Today I am caring for prisoners in jail; I am evangelizing the disenfranchised in Nepal; I am praying over the sick child in the hospital; I am serving the recovering victims of sex trafficking; I am standing against racial injustice; and I am caring for widows. And I am doing so much more. How? I am doing all of this because I am part of the living body of Christ. God's Spirit has united me to Christ and, because of that union, to my sisters and brothers of the faith. We are one. I am part of the church, both local and global. Obviously I can't personally do all of these things in a single day, nor even in a single lifetime; however, my church actively pours itself out in love for our neighborhood, the larger city, and farther as we extend ourselves out to the world. Our church is just one of the vast number of churches scattered throughout the world. As part of God's church, we have people doing prison ministry, caring for children, feeding the hungry, praying, preaching, and caring for orphans and widows. I am not the body—I am just a part of it. But together, the body works well and reflects the Messiah's heart as it participates in his actions of love, healing, and service. As part of the church that is reigned over by the ascended Christ and empowered by his Spirit, we are collectively able to do even greater deeds than Jesus did before his death and resurrection (John 14:12).[7] God now normally (though not exclusively) does his redemptive work in and through us, his church.

I am not the Messiah. And neither are you. Nor is your pastor. But *together*—resting in the finished work of Christ and empowered by the Spirit—*together* we carry out the Father's compassion and love by participating in his holy work. We do this as the body of Christ. We are sheep, and because the Shepherd loves us, we *together* follow and imitate him.

Together, We Care for God's World

Matt works in college ministry. That is not only time-consuming but also emotionally demanding. He can't do all the other things listed in Matthew 25. But then again, Susan, who is a gifted lawyer in Chicago, can't minister to needy college students on a secular campus. Yet she does minister to those students, not because she is personally there doing the work, but because she is connected to Matt by the Spirit. In our union with Christ, we benefit from the vicarious work of Christ. But we also benefit in some vicarious way from the work of our sisters and brothers. This has nothing to do with our justification, but it has everything to do with being a part of God's living church.

I can't pray for everyone who needs prayer, but as part of this body, we can pray together for all who need prayer. I don't do nearly the amount of direct poverty alleviation that I would like, but other believers do. Only when we live in our interconnectedness will we stop belittling those with "secular" vocations who honor Christ as painters and teachers, as landscapers and homemakers, as politicians and software engineers. Rather than disparage someone else's work, we can see it as part of the whole, and thus we are liberated to really celebrate all manner of vocations and labor. Scottish theologian John Baillie (1886–1960) captures this spirit when he prays, "O Lord of the vineyard, I beg Thy blessing upon all who truly desire to serve Thee by being diligent and faithful in their several callings, *bearing their due share of the world's burden*, and going about their daily tasks in all simplicity and uprightness of heart."[8] He goes on to pray for those in different vocations, from farmers to shepherds, from those who go into dark mines to those employed in factories or the marketplace. Whether you buy or sell, use pens or the plow, tend the hearth or the child, each is enabled to use their labor to honor God and for the common good.

Baillie understood how God normally works in his world and through his people: he works by employing *all* his people, with their various gifts and callings. But notice the key—no individual is to carry the weight of the world. It can and will crush any and each of us if we try to carry it alone. Each believer, following the Messiah, is to "[bear] their due share of the world's burden." And each one of our "due shares" will look different and unique according to our various gifts, capacities, and callings. It takes all of us to represent the one Christ. We bear one another's burdens (Gal. 6:2), denying ourselves as we serve others (Matt. 16:24), and thus willingly sharing in the sufferings of Christ (1 Pet. 4:13). We are his body, so we need not be ashamed of our smallness, of our limits. Instead, we can be encouraged to do our work well and diligently and to pray and be thankful for others who also carry on good work.

Only when we truly believe that we are interconnected can we move away from a position of begrudging requests for financial support from pastors, missionaries, and ministries who spend the majority of their days devoted to particular efforts the church deems needed. Rather than being embarrassed when asking for support, those speaking might be encouraged to know that they are offering the rest of us a way to do what we could not do without them. When I give or pray, for example, a small part of me is allowed to participate in this larger work. The body is living and active. But I am also liberated to know that I am not the whole body, so I don't personally need to go to every event, financially support every wonderful ministry, or pray for every need in the world. Things can be wonderful and important to God without being something that I personally must do or even know about.

Accepting our finitude and affirming our interdependence as the people of God move us from guilt to liberty, from being overwhelmed to being energized, from passivity to activity. God never expected each of us to do everything—he is the one who gave us our limits, after all. He also uniquely gifted and called each of us to some form of service and love. This is not reserved simply for the "spiritual" people in full-time ministry.

God also understands our limits and our complex webs of obligations. He is the one who gave you children to feed, crops to be harvested, a body to nourish and clothe, and relationships to dwell within. We can value our respective vocations, recognize differences in gifts and skills, honor different personalities, and foster the arts even as we give attention to social injustices. But such a full vision can be honored only if we take more seriously the *whole* body of Christ.

We are not rugged individuals; we are an interconnected body. Jesus does not overburden his flock; he affirms who they are in their life as a whole. "I am in you and you are in me," he says, which is also true of our participation in each other as a body. A part is not the whole; nor should the whole be reduced to the part. This is why we weep with those who weep, we celebrate with those who celebrate. We serve and we feast, we rest and we labor, we love and we sacrifice. Living in Christ means that we imitate him: but it takes the *whole* church to fully reflect the Messiah.

Only Jesus is his whole body. Only he is the Messiah. The rest of us don't have to be him; we just have to be *in* him, united to one another as his body. With this in mind, I would like to turn more specifically to ministry leaders and their congregations.

A Word to Ministry Leaders and Their Congregations

Ministry leader, your work is very important, but unrealistic expectations produce unhealthy problems and often drive pastoral burnout.

While the language of "self-care" is often viewed with great suspicion and nervousness by some Christians in general, and pastors in particular, growing research shows that recognizing one's needs and limits is essential for the long-term health of those in ministry. We can also describe this self-care theologically as a proper appreciation of our creaturely finitude—what I called *humility* in chapter 6. When we—including pastors, leaders of nonprofits, and other ministry leaders—ignore the very real limits of our creaturely resources, the consequences are devastating, especially for those in leadership.

Ministry leaders too often translate their sense of God's calling to serve Christ and his kingdom into an appetite or obligation to accomplish endless goals, making it difficult for themselves to say no. Low levels of guilt are a constant companion. There is always more they could do. How can a pastor, who is modeling Christ's sacrificial love, ever be heard saying no? Shouldn't you be willing to die for others? Doesn't this vocation mean always doing what is asked or required? In their helpful book *Resilient Ministry*, Bob Burns, Tasha Chapman, and Don Guthrie use the results of their research to produce practical advice that will help pastors avoid burnout. They mention the commonly used pastoral refrain, "I'd rather burn out than rust out in the service of the Lord," which goes back to the nineteenth-century Welsh preacher Christmas Evans. They also comment, however, that one original listener drew from Acts 20:24 to respond, "I want neither to burn out nor rust out. I want to finish out the race."[9] If we only think about short-term concerns, we will not finish the race.

Most of us agree we don't want our pastors to burn out. We don't want to have unrealistic expectations of them, and we don't want them to have unrealistic expectations of themselves. In practice, however, we often do pack so much into our expectations that they become impossible. Try adding up the hours. How many hours of spiritual guidance should the pastor offer each week? Who gives premarital or grief counseling? Who counsels the struggling marriages on the verge of collapse? Who should visit those in the hospital or sick at home? Many recipients of these services don't want just anyone; they want their pastor. How many hours of sermon preparation should be done each week? How much should pastors keep up with current events? How much should they know and study current issues that congregation members are wrestling with? How many small "talks" should the pastor give each week, whether for Sunday school, a devotional at the local retirement home, or a special talk to the kids? How many hours in prayer? What role must the pastor play in administration? How much time should be spent crafting and pushing a vision that advances the church's missional concerns amid their particular setting and congregation? Letters need to be written, meals need to be shared, funerals need presence, and weddings require planning and participation.

These are all good and important activities. And we could add many others to the list. Just ask your pastor: my guess is that you will be surprised at all they do in any given week. If they make a thorough inventory, even *they* might be surprised at all they have tried to do in a week. Most of us don't realize half of what fills their days. But who can do it all? And outside of the most affluent churches, many pastors have very little paid help. Sure, megachurch leaders can afford to specialize, but most local pastors are the go-to person, not only for prayer and counsel, but also for everything else in the local church. *Christianity Today* reports that in 57 percent of churches in America, fewer than one hundred people attend services on any given Sunday.[10] The majority of churches don't have huge staffs and resources, which means pastors face more obligations than they can possibly fulfill. Pastors of large churches and those of small churches often face different types of demands, but many appear to share a sense of feeling constantly exhausted and spread too thin.

> I wonder how much more effective our churches would be if we made the pastor's spiritual health—not his or her efficiency—our number one priority.
>
> Philip Yancey, in *Christianity Today*, 2001

Amid the avalanche of requests and needs, how can the pastor ever say no with a clear conscience? As the research of *Resilient Ministry* clearly demonstrates, "Self-care requires limits and rhythms."[11] But it can be hard for the congregation to honor such limits, and often it is even harder for the ministry leader to keep them. Few have expectations as unrealistic as pastors and ministry leaders have of themselves.

Francis of Assisi (1181–1226) also struggled with the endless demands placed on him. He had many skills, but organization and preaching were two difficult areas for him. People flocked to him, often inspired by his simplicity of life and how he modeled sacrifice, prayer, and service. But as his little group of followers kept expanding, he knew he needed help. Francis traveled to Pope Honorius, whom he recognized as having authority over him. But knowing how busy the pope was, Francis asked only that he would give him "many popes" who could provide him with needed advice, because he was trying to carry all the weight of leadership on his own.[12] Francis needed others with gifts he didn't have, to give him guidance. The pope assigned Cardinal Hugolino to help him, after which Francis "wasted no time in unburdening himself of his problems to Hugolino, his new 'pope.'"[13] When we think that being in charge means being alone, that we by ourselves bear all the authority and all the responsibility, it crushes us. It leads to arrogance and isolation. We need others, including authorities over us. Others see our blind spots, hear our sadness, and help God's people in ways we cannot.

Later, Francis appointed others as leaders, even trying to put himself under their authority.[14] Although his charisma meant that he really was still in many ways the leader even when he was not in front, he fought for a healthy situation both for himself and for those he was supposed to be leading. Too many were looking to him alone. Although inconsistent and far from perfect, Francis often appeared to recognize his own needs as well as his dependence on others. He sought those with different gifts and temperaments, and in the end this larger leadership group produced the Franciscan order. If you were to ask Francis who did the work, he would definitely say, Jesus; however, he realized that Jesus works through his church and not simply through single individuals.

Philip Yancey once wrote, "I wonder how much more effective our churches would be if we made the pastor's spiritual health—not his or her efficiency—our number one priority."[15] For pastors to flourish, they need external and internal harmony: the congregation and their own psychology must allow them to recognize that being finite is not sinful. It is not wrong to rest, to sleep, to laugh, to forget, to say no. "Limits are linked to life rhythms. Certain rhythms—like sabbath, exercise, friendship and contentment in calling—create patterns of healthy living."[16] But one cannot honor the Sabbath without taking time away from "work," and one cannot enjoy the refreshment of friendship without making it a distinct goal rather than an often-neglected option. As Peter Scazzero demonstrates, trying to separate our emotional health from our spiritual health is destructive to both; this mistake is painfully common in the church and especially among church leaders. Too often we confuse busyness with honoring God or confuse checking off to-do lists with spiritual health.[17] Gregory the Great (540–604) encouraged the minister to "not relax his care for the internal life while he is occupied by external concerns, nor should he relinquish what is prudent of external matters so as to focus on things internal."[18] We need to be holistic. And let us beware that if we neglect our own internal worlds we will usually undermine our ability to love well and wisely the very people we hope to serve.

Now let's consider an example of how commonplace and practical this can be. Like many of us, pastors sit a lot. They often don't just sit at their desk—they also meet people for breakfast, lunch, coffee, and so on. They are present to listen, to comfort, and to care. But often what they are hearing is highly emotionally charged, stressful, and relationally complicated. They listen to confessions, absorb angry outbursts, witness debilitating fears, and encounter hardened hearts, all in the course of one day. Rae Jean Proeschold-Bell, who served as a lead researcher on a massive study of Methodist clergy, observed that pastors feel pressure to care for others nonstop: "The sacred nature of their work combined with the many roles they play makes pastors reluctant to take breaks, especially if there is no co-pastor in their church to provide back-up." The results of this study are sobering as they reveal some of the concrete consequences of pretending ministry leaders don't have limits. The relentless stress and the constant link between food and church meetings has the result that "78 percent of pastors are overweight or obese, which then makes them vulnerable to chronic diseases." The research has "documented above-average rates of depression, obesity and several chronic diseases for clergy."[19]

Our bodies can only absorb so much pain and trauma, can only sit for so long, can only eat so much food; as Bessel van der Kolk declares, "The body keeps the score."[20] Exercise—in whatever form—may feel like a wild luxury for most pastors (and even for the rest of us!), but in truth, our sedentary habits make it a necessity for long-term health. Creatures need movement, and exercise refreshes the mind and brings needed renewal. Amid the noise and busyness, a walk or a run can clear the mind, calm the anxieties, and quiet the soul, allowing a person to recognize God's prompts and receive God's comforts more readily. But when we exercise or sit quietly in a park, we often don't feel that we are "doing anything." Exercise and rest thus cease to be genuine goals, and instead we fill up our calendars with what we imagine is a more productive use of our time. Eventually this mistake catches up with us.

There are consequences to neglecting such essentials as rest, exercise, and friendship. How might we, in a nonjudgmental way, love our pastors enough to help protect them and empower them to live within a healthier vision that encourages long-term sustainable ministry? We look to our pastors to model the Christian life. If physical, emotional, or relational health is not honored by our minister, it will be harder for us to value it in our lives. And for the pastors themselves, might true "self-denial" result in denying oneself the illusion of trying to do everything, to be everywhere, to solve all problems and help all souls? It can be painful to say no, and strangely enough, it can even feel like dying to self. It takes real faith to depend on God to care for others when you cannot.

For the sake of ministry leaders, for our sake, and for the sake of the kingdom, let us deal with the full humanity of ministry leaders, reminding them and ourselves that they are creatures and not the Creator, that their finitude is not a sign of sin but the reality of faithful, creaturely dependence.

As much as ministry leaders speak about God's grace, it can be hard for them to rest in that grace themselves. It is not that they don't believe what they are telling other people, but as I have written about elsewhere, there are gospel truths that become more believable when we hear them from others who are speaking directly to us.[21] They tell me not simply that God loves "the world" but that he loves *Kelly*, and that God is happy for *me* to rest, for *me* to let others carry the weight, to trust him that he is God and I am not. I can trust their words far more than I can trust myself as I am staring at a mirror trying to convince myself that rest is acceptable.

Because of the endless needs, limited time, and ministry leaders' personal sense of both responsibility and inadequacy, this change will require that we as congregation members tell our pastors, "Well done, good and faithful servant." Sometimes the only way they will believe that God thinks this of them is for the words to come from our mouths first, not in false flattery, but in genuine appreciation. If they come to genuinely believe *we* think they are good and faithful, even in light of their limits, weaknesses, and sin, then they might gain the courage to believe that their Father actually thinks that of them as well. We need one another, especially for faith, hope, and love.[22]

Taking Jethro's Advice

Exodus 18 tells us about Moses's father-in-law, Jethro, who visited the leader of the Israelites in their wanderings. What Jethro found disturbed him: "The people stood around Moses from morning till evening" (18:13). When he asked why Moses was doing this, Moses replied, "Because the people come to me to inquire of God" (18:15). Who can argue with that? What ministry leader would not be sympathetic to this answer? When people in your church or ministry want to ask about God or his ways, shouldn't the ministry leader *always* personally be willing to stay and answer? Sure, you can skip a meeting about planning the Christmas pageant, but you certainly cannot decline an opportunity to talk with those who want to ask for guidance about God or about how his Word applies to some problem they are facing.

Jethro sees all of this and offers an unambiguous response: "What you are doing is not good" (Exod. 18:17). This echoes God's comment when, seeing Adam without others of his kind, God declares, "It is not good that the man should be alone" (Gen. 2:18).[23] God created us for relationships, for mutual dependence, for love. No single leader is meant to carry all the others. Jethro advises the division of labor: a recognition of giftedness but also limitations and difference, seeing that Moses alone cannot and should not carry all the burdens of the whole community (Exod. 18:19–27).

This brings us back to examining the connections between individuals and the community, between pastors and parishioners, between responsibility and mutual dependence. I want to step back and think about this mutual dependence in a way that I hope will tie together all we have talked about thus far: it takes the *whole* church to be the one body of Christ. Our interconnectedness is good not just for leaders but for the entire congregation.

COVID, the Church, and Needing Each Other

I originally wrote this chapter during an intense period when the COVID pandemic was shutting down everything in the part of the world where I live.[24] Many shelter-in-place orders and requirements for face masks and social distancing—all of which increased our feelings of isolation—were still in effect. We were all starting to feel some of the consequences of these new restrictions. It is easy to imagine we don't need others until we have to actually live without them. Especially during extended periods of at-home isolation, we started to realize how much we miss the physical touch of friendly hugs and handshakes when they are absent and how hard it is to read people when you can't even see most of their face, or when they are only tiny images on a screen. Singing in church and chatting after the service may have seemed nice before this, but not essential; yet, in their absence, we strongly feel the lack. Standing alone in front of a TV screen, I found singing so painful; our voices alone tried to fill the empty air of the family room, and it just didn't seem right in the absence of the rest of the church. We need the presence of others, not just to say hello, but to sense their bodies, to hear their voices, to draw on their life. We need real bodies in real worship, whether a house church of fifteen or a congregation of three hundred. We need others, and others need us. Why? Because we were created for communion, not just with God, but with one another. We were created to belong. The church is meant to be an oasis from the confusion of the everyday, a pointer toward the new earth. But that vision becomes much harder to sustain when we are separated, isolated, and struggling. This is a problem not just for pastors but for all of us.

Many have looked to the flu pandemic of 1918 for understanding, but my mind has returned again and again to the World War II bombings of London from September 1940 to May 1941. Although experiencing COVID quarantines and shutdowns is not the same as being targets of a bombing campaign, there are some meaningful parallels. As others have noted, the pandemic is waged by an invisible enemy. Rather than bombs falling from planes, we face microbes on surfaces or in the air we breathe. Rather than the horror of indiscriminate bombing destruction, we feel the panic of watching friends and relatives and neighbors die.

Charles E. Fritz, an American sociologist and early developer of disaster research, was posted in England by the United States Strategic Bombing Survey. His task was to understand if the "London Blitz" and the massive bombings in Berlin were effective. Fritz found that, rather than destroying morale, they achieved the opposite. Communities subjected to bombing campaigns became *more* unified in their resistance. Fritz observed that, rather than panicking, "people overwhelmingly devoted their energies toward the good of the community rather than just themselves."[25] Sadly, some of what has started to happen during COVID-19 has been the opposite, in that we have allowed the frustrations and difficulties to drive us apart rather than to unite our hearts even when we can't be physically together.

Fritz eventually concluded that disasters, whether created by people or nature, provide an opportunity to create what he called a "community of sufferers" and that this "allows individuals to experience an immensely reassuring connection to others."[26] In the midst of these terrors and threats, "class differences are temporarily erased, income disparities become irrelevant, race is overlooked, and individuals are assessed simply by what they are willing to do for the group."[27] One of the challenges with COVID-19 is that much of the suffering has heightened disparities between people in different income, racial, and social groupings. It has threatened to pit people against one another, rather than bringing them together. In our currently polarized world, these tensions only increased division rather than brought unity. At its best, the church has sought to draw hearts together even when physical proximity has not been possible, showing a shared love that moves people to sacrifice and service. Sadly, too often we have not been at our best.

Longing to Belong

Award-winning journalist and war correspondent Sebastian Junger made some observations that resonate with those of Charles Fritz. He saw that many veterans returning from the battlefield unexpectedly wanted to go back into combat with their fellow troops even though it meant leaving the safety of home. Their shared experience of life-threatening situations connected them with each other in a way rarely felt in civilian life. They had a strong and clear sense of belonging and interconnectedness: after that, they didn't want to go back to disconnected living, even if it meant they had to return to battle to find that sense of belonging again. I think those who experience such longings have discovered an important aspect of their humanity. Our civilization has divided us into disconnected silos: we live in proximity without true community. The soldiers had lived in genuine community.[28]

The Christian account of human flourishing is grounded in the idea of love: love for God and love for neighbor, with implications for how one relates to the earth and even to one's self. That was how we were created, but sin has ravaged every one of those relationships.

Even in our fallen world, faithfulness to Christ would mean that the church provides a space for God to realign our loves to our created purpose. Faithfulness in the church would make it a place where our shame and guilt before God can be addressed and overcome. The church, at its best, realizes

God's relational design for humans, not simply promoting programs but promoting shared lives. Unfortunately, the church is often not at its best.

The gospel entrusted to the church preaches a grace that restores and unites neighbors who are not naturally drawn together. When we gather, we do so not because we are so similar but because our Creator Lord calls us out of our differences to unite together in worship.

Longing to Be Needed

In addition to demonstrating the human need to belong, Junger captures another powerful human drive when he concludes, "*Humans don't mind hardship, in fact they thrive on it; what they mind is not feeling necessary.* Modern society has perfected the art of making people not feel necessary."[29] I think he has perfectly captured the problem here, which also points, in my mind, to why we must rely on the *whole* church. Too often our world tells people they are not needed, that they are only important as consumers. One reason that it's difficult to find volunteers in our churches may be that people don't believe they really are needed and that, until they have tasted the good of mutual dependence, they don't know what they are missing.

Many of us feel unnecessary, not needed, and disconnected. The one thing that was *not* "good" in Genesis 1 was human isolation. We were designed by the Creator for being-in-communion. Think about the very young and the very old in our lives. Are we communicating to them that they are needed, or that they are merely vulnerable? What are we unintentionally communicating to the nonclergy in our churches about their importance to the life of our congregation? God made us for community and interdependence; God created us for mutual neededness.

Given the strange nature of the COVID crisis and the shelter-in-place orders, we have faced a second threat beyond sickness: we didn't even *have* one another. We need to be needed, and yet the natural ways we might care for others and receive their company and care became impossible for us. Rules about home isolation and social distancing tempted us to draw even more inward, to face this despair and hardship alone. But we must courageously resist isolation, not by violating any government's sober and helpful instructions, but by learning afresh to cultivate communion with God and neighbor even in strange seasons like this one. With all of the disunity social media and certain forms of technology can foster, we can use technology for good. The church can pray together even when they are not physically together, texting one another words of encouragement and prayers of concern. Calls and video chats are not nearly as nice as warm hugs, but they can meaningfully convey shared life even in a world that so often pushes us toward isolation. Just ask the persecuted church around the world, since they have had to depend on such less-than-ideal situations for a long time. Handwritten notes dropped in a mailbox, homemade banana bread left on the front porch, or a knitted scarf can be an intentional gift that communicates thoughtfulness and love despite distance. Imposed time at home, for whatever reason, doesn't have to only consist of bingeing Netflix, but can provide an opportunity for some intentional time away from the hurry of life, turning for a season to more time filled with quiet, slower tasks, and prayer. Take a long and unhurried walk. Let your mind wander to different needs you've normally not had time to pray for, remember that buddy from high school who has fallen away from the faith or your friend's struggles at work or at home. Go sing hymns outside the windows of the nearest nursing home. Go sit in the woods or by a pond and just be still. Memorize Scripture—better yet, memorize Scripture with friends. Sing. Write poetry, read fiction, journal your prayers to God and send a text to a friend you are thinking about. Countless other examples could be given.

COVID has reminded us how important it is to belong and to be needed, that church is not about a few paid people doing everything, but all of us participating in some way. More than ever, the pandemic forced us to face our limits and recognize afresh how dependent we are on each other. More than ever, it made it difficult to use our gifts for the good of others and to find opportunity to receive what others have to give. Pastors, at their best, can model this *dependence* for us. COVID has reminded us that neither our pastors nor we ourselves are self-sufficient. Only God is self-sufficient. All humans, including ministry leaders, are wonderfully and necessarily dependent creatures. We need to be needed, and we need to receive what others can give, and that mutual dependence is a good thing.

Praise God. It takes the *whole* church to be the one body of Christ.

Given that we are but part of the whole, what are patterns of life we might practice that can help each of us develop a healthier appreciation of our finitude? What are practical ideas that might help reshape our lives to reflect the good of human limits? To these pastoral questions we devote an extended discussion in the last chapter.

10

how do we faithfully live within our finitude?

rhythm, vulnerability, gratitude, and rest

> Time is God's gift. Only time given and received as a gift is real time.
>
> Eberhard Busch, *The Great Passion*

Our lives have a definite shape as well as definite limits. We go through seasons, we are not self-sufficient, we depend on God for relief and provision, and we grow weary. A faithful life embraces its rhythms, recognizes its vulnerability, expresses both lament and gratitude, and rests in confidence in our faithful God.

A Scrapbooker?

When I was little, I was a "pretty good" kid from a stable home, who regularly attended a local Roman Catholic church with my family. As my elementary-school years were ending, attending church became less and less a part of my life, and yet I began to experience new longings for meaning. That summer I stood next to a large trampoline—this was a relatively rare thing back then—watching friends bounce up and down, flipping and laughing, and we started talking about what it would be like to go to middle school that coming fall. My guess is we were all feeling pretty anxious about it, but I'm sure we wanted to pretend it was no big deal. We knew some older kids who seemed to become seriously troubled youths after they went to junior high. But not us, right? I clearly recall thinking, if not outright saying: "That won't be me." I was probably eleven or twelve at the time.

But the truth is, new longings and desires were just starting to grow in me. Yearnings for acceptance, purpose, and a larger story were starting to drive me, even if I couldn't articulate them back then. I know this sounds melodramatic—which it may have been, given my age—but it was true. It didn't take long in middle school for me to decide life was short and I should live it to its fullest, taking everything I could get from it. This was the same time that movies like *Sixteen Candles* and *Ferris Bueller's Day Off* came out, and in my California setting this zeitgeist quickly became my worldview. Life was meant to be seized without limitation and without consequence.

Before I was halfway through seventh grade, I was pushing against most restraints on me, and by the time I was in eighth grade, I was regularly smoking marijuana, drinking, and partying with peers and those much older than me. At the same time, I also started making scrapbooks for myself—probably the only guy I knew who was doing that. Certainly none of my partying friends did, even though they populated my pictures and the events I memorialized. I don't think I understood it at the time, but it is likely the outworking of my sense that "this is all there is." We have this life and that's it, so I needed to live in an extreme way and I should keep a record of as much of it as possible—my life receipts (scrapbooks!) would validate my existence. It was as if I needed to prove to myself and everyone else that my life mattered.

By the middle of my freshman year in high school, through the ministry of a Baptist youth group and other providential events, faith became real to me and I became a follower of Jesus. Not long afterward, I stopped making photo albums and keeping memorabilia. This happened naturally, without my even thinking about it at the time. Only decades later could I look back and make more sense of that significant change. Now please don't be offended if you're a big scrapbooker; but for me, with my particular history, this evolution represented a healthy development.

The burden of making this life *everything* was starting to lift. My horizon had profoundly expanded. Now there was so much more to life than three score years and ten. There were still endless things I wanted to do, see, and accomplish, but it felt different. Accumulating and archiving events and memories to give my life meaning no longer mattered as much as it had. I had begun to discover my life *already* had meaning, and I didn't have to make it so. God had given my life and story purpose beyond anything I could conjure up on my own. Thankfully, I didn't need to squeeze an eternity's worth of life into my adolescence: I was now liberated to see my life against the backdrop of God's good and trustworthy eternality. While I still struggle to keep a healthy perspective, I now recognize that this shift first occurred as I embraced the promises of God.

Kate Bowler, in her moving memoir *Everything Happens for a Reason, and Other Lies I've Loved*, walks readers through her heartbreaking struggle with cancer (among other things).[1] She mentions her love of anticipating "the next thing," always planning, always improving, always making things better. She was constantly planning for the future, longing for what was to come. While there can be much good in anticipation, she came to see that there might be a dark side to it at times, a side she calls "the sin of arrogance, of becoming impervious to life itself." She adds, "I failed to love what was present, and decided to love what was possible instead. I must learn to live in ordinary time, but I don't know how."[2] While our circumstances were different, I believe that Bowler and I both sensed a fairly common challenge: to appreciate the present, to honor our limits even as we invest and seek to grow, and to love what God has given rather than feeling angry about what is withheld or anxious about what is to come.

In this last chapter I want us to consider the question, How are we to live in this ordinary time? Although this could easily become a second book, I have decided to focus on four key ideas here:

1. *Embrace the rhythms and seasons of life*
2. *Recognize vulnerability*
3. *Express lament, cultivate gratitude*
4. *Rest: honor sleep and sabbath*

Examining these ideas can, I hope, help us gain a healthier appreciation of both our fullness and our finitude even in a culture that constantly wants us to enlarge the first and ignore the second. We hope to avoid trying to ask too much of every single moment or simply living for the future.

Because the finitude of this chapter does not allow me to explore at length various classic Christian practices (e.g., fasting, prayer, solitude, silence), let me instead just recommend a few useful books that might help the interested reader explore these practices more fully. From the sixth-century *Rule of Saint Benedict* to the sixteenth-century Book of Common Prayer, the church in her different expressions has often found help from practices that slow us down, both as particular Christians and as communities, helping us recognize God's presence and increase our awareness of our dependence on the Creator and the rest of his creation. Popular twentieth-century volumes that introduced many believers to similar ideas include Richard Foster's *The Celebration of Discipline* and Dallas Willard's *The Spirit of the Disciplines*: both of them continue to profit their readers, not only because of their clarity of expression and desire to take the Christian faith seriously, but because they give an alternative to the increasingly chaotic and self-absorbed tendencies of our culture. More recently, I have been delighted by the warm response to such volumes as Tish Harrison Warren's wonderfully written *Liturgy of the Ordinary* as well as accessible and practical volumes like John Mark Comer's *The Ruthless Elimination of Hurry*, David Murray's *Reset*, and Justin Whitmel Earley's *The Common Rule*; each of these, in its own way, seeks to help us become more aware of God throughout our days.

Beyond merely providing a longer reading list or detailing all the practices that might be helpful, I want to spend some time reflecting on the four key ideas mentioned above: rhythm, vulnerability, lament and gratitude, and rest. My prayer is that these reflections will provide a nourishing and practical conclusion to this book on how our limits are part of God's good design for us, a design that can lead us into greater faithfulness here and now, even in a sinful and exhausting world. Given the extended discussion in this particular chapter, readers may find it useful to take each of the four sections slowly, one at a time, maybe pausing for a day or two after each one to consider how it might relate to your life.

1. Embrace the Rhythms and Seasons of Life

Might one of our great challenges be that when we judge how we are doing, we try to assess the whole by only looking at a part? What I mean is this:

we imagine what a faithful and rich life looks like, and then on any given morning, we dislike the person we see staring back at us from the mirror. We see bags under our eyes and anticipate a day of laying bricks or cleaning or being stuck in endless and unfruitful meetings. We don't feel strong or triumphant; we don't feel significant or accomplished; we just feel small and tired.

How are we to know if we are faithful? Well, we probably need to be more realistic about what to expect of ourselves in any given day, week, month, and year; but we also need to look beyond the immediate to a greater horizon. When we step back to imagine things from God's perspective, we might get a fresh view of what a faithful and rich life looks like: my guess is that it is much slower, more ordinary and earthy, but also more beautiful than we anticipate. Let me explain.

Can We Have It All?

In 2012 Anne-Marie Slaughter wrote "Why Women Still Can't Have It All" in the *Atlantic*, and a series of articles and reflections by others furthered the discussion.[3] The authors were, in various ways, wrestling with the myth of trying to "have it all." Most of them focused on women, often describing a specific woman who was trying to accomplish good goals but was also finding that her own ambitions and the expectations laid on her by others were more than she could meet. This was usually some combination of career, marriage, starting a family, caring for children, being physically healthy, keeping social connections, caring for extended family such as aging parents, keeping up a home, staying intellectually engaged, and sleeping more than five hours a night. Please don't read this list and say, "Well, that is dumb, they shouldn't care about [insert rejected item here]." There is nothing wrong with anything in this list—nor should we see ourselves as immune to such expectations, because we're not. The problem isn't the items on this list; it's that no one person can do them all well at the same time.

And let's be clear, this is not just a woman's problem. We do have a stereotype of men from the 1950s who went to the "office" during the day to "work," came home at night, and then were "done." Food would be prepared, house cleaned, shopping accomplished, kids in order, all before Dad arrived home. However much that may or may not have happened in the 1950s, it is certainly not the case for most men I know today. Guys have tried many different methods, with varying degrees of effort and success, to become better partners, more understanding and helpful. This is a beautiful thing. It is true that studies show women still bear a much higher percentage of the housework and child-related care than men, even when the women have jobs outside the home like the men. This is often not good or right. But even granting that legitimate point, I also know many conscientious men who are seeking to be far more attentive, helpful, and engaged. All of that is positive. But it also means that, just as women are struggling to "have it all," so too are men becoming exhausted and frustrated by the realization that they can't "have it all" either.

To be more engaged at home means having less time for work. Do I choose friendships or exercise, sleep or prayer, sports or church activities? No one can have it all! It's no longer hard to imagine that men are beginning to mirror burdens similar to those women have faced for longer: careers needing investment, health declining if ignored, friendships neglected or never developed, children not given the attention desired, and the list could go on and on.

Who can have it all? We laugh because it is ludicrous, but even as we chuckle, we plan our next day with the expectation that we can and will excel at our job, spend quality time with our family, renew our bodies through physical fitness, eat healthy meals, do the laundry, and . . . And in the middle of all this we expect to be joyful, patient, interesting, and kind. Very few of us lay our heads on the pillow at night and feel that we have conquered the day. It just doesn't happen, does it? The cumulative effect of exhaustion and unrealistic expectations paralyzes and wears down our minds, bodies, and relationships. Often we find ourselves feeling that we are failing at everything. Instead of crushing the day, we feel crushed by it. While none of us tend to meet all of our expectations in a single day, does that mean we don't succeed at any of them? A woman may in fact have a day at work filled with triumph! Her boss and colleagues praise her for her excellent contributions and her invaluable presence in the organization. But then, that same night she forgets about one of her kids' games, doesn't go for an evening walk with her friend, and spends too much time unwinding online. Perhaps the next day she puts in her eight hours at work but leaves the office feeling totally frustrated and feeling that she didn't make any progress on her projects; yet that evening she has a great time with the family at the church's communal Wednesday night dinner, laughs heartily with her children, and is even able to read a bit of a novel. Men have the same kinds of experiences, of course—they also have spouses, children, jobs, bodies, and relationships. This is not a problem for only one sex; it is *our* problem together!

Trying to "have it all"—*all at once*—sets us up for frustration and failure. A healthy view of our finitude allows us to step back, take a breath, and think about the importance of different seasons in life, the rhythms of our bodies and our days, our months, and our years. Appreciating such divinely created rhythms helps us avoid the perpetual frustration and self-condemnation that grow from mistaking our limits for sin. My guess is that we should do less than we would like and that we will be surprised that pushing for less might accomplish more.

Not Every Day or Season Is the Same

I first heard the phrase "productivity shame" from Jocelyn K. Glei, as she explored how many of us perpetually set unrealistic goals and then feel guilty about not meeting them. This resonated deeply with me. Even though I should know better by now, I still do it all the time. I am notorious for this even with my kids, who learned when they were little that when dad made a list of chores for a Saturday morning it inevitably required mom to come and cross items off if it was to be just a "morning" and not a full day of work. Mostly, however, I inflict this problem on myself rather than on others.

As I sit down and map out my week, my to-do list for Monday usually contains a whole week's worth of work; and yet somehow I still stand baffled when I end my day feeling defeated for getting "so little done." I sabotage myself. I deny my very real creaturely limits and the rhythm of human life as God designed it. I let endless demands, rather than a realistic and healthy consideration of my limits and rhythms of life, dictate my expectations. When I follow the temptation to deny my finitude, it hurts me, my relationships, and even my work. As Glei reflects, "Creative labor has its own pace, and all you can do for the most part is show up and be present and ready to execute, if and when the insights come. But how you feel about that work and how you feel about that pace is completely within your control—it is about mindset and expectations."[4] When my expectations ignore my limits, I am sinning, for I am trying to act as a god rather than as a human, infinite rather than finite. Harmonizing our expectations with the seasons and rhythms of life is fundamental to a faithful life.

Trying to "have it all" pushes us to expect that every day we should experience the whole of life and not just a part. So we take the hopes and ambitions of a lifetime, of a year, of a month, of a week, and we shove them into each and every day. That, as I well know, is a recipe for disaster. Rather than cultivating a life of gratitude and joy, it produces frustration and resentment. What if we (re)learned how to live by the seasonal nature of life? What if we learned to appreciate the rhythms of the day, of the weeks, of the years? The Christian tradition actually has a distinctive view of time. So many of us live, however, in denial or neglect of the Christian calendar. Sure, we celebrate Christmas and Easter, but besides hearing a special sermon on those days, have we allowed those distinct time periods to reshape our lives?

Life in ancient Israel was shaped by feasts and festivals, sacrifices and Sabbaths. There were different times and seasons that shaped the vision, expectation, and pattern of Israelites' lives. Christians have likewise followed a distinctive calendar through the centuries. Many churches visually demonstrate this movement in their congregations by displaying different colors and patterns: for example, in some traditions purple is used for key parts of Advent and Lent, rose/pink for the third and fourth Sundays during Lent, red for Good Friday and Passion Sunday, green for Ordinary Time (the largest part of the calendar!), and white or gold for Easter and Christmas seasons.[5] And each of these colors and times corresponds to the different expectations for each of those seasons. While different Christian traditions don't always use the exact same colors, the basic intent is similar. The green of Ordinary Time points to the good of normal life, anticipation, and growth, while red can signify both the depth of God's love and the idea of Christ's passion; white and gold are meant to lift the spirit, pointing not just to joy and glory but also to purity and freedom in Christ; purple often indicates preparation and sacrifice, while black is normally linked with mourning and death. Along these lines, Lent and Advent call us to reflect and repent, preparing for what God has done and is doing. Holy Week and Pentecost encourage us to consider Christ's sacrifice for us, while the final Sundays of Lent encourage a sense of anticipation (the time of waiting is about to end!). The long seasons of Ordinary Time remind us of plants and trees, encouraging us to lay down roots and grow and to have hope for this life as well as the next. Finally, Christmas and Easter call us to joy and purity, cultivating a greater awareness of God's presence and life-giving care.

Beyond a liturgical calendar, however, we would do well to honor the common pattern of everyday life. Different times of life bring different callings. An adolescent is different from an elderly grandparent, a teenager from a middle-aged mom, a painter from a politician: each has dignity, each has stuff to "do," and therefore each should have different expectations. They should continue to employ their respective gifts, to sacrifice for others, but also recognize their limits and dependence on others. Parenting a newborn is different from being the parent of a thirty-year-old. A family may decide that the season of raising little ones requires that one parent always be at home, and so, through creative organization and sacrificial budgeting, they figure out how to make that happen. Whether it means both parents' employment is more limited, or that they divide responsibilities so one person's career helps make it possible for the other to be home, they make adjustments in light of the season of life. What may be healthy in one season can be unhealthy in another. Only when we appreciate our finitude and the rhythms of life can we embrace such seasons without growing resentful or despairing.

We can all do hard things for a time, but we can't perpetually live on high alert. Soldiers can be under fire during a skirmish, but unceasing fire erodes their bodies and souls. Students can push themselves during midterms and the occasional late-night study session, but if four hours of sleep become the norm, they will eventually crash and burn. Entrepreneurs can pour themselves into their startups, but if the demands never lighten and the seasonal self-denial becomes constant and year-round, then relationships start to wither and die. Unrealistic expectations hurt ourselves and others. We need to be more honest about the demands we face, about how long things take and what we can and cannot do on any given day, or week, or season of life.

This brings me to our next key idea: vulnerability.

2. Recognize Vulnerability

Brené Brown gave a TED Talk called "The Power of Vulnerability" in 2010.[6] It has been watched over fifty-three million (!) times as of May 2021. Brown's research concerning shame has produced many helpful books and promoted much-needed discussions. Her basic thesis is that pretending to be invulnerable fails, producing lives suffocated by fear and shame, and that only by being more honest, more open, and more realistic about our struggles and limits can we experience any sense of wholeness. I obviously share many of her concerns.

Christian psychiatrist Curt Thompson has also argued that the remedy to shame is to admit our vulnerability—that is, to recognize that we are not self-sufficient, that we are subject to coming up short, that we need others, that we're susceptible to attack and even failure; only by recognizing this state of our vulnerability can we be fully known.[7] We tend to think of vulnerability, however, as an occasional feeling, as when we lose our job or someone breaks up with us. Yet as Thompson rightly explains, "Vulnerability is not something we choose or that is true in a given moment, while the rest of the time it is not. Rather, it is something we *are*. This is why we wear clothes, live in houses and have speed limits. So much of what we do in life is designed, among other things, to protect us from the fact that we are vulnerable at all times. To be human *is* to be vulnerable."[8] Just like humility, discussed in chapter 6, vulnerability is a real aspect of our creaturely limits and interdependence. To recognize our vulnerability is to confess that we are creatures rather than the Creator. But we fear that admitting vulnerability will either make us targets for predators or cripple us with anxiety, so instead of seeing it as something to accept and even celebrate, we try to deny or overcome it.

Although these ideas resonate with some people, others find them very discomforting. For example, when you hear the word *vulnerable*, does it sound more feminine than masculine to you? Why is this word associated more often with women than with men? It shouldn't be. To be vulnerable, to have weaknesses and needs, is not just a trendy idea; it is part of how God made us. Brené Brown, in her audio series *Men, Women, and Worthiness*, admits she was forced to see how uncomfortable we are when applying this idea to men.

Brown tells the story of being at a book signing where a woman and her husband approached her with books to get autographed for the mom and three daughters.[9] After Brown signed the books, the wife turned to leave and said, "Come on, hon," to her husband. "No," he replied, "I want to talk with her for a second." The woman insisted that they move on. Again he stubbornly said, "No, I need to ask her something." So the flustered wife agreed, but said she would wait for him in the back.

Uncomfortable, Brown just waited. The guy then looked at her and said, "I really love all this stuff you're talking about, this shame, and being perfect, and having to be someone we're not, and having to reach out. It is really powerful. But I never heard you mention anything about men." She felt relieved, knowing she could get out of this: "I don't study men." He immediately responded, "That's convenient." Nervously, she asked, "Why convenient?" "It's convenient you don't talk about men," he said, "because when we reach out, when we tell our stories, when we share our shame experiences, we get the emotional [s—] beat out of us." Stunned, Brown was about to reply when he added, "Before you say anything about those dads, and those coaches, or about those bosses and mean bully friends, let me explain this to you. My wife and my three daughters you just signed books for, they would rather see me die on top of my white horse rather than see me fall off." And then he just left.

Once you see the truth, you can't unsee it.

Before any reader simply dismisses this view of men as coming only from one end of the political spectrum, I will say I have seen it strongly affecting people on both the left and the right. Though the two sides have different rhetoric about men and women, it is rare for men anywhere to feel they can safely admit their shortcomings, their weaknesses, their needs. Yet, if vulnerability is part of the human condition, then it is healthy for all people to recognize, men and women, rich and poor, young and old.

So is this emphasis on vulnerability merely a modern trend? How often do the words *vulnerable* or *vulnerability* show up in Scripture? You won't find them there. Millennia ago, *vulnerable* referred to weaknesses in a fortress or army, not a person. Applying this term to one's personal weaknesses, dependence, or needs is a fairly modern usage, and yet the term now, as Brown's work demonstrates, resonates deeply with many people. While the use of the term may be recent, the fundamental truth behind it is not.

I believe that recognizing one's vulnerability before God and others is fundamental to a Christian understanding of being human. Although the word is absent from the Bible, both testaments affirm that we are, in fact, vulnerable to failure, external attack, and internal weaknesses. From the air we breathe to the water we drink, from our relationships to our employment, from our minds to our wills, everything about us points to our dependence on God, others, and the earth. We are creatures, and thus we are necessarily vulnerable. But our modern world tempts us in countless ways to pretend this is not the case. I might imagine I don't need anything or anyone, but trying to live this falsehood is devastating, and we can feel it. Using the term *vulnerability* now is simply a way of putting fresh words to human experience, an experience that has always been true.

Some segments of the church are deeply uncomfortable with admissions of vulnerability. Having considered this for some time, I believe that (1) the decline in the role of confession and (2) the loss of extended times of prayer have contributed to this problem. By "confession" I don't particularly mean the Roman Catholic practice of formally entering a confessional booth with a priest, so much as the congregational practice of regularly confessing our sins to God and acknowledging our wrongs against one another as part of our worship services. This practice of corporate confession of sin reminds us that we have a problem with sin and failure: without that reminder we open ourselves to the error of seeing God and the gospel as means of self-help rather than the source of our life. Not only do we start to imagine that we haven't sinned—or at least not very badly—but also we begin to think that we aren't needy. We begin to see God and others as a bonus to our lives, meant to enrich us, whereas confessing our dependence on the care, provision, and grace of others can make us deeply uneasy or even suspicious. So we avoid it. Similarly, when we neglect private and corporate prayer, we deprive ourselves of necessary reminders that we are indeed vulnerable—not only have we sinned, but we need the acceptance and love and help of God and each other. When prayer ceases, the weight on my shoulders increases: there is often a direct correspondence between my sense of vulnerability and my practice of prayer. Those who do not sense their vulnerability rarely pray; those who cultivate an awareness of it have a hard time not praying.

> We are constantly tempted, as Adam was at the beginning, to think that we are actually sufficient unto ourselves, that we have life in ourselves.
>
> John Behr, *Becoming Human*

As we move away from the regular practice of confession and extended times of prayer in our congregations, our homes, and our friendships, the reality of our vulnerability does not change, but our perception of it does.

I should clarify that by *vulnerable* I don't mean that humans are fragile: one can sympathize with the "antifragility" movements that call for greater resilience in youth, and yet at the same time also affirm the need to recognize our vulnerability.[10] Parents who overprotect children imagine they can somehow shield the child from all difficulties and hardships: but they and their children are inherently vulnerable creatures, not fragile but limited, flawed, even subject to failure and susceptible to attack. Ironically, the admission of our vulnerability can help us find where to strengthen ourselves and our children, and it can lead us to learn how to depend on each other and on God. Bumps and bruises, disappointments and challenges all teach us what our limits are and how to respond to them. At its best, admitting our vulnerability enables a healthy, honest, and accurate assessment of our existence, which includes authentic dependence on God, neighbor, and the earth.

Here, two temptations often arise. First, as we have discussed, we can try to avoid or ignore our vulnerability. But, if we are honest, we know we can't eat, flush our toilet, or stay clothed without the work of others. We can't flourish emotionally and relationally and vocationally without others. We need, and so we are vulnerable. The church exists as an expression of our need for God and one another.

A second temptation is to abuse the weaknesses of others by manipulating them. Chuck DeGroat has coined the term "fauxnerability"[11] to describe the act of appearing to admit sin, weakness, or need in a shallow way that doesn't really put the speaker at any risk. DeGroat's extensive work on narcissism has demonstrated how subtle forms of this practice can devastate the church.[12] We have seen fallen megachurch pastors or actors or politicians use this technique to exploit or control others, to get people to feel bad for them and secure support. While I strongly believe Christians must be empathetic and gracious people, we should recognize the difference between the quest for unhealthy attention and genuine godly openness. The first enables the manipulation of crowds, while the second opens the way to life-giving connection with others. A healthy doctrine of the church, the body of Christ, will guide us to see warning signs and know true admissions of vulnerability from their false imitation.

Encouraging life together, the apostle Paul calls us to "let love be genuine" as we engage one another with sibling affection, seeking to "outdo one another in showing honor" (Rom. 12:9–10). One reason that it can be so hard for us to honor others is that we want to be the hero, to imagine we do not depend on others—we want to pretend that we have no need to admit we are vulnerable. Paul encourages each member of the body "not to think of himself more highly than he ought"; instead, by a "sober judgment" each believer should recognize not just their gifts but also their dependence on others (12:3–8). We might like the idea that others need us, but we hate the idea that we need them: if you need others, then you should honor them, and this means that you may have to let go of your own opinions in favor of theirs! You might be wrong—and no one wants to admit that. But in a healthy church we learn to give way to others and honor them, and then we are prepared to practice this more faithfully in the world.

When we honor our neighbors and colleagues, it means we recognize their strengths, we value their contributions, and we affirm that sometimes they are right when we are wrong. This reflects the shape of the interconnected world God created and loves. Think about how many people started praising elementary teachers during COVID-19 lockdowns when they had to start teaching their own children. There were calls for teacher pay increases, for realizing the challenge of being a third-grade teacher, and a new recognition for how dependent we were on people we previously took for granted. Until we recognize our vulnerability—that we don't have what it takes—we can easily undervalue elementary teachers (or anyone else) in our lives. God has made us dependent on his good work and gifts in others, so that affirming those gifts and encouraging them is no more than a realistic approach to life.

Before God we are always the ones in need. He alone is our safe shelter and security. He has no needs, so we can be fully honest before him, knowing he will always faithfully care for us and never manipulate or abuse us. But when we are not honest before God about our needs and weaknesses, our frustrations and fears, can we really rest in his grace and patience? This takes us to lament and gratitude.

3. Express Lament, Cultivate Gratitude

Tabitha, my wife, is deeply thankful to God for the opportunities he has given her, including her education, working at the American Embassy in London, holding various meaningful positions in the workforce, and having two amazing children and a decent husband. She is thankful for the right to own land and to vote. Only those ignorant of history don't appreciate how recent some of these opportunities are for women. And yet, along with most women she knows, she still faces countless challenges. Widespread negative assumptions about women persist in our society, such as unfounded beliefs that women can't handle pressure, can't drive properly, or are less intelligent; on top of which they have to deal with mansplaining when a man talks down to the woman in front of him, who may in fact know more about the topic than he does. It's not pretty, but it happens a lot and remains far more common than we would like to admit.

So should Tabitha and other women in America be thankful or upset? Should the fact that there is much to be grateful for mean that speaking up about continuing problems is no more than complaining? Are they ungrateful? Or might it be that living in a fallen world requires us—or at least Christians—to tell the truth about what we see and experience?

One of the remarkable things that Scripture affirms is that two conflicting factors in life can be true at the same time: problems and frustrations coexist with gifts from God. To recognize and affirm them both often requires courage and patience: choosing one over the other may be easier, but facing complexities is also part of living in a vast and layered world. Instead of denying one side of the tension, we turn it over to the triune God, who still takes care of us and handles the complexities that are beyond us. How do we do this? Through lament and gratitude.

Don't Pick between Lament and Gratitude

Both our secular culture and the church often push us to choose between things that are equally true. I want you to see that there are times when you should not make that kind of choice (which is itself a choice!). Dichotomies and tensions are constantly before us, asking us to pick a winner: the individual or the community, grace or effort, piety or cultural engagement, love or justice, lament or gratitude. What if instead of choosing an unrealistic oversimplification, we choose what I call *biblical realism*. This posture allows us to express both lament and gratitude, each a genuine part of our experience and neither canceling out the other.

We develop biblical gratitude and joy not by ignoring the bad but by making sure our vision is not reduced to a single mood. This helps us resist two pressures. Some people tell Christians that we are supposed to be joyful and filled with gratitude, but their approach to pain and suffering is simply to deny it. This refusal of the real is neither honest nor helpful. Others, however, are so aware of the hurts and problems in this life that Christian expressions of joy or gratitude appear to them as naive at best, or coldhearted at worst.

But what if you don't have to pick between lament and joy?

As we experience or witness hardship, injustice, and suffering, it is appropriate that we express honest lament. Such expressions do not undermine faith in God, but actually express our faith—you don't voice frustration, confusion, and pain to someone who isn't there. As the psalmist says, "*My* God, *my* God, *why* . . ." (Ps. 22:1; emphasis added): this is not a distant deity, but David's God, the Lord of the Covenant, Israel's Sovereign King, who is present and listening, as the rest of the psalm testifies. This is the Almighty, who has made promises, who is good and trustworthy. This is *my* God. *I*, as an individual, and *we* as a people, cry out to this God and no other. And so when we hurt, when we have deep questions, when we see atrocities and experience slights, we lament, believing his presence, compassion, and power can truly handle and absorb our raw emotions without being overwhelmed by them.

Despite pressures from both outside and within the church, lament and thanksgiving are not in a contest. The Bible calls us to both. Don't pick between Psalm 22 and Psalm 23: believers are allowed to cry out, "My God, my God, why have you forsaken me?" in their distress, and at the same time confidently declare, "The Lord is my Shepherd." These expressions are not tied to good and bad times, but to the one God, who is present in both: we gain confidence in God's kindness and provision when we "walk through the valley of the shadow of death." If we try to choose one and not both, we risk turning our laments into hopeless despair or reducing divine promises to shallow clichés. When we engage both lament and gratitude, then each becomes stronger and truer.

Now to the key point: *Lament and gratitude are mirror concepts that highlight the same fundamental truth: we are dependent on the God who rescues us*. Only when we accept our creaturely finitude will this make sense to us. When things are hard, troubling, and wrong, we lean on God, voicing our fears and frustrations to the Creator and Sustainer. We depend on him to make right what is wrong, to heal what is diseased, to reconcile what is broken, to forgive what sins have been committed. Likewise, when a newborn is put into the embrace of her mother, when a scrumptious meal feeds the body and laughter strengthens the soul, when injustice is corrected, and when our work is done well—in all of this we rejoice and express gratitude, for it reminds us that God is the Giver of all good gifts and that we depend on him for life, breath, and our very existence. Many of us have experienced complex moments that are filled with seemingly inconsistent emotion. We might be thankful for a loved one's peaceful passing, while still experiencing the depth of sorrow and loss. We may be overjoyed that our child got into college, while simultaneously feeling a knot in our stomachs as we cannot imagine how we will pay for it. We can be happy for a friend's promotion at the same moment that we feel the pain of being passed over ourselves. God created in us such an intricate web of emotional response that we can experience complexities so rich that they seem beyond all possibility. But don't miss the beauty: *Lament and gratitude together not only recognize our dependence on God; they also deepen our sense of his faithfulness.*

Because we live in a fallen and hurting world, and yet a world where God remains present and active, God's children may express both lament and gratitude, questions and confidence. Just as believers rightly voice their concerns, confusions, and frustrations to the God who sees and understands, so those same believers freely offer praise and thankfulness to the God who is good and active, trustworthy and kind. Rather than opposing each other, these senses go together: "I will rejoice and be glad in your steadfast love, *because* you have seen my affliction" (Ps. 31:7–9; emphasis added). Here the psalmist feels that his life is spent in weakness, sorrow, and sighing, and yet he looks to both the present and the future as times when God not only hears his people's concerns but acts to care for them. He is present. He knows our weaknesses and needs.

A few years ago a dear friend spoke in chapel and shared a "generational testimony" of sorts.[13] She pointed out that, as an African American woman, she finds her faith strengthened by the fact that God could make himself so powerfully known and so tangibly close even to the enslaved. Her four-times-great-grandmother's family had endured slavery and treacherous treatment—often by those who claimed to be Christians—and yet left a legacy of faith to her. Despite the injustice that defined their lives, this family came to be convinced that God heard their cries and loved them. They believed God was good, he was with them, and so he could be praised; not because *things* were good, but because *he* was! The same person who laments is also the one who can praise and express deep thanksgiving. Depending on your tradition, you might be quicker to choose one side or the other. The challenge I encourage you to embrace is to hold both things together, just like my friend and her family.

Because I have written extensively about lament elsewhere, I will concentrate more here on how to cultivate gratitude.[14] This also makes sense because, while lament is a proper expression for us in our fallen world, even an unfallen world would resound with gratitude. Thanksgiving is proper and intrinsic to human existence.

Gratitude: An Awareness That God Is Near

The Bible uses a cluster of words related to the idea of thankfulness: *rejoice*, *praise*, *joy*, *thanksgiving*, *gratitude*, and others. While each word could be distinguished from the others, they are in the same theological and existential family. These words all point to our recognition that God is the great Giver, for "*from* him and *through* him and *to* him are all things" (Rom. 11:36; emphasis added). Recognizing and confessing his faithfulness provokes praise and admiration, thanksgiving, and a disposition of gratitude. All of these ideas illuminate dynamics of living within a healthy sense of appreciation for God, others, and the rest of creation.

Given our limited space here, we will restrict ourselves to a brief look at Paul's advice in Philippians 4. Here the apostle sketches out the believer's life of gratitude. Rejoicing and being grateful go a long way toward shaping a healthy appreciation of our creaturely finitude and rightful dependence on God. "Rejoice in the Lord always; again I will say, Rejoice. Let your gentleness be known to everyone. The Lord is near. Do not worry about anything, but in everything by prayer and supplication with thanksgiving let your requests be made known to God. And the peace of God, which surpasses all understanding, will guard your hearts and your minds in Christ Jesus" (Phil. 4:4–7 NRSV). Paul begins with the imperative "Rejoice!" This is less of a request and more of a directive. We are to be the kind of people who rejoice, who praise God in all seasons.

A Christian college professor I know—who is allergic to shallow spirituality—doesn't always pray before his classes, but when it is terribly wet, windy, and miserable outside, then he normally offers thanksgiving to God. For him it is important to make sure that he and his students don't reduce God's providence to seasons of prosperity. God cares for us at all times, whether we see tornados or blue skies. Similarly, in connection with our constant creaturely dependence on God, the apostle Paul does not restrict rejoicing to enjoyable circumstances. How could he do so without ignoring or lying about the genuine hardships of life?

Paul's answer is as simple as it is transformative: "The Lord is near" (Phil. 4:5b). There is some debate about what the "near" means here, whether it refers to the Lord's expected coming, which could be very soon (near in *time*), or to the idea that he is currently with us (near in *space*).[15] But why choose? As Gordon Fee argues, Paul is probably here using an "intentional double entendre": in other words, the Lord's being "at hand" includes both of these ideas.[16] I would add that Paul here exemplifies the believer who lives in the "fear of the Lord" in the way we have discussed in chapter 7. Remember, this is not so much about living in fear of divine punishment but about living in awe of divine presence. This is what separates the foolish from the wise: one ignores God while the other lives in constant awareness of his nearness. It makes sense that Paul then adds that our "gentleness"—or it can be translated as "reasonableness"—should be "evident to all" (4:5 NIV). Those who really believe God to be "near" are not panicked people, not cruel or easily angered, but reasonable or even gentle.

Because of the promise that *the Lord is near*, Paul encourages us not to be anxious. Why? Not because we will escape difficulty, or because we can predict how everything will work out (we are still finite). No, we can only cease to be anxious because the infinite God is with us in every situation. We are not alone. We are not orphans. Consequently, because we know our loving, holy, and attentive Father is at hand, we do not reserve our prayers and petitions for special occasions but offer them throughout our days. We offer prayers "with thanksgiving" because we are confident in the character of the One we are addressing. We present our requests not to a nameless void, not to a vague power, but to the Father of our Lord Jesus Christ, who has given us his Spirit. He is *our* God! While we are finite, he is infinite, good, wise, and faithful. And so we make our request to him, confident that he is near.

How might our lives be changed if we just chewed on simple promises like "The Lord is near" as a cow chews on her cud? We sometimes make meditating on Scripture sound too difficult, too sophisticated, too spiritual for those of us who are not supersaints. But meditating is just taking a biblical truth (e.g., "The Lord is near") and savoring it throughout our day, thinking about it, resting in its assurance, allowing the thought to run over us like a purifying stream on a hot summer day. These truths often take a while to move into our souls, so we must spend time with and rest in them. Beloved, *the Lord is near*. Only because of this can we be thankful even during times that may also warrant lament.

This then provides the "peace of God," which goes beyond our ability to understand how all the pieces fit together (Phil. 4:7). God's peace "will guard your hearts and your minds in Christ Jesus." The phrase "in Christ Jesus" easily passes by our eyes, but we should not miss the content: Paul grounds his confidence and peace in the person and work of Jesus the Messiah. Elsewhere, when writing to the Thessalonians, Paul similarly declares, "Rejoice always, pray without ceasing, give thanks in all circumstances; for this is the will of God *in Christ Jesus* for you" (1 Thess. 5:16–18 NRSV; emphasis added). When things are awful in our lives and we look at the tragedies and hurts, we are tempted to hopelessness. What, then, does Paul mean when he tells us to rejoice?

Don't listen to people who tell you to look at terrible events and pain and call them "good." That is not what Paul is saying. The good, the confidence, the rejoicing is not about the circumstances, but about God's faithfulness and presence, which is most clearly seen in the life, death, and resurrection of Christ. Jesus the Messiah is the reason we can be grateful no matter the circumstances. Elsewhere Paul encourages the Ephesians not to get drunk with wine, but instead be filled with the Spirit (i.e., God's presence), by cultivating a life of "psalms and hymns and spiritual songs" and by "giving thanks always and for everything to God the Father in the name of our Lord Jesus Christ" (Eph. 5:19–20). Rather than anchoring our thanks and gratitude in our ever-changing circumstances, Paul ties them to the faithfulness of the triune God: the Spirit dwelling in us reminds us of the love of the Father and the grace of the Son. This is not naive optimism nor ignorant cliché, but confident hope in the infinite God of Israel, who has been and always will be faithful (Heb. 11).

Christians are remarkable and different because we are encouraged to resist picking between honest assessment of hardships and hopeful confidence in God's presence. After all, Paul wrote this encouragement while in prison. The joy he spoke of was not restricted to the absence of genuine challenge and injustice. As New Testament scholar Lynn H. Cohick rightly reminds us, "The source of the Philippians' joy is participating in God's unfolding story of redemption," and then she adds, "This joy comes not from achievement but from abiding with God, no matter what."[17] Christians do not have to pick between lament and gratitude because we recognize not only that we are vulnerable creatures living in a fallen world but also that our God is infinite, wise, good, and present, filled with compassion and care for his people.

Remember, Look, Identify

Paul calls us to practice gratitude as a consistent way of life amid the limits of life. Breaking it down into three movements gives us a useful and workable approach to instilling this practice into our daily routine: we remember, look, and identify.

To be a grateful people, we first need to *remember* what God has done in salvation history. From the exodus onward, remembrance has always been a key practice for God's people. Remember what God has done. Exodus always precedes Sinai: deliverance always comes before, and informs, commands. We easily lose this, so we must constantly remind ourselves that Jesus is the Messiah, our Savior and Risen Lord. Never forget. Remember.

Christians are not merely historians, however, since we also *look* to the present. God continues to be among us and active in and through us. Not only did God work yesterday, but he still works today. He constantly brings salvation and liberating transformation to his people. We look not simply for God's power in the sunrise or as we stand in awe before the vast ocean. We also look for signs of hope amid the ashes, for his presence and kindness in unexpected places, not because he delights in pain and suffering, but because Christ is the sympathetic high priest and our God promises to make all things new. There in the ashes, we proclaim a gospel of hope because Christ is the Lord there, too: no place is beyond his grasp, his renewal, his redemption.

Further, we do not merely *remember* what God has done and *look* for what he is doing, but we also *identify* the works of God that remind us of his character, activity, and presence. To identify is to name these works as his: he did *that*, and *this*, and we will remember it and give thanks. When Paul calls us to "continue steadfastly in prayer," he adds, "being watchful in it with thanksgiving" (Col. 4:2). If we are not watchful, we will not identify what God is doing, and when that happens, we cease to be a grateful people. When thanksgiving is replaced with grumbling, we start to imagine God is distant and cruel rather than present and concerned. We may remember that Daniel prayed three times a day, but during those prayers he also "gave thanks" (Dan. 6:10). He cultivated a disposition of gratitude partly because he realized how little control he had in this world.

> As for me, I call to God,
> and the Lord saves me.
> Evening, morning and noon
> I cry out in distress,
> and he hears my voice.
> Psalm 55:16–17 NIV

When Tabitha and I lived in London, we were part of Goodenough College, which is a historic postgraduate residence with rich history, reflected in some amazingly old and beautiful tables. We eventually discovered that on one leg of each of the hand-carved tables was a little mouse chiseled out of the wood. The uninformed would never know, but those who looked could eventually locate the carvings. Each mouse identified the artisan who built the table, provoking the observer to gratitude for their excellent craftsmanship.

Paul calls us to practice thanksgiving by seeking to identify the fingerprints of God's work. He exhorts the beloved: "Whatever is true, whatever is honorable, whatever is just, whatever is pure, whatever is lovely, whatever is commendable, if there is any excellence, if there is anything worthy of praise, think about these things" (Phil. 4:8). Identifying these traits reminds us of the good Creator and Sustainer, who has not abandoned his world to evil and misery, but remains present and active.

We push against despair with gratitude and thanksgiving. Finding the fingerprints of God around us requires practice, intent, and perhaps some training. Those who attend to the path will find plenty of reasons to be grateful and rejoice, but those who stop looking will only grow further disillusioned and distressed.

Gratitude Is Natural and Good for Limited Humans

Over the past twenty-five years a movement called "positive psychology" has developed the idea that the discipline of psychology had become very good at diagnosing problems and mental challenges but had not given sufficient attention to positive traits. Thus research began into more classic conceptions—often going back to Aristotle—of characteristics thought to accompany what used to be called the "good life," what Aristotle used to call *eudaimonia*, or what many today call "human flourishing."

While countless studies emerged from positive psychology on everything from happiness to forgiveness, one area that Robert Emmons from the University of California, Davis, and others focused on was gratitude.[18] Emmons, who happens to be a Christian, realized that few people had studied gratitude from a psychological perspective, and he was interested to see if it might be possible to empirically observe benefits from practicing acts of thankfulness and cultivating a disposition of gratitude. What he and others have gone on to find probably shouldn't surprise us: gratitude is essential to the good and virtuous life.

Whether measured as a trait or a mood, gratitude is consistently linked with all kinds of positive benefits. Researchers found that "highly grateful people, as compared to their less grateful counterparts, tend to experience positive emotions more often, enjoy greater satisfaction with life and more hope, and experience less depression, anxiety, and envy. They tend to score higher in pro-sociality and be more empathic, forgiving, helpful, and supportive as well as less focused on materialistic pursuits."[19] If someone keeps a simple gratitude journal for a month, we can measure changes from lower blood pressure to improved immune systems, from better sleep to increased energy levels.[20] Seems crazy, right?

Christians, of course, didn't need positive psychology research to tell us that gratitude is vital to the Christian life.[21] We have been commanded to rejoice, but here is the key: our rejoicing does not mean that we ignore evils, harden our hearts, or withdraw from the difficulties of pain and sufferings. No, we rejoice because *God is near*.

We rejoice because we remember what God has done, we look for what he is doing, and we identify his presence and kindness in whatever is good, noble, just, peace producing, and worthy of praise. Sometimes we give thanks for the brave young girl who stands up to the bully, or for the baker who offers stunningly good sourdough bread. We are grateful to God for friendships; for those who are willing, as Jeremiah says, to "[defend] the cause of the poor and needy" (Jer. 22:16 NIV); and for acts of gentleness in a hostile world. We are grateful for the cool glass of water and the kind word, for the warmth of the sun and for a well-built automobile. We don't need to be infinite to recognize God's good presence and action, and this perception brings us confidence and comfort even in the midst of our finite and fallen lives.

Most of all, we are a grateful people because we are confident of who God is and that God is with us, because we see Christ and are filled with his Spirit. The wickedness, the sadness, and the frustrations all remain worthy of our laments and action, but the laments are not all there is: Christ did not merely die; he rose, and he will come again. Christ is with us, God is near, and that is a fact always worth chewing on.

4. Rest: Honor Sleep and Sabbath

Until we believe the good news that the Creator is also the Redeemer, that we are not abandoned, alone, or left to our sins; until we believe that God is near, compassionate, quick to forgive, and abounding in love—until we believe these things, we cannot and will not rest. But when we do rest in that kind of trust in God, we also begin to have a healthy view of our finitude. This takes us to our final reflections on sleep and the value of Sabbath rest, two elements that reflect our finitude and our relationships, both part of God's original creation and therefore good and very good (Gen. 1:31).

Sleep as a Spiritual Discipline

We don't tend to address sleep as a spiritual topic, but see it only as a physical reality: we go through our days, and whenever we are finally done and tired, we go to sleep. There is nothing more to it really, is there? Maybe there is: when we are deprived of sleep for an extended time, we quickly see just how essential it is to human existence—not only do we get grumpy and often sick, but our hearts also grow more open to sin, doubts, self-condemnation, and fears.

Although sleep is a blessing, struggling to sleep is not necessarily linked to a moral cause. Problems with sleeping occur for all kinds of reasons at many different ages. Recent studies suggest that environmental factors contribute to sleep troubles,[22] but these are not caused only by pesticides. Research—although this seems like fairly common sense—has recently shown that family and other relationships have either a positive or a negative effect on one's ability to sleep, with the negative seeming to have more consequences than the positive.[23] One study looked at how religious cognitions—in this case, a secure attachment to God and assurance of salvation—actually helped lessen the power of stressful events disturbing a person's sleep quality.[24] The environment, relationships, and even beliefs can all affect the quality of our sleep.

Basic sleep hygiene can help many of us. Simple habits, such as keeping a schedule, reducing caffeine and alcohol, putting away screens, getting exercise, and trying to create a quiet dark space have all been shown to be helpful. But I am more interested here in examining why sleep matters theologically than in giving advice for increased ability to sleep.

Sleep reminds us every day that we are creatures rather than the Creator. God never sleeps. We usually take that for granted, but we should stop and think about it for a minute. Never. Ever. Sleeps. This gives profound comfort to vulnerable creatures who live in a hostile world. When you are on the front lines, you can't sleep unless someone is there to watch your back. If we don't believe in God, sleep can terrify us because it means that no one is looking out for us. Sleep reminds the believer that we don't sustain the world, but that God does. "My help comes from the LORD, who made heaven and earth. He will not let your foot be moved; he who keeps you will not slumber. Behold, he who keeps Israel will neither slumber nor sleep" (Ps. 121:2–4). We can sleep because God doesn't: "In peace I will both lie down and sleep; for you alone, O LORD, make me dwell in safety" (Ps. 4:8; cf. 46:10–11).

Unlike God, we need sleep, and that is a good gift. Our culture unfortunately links sleep with weakness. I recently heard that a famous entertainer only sleeps three to five hours a night, and it astounded me. While different individuals need different amounts of sleep, we can't really be blamed for forming the impression that only wimps need sleep and can't keep working or studying. Current technologies lead us to believe that a short charging session is all that's needed, but unlike machines, humans need sleep.

Jesus slept. The Gospel writers seldom mention this aspect of Jesus's life because, like his need to urinate, they assume it. We know he grew tired and weary from his pilgrimages (John 4:6). Once he was so exhausted he slept in a boat being tossed about amid a violent storm (Matt. 8:24; Mark 4:38–39). As a man, Jesus couldn't endlessly keep going: he needed sleep! And, although Jesus valued sleep, he was also willing to go without it during particularly challenging times. Like a firefighter facing a raging blaze or a parent of a crying newborn, sometimes Jesus was called to deny himself the usual amount of sleep. Whether praying all night before picking the twelve disciples (Luke 6:12–13) or struggling throughout the evening in the garden of Gethsemane (Matt. 26:36–46; cf. Mark 14:32–42), Jesus experienced times he couldn't or didn't sleep. We read that during his struggle in that garden Jesus "began to be sorrowful and troubled" (Matt. 26:37). This reminds us that feeling so "troubled" and even "sorrowful" that you can't sleep is not necessarily sinful. Jesus did it without sinning, and there are times that we can do it too. It can represent the right response to real difficulties and provide an opportunity for us to be with God in a special way.

> Since the body is the location in which spirituality is lived out, the richness of our spiritual life depends on how we view life cycles, aging, beauty, intimacy, illness, and finally our own death.
>
> Lillian Calles Barger, *Eve's Revenge*

My own struggles with sleep have often revealed that either I am failing to trust in God's faithfulness or I am tempted to feel that God has left me as an orphan (John 14:18). I start to act as if the weight of the world rests on my shoulders. Concerns about my children, spouse, or church, fears about the future and finances, health and happiness—they all weigh on me. This weight inevitably wakes me up and then keeps me from sleep. I can't sleep because I feel a need to constantly watch my back, prepare, and be ahead of the game. When I feel like an orphan or ignored by God, sleep becomes elusive to me.

There are various causes that wake us up in the middle of the night. The theological question isn't how well you sleep or whether you wake up, but when you do wake up, to whom do you turn? Our worries and sorrows crush us if we are alone, but with God we find comfort and rest.

Sometimes sleeplessness is part of our lament. During times of lament, the psalmist feels as if God is hiding his face from the psalmist's distress (Ps. 102:2). His affliction and struggle cause him to imagine that God is ignoring him, and yet he does not run from God but cries out to him: "I lie awake; I am like a lonely sparrow on the housetop" (102:7). Then he remembers Yahweh's goodness and power: God is "enthroned forever" (102:12), and "he regards the prayer of the destitute and does not despise their prayer" (102:17).

We can sleep because of divine faithfulness. "Because of the Lord's great love we are not consumed, for his compassions never fail. They are new every morning; great is your faithfulness" (Lam. 3:22–23 NIV). Or as Jeremiah awakes after a dream in which God's promised mercies were at the forefront of his mind, his sleep has brought hope and replenished his soul (Jer. 31:25–26). At other times God wakes us up in order to rescue us, as when he cared for Peter when he was surrounded by soldiers in a prison (Acts 12:6–7). Or when he awakens King Ahasuerus, who then has the "book of memorable deeds" read to him in the middle of the night; the result is that Mordecai's forgotten good actions are remembered and then rewarded (Esther 6:1–13): this awakening ended up saving thousands of lives! Sometimes when we can't sleep, God teaches us, counseling us in the dark quiet of the night when we can finally hear him (Ps. 16:7–8). This is partly why "sleeping on things" can serve as an act of faith, as God "instructs" our hearts.

Wrestling with God at night can involve a true spiritual battle: for some of us it is also a medical struggle as sickness or pain keeps us awake. Again, the psalmist models for us this experience of depending on God in the dark. Despite his desire for sleep, he tells God, "You hold my eyelids open; I am so troubled that I cannot speak" (Ps. 77:4). In his "day of trouble" he seeks God even into the late night (77:2–3). In the dark of night, he confesses his confusion and his struggle to recognize God's provision. The questions pour out:

> Will the Lord spurn forever,
>   and never again be favorable?
> Has his steadfast love forever ceased?
>   Are his promises at an end for all time?
> Has God forgotten to be gracious?
>   Has he in anger shut up his compassion? (77:7–9)

The question for the psalmist and for us is this: *Will our circumstances or God's promises shape us?* Facing an uncertain future, the psalmist reminds himself of what he knows:

> I will remember the deeds of the LORD;
>   yes, I will remember your wonders of old.
> I will ponder all your work,
>   and meditate on your mighty deeds. (77:11–12)

He comforts himself by remembering God's words and actions: God has always been present and working, "yet [his] footprints were unseen" (77:19). Even if we don't notice him, that doesn't mean God wasn't there.

Sleep is a spiritual discipline that daily reminds us of our lack of control. Just as a king is not saved simply by the size of his army or a warrior by his strength alone (Ps. 33:16–18), so sleep reminds us daily that we can't rescue ourselves: we are never strong enough, we never know enough, we never can do enough to eliminate our vulnerability. And so *sleep is an act of faith*. It requires us to see our finitude as a good part of God's design for us.

According to Christian practice, preparing for sleep also prepares us for death. Not only was sleep a common way people described death (John 11:11; 1 Cor. 11:30; 15:6), but Christians were those who "have fallen asleep in Christ" or "in him" (1 Cor. 15:18, 20). In Christ we sleep, and in Christ we will rise (1 Thess. 4:14–15). So how might connecting sleep with death actually prove helpful to us? I grew up knowing the children's prayer put on endless plaques and framed art work: "Now I lay me down to sleep, I pray the Lord my soul to keep. If I should die before I wake, I pray the Lord my soul to take." It sounds grim, but it originated in a time of high infant mortality rates and confirmed human vulnerability, dependence, and need.

Because going to sleep is both a time of ending one day and beginning a renewal for the next, the time just before sleep is a good moment for the practice called a "daily examination," or sometimes just called "examen." Various groups within the church, from monasteries to the Puritans, have followed similar practices, so I would like to outline a very simple practice that can be used to prepare for sleep each night. Those who want a fuller model could look to the classic Ignatian Exercises,[25] but this is a short and memorable version easily practiced by any believer. I encourage you to briefly do three things each night: *review*, *remember*, and *rest*.

- First, *review*: Take a moment to review your day, noting gifts, expressing gratitude, asking for forgiveness, strength, and wisdom in due measure.
- Second, *remember*: God is compassionate, he loves his children, he is near and working. Remember that he will never leave or forsake you or his church. Remember his promises and that the gospel is genuinely good news.
- Third, *rest*: It is finished. The day is done, so lay it at the feet of God. You don't need to do anything else today. But more importantly, your sins are covered, so rest in that assurance. Do not let them taunt you or linger in your head and heart: Jesus declared, "It is finished." Be confident that his mercies will be new yet again tomorrow morning when you rise, no matter what uncertainties you face and what weaknesses you feel.

Review, remember, and rest. This takes us from the daily pattern of sleep to the weekly promise of Sabbath rest.

Sabbath as Subversive Spirituality

Some people have the impression that Christianity is mostly about a list of "to-dos." But one of the most attractive things about our faith has always been its revelation that there are things you *don't* have to do. For example, in the ancient Roman world, Christianity was appealing to many because it said, "You *don't* have to have sex with just anyone."[26] In that pagan society where women and young children were often reduced to sexual objects for men in power, the Christian faith radically declared, "No." God was on their side in their refusals. Believers were not even required to get married. Sex was a gift for a covenantal and safe relationship in which its goodness could be enjoyed and fostered. But when this good gift was perverted and distorted, Christians could and should be free to say no. We see this distorting pattern again and again, that good gifts become tyrannical when demanded. Similarly, the Christian faith says you don't have to worship Caesar, nor can the state require your unquestioning allegiance—only Jesus is your Lord. In its view of the world around us, from the food we eat to the clothes we wear, Christianity was stunningly liberating in terms of what you were *not* required to do.

One of the most countercultural and radical ideas in the Bible, when compared to the ancient world, is the Sabbath. One day a week you do not have to work. The Jews were thought lazy because of it.[27] While those in power could rest when they wanted, slaves and peasants were often unprotected from demands for endless labor, a terrible burden still on the poor of our day who have multiple jobs to make ends meet or are trapped in other modern forms of slavery.

If there were anyone who could legitimately ask for unceasing industry, it would be the Creator of heaven and earth. Yet from the beginning Yahweh said he and his people would reject that notion. From its foundation in the opening creation narrative (Gen. 2:1–3) to its inclusion as one of the Ten Commandments (Exod. 20:8–11), the call to rest from one's regular labor was a defining characteristic of the Creator God and his worshipers. Strong and weak, rich and poor, male and female, all were to be free at least one day in seven, free for unhindered worship, refreshment, and renewal. Amid the endless demands of life and labor, one day a week was treated as different, reminding Israel that God, not creatures, upholds the world and calls it good. We were designed not only to work but also to rest, just as God rested after six days of creative work. Yahweh looked back at his creation in delight and satisfaction, declaring the seventh day as holy, different, set apart.[28]

The Sabbath was not instituted to make you feel guilty but to make you feel known and loved. It was meant to reorient your view and experience of God and his world. As Jesus later explained, "The sabbath was made for man, not man for the sabbath" (Mark 2:27). Contradicting our temptation to imagine that God's love for us depends on our productivity, one day a week he says, "Stop; look up; look around; lift your heart; delight and rest." Without this rhythm we easily stick to our labor and make it our lord; we start to worship the creation rather than the Creator. This is why you and I must rest, not because God needs us, but because we need him. When we ignore our need to rest, we ignore our limits, and we end up ignoring God.

Christian conceptions of the Sabbath are not exactly the same as those of the ancient Jews, although they are deeply related. First, not all Christians have even agreed on whether the Sabbath has ongoing significance for them. Second, does it matter which day churches gather and encourage rest? Moving from Sabbath to Lord's Day, followers of Jesus started to celebrate their corporate gatherings for worship on Sunday rather than Saturday. As Justo L. González has demonstrated, a wide variety of attitudes and practices for the Lord's Day have shown up in the history of the church.[29] Even in those communities, like the Reformed tradition, that have tended to affirm the ongoing importance of the Sabbath, there has been much debate: Is this simply a principle about setting apart one day in seven, or is honoring a specific day of the week important? For these and other reasons, Sabbath observance has been a debated topic from the days of Jesus to the sixteenth and seventeenth centuries and, in some communities, even in our day. This chapter is less interested in these debates and more interested in the promises of rest that were originally linked with the Sabbath.

For many who have grown up in legalistic settings where adherence to the Sabbath was demanded in a crushing and solemn way, there is no joy or delight in this day. But when I encounter Christians in our modern world who have never really been introduced to the biblical promise of a day of rest, this sounds to them like one of the most radical and liberating ideas they have ever heard. They just cannot believe it could be possible. "You don't have to work for a whole day?"

The idea of not doing homework can sound crazy to high school and college students. Not studying on Sunday might even make them feel morally guilty: when asked, many will admit that they suspect that God is disappointed with them—or at least their parents are!—for not cramming on Sunday. But what if the moral shortcoming isn't that they take a day off from their regular work but that they imagine they can and should work constantly? What if we believed that what was offensive to God was not that we stopped working before dinner, or didn't do our regular work on Sunday, but that we imagine we can and should *always* be working. Or maybe God is less offended and just raises an eyebrow at our naivete.

How luxurious does this sound? You get a full night of sleep; next you take time to gather with God's people to sing, pray, and receive the Word and sacrament; and then you eat a slow lunch with others, go for a walk, take a guilt-free nap, and spend time with family or friends, reading or resting or whatever. You get a whole day of rest and worship. What if I told you this is not a luxury, but a fundamental aspect of how God made you? I worry that ignoring our need for such a pattern of rest means that we are functionally pretending to be the Creator and the Sustainer. And this sets me—and *you*—up for not just endless exhaustion but also increased feelings of condemnation and despair.

Christ Is Our Rest

Thought leaders and self-help gurus in our day call for people to slow down from the frantic pace of modern life. You don't need to be a Christian to see the problem. Some call for shorter work weeks or fewer hours devoted to paid labor each day. Some encourage yoga, mindfulness techniques, and exercise regimes. Yet, as helpful as any of those things may be, I think they will all ultimately leave you wanting, longing, and unsettled.

> The Stoics say, "Retire within yourselves; it is there you will find your rest." And that is not true.
>
> Others say, "Go out of yourselves; seek happiness in amusement." And this is not true. Illness comes.
>
> Happiness is neither without us nor within us. It is in God, both without us and within us.
>
> Blaise Pascal, *Pensées*, no. 465

This is because true human rest is not a form of self-isolation, but is necessarily tied to God's rest. We were created in his image and likeness. This includes our call to the dignity of labor, participating in the motions and movement of creation; but it also means we were made to rest, to connect, to worship and sleep. According to Genesis, the foundation of our call to rest is that *God* himself rested (Gen. 2:3). Because God looks at his good creation and rests in his finished work, humanity can rest as well. Our rest is directly linked to his rest, and therefore it is also linked to fellowship with him.

We now find it difficult to rest. The goodness of creation and the rhythm of productivity and peace are clouded over by our estrangement from God.

We are confronted not only by limits but by our sins, the ways we have hurt others, disappointed ourselves, and ignored our Creator. This situation creates in us an endless striving. We want approval and we want security, but they easily elude us.

The author of Hebrews encourages us, therefore, not to harden our hearts, but to turn again in trust to God. To enter into God's rest is to abide in Christ, to be found in him. The Gospels show us that the Creator is also the Redeemer. Jesus, the incarnate Son of God, has done the work of new—and thus renewed—creation. Therefore, after his life and death, the Messiah also rose from the grave and ascended into the heavens. And in his rising we encounter not only the beginning of a new creation but also a fresh invitation to rest. The work of redemption is now completed in Christ, so that "it is finished." There is nothing else to be done: your sins are taken away. Our rest is not located and secured simply in creation, but in redemption and the promises yet to be fulfilled. We enter into God's rest, the same God who entered into our world and did what we could not do, so that now we might enter again into the very rest of God (Heb. 4:9–11). As John Murray concludes, "The Sabbath is not only a memorial of creation completed and redemption accomplished; it is also the promise of a glorious prospect, the foretaste of the Sabbath rest that remains for the people of God."[30]

• ● •

Beloved, you and I are secure in the love of the Father, the grace of the Son, and the fellowship of the Spirit. May this security allow us to celebrate our limits as part of God's good work. May this security drive us back to our God, to one another, and even to our right dependence on the rest of creation. May this security encourage our work, liberate our rest, and free us to love and serve others. God made us to be limited creatures, able to freely participate in his work, confident in his presence, and grateful for his promises and provision. Let us appreciate the goodness of our finitude as we rest in the love and provision of our infinitely good God. May it be so.

acknowledgments

IT IS NO EXAGGERATION to say that I have been thinking about this book in some way for over twenty years. Going back to my time working under my *Doktorvater* Colin Gunton, he helped open up for me the significance of the doctrine of creation in ways I had not considered before. At the same time, my research into John Owen's (1616–83) anthropology led me to become deeply interested in how a healthier view of creation and humanity could be transformative for our lives. Although it always lingered in my mind, and occasionally revealed itself in public lectures I would give, other writing projects always seemed to require more attention. Then, after facing my wife's cancer and subsequent chronic pain, with her encouragement I wrote *Embodied Hope: A Theological Meditation on Pain and Suffering* (InterVarsity, 2017). Researching that book was a tremendous help to me and my family, and so we prayed the fruit of that labor might be useful to others. But it also prepared us for this book.

I became convinced that it was time for me to more fully explore the *good* of being a human creature. Suffering and pain always need our attention and compassion in this broken world, and lament and hope are required in the midst of it. But I also had a growing sense of clarity that part of the contemporary Christian challenge is related to our discomfort with simply being human. Not many of us claim to be God, but our unrealistic expectations for our work, our children, our bodies, our churches—for just about every aspect of our lives—show that we actually do imagine that we are God. We act as if we should never grow tired or weary, that we could and should always do more and be more. Not only do secular self-help books sell time-management as the main answer, but I also found that Christians often naively agree with this model, only in a "Christianized" form. "Baptizing" such notions sometimes makes them more potent and potentially more dangerous. In our culture, it's easy to tell yourself that God always wants you to change the world. The Bible says you should die to yourself, so how can you ever say no when you see a need? "Don't waste your life, but use every second to its maximum potential." Such thoughts, especially when delivered with passion and biblical citations, are powerful and moving. The problem is that the eventual pressure and consequences can be devastating. Without exaggeration, I have seen marriages fall apart, ministries destroyed, children neglected, bodies broken, and souls withered because of this attitude. And I suspect you have seen this too.

Speaking of salvation without connecting it to the doctrine of creation cripples our ability to make sense of our human limits. I have found that Christians often think of the limitations that God has given them as sinful rather than a part of the good of God's creation. What makes me so passionate about this topic is the fact that I wrestle with this myself: I sometimes feel guilty about how much I cannot do, all the places I cannot be, all the weaknesses and limits that I have. I am always tempted to respond by trying harder, by doing more, by pushing myself to show up to everything. This is where our family journey of suffering has brought unexpected help to me. As a family and as individuals, Tabitha and I had to significantly cut back. We said and continue to say no to so much. At first we cut a few things out, but it became clear that more and more needed to be trimmed from our lives. Tabitha often says that the biggest casualty of chronic pain has been our limitation of opening our home in hospitality as we had been accustomed to. We could help at church, we could be good employees, we could try to be faithful friends, but we would need to slow way down and be more discerning. It has taken me years not to feel guilty about having so many evenings in a week when my only obligation is to make dinner or clean up, but not also rush out the door. And to be honest, as I hear about all that others are doing, I still often am tempted to feel guilty, guilty about my very human limitations.

But then Tabitha reminds me that it is enough because it is all we can do. Put another way, it is all we can do, so it is enough. I like the saying that circulates: "You are enough." However, as a theologian, I would prefer to put it much less poetically: "You are *not* enough, and that is exactly why you *are* enough!" In other words, only when we realize that the world does not depend only on us, but on God and on others, and that we only play a small (but significant!) role—only then can we be truly liberated to see that "I am enough." Why? Because I am God's child, and I am connected to his church and world. I have much to offer, but I don't have everything. And God doesn't expect me to, either.

This brings me to my favorite part of writing books: thanking people. And if you get mad about how long this acknowledgments section is, please read chapter 6 again, and then you will see that I feel not only obligated but joyful for the chance to name others. The only problem is that I can't say something about each of them, and I inevitably leave people out who have been so incredibly helpful along the way. While I cannot name everyone properly, what follows is a taste of many who spoke into this part of my journey and this book, shaping it and giving it life.

To begin, I would like to thank students, faculty, staff, and alumni at Covenant College, which is the birthplace for much of this material and has continued to offer insightful feedback and much needed encouragement; recognizing our "finitude" now feels like part of our campus culture, and I am so thankful for that! I also benefited from interaction and feedback from people at other institutions, but especially those at Moore Theological College in Australia, Christ College in Sydney, Colorado Christian University, Beeson Divinity School, and many churches who heard early ruminations of this material. A vibrant and faithful group of Kingdom Class Sunday School participants from Lookout Mountain Presbyterian Church in Lookout Mountain, Tennessee, took months and months to listen to my ideas and help me understand how they might relate to their different vocations and the church—Sunday mornings with you all has been rich beyond measure.

There were many who not only heard samples of this work but also were willing to read drafts and give constructive feedback. Thanks to Dan Treier, Michael Allen, Marie Bowen Fennema, Joe Novenson, and Ty Kieser for reading through the manuscript before submission: that was a massive gift to me. Henri Lowe not only carefully read the entire manuscript; she also tirelessly helped me hunt down sources like a champion. Others who read significant portions and offered helpful early feedback include Kathy Ward, Ed Gerber, Kathryn Andrews, David Kraus, and so many others (many whose names appear elsewhere on these pages). When Hebrews speaks of "entertaining angels unaware," that is how I think of John Yates coming into my life years ago (a story too long for here): John, yet again you carefully read every word and chapter, offering wonderful—even if sometimes painful—editorial critique on the various drafts. You somehow improve my manuscripts and also lift my spirits. I owe a great debt to you.

This book would not be in your hands if I had not received several grants that generously helped fund the research that made the book possible. While the opinions expressed in this publication are mine, and do not necessarily reflect the views of the John Templeton Foundation or any other foundation, this book was partly made possible through a generous grant from the John Templeton Foundation. I have the privilege of being part of a core research team of psychologists, theologians, and philosophers who are exploring "Christian meaning-making in suffering and its relationship to flourishing":[1] Elizabeth Hall, Crystal Park, Jason McMartin, Jamie Aten, Laura Rosemary Shannonhouse, Eric Silverman, and Robert C. Roberts, you all have taught me so much, and it has been one of my professional joys to be working alongside you through these years.

Jim Seneff, through the ups and downs of life, through the debates and conversations, through the tears and deep laughter, you have been one of my most consistent encouragers, believing in me and my work since I was in my early 20s: I am deeply thankful for you. Robert A. Emmons, I have so benefited from your excellent questions and deep passion for research and its applications to real life. Bob Hosack, you have been more of a friend and not just an editor: thank you for not only believing in this book from early on, but also for being very patient with me about it, so that I could do it when the time was finally right. And I am grateful to the whole Brazos team.

Working in the various contexts of Covenant College, churches, and friendships near and far, there are more people than I can possibly thank in detail. But here are the names of people who all have offered their wisdom, prayers, stories, encouragement, and laughter, each in a particular way during the writing of this book. Besides the Templeton team, I am grateful to Mike Rulon and Carole Yue at Covenant for helping me navigate the field of psychology; I'm grateful for Matt Vos and his trusted advice in all things sociology; and while my whole department of Biblical and Theological Studies has been hugely helpful, Scott Jones, Herb Ward, Jeff Dryden, and Hans Madueme have, in particular, brought needed insights and timely encouragement. Others who offered prayers, needed wisdom, a listening ear, and valuable feedback include Stephanie Formenti, Cameron

Clausing, Jerilyn Sanders, Scott Swain, Tanya and Mike Hsu, Elissa and Noel Weichbrodt, Liz and Todd Crusey, Sarah and Mark Huffines, Eddie Jacks, Chuck DeGroat, Matthew Trexler, K.J. and Ryan Ramsey, John Rush, Keith Plumber, Ron Thomas, Steffan Nunn, Olivia and Nate Oster, Katya Covrett, Beth and Paul Nedelisky, Kevin Smith, Alicia Zanoni, Lynn and Jeff Hall, Beth and Joseph Wingfield; Christiana Fitzpatrick, Sarah and Wes Robbins, Nola and Brian Hecker, Stephanie and Everett Pierce, Wendy and Derek Halvorson, Beth and Chris Bailey, Jodi and Eric Blick, Mary Vassar and Frank Hitchings, Aimee Byrd, Wim Codington, Jen Allen, Bill Davis, Grant Lowe, Esther Pruitt, Mark Perry (thanks for writing the music!), Riley Shannon, Caroline Davis, Nesha Evans, Makayla Payne, Michal and Bob Parsley, Aaron Tolson, Brian Salter, Chad Middleton, Justin Borger, Claire Slavovsky, Hannah Bloomquist, Brian Fikkert and the whole team at the Chalmer's Center, Kathryn Dodd Shumate, Jenny and Charlie Whitener, Liz Edrington, John Holberg, Jonathan Parker, Jennifer West, Jenny-Lyn de Klerk, Donald Guthrie, Adam Neder, Miroslav Volf, Ruth Haley Barton, Todd Billings, and so many more I would like to thank by name.

Jay Green and Jeff Morton, deep friendship is a true gift from God, and I continue to feel deep gratitude for being able to navigate life with you two close at hand. Extended family has continued to offer constant support even when times have been difficult. We can never say "I love you" enough: Gary and Linda, Danny and Emily, John and Lynne, Ming and Jennifer, and David and Jennifer.

Tabitha, your courage, humor, sharpness of mind, and deep love have been such gifts in this adventure of life together, and I don't know what I would do without you. Margot, it is amazing to watch you grow from a little girl to a young woman: you are an amazing mixture of strength, brilliance, and energy, and it is a joy to see you become the person God is calling you to be.

Finally, it brings such a big smile to my face and heart to dedicate this book to Jonathan, my son. I'll never forget welcoming you, my firstborn, into the world and just losing it with tears of joy. From that day to this I continue to stand before God grateful beyond words for you. God has given you a great mind, strong empathy, incredible relational skills, and a heart for the vulnerable. Even with the various challenges you have faced, including the painful process of going through school while dealing with serious dyslexia and dysgraphia, you keep fighting not to lose heart, but instead to love others and to grow (and giving me permission to speak about them is an extension of that). I so often want to protect my children from the challenges of life, and quickly remember that I cannot. Jonathan, you have helped me see with even greater clarity what is true about *all of us*: we each face serious challenges and are wonderfully dependent, limited, and blessedly vulnerable. None of us escapes finitude. You have also taught me a great deal, sometimes helping me to chill out, or find our way home when lost in Edinburgh, or notice what I might otherwise miss. Throughout this project in particular, you made me a better listener, especially to voices I wouldn't naturally hear. This includes listening to music where the theme of finitude is powerfully wrestled with and engaged. For example, because of you I have often had on repeat such songs as "It's Alright" by Mother Mother and "Human" by John Bellion, plus many others. Jonathan, trying to find words to express my love for you feels like an impossibility, because I know there is no way that they can do justice to how much I love you. But know this, you are my beloved son, and I thank God for you. Jonathan, you are enough. We all are enough. Praise God.

notes

Chapter 1 Have I Done Enough?

1. Martin Luther King Jr., "Shattered Dreams," in *Strength to Love* (Boston: Beacon, 1981), 94.

2. While it may surprise some, classic Reformed scholastic theology affirmed that human creatures were made "material, dissoluble, mortal," and yet, "by this it is only acknowledged . . . that man's body could die, not that it had to die." Johannes Heidegger, *Corpus Theologiae* (1696), 6:92, quoted in Heinrich Heppe, *Reformed Dogmatics* (Grand Rapids: Baker, 1978), 231.

3. Thomas Merton, *Conjectures of a Guilty Bystander* (New York: Image Books/Doubleday, 1965), 81.

4. See Kelly M. Kapic, "Anthropology," in *Christian Dogmatics: Reformed Theology for the Church Catholic*, ed. Michael Allen and Scott R. Swain (Grand Rapids: Baker Academic, 2016), 165–93. For further discussion on this, see, e.g., Brian Brock and John Swinton, *Disability in the Christian Tradition: A Reader* (Grand Rapids: Eerdmans, 2012); Hans S. Reinders, ed., *The Paradox of Disability: Responses to Jean Vanier and L'Arche Communities from Theology and the Sciences* (Grand Rapids: Eerdmans, 2010).

5. Kelly M. Kapic, *A Little Book for New Theologians* (Downers Grove, IL: InterVarsity, 2012).

6. For more on my approach to the problem of suffering and pain and how they relate to the tragedy of sin, see *Embodied Hope: A Theological Meditation on Pain and Suffering* (Downers Grove, IL: InterVarsity, 2016).

7. Gerhard von Rad, *Old Testament Theology*, vol. 1, *The Theology of Israel's Historical Traditions*, trans. D. M. G. Stalker (New York: Harper & Row, 1962), 155.

8. I have expanded on this theme more fully in *The God Who Gives: How the Trinity Shapes the Christian Story* (Grand Rapids: Zondervan, 2018), esp. chaps. 1–2.

9. Von Rad, *Theology of Israel's Historical Traditions*, 160.

Chapter 2 Does God Love . . . Me?

1. For those interested, a book with this title came out recently, but this chapter was already written before that book was published or came to my attention. Having said that, I am delighted to point people to a volume with similar concerns. See Cyd Holsclaw and

Geoff Holsclaw, *Does God Really Like Me? Discovering the God Who Wants to Be with Us* (Downers Grove, IL: InterVarsity, 2020).

2. Alicia Zanoni, author and illustrator, "I Like You, Samantha Sarah Marie," unpublished manuscript. Used with permission. For more on Zanoni and her artwork visit http://www.aliciazanoni.com/.

3. Zanoni, "I Like You."

4. Even post-Christian culture, in the West in general and in America in particular, has retained the idea that God is love. But if one were to ask how people know this to be true apart from Christianity, the answers are less than obvious. There are plenty of cultures and religions that certainly don't think of the Divine as "love" and "loving." Often what we find here is more a borrowing of Christian ideas without their theological foundations or context. In truth, this makes such concepts fairly hollow and unstable: unless people are confronted by the God who is love, the concepts simply cannot and will not last.

5. E.g., Benedict Carey, "Getting a Handle on Self-Harm," Health, *New York Times*, November 11, 2019; Ana Homayoun, "What's Worrying Teenagers Right Now," *New York Times*, June 11, 2020; Madeleine George, PhD, "The Importance of Social Media Content for Teens' Risks for Self-Harm," *Journal of Adolescent Health* 65, no. 1 (July 2019): 9–10.

6. Shauna Niequist, *Present over Perfect: Leaving Behind Frantic for a Simpler, More Soulful Way of Living* (Grand Rapids: Zondervan, 2016).

7. Rightly understood, these three things (mental, physical, and relational) are not easily disentangled.

8. Friedrich Nietzsche made a similar critique for very different reasons. For Nietzsche's discussion of the herd mentality and morality that he believed characterized his modern society, see, e.g., "The Natural History of Morals," chap. 5 in *Beyond Good and Evil*, trans. Helen Zimmern (Leipzig, 1886), esp. sections 191, 199, 201, and 202, https://www.gutenberg.org/ebooks/4363.

9. We will return to this in a later chapter on our struggle to be comfortable with our bodies.

10. E.g., see Benoit Denizet-Lewis, "Why Are More American Teenagers Than Ever Suffering from Severe Anxiety?," *New York Times*, October 11, 2017; "How 'Likes' Affect Teenagers' Brains," Science and Technology, *Economist*, June 13, 2016; Tara Parker-Pope, "Teenagers, Friends and Bad Decisions," Well, *New York Times*, February 3, 2011; Jan Hoffman, "Teaching Teenagers to Cope with Social Stress," Health, *New York Times*, September 29, 2016.

11. E.g., see Perri Klass, MD, "When Social Media Is Really Problematic for Adolescents," Family, *New York Times*, June 3, 2019; "Cutting Adolescents' Use of Social Media Will Not Solve Their Problems," Leaders, *Economist*, January 11, 2018; Ana Homayoun, "The Secret Social Media Lives of Teenagers," Family, *New York Times*, June 7, 2017; "What Students Are Saying about How Much They Use Their Phones, and Whether We Should Be Worried," Learning Network, *New York Times*, February 6, 2020; "How Children Interact with Digital Media," Special Report, *Economist*, January 3, 2019.

12. Here one might think of Jesus's response to the onlooker who called him good: "Why do you call me good? No one is good except God alone" (Mark 10:18; Luke 18:19). Though sometimes the inference is suggested, clearly Jesus is not claiming to be a sinner himself: see B. B. Warfield, "Jesus' Alleged Confession of Sin," *Princeton Theological Review* 12 (1914): 177–228. It is a violation of the passage to remove this remark "none is good" from its setting. Furthermore, there is good reason to believe that, when Jesus responds to the rich young man by demanding the weight and seriousness of the question of eternal life that was asked of him, the young man has been employing flattery (Larry W. Hurtado, *Mark*, NIBC (Peabody, MA: Hendrickson, 1989), 164. Fallen humanity is not "righteous," since "none is righteous,

no, not one" (Rom. 3:10). The fundamental point seems to be that humans are sinful and need redemption, for nothing in them alone can right the wrongs of their rebellion against God. But to claim this means humans are void of any positives is problematic. Is Jesus or Paul really arguing here that humans are *utterly* sinful, to the extent that everything about them is *only* evil (*utter* depravity)? If so, that is far different than historic claims of "total depravity," which refer to how sin affects humans in their totality, with no aspect of the human person (mind, will, affections, body, relationships) free from the tentacles of sin. That doctrine was not meant to assert that humans are entirely and completely evil. Brains and bodies, affections and aptitudes, are gifts from God that have all now (sadly!) been infected by the corrosive powers of sin. While that doesn't mean brains and bodies are inherently bad, it does mean there is disharmony and even rebellion where there used to be shalom. It is just this kind of misunderstanding that Augustine and others tried to resist when they framed sin as "privation," since sin was always dependent on some underlying original good. Our original righteousness—our original right relations with God and neighbor—has been compromised, and we now live with the devastating effects. But that is no reason to claim that Tom or Tina has no "good" in them. Scripture and human experience remind us that sinners are capable of, and do implement, positive actions, but that such glimmers of original desire and purpose do not make one right with the holy and loving Lord; only union with Christ by the Spirit accomplishes that.

13. We will talk more about the challenges of being "seen" in a later chapter that touches on diversity.

14. We will return more fully to this idea of God's ability or inability to be in the presence of sin when we talk about the work of the Holy Spirit in a later chapter.

15. John Owen, *Communion with the Triune* God, ed. Kelly M. Kapic and Justin Taylor (Wheaton: Crossway, 2007), esp. 105–32.

16. Morna D. Hooker, "Interchange and Atonement," *Bulletin of the John Rylands University Library Manchester* 60, no. 2 (Spring 1978): 480.

17. Westminster Confession of Faith (1646), chap. 15 ("Of Repentance unto Life"), sec. 1.

18. Constantine R. Campbell, *Paul and Union with Christ: An Exegetical and Theological Study* (Grand Rapids: Zondervan, 2012), 414.

19. E.g., the temple imagery, the vine/branches, and unity texts in John 1–4, 15, 17; the brotherhood of Jesus in Heb. 2:11; 1 Pet. 1:1–12; 2 Pet. 1:3–4; 1 John 4:7–16; the bridal imagery of Rev. 19–22.

20. Grant Macaskill, *Union with Christ in the New Testament* (Oxford: Oxford University Press, 2013), 298.

21. The "Servant Songs," as they are now commonly known, are Isa. 42:1–4; 49:1–6; 50:4–7; 52:13–53:12.

22. Macaskill, *Union with Christ*, 299.

23. We receive all of the blessings out of our union with Christ, according to Paul. This includes the idea of being chosen, redeemed, reconciled, and sealed (Eph. 1:3–13).

24. John Calvin, *Institutes of the Christian Religion*, ed. John T. McNeill, trans. Ford Lewis Battles (Philadelphia: Westminster, 1960), 3.1.1 (p. 537).

25. Macaskill, *Union with Christ*, 221.

26. Susan Eastman, "Double Participation and the Responsible Self in Romans 5–8," in *Apocalyptic Paul: Cosmos and Anthropos in Romans 5–8*, ed. Beverly Gaventa (Waco: Baylor University Press, 2013), 98.

27. Charles Spurgeon, "Christus et Ego," sermon no. 781 in *Spurgeon's Sermons*, ed. Anthony Uyl, 13:1867 (delivered on Lord's-day Morning, November 17, 1867, at the Metropolitan Tabernacle, Newington), https://www.ccel.org/ccel/spurgeon/sermons13.liv.html.

28. Spurgeon, "Christus et Ego."

29. Martin Luther, *Commentary on the Epistle to the Galatians* (1535), trans. Theodore Graebner (Grand Rapids: Zondervan, 1949), 78. I like this translation/paraphrase of this part, but for accuracy—though definitely more awkward sounding—cf. Martin Luther, *Lectures on Galatians*, in *The Works of Martin Luther*, ed. J. Pelikan, H. Oswald, and H. T. Lehmann (Saint Louis: Concordia, 1999), 26:167.

30. Luther, *Lectures on Galatians*, 167. This newer translation reads well here.

31. For similar concerns raised, see, e.g., Adam S. McHugh, *Introverts in the Church: Finding Our Place in an Extroverted Culture* (Downers Grove, IL: InterVarsity, 2009); see also Susan Cain, *Quiet: The Power of Introverts in a World That Can't Stop Talking* (New York: Broadway Books, 2013).

32. John Owen, *Doctrine of the Saint's Perseverance*, in *The Works of John Owen*, ed. William H. Goold, 24 vols. (Edinburgh: Johnson & Hunter; 1850–55; repr., London: Banner of Truth, 1965), 11:336.

33. Owen, *Doctrine of the Saint's Perseverance*, 336.

34. Owen, *Doctrine of the Saint's Perseverance*, 337.

35. Macaskill, *Union with Christ*, 300–301.

36. Heidelberg Catechism, Q&A 75 (emphasis added). See also Q&A 52, 60.

37. Heidelberg Catechism, Q&A 21.

Chapter 3 Are the Limits of My Body Bad?

1. There is a great amount of literature (and debate) about the role, accuracy, and extent of oral culture in the ancient world in general, and Israel in particular. See, e.g., David M. Carr, *Writing on the Tablet of the Heart: Origins of Scripture and Literature* (Oxford: Oxford University Press, 2005), esp. chaps. 10–12; M. S. Jaffee, *Torah in the Mouth: Writing and Oral Tradition in Palestinian Judaism, 200 BCE–400 CE* (Oxford: Oxford University Press, 2001); Robert D. Miller II, "Orality and Performance in Ancient Israel," *Revue des sciences religieuses* 86, no. 2 (2012): 183–94. For more focus on Christian oral transmission, see, e.g., Richard Bauckham, *Jesus and the Eyewitnesses: The Gospels as Eyewitness Testimony*, 2nd ed. (Grand Rapids: Eerdmans, 2017).

2. It must be admitted that most of the material we have about Marcion and his followers' opinions comes from their opponents, and so there are likely historical misrepresentations. But for a classic and full treatment in primary source material, see esp. Tertullian, *The Five Books against Marcion*. (This work can be found in *The Ante-Nicene Fathers* [*ANF*] series, vol. 3, pp. 269–474. This series can be found in the Christian Classics Ethereal Library at https://ccel.org/ccel/schaff/anf-series/anf-series. Hereafter, references to *ANF* will be styled *ANF* 3:269–474 and will appear in parentheses following the primary citation.) For recent scholarship trying to offer a more generous view of Marcion and warn against potential misrepresentations of him, see Judith M. Lieu, *Marcion and the Making of a Heretic: God and Scripture in the Second Century* (Cambridge: Cambridge University Press, 2015); see also R. Joseph Hoffman, *Marcion: On the Restitution of Christianity; An Essay on the Development of Radical Paulinist Theology in the Second Century*, American Academy of Religion Academy Series (Chico, CA: Scholars Press, 1984). For warnings about overestimating Marcion's impact, see E. C. Blackman, *Marcion and His Influence* (Eugene, OR: Wipf & Stock, 2004).

3. Origen, for example, observes how Marcion and Gnostics contrast the New Testament "compassionate" God with the judgmental "God of this world," who created materiality and is therefore associated with evil. The God of the law and prophets becomes strongly juxtaposed with the God of Jesus the Messiah: The Creator is evil, while the Redeemer is good. See Origen, *De principiis* 2.5.1–2 (*ANF* 4:278).

4. It is assumed that Marcion would similarly have to deny the physicality of Jesus's death, but the evidence we have focuses on his problems with Jesus's birth; therefore, this

event begins to represent his concern with the Christ's apparent connection to the material, physical world.

5. Similarly, Jesus "appeared in a phantasm of a body, and it is the soul only which he will save, the flesh being incapable of salvation" (Ernest Evans, introduction to *Tertullian's Treatise on the Incarnation*, ed. and trans. Ernest Evans [London: SPCK, 1956], xxvii).

6. The Gnostic and Marcionite reduction of Jesus's humanity to "appearance and not reality" was commonly condemned by early church leaders—e.g., Novatian, *The Trinity* 10 (*ANF* 5:619–20). Debate existed as to whether signs of early docetism can be traced all the way back into the Christian canon (e.g., John). There is good reason to resist this conclusion, though there was reasonable ground for later developments of this phenomenon. For a sampling of further background discussions on these questions, see also Reimund Bieringer, Ines Jager, Jens Schroter, and Joseph Verheyden, eds., *Docetism in the Early Church*, in Wissenschaftliche Untersuchungen zum Neuen Testament (Tübingen: Mohr Siebeck, 2018).

7. I will focus on the virgin birth below, but for more on the resurrection, see, e.g., Tertullian, *On the Resurrection of the Flesh* (*ANF* 3:545–94).

8. Irenaeus of Lyons, *Against Heresies: Book 3*, trans. and ann. Dominic J. Unger, Ancient Christian Writers 64 (New York: Newman Press, 2012), 3.11.3 (p. 53).

9. Irenaeus, *Against Heresies* 3.11.2–3 (Unger, p. 53).

10. Irenaeus, *Against Heresies* 3.11.3 (Unger, p. 53).

11. See, e.g., Irenaeus, *Against Heresies* 1.272–74; 2.30.9; 3.11.12. For helpful background, see John Behr, *Irenaeus of Lyons: Identifying Christianity*, Christian Theology in Context (Oxford: Oxford University Press, 2013); see also Sara Parvis and Paul Foster, eds., *Irenaeus: Life, Scripture, and Legacy* (Minneapolis: Fortress, 2012).

12. Tertullian, *On the Flesh of Christ*, chap. 1 (*ANF* 3:521) (emphasis added).

13. E.g., Nigel M. de S. Cameron, *Complete in Christ: Rediscovering Jesus and Ourselves* (London: Paternoster, 1997), esp. chap. 1.

14. Donna-Marie Cooper, "Was Tertullian a Misogynist? A Re-Examination of This Charge Based on a Rhetorical Analysis of Tertullian's Work" (PhD thesis, University of Exeter, 2012).

15. Tertullian, *On the Flesh of Christ*, in *The Christological Controversy*, Sources of Early Christian Thought, ed. and trans. Richard A. Norris Jr. (Philadelphia: Fortress, 1980), 67.

16. For a classic defense of the historical and theological significance of the virgin birth, see J. Gresham Machen, *The Virgin Birth of Christ* (London: James Clarke, 1958), and New Testament scholar Brandon D. Crowe's accessible booklet *Was Jesus Really Born of a Virgin?* (Phillipsburg, NJ: P&R, 2013).

17. This is part of what is so remarkable—and noteworthy—about young Jesus's time in the temple. He remained behind, and his mother eventually found him not with the traveling party, but back at the temple with the rabbis. Immediately after this episode, we are told that he obeyed his parents—in other words, the episode pictures him as a consistently faithful child. This scene was surprising because it was far out of the ordinary pattern of his childhood; thus, it is worth retelling. What do we discover? Not a denial of Jesus's humanity, but an indication that his "origin" or reality is not merely traceable to Mary and Joseph, for Jesus speaks of the temple as his Father's house (Luke 2:49).

18. For more on this difference and debate, see Willem Balke, *Calvin and the Anabaptist Radicals*, trans. William J. Heynen (Grand Rapids: Eerdmans, 1981), 206. See also Calvin, *Institutes*, 2.14.1 (pp. 482–83).

19. For more on the Radical Reformation approach to the "heavenly flesh" doctrine and some historical attempts to defend it against Arianism (e.g., Schwenckfeld), see Stephen H. Webb, *Jesus Christ, Eternal God: Heavenly Flesh and the Metaphysics of Matter* (Oxford: Oxford University Press, 2012), esp. chap. 6.

20. See, e.g., Jaroslav Pelikan, *Mary through the Centuries* (New Haven: Yale University Press, 1996), esp. 39–54.

21. Tertullian uses vivid language: "That which through that sex [i.e., Eve] had gone astray into perdition should through the same sex [Mary] be led back again into salvation. Eve had believed the serpent: Mary believed Gabriel" (*De Carne Christi* 17 [Evans, *Tertullian's Treatise*, 61; cf. *ANF* 3:536]). See also the earlier similar statements by Justin Martyr, *Dialogue with Trypho the Jew* 100; Irenaeus, *Against Heresies* 3.22.4.

22. Richard Bauckham, *Gospel Women: Studies of the Named Women in the Gospels* (Grand Rapids: Eerdmans, 2002), 66.

23. We are not saying that the incarnation is a matter of fitting the infinite God into a finite human being. Far from it! There is a long theological debate here that I am sidestepping. The argument comes down to this Latin clause: "Finitum non capax infiniti" (The finite is incapable of the infinite). This approach is how many patristic and, later, Reformed theologians protected the full humanity of Jesus. The point was that, for the Savior to be genuinely human, his human nature must be finite. Obviously, this is an extremely technical (although important) debate, but one I cannot get into here. For more, see Richard A. Muller, *Dictionary of Latin and Greek Theological Terms* (Grand Rapids: Baker, 1985), 119, and for more on the *extra calvinisticum*, see 111; Andrew M. McGinnis, *The Son of God beyond the Flesh: A Historical and Theological Study of the Extra Calvinisticum* (London: Bloomsbury T&T Clark, 2016); E. David Willis, *Calvin's Catholic Christology: The Function of the So-Called Extra Calvinisticum in Calvin's Theology* (Leiden: Brill, 1966).

24. Tertullian, *On the Flesh of Christ* 4.2 (Norris, *Christological Controversy*, 68).

25. Tertullian, *On the Flesh of Christ* 9 (*ANF* 9:530).

26. Tertullian, *On the Flesh of Christ* 5.1 (Norris, *Christological Controversy*, 69).

27. And later, "Was not God truly crucified? And being truly crucified, did he not truly die? And having truly died, was he not truly raised?" (Tertullian, *On the Flesh of Christ* 5.2 [Norris, *Christological Controversy*, 69]). How is this all possible? Only because the Son of God truly took our nature (Tertullian, *On the Flesh of Christ* 5.5 [Norris, *Christological Controversy*, 70). Here we encounter the beginning of the Chalcedonian formulation. Notice how Tertullian holds two truths together, though seemingly impossible. He is here pointing to the doctrinal development that argues for the integrity of each nature preserved through the unity of the natures in the one person of Christ.

28. Tertullian, *On the Flesh of Christ* 4 (*ANF* 3:524).

29. Tertullian, *On the Flesh of Christ* 4 (Evans, *Tertullian's Treatise,* 15) .

30. Tertullian, *On the Flesh of Christ* 4.5 (Norris, *Christological Controversy*, 68).

31. Tertullian, *On the Flesh of Christ* 4.3 (Norris, *Christological Controversy*, 68).

32. Tertullian, *On the Flesh of Christ* 4 (Norris, *Christological Controversy*, 68).

33. For more on these allusions, and for demonstrations on how Mark and Luke appear to show similar allusions, though far less overtly, see Sean M. McDonough, *Christ as Creator: Origins of a New Testament Doctrine* (Oxford: Oxford University Press, 2009), esp. 19–22, with 212–22 focused on John's handling of this material.

34. Basil, *Epistle 261*, cited by Peter C. Bouteneff, *Beginnings: Ancient Christian Readings of the Biblical Creation Narratives* (Grand Rapids: Baker Academic, 2008), 132.

Chapter 4 Why Does Physical Touch Matter?

1. Matthew Block, "The Spiritualist Origins of 'You Don't Have a Soul. You Are a Soul,'" *First Things*, January 13, 2014, https://www.firstthings.com/blogs/firstthoughts/2014/01/the-spiritualist-origins-of-you-dont-have-a-soul-you-are-a-soul.

2. The one exception to this is the "unnatural" intermediate state. Cf. Karl Barth, who, deriving his anthropology (view of humans) primarily from Christology (view of Christ),

writes, "Jesus . . . is one whole man, embodied soul and besouled body: the one in the other and never merely beside it" (*Church Dogmatics*, III/2 [Edinburgh: T&T Clark, 1960], 327, in §46, "Man as Soul and Body"). Cautioning his readers against attempts to separate these, he also writes, "Soul can awake and be only as soul of a body. Soul presupposes a body whose soul it is, i.e., a material body which, belonging to the soul, becomes an organic body. . . . Hence every trivialisation of the body, every removal of the body from the soul, and every abstraction between the two immediately jeopardises the soul. Every denial of the body necessarily implies a denial of the soul" (373).

3. Lilian Calles Barger, *Eve's Revenge: Women and a Spirituality of the Body* (Grand Rapids: Brazos Press, 2003).

4. Barger, *Eve's Revenge*, 101.

5. E.g., Michel Onfray, *In Defence of Atheism: The Case against Christianity, Judaism and Islam*, trans. Jeremy Leggatt (London: Serpent's Tail, 2007), 135, writes, "Starting from his own dilapidated physique, Paul militated for a world that resembled him. His hatred of self turned into a vigorous hatred of the world and all its concerns: life, love, desire, pleasure, sensations, body, flesh, joy, freedom, independence, autonomy. There is no mystery about Paul's masochism."

6. Contrary to such charges, for a strong affirmation of the body by conservative authors, see, e.g., Timothy C. Tennent, *For the Body: Recovering a Theology of Gender, Sexuality, and the Human Body* (Grand Rapids: Zondervan, 2020); Nancy Pearcey, *Love Thy Body: Answering Hard Questions about Life and Sexuality* (Grand Rapids: Baker Books, 2018).

7. See infographics provided by USC Dornsife in "Thinking vs Feeling: The Psychology of Advertising," USC Dornsife, https://appliedpsychologydegree.usc.edu/blog/thinking-vs-feeling-the-psychology-of-advertising/; Louise Story, "Anywhere the Eye Can See, It's Likely to See an Ad," *New York Times*, January 15, 2007, https://www.nytimes.com/2007/01/15/business/media/15everywhere.html.

8. Readers are encouraged to watch a series of four short videos, produced by Dove, on "real beauty": (1) "Dove Real Beauty Sketches: You're more beautiful than you think (3mins)," 3:00, YouTube, posted by Dove US, April 14, 2013, https://www.youtube.com/watch?v=XpaOjMXyJGk; (2) "Dove Evolution," 1:14, YouTube, posted by Tim Piper, October 6, 2006, https://www.youtube.com/watch?v=iYhCn0jf46U; (3) "Dove Change One Thing: How our girls see themselves," 1:12, YouTube, posted by Dove US, September 29, 2015, https://www.youtube.com/watch?v=c96SNJihPjQ; (4) "Dove – Onslaught," 1:19, YouTube, posted by bornsquishy, April 3, 2008, https://www.youtube.com/watch?v=9zKfF40jeCA. See also Aerie, which vowed to end their practice of retouching images and photo-shopping models; however, legitimate questions remain. See Shannon Palus, "Photoshop Isn't the Problem," *Slate Magazine*, December 10, 2018, https://slate.com/technology/2018/12/aerie-no-airbrushing-ads-jameela-jamil-authenticity.html.

9. E.g., "Lili Reinhart On Unrealistic Body Standards and 'Trying to Navigate My Fluctuating Weight,'" *Shape*, November 13, 2018; Lauren Alexis Fisher, "'We're So Hungry!' Jameela Jamil Gets Real about the Effects of Photoshop," *Harper's Bazaar*, January 31, 2019; Laura Byager, "Jameela Jamil Goes Viral with Her Comments about 'Why Airbrushing Should Be Illegal,'" Culture, *Mashable*, December 3, 2018, https://mashable.com/article/jameela-jamil-photoshop-viral-tweets/.

10. Payam Ebizadeh, "Fifty Is the New Thirty: See the Reasons Why," *Splash Magazines*, July 18, 2018, https://splashmags.com/index.php/2018/07/12/fifty-is-the-new-thirty-see-the-reason-why/.

11. Some psychologists have observed, e.g., a paradox with regard to shopping: while women often find the ritual of going clothes shopping both pleasurable and necessary, the process also produces for many an "internalized attribution style" that can generate terrible

feelings of insecurity. E.g., "the conceptual process of trying on a swimsuit can have a serious impact on a woman's sense of wellbeing." Objectification of our bodies tends to undermine not only our self-acceptance but also our relationships. See Marion Kostanski, "Beyond the Media: A Look at Other Socialization Processes That Contribute to Body Image Problems and Dysfunctional Eating," in *Body Image: Perceptions, Interpretations and Attitudes*, ed. Sophia B. Greene (New York: Nova Science, 2011), 122.

12. For more on the early history of this shift, see John Pettigrew, *Brutes in Suits: Male Sensibility in America, 1890–1920* (Baltimore: Johns Hopkins University Press, 2007); for more recent and accessible treatment that covers up to the end of the twentieth century, see Lynne Luciano, *Looking Good: Male Body Image in Modern America* (New York: Hill and Wang, 2001).

13. Luciano, *Looking Good*, 179.

14. Luciano, *Looking Good*, 180.

15. Historically, this is nothing really new, but a return to the old, for, while women have faced consistent objectification, men have also faced objectification in varying degrees throughout history. This renewed objectification of the male simply returns us to such periods as ancient Greece.

The topic of male objectification proves both interesting and controversial. Some groups, including Christian groups, feminist groups, and intersections of the two, argue that objectification of the male, particularly notable in advertising and movies, is as degrading and dehumanizing as objectification of the female. Other groups, however, argue that objectification of the male, while negative, cannot be paralleled with objectification of the female, due to the argued inherent power structure evinced by male objectification of the female body. Cf. Peter Lucas, "Why the Sexual Objectification of Men Isn't Just a Bit of Fun," *The Conversation*, September 18, 2018, https://theconversation.com/why-the-sexual-objectification-of-men-isnt-just-a-bit-of-fun-103145; Benjamin Caven-Roberts, "'Hunkvertising' Is the Trend Advertisers Are Obsessed With," *Business Insider*, August 18, 2015, https://www.businessinsider.com/advertisers-obsession-with-huge-male-muscles-in-ads-2015-8.

16. Bryan T. Karazsia and Kathryn Pieper, "A Meta-Analytic Review of Sociocultural Influences on Male Body Image," chap. 8 (pp. 153–72) in Greene, *Body Image*. See also Tamara Y. Mousa and Rima H. Mashal, "Negative Body Image Perception and Associated Attitudes in Females," chap. 15 (pp. 255–62) in Greene, *Body Image*; Nancy Xenakis and Judith Goldberg, "Body Image in Young and Adult Women with Physical Disabilities," chap. 16 (pp. 263–68) in Greene, *Body Image*.

17. See also Shakespeare's "Sonnet 130," which wonderfully—and uncomfortably—denounces an idealistic, unrealistic view of lovers perpetuated in Renaissance poetry, by reminding us that we "tread on the ground," which is not only beautiful but also real. Thanks to Marie Bowen for first bringing this to my attention.

18. For background, see *2017 Report on International Religious Freedom: Saudi Arabia* (Washington, DC: U.S. Department of State, 2018), https://www.state.gov/reports/2017-report-on-international-religious-freedom/saudi-arabia/.

19. See, e.g., Bart Wagemakers, "Incest, Infanticide, and Cannibalism: Anti-Christian Imputations in the Roman Empire," *Greece & Rome* 57, no. 2 (2010): 337–54; Marcus Minucius Felix, *The Octavius of Minucius Felix*, esp. chaps. 9, 10, 28, trans. Robert Earnest Wallis (*ANF* 4:177–78, 190–91). Minucius Felix lived from ca. 160 to ca. 250.

20. Justin Martyr, *The First Apology* 65 (*ANF* 1:185).

21. Tertullian, *On Prayer* 18 (*ANF* 3:686–87).

22. Daniel B. Hinshaw, *Touch and the Healing of the World* (New York: St. Vladimir's Seminary Press, 2017), 118.

23. Warnings of potential abuse and how to guard against it can be found in early church leaders, such as Athenagoras, *A Plea for Christians* 32–35 (*ANF* 2:146–47). For an excellent recent book navigating these challenges, see Lore Ferguson Wilbert, *Handle with Care: How Jesus Redeems the Power of Touch in Life and Ministry* (Nashville: B&H, 2020).

24. *Apostolic Constitutions* (*ANF* 7:422).

25. Rodney Stark, *The Rise of Christianity* (Princeton: Princeton University Press, 1996), esp. chap. 5 (pp. 95–128); Mike Aquilina and James L. Papandrea, *How Christianity Saved Civilization* (New York: Image Books, 2015; repr., Manchester: Sophia Institute, 2018), esp. chap. 3, which contrasts the early church's views of the home against those of the Roman world in particular, pp. 57–77.

26. John Paul II, *A Theology of the Body: Man and Woman He Created Them*, trans. Michael Waldstein (Boston: Pauline Books and Media, 2006), 6.3, p. 152.

27. Adam is "a body among bodies" who then "discovered the meaning of his own bodiliness" (John Paul II, *Theology of the Body* 6.4, p. 153).

28. John Paul II, *Theology of the Body* 6.3–4, pp. 152–53.

29. Sharon K. Farber, "Why We All Need to Touch and Be Touched," *Psychology Today*, September 11, 2013; Joe Fortenbury, "Fighting Loneliness with Cuddle Parties," Health, *Atlantic*, July 15, 2014; Jonathan Jones, "Why Physical Touch Matters for Your Well-Being," Mind and Body, *Greater Good Magazine*, November 16, 2018; Sirin Kale, "The Life of the Skin-Hungry: Can You Go Crazy from a Lack of Touch?," Identity, *Vice*, November 8, 2016. On solitary confinement, see "Solitary Confinement Should Be Banned in Most Cases, UN Expert Says," *UN News*, October 18, 2011, https://news.un.org; J. Wesley Boyd and Gali Katznelson, "Solitary Confinement: Torture, Pure and Simple," *Psychology Today*, January 15, 2018.

30. Bessel van der Kolk, *The Body Keeps the Score: Brain, Mind, and Body in the Healing of Trauma* (New York: Penguin, 2015), 217.

31. See the testimony of Carolyn Holderread Heggen in Mark Openheimer's "A Theologian's Influence, and Stained Past, Live On," *New York Times*, October 11, 2013, section A, p. 14. Heggen also wrote the book *Sexual Abuse in Christian Homes and Churches* (Harrisonburg, VA: Herald Press, 1993), though she doesn't single Yoder out in that volume.

32. For the official statement from L'Arche, see https://www.larcheusa.org/news_article/findings-of-larche-internationals-inquiry-into-jean-vanier/.

33. For an interview I recently did for *Christianity Today* on this situation, see Morgan Lee, "Don't Diminish Ravi Zacharias's Abuse with "We're All Sinners," February 17, 2021, *Quick to Listen*, podcast, 1:08, https://www.christianitytoday.com/ct/podcasts/quick-to-listen/ravi-zacharias-sexual-abuse-sin-grace-mercy-podcast.html.

34. For example, I am a strong advocate of churches having strong, clear, and faithfully followed child protection policies. These are crucial and are, reportedly, the primary deterrent against harming the vulnerable in our churches. But the point of policies is not to make those who minister become so nervous they avoid caring for children or fear a child's hug. Rather, the point of these policies is wisdom, transparency, and accountability, because we are not Jesus.

35. Cf. Ben Witherington III, *Women in the Earliest Churches*, Society for New Testament Studies Monograph Series 59 (Cambridge: Cambridge University Press, 1988).

36. For probably the best source on women in the Gospels, with extended discussion of their importance for the resurrection narratives, see Richard Bauckham, *Gospel Women: Studies of the Named Women in the Gospels* (Grand Rapids: Eerdmans, 2002).

37. Augustine, *Sermon 115*, in *Sermons on the New Testament: 94A–147A*, The Works of Saint Augustine III/4 (New York: New City, 1992), chap. 4, p. 200.

38. Augustine, *Sermon 115*, chap. 4, p. 201.

39. Craig S. Keener, *The Gospel of John: A Commentary* (Peabody, MA: Hendrickson, 2003), 1:600.

40. Keener, *Gospel of John*, 1:621.

41. Wilbert, *Handle with Care*, 219.

Chapter 5 Is Identity Purely Self-Generated?

1. Stanley Hauerwas and William H. Willimon, *The Truth about God: The Ten Commandments in Christian Life* (Nashville: Abingdon, 1999), 68.

2. Jean-Paul Sartre, *Existentialism Is a Humanism*, trans. Carol Macomber (New Haven: Yale University Press, 2007; first published as *L'existentialisme est un humanisme* [Paris: Gallimard, 1947]), 20.

3. Sartre, *Existentialism Is a Humanism*, 22 (emphasis added). The full quote is as follows: "There is no human nature since there is no God to conceive of it. Man is not only that which he conceives himself to be, but that which he wills himself to be, and since he conceives of himself only after he exists, just as he wills himself to be after being thrown into existence, *man is nothing other than what he makes of himself*. That is the first principle of existentialism."

4. Alasdair MacIntyre, *After Virtue: A Study of Moral Theory*, 3rd ed. (Notre Dame, IN: University of Notre Dame Press, 2007), 58–59. See also Carol A. Newsom, "Models of the Moral Self: Hebrew Bible and Second Temple Judaism," *Journal of Biblical Literature* 131, no. 1 (2012): 5–25. Thanks to Scott Jones for pointing me to Newsom.

5. This social order (with its various problems) has been replaced in modernity: "We have moved from a hierarchical order of personalized links [e.g., peasants were connected to, but also under, lords who were under kings] to an impersonal egalitarian one [there are no necessary relations]; from a vertical world of mediated-access to horizontal, direct-access societies" (Charles Taylor, *Modern Social Imaginaries* [Durham, NC: Duke University Press, 2004], 158).

6. Samuel Waje Kunhiyop, *African Christian Ethics* (Kenya, Nigeria: Hippo Books, 2008), 24.

7. Kunhiyop, a missiologist with extensive research into the culture and history of Africa, reflects on the significance of the communal. He quotes missionary John Taylor, and what Taylor says actually applies to all of us, whether we realize it or not. "Every man is born into a community. He is a member of a family and he grows up inheriting certain family characteristics, certain property, certain obligations; he learns certain family traditions, certain patterns of behavior, and certain points of pride. In the same way, also, he is a member of a particular clan, tribe, and nation, and these will give him a particular culture and history, a particular way of looking at things, probably a particular religion. It is in such ways that every human being belongs to his own environment. He has his roots in a particular soil; he cannot be transplanted to a different soil without feeling the change very deeply; and if he is left with his roots in no soil his personality will become weak and unhappy and sick. Men and women who do not live in a community and feel that they belong to it are not completely human. Something essential is missing, something which God has ordained for them as necessary for their true life. 'It is not good for the man to be alone' (Gen. 2:18)" (John V. Taylor, *Christianity and Politics in Africa* [Harmondsworth: Penguin, 1957], 35, quoted in Kunhiyop, *African Christian Ethics*, 67). As Taylor notes, we all find ourselves located within a particular time, place, and people.

8. This translation follows Bonhoeffer's German text rather than a standard English one.

9. For this sermon, see Dietrich Bonhoeffer, *Barcelona, Berlin, New York, 1928–1931*, ed. Clifford J. Green, trans. Douglas W. Stott, Dietrich Bonhoeffer Works 10 (Minneapolis: Fortress, 2008), 532–35.

10. His father was a professor of psychiatry and neurology at the University of Berlin. For more on his complicated view of and engagement with psychology, see Clifford J. Green, "Two Bonhoeffers on Psychoanalysis," in *A Bonhoeffer Legacy: Essays in Understanding*, ed. Abram John Klassen (Grand Rapids: Eerdmans, 1981), 58–75.

11. Cf. Clifford J. Green, *The Sociality of Christ and Humanity: Dietrich Bonhoeffer's Early Theology, 1927–1933* (Missoula, MT: Scholars Press, 1975).

12. E.g., "When Christ comes 'into' us through the Holy Spirit, the church comes 'into' us. . . . Faith acknowledges God's rule and embraces it; love actualizes the Realm of God" (Bonhoeffer, *Sanctorum Communio: A Theological Study of the Sociology of the Church*, Dietrich Bonhoeffer Works 1 [Minneapolis: Fortress, 1998], 165).

13. Emerging views of self-development as framed by early sociologists like Émile Durkheim (1858–1917), Jean Piaget (1896–1980), Charles Cooley (1864–1929), and George Herbert Mead (1863–1931) represent the kind of thinking that would have shaped Bonhoeffer's awareness of this social dynamic. While we don't know if any of these early sociologists were in Bonhoeffer's mind at this time, their work was gaining attention. Mead, for example, argued that the self emerges from social interactions following a threefold pattern: imitation, role-playing, and games in which a young person discovers that others have opinions and can take on multiple roles at different times. This led Mead to make a distinction between "I" and "me": the latter was what might be called the "social self," while the former was a response to these data—the true self was apparently found somewhere in this dynamic between the two. Mead wrote influential essays during his life (e.g., his 1913 "The Social Self"), but it would not be until his students later gathered his work that full-length books of his were published. See, for instance, George Herbert Mead, *Mind, Self, and Society*, ed. Charles W. Morris (1934). I am thankful to sociologist Matt Vos for pointing me to the relevant discussions and literature.

Cooley similarly observed the "looking glass" phenomenon, in which people view themselves through the lens of how others see them. This is particularly tricky, since, as Cooley is aware, there is often a difference between how others perceive us and how we *imagine* others perceive us—they are rarely the exact same thing. He first advocated this theory of the "looking-glass self" in Charles H. Cooley, *Human Nature and the Social Order* (New York: Scribner's, 1902), esp. 183–84.

Although these early-twentieth-century thinkers are now dated, their influence remains with us. For an example of a neo-Piagetian perspective that also engages the other theories of "self" formation, see Robert Kegan, *The Evolving Self: Problem and Process in Human Development* (Cambridge, MA: Harvard University Press, 1982), with a helpful chart on 86–87.

14. Bonhoeffer, *Barcelona, Berlin, New York*, 532.

15. Bonhoeffer, *Barcelona, Berlin, New York*, 532.

16. Bonhoeffer, *Barcelona, Berlin, New York*, 532–33.

17. Charles Marsh, *Strange Glory: A Life of Dietrich Bonhoeffer* (New York: Knopf, 2014), 71–72.

18. This is exactly the story Charles Taylor masterfully lays out in his philosophical history, *Sources of the Self: The Making of Modern Identity* (Cambridge, MA: Harvard University Press, 1989).

19. Bonhoeffer, *Barcelona, Berlin, New York*, 533.

20. Bonhoeffer, *Barcelona, Berlin, New York*, 533.

21. Much like our discussion of Gal. 2:20, Bonhoeffer uses the strong language of "new" right next to the language of "cleanse"; he is not advocating self-hatred or the notion of God's destroying the ego, but he does not flinch from the problem of a disordered self.

22. Bonhoeffer, *Barcelona, Berlin, New York*, 534.

23. Rather than seeking a path of perfection, the ego is given to God, and the other is redeemed "only through God" (Bonhoeffer, *Barcelona, Berlin, New York*, 534).

24. Bonhoeffer makes the connections clear between loving God and neighbor and then adds, "You have found the ego for which you have been searching since you were young; you—no, God has become Lord over your ego; you—no, God has torn you from the distress of the life of the ego and liberated you. You have lost your soul to God—no, God has lost his love to you; you have penetrated into God's—no, God has penetrated into your life" (Bonhoeffer, *Barcelona, Berlin, New York*, 535).

25. Echoing Paul's statement in Gal. 5:1, Luther creates a diagram and then explains: "For he who is free from sin has become a slave of righteousness; but he who is the slave of sin is free from righteousness, and *vice versa*" (Martin Luther, *Lectures on Galatians—1535: Chapters 5–6; Lectures on Galatians—1519: Chapters 1–6*, ed. Jaroslav Pelikan and Walter A. Hansen, trans. Richard Jungkuntz, Luther's Works 27 [Minneapolis: Fortress, 1964], 326).

26. Martin Luther, "The Freedom of the Christian," in *Martin Luther's Basic Theological Writings*, ed. Timothy F. Lull (Minneapolis: Fortress, 1989), 596.

27. Augustine, "Fifth Homily," in *Homilies on the First Epistle of John*, ed. Daniel E. Doyle and Thomas Martin, trans. Boniface Ramsey, The Works of Saint Augustine III/14 (Hyde Park, NY: New City, 2008), 77.

28. James Wetzel, "Sin," in *Augustine through the Ages*, ed. Allan D. Fitzpatrick (Grand Rapids: Eerdmans, 1999), 800.

29. See also Etienne Gilson, who quipped, "The more a doctrine tends to be built around charity [love] the more Augustinian it is" (*The Christian Philosophy of Saint Augustine* [New York: Random House, 1960], 238).

30. See Kelly M. Kapic, "The Place and Purpose of the Law/Gospel Distinction in Reformed Theology and Ministry," in *God's Two Words: Law and Gospel in Lutheran and Reformed Traditions*, ed. Jonathan Linebaugh (Grand Rapids: Eerdmans, 2018), 129–51.

31. Knowing this can help contemporary readers better understand classic and medieval traditions, which speak of objects moving according to the divine loves that pull them, and in this way speak of love in the same way as we speak of the "law of gravity." We think that, because we give phenomena scientific names, we have said something truer than the ancient descriptions of things; but that, I'm afraid, says more about our chronological snobbery than it does about a truer depiction of the world. The blind bias of our day that has come to believe scientific descriptions are truer than ancient ones has failed to understand how language, science, and the world work—but that is a discussion for another day. See G. K. Chesterton, C. S. Lewis, and Jacques Ellul.

32. Eberhard Bethge, "Letter from Nov. 30, 1943, Berlin-Charlottenburge," in Dietrich Bonhoeffer, *Letters and Papers from Prison*, Dietrich Bonhoeffer Works 8, 209.

33. Bonhoeffer, *Letters and Papers*, 208.

34. Bonhoeffer, for example, explicitly worried that his fiancée was getting a skewed perspective of him as a holy martyr, and that this was far from the whole story.

35. Dietrich Bonhoeffer, "Letter to Eberhard Bethge, Dec. 15, 1943," in *Letters and Papers*, 220.

36. Thanks to Scott C. Jones for this fresh translation of Bonhoeffer's poem, and for helpful encouragement and feedback from Hermann Spieckermann and Tom Neiles. It originally comes from Dietrich Bonhoeffer, *Widerstand und Ergebung*. A copy of the original German poem, including a picture of it, can be found at https://www.dietrich-bonhoeffer.net/predigttext/wer-bin-ich/. For a different translation, see Bonhoeffer, "Who Am I," in *Letters and Papers*, 459–60.

37. Bonhoeffer, *Letters and Papers*, 221. Elsewhere Bonhoeffer complains, "To psychologize and analyze people, as has become fashionable these days, is to destroy all trust" (*Fiction from Tegel Prison*, Dietrich Bonhoeffer Works 7 [Minneapolis: Fortress, 2000], 65, noted in *Letters and Papers*, 221n18).

38. Søren Kierkegaard, following a classic tradition that sees the fundamental problem as sin itself, and not just *sins*, explains, "The state of sin is the sin; the particular sins are not the continuance of sin but the expression for the continuance of sin; in the specific new sin the impetus of sin merely becomes more perceptible to the eye. The state of sin is a worse sin than the particular sins; it is the sin" (*The Sickness unto Death*, ed. and trans. Howard V. Hong and Edna H. Hong, Kierkegaard's Writings 19 [Princeton: Princeton University Press, 1980], 106).

39. Martin Luther wrote, "We do not consider it a special honor that we are God's creatures: but because someone is a prince or a great lord, men stare and gape, although the man's office is merely a human creation, as Peter calls it (1 Pet. 2:13), and an imitation. For if God had not previously produced His creature and made a man, it would be impossible to make any prince. And yet all men grasp for such an office as if it were a precious and great thing, whereas the fact that I am God's work and creature is much more glorious and great. Therefore menservants, maids, and everybody ought to interest themselves in this high honor and say: I am a human being; this is certainly a higher title than being a prince, for God did not make a prince; men made him. But that I am a human being is the work of God alone." Quoted in Ewald M. Plass, *What Luther Says* (St. Louis: Concordia, 2006), 877.

40. *The Book of Common Prayer*, "A Penitential Order: Rite One" (New York: Oxford University Press, 1979), 321.

41. See Søren Kierkegaard, *The Sickness unto Death: A Christian Psychological Exposition for Upbuilding and Awakening*, ed. and trans. Howard V. Hong and Edna H. Hong, Kierkegaard's Writings 19 (Princeton: Princeton University Press, 1980).

42. While this is not his real name, this is a real person and this account reflects, to the best of my ability, our actual conversation.

43. I am well aware of recent trends that argue against this pointing toward internal Christian struggles, but I believe Dunn, Bruce, Cranfield, and others still make a compelling case. Further, much of church history has accepted this interpretation, even before the hyperpsychologizing of modernity.

44. Susan Eastman, "Double Participation and the Responsible Self in Romans 5–8," in *Apocalyptic Paul: Cosmos and Anthropos in Romans 5–8*, ed. Beverly Gaventa (Waco: Baylor University Press, 2013), 101.

45. Eastman, "Double Participation and the Responsible Self," 101.

46. E.g., John Owen's *Indwelling Sin*, in *Overcoming Sin and Temptation: Three Classic Works by John Owen*, ed. Kelly M. Kapic and Justin Taylor (Wheaton: Crossway, 2006), 229–407.

47. J. de Waal Dryden calls this a "dialectical tension" in "Revisiting Romans 7: Law, Sin, and Spirit," *Journal for the Study of Paul and His Letters* 5, no. 1 (2015): 139.

48. C. K. Barrett, *The Epistle to the Romans*, Black's New Testament Commentary (Peabody, MA: Hendrickson, 1991), here quoted by Dryden, "Revisiting Romans 7," 141n27.

49. Dryden, "Revisiting Romans 7," 141.

50. "So the true self, ontologically severed from sin, experiences the Law no longer through guilt and shame but through the life-giving freedom of the Spirit" (Dryden, "Revisiting Romans 7," 154).

51. Eastman, "Double Participation and the Responsible Self," 108.

52. Eastman, "Double Participation and the Responsible Self," 107.

53. See also Old Testament scholar J. Gordon McConville's distinction: "Selfishness is of course an inescapable fact of experience. In biblical perspective, however, it is not defined by biological determinism, but always lies under the prophetic call to repent" (*Being Human in God's World: An Old Testament Theology of Humanity* [Grand Rapids: Baker Academic, 2016], 67).

Chapter 6 Have We Misunderstood Humility?

1. Alasdair MacIntyre, *After Virtue*, 3rd ed. (Notre Dame, IN: University of Notre Dame Press, 2007), 184.

2. Regarding the word family of the Greek word *tapeinos* (ταπεινός = low, lowly, poor, etc.), see also H. H. Esser's comment: "In the Gk. World, with its anthropocentric view of man, lowliness is looked on as shameful, to be avoided and overcome by act and thought. In the NT, with its theocentric view of man, the words are used to describe those events that bring a man into a right relationship with God and his fellow-man" (*The New International Dictionary of New Testament Theology*, ed. Colin Brown [Grand Rapids: Zondervan, 1975], 2:260).

3. See also Aristotle, *Nicomachean Ethics* 4.3 (esp. 1125.16). Here the extremes are *vanity* on the one hand and *humility* on the other, with appropriate *pride* serving as the mean. What he means by humility, however, is part of the debate, since his understanding and the Christian conceptions are different—sometimes looking at the two on the subject can be like comparing apples to oranges. Despite this seeming disparity, Aquinas, for example, happily draws from Aristotle when he advocates Christian humility.

4. There's a quip, attributed both to John Bright discussing Benjamin Disraeli and to William Cowper, that runs, "He is a self-made man who worships his creator."

5. Randall Collins, *The Sociology of Philosophies: A Global Theory of Intellectual Change* (Cambridge, MA: Harvard University Press, 1998).

6. Collins, *Sociology of Philosophies*, 74.

7. Alister E. McGrath, *Luther's Theology of the Cross: Martin Luther's Theological Breakthrough*, 2nd ed. (London: Wiley-Blackwell, 2011), 193 (see also 32–33, 94–95).

8. Wilson and Presley did later become friends, and a widely circulated anecdote reports Wilson's graciously adding that he learned as much from Elvis as Elvis did from him (Tony Douglas, *Jackie Wilson: Lonely Teardrops* [New York: Routledge, 2005], e.g., 48–49). Even when others ignored it, Elvis himself did humbly acknowledge his debt to others.

9. Bernard of Clairvaux, *The Twelve Degrees of Humility and Pride*, part 1, chap. 1, trans. Barton R. V. Mills (CreateSpace, 2010), 11 (emphasis added).

10. Bernard was building on the sixth-century *Rule of Saint Benedict*, in which Benedict, the father of Western monasticism, states twelve steps of humility (see *The Rule of St. Benedict*, trans. Anthony C. Meisel and M. L. Mastro [New York: Image Books, 1975], 56–61). Benedict offers useful wisdom regarding our need to walk humbly before God, but his dominant emphasis is on sin. Still, at the end of his reflections, Benedict concludes that the monk will "find that perfect love of God which casts out fear, by means of which everything he had observed anxiously before will now appear simple and natural," adding that the monk will "no longer act out of the fear of Hell, but for the love of Christ, out of good habits and with a pleasure derived of virtue," and that "the Lord, through the Holy Spirit, will show this to His servant, cleansed of sin and vice" (61).

11. This story and the responses come from *The Desert Fathers: Sayings of the Early Christian Monks*, trans. Benedicta Ward (London: Penguin, 2003), 154 ("Humility," no. 19).

12. I have purposefully decided not to include the author or book title here as I do not want to draw negative attention to the person.

13. Thomas Aquinas, *Summa Theologica*, trans. Fathers of the English Dominican Province (New York: Benziger Brothers, 1948), II-II, q. 161, art. 1 (p. 1842).

14. Aquinas, *Summa Theologica*, II-II, q. 161, art. 2, I answer that (p. 1843).

15. Aquinas, *Summa Theologica*, II-II, q. 129, art. 3, reply to obj. 4 (p. 1724). There is some debate about how to understand *defectus* in Aquinas, but it can be argued that the term points toward "negation that is not yet a privation," or, put differently, it points to an absence of something, but not necessarily to sin or evil. See Bernadette E. O'Connor, "Insufficient Ado about the Human Capacity for Being and Maritain's Dissymmetry Solution," in

Aquinas and Maritain on Evil: Mystery and Metaphysics, ed. James G. Hanink (Washington, DC: American Maritain Association, 2013), 155–69, but 157n8 is where more on this can be found. This distinction can make a significant difference in how one treats our limits and the challenge of confusing finitude and sin. I should also add that maybe my greatest debt for understanding this material in Aquinas is to Mary M. Keys, whose nuanced and insightful essay is the best I read: Mary M. Keys, "Aquinas and the Challenge of Aristotelian Magnanimity," in *History of Political Thought* 24, no. 1 (Spring 2003): 37–65.

16. See also Robert Miner, *Thomas Aquinas on the Passions: A Study of Summa Theologiae, Ia-IIae, 22–48* (Cambridge: Cambridge University Press, 2011), 245. For a lengthy essay arguing that similar misunderstandings have made people mistakenly accuse Aquinas of treating women as "less than men," see Michael Nolan, "The Aristotelian Background to Aquinas's Denial that 'Woman Is a Defective Male,'" *The Thomist* 64 (2000): 21–69.

17. Aquinas, *Summa Theologica*, II-II, q. 161, art. 2, reply to obj. 2 (p. 1843). He later adds, "Excessive self-confidence is more opposed to humility than lack of confidence is," q. 161, art. 2, reply to obj. 3 (p. 1843).

18. G. K. Chesterton, *Saint Thomas Aquinas: "The Dumb Ox"* (Garden City, NY: Image Books, 1956), 90. I am here drawing these quotes from Mary M. Keys's wonderfully stimulating essay, "Statesmanship, Humility, and Happiness: Reflections on Robert Faulkner's *The Case for Greatness*," in *Perspectives on Political Science* 39, no. 4 (October–December 2010): 194.

19. Mary Keys—one of the most able interpreters of Aquinas on this—nicely captures this twofold dynamic: "Magnanimity aids a person in daring good and great deeds according to true dictates of reason and despite formidable dangers and difficulties; humility keeps this passion for greatness from feeding the flame of hubris and motivating irrational, vicious action under the cloak of what seems honorable and outstanding" ("Statesmanship, Humility, and Happiness," 195).

20. Sheryl Overmyer, "Exalting the Meek Virtue of Humility in Aquinas," *Heythrop Journal* 46 (2015): 659.

21. See also the following: "For just as the magnanimous man tends to great things out of greatness of soul, so the pusillanimous man shrinks from great things out of littleness of soul" (*Summa Theologica*, II-II, q. 133, art. 2, I answer that [p. 1738]).

22. See, e.g., Aristotle, *Nicomachean Ethics* 4.3–4.1123a–1126a.

23. Aquinas, *Summa Theologica*, II-II, q. 133, art. 1 (pp. 1736–37).

24. *Summa Theologica*, II-II, q. 133, art. 1, reply to obj. 3 (p. 1737).

25. Aquinas has great respect for and owes a great debt to both Aristotle and Benedict of Nursia (480–547), and he draws these two thinkers (and others) together in an innovative manner, offering what I believe is a somewhat fresh proposal. I am highlighting his work because he appears to place humility within the context of creaturely finitude rather than isolating it within the context of human fallenness. He treats humility as the ability to recognize one's limits and restrain one's appetites accordingly (*Summa Theologica*, II-II, q. 161, art. 1, reply to obj. 3 [p. 1842]). Right reason avoids naive assumptions of self-sufficiency while also remaining open to doing "great things," even though they might be difficult (e.g., magnanimity). See also *Summa Theologica*, II-II, q. 161, art. 1, I answer that (p. 1842).

Later, when he is both building on and gently reacting to the "Twelve Degrees of Humility" outlined in Benedict's *Rule*, Aquinas highlights three aspects of handling one's own "deficiency": (1) acknowledge your shortcomings, (2) confess "oneself incapable of great things" (apart from God), and (3) "count others before oneself" (Aquinas, *Summa Theologica*, II-II, q. 161, art. 6, I answer that [p. 1847]). It is widely noted, I should add, that Aquinas, for example, flips the order originally found in Benedict, so that Aquinas begins where Benedict ends, and vice versa.

26. God is not the author of sin; instead, sin grew out of the humans' rejection of the limits God placed on them (see Gen. 2:16–17; 3:1). In a very Augustinian manner, Aquinas believes that sin grew out of the fall and has since been fostered by sinful impulses and actions.

27. Aquinas, *Summa Theologica*, II-II, q. 161, art. 6, reply to obj. 2 (p. 1847).

28. Aquinas, *Summa Theologica*, II-II, q. 161, art. 3 (pp. 1843–44). Aquinas puts it thus: "A man may esteem his neighbor to have some good which he lacks himself, or himself to have some evil which another has not: by reason of which, he may subject himself to him with humility," I answer that (p. 1844).

29. This is quoted and styled after his prayer "On Acquiring the Virtues," in *The Aquinas Prayer Book: The Prayers and Hymns of St. Thomas Aquinas* (Manchester: Sophia Institute, 2000), 35. In Alasdair MacIntyre, *Dependent Rational Animals* (Chicago: Open Court, 1999), xi, MacIntyre paraphrases this prayer (and is then referenced by others, such as Keys), but none appear to quote or cite the original source.

30. Aquinas, *Summa Theologica*, II-II, q. 129, art. 3, reply to obj. 4 (p. 1724).

31. Aquinas, *Summa*, II-II, q. 161, art. 5 (pp. 1845–46).

32. John Calvin, *Institutes of the Christian Religion*, ed. John T. McNeill, trans. Ford Lewis Battles (Philadelphia: Westminster, 1960), 3.7.1 (p. 690).

33. Calvin, *Institutes*, 1.17.2 (p. 212).

34. Along these lines, it has been argued that humility was a necessary prerequisite for faith in Luther's view, although Luther does not simply reduce faith to humility. You can't skip humility, and a Christian version of it always starts with one's awareness of one's small creaturely place before the Holy Creator Lord. See, e.g., Berndt Hamm, "Why Did 'Faith' Become for Luther the Central Concept of the Christian Life?," in *The Reformation of Faith in the Context of Late Medieval Theology and Piety: Essays by Berndt Hamm*, ed. Robert J. Bast (Leiden: Brill, 2004), 169–71 (see esp. n. 41). The chapter covers 153–78.

35. Calvin, *Institutes*, 3.7.2 (p. 691).

36. Calvin, *Institutes*, 3.7.2 (p. 691).

37. Calvin, *Institutes*, 3.7.4 (p. 693).

38. Calvin, *Institutes*, 3.7.4 (p. 693).

39. Calvin, *Institutes*, 3.7.4 (p. 694).

40. Calvin, *Institutes*, 3.7.4 (p. 693).

41. Calvin, *Institutes*, 3.7.4 (p. 694).

42. Calvin, *Institutes*, 3.7.4 (p. 694).

43. Calvin, *Institutes*, 3.7.4 (p. 694).

44. Calvin, *Institutes*, 3.7.4 (p. 694).

45. Calvin, *Institutes*, 3.7.5 (p. 695).

46. Calvin, *Institutes*, 3.7.5 (p. 695).

47. Aquinas, *Summa Theologica*, II-II, q. 161, art. 3, reply to obj. 1.

48. Calvin, *Institutes*, 3.7.5 (p. 695).

49. Calvin, *Institutes*, 3.7.5 (p. 695).

50. Justin L. Barrett, "Give Up Childish Ways or Receive the Kingdom like a Child? Spiritual Formation from a Developmental Perspective," in *Psychology and Spiritual Formation in Dialogue: Moral and Spiritual Change in Christian Perspective*, ed. Thomas M. Crisp, Steven L. Porter, and Gregg A. Ten Elshof (Downers Grove, IL: IVP Academic, 2019), 254–68, and Barrett's *Born Believers: The Science of Children's Religious Belief* (New York: Free Press, 2012), 144–47, 175.

51. H.-H. Esser, "ταπεινός [*tapeinos*]," in Brown, *New International Dictionary of New Testament Theology*, 2:262.

52. Do note, the similarities are more conceptual than linguistic.

Chapter 7 Do I Have Enough Time?

1. Cf. Tim Keller, *Counterfeit Gods: The Empty Promises of Money, Sex, and Power, and the Only Hope That Matters* (New York: Penguin, 2011).

2. Augustine, *Confessions*, trans. Henry Chadwick (Oxford: Oxford University Press, 1991), 11.14 (17), 230.

3. While there is some debate about whether creation ex nihilo was originally intended when the opening chapters of Genesis were written (see, e.g., the Jewish scholar Jon Levenson, who doesn't read them in terms of creation ex nihilo), by the time of Second Temple Judaism, we see what appears to be a clear affirmation of it—e.g., 2 Macc. 7:28. However, other Jewish scholars do think that even the Genesis text contains "intimations" of the idea of creation ex nihilo and that the point is there is "no human parallel." See Nahum Sarna, *The JPS Torah Commentary: Genesis* (Philadelphia: Jewish Publication Society, 1989), 5. See also Gen. 1:1–2; Heb. 11:3; John 1:3; Rev. 4:11; Ps. 104:24.

4. E.g., Augustine, *Confessions*, trans. Maria Boulding, in *The Works of Saint Augustine: A Translation for the 21st Century* I/1 (New York: New City Press, 1997), 12.15.20–21 (pp. 323–24).

5. Barbara Adam, *Time* (Cambridge: Polity Press, 2004), esp. 102–12.

6. For the biblical texts and background for such divisions along natural lines, see Roland de Vaux, *Ancient Israel: Its Life and Institutions*, trans. John McHugh (Grand Rapids: Eerdmans, 1997), 182; for a full treatment on the divisions of time in ancient Israel and neighboring lands, see 178–94.

7. Aristotle, *Physics* 4.10–13.

8. See, e.g., Augustine, *Confessions*, books 11–12.

9. Jeffrey L. Singman, *Daily Life in Medieval Europe* (Westport, CT: Greenwood, 1999), 223.

10. Hendrik Spruyt, *The Sovereign State and Its Competitors: An Analysis of Systems Change* (Princeton: Princeton University Press, 1996), 70.

11. For a recent attempt to encourage Christians to let the Christian calendar guide their view of time, see, e.g., Bobby Gross, *Living the Christian Year: Time to Inhabit the Story of God* (Downers Grove, IL: InterVarsity, 2009).

12. Singman, *Daily Life in Medieval Europe*, 223–24.

13. Gerhard Dohrn-van Rossum, *History of the Hour: Clocks and Modern Temporal Orders*, trans. Thomas Dunlap (Chicago: University of Chicago Press, 1996), 33–35. For more of Rossum's excellent and balanced treatment of time in this period, see all of chap. 3, esp. 33–39.

14. Rossum, *History of the Hour*, 36. Although there was talk of "punctuality," this was linked to the "collective conduct." Benedict valued rhythms of prayer and work; thus, throughout the day, and at different "hours," the monks would gather to offer up praise and petitions.

15. John Swinton, *Becoming Friends of Time: Disability, Timefullness, and Gentle Discipleship* (Waco: Baylor University Press, 2016), 25. See also Neil Postman, *Technopoly: The Surrender of Culture to Technology* (New York: Vintage Books, 1993), 14.

16. George Woodcock, "The Tyranny of the Clock" (1944), reprinted in *Time: Documents of Contemporary Art*, ed. Amelia Groom (Cambridge, MA: MIT Press, 2013), 65.

17. Woodcock, "Tyranny of the Clock," 65.

18. Leofranc Holford-Strevens explains as follows: "It made no sense that a train travelling at a given speed so many miles due west should appear to complete them sooner than one travelling at the same speed an equal number of miles due east" (*The History of Time: A Very Short Introduction* [Oxford: Oxford University Press, 2005], 11).

19. Robert Hassan, *The Age of Distraction: Reading, Writing, and Politics in a High-Speed Networked Economy* (London: Transaction Publishers, 2012), xiii.

20. The eight points, which he unpacks, can be summarized as follows: (1) "the African notion of *the active presence of the Creator God in the world*"; (2) "the African *unified sense of reality*"; (3) "the African notion of *life as the ultimate gift*"; (4) "the concept of *the family and community as the place to be born, live, and die*"; (5) "the African concept of *the nature and role of ancestors*"; (6) "the place of *oral tradition in African life*"; (7) "the African notion of *the sanctity of nature and environment*"; and (8) "Africa's notion of *time*" (Nwaka Chris Egbulem, "Mission and Inculturation: Africa," in *The Oxford History of Christian Worship*, ed. Geoffrey Wainwright and Karen B. Westerfield Tucker [Oxford: Oxford University Press, 2006], 680–81).

21. Egbulem, "Mission and Inculturation: Africa," 681–82.

22. Besides Swinton, *Becoming Friends of Time*, see also Brian Brock, *Wondrously Wounded: Theology, Disability, and the Body of Christ* (Waco: Baylor University Press, 2020); William C. Gaventa, *Disability and Spirituality: Recovering Wholeness* (Waco: Baylor University Press, 2018).

23. See, e.g., Barbara Adam, *Timewatch: The Social Analysis of Time* (Cambridge: Polity, 1995), esp. chap. 4; see also Anthony Giddens, *A Contemporary Critique of Historical Materialism: Power, Property and the State* (London: Macmillan, 1981), who makes these connections between time, production, and expectations throughout his book.

24. Barbara Adam, *Time* (Cambridge: Polity, 2004), 39.

25. Judy Wajcman, *Pressed for Time: The Acceleration of Life in Digital Capitalism* (Chicago: University of Chicago Press, 2015), 31.

26. From lives saved because a phone call was placed, to someone with physical limitations now being able to easily send voice texts, the smartphone has brought many positive benefits to our lives.

27. For helpful background that seems more balanced and data-informed, see, e.g., Robert Goodin, James Rice, Antti Parpo, and Lina Eriksson, *Discretionary Time: A New Measure of Freedom* (Cambridge: Cambridge University Press, 2008); John Robinson and Geoffrey Godbey, *Time for Life: The Surprising Ways Americans Use Their Time* (University Park: Penn State University Press, 1997); Jonathan Gershuny, "Busyness as the Badge of Honor for the New Superordinate Working Class," *Social Research: An International Quarterly* 72, no. 1 (2005): 287–314.

28. Wajcman, *Pressed for Time*, 64.

29. See also Wajcman, *Pressed for Time*, 66.

30. Wajcman, *Pressed for Time*, 111–35.

31. See also Robert Hassan, *Chronoscopic Society: Globalization, Time and Knowledge in the Network Economy* (New York: Peter Lang, 2003), 236.

32. See Hassan, *Age of Distraction*, chap. 5.

33. See Nicholas Carr, "Is Google Making Us Stupid? What the Internet Is Doing to Our Brains," in *Atlantic Monthly*, July/August 2008; see also the more extensive study in N. Carr, *The Shallows: How the Internet Is Changing the Way We Think, Read and Remember* (London: Atlantic Books, 2010).

34. Cal Newport, *Deep Work: Rules for Focused Success in a Distracted World* (New York: Grand Central Publishing, 2016); see also his more recent volume, *Digital Minimalism: Choosing a Focused Life in a Noisy World* (New York: Penguin, 2019).

35. E.g., Daniel T. Willingham, "The High Price of Multitasking: How to Calm the Inner Frenzy," Opinion, *New York Times*, July 14, 2019; "The Perils of Multi-tasking," *1843*, May 10, 2006; Steve Lohr, "A Warning on the Limits of Multitasking," International Business, *New York Times*, March 25, 2007; Ruth Pennebaker, "The Mediocre Multitasker," Week in Review, *New York Times*, August 29, 2009; Alina Tugend, "Multitasking Can Make You Lose . . . Um . . . Focus," Shortcuts, *New York Times*, October 24, 2008.

36. Wajcman, *Pressed for Time*, 3.

37. John O'Donohue, *To Bless the Space between Us: A Book of Blessings* (New York: Doubleday, 2008), immediately preceding the poem "To the Exhausted."

38. See Matthew Ratcliffe, *Experiences of Depression: A Study in Phenomenology* (Oxford: Oxford University Press, 2014), 174–200.

39. For a powerful and helpful book on PTSD with many empirically grounded (and often surprising) suggestions for moving forward, see Bessel van der Kolk, *The Body Keeps the Score: Brain, Mind, and Body in the Healing of Trauma* (New York: Penguin, 2015).

40. Robert Erle Barham, "Seeing the World through Poetry," (chapel talk, Covenant College, February 12, 2020), YouTube video, 22:34, posted by Covenant College, February 12, 2020, https://youtu.be/H6mYVmqYZDA.

41. Chuck DeGroat, *Wholeheartedness: Busyness, Exhaustion, and Healing the Divided Self* (Grand Rapids: Eerdmans, 2016).

42. Alexander Schmemann, *For the Life of the World: Sacraments and Orthodoxy* (New York: St. Vladimir's Seminary Press, 2018), 140.

43. Schmemann, *For the Life of the World*, 143.

44. Bruce K. Waltke, "The Fear of the Lord: The Foundation for a Relationship with God," in *The Dance between God and Humanity* (Grand Rapids: Eerdmans, 2013), 282–300.

45. Waltke, "Fear of the Lord," esp. 295–96.

46. Peter Lombard, *The Sentences, Book 3: On the Incarnation of the Word*, trans. Guilio Silano, Mediaeval Sources in Translation 45 (Toronto: Pontifical Institute of Mediaeval Studies, 2008), 34.3 (p. 138; emphasis added).

47. For example, in 2010 Nikki Waller reported on research that showed that as people in America earned more money, their happiness increased—that is, until they reached $75,000 a year; after that point it was true that "stuff" increased, but "happiness did not" ("Magic Number for Happiness: $75,000 a Year," *Wall Street Journal*, September 12, 2010; cf. Jo Craven McGinty, "On Gauging the Pursuit of Happiness," *Wall Street Journal*, August 21, 2015; "Economic Growth Does Not Guarantee Rising Happiness," Graphic Detail, *Economist*, March 21, 2019, https://www.economist.com/graphic-detail/2019/03/21/economic-growth-does-not-guarantee-rising-happiness.

Chapter 8 Why Doesn't God Just Instantly Change Me?

1. E.g., Sandra Fleishman, "No Need to Be Ugly," *Washington Post*, November 16, 2002.

2. For this story and his relevant reflections, see Gary S. Selby, *Pursuing an Earthy Spirituality: C. S. Lewis and Incarnational Faith* (Downers Grove, IL: InterVarsity, 2019), chap. 7.

3. See E. Randolph Richards and Brandon J. O'Brien, *Misreading Scripture with Western Eyes: Removing Cultural Blinders to Better Understand the Bible* (Downers Grove, IL: InterVarsity, 2012), 93, 215–16.

4. See the excellent and well-balanced essay by M. C. Steenberg, "Children in Paradise: Adam and Eve as 'Infants' in Irenaeus of Lyons," *Journal of Early Christian Studies* 12, no. 1 (Spring 2004): 1–22.

5. Peter C. Bouteneff, *Beginnings: Ancient Christian Readings of the Biblical Creation Narratives* (Grand Rapids: Baker Academic, 2008), 80.

6. Irenaeus, *Adversus haereses* 4.38.3, also quoted by Steenberg, "Children in Paradise," 1.

7. Gregory of Nyssa, *On the Making of Man*, trans. H. A. Wilson, in *Nicene and Post-Nicene Fathers*, Series 2 (Peabody, MA: Hendrickson, 1994), 5:387–427. *The Nicene and Post-Nicene Fathers (NPNF)* series can be found in the Christian Classics Ethereal Library at https://ccel.org/ccel/schaff/npnf102/npnf102.

8. Gregory of Nyssa, *On the Making of Man* 2 (*NPNF*, Series 2, 5:390); here I have quoted the fresh translation by Robert Louis Wilken, *The Spirit of Early Christian Thought* (New Haven: Yale University Press, 2003), 149.

9. Wilken, *Spirit of Early Christian Thought*, 149.

10. Quoted by Wilken, *Spirit of Early Christian Thought*, 150.

11. Wilken, *Spirit of Early Christian Thought*, 154. The quote in the previous sentence also is Wilken's.

12. Wilken, *Spirit of Early Christian Thought*, 155.

13. Geerhardus Vos, *The Pauline Eschatology*, ed. Richard Gaffin (Phillipsburg, NJ: P&R, 1986), 82, editor's note 14.

14. The following paragraphs in the next few pages are taken, with some significant modification, from my chapter, "Theological Anthropology," in *Christian Dogmatics*, ed. Michael Allen and Scott Swain (Grand Rapids: Baker Academic, 2015), 165–93, copyright © 2016. Used by permission of Baker Academic, a division of Baker Publishing Group.

15. Geerhardus Vos, *The Eschatology of the Old Testament*, ed. James T. Dennison Jr. (Phillipsburg, NJ: P&R, 2001), 73–76.

16. Vos, *Eschatology of the Old Testament*, 74.

17. See also Henri J. M. Nouwen, *Adam, God's Beloved* (Maryknoll, NY: Orbis Books, 1997); Thomas E. Reynolds, *Vulnerable Communion: A Theology of Disability and Hospitality* (Grand Rapids: Brazos, 2008).

18. John Swinton, *Becoming Friends of Time: Disability, Timefullness, and Gentle Discipleship* (Waco: Baylor University Press, 2016). This paragraph, with minor alteration, originally appeared in my article "Learning to Value Limits: A Brief Bibliographical Reflection," in *Didaktikos: Journal of Theological Education* 1, no. 3 (March 2018): 38–40.

19. For Emily's story and reflections on learning from her son, see Emily Colson, *Dancing with Max: A Mother and Son Who Broke Free* (Grand Rapids: Zondervan, 2010).

20. Jonathan Aitken, *Charles W. Colson: A Life Redeemed* (Colorado Springs: Waterbook, 2005), 370.

21. Eusebius, *Church History* 3.25, in *NPNF*, Series 2, 1:157.

22. See, e.g., the helpful discussion of *anakephalaiōsis* (recapitulation) in Robert M. Grant, *Irenaeus of Lyons*, Early Church Fathers (London: Routledge, 1997), 50–53.

23. See, for example, how the Hebrew adjectives *tāmîm* and *tām* convey this idea of being complete and, thus, blameless, in the *Theological Lexicon of the Old Testament*, ed. Ernst Jenni and Claus Westermann, trans. Mark E. Biddle (Peabody, MA: Hendrickson, 1997), 3:1424–28. While *teleios* is not often the Septuagint's choice for translating these words, in the New Testament *teleios* is the preferred term used by the author of Hebrews and other authors to convey a similar idea of whole or complete, linked with blameless. See G. Delling, "τέλος κτλ. [*telos* etc.]," in *Theological Dictionary of the New Testament*, ed. Gerhard Kittel and Gerhard Friedrich, trans. Geoffrey W. Bromiley (Grand Rapids: Eerdmans, 1972), 8:49–87.

24. For more on the complexities of this verse and the different ways *teleios* is employed in Hebrews, see Paul Ellingworth, *Commentary on Hebrews*, New International Greek Testament Commentary (Grand Rapids: Eerdmans, 1993), 157–63.

25. See also Moisés Silva, "Perfection and Eschatology in Hebrews," *Westminster Theological Journal* 39 (1976): 60–71.

26. Anthony A. Hoekema, *Saved by Grace* (Grand Rapids: Eerdmans, 1989), 192–93. See the rest of Hoekema's chap. 12 for both this helpful distinction and an excellent overview of the issues related to common discussions about sanctification.

27. Ralph P. Martin, *2 Corinthians*, Word Biblical Commentary 40 (Waco: Word, 1986), 72, Accordance electronic ed. See also A. R. C. Leaney, "Conformed to the Image of His Son," *New Testament Studies* 10 (1963–64): 470–79.

28. John Owen, *Pneumatologia*, in *The Works of John Owen*, ed. William H. Goold, 24 vols. (Edinburgh: Johnson & Hunter; 1850–55; repr., London: Banner of Truth, 1965), 3:386. This immediately follows a much longer definition: "Sanctification is an immediate work of the Spirit of God on the souls of believers, purifying and cleansing of their natures from the pollution and uncleanness of sin, renewing in them the image of God, and thereby enabling them, from a spiritual and habitual principle of grace, to yield obedience unto God, according unto the tenor and terms of the new covenant; by virtue of the life and death of Jesus Christ. Or more briefly:—It is the universal renovation of our natures by the Holy Spirit into the image of God, through Jesus Christ."

Elsewhere Owen describes sanctification as "the immediate work of God by his Spirit upon our whole nature, proceeding from the peace made for us by Jesus Christ, whereby, being changed into his likeness, we are kept entirely in peace with God, and are preserved unblamable, or in a state of gracious acceptation with him, according to the terms of the covenant, unto the end" (*Pneumatologia*, 369).

29. As the Westminster Larger Catechism puts it, God's "Spirit infuseth grace, and enableth [us] to exercise thereof" (Q. 77). While early Protestants did not use the language of "infuse" in terms of justification (as Roman Catholics did), they nevertheless employed this term in regard to sanctification. Knowing this distinction could help the different traditions better understand one another.

30. E.g., Owen, *Communion with God*, in *The Works of John Owen*, ed. William H. Goold, 24 vols. (Edinburgh: Johnson & Hunter, 1850–55; repr., London: Banner of Truth, 1965), 2:258. For an excellent sampling of seventeenth-century Enthusiasm, see Geoffrey F. Nuttall, *Studies in Christian Enthusiasm: Illustrated from Early Quakerism* (Wallingford, PA: Pendle Hill, 1948). The early Quakers are the most famous of the "Enthusiasts." See also Hugh Barbour, *The Quakers in Puritan England* (New Haven: Yale University Press, 1964); Barry Reay, *The Quakers and the English Revolution* (London: Temple Smith, 1985), esp. 35–37.

31. John Stott, "Basic Stott," interview with Roy McCloughry, *Christianity Today*, January 8, 1996, 32.

32. N. T. Wright, *After You Believe: Why Christian Character Matters* (New York: HarperCollins, 2010), 197.

Chapter 9 Do I Need to Be Part of the Church?

1. For more on the need to be more holistic in thinking about "poverty," see Brian Fikkert and Kelly M. Kapic, *Becoming Whole: Why the Opposite of Poverty Isn't the American Dream* (Chicago: Moody, 2019).

2. E.g., Timothy C. Tennent, *Theology in the Context of World Christianity: How the Global Church Is Influencing the Way We Think about and Discuss Theology* (Grand Rapids: Zondervan, 2007), 15.

3. For an excellent and balanced treatment of this idea and how the church can participate without being co-opted by non-Christian social and political concerns, see Jake Meador, *In Search of the Common Good: Christian Fidelity in a Fractured World* (Downers Grove, IL: InterVarsity, 2019).

4. Cake, "Sheep Go to Heaven," by John McCrae, track 1 on *Prolonging the Magic*, Capricorn Records.

5. For the background information and the following quotes from C. T. Studd, I am drawing from Gerald L. Sittser, *Water from a Deep Well: Christian Spirituality from Early Martyrs to Modern Missionaries* (Downers Grove, IL: InterVarsity, 2007), 264–68.

6. Irwyn L. Ince Jr., *The Beautiful Community: Unity, Diversity, and the Church at Its Best* (Downers Grove, IL: InterVarsity, 2020).

7. See, e.g., Patrick Schreiner, *The Ascension of Christ: Recovering a Neglected Doctrine* (Bellingham, WA: Lexham, 2020).

8. John Baillie, *A Diary of Private Prayer* (New York: Charles Scribner's Sons, 1955), 81, day 19 (emphasis added).

9. For this story and these quotes, see Bob Burns, Tasha D. Chapman, and Donald C. Guthrie, *Resilient Ministry: What Pastors Told Us about Surviving and Thriving* (Downers Grove, IL: InterVarsity, 2013), 61.

10. Aaron Earls, "The Church Growth Gap: The Big Get Bigger While the Small Get Smaller," *Christianity Today*, March 6, 2019.

11. Burns, Chapman, and Guthrie, *Resilient Ministry*, 99.

12. Augustine Thompson, *Francis of Assisi: A New Biography* (Ithaca, NY: Cornell University Press, 2012), 74.

13. Thompson, *Francis of Assisi*, 74.

14. For more on this struggle in Francis's life and ministry, see esp. Thompson, *Francis of Assisi*, 72–114.

15. Philip Yancey, Back Page, *Christianity Today*, May 21, 2001, 104.

16. Burns, Chapman, and Guthrie, *Resilient Ministry*, 99.

17. Peter Scazzero, *The Emotionally Healthy Leader: How Transforming Your Inner Life Will Deeply Transform Your Church, Team, and the World* (Grand Rapids: Zondervan, 2015); see also Scazzero, *Emotionally Healthy Spirituality: It's Impossible to Be Spiritually Mature, While Remaining Emotionally Immature*, rev. ed. (Grand Rapids: Zondervan, 2017).

18. Gregory the Great, *The Book of Pastoral Rule*, trans. George E. Demacopoulos (Crestwood, NY: St. Vladimir's Seminary Press, 2007), 49.

19. These quotes come from "Clergy Intervention Program Reduced Health Risk Factors," Campus, Medicine, *Duke Today*, June 19, 2017, https://today.duke.edu/2017/06/clergy-intervention-program-reduces-health-risk-factors.

20. While the book talks about therapists helping those who are facing personal trauma (e.g., PTSD), the central idea behind the book—that the body absorbs far more than we realize—is of great import for all involved in ministry. See Bessel van der Kolk, *The Body Keeps the Score: Brain, Mind, and Body in the Healing of Trauma* (New York: Penguin, 2015).

21. See Kelly M. Kapic, *Embodied Hope: A Theological Meditation on Pain and Suffering* (Downers Grove, IL: InterVarsity, 2016), esp. 138–48.

22. For more on the communal nature of faith, hope, and love, see Kapic, *Embodied Hope*, 121–32.

23. Justin Borger, a friend, former student, and now pastor, helped me make these connections as we spoke about this passage in Exodus. I am so grateful for his faithful help and prayers.

24. Some of the following material comes from my essay "Belonging in a Time of Isolation," Christian Living, Gospel Coalition, April 14, 2020, https://www.thegospelcoalition.org/article/belonging-in-isolation/.

25. Sebastian Junger, *Tribe: On Homecoming and Belonging* (New York: Twelve Hachette Book Group, 2016), 52.

26. See Charles Fritz, *Disasters and Mental Health: Therapeutic Principles Drawn from Disaster Studies* (Newark: University of Delaware Disaster Research Center, 1996). Here the quotes come from Junger's engagement with Fritz's work; see *Tribe*, 53.

27. Junger, *Tribe*, 54.

28. Junger, *Tribe*, 48–55.

29. Junger, *Tribe*, xvii (emphasis added).

Chapter 10 How Do We Faithfully Live within Our Finitude?

1. Kate Bowler, *Everything Happens for a Reason, and Other Lies I've Loved* (New York: Random House, 2018).

2. See Bowler, *Everything Happens for a Reason*, 156.

3. Anne-Marie Slaughter, "Why Women Still Can't Have It All," *Atlantic*, July/August 2012.

4. Jocelyn K. Glei, "Productivity Shame," *HurrySlowly*, podcast, May 14, 2019, https://hurryslowly.co/216-jocelyn-k-glei/.

5. For a detailed outline of how the different liturgical colors are used by different denominations and traditions, see "Liturgical Colors, Revised Common Lectionary," Vanderbilt Divinity Library, accessed May 13, 2021, https://lectionary.library.vanderbilt.edu/liturgical-colors.php.

6. Brené Brown, "The Power of Vulnerability," TED video, 19:43, June 2010, https://www.ted.com/talks/brene_brown_the_power_of_vulnerability?language=en.

7. Curt Thompson, *The Soul of Shame: Retelling the Stories We Believe about Ourselves* (Downers Grove, IL: InterVarsity, 2015), esp. chap. 6.

8. Thompson, *Soul of Shame*, 120.

9. See Brené Brown, *Men, Women, and Worthiness: The Experience of Shame and the Power of Being Enough*, Sounds True, 2012, audio download; the story starts about minute 19:30 of the audiobook. No printed version available.

10. See Greg Lukianoff and Jonathan Haidt, *The Coddling of the American Mind: How Good Intentions and Bad Ideas Are Setting Up a Generation for Failure* (New York: Penguin, 2018), esp. chaps. 1, 6–12.

11. Chuck DeGroat, "Vulnerability and Fauxnerability: Learning the Difference Is Essential for a Leader," *In All Things*, September 25, 2018, https://inallthings.org/vulnerability-and-fauxnerability-learning-the-difference-is-essential-for-a-leader/.

12. Chuck DeGroat, *When Narcissism Comes to Church: Healing Your Community from Emotional and Spiritual Abuse* (Downers Grove, IL: InterVarsity, 2020).

13. Jerilyn Sanders, "How Did I Get Here?," chapel talk, Covenant College, March 30, 2015, YouTube video, 24:32, posted by Covenant College, March 30, 2015, https://youtu.be/saQQLf1s4p8.

14. For more on my approach to lament, see Kelly M. Kapic, *Embodied Hope: A Theological Meditation on Pain and Suffering* (Downers Grove, IL: InterVarsity, 2017), esp. chaps. 1–3.

15. Fritz Reinecker, *Linguistic Key to the Greek New Testament*, trans. by Cleon L. Rogers (Grand Rapids: Zondervan, 1980), 560.

16. Gordon Fee, *Philippians*, IVP New Testament Commentary Series (Downers Grove, IL: InterVarsity, 1999), 407.

17. Lynn H. Cohick, *Philippians*, ed. Tremper Longman III and Scott McKnight, Story of God Commentary 11 (Grand Rapids: Zondervan, 2013), 219.

18. A robust example of the early and formative work in this area is Robert A. Emmons and Michael E. McCullough, eds., *The Psychology of Gratitude*, Series in Affective Science (New York: Oxford University Press, 2004).

19. Giacomo Bono, Mikki Krakauer, and Jeffrey J. Froh, "The Power and Practice of Gratitude," in *Positive Psychology in Practice: Promoting Human Flourishing in Work, Health, Education, and Everyday Life*, ed. Stephen Joseph (Hoboken, NJ: John Wiley & Sons, 2015), 561.

20. See, e.g., Robert A. Emmons, *Thanks! How the New Science of Gratitude Can Make You Happier* (Boston: Houghton Mifflin, 2007); Emmons, *The Little Book of Gratitude: Create a Life of Happiness and Wellbeing by Giving Thanks* (London: Gaia Books, 2016); Emmons, *Gratitude Works! A 21-Day Program for Creating Emotional Prosperity* (San Francisco: Jossey-Bass, 2013).

21. For some legitimate cautions about aspects of overstatements or misapplications of empirical science in general and positive psychology in particular, see James Davison Hunter and Paul Nedelisky, *Science and the Good: The Tragic Quest for the Foundations of Morality* (New Haven: Yale University Press, 2018).

22. E.g., Ivy Shiue, "Urinary Arsenic, Pesticides, Heavy Metals, Phthalates, Polyaromatic Hydrocarbons, and Polyfluoroalkyl Compounds Are Associated with Sleep Troubles in Adults: USA NHANES, 2005–2006," *Environmental Science & Pollution Research* 24, no. 3 (2017): 3108–16, https://doi.org/10.1007/s11356-016-8054-6.

23. Jennifer A. Ailshire and Sarah A. Burgard, "Family Relationships and Troubled Sleep among US Adults: Examining the Influences of Contact Frequency and Relationship Quality," *Journal of Health and Social Behavior* 53, no. 2 (2012): 248–62, https://doi.org/10.1177/0022146512446642. Religious cognitions, they conclude, often served as a kind of "buffer against stress-related sleep disturbance."

24. Christopher G. Ellison, Reed T. Deangelis, Terrence D. Hill, and Paul Froese, "Sleep Quality and the Stress-Buffering Role of Religious Involvement: A Mediated Moderation Analysis," *Journal for the Scientific Study of Religion* 58, no. 1 (2019): 251–68, https://doi.org/10.1111/jssr.12581.

25. Ignatius of Loyola, *The Spiritual Exercises of St. Ignatius*, trans. Louis J. Puhl (New York: Vintage Books, 2000).

26. Beth Felker Jones, *Faithful: A Theology of Sex* (Grand Rapids: Zondervan, 2015).

27. Mike Aquilina and James L. Papandrea, *How Christianity Saved Civilization* (New York: Image Books, 2015; repr., Manchester: Sophia Institute, 2018), 88.

28. For further stimulating and helpful discussion on the Sabbath and its ongoing relevance, see Marva Dawn, *The Sense of Call: A Sabbath Way of Life for Those Who Serve God, the Church, and the World* (Grand Rapids: Eerdmans, 2006); Norman Wirzba, *Living the Sabbath: Discovering the Rhythms of Rest and Delight* (Grand Rapids: Brazos, 2006).

29. Justo L. González, *A Brief History of Sunday: From the New Testament to the New Creation* (Grand Rapids: Eerdmans, 2017). See also the older but very helpful volume edited by D. A. Carson, *From Sabbath to Lord's Day* (Grand Rapids: Zondervan, 1982).

30. John Murray, "The Sabbath Institution," in *Collected Writings* (Edinburgh: Banner of Truth, 1976), 1:216. See also his brief essay in the same volume: "The Pattern of the Lord's Day," 219–24.

Acknowledgments

1. "Christian Meaning-Making, Suffering and the Flourishing Life," John Templeton Foundation, accessed April 30, 2021, https://www.templeton.org/grant/christian-meaning-making-suffering-and-the-flourishing-life.

scripture index

subject index

To Cathy, Jason, Justin,
and Vanessa

Contents

Preface

If a man will begin with certainties, he shall end in doubts; but if he will be content to begin with doubts, he shall end in certainties.
FRANCIS BACON

The real estate industry has been severely affected by the events of the past few years. In the late 1970s, soaring construction costs began pricing housing beyond the reach of much of the potential market. An intense period of undisciplined commercial property lending and investment in the early 1980s created overbuilt situations in most urban areas, many of which still exist today. Increasingly stringent environmental and social legislation has produced significant changes as to where and in what manner development should occur. Energy conservation has also affected real estate in terms of the location of new projects and the way in which they are planned and designed. Government fiscal policy has changed significantly, removing or modifying many of the favorable tax advantages that real estate has enjoyed in the past.

What of the future? Will the national economy experience continuing periods of economic growth, perhaps accompanied by renewed inflation, or are we in for a period of slow, possibly negative, economic growth, haunted by the specter of possible depression? On the local scale, which urban areas will continue to grow and which will stagnate? Will environmental legislation continue to restrict new development, or will the pendulum swing back in favor of the developer? What will be the life-style preferences of individual Americans, and how will they affect the demand for various land uses? What will be the role of developers, brokers, architects, contractors, financial institutions, asset managers, and others in the somewhat confusing real estate community of the future?

It was against a similar backdrop of uncertainty that this book was originally written in 1976. My objective in writing the original book was not to establish certainty—but rather to *reduce uncertainty to a manageable level where effective decisions could be made.* For over 10 years, developers, investors, students, and others have used the book to help them grapple with real estate decisions. The extensive popularity of the book over the years is a testimony to the timelessness of this message.

In this revision, I have tried to shed some light on the rapidly changing social and economic forces now affecting real estate. More important, the book provides readers with a basic framework of understanding whereby they can make their own observations about these forces and relate these observations to the specific decisions faced in their real estate operation.

Effective decision making, however, is based on more than an understanding of broad social and economic forces. It also requires a systematic program of collecting and evaluating market, financial, and physical data which bear directly on a specific decision that must be made. This book reviews many traditional analytic methods as well as some new and innovative ones.

But even the most sophisticated analytic program ultimately requires subjective judgment. While this book can't provide sound judgment, for that can only come through experience, it does indicate the key points in the decision-making process when judgment is required and the various trade-offs that must be considered. It also outlines methods of monitoring the decision once it has been made so as to be certain that the project continues to be consistent with unfolding realities.

The major focus of the book is on the creation of new real estate values through the property development process. Most of the analytic techniques, however, apply equally well to investment in existing improved properties. There is also some application to raw land purchased on a speculative basis for future development.

Many who read the book will be totally new to the property development field, perhaps university students contemplating real estate as a career. Others will be knowledgeable in one or more aspects—marketing, finance, planning and design, construction, brokerage, property management—but will desire a broader understanding of how their specialty relates to the total development process. Still others will be experienced developers and investors, many with an implicit understanding of much of what is in the book, but they will be pleasantly surprised to see it in explicit form for the first time. For all, it is hoped, the book will contribute to their overall ability to make more effective decisions in a time of growing uncertainty.

The revision of this book involved the contributions of many individuals. I am particularly indebted to Jeannine Marschner who provided invaluable assistance in researching, updating, writing, and editing the final version. Also, Martha Jewett of McGraw-Hill, who ever so patiently prodded and cajoled me to get the revision underway and then provided the support necessary to see that it was accomplished.

I also wish to acknowledge the efforts of the individuals listed on pp xvii and xviii who reviewed various portions of the book. I particularly want to thank Harry Newman, Rick Peiser, Joel Peterson, Gary Rosenberg, Lynne Sagalyn, Tom Swift, and Jim Webb, who reviewed the entire book, as well as Tony Downs, Dick McElyea, Bill Murray, and Rollie Warner, who reviewed multiple chapters. Jim Strahorn was also a great resource for the computer graphics developed for Chapter 14.

Finally, a special acknowledgment to my wife Jacqueline, who endured the many early mornings and weekends necessary to pull the effort together. Without the assistance and support of these people, the revision of the book would not have been possible.

JOHN MCMAHAN

Reviewers

Bruce A. Batty
Chief Financial Officer
Tooley & Company
Los Angeles, California

Richard S. Banwell
Hardison, Komatsu, Ivelich & Tucker
San Francisco, California

Steven B. Brabant
V.P. Real Estate Council
The Boston Company
Los Angeles, California

Michael P. Buckley
President
Halycon
Hartford, Connecticut

Thomas C. Clark
Executive Vice President
McMahan Real Estate Advisors, Inc.
San Francisco, California

Anthony Downs
Senior Fellow
The Brookings Institution
Washington, D.C.

Greg Dresdow
Tax Partner
Arthur Anderson & Co.
San Francisco, California

Thomas J. Flynn
Chairman
Blackman Garlock Flynn & Co.
San Francisco, California

Briana M. Finley
President
Lacor
Pasadena, California

Susan L. Giles
Partner, Director of Real Estate
Arthur Young
San Francisco, California

James L. Grasscamp (Deceased)
Chairman, Real Estate and Urban Economics
University of Wisconsin
Madison, Wisconsin

Lisa Grubbs
Director of Marketing
Kaufman & Board of Southern California, Inc.
Los Angeles, California

George Ivelich
Vice President
Hardison, Komatsu, Ivelich & Tucker
San Francisco, California

William C. Lazier
Lecturer
Stanford University
Stanford, California

Richard J. McElyea
Executive Vice President
Economics Research Associates
San Francisco, California

Mike Miles
Professor
University of North Carolina
Chapel Hill, North Carolina

William G. Murray, Jr.
Partner
Morrison & Foerster
San Francisco, California

Harry Newman, Jr.
President
Newman Properties
Long Beach, California

Richard Peiser
Director
Lask Center for Real Estate Development
University of Southern California
Los Angeles, California

Joel C. Peterson
National Managing Partner
Trammell Crow Company
Foster City, California

Gary A. Rosenberg
Chairman of the Board & Chief Executive Officer
UDC Universal Development L.P.
Chicago, Illinois

Judith M. Runstad
Attorney at Law
Foster, Pepper & Riveria
Seattle, Washington

Lynne B. Sagalyn
Associate Professor of Planning and Real Estate Development
Massachusetts Institute of Technology
Cambridge, Massachusetts

Norman A. Spencer
Director of Marketing
Gerald D. Hines Interests
San Francisco, California

James Strahorn
Strahorn & Associates
Menlo Park, California

Thomas B. Swift
Executive Vice President
Gerald D. Hines Interests
San Francisco, California

William L. Tooley
Chairman
Tooley & Company
Los Angeles, California

Rollin M. Warner
Dean of Students
Towne School
San Francisco, California

James R. Webb
Visiting Texas Real Estate Research Center
Professor
The University of Texas at Austin and Executive Director of the American Real Estate Society
Austin, Texas

Introduction

In a nationwide survey conducted several years ago, a major pollster asked Americans to list their most favored forms of investments. To the surprise of many, particularly those on Wall Street, the answer was not stocks and bonds but real estate. What's astonishing is that there *was* any surprise. Real estate has always held a very special place in the hearts of most Americans. Great personal fortunes have been based upon it, institutions have been built around it, and governments have risen and fallen over its use. In fact, real estate has been the premier investment for Americans since the *Mayflower* landed at Plymouth Rock.

The history of America's romance with the land is long and colorful. Several of the founding fathers speculated in land. Many of the largest cities in the United States began as land promotions. Land provided the motivating force behind the development and expansion of the canal and railroad systems. Florida and California would probably be largely swamps and deserts today if they hadn't fallen prey to the land speculators.

The people who developed and speculated in land were equally colorful: John Jacob Astor, who made millions buying up farmlands in Manhattan; Jay Cooke, who helped to finance the Civil War but couldn't pull off one of the largest land speculations of all; Henry Flagler, who almost single-handedly built Florida; the Van Sweringen brothers, who developed Shaker Heights, the granddaddy of modern suburbs, near Cleveland; Harry Black, who pioneered in high-rise construction; the Levitts, who made mass-produced suburbs a reality; and William Zeckendorf, who began revitalizing America's central cities. Many of these colorful individuals created vast fortunes through real estate; others died penniless. All had a certain style and a vision of America's future.

What is real estate, this mystical entrepreneurial pursuit that has attracted so many through the years? Many definitions have been proposed, varying with the viewpoints of the persons or disciplines involved. Geographers and cartographers tend to see real estate as a physical entity that can be seen, felt, and measured. Lawyers view it as a "bundle" of legal rights related to land and its use. To economists, real estate is the economic value created by activity associated with land and its improvements. In reality, real estate is all of these: it is the *economic exploitation of legal rights to the land.*

Let's explore this concept a bit further. Certainly, land is the foundation of all real estate activity. Physically, land is the outer crust of the earth's surface, including soil and vegetation. Land has certain unique characteristics. For instance, it is *durable;* except for drastic acts of God, such as earthquakes and other cataclysms, land is virtually indestructible. It is also *immobile*; unlike tools, machinery, buildings, and other items which can be moved from place to place, the location of land is fixed. Finally, land is *nonsubstitutable*; every parcel of land has physical characteristics which make it absolutely unique and discernible from all other land parcels.

These characteristics make it possible to ascribe certain *legal rights* to individual parcels of land. This bundle of legal rights has evolved through the years and affects virtually every aspect of real estate. Certain legal instruments establish the rights of ownership to land and improvements. Other instruments protect the rights of those who participate in the construction process or who lend monies using real estate as collateral. Still other instruments deal with the relationship between those who own real estate and those who utilize it on a day-to-day basis, if they are other than the owner.

These legal rights are of little value, however, unless they are *exploited economically.* In urban areas, exploitation usually occurs through the construction and sale or lease of a building, or portion thereof, to a user. The user may be an individual or a family for a home or an apartment, a retailer for a store or shopping center, a business or government operation for an office or industrial building, or an operator for a hotel or motel. The buildings built for these users are referred to as *improvements,* reflecting the historical view that land values are enhanced, or improved, through the construction and use of buildings.

The improvement of raw land occurs through the *development process.* Real estate development is a highly creative process in which physical ingredients such as land and buildings are effectively combined with financial and marketing resources to create an environment in which people live, work, shop, and relax. At its best, the development process is *synergistic,* that is, the ultimate combination of resources has a greater value than the sum of the individual parts.

The degree to which synergy exists in a real estate project is partly a result of the location and character of the land involved. Some parcels are so well located or have such great physical beauty that value will be created under virtually any development program. Most parcels, however, aren't so fortunate and require the utmost in *creative skills* on the part of the developer to marshall the necessary resources and skillfully weave them together into a finished product that is economically sound, aesthetically pleasing, and environmentally responsive.

These creative skills are built upon an understanding, explicit or implicit, of the *fundamentals* of the development process. These fundamentals—market research, finance, planning and design, construction, marketing, and property management—must be intrinsically sound and interrelate in such a manner that the overall project becomes a viable entity. A weakness or failure in any one area can ultimately prove the undoing of the total effort.

This book is about the fundamentals of the real estate development process. After the historical and economic stage has been set, the book pursues each of the fundamentals in a step-by-step fashion in much the same manner that a well-organized developer would approach a new project. The emphasis throughout is on the important role played by each of the fundamentals and how they mesh into a smoothly functioning process.

PART 1

Historical Perspective

1 The Inalienable Right

It clearly appears to me that the two great objects of America must be the settlement and cultivation of good lands and the establishment of manufactures. If we review the rise and progress of private fortunes in America, we shall find that a very small proportion of them has arisen or been acquired by commerce, compared with those made by prudent purchases and management of lands. SILAS DEANE, 1783

Americans historically have viewed as an inalienable right the private ownership of land, whose use is to be determined exclusively by its owner. The origins of this deep-seated conviction aren't entirely clear. Perhaps it was in reaction to the European heritage, which allowed only a few people to own land. Possibly it was linked to the ingrained American belief in the freedom of the individual. Or maybe there was so much land that no one questioned the right of individuals to do as they wished with their own property. Whatever the origins, the history of real estate in the United States, until very recently, has been the story of private ownership and development of land.

"Religious freedom is my immediate goal, but my long-range plan is to go into real estate."

Land for All

For the first hundred years after the Revolution, America was one great land speculation. Everybody was involved: European nobility; the founding fathers; merchants; investment bankers; railroad tycoons; government officials; and, as speculation became better organized, many average Americans. Great fortunes were won and lost as land bubbles formed and burst. New cities appeared and disappeared almost overnight. Canals were extended, railroads built, and even wars financed—all on the basis of investors' anticipations regarding the future value of land.

The Land Companies

Actually, private speculation in land had trouble getting started because so much land was given away by the king of England in order to promote settlement. Gradually, the amount of free land diminished in the East, and speculators' sights turned toward land west of the Alleghenies. "Land companies" were formed, and land grants were obtained to settle this land—until the British forbade colonial governors to make grants to individuals (the latter, incidentally, a factor leading to the Revolution).

After the Revolution land speculation resumed and in a few years reached boom proportions. It was fed not only by new lands in the West but also by the confiscation of Tory holdings and the issuance of "land warrants" to returning soldiers. The boom collapsed around 1800, largely because there was simply too much land for the arriving settlers.

Town Jobbing

As America moved into the nineteenth century, land speculation was at a low ebb. To stimulate new interest, Congress passed legislation reducing the minimum for single-purchase tracts from 640 to 320 acres. The federal government then opened up scores of land offices to facilitate the sale of government lands to settlers. Private land companies decided to accelerate their own efforts by creating "new towns" where entire cities would be laid out and sold to potential investors. This "town jobbing" resulted in the creation of Cleveland, Cincinnati, Toledo, and many smaller Ohio cities. Other entrepreneurs were active in the older cities of the Northeast. One was John Jacob Astor, who accurately foresaw that Manhattan could only expand northward and invested in farms and swamp land in the area that is now midtown Manhattan.

Canals and Railroads

Transportation has always played an important role in the development of land in America. Proximity to good harbors was critical to the growth of cities in the early colonial period. Later, the development of an extensive canal system brought transportation into the interior and opened up vast new areas. In 1825, the opening of the Erie Canal spurred the growth of New York City and of communities along the canal route. Following the Panic of 1837, however, the recovering

OBSERVATIONS

ON THE

North-American Land-Company,

LATELY INSTITUTED IN

PHILADELPHIA:

Containing an Illuſtration of the Object of the Company's Plan, the Articles of Aſſociation, with a ſuccinct Account of the States wherein their Lands lie:

TO WHICH ARE ADDED,

Remarks on AMERICAN LANDS in general, more particularly the Pine-Lands of the Southern and Weſtern States, in Two Letters from *Robert G. Harper, Eſquire,* Member of Congreſs, for SOUTH CAROLINA, to a Gentleman in Philadelphia.

LONDON:

PRINTED, BY H. L. GALABIN, INGRAM-COURT,
FOR C. BARRELL AND H. SERVANTE', AMERICAN AGENTS,
NO. 6, INGRAM-COURT, FENCHURCH-STREET:
SOLD ALSO BY J. DEBRETT, PICCADILLY; J. JOHNSON, NO. 72,
ST. PAUL'S CHURCH-YARD; AND W. RICHARDSON,
UNDER THE ROYAL EXCHANGE.

M.DCC.XCVI.

Figure 1-1. Offering circular of the North American Land Co. *(Rare Book Division, The New York Public Library, Astor, Lenor, and Tilden Foundations)*

Figure 1-2. Land sale at Monrovia, California, late 1880s. *(Title Insurance and Trust Company, Los Angeles, California; Collection of Historical Photographs)*

economy saw greater promise in the emergence of the more competitive railroads, and little new canal construction occurred after 1850.

Nothing influenced land speculation in the United States as much as the development of the railroads. Although the first operating American railroad was the Baltimore and Ohio in 1830, railroad growth really got moving several years later when Congress provided grants of land along the right-of-way.

The success of the Illinois Central Railroad, which had obtained a grant from the state of Illinois, motivated other financiers and those in different geographic areas, especially in the West, to press for grants. The Union Pacific, Northern Pacific, Central Pacific, Atlantic and Pacific (which later became the Santa Fe), Southern Pacific, Oregon and Pacific, and other railroads received land grants of more than 91 million acres from the federal government.[1]

Florida and California

Florida's and California's enticements were not land for agriculture but sunshine. To these sunny climes came thousands from the North and

[1]Roy M. Robbins, *Our Landed Heritage, The Public Domain.*

Midwest: tourists, settlers, the elderly, and of course, land speculators.

Land activity began booming in Los Angeles when the Southern Pacific line, linking the city with the East, was completed in 1882. Within 3 months town jobbers had marked off thirteen new town sites along the rail lines. But by 1888 it was largely over. Of the hundred-odd new towns plotted between 1884 and 1890, sixty-two had vanished.

Florida experienced a similar boom after the arrival of Henry Flagler, who built a series of hotels catering to wealthy folk from colder regions. Starting in St. Augustine and extending both his hotels and his narrow-gauge railroad southward, Flagler built an empire all the way to Key West. The real estate he acquired was ultimately more profitable than the railroad itself.

America Urbanizes

At the beginning of the nineteenth century, land speculation centered on land for agriculture; by the end of the century, the emphasis was on land for cities. America's cities grew dramatically during the 1800s. In 1790, only one out of thirty Americans lived in towns and cities; by the end of the nineteenth century, one out of three did. In 1800, only 6 cities had populations of 8000 or more; by the end of the century, there were almost 500.[2] America was urbanizing at a rapid pace.

The Move to the Cities

Several factors enticed people to the cities. Rural areas were continually subject to extended depressions; the cities offered jobs. Many of the conveniences of the city—electricity, trolley cars, telephones—had not reached the countryside. To the rural American, the cities promised excitement and economic opportunity.

America's urbanization was also accelerated by greatly expanded immigration, particularly from Europe. These immigrants concentrated in the large cities. By 1890, one-fourth of Philadelphia's and one-third of Chicago's residents were foreign born. In New York City, four out of five were either of foreign birth or foreign parentage.[3]

The crush of humanity into the cities created slum areas and fostered

[2]*1776–1936,* University of Nebraska Press, Lincoln, 1942, p. 223 (paperback). John M. Blum et al., *The National Experience,* 3d ed., Harcourt Brace Jovanovich, New York, 1973, vol. 2, p. 441.

[3]Ibid., p. 445.

the development in 1879 of the "railroad" apartment building, which allowed developers to crowd several families onto a single site. By 1890, 37,000 tenement buildings had been built in New York City alone—housing more than half of the city's population.[4]

The Emergence of the Skyscraper

The rapidly escalating cost of urban land forced developers to discover ways of increasing the intensity of commercial properties as well. Chicago, led by the vision of architect Louis Sullivan, was the first city in which skyscraper construction was used. In 1892, the Masonic Temple rose twenty-one stories. Not to be outdone, New York surpassed Chicago in 1899 with the construction of the St. Paul Building. Opposition to skyscrapers raged as buildings grew higher. New York's Flatiron Building, completed in 1902, generated much controversy, but its great commercial success encouraged other Manhattan real estate entrepreneurs. As a result, New York became the worldwide center of real estate development and speculation. The Woolworth Building, costing $13.5 million, opened in 1913 and remained the world's tallest building until the Empire State Building was completed almost two decades later.

Real estate activity in New York and other cities was curtailed by World War I and the postwar depression. It resumed in the early 1920s as America headed for its greatest binge yet. Land speculation also reached new heights in Florida (shortly afterward it was devastated by a hurricane), California, and New York. Residential developments and office-building activity continued unabated.

Several men left their mark on Manhattan and the nation's real estate community during the 1920s. Harry Black, the developer of the Flatiron Building, established high-rise construction as a viable method of providing space in major urban areas. Ellsworth Statler developed a national chain of major hotels. Fred French pioneered the concept of large, in-town residential communities with his Tudor City development on the east side of Manhattan, opening up the area for the extensive development activity that would follow World War II.

The Rail Suburbs

As new migrants from rural America and Europe crowded into the cities, the wealthy moved out. The advent of good passenger rail service

[4]Ibid., p. 446.

Figure 1-3. Flatiron Building, New York City, 1904. *(United Press International Photo)*

allowed the wealthy to live in the suburbs and work in the central city. The first truly modern rail suburb was Branch Hill, developed in 1887, 20 miles from Cincinnati. Soon, rail suburbs sprang up around New York, Chicago, Boston, Philadelphia, and other cities.

One of the most famous rail suburbs was Shaker Heights, near Cleveland. Developed in the early 1900s by the Van Sweringen brothers, Shaker Heights was one of the most successful suburban developments of the 1920s. Its innovative planning and design, including beautiful landscaping and community facilities, set the standard for later suburban development.

Perhaps the most ambitious suburban rail promotion was that of Henry Huntington in Los Angeles. Between 1901 and 1920 Huntington laid almost 1200 miles of track for his famous "red cars," which connected virtually all of the small towns in the Los Angeles basin. Land serviced by the system increased in value, and Huntington and others reaped huge profits.

Depression and War

The crash of the stock market in 1929 dried up funds for many of the ambitious projects that had just recently been announced. It became

Figure 1-4. Shaker Heights, Ohio, 1926. (Plain Dealer, *Cleveland*)

difficult to lease completed projects, and many buildings were foreclosed. The Empire State Building, almost one-third vacant, soon became known as the "Empty State Building." Land values plummeted.

During the Depression, only a few projects proceeded. French developed another residential project, Knickerbocker Village, in a slum-infested area of the lower east side. Rockefeller Center, originally conceived in 1926 as a single building to replace the Metropolitan Opera House, grew to ten buildings by 1935, introducing many precedent-setting ideas: a large open plaza, the use of a private street, underground concourses, and large underground parking facilities. It ultimately became the prototype for other large-scale, multiuse projects throughout the country.

When the United States entered World War II, unemployment vanished almost overnight. Consumer goods became scarce and were rationed. Except for building related to the war effort, new construction fell to virtually zero. During the war, several factors developed which would profoundly affect real estate in postwar America. First, overall economic activity increased dramatically. Much of the increase went toward war production, but the experience of living with an expanded economy, which would be able to handle greater domestic production after the war, proved infectious. Second, social patterns changed: marriages increased, women went into the labor force, racial barriers were eased, and people adapted to a more transitory way of life. Third, the lack of domestic construction, combined with the lower construction levels of the Depression years, led to strong pent-up demand, particularly for housing.

Suburbia Dominant

No factor was to affect postwar real estate more than America's love affair with the automobile. Mass ownership of the automobile opened up entirely new opportunities: residential suburbs in areas totally unrelated to rail service, suburban shopping centers that would literally become "new downtowns," industrial and office parks that would ultimately shift the majority of jobs to the suburbs, and large multiuse complexes that would effectively incorporate a variety of activities in a single synergistic hub.

Suburban Residential Development

The rail suburbs at the turn of the twentieth century consisted of relatively large homes directed primarily toward the wealthy. Only the limited amount of land along the railroad was available for their development. In suburban communities, land was generally valued according to its proximity to rail commuter stations.

Mass ownership of the automobile changed this pattern. No longer was it necessary to live along the rail line. With World War II over, the combination of the automobile, higher personal incomes, and pent-up wartime demand appeared to provide all of the ingredients for a postwar suburban housing boom.

But this did not occur. In 1947, housing starts were little better than in 1946; prices, however, were up substantially. It was evident that both the production and the financing of housing had to be made more efficient if any form of mass housing production were to occur. Responding to the need, Congress, which had established the Federal Housing Administration (FHA) in 1934 but had insufficiently funded it, substantially increased FHA's appropriation and also established the Federal National Mortgage Association (FNMA, nicknamed "Fannie Mae") to assure a second money market for FHA loans. The Veterans Administration also guaranteed mortgage loans to U.S. war veterans.

Beset by rising labor and materials costs, the private housing industry was forced to improve production efficiency. On Long Island, New

York, builder William Jaird Levitt decided to adapt mass production techniques to housing. Levitt and Sons acquired acreage near Hicksville, Long Island. Wishing to sell a house for under $8000 and still make a profit, they designed a more efficient unit, used prefabricated material, broke the house-building process into components, utilized nonunion labor, and began a vertical integration process to eliminate the middleman. Directing sales primarily toward returning veterans, the Levitts sold over 17,000 units in Levittown by the time the project closed out in 1951. They went on to apply this successful formula elsewhere in the United States and Europe.

Not all who moved to the suburbs wished or could afford to live in a single-family home, yet they didn't want the conformity of a high-rise apartment. The solution was the garden apartment, which combined the convenience of apartment living with the openness of suburban life. This gave a boost to multifamily construction, which accounted for more than one-third of annual private housing starts by 1965, and 36 percent of all private housing starts during the 1970s.[5]

The Suburban Shopping Center

As central city merchants watched their customers flee to the suburbs, they reluctantly decided they had better follow. Before long, suburban stores were outselling those in the central city.

The first suburban branch stores, along with the stores of local merchants, were generally located in strips on both sides of major arterials. As the number of merchants increased, however, the strip became too long for easy shopping, parking was a serious problem, and traffic congestion threatened to stifle business activity.

The answer was to assemble the merchants' stores in a planned "center" owned by a single developer. The first major regional center was Northgate near Seattle, Washington, and others were developed in suburban areas throughout the nation: Shoppers' World near Framingham, Massachusetts; Roosevelt Field on Long Island; Cross County in Yonkers, New York; Hillsdale south of San Francisco; and Northland Center in the Detroit suburbs.

The single responsibility for planning and development provided shopping center developers with a unique opportunity to overcome a problem faced by all retailers—inclement weather. In 1956, the nation's first major enclosed mall center, Southdale, opened in Edina, Minnesota. Southdale also introduced the concept of having more than

[5] U.S. Bureau of the Census, *Construction Reports,* series C20.

(a)

(b)

Figure 1-5. Farmland becomes suburbia: Valley Stream, Long Island, New York, 1933 (*a*) and 1959 (*b*). *(Jones Beach State Parkway Authority)*

Figure 1-6. The nation's first enclosed mall shopping center: Southdale Center, Edina, a suburb of Minneapolis, Minnesota. *(Dayton Hudson Properties)*

one department store in the same center, a revolutionary thought for retailers at the time. Other enclosed mall centers followed: Cherry Hill near Pennsauken, New Jersey; Topanga Plaza in Los Angeles; and Eastridge near San Jose.

Industrial Parks

Not too long after consumers and businesses began moving to the suburbs, industry followed suit for several reasons: land was cheap and could be assembled in large parcels, buildings could be constructed on a single floor to allow more efficient flow processing, adequate parking could be readily provided, and, importantly, many executives lived in the suburbs and could avoid the commute to the central city.

The first firms to build new facilities in the suburbs were large manufacturers. Smaller firms, wishing to be nearby, purchased land or leased buildings from local developers. Little regard was given to problems such as air pollution, waste disposal, parking, traffic, aesthetics, or interfaces with other uses, such as residential.

Sensing an opportunity, several developers began creating industrial "districts" and "parks" where industry could purchase or lease land and buildings within a planned environment which would regulate each firm's operation according to certain minimum standards. The first major postwar industrial park, the New England Industrial Center near Boston, opened in 1953. The same year, Windsor Properties began developing the Brookhollow Industrial District outside Dallas. Other industrial parks were developed throughout the United States, the majority of them located in the suburbs.

Office Parks

Eventually research and development (R&D) firms decided to follow manufacturing firms to the suburbs. As problems in the central city grew, more and more manufacturers moved their office operations to the suburbs. It wasn't long before suburban office parks developed that limited manufacturing and distributive uses. The first of these was Mountain Brook Office Park near Birmingham, Alabama, which opened in 1952. Three years later, the Middlesex Mutual Trust Company opened the Hobbs Brook Office Park on Route 128 in Waltham, Massachusetts. Suburban office parks developed in other areas: Del Amo Financial Center in Los Angeles, Executive Park near Atlanta, Gamble Center and Norman Center in the Minneapolis suburbs, Ward Parkway Office Center near Kansas City, Oakland Office Research and Industrial Park in Bergen County, New Jersey, and the Denver Technological and Executive Park, one of the finest early examples of office park development.

Mixed-Use Developments

As residential, commercial, industrial, and finally, office firms moved to the suburbs, developers in certain sections of the country began creating large, mixed-use projects which could house a number of land uses within the framework of an overall master plan. The various uses could thus complement one another in a synergistic fashion, bringing the developer a greater return than would single-use development.

One of the earliest was Oak Brook, which opened in the Chicago suburbs in 1960. This project combined residential, commercial, hotel, industrial, and office uses. On a more urban scale, Galleria Post Oak in suburban Houston opened in 1969, connecting a shopping mall, office buildings, and a 450-room luxury hotel.

(a)

(b)

Figure 1-7. Pioneer industrial and office parks. (*a*) New England Industrial Center, Needham, Massachusetts and (*b*) Mountain Brook Office Park near Birmingham, Alabama. Note the similarity in layout except for the taller buildings in the office park. *[(a) Cabot, Cabot & Forbes and (b) Jackson Company]*

The Search for Alternatives

By 1970, the dominance of suburbia was complete. In some suburbs, whole new "downtowns" were being created around major regional shopping centers and mixed-use complexes. As suburbs began to emulate the central cities, they also fell prey to many city-like problems: air and noise pollution, traffic congestion, waste disposal, and what many had come to the suburbs to avoid—crime. The search began for alternatives to the dominance of suburbia. There were clearly three: (1) improve conditions in the central city, (2) make the suburbs more livable, or (3) develop totally new towns.

The Struggle to Revitalize the Central City

In the view of central city residents, suburbs might have the problems, but they also had the resources—people, jobs, retail sales. The central cities, on the other hand, had greater problems and dwindling resources. The problem was further compounded by an influx of millions of poor, largely rural families. Often without jobs or even the skills to get jobs, they lived in the deteriorating housing that the middle class had left behind in its flight to suburbia.

Urban Renewal. Increasingly, beleaguered cities turned to the federal government for assistance. The Housing Act of 1949 was the first federal program to address the task of urban renewal. The Housing Act of 1954 emphasized the rehabilitation of existing structures and the conservation of neighborhoods, offered funds to guarantee bank loans for these purposes, and emphasized commercial and industrial uses over residential. In 1959, cities were encouraged to plan more comprehensively for redevelopment activities through a Community Renewal Plan (CRP). In 1966, assistance for expanded social and economic activity was enacted under the "Model Cities" program.

The Housing Act of 1968 established 10-year housing production goals and sought to eliminate all substandard housing. The Act also introduced government guarantees for financing and developing new towns and established a national housing "partnership" to attract more private funds into low- and moderate-income housing.

Many cities throughout the nation took advantage of the various federal urban renewal programs. One of the earliest and most successful programs was undertaken in Philadelphia, where the rebuilding requirements of the central city were carefully meshed with the restoration of the city's historic buildings. Boston used urban renewal to rebuild its Government Center, thereby spurring private redevelopment. Under San Francisco's renewal program a large portion of the Embarcadero and Western Addition was rebuilt.

Other cities with comprehensive urban renewal programs for their central cities included New York, Chicago, Minneapolis, St. Paul, Washington, D.C., Hartford, Richmond, Portland, and Cincinnati. Some cities, notably Cleveland, St. Louis, Detroit, and Newark, were not as successful: large amounts of cleared acreage stood vacant, with little or no developer interest. By 1972 the federal government had spent $10.9 billion on 2481 urban renewal projects, with many more billions spent in private construction. In 496 completed projects, assessed values had increased 228 percent over pre-redevelopment levels on one-third less taxable land area.[6] Still, urban renewal was considered by many to have been a failed policy that did not address the root causes of urban deterioration. Instead, critics claimed, it resulted in the wholesale destruction of neighborhoods, displacing the very people it was intended to help.

Public and Private Partnerships. In the face of this criticism, urban renewal gave way to new strategies for redeveloping the nation's cities that relied more on partnerships between private enterprise and federal, state, and local governments. Under President Ford, the Community Development Act of 1977 was signed into law and the Community Development Block Grant (CDBG) program was formed. Under the program, individual cities applied for grant money which was used for restoration and upgrading of existing buildings rather than tearing down slums.

Many of these projects were carried out under the Urban Development Action Grant (UDAG) title of the 1977 Act, which provided grants for commercial and industrial projects that promised to boost real estate taxes and create new jobs. Tax incentives encouraged the renovation of older buildings. Between 1978 and 1983, the UDAG program provided $3 billion in grant monies to urban communities.

The Housing and Community Development Act of 1977 sought to further stimulate private investment in urban revitalization. The Act extended the CDBG program, targeting funds primarily for capital projects to conserve energy and correct violations of health and safety codes.

[6]U.S. Department of Housing and Urban Development, *1972 HUD Statistical Yearbook,* 1974.

(a)

(b)

Figure 1-8. Independence Mall, Philadelphia, Pennsylvania, before (mid-1950s) redevelopment (*a*) and after (1973) redevelopment (*b*). Note Independence Hall in the foreground. *(Development Authority, City of Philadelphia)*

State and local governments helped as well, providing direct aid and tax incentives to spur private development efforts. As a result, a number of cities, including Newark and St. Louis, that had been devastated by urban renewal became revitalized.

Historic Preservation. Some of the thrust for redevelopment in the central cities came from a revival of interest in preserving historic buildings. In 1965, New York State passed the Landmarks Preservation Law, restricting changes that could be made to designated historic buildings. This spurred Congress, in 1966, to establish the National Register of Historic Places and begin providing grants to the states for preservation of historic sites. The movement grew and spread, until today it would be difficult to find any city, small or large, that has not undertaken at least one historic renovation project.

Much of the preservation movement involved the *adaptive use* of a building to a new use more compatible with current market conditions. The prototype for adaptive use projects was Ghirardelli Square, an abandoned chocolate factory in San Francisco that reopened as a specialty shopping center in 1964. Today, nearly every major city around

Figure 1-9. St. Louis Union Station, one of the largest adaptive use projects in the country. Originally a thriving railroad terminal dating to 1894, the station, a certified National Historic Landmark, was reopened in 1985 as a hotel-retail complex, after a $150 million development effort. *(St. Louis Union Station)*

the country boasts a renovated old theater, factory, train station, or office building that would almost certainly have been razed 20 years ago.

Federal tax laws over the past decade helped to make the preservation movement possible. The Economic Recovery Tax Act (ERTA) of 1981 allowed an income tax credit of 25 percent of the cost of renovating certified historic structures. Nonhistoric buildings more than 30 years old could qualify for income tax credits up to 20 percent if they were put to commercial use. Under the Tax Reform Act of 1986, tax credits were reduced but not before significant progress was made: since 1981 an estimated $11 billion has been spent to renovate some 17,000 historic buildings in 1800 cities and towns.[7]

The preservation movement has not been without its critics, who charge, among other things, that rent increases in historic areas drive up prices and result in *gentrification,* the taking over of poor neighborhoods by upwardly mobile, usually young, homeowners. Nevertheless, few critics would deny that the move to preserve the architectural heritage of the American city has added to the appeal of urban living.

New Urban Developer. The efforts of the central cities to revitalize themselves created a new breed of urban developer—aggressive, resourceful, and adept at conceiving large projects requiring a close working relationship between the private and public sectors. Probably the most famous of these was William Zeckendorf, who, in addition to his activities in New York City, contributed significantly to Place Ville Marie in Montreal, Mile High Center in Denver, and L'Enfant Plaza in Washington, D.C. Zeckendorf's high-flying bubble burst in 1965, but in 20 frantic years he had radically altered the face of many U.S. cities and proved that the central city could survive and regain its place as the vital center of a metropolitan area.

Zeckendorf's legacy has been carried forward by other creative, farsighted men, among them John Portman, with Peachtree Center in Atlanta; Trammell Crow, with Embarcadero Center in San Francisco; Donald Knudsen with Gateway Center in Minneapolis; Arthur Rubloff, with Carl Sandburg Village in Chicago; and James Rouse with Baltimore's Harborplace and Boston's Faneuil Hall Marketplace.

[7]Kurt Anderson, "Spiffing Up the Urban Heritage," *Time,* November 23, 1987, p. 79.

Figure 1-10. Montreal was one of the early leaders in the trend toward mixed-use developments. Place Ville Marie, opened in 1962, is noted for its crucible-form central office tower and three-story underground shopping concourse. *(Trizec Equities Limited)*

New Alternatives in Suburban Residential Development

A second alternative was to improve the suburbs themselves. While progress was made in the areas of shopping centers and industrial parks, suburban residential development continued to reflect the depressing "cookie cutter" subdivisions of the initial postwar years, with their inefficient provision of public amenities. In attempting to solve these problems, land planners evolved the "cluster" concept, which maintained the same basic density levels as single-family subdivisionsbut clustered housing units together in groups, thereby reducing public service costs and allowing for the development of additional usable

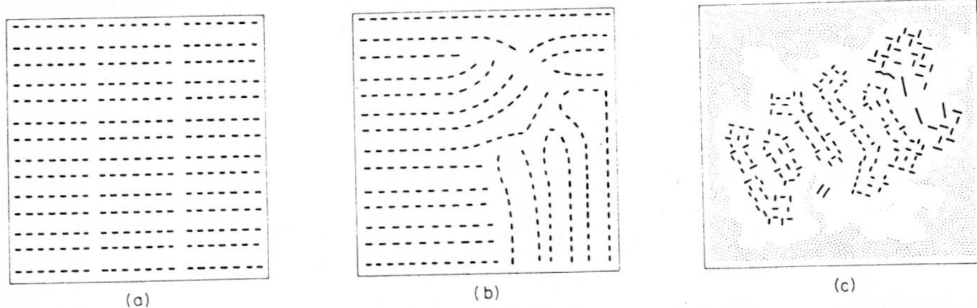

Figure 1-11. Various approaches to subdivision planning. (*a*) Traditional "grid" street pattern, (*b*) curvilinear or "contour" pattern, and (*c*) "cluster" pattern.

open space. While clustering solved the design problem, there was still the question of how ownership of these units could be legally recognized.

The Housing Act of 1961 provided the solution. Section 234 extended FHA mortgage insurance guarantees to a new form of housing ownership called condominiums. The condominium concept called for individual ownership of air space within each unit and collective ownership of common areas, such as walkways, swimming pools, and open areas. A mortgage would be issued to each individual owner, with the costs of common area maintenance paid monthly on a pro rata basis. Condominiums were slow to gain acceptance. Lenders were often reluctant to lend against air space, buyers were confused about the new concept, and marketing efforts were often discouraging. In many cases, cities were reluctant to approve condominiums, which seemed to many a ruse for higher density. The concept finally caught on, however; by 1973 the annual production of condominium units was a major component of new housing starts in many urban areas and remains so today.

The development of the condominium was critical to the implementation of new planning techniques because it freed the building from a single parcel of land, allowing for more efficient clustering of units. The legal concept of the condominium and the physical concept of cluster housing were finally pulled together through the development of a new model zoning ordinance called a planned unit development (PUD). The ordinance provided cities with a comprehensive package for cluster development. Despite opposition from many communities, the PUD concept took hold in the 1960s. PUDs lost some popularity during the mid-1970s, when high interest rates made large residential projects more difficult to build, but today they are regarded as a major tool in improving the residential environment of the suburbs.

The Total Alternative: New Towns

Important as PUDs were, many believed that what was needed was a totally "new" town in which the development of *all* land uses and activities could be carried out under comprehensive planning and management control. England, the Scandinavian countries, France, Canada, Israel, the Netherlands, Germany, India, Brazil, and the Soviet Union had utilized government-sponsored new towns extensively since World War II to redistribute population. Early new town development in the United States was largely a private effort. In southern California, postwar population growth extended suburban frontiers far beyond the central city. Lying in the path of this "sprawl" was a series of large land holdings, many dating back to early Spanish land grants. These ranches were being used for agriculture and other relatively low-intensity uses. With approaching urbanization, increasing property taxes made it difficult to profit from these uses. This squeeze, combined with the owners' awareness of the opportunities for potential profits from land development, led several large ranches to begin preliminary land use planning.

The largest was the Irvine Ranch, which covered more than 100,000 acres of land in Orange County, California. Development began on the ranch in 1962 and a part of it was incorporated as the City of Irvine in 1971. The Irvine Company, developers of the community, donated 10,000 acres for a new campus of the University of California. The development also encompasses several large residential neighborhoods, a major regional shopping and office center, an airport, and two large industrial parks. Today Irvine covers 28,000 acres of land, has a population of 99,000, and employs 100,000 workers. Other large developments in California were Janss/Conejo, Valencia, Laguna Niguel, Westlake Village, Mission Viejo, Rancho Bernardo, Rancho California in the south, and Foster City in northern California.

In the East, two major new towns were emerging near the nation's capital. The first of these, Reston, was begun by Robert E. Simon in 1963 on 7400 acres of rolling countryside in Fairfax County, Virginia. In 1967 Simon was bought out by his financial partner, Gulf Oil Corporation, which largely continued Simon's original plan. In 1976 Reston Land Corporation, a Mobil Oil subsidiary, took over the development role. Reston now houses a population of 50,000 and more than 1000 businesses.

The second major new town in the East was Columbia, located on 14,000 acres in Howard County, Maryland. Developed by James W. Rouse, Columbia's goals were social as well as economic, providing a

Figure 1-12. Lake Anne Village Center, Reston, Virginia. The shopping area at the left, the high-rise apartment building at the right, and townhouses, condominiums, and single-family homes nestle around the 27-acre lake. *(Reston Land Corporation)*

complete range of housing to meet the needs of all potential residents. In addition to residential uses, 20 percent was set aside for business and industry, 36 percent for open space and recreational areas, and the rest for cultural, medical, educational, and other facilities. Columbia's population has grown to 67,000 and the community provides jobs for 42,000 workers.

Although much of the early effort was private, the federal government finally got involved through the Housing Act of 1968. Title VII of the act authorized the Department of Housing and Urban Development (HUD) to guarantee financing for land acquisition and development by new town developers. In return, the developers had to demonstrate the validity of their planning, scheduling, financial resources, and development capability. Plans that were approved could receive up to $50 million in federal guarantees for the purchase of land, installation of public services, and for planning and management activities. Approximately fifteen new towns were announced under this program, including Park Forest South near Chicago and the Woodlands near Houston. The Woodlands in particular was successful, today incorporating 25,000 acres of land, supporting a population of 20,000 and providing 6000 jobs for area residents.

Not all new towns were in the suburbs. The idea of the "New Town

Intown" was introduced by Dr. Harvey Perloff, former Dean of the School of Architecture and Urban Planning at the University of California at Los Angeles. The concept involved redevelopment and rehabilitation within the boundaries of the central city. To that end, the Urban Growth and Community Development Act of 1970 provided funds for the New Town Intown program until the early 1980s. Projects undertaken under the Act were Cedar-Riverside in Minneapolis and Roosevelt Island in New York.[8]

Changing Leisure Patterns

As the nation struggled to find viable methods for dealing with urban and suburban growth, major changes were taking place in the way Americans spent their leisure time. Personal incomes were rising substantially and the work week was shrinking. Greater affluence postponed entry into the labor force and encouraged earlier retirements. The advent of jet travel expanded the geographic scope of leisure opportunities. America was slowly relaxing its work ethic.

The Public Lodging Industry Comes of Age

Increased travel meant people had to have a place to stay. As a result of the Depression and war, however, America's stock of guest rooms was old and largely obsolete. The process of creating new public lodging facilities geared to changing postwar patterns began.

One man soon emerged as the leader in new hotel development and management. In the early years after the war, Conrad Hilton purchased and renovated older hotels such as the Plaza and Waldorf Astoria in New York City, the Stevens and Palmer House in Chicago, and the Town House in Los Angeles. He introduced his famous "digging for gold" program, which converted unoccupied space to profitable use. His success continued, and during the 1950s he expanded to a worldwide operation.

Other hotel chains in the United States were expanding operations. Sheraton, utilizing a franchise approach, built new facilities in virtually every major American city. Western International (now Westin) expanded out of the Pacific Northwest into San Francisco, the Southwest,

[8]Arthur Gallion and Simon Eisner, *The Urban Pattern: City Planning and Design*, 5th ed., Van Nostrand Reinhold, New York, 1986, pp. 561–562.

Figure 1-13. Atrium lobby of Hyatt Regency Hotel, Atlanta, Georgia. *(Hyatt Corporation)*

and, ultimately, Chicago and New York. Hyatt joined with architect-developer John Portman in introducing then-radical concepts of hotel design in Atlanta, Chicago, and San Francisco.

The hotel industry failed to note, however, the impact of the automobile on real estate in postwar America. The automobile opened up travel to a new generation of Americans, many of whom, traveling with families, could not afford hotel accommodations. Furthermore, after a hard day's journey such travelers weren't interested in the prestige and full service provided by traditional hotels. They wanted cheap, clean rooms which were located near the highways on which they were traveling.

The answer was the motel. Although several thousand tourist courts had operated prior to World War II, the expanding postwar highway construction program as well as pent-up travel demand from gas rationing and other wartime restrictions caused the phenomenal growth of the motel industry. By 1954, over half the nation's guest rooms were in motels which accounted for 16 percent of total industry sales.[9]

[9]Howard E. Morgan, *The Motel Industry in the United States: Small Business in Transition,* Bureau of Business and Public Research, University of Arizona, Tucson, 1964, p. 187.

Several enterprising entrepreneurs saw exceptional opportunities in the rapid growth of the motel industry. One such man was Kemmons Wilson, founder of the Holiday Inn chain. He hit on a successful formula that appealed to a large segment of the American motoring public, particularly families and the commercial traveler. The formula combined many of the conveniences of hotels—large rooms, double beds, telephone and television, restaurants, and swimming pools—with motel features not offered by most hotels—accessibility to major highways, parking, lower rates, no charge for children under 12, a computerized reservation system, and an informal atmosphere that made the road-weary traveler feel welcome.

The success of the Holiday Inns led to a series of other major motel chains including Ramada Inns, Quality Courts, Best Western, and Howard Johnson. Finally recognizing that motels were here to stay, several of the major hotel chains—Hilton, Sheraton, Hyatt, and Marriott—began developing "inns" at locations near airports and major sources of activity.

As the hotel chains entered the field, motels looked increasingly like hotels. The original concept of the motel, that is, simple, cheap lodging, seemed to get lost in the shuffle. It was only a matter of time, therefore, until the wheel turned full circle and the "budget" motel was introduced. One of the major pioneers of this concept was Motel 6 in California, which offered a basic room for $6 per night, regardless of season or location. Its rates were kept low by construction and design innovations, labor-saving operating techniques, and a continuing refusal to get into the restaurant or convention business.

In recent years the lodging industry has become increasingly competitive, partly in response to a wave of overbuilding, and market segmentation, involving increasingly aggressive marketing techniques and service improvements, has become an important factor in the success of the individual players in the marketplace.

Divots, Sitzmarks, Catwalks, and Double Faults

As Americans experienced greater leisure time, they turned more and more to participation in athletic activities: golf, skiing, boating, and tennis. Initially, facilities for these activities were developed exclusively for the purpose of the sport. As the facilities grew in scale, however, developers began to see the profit potential in utilizing participation sports to sell real estate.

Golf was the first major participation sport to gain extensive acceptance after World War II. The number of golf courses in the United

States increased from 4808 in 1945 to 11,134 in 1974.[10] Golf courses were developed in sprawling suburban areas as well as resort areas. Palm Springs, California, as an example, became a major resort largely through the development of a series of fine golf courses. In urban areas, golf courses were tied in with new residential subdivisions. Developers soon realized that, while they might not make money on a golf course operation, they could more than pay for the cost of the course through higher residential land values.

Another sport that took off after World War II was skiing. With the refinement of the mechanical lift, downhill skiing was suddenly less arduous and much more appealing to Americans with newly found leisure time. Traditional ski resorts such as Stowe, Sun Valley, Aspen, and Lake Tahoe expanded operations. Entirely new projects were developed: Snowmass-at-Aspen and Vail in Colorado, Sugarbush in Vermont, Park City and Snowbird in Utah, and Killington, Stratton, and Waterville Valley in New England. It was clear to the developers that the profit was not on the slopes but at the bottom of the hill, in the form of hotels, restaurants, and other service facilities, as well as the sale of second home lots and condominiums.

Americans also took to the water. As the sale of pleasure boats increased, entrepreneurs began developing marinas and other facilities. In areas such as Florida and California, boating was tied into residential and commercial real estate developments. Marina del Rey in California, one of the largest marinas in the nation, was financed largely on the basis of increased real estate values. In inland areas, marina development activity concentrated on lakes and rivers, where the promise of boating activity was often one of the major lures in attracting prospective residential buyers.

Tennis boomed in the 1970s as well. As a result, tennis clubs, both outdoor and indoor, were established in virtually every city in the country. In California and Texas, "tennis ranches" emerged, in which a noted professional saturates hardy guests in dawn-to-dusk tennis instruction. In terms of real estate, tennis was attractive not only as a direct investment but also as a means of selling houses and renting apartments. Subdivisions that in the past would have used a golf course as a marketing tool now began turning to tennis. The fact that tennis requires much less land and capital investment than golf has also influenced this trend.

The growing emphasis on physical fitness in the 1980s has led to yet another type of resort activity, namely, the health and fitness center.

[10]National Golf Foundation, *Information Sheet,* Golf Facilities in the United States, Chicago, 1974.

Figure 1-14. Harbour Town in Sea Pines Plantation, Hilton Head Island, South Carolina. *(Sea Pines Plantation Company, Inc.)*

The Snowmass Club in Colorado is one example of a resort facility that capitalized on America's fitness craze. The Club combines the luxury of a first-class resort with a fully equipped health spa. Guests can choose from a wide array of exercise classes. A staff physiologist is on hand, and the dining room offers nutritionally sound meals.

The combination of increased travel and greater emphasis on participation sports ultimately led to the reintroduction of "destination resorts," where harassed urban dwellers can select from a wide variety of sporting activities at a single location. Destination resorts date back to the late 1800s and early 1900s. In those days, resorts such as Broadmoor in Colorado, Biltmore in Arizona, and Homestead in Virginia relied on rail transportation to bring guests to their facilities. Today, many destination resorts are located in tropical vacation spots: Caneel Bay in the Virgin Islands, Dorado Beach in Puerto Rico, and Mauna Kea, Kaanapali, and Waikoloa in Hawaii.

The Boom in Second Homes

The idea of a second or "country" home was not new to postwar America: the wealthy had owned them for years. But with rising incomes, more middle-class Americans could enjoy the luxury of a second home. This trend was further encouraged by tax advantages which allowed the owner to deduct many of the costs of ownership if the units were rented a certain portion of the year (recent changes in the tax laws have limited these deductions). Another factor was earlier retirement ages; the second home allowed a smooth transition between employment and retirement.

Initially, second homes were developed by local builders in areas near major urban areas. As travel times decreased, however, second homes began emerging in more remote areas, often connected with major sporting activities: Sun Valley, Stowe, Lake Tahoe, Aspen, Vail, and others.

For those who could not afford a second home, the concept of timesharing provided a way to own a piece of property for a limited number of days each year. The idea started in Europe in the 1960s, and in 1969 the first U.S. timeshare resort, Kauai Kailani, opened in Hawaii. Since then everything from hotels and motels to lodges, villas, and recreational vehicle parks have taken advantage of the concept.

It was only a matter of time before projects that combined the features of a destination resort with a second-home community evolved: Sea Pines Plantation in South Carolina, Sunriver in central Oregon, New Seabury on Cape Cod, Amelia Island in Florida, and Big Sky in Montana. Well planned and heavily financed, these projects often appealed to wealthy individuals who were repulsed by the land use hodgepodge of older resorts. Most of the projects emphasized strong architectural design and harmony with nature. While a portion of the income was generated from resort-type operations, the profit was clearly in the development and sale of second homes.

The boom in second homes created an even greater boom in land speculation. Promoters, who offered liberal financing and used high-pressure sales tactics, began carving up Lake Tahoe, the Poconos, the Florida coast, and much of the state of Vermont. Initially, most of these promoters were local operators; gradually, large corporations such as Boise Cascade, ITT, International Paper, GAC, General Development, American Standard, and Dart Industries moved in to dominate the industry. The general reputation of these firms didn't stop the public from worrying about the sales tactics and the environmental impact of land speculation in second home areas. Finally, Congress passed the Land Sales Full Disclosure Act of 1968, which required developers to register information on subdivisions of more than fifty lots. Two years later, as a result of the Housing and Urban Development Act of 1970, HUD began investigating abuses within the industry. This was only one of many indications that the development of real estate was becoming less of an inalienable right and more of a negotiated privilege offered or withheld by governmental agencies.

2
The Ground Rules Change

Let us tell the developers and let us tell the rest of the country right here and now that Vermont is not for sale.

THOMAS P. SALMON,
Governor of Vermont,
January 1973

HUD's investigation of second home development practices was but one example of the fact that governmental agencies at all levels were taking a much broader role in real estate development in the late 1960s and early 1970s. As noted in Chapter 1, government has always been involved in land development in America. Historically, however, government *encouraged* development through a variety of devices: granting land to the early land companies; developing transportation facilities such as canals, railroads, and the interstate highway system; expanding home ownership through such vehicles as homesteading, FHA, and favorable income tax treatment; and subsidizing the central cities through urban renewal, private-public partnerships, and public housing. This policy of encouraging development directly affected Western expansion, the settlement of the cities, and the explosive growth of the suburbs.

Implicit in governmental support of development has been the tacit presumption that "growth is good" in that it creates employment opportunities, increases property values, and provides greater public revenues. Less obvious have been the attendant problems of growth: overcrowded housing, traffic congestion, crime, air pollution, and unsightly urban sprawl.

In recent years, increasing numbers of Americans have questioned the "growth-for-growth's sake" concept. Many have suggested that government should take a stronger role in limiting, or at least directing, the location, magnitude, and quality of land uses. The "inalienable right" of landowners to develop their property as they personally desire is coming into question.

The Evolution of Planning and Zoning in America

City planning goes back a long way in America. Most New England towns had a village square, or common, in the center of town. The Dutch planned New Amsterdam in 1660 in a pattern similar to the Dutch towns they knew best. Williamsburg, laid out in 1699, was planned on the scale of English towns. In 1682, William Penn commissioned a plan for Philadelphia, with two major streets crossing in the center of the city to form a public square. The streets divided the city into four separate quadrants, each with its own public park. In 1733, Oglethorpe laid out Savannah on a somewhat similar basis. Washington and Jefferson adopted a plan for the new capital in Washington, which was based on a classical plan prepared by a French designer, Major Pierre Charles L'Enfant, in 1791. The L'Enfant plan, patterned after French cities, called for a series of wide, radial boulevards, with the traditional gridiron layout superimposed on them.

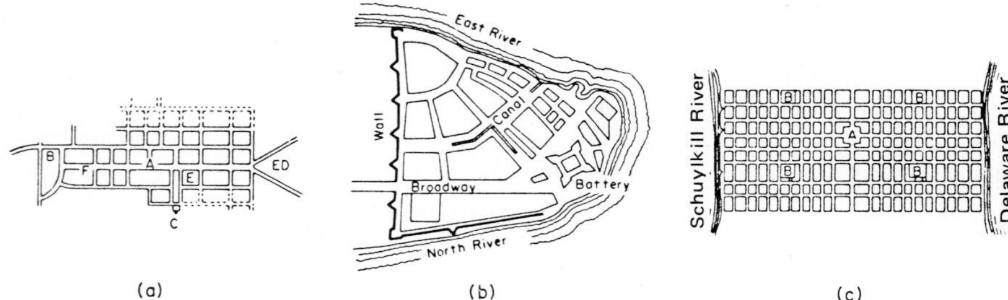

Figure 2-1. Early U.S. planning efforts. (*a*) Williamsburg, Virginia, 1699. A, Market Square; B, the Capitol; C, the Governor's Palace; D, College of William and Mary; E, Bruton Parish Church; F, Duke of Gloucester Street. (*b*) New Amsterdam (New York City), New York, 1660. (*c*) Philadelphia, Pennsylvania, 1682. A, City Square; B, parks.

Coping with Industrialization

Despite the visionary proposals of many planners in the early 1800s, the pressures of industrialization were catching up with the cities. As more and more people came to the cities to find jobs, pressure on land values intensified. In 1811, New York rejected a proposal based on the L'Enfant plan and decided to replan the rest of Manhattan on a very tight gridiron, allowing virtually no open space (Central Park wasn't set aside until 45 years later). This emphasis on economy set the stage for the planning of most new cities in the next 40 to 50 years. The only plan that remained relatively untouched was Washington, D.C.'s, where industry and commerce were largely excluded.

With the growth of industrialization, sanitary conditions in the cities began to deteriorate. By 1840 the typical American city was littered with garbage, and deadly diseases were commonplace. A sanitary reform movement focused public attention once more on the need for city planning to alleviate sewage and drainage problems.

In the second half of the nineteenth century, European cities started responding to the pressures of industrialization. In 1853, Napoleon III started a 17-year program to open up a series of broad avenues through Paris. In England and Germany, industrialists began to develop "model towns" for their workers. In 1870, Sweden established a program to lend public funds to nonprofit "public utility companies" engaged in housing. Germany and the Netherlands enacted similar legislation shortly thereafter. The British Housing Law of 1890 empowered local governments to condemn land and buildings in order to develop housing for the working class.

Progress was slower in the United States. In 1857, Frederick Law Olmsted won a competition to design Central Park in New York City. He later designed parks in Buffalo, Detroit, San Francisco, Chicago, Montreal, and Boston. In 1867, New York passed the first law to regulate tenement building. The Boston Cooperative Company started a rental housing program for the urban working class in 1871. Eight years later, the Washington Sanitary Improvement Company was formed to provide housing to low-income workers in the nation's capital.

City Beautiful

In 1893, the World's Columbian Exposition, an international fair held in Chicago, captured the imagination of cities around the country. The fair, on a site which ultimately became Jackson Park, attempted to show

America's industrialized cities the importance of good planning and architecture. The physical layout of the fair site was classical, with grand boulevards and imposing exhibition buildings. Leaders of other cities went home with glowing reports of the "City Beautiful." Daniel H. Burnham, the exposition's chief architect, prepared a plan for San Francisco after the earthquake and fire of 1906. Three years later, he developed a plan for Chicago. Other planners and architects developed similarly grandiose plans for other American cities.

Although the City Beautiful movement has been criticized as a cosmetic approach to city problems, it did arouse Americans' interest in urban planning. Planning organizations sprang up in most major cities. In 1909, the first national planning conference was held. In 1913, Massachusetts became the first state to require that all cities with a population of over 10,000 establish a planning board to oversee city planning. By then, eighteen U.S. cities had official planning boards.

This national interest in planning, however, began to conflict with the growth of America's cities. At a time when land values in most American cities were soaring because of unprecedented industrial and commercial growth, implementation of such visionary plans seemed exceedingly difficult. A more realistic way of reconciling private property rights with broader public planning concerns was needed.

Zoning

The answer was zoning. Zoning is the application of the "police power" of the government to the use of land and improvements. The concept was not totally new, although most of its early applications concerned dangerous or obnoxious land uses. Boston, as an example, prohibited the storage of gunpowder near the center of town. New York, as a result of a series of tenement fires, passed laws limiting certain types of construction. In 1895, Los Angeles prohibited the operation of a steam shoddying plant within 100 feet of a church. In almost all these cases, zoning laws were used to prohibit certain activities in the zoned areas; other areas of the city were allowed to develop as they might.

In the early part of the twentieth century, zoning was also used to enhance land values. Local governments, often working closely with land developers, would "spot-zone" properties for land uses that would bring the highest current price. However, undesirable development on the spot-zoned parcel could cause other owners to suffer decreases in property values. As a result, public officials were pressured to provide zoning on a more comprehensive basis.

In 1891, Boston passed an ordinance limiting building height. In 1909, Los Angeles was divided into seven industrial districts; the rest of the city was declared residential. The most comprehensive attack on the problem of zoning, however, occurred in New York City. Under the leadership of a local attorney, Edward M. Bassett, New York enacted the nation's first comprehensive zoning ordinance in 1916. With certain modifications, the ordinance was adopted by other cities, and several court tests of the law established the legality of zoning.

One of the most important of these court tests occurred in 1926 in Euclid, Ohio. In this case,[1] the Supreme Court of the United States held that a community had the right and responsibility to determine the uses of land within its boundaries, provided such determination did not upset the orderly growth of the region or nation. This decision provided communities with the necessary tools to implement comprehensive planning activities.

SZEA and SPEA

Interest in planning, meanwhile, was increasing throughout the country. On the national level, the U.S. Department of Commerce developed two major pieces of model legislation. The first, formulated in 1922, was the Standard State Zoning Enabling Act (SZEA). This act enabled local governments to control the height, area, bulk, location, and use of buildings. It also allowed local jurisdictions to divide their land area into zones or districts with varying regulations (e.g., residential, commercial, industrial), as long as the properties within the districts were treated uniformly. In 1928, the second model act appeared. The Standard City Planning Enabling Act (SPEA) outlined a "master plan" for communities, which would be prepared by a planning commission. The Act discussed provisions for approval of all public improvements by the commission, procedures for subdividing land, and participation of the local jurisdiction in the regional plan.

These two pieces of model legislation were gradually adopted by virtually every state and local government in the country, providing the basis for our current laws regarding planning and zoning. Basically, these laws prohibit undesirable land uses by stipulating that landowners can develop their land as they see fit, provided such development isn't specifically restricted by state and local legislation.

Regional and Local Planning

Planning was also proceeding at the regional and local levels. Henry Wright and Clarence Stein produced a plan for the state of New York,

[1]Euclid v. Ambler Realty Co., 272 U.S. 365.

clearly establishing the relationship between industrialization, transportation, and land use. In 1928, a plan for metropolitan New York was developed for the Regional Planning Association of New York by the Scottish planner Thomas Adams. The same year, Benton MacKaye published *The New Exploration: A Philosophy of Regional Planning,*[2] which established many of the fundamental principles of regional planning.

In 1933, the National Planning Board was established to coordinate planning activities throughout the nation. A year later, it became the National Resources Board and initiated a series of regional plans, generally following the guidelines of Wright and MacKaye. Many of these ideas were utilized in the development of the Tennessee Valley Authority (TVA), which encompassed seven states and 2 million people and was by far the largest and most significant regional planning program undertaken in America up to that time.

Planning progress was also being made abroad. In 1937, Le Corbusier published *Le Plan de Paris,* illustrating how Paris could be rebuilt without losing its historic monuments. In England, the 1940 *Report of the Royal Commission on Distribution of Industrial Population* established many of the concepts of English new towns. In 1943, Sir Patrick Abercrombie and J. H. Forshaw published the *County of London Plan,* which demonstrated how London could be successfully rebuilt after the war.

In the United States, postwar pressures for housing consumed large amounts of suburban land, often with little or no planning. In the central cities, the neglect and decay of the Depression and war years forced most major cities to replan and rebuild in order to survive. Recognizing this need, the federal government passed the Housing Act of 1949, which attacked both planning and rebuilding problems. The urban renewal program was established to handle the problem of rebuilding the central cities. Planning was encouraged through Section 701, which provided federal funding for state and local planning activities. This infusion of monies enabled many communities to hire professional planners and begin formulating effective plans for transportation and land use development.

The Environmental Movement

By the 1960s many communities, particularly those in high-growth areas, became concerned that planning alone would not assure quality

[2]Rev. ed., University of Illinois Press, Urbana, Ill., 1962 (paperback).

development in the remaining developable land areas and maintenance of open space in undeveloped areas. Conservationists were particularly concerned about such mountain recreation areas as Lake Tahoe, the Adirondacks, Vermont, and the Colorado Rockies and for coastal wetlands in areas like California, Florida, Massachusetts, New York, and the Carolinas. In addition to planning, a basic change in the legal view of the ownership of land seemed necessary.

Problems with Traditional Land Ownership

In 1963, the American Law Institute began investigating the legal structure of land ownership, land use, planning, and zoning as it was being practiced in the United States. The institute identified five major problems with the existing system:

- Exclusive dependence on zoning was an ineffective method of obtaining desirable land development.
- The unrestricted granting of power over land use to the smallest unit of government (e.g., town, village, city) distorted metropolitan growth, rendering the small governmental unit almost impotent in attacking regional problems such as pollution, transportation, and housing.
- Ordinances enacted at the local level dealt ineffectively with large-scale development, particularly in suburban communities.
- The forces of urban growth were too dynamic to be properly controlled by the development of a "static master plan."
- Local zoning control created an administrative process which ran counter to general concepts of fairness and orderly procedure.

The institute then drew up a new model land development code to replace the SZEA legislation and SPEA local ordinances of the 1920s.

Responses at the State and Regional Levels

While the institute was working on the new land use code, a series of court decisions and laws at the regional and state levels directly affected land development. Hawaii was one of the first states to act, partly in response to fraudulent land sale practices by developers in the 1950s. In 1961, Hawaii divided all land in the state into three districts: urban,

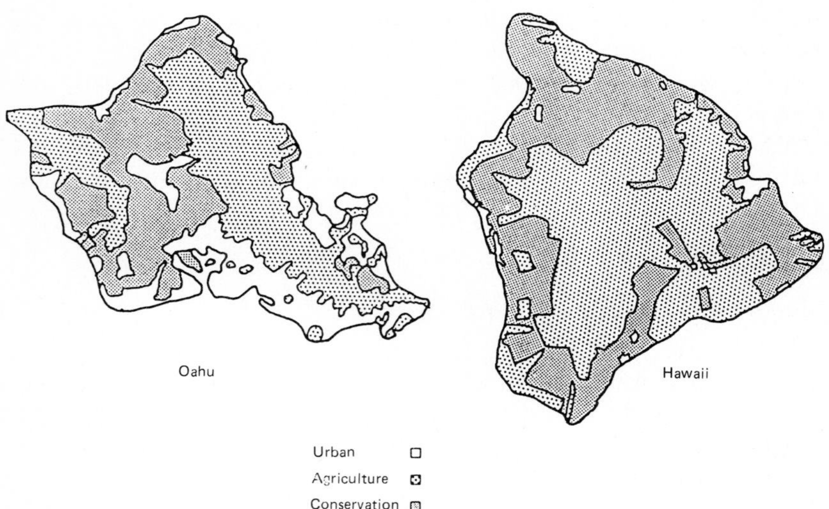

Figure 2-2. Hawaii land-use districts. Of Hawaii's eight major islands, Oahu is the most urbanized, Hawaii one of the least. *(Reprinted with permission from* Land Growth & Politics, *John M. DeGrove, 1984 by the American Planning Association, 1313 E. 60th Street, Chicago, Illinois)*

agriculture, and conservation. Land in the last two districts was strenuously protected against development pressures. Despite stricter criteria for district boundary changes embodied in 1975 legislation, the pressure for converting land to urban use has continued to steadily increase in Hawaii. Between 1962 and 1980, 40,500 acres of land changed from agricultural to urban use.[3]

In 1965, California passed the Williamson Act, authorizing counties to designate special agricultural preserves. Owners of farms of over 100 acres within these preserves received favorable property tax treatment, provided they maintained the land in a "use not incompatible with agriculture" for at least 10 years. Many counties immediately took advantage of the new law; two-thirds of Marin County's 300,000 acres were placed in such a preserve.

Since the 1960s, there has also been an ongoing battle in California to protect the coastline. Under the California Coastal Zone Conservation Act of 1972, a permanent state commission and six regional commissions were formed to develop and carry out a long-term plan for the California coastline. In 1976 the legislature gave local government the

[3]John M. DeGrove, *Land Growth &Politics,* American Planning Association, Chicago, 1984, pp. 9–63.

prime responsibility for managing the coast. By mid-1982 there were twenty-seven local coastal plans in place.[4]

In 1963 the Massachusetts legislature enacted the Coastal Wetlands Protection Act, which placed permanent restrictions on private coastal wetlands, provided the owners of the properties consented. The owners were not compensated for the restrictions, although they had the right to appeal; only a few did so.

Back in the West, the San Francisco Bay Conservation and Development Commission was formed to regulate land and water use around the Bay. At Lake Tahoe, the Tahoe Regional Planning Association (TRPA) was formed to deal with lake pollution, landfill, and other problems besetting the "Lake in the Sky." It took until 1984 for TRPA to come up with a regional plan, and pro- and antigrowth factions continue their ongoing debate about the future of development in the area.

In 1970, Vermont enacted Act 250, the State Land Use and Development Plan. This act established a state environmental board to regulate development. To secure approval of the board, projects had to pass a variety of tests to ensure they would not generate undue environmental problems such as water or air pollution and that they wouldn't put too great a burden on public services or adversely affect the aesthetics of an area. Also, development had to proceed according to a duly adopted plan and had to conform to existing local or regional plans. The legislation enacted a stiff capital gains tax on real estate transfers in 1973. The tax penalizes short-term investment and was designed to discourage speculation. However, the tax has not been successful in curtailing speculation, since profits often exceed the tax imposed.

In 1971 a major drought spurred Florida's political leaders to look seriously at the environmental problems created by the rapid urbanization of the state. In April 1972, the legislature passed four major land use laws. The most important of these, the Environmental Land and Water Management Act, established state control over those land use decisions having an impact outside local areas.

In 1986, in response to continuing rapid expansion, Florida saw the need to coordinate its efforts. The state took an integrated approach to land use management, establishing a state plan and requiring that local plans be approved by the state planning agency. The new approach is embodied in two laws passed in 1985, the State Comprehensive Plan Act and the Growth Management Act.

Florida's state plan requires localities to undertake capital improvement projects and tightens development restrictions in the coastal zone,

[4]Ibid., pp. 177–234.

THE FAR SIDE By GARY LARSON

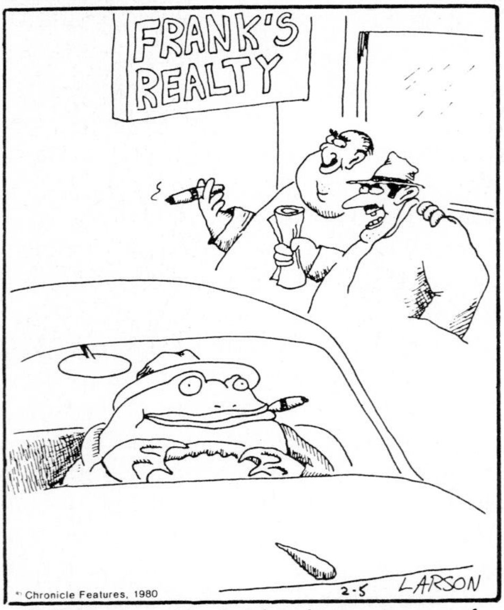

Well, another sucker just bought twenty acres of swampland.

where 80 percent of new growth occurs. The state earmarked funds to assist local governments in developing and implementing their plans. Local communities that don't invest the required amount in their capital improvement programs risk being cut off from a variety of state funds.

Attempts to Control Growth at the Local Level

While many of the early efforts occurred at the state and regional levels, several municipalities also struggled with the problems of rapid development. Ramapo was a semirural community, 25 miles north of New York City, which experienced explosive growth in the late 1950s and early 1960s as a result of the opening of the New York Thruway and the Palisades Parkway. In order to deal with the problems caused by this growth, in 1966 Ramapo adopted a comprehensive plan to control housing density. Ramapo then declared a moratorium on development, allowing selective developments to proceed in accordance with an 18-year capital budgeting program, covering construction of streets, sewers, public parks, and other public facilities. To obtain a special use permit, a developer had to demonstrate that these facilities would be in place by the time the project was completed. If they were not in the capital budget, the developer had to pay for the improvements or abandon the project.

Although Ramapo lost an initial court test, its development control ordinances were finally upheld in a 1972 decision by the New York State Supreme Court. But an economic recession coupled with cutbacks in federal funds for much-needed sewer work slowed growth naturally. In 1983 the controlled growth program was repealed, 4 years before the 18-year capital budgeting program would have ended in 1987.

Boulder, Colorado, also took steps to control development. In 1967, the town's voters approved a greenbelt purchase program financed out of a local sales tax. In 1971, a charter amendment to fix a maximum population for the city was narrowly defeated. However, the voters overwhelmingly approved a city council resolution to maintain growth levels well below those experienced in the 1960s and to undertake a study to determine the city's optimum population size. This study was completed in November 1973. The city slowed growth by levying development fees on commercial and industrial developers. Hookup fees for residential development also were raised substantially. In addition, Boulder began purchasing open space on all sides under the greenbelt program instituted in 1967.

In 1976 Boulder enacted a strict growth control ordinance that limited growth in the community to 2 percent per year. The ordinance stands to this day; the 2 percent growth level is maintained through the allocation of residential building permits. Also, parcels of developable land were subdivided to such an extent that large developers no longer found it profitable to undertake projects in the area. By the mid-1980s these restrictions, coupled with a weak economy, resulted in growth levels below those mandated by controls. In 1985, 95 percent of the available building permits were allocated; in 1986 only 60 percent of the permits authorized were distributed.[5]

In the early 1970s, Petaluma, California, began taking measures to curb its rapid growth. Petaluma is part of a rapidly growing suburban area north of San Francisco. The city's general plan, developed in 1962, encouraged the growth of the area. But the flood of newcomers between 1968 and 1972—2000 new residents annually—prompted Petaluma to establish a growth management program. In 1972 a 5-year environmental design plan was published, which drastically limited new

[5]Planning Department, City of Boulder.

housing and enacted strict criteria for evaluating new development. Petaluma was sued in 1973 as a result, but the Supreme Court in 1976 upheld the so-called "Petaluma Plan." In 1977 a second ordinance, similar to the first, was enacted, but by this time many developers had chosen to avoid Petaluma. As a result of the city's growth strategy, the population increased only 2.5 percent annually between 1976 and 1986, well below the 5 percent limit imposed by the plan.

In addition to citywide growth control measures, some communities have sought to alleviate the problems of crowded downtown areas by imposing controls on commercial development in those areas. In San Francisco, The Downtown Plan was enacted in 1985 to control the development of new commercial properties. The plan was drawn up partly in response to the adverse impact of certain commercial developments on local housing and transportation. Under The Downtown Plan, the costs of such adverse impacts must be incorporated into the cost of commercial developments, along with the responsibility of providing certain social amenities. For example, a $5.00 per square foot transportation fee and $5.39 per square foot housing fee are now automatically added to the cost of new commercial development projects. Developers in certain cases must provide for day-care facilities. One percent of each project's costs must be contributed toward public art. Additional open space requirements and performance standards involving sun, shadow, and wind impacts of new buildings are also part of The Downtown Plan.

In November, 1986, 1 year after The Downtown Plan was enacted, voters approved Proposition M, which incorporated citywide growth limits and imposed further restrictions on real estate development in San Francisco. Proposition M limits new commercial development to 475,000 square feet a year and incorporates a long list of criteria that developers must meet in order to receive approval for real estate projects, including, among other things, provisions for adding to the supply of affordable housing, maintenance of neighborhood housing, and design that does not obstruct sunlight or city views.

Together, The Downtown Plan and Proposition M represent two of the most aggressive attempts by a community to control the amount and direction of local growth.

California has been the leader in the slow-growth movement. Even in Los Angeles, where the notion of growth-for-growth's sake has been a given for years, voters passed Proposition U in 1986. The measure halves the allowable size of new buildings on much of the city's commercial land. In August 1987, San Diego set a temporary limit on new housing of 8000 units per year to curb runaway growth. Dozens of other smaller California cities have initiated slow-growth legislation.

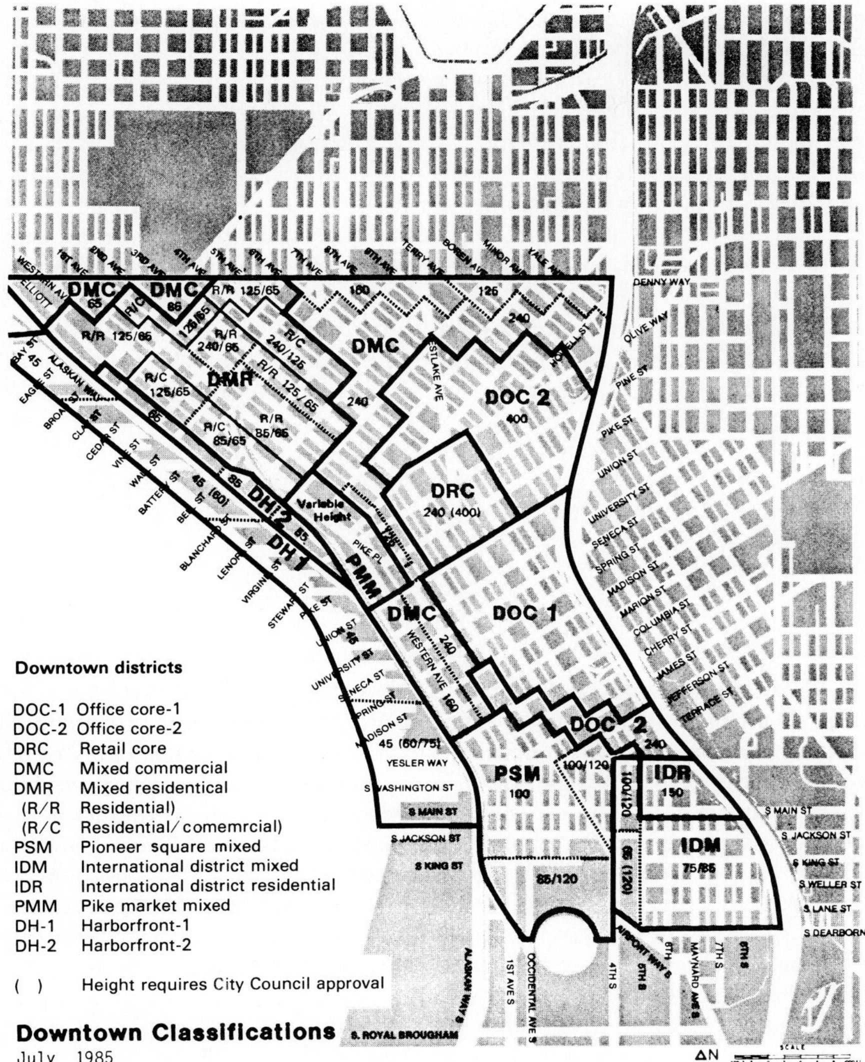

Figure 2-3. Seattle Downtown Plan, 1985. *(City of Seattle Office for Long-Range Planning)*

While San Francisco was unveiling its Downtown Plan, Seattle was developing one of its own. Fearing the imposition of similar restrictive measures, the Seattle business community, in cooperation with city planners, developed a comprehensive incentive program with limited restrictions. While the program contains housing fee requirements, it is less restrictive than the San Francisco plan.

The Seattle plan adopts a two-tier incentive approach. Developments in excess of a floor area ratio (FAR)[6] of 10 must include on-site amenities which relate to the site topography, location, or sensitivity. For example, for a development located on a steep grade, bonuses are awarded for hill climb assists and hillside terraces. In order to develop in excess of 15 FAR up to the maximum 20 FAR limit imposed by the program, the developer must provide housing or pay into a housing fund.

The Seattle plan incorporates the spirit of the City Beautiful movement by encouraging amenities which complement the overall city plan, while producing the social services and housing benefits sought by San Francisco's Downtown Plan.

San Francisco's legislation has served as a model for other cities in their efforts at curbing growth. Boston, New York, and Portland have also followed the lead of San Francisco in enacting legislation to limit commercial development.

Exactions and Development Fees

San Francisco also has been in the forefront of a growing trend among cities to require developers to help pay for the costs, both direct and indirect, associated with their projects. In the 1970s, many cities that were experiencing rapid growth found they could no longer afford to finance the infrastructure needed to support new development. The federal government had reduced funding in this area, and many states followed suit. Local voters rebelled against tax increases and voted against issuing bonds to pay for growth. In the late 1970s and early 1980s, some of these communities attempted to shift more of the burden of infrastructure financing to developers through the assessment of development fees.

The idea of developers helping to pay for the infrastructure surrounding development is not new. Over the years, developers have been asked to "voluntarily" construct such things as roads and sewage systems and dedicate them to the local jurisdiction. These payments-in-

[6]The floor area ratio is the ratio of the total square footage of a building to the total square footage of the land on which it is situated. For example, a FAR of 12 would permit the development of a 1.2-million-square-foot building on a land parcel of 100,000 square feet.

kind are known as *exactions*. In many cases, communities discovered it was inefficient to require exactions. Some developments were so small they could not supply enough land for dedication, or a community might end up with a number of small parks, one provided by each development, rather than more carefully planned larger parks. As a result, cities began replacing exactions with development fees, which could be pooled and used to build the required infrastructure in a more integrated fashion.

Prior to World War II, developers were generally asked to pay only for infrastructure that affected the residents of their developments. But eventually they were asked to help pay for facilities that benefited the entire community. Such off-site infrastructure might include libraries, parking facilities, schools, or storm drainage systems. In some cases, communities give "development credits" to developers who come up with ways to reduce traffic congestion and otherwise mitigate the need for new roads.

Over the years, cities have greatly expanded the definition of "infrastructure"; development fees are now used to support everything from street building to the purchase of police cars. In some cases the legality of development fees assessed by cities is questionable, but often developers would rather pay them than incur the greater expenses that are involved in litigation and delay of the project.

In 1976 the courts instituted the concept of *rational nexus* to determine the maximum fee communities can charge developers for off-site infrastructure. Under this concept, developers can be charged only for the portion of municipal capital facilities that serve their developments. Also, fees collected from developers cannot be used to build capital projects that support the population outside the development project. Case law also makes it illegal for communities to "double charge" developers for the same infrastructure by requiring both exactions and development fees. But despite restrictions in what cities can legally charge developers, there has been an increase in the amount of "voluntary contributions" required.

It should be noted that development fees and exactions have an impact on limiting the competition among developers and an exclusionary effect on housing markets. Forcing developers to maintain higher standards and incorporate into their projects infrastructure such as parks limits the competition among developers to those large enough to provide such amenities. To the extent that development fees can be passed along to the consumer (which depends on market demand in the surrounding area), they exclude certain segments of the population that cannot afford to absorb the fees.

Broadening the Geographic Planning Unit

There were also attempts to broaden the geographic base of the local planning unit. The U.S. Demonstration Cities and Metropolitan Development Act of 1966 required that local governments who applied forcertain types of federal grants-in-aid be subject to review by "an areawide agency designated to perform metropolitan or regional planning for the area within which the assistance is to be used." Metropolitan areas responded by forming "councils of government" (COGs), loosely organized confederations of local jurisdictions. The COGs were strengthened somewhat by the U.S. Intergovernmental Cooperation Act of 1968, which broadened the areas subject to COG review to include virtually all federal grants-in-aid. The next year, the Office of Management and Budget issued Circular A-95, bringing state governments into the review process simultaneously with the COGs. Many saw this as a recognition that the powers of the COGs to deal with regional planning problems were limited.

Several metropolitan areas, recognizing this same problem, attempted to enlarge the basic unit of government through city-county consolidation. San Francisco had operated as a consolidated unit for years. Other areas which adopted this approach were Nashville-Davidson County, Tennessee; Indianapolis-Marion County, Indiana; Jacksonville-Duval County, Florida; and the city and borough of Juneau, Alaska. The trend toward consolidation peaked in the mid-1970s. By 1975, according to the National Association of Counties, over twenty counties were consolidated or considering it, and this figure has not increased appreciably since that time. Part of the reason is that local voters have consistently vetoed attempts at consolidation, preferring not to change the structure of government unless there was an overwhelming reason to do so.

As an alternative to county consolidation, many communities have chosen to simply consolidate certain functions that could more effectively be carried out at the county level. For example, in Broward County, Florida, voters transferred responsibility for planning and land use control from local municipalities to the county. Minneapolis and St. Paul established the Twin Cities Metropolitan Council to deal with transportation, sewage disposal, air pollution, and other regional problems.

Despite examples such as these, relatively little regional planning has been implemented. One reason is that local governments fear losing power to the regional planning group. In the early 1970s, for example,

California attempted to develop planning districts based on common economic, social, and cultural interests. The project failed badly; local communities resented the state's initiative.[7]

Environmental Impact Legislation

In addition to encouraging regional governments, the federal government attempted to come to grips with the impact of development on the environment. The problem was particularly acute in the case of federally funded projects, such as flood control, airports, highways, and other public works that tend to significantly affect the ecology and environment of the area in which they are developed.

Recognizing this problem, Congress passed the National Environmental Policy Act (NEPA) of 1969, which required federal agencies to file an Environmental Impact Report (EIR) with the Council on Environmental Quality (CEQ). In the statement, the agency was required to include:

[7]Gallion and Eisner, op. cit., p. 545.

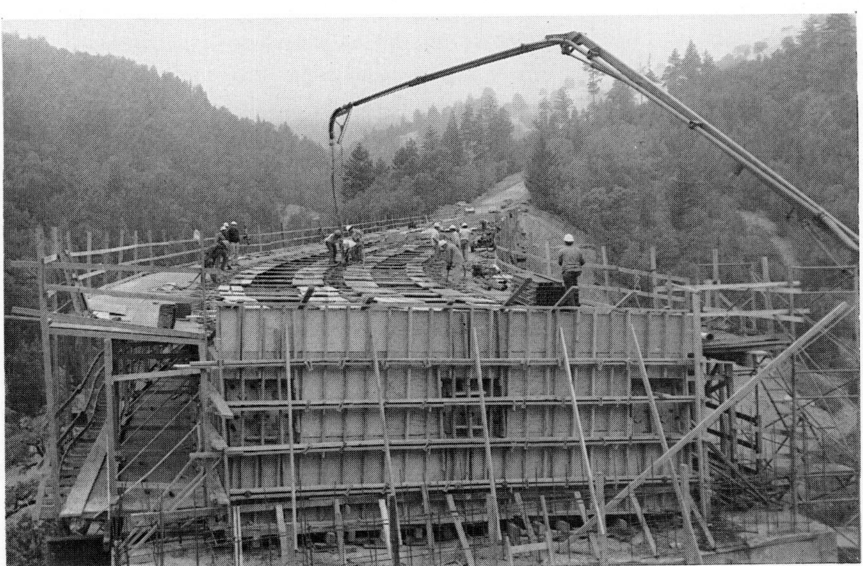

Figure 2-4. Federal agencies must submit Environmental Impact Reports before undertaking environmentally sensitive projects such as this dam being built by the Army Corps of Engineers. *(U.S. Army Corps of Engineers)*

- A detailed description of the proposed action
- A discussion of direct and indirect impacts that might result from the action
- Identification of unavoidable adverse environmental effects
- An assessment of feasible alternatives to the proposed action
- A description of cumulative and long-term effects of the action on the earth's resources
- Identification of any irreversible commitment of resources that might result from the action

Federal "actions" have been broadly interpreted to include approval of a federal permit or license, a grant-in-aid, policy determinants, provisos and regulations, and proposed legislation. As a result, many state and local projects, particularly those involving federal grants-in-aid, require EIRs. Several states require EIRs for all public projects, regardless of federal involvement.

Many other states have enacted their own versions of NEPA. The experience in some of these states has been that environmental review of projects on an ad hoc, case-by-case basis results in use of the statutes as popularity contests for individual projects. This approach is a poor substitute for much needed comprehensive planning.

Since 1969, a considerable amount of time and effort have been spent searching for a practical, effective way to meet the requirements of the law. The legislation's broad wording has posed many problems of interpretation; determining which "actions" should require an impact statement has also posed a problem; and some agencies have actually used the impact report to confuse the public and the courts. On the positive side, however, environmental issues have been drawn into the planning process in such a way that they can be dealt with before the project is too far committed.

Citizens' groups have used the environmental impact requirement to slow or stop proposed projects; the courts have generally supported them. In 1970, conservation groups were successful in blocking construction of the Alaska pipeline because of failure to meet environmental impact requirements. Construction of a nuclear power facility on Chesapeake Bay was halted in 1971 as a result of deficient EIRs. A landmark case in terms of land development was the *Friends of Mammoth v. Mono County* decision,[8] in which the California Supreme Court extended the state law requirement for environmental impact reports to

[8]C3d 247, 104 Cal Rptr 761, 502 P2d 1049.

private development. This decision immediately affected development activity in California, as developers scurried to produce impact reports. Some suspended or shut down operations in the state.

To this day the Sierra Club and other environmental groups are involved in a wide range of lawsuits aimed at preventing development that threatens the environment. Clearly, the environmental movement and its impact on the regulation and control of land use in this country will continue to be felt for years to come.

Other Federal Legislation

The EPA has made other attempts to control land use. One such attempt emerged from an unexpected source. The Clean Air Act of 1970, as amended, required states to show how they intended to ensure maintenance of ambient air quality standards once the standards had been achieved. In 1974, the required review process was extended to cover not only direct sources of air pollution, such as power plants, but "indirect sources," where a concentration of motor vehicles might adversely affect air quality. The new regulations would affect all large private projects, not just those that were federally funded, and especially shopping centers.

This attempt at regulating private development ultimately ended in failure. As a result of strong criticism, particularly from the development community, the initiation date of the regulations was postponed several times. Finally, the new review procedures were largely invalidated under the Clean Air Act Amendments of 1977. Recently, the EPA has been studying another issue that may have major ramifications for the development community. In October 1987 strict regulations were set forth for management of asbestos hazards in public schools. By the end of 1987, the EPA was considering extending these regulations to include commercial development. Such legislation would have far-reaching effects on the development community. Nearly one million commercial and public buildings could be affected by the regulations, and the cost of compliance would be enormous.

Land Use and the Courts

Federal, state, and local legislation have had a major impact on land use in the United States. But many of the deciding battles over the right to develop land or to prevent development have been fought in the courts. In the 1960s, these cases often involved challenges to local exclusionary ordinances that violated the civil rights of minorities and the poor by denying them access to housing. In the 1970s, the federal courts decided many land use cases involving violation of environmental laws. In the 1980s, many of the land use cases involved local governments being sued for violation of property rights.[9]

The majority of this land use litigation has taken place in state courts. The U.S. Supreme Court has consistently failed to take firm stands on land use issues and has often given cases back to the states, citing precedents dictating that the Supreme Court cannot rule on unsettled state law issues and should not interfere with important state policies.

In recent years, though, landowners and local governments have turned to the U.S. Supreme Court for a definitive ruling on the so-called "taking issue," the debate over whether or not zoning laws and regulations constitute "taking" of property and thus require compensation to owners under the Fifth Amendment. Over the past few years the Supreme Court has looked at several cases involving the taking issue, but in each instance the issue remained unresolved because of procedural problems. In June of 1987, however, the Court ruled in favor of landowners in a similar case;[10] how future cases will be interpreted by the Court remains to be seen.

Regardless of how particular land use cases are decided in the courts, the land use issues that have arisen since the 1960s will continue to have a great impact on the real estate development process in the coming years. Private developers must now demonstrate that their projects will not adversely affect the environment and quality of life around the development and that they contribute to improving public amenities such as housing and day-care facilities. Local governments, on the other hand, must justify regulations restricting land use, relying on sound rationales rather than simply administering land use controls at will.[11] For all, in the 1980s and beyond, the ground rules governing real estate development have irrevocably changed.

[9]Donald G. Hagman (ed.), *Land Use and Environment Law Review 1982,* Clark Boardman Company, New York, 1982, p. xvii.

[10]*First Evangelical Lutheran Church of Glendale v. County of Los Angeles,* U.S. Supreme Court, decided June 9, 1987, No. 85– 1199, 55 U.S.L.W. 4781.

[11]*Nollan v. California Coastal Commission,* 55 US Law Week 5145 (1987).

3
Restructuring of the Industry

Real estate is the last of the nineteenth-century industries.
ANONYMOUS

Increasingly stringent environmental legislation wasn't the only problem facing the real estate industry in the 1970s and 1980s. Land and building costs in urban areas were increasing faster than personal income, thus excluding a sizable percentage of the population from the private housing market. In addition, the growing size and complexity of real estate projects required broader sources of financing and larger, more complex organizational structures than had traditionally been available.

Real estate, however, historically had not been an industry which adapted to rapid change. The explosive growth of the nation and the seemingly unlimited supply of land had worked to postpone structural changes that occurred in virtually every other American industry. In 1968, the real estate industry was in many ways not much different structurally from what it had been at the turn of the century: fragmented, small scale, undercapitalized, and managed on a highly informal basis. During the following 20 years (1969–1988), however, outside forces and internal leadership would play a major role in reshaping the real estate development process and the organizational structure of development and investment firms.

Responding to the Consumer

The Search for Lower Housing Costs

In the early 1970s, more and more Americans were driven out of the single-family market because of continuing increases in land, labor, and materials. This trend continued in the next decade. In 1980, the home-ownership rate was 65.6 percent. That figure declined slightly between 1980 and 1987, when the rate was 64.0 percent.[1] Chapter 1 discussed attempts to offset increasing land costs through cluster housing, PUDs, and other forms of more intensive land use. Combating spiraling labor and material costs, however, required more than improved design. Fundamental changes in the housing production process were necessary to bring housing costs back in line with the buyer's ability to pay.

The growth in the use of mobile homes suggested one solution to the problem. Starting with retirees who moved to the sunbelt states, mobile home ownership spread throughout the nation. In 1960, 103,700 mobile homes were shipped, representing 7.4 percent of all new housing units built in that year.[2] By 1972, annual production of mobile homes had risen to 576,000 units, with 5 million Americans living in approximately 2.1 million mobile homes.[3]

Seeing the explosive growth in mobile home sales, many believed that the answer to increasing housing costs lay in applying mass-production techniques on a broader scale. In 1969 the federal government initiated the "Operation Breakthrough" program to promote the concept of modular housing. Several cities participated in the program and twenty-two firms were granted contracts to develop modular homes. But local opposition, bottlenecks in contract negotiations, and Congressional funding cuts doomed Operation Breakthrough. By 1973, the project had lost its momentum. In all, just 2794 housing units were developed.[4]

Modular housing suffered other setbacks. State laws restricted transportation of modular units across state lines. Compliance with varying local building codes increased costs. Industry expectations were high and stocks of modular manufacturers were overpriced. Builders ran

[1]Savings Institutions Sourcebook, 1988, Table 47, p. 44 and U.S. Bureau of the Census.

[2]U.S. Bureau of the Census, *Historical Statistics of the United States: Colonial Times to 1970,* series N 170, pp. 639–640.

[3]*Federal Reserve Bulletin,* December 1973, p. A63.

[4]*Operation Breakthrough—Lessons Learned about Demonstrating New Technology,* Report to the Congress by the Comptroller General of the United States, November 2, 1976, p. 10.

(a)

(b)

Figure 3-1. Evolution of the mobile home. (*a*) 1937 Schult Homes sports model compact trailer, which included such amenities as chemical toilet and permanent bed with box spring and mattress *(Schult Homes)* and (*b*) the modern manufactured home. *(Manufactured Housing Institute)*

into financing problems. Manufacturers overproduced, creating unwanted inventories. But the basic problem was that modular housing did not result in a reduction in total housing costs, only in certain components such as roof trusses and wall sections. Industrial production of these and other components was quickly absorbed into the on-site construction industry wherever efficiencies could be demonstrated.

By the mid-1970s, it was increasingly evident that modular housing was falling far short of the goals that had been set by the government and industry leaders. Manufactured housing continues to maintain a stable market share, accounting for 12 percent of new home shipments in 1986.[5] It has become increasingly clear, however, that mass-produced housing has not been the panacea many had sought.

Dealing with Demographic and Life-Style Change

The real estate industry also attempted to adjust to changes in demographic patterns and consumer life-styles. In terms of housing, large numbers of young single people spurred the demand for large apartment complexes with a wide assortment of amenities. As these individuals became older and started to establish households, demand developed for condominiums and small "starter" houses. The growth of the elderly population led to an increase in demand for retirement housing and extended care facilities. Traditionally, elderly people lived with younger family members, but the trend in recent years has been toward independent living. The younger segment of the elderly population often maintained their own homes or moved into completely independent retirement communities. The oldest segment of the population, those 85 and over, increased demand for nursing homes. For those elderly who required living assistance but were not in need of medical care, the congregate care facility became an increasingly popular choice.

The growing participation of women in the labor force added to the demand for office space and day-care facilities both on and near the work premises. The concerns of a younger work force about its health led to the development of gyms, swimming pools, running tracks, and health spas in some suburban office parks.

The growth of single-parent homes and two-earner households reinforced the need for convenient shopping. Neighborhood "super stores" became popular, as did strip retail centers, where busy consumers could stop and shop on the way home from work. Catalog shopping became increasingly popular. Super-regional centers evolved out of the regional shopping center, guaranteeing the busy consumer one-stop shopping. Single-parent homes were often less affluent, and so more affordable goods were needed; this helps to explain the growth of discount houses and the popularity of off-price shopping centers.

As more and more women entered the labor force, the number of

[5] *Federal Reserve Bulletin,* October 1988, p. A49.

affluent two-income housing units grew, and this helped fuel the demand for upscale, specialty shopping. By the late 1980s, a substantial number of the 80 million baby boomers (those born between 1946 and 1964) were reaching middle age and the peak of their earning power, thus adding to the demand for upscale specialty shops.

An increase in immigration and growth in ethnic households, especially Asian and Hispanic, changed retail patterns as well. Retailers, particularly in areas such as Los Angeles, found they had to cater to the different life-style and cultural patterns of the immigrant population in order to be successful. Increasingly, retailing was becoming more specialized, focusing on smaller and better-defined segments of the consumer population.

Developments in the hotel and resort industry followed changes in demographic patterns and leisure preferences as well. As trends in participation sports evolved, resort facilities began offering everything from golf courses to tennis facilities to health and fitness centers.

Broadening the Financial Base

The Traditional Real Estate Capital Market

The financing pattern of real estate for the first 20 years after World War II was fairly straightforward. Long-term residential construction was financed largely by mutual savings banks and savings and loan associations, often with mortgages insured by the federal government. Long-term financing of commercial and industrial buildings was largely undertaken by the nation's insurance companies. Short-term, or "interim," financing for virtually all types of construction was undertaken by commercial banks. A continuing surplus of mortgage funds made it possible for many developers to "mortgage out" on their projects—little or no equity capital was required. Equity capital that did have to be raised usually came from syndicates composed of a relatively few wealthy investors often seeking the tax advantages of real estate development.

The investment policies of the institutions tended to nudge local real estate markets toward equilibrium and avoided major episodes of over- or underbuilding. Long-term lenders, such as insurance companies, generally required new building projects to have 25 to 50 percent of the space preleased before proceeding. If vacancy in a local market increased significantly, institutions stopped lending in that market until the oversupply was reduced. Construction lenders, such as banks, generally required "take out" commitments by permanent lenders before providing construction funds. Thrifts were largely restricted to residential lending.

This simple framework served the nation well in the relatively calm years after the war. Strong economic growth, coupled with low inflation and a housing demand backlog, produced an environment in which most of the players prospered and were generally uninterested in altering the cozy world in which they operated.

A Period of Change: 1968–1987

During the next 20 years, the U.S. real estate capital market went through a dramatic change as the direct or indirect result of several major events that occurred in the economy or society at large.

Inflation. Probably the single most important factor influencing the real estate capital market was the emergence of double digit inflation in the mid-1970s. For the first time since World War II, inflationary expectations influenced investor attitudes. Savers became less interested in fixed-rate passbook accounts or life insurance policies with seriously eroding face values. Mortgage lenders watched in dismay as long-term real interest rates turned and stayed negative for over 2 years (i.e., 1979 to 1980).[6] Pension fund managers became concerned with their ability to fund retirement liabilities.

Inflation also decimated the stock and bond markets and forced investors to look elsewhere for an investment that would provide a hedge against inflation. Creative real estate attorneys began tying operating costs and rents to inflation indices and this, coupled with rapidly rising construction costs, made real estate the preferred hedge. Large amounts of new capital, most notably from pension funds, began pouring into real estate equities.

Inflation also introduced a new way of thinking to the real estate community—one in which projects that were not initially feasible proceeded in expectation of future inflationary rental increases. This attitude had an impact on the overbuilding cycle of the 1980s.

Deregulation. In the late 1970s, Congress began deregulating America's financial institutions. As a result, commercial banks were allowed to operate in geographical areas other than their traditional mar-

[6]For an excellent discussion of the impact of inflation on the mortgage markets, see "How Inflation Erodes the Income of Fixed-Rate Lenders" by Anthony Downs and S. Michael Giliberto, *Real Estate Review,* Spring 1981.

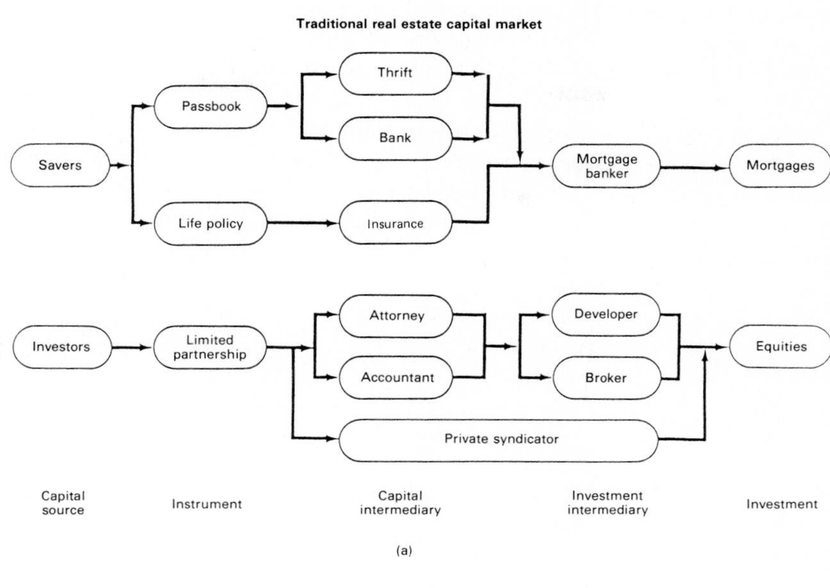

(a)

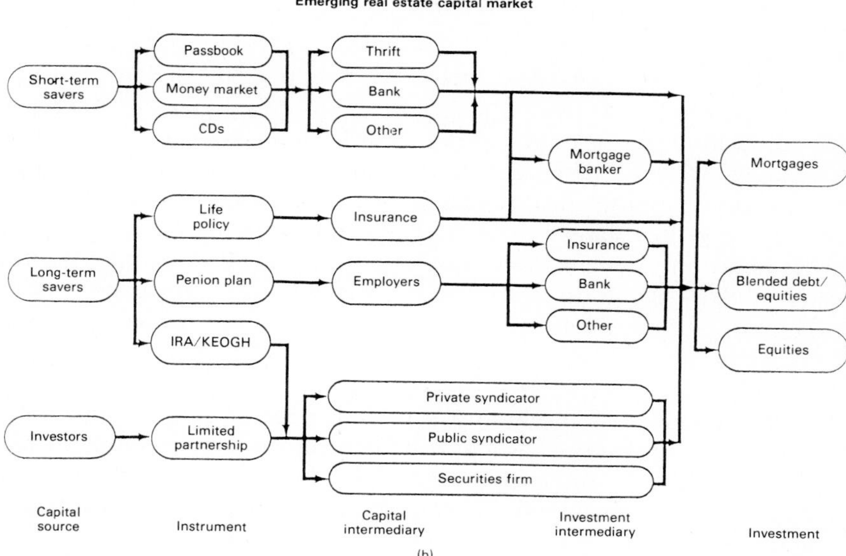

(b)

Figure 3-2. The changing real estate capital market.

kets and construction lending rapidly took on a national and, ultimately, international flavor. Thrift institutions, previously restricted to residential lending, were allowed to invest up to 10 percent of their assets in commercial properties.

Deregulation had a more fundamental impact on the housing market. Prior to deregulation, interest-rate ceilings had been imposed on the savings accounts of thrift institutions. Traditionally, thrifts borrowed money for the short term and used it to make long-term loans at fixed rates. When interest rates rose, customers withdrew their savings and put their money in higher-yielding accounts of other institutions. This process was known as *disintermediation,* literally "bypassing the intermediary," the financial institution. As a result, thrifts would periodically run short of funds to lend for housing, creating a "credit crunch" and slowing construction activity during periods of high interest rates.

Under deregulation, interest ceilings were lifted and thrifts were allowed to compete on an equal footing with other financial institutions for savings deposits, enabling them to continue making mortgage loans when interest rates rose. Thrifts were in fact more than equal in their ability to raise funds under deregulation, since they combined market interest rates with federal deposit insurance guarantees. As a result, they began attracting large pools of funds, some of which were invested in land speculation or commercial loans that were outside of the thrifts' areas of expertise. These bad investments helped to weaken the thrift industry in the mid-1980s.

Deregulation also brought about a shift from fixed- to variable-rate mortgages. While the lifting of interest-rate ceilings allowed the thrifts to compete with other institutions, it also meant that in times of rising interest rates they had to offer higher rates, while continuing to earn lower yields on their portfolio of long-term fixed-rate mortgages. As a result, thrifts began to shift toward variable-rate mortgages which would bring their long-term earnings more in line with short-term interest-rate fluctuations.

Spread Financing. Largely as a result of inflation and deregulation, many financial institutions began restructuring their investment portfolios in the late 1970s and early 1980s. This strategy involved not only an attempt to match various levels of risk but the maturity of assets and liabilities as well. The result was profit made on the "spread" between the return of the asset and the cost of the liability. If individual matchups were successful, the thinking went, the overall performance of the portfolio also would be successful.

The impact of this strategy on real estate was to tie the availability and terms of mortgage financing to the broader capital market and thus make real estate financing more volatile. In terms of permanent financing, the maturity and rate charged for a mortgage loan often became linked to the maturity and rate paid on a Guaranteed Investment Contract (GIC). Construction financing became linked to the prime rate, LIBOR, or some other "floating" index.

This new level of volatility made it difficult to plan and execute real estate projects that might take 2 to 5 years to complete. The maturity of permanent financing dropped from 25 to 30 years to 7 to 10 years. In periods of rapidly escalating inflation, reserves for construction interest often proved inadequate, with the developer in default before construction was complete.

Tax Legislation. In the 1960s and 1970s real estate received a moderate tax subsidy through the deduction of interest and depreciation. Some industry elements, such as low- and moderate-income housing and historic preservation, were singled out for special treatment, but with the exception of single-family housing, real estate was not treated much differently than other investment assets.

This changed in 1981, however, when Congress provided the real estate industry with a windfall by substantially reducing the recovery period for the depreciation of investment assets. In addition, the industry was granted an exemption from new at-risk rules which would limit deductions to the amount of funds invested. These factors made real estate a very attractive investment vehicle for taxable investors, and funds flowed freely into the industry. Although the recovery standards were modified somewhat by the tax bill of 1984, the subsidy still was significant, particularly when compared with other types of investments. Congress reversed itself in 1986 and took away virtually all subsidy from real estate, but not before the industry received a major infusion of new equity capital.

Securitization. Wall Street has been periodically preoccupied with the desire to provide liquidity (and tradeability) for illiquid assets such as real estate. The mortgage bonds of the 1920s were an early attempt to tackle this problem. While they provided a substantial infusion of real estate capital, they were a factor in the later collapse of the real estate market and subsequent Depression. A more recent attempt to provide liquidity to real estate markets was made in 1960, when Congress created a new investment vehicle, the Real Estate Investment Trust (REIT), to allow "pass through" tax treatment for trusts which met certain standards and conditions. REITs seemed to offer a panacea for real estate finance. For the first time, large numbers of small investors could invest in real estate on a national basis. Illiquid assets could now be turned into securities that would trade as easily as common stocks.

REITs were not the panacea the industry had hoped for. Shortly after their introduction, the stock market, and REITs shares along with it, declined sharply. REITs came back in the late 1960s and did exceptionally well in the early 1970s until interest rates tightened in 1973, loans went sour, and the bottom dropped out of the REIT market once more. In the 1980s, REITs experienced yet another comeback as investment vehicles in the growing secondary market.

Attempts were also made to expand the secondary market for residential mortgages. The secondary market is made up of investors who buy and sell mortgages originated by a third party. The development of this market allowed a much broader array of investors to participate in

"Looks like the small investor is finally getting back into the market."

the real estate marketplace and expanded the pool of capital funds available for development projects.

By 1986, 45 percent of all new single-family mortgages were securitized.[7] Commercial real estate debt was first transformed into mortgage-backed securities in 1984; nearly $1.2 billion of commercial properties was securitized in that year. In 1985, more than $6 billion of new commercial issues came to market.[8]

Internationalization. The OPEC oil embargo in 1973 shifted attention to the rapid accumulation of capital by OPEC countries and the need to recycle funds into U.S. investments, including real estate. The Arabs and Iranians, in particular, were identified as potential buyers of U.S. real estate. While investments never reached the levels anticipated, there was extensive Arab investment in Atlanta, Houston, Salt Lake City, and throughout California.

Canadian development companies also purchased extensive land holdings in California, Arizona, and Texas for an often ill-fated expansion of their development activities. Canadian investors, such as Olympic and York, purchased undervalued office buildings in New York and other cities. European banks and pension funds invested funds in projects throughout the United States. Australian development and investment companies initiated operations in the western states, particularly California. Individual investors from Hong Kong, Singapore, and Latin America bought properties in Florida, Texas, and California.

The Japanese, who had cautiously begun investing in U.S. real estate 15 years earlier, increased the pace in the mid-1980s, buoyed by a growing trade surplus. A shortage of real estate investment opportunities in Japan and an attractive exchange rate accelerated this process, which was directed primarily at "trophy" office buildings in major U.S. cities. In 1986, Shuwa Investment Company acquired Arco Plaza in Los Angeles for a reported $620 million and the ABC Building in New York for $175 million.

In 1987, several Japanese banks began competing directly with U.S. banks and insurance companies for mortgage financing of major properties. With a lower cost of capital, the Japanese banks proved to be formidable competitors, much to the delight of American developers. The

[7]Kenneth T. Rosen, "Securitization and the Mortgage Market," *Bond Market Research—Real Estate,* Salomon Brothers Inc, New York, August 1987.

[8]Ibid., p. 6.

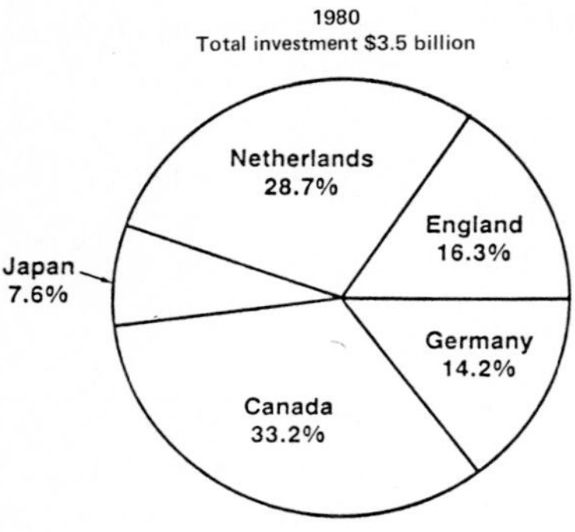

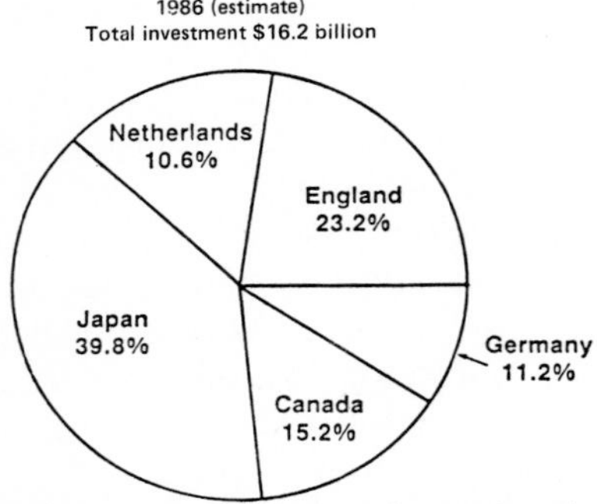

Figure 3-3. The five most active foreign investors in the U.S. real estate market, 1980 and 1986. *(Goldman Sachs, U.S. Department of Commerce)*

lower cost of Japanese capital also provided attractive marketing opportunities for Wall Street firms seeking investors for securitized offerings.

By 1988, the U.S. real estate capital market had been significantly broadened to a worldwide market with new, more complicated financing instruments than ever before. With these changes has come increased volatility and greater difficulty in reaching market equilibrium, as demonstrated in the overbuilding of the 1982 to 1986 period.

Reshaping the Real Estate Organization

While the real estate capital market was broadening, changes were also occurring in the way in which real estate was developed and managed.

The entry of public corporations and Canadian development companies resulted in significant changes in organizational structures and led to the rise of the national development firm. The emergence of absentee ownership resulted in the creation of the real estate investment advisory industry.

In Search of Bookable Earnings

Over the years, many public corporations had owned or managed their own plants, warehouses, or other properties or had acquired land in the course of their operations. But it wasn't until the 1960s that public corporations began participating in real estate development for other users.

Corporations had many reasons for getting into real estate. For landowning companies such as the railroads and agribusiness firms, real estate development was one way to realize a greater return on underutilized assets. Other firms used real estate as a vehicle for advertising their products, such as steel, aluminum, concrete, or wood. Some firms, already using real estate in their daily operations, decided to integrate vertically. For example, retailers who had leased space in shopping centers began developing their own centers. Airlines developed or purchased hotel operations. Financial institutions, long engaged in the real estate lending business, began buying and developing their own properties.

While many corporations had a specific reason for entering the real estate marketplace, many firms with no direct reason for participating, other than to diversify and raise price/earnings ratios, got into real estate in the late 1960s. When the "pooling of interest" ruling[9] changed in the fall of 1970, the use of acquisitions as a means of entry into real estate dropped off significantly, and the lure of real estate as a new area of diversification for the public corporation substantially diminished. This disenchantment was followed by a shakeout period, during which many corporations got out of the industry altogether. With the exception of housing, direct corporate involvement in the industry since the mid 1970s has been substantially reduced. Although begun with great fanfare, the attempt of the public corporations to join the ranks of the real estate community largely ended in failure. Many of the mana-

[9]The "pooling of interest" allowed acquiring corporations to include the earnings and assets of acquired corporations in their financial statements. In October 1987, tax accounting rules were changed to severely restrict the use of pooling of interest.

gerial techniques introduced by the public corporations, however, would prove an enduring and constructive legacy.

The Canadians Move South

Another force shaped the U.S. real estate community in the mid-1970s and formed a model for national development firms in this country. Canadian developers, flush with cash and facing a scarcity of projects in their own country, began crossing the border and actively participating in U.S. real estate markets. Canadian banks played a major role in supporting the development companies, providing a steady line of credit for development projects. This allowed the Canadians to move fast and buy up properties far more quickly than Americans could. Favorable tax laws also allowed Canadian developers tax deferrals and ensured ongoing cash flow.

As a result of fierce competition for a limited market in Canada, the Canadians were experienced competitors. Those development companies that survived were among the most innovative, and this won them many competitions to build projects in the United States.

Unlike U.S. development companies, the Canadians were accustomed to operating on a large scale. The major Canadian developers had offices throughout Canada and set up a similar structure in the United States, enabling them to maintain a presence in several local markets and move resources wherever they were needed to pursue the project at hand. The sheer size of the Canadian firms enhanced their competitive stance. As projects became larger and more complex, it became increasingly clear that only those organizations with extensive resources could hope to compete effectively.

Not all of the Canadian firms succeeded. Several paid too much for land and their projects never had a chance to reach the market. Others stretched their resources too thin and declared bankruptcy or abandoned their U.S. operations. Even some of the successful firms, such as Cadillac Fairview, decided to sell off their operations and pursue other interests.[10] But despite the mixed results of their efforts, the Canadian developers made a lasting impact on the organizational structure and scale of operation of U.S. real estate.

The Rise of the National Developer

As discussed previously, the real estate industry in the United States had traditionally been dominated by a large number of small, localized

[10]The $5 billion sale of assets by Cadillac Fairview to JMB Realty Corporation in November 1987 was the largest real estate transaction in history.

development firms. Over the years, however, the scope of development projects broadened, and larger organizations were required in order to attract sufficient financing and muster internal resources to undertake complex projects, as the Canadian firms had amply demonstrated. As a result, a number of national development firms evolved in the U.S. marketplace.

One of these firms was created by Trammell Crow, who established partnerships with local entrepreneurs in cities throughout the country. Trammell Crow recognized the importance of ongoing funding to remain competitive. As a result, his organization, along with other national developers, began linking up with financing sources. The company established an investment banking unit and formed a limited partnership to raise equity financing.

Several other national development companies emerged. The Rouse Company is the country's largest publicly traded development firm. Founded by James Rouse, the company pioneered a string of major, high-profile projects, including the highly successful Faneuil Hall Marketplace in Boston and the new town of Columbia, Maryland. Another major national developer, Gerald Hines Interests, evolved out of the Houston marketplace and has had a major impact on transforming the skylines of many American cities. Other national development firms include The Edward J. Debartolo Corporation, Melvin Simon & Associates, Inc., The Hahn Company, and The Taubman Company, Inc., in shopping center development; Olympia & York, Metropolitan Structures, Inc., and JMB Realty Corporation in office buildings; Cabot, Cabot, & Forbes in industry; Lincoln Properties, in apartments; and U.S. Home Corp., Ryan Homes, Inc., and UDC-Universal Development in single-family residential development.

The Investment Advisory Industry

As noted earlier, rapidly increasing inflation in the 1970s attracted pension funds to real estate investment. At the same time, foreign nationals also discovered the attractions of U.S. real estate. Both of these investor groups were generally risk averse and had little real estate experience. Furthermore, investors were often located thousands of miles from the properties they were acquiring. As a result, a need arose for someone to acquire, manage, and dispose of assets on a local basis. The real estate investment advisory industry evolved to serve this need. Initially, the new industry was dominated by insurance companies (Equitable, Prudential, Aetna, and New England Life) and banks (Wachovia, First Chicago, Morgan Guaranty). Eventually, entrants also included firms from related fields such as mortgage bankers (Heitman, Lomas &

Nettleton, Eastdil, FIA), syndicators (JMB, Balcor), developers (LaSalle Partners), security managers (Rosenberg, TCW, Boston Company), foreign advisers (Jones Lang Wooton, Richard Ellis, Lehndorf & Babson), real estate brokers (Coldwell Banker), as well as start-up entrepreneurial firms (Aldrich, Eastman & Waltch, J. W. O'Connor).

By mid-1988, there were over 100 investment advisory firms, managing over $311 billion in assets.[11] Most of these firms provided a full range of services including finding and evaluating properties, acquisition, negotiation and due diligence, portfolio management, property management, and disposition services. Most of the properties acquired were fully leased lower-risk investments, although some managers entered into higher-risk investment structures and, in a few cases, took development risks. Since most of the clients were tax exempt or low-tax investors, leverage was seldom used, most properties being purchased on an all-cash basis.

The growth of investment advisory activities helped to change the thinking of many in the real estate industry. For the first time, real estate practitioners begin looking at real estate from a portfolio as well as a property point of view. As a result of institutional policies and a rigorous regulatory process, the overall professional quality of real estate transactions improved, as did the quality of individuals attracted to the industry.

Developers increasingly looked to the investment advisory firms and their clients to provide "take out" financing or acquire the project upon completion. With the separation of the production and ownership process, many developers became merchant builders, developing for sale rather than ownership.

This new era of absentee ownership had considerable consequences for the long-term quality of real estate product but, at the same time, introduced significant management opportunities for nonproduction players. How the development process will evolve under this new structure remains to be seen. One thing is certain: the fragmented, small-scale, undercapitalized, and loosely managed industry of the late 1960s has been irrevocably altered. By 1988, real estate had caught up with the realities of the modern marketplace.

[11] *Pensions and Investment Age*, September 19, 1988, p. 14.

PART 2

The Economics of Real Estate

4
The Economics of Real Estate at the National Level

You won't have any trouble in your country as long as you have few people and much land, but when you have many people and little land, your trials will begin.
Thomas Carlyle's advice to America when it was a nation of 25 million

In the historical tapestry of real estate, a recurrent thread is the relationship between events at the national and the local levels. The economics of real estate development do not exist in a vacuum but are an integral part of the overall national economy (and increasingly, the international economy). There are fundamental relationships that cause changes in the economy at the national level to bear on real estate at the local level.

Unfortunately, developers often overlook these relationships. It isn't always clear what local real estate markets have to do with the national economy; changes in the economy may not affect local real estate for some time or may take forms that aren't immediately recognizable.

Also, more than just economic factors play a part: demographic trends and changes in life-styles may have an important effect.

If we view real estate as a series of socioeconomic forces (demand) creating pressure on a relatively limited resource (land), we can get a somewhat clearer perspective. At the national level, demand and supply are seldom in equilibrium; the disparities often last for years. Whether or not national equilibrium is achieved matters little to the developer. Most important is discerning broad, long-term national demand and supply trends which ultimately will have an impact on local real estate development.

National Demand Patterns

Demand for real estate at the national level is influenced by national population growth and demographic change, coupled with expanding employment opportunities and rising per capita incomes.[1] Increases in population create an increased demand for housing. Greater numbers of people with rising incomes require a greater amount of goods and services, thereby creating demand for shopping centers and other commercial facilities. Population growth, accompanied by increased levels of employment, creates a demand for new offices and industrial buildings.

Population Growth

Population growth is a function of the existing level of population, or *base,* and the annual *rate* at which new people are added to the base. Change in the annual rate and immigration are the major factors affecting population growth today. Population growth rates are a function of the number of births (*fertility*)[2] versus deaths (*mortality*). *Migration* patterns can also affect the population growth of individual countries. In essence, the population increases when the number of people being born or immigrating is ultimately greater than the number dying or emigrating.

The world's population is growing at a rapid rate. From 1983

[1]If per capita incomes are falling, increasing population merely results in overutilizing existing real property resources. This is illustrated by overcrowded housing conditions in many underdeveloped countries.

[2]Fertility rates in themselves don't tell the whole story. The key factor is the *net reproduction rate,* which is the average number of girl babies that will be born to a representative newly born girl in her lifetime. If the rate is greater than 1.0 over an extended period of time, population will grow; if less than 1.0, it will ultimately decline.

through 1986, world population grew at an annual rate of 1.6 percent. At that rate of growth, the world would double its population in just 43.3 years.[3] Life expectancy continues to increase in both the developed world and in underdeveloped countries. In underdeveloped countries, recent improvements in public health have had dramatic results in extending longevity. While life expectancy in developing countries stood at just 57 years in 1985, far below the figure for developed nations (73), that gap is expected to narrow. By the year 2000, life expectancy in the developing countries should reach 63.5 years, versus 75.4 for the developed world.[4]

In contrast to underdeveloped countries, the population growth rate of the United States has been in a long-term decline since 1800. The growth rate was approximately 3.3 percent in the second decade of the nineteenth century. By 1900, the rate had dropped to 2.1 percent; by the 1930s, to 0.7 percent. Following World War II, the growth rate increased to 1.8 percent, and then it began to fall until it reached approximately 0.75 percent in the mid-1970s.[5] The rate began increasing slightly in the mid-1970s and into the 1980s. The average annual rate of growth between 1980 and 1987 was 0.99 percent, higher than the early 1970s rate but still well below the rates of 1.26 percent for the 1960s and 1.71 percent during the 1950s baby boom.[6]

This long-term decline may come as a shock to many who have been hearing of a pending population disaster. This confusion is the result of three factors. First, most of those predicting population growth problems are referring to the *underdeveloped* countries. Second, the growth rate may be declining, but the base is so large that there will still be substantial increases in the total population for years to come. Third, many of the problems created by U.S. population growth are related more to the geographic *distribution* of the population than to its overall size.

Let's explore the major elements of population growth as they relate to the United States. Immigration has long been a source of population increase, accounting for 40 percent of the country's population growth in the first decade of this century. During the 1930s, immigration levels dropped to virtually zero; they rose again after World War II, and ac-

[3]Henry S. Shryock, Jacob S. Siegel and Associates, *The Methods and Materials of Demography,* vol. 2, U.S. Bureau of the Census, 1980, p. 386.

[4]*World Population Trends, Population and Development Interrelations and Population Policies: 1983 Monitoring Report.* Vol. I: *Population Trends* (United Nations publication, Sales No. E.84.XIII.10), p. 21.

[5]U.S. Bureau of the Census, *Current Population Reports,* ser. P-25, no. 545, 1975.

[6]U.S. Bureau of the Census, *United States Population Estimates and Components of Change: 1970 to 1986,* ser. P-25, no. 1006, 1986.

Table 4-1. World Population Characteristics, 1975 to 1986, and Projections to 2000

Item	Unit	1975	1980	1983	1984	1985	1986	1990	1995	2000
World total	Millions	4103	4473	4710	4787	4865	4944	5271	5708	6159
Population per sq mi	Number	78	85	90	91	93	94	101	109	117
Males	Millions	2056	2244	2363	2403	2443	2483	2649	2870	3099
Females	Millions	2047	2229	2345	2383	2422	2461	2622	2837	3061
Under 5 years old	Percent	13.6	12.3	12.0	11.9	11.8	11.7	11.4	11.2	10.8
5 to 14 years old	Percent	23.5	23.4	22.5	22.2	21.9	21.6	20.6	20.0	19.6
15 to 64 years old	Percent	57.4	58.6	59.8	60.2	60.6	60.9	62.1	62.6	63.0
65 years old and over	Percent	5.5	5.7	5.7	5.7	5.7	5.8	6.0	6.3	6.6
Median age	Years	21.6	22.4	22.9	23.1	23.3	23.5	24.2	25.3	26.4
More developed regions	Millions	1096	1136	1159	1166	1173	1180	1208	1240	1268
Less developed regions	Millions	3007	3336	3551	3621	3692	3763	4063	4468	4891

SOURCE: *Statistical Abstract of the United States, 1987.*

counted for about 16 percent of the population growth during the 1960s.[7] Immigration has been on the rise in recent years. In 1985 there were 577,000 legal immigrants, representing about 26 percent of that year's growth.[8] This was down from 33 percent in 1980 but considerably higher than the 1970 rate of 17 percent.[9]

Improved mortality has also contributed to the nation's population growth. The average mortality age at the present time is approximately 73 years—considerably greater than the 47 that was average at the turn of the century. Since the beginning of the twentieth century, the death rate has fallen from about 17 per 1000 population to approximately 9 per 1000 in 1984.[10]

Changes in the fertility rate, however, have been the major factor affecting population growth in this country. Since 1800, U.S. fertility rates have been in a long-term decline, *with one notable exception*—the period after World War II. After the war, large families became very popular among the middle class, who were experiencing rising levels of affluence.[11] In 1957, fertility rates began to turn downward once more, continuing to decline until 1976, turning up and remaining slightly higher since then. From a peak of 3.5 children per lifetime for each woman in the last half of the 1950s, the lifetime fertility rate started its decline to a rate of 1.7 during the first half of the 1980s.[12]

As noted in Chapter 3, many corporations entered real estate in the late 1960s, partly because a housing boom was predicted for the 1970s, based on an "echo boom" from the aberration in fertility rates during World War II. As war babies married and had children of their own, increased demand for new housing was anticipated. There was, in fact, some evidence of an echo boom, as birth rates increased to 18.2 per 1000 in 1970 after reaching a low of 17.5 in 1968. In 1971, however, the birth rate fell back to 17.3 and people began talking about the "birth dearth."

Increasing numbers of women in the childbearing age group were being offset by fewer children per woman for three reasons: (1) women

[7]Ibid.

[8]U.S. Bureau of the Census, *Current Population Reports,* ser. P-23, no. 150, 1987. This does not include illegal immigrants, which could increase these figures substantially.

[9]*Current Population Reports,* ser. P-23, no. 150, op. cit.

[10]*Population and the American Future,* Report of the Commission on Population Growth and the American Future, New American Library, New York, 1972, p. 12; and U.S. Bureau of the Census, *Current Population Reports,* ser. P-25, no. 971, 1985.

[11]Paul A. Samuelson, *Economics,* 9th ed., McGraw-Hill, New York, 1973, p. 32.

[12]U.S. Bureau of the Census, *Current Population Reports,* ser. P-25, no. 1006, 1987.

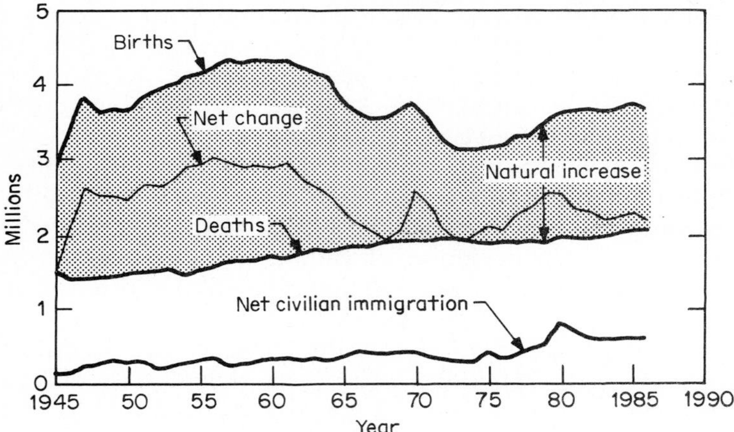

Figure 4-1. Components of U.S. population change, 1945–2000. *(U.S. Bureau of the Census)*

were having children at an older age, (2) small families became popular, and (3) contraceptive techniques had improved.[13] Despite the slight rise since the late 1970s, noted earlier, American fertility has remained relatively low and stable. Total fertility rates[14] peaked in 1957 at 3.8, declining steadily until they reached a low of 1.7 in 1976; since 1976 the fertility rate has risen only slightly, hovering around the 1.8 level since 1979.[15]

By the end of 1987, the total population of the United States had reached nearly 245,000,000, and the population is expected to continue growing into the next century. If current fertility patterns persist, annual births would continue to outnumber deaths until about 2030. Even then, immigration could cause continued growth in the population.[16]

[13]*Population and the American Future,* Report of the Commission on Population Growth and the American Future, New American Library, New York, 1972, pp. 14–15.

[14]The total fertility rate represents the average number of children a woman would have during her lifetime, based on childbearing rates in the survey year.

[15]*Current Population Reports,* Series P-23, no. 150, op. cit., pp. 42–43 and U.S. Bureau of the Census, *Historical Statistics of the United States: Colonial Times to 1970,* Series B11-19, p. 50.

[16]Ann Cooper and Julie Kosterlitz, "Coming of Age," *National Journal,* vol. 18, no. 10, March 8, 1986, p. 548.

Population Characteristics

Demand for real estate is determined not only by the sheer number of people but also by shifts in the nature, or *demographics*, of the population. Demographic factors of greatest consequence are changes in the age composition of the population and changing patterns of marriage and household formation. These factors are not only highly interrelated but also affected by changes in the economy and life-style patterns.

Age. The median age of Americans has been increasing steadily since the turn of the century, with the exception of the post-World War II aberration created by the baby boomers. By 1985, the median age of the population was 31.5 years, and it is expected to rise, reaching 36.3 years at the turn of the century and 40.8 years by 2030.[17]

The changes in the age structure of the population also point to an increase in numbers of elderly citizens. Currently 12 percent of the population are 65 years of age and over; that figure is expected to reach 13 percent by the year 2000 and 21 percent in 2030, as the baby boomers become senior citizens. By 2030, the population 65 years and over will more than double (65 million versus 29 million) in 1985.

Marriages. The number of marriages declined in 1974, the first time since World War II, closely paralleling the continuing increase in the nation's divorce rate during the 1970s. The median age of first marriage has increased since 1970; by 1985 it had reached 25.5 years for men and 23.3 for women. There has also been a rise in the percentage of young adults who have never married. In 1970, 19.1 percent of men in the 25 to 29 age bracket and 10.5 percent of women had never married; in 1985 those figures rose to 38.7 percent and 26.4 percent, respectively.[18]

Households. The total number of households in the country increased by about 1 million a year during the 1960s. The average population per household declined from 3.33 in 1960 to slightly under 3.0 persons by the mid-1970s.[19] By 1985 average household size had de-

[17]*Current Population Reports,* ser. P-23, no. 150, op. cit.

[18]Ibid.

[19]U.S. Bureau of the Census, *Current Population Reports,* ser. P-20, no. 279, 1985.

clined even further, to 2.69.[20] This is a result not only of lower birth rates but also of an "uncoupling" phenomenon, that is, individuals tending to set up separate households. There are several reasons for this: young people leaving home at an earlier age, increased divorce rates, parents not living with their children, and overall greater affluence levels.

New household formations declined dramatically and unexpectedly in the early 1980s. An average of only 1.2 million new households was formed between 1980 and 1985. The drop was caused by a combination of factors, among them a severe recession and more conservative social attitudes that encouraged young adults to stay at home longer.[21]

The Census Bureau projects a 22 percent increase in the number of households formed between 1985 and the turn of the century, an average gain of at least 1 million households a year. Nonfamily households should increase at nearly 3 times the rate of family households (40 versus 15 percent).[22] Households headed by persons in the 45 to 54 age range are expected to grow by 71 percent by the year 2000. There will also be an increase in households headed by people 75 and older; nearly 4 million such households are expected to be formed by the end of this century.[23]

How will these trends affect the housing market? The 20- to 29-year-old age group, a primary source of new household formations, will shrink rapidly through the turn of the century, depressing demand for new housing. However, this could be mitigated if the current trend of marrying at a later age continues, leading to increased demand for housing for single adults. Housing for the elderly should also grow to accommodate the increases in the population of householders 65 years and older.

Employment

The level and nature of national employment are important to real estate for two major reasons. First, the overall level determines to some degree the level of total household income that will be available for

[20]*Current Population Reports,* ser. P-23, no. 150, op. cit.

[21]*American Demographics,* April 1987, pp. 30–31.

[22]Based on middle series projections, U.S. Bureau of the Census, *Current Population Reports,* series P-25, no. 986, 1985.

[23]Based on middle series projections from "Projections of the Number of Households and Families: 1986 to 2000," *Current Population Reports,* Series P-25, U.S. Bureau of the Census, no. 986, 1986 and estimates from March 1985 *Current Population Survey,* U.S. Bureau of the Census.

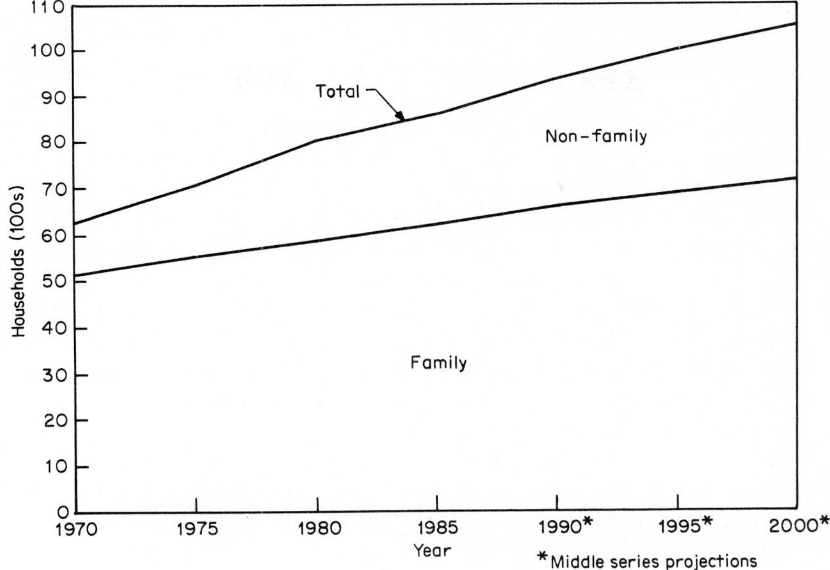

Figure 4-2. U.S. households, 1970–2000. *(U.S. Bureau of the Census)*

housing and retail expenditures. Periods of rising employment generally mean periods of rising total incomes; periods of continued high unemployment depress household incomes and reduce people's capacity to spend for housing and retail items. Second, shifts in long-term employment patterns can ultimately affect the nature of real estate demand. For example, the gradual shift from blue- to white-collar employment has significantly influenced the type of space provided in industrial parks.

In 1987, there were approximately 122 million Americans in the total labor force, representing 65.9 percent of those people who could join the labor force if they so desired. This percentage, or *participation rate,* has remained stable, hovering in the 60 to 65 percent range since the end of World War II. The degree of participation by various groups, however, has varied considerably. In general, women have increased their participation at the same time that early retirement has reduced the participation rate of men over 55. Although the participation rate of women in the work force has leveled off in recent years, the absolute number of women entering the work force is still substantial. There were 1.3 million new women workers in 1985, 1.4 million in 1986, and

1.2 million in 1987.[24] The participation rate of teenagers has been up and down. The rate for men in the 20 to 24 age group declined during the Vietnam war years but began rising again in the 1970s, following elimination of the draft.

According to the U.S. Bureau of Labor Statistics, the labor force is expected to reach nearly 123 million by 1990 and 129.2 million by 1995. That represents a total increase of 13.7 million workers, an average of more than 1 million workers each year. While the absolute increase is substantial, it represents a 12 percent growth rate that is just slightly more than half as large as the 21 percent rate for the previous 10-year period, 1975 to 1985, when 22.5 million people were added to the labor force.[25] This is primarily a reflection of the continued aging of the general population; fewer new workers are entering the job market than in the peak years of the baby boomers' entry into the work force.

During the 1970s large increases in the labor force prompted many observers to worry about the economy's ability to expand and absorb new workers. Now the tide has turned, and a shortage of labor is predicted. With the baby boom generation entering middle age, the potential pool of new entrants into the labor market is rapidly shrinking. The effects of this shift are particularly hard-hitting for businesses, such as fast-food chains, that rely on employing young, low-wage workers.

Many other factors influence the nature and overall level of employment. Foreign competition, demands for a changing mix of goods and services, educational levels, and the state of the national and international economies are just a few of the factors that help to determine the unemployment rate at a particular time. Since World War II, unemployment has ranged from a low of 2.9 percent to a postwar high of 9.7 percent in 1982 before declining to a level of 6.2 percent in 1987.[26]

Income

Per capita income is particularly important in determining the demand for housing, retail, and transient commercial facilities. In the United

[24]U.S. Bureau of Labor Statistics, *Monthly Labor Review,* December 1986, p. 58, August 1987, p. 74, and October 1988, p. 65.

[25]U.S. Department of Commerce, *Statistical Abstract of the United States,* 1987, Table 639, p. 376.

[26]U.S. Bureau of Labor Statistics, *Monthly Labor Review,* vol. 110, no. 10, October 1988, p. 66.

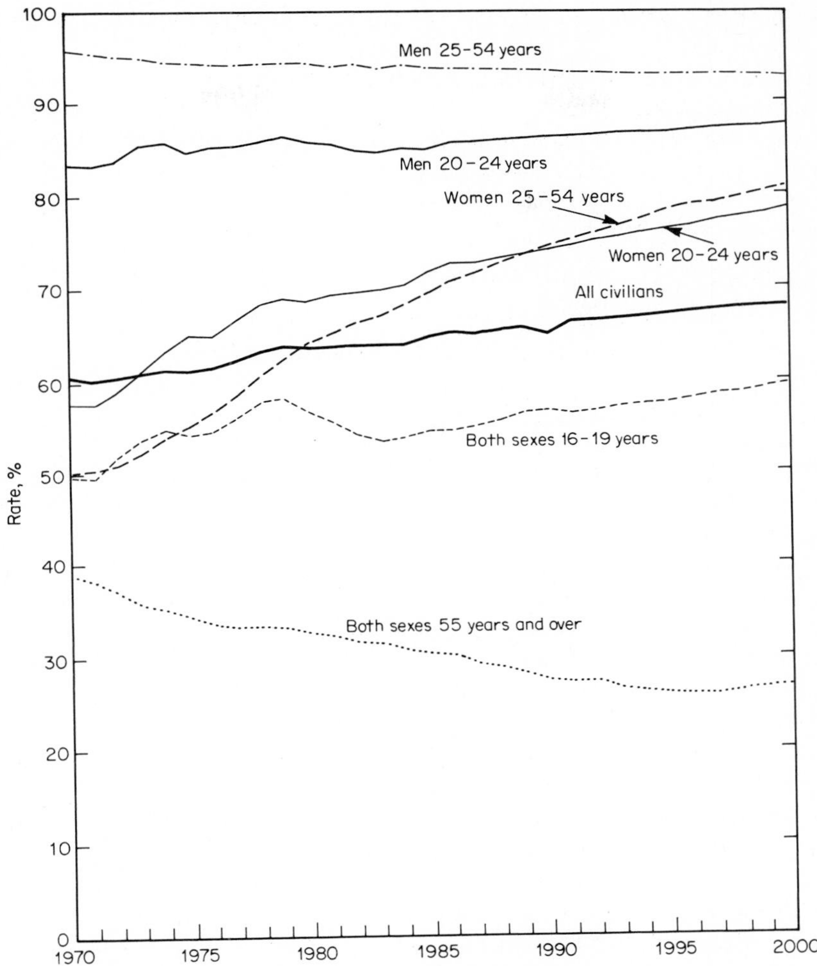

Figure 4-3. Civilian labor force participation rates: 1970–2000. The rate is for the civilian labor force as a percentage of civilian noninstitutional population in the group specified. Data for 1987–2000 represents middle series projections. *(U.S. Bureau of Labor Statistics)*

States, real per capita disposable income in 1987 was $10,947.[27] This figure has been rising, between 1 and 2 percent annually, since 1970. Income is unevenly distributed; in 1984, for example, individuals who constituted the lowest 20 percent in terms of annual income received

[27]U.S. Department of Commerce, *Survey of Current Business,* December 1987, p. 6.

only 2.9 percent of total U.S. income; the highest 20 percent received 47.8 percent.[28]

The level of real income determines the amount of funds that will be available for housing and retail expenditures. It also affects real estate indirectly through changes in the level of business activity that alter demand for industrial and office facilities.

Household Expenditures for Real Estate Goods and Services

Most households try to provide for their future needs by setting aside a portion of their disposable incomes in the form of *savings*. The remainder is spent for goods and services. The relationship between the amount spent and total disposable income is called the *propensity to consume,* which varies with the level of disposable income, the degree to which prior debt is being retired, and household expectations about the levels and stability of future income. In general, households are more inclined to consume when they expect good times ahead or when they expect inflation to be so severe as to encourage hoarding against future price increases.

The demand for real estate goods and services is created by household expenditures in three major areas: (1) housing, (2) retail commercial activities, and (3) transient commercial activities.

Housing. Households traditionally have spent approximately 25 to 30 percent of disposable income on housing. Because of escalating housing costs, in recent years households have been spending 30 to 40 percent of disposable income on housing. The major portion of these expenditures takes the form of mortgage payments or rent. Payments on mortgages reflect demand for ownership housing, single-family and condominiums. The price of ownership housing, in turn, is influenced by the cost of mortgage financing and the term over which the mortgage is repaid. For example, increases in interest rates reduce the price that a household is able to pay for housing, longer repayment periods increase the potential price of housing, and lower down payments increase the price a household can afford.

Rental payments reflect a demand for apartment and single-family

[28]U.S. Bureau of Labor Statistics, *Consumer Expenditure Survey,* 1984, Bulletin 2267, 1986.

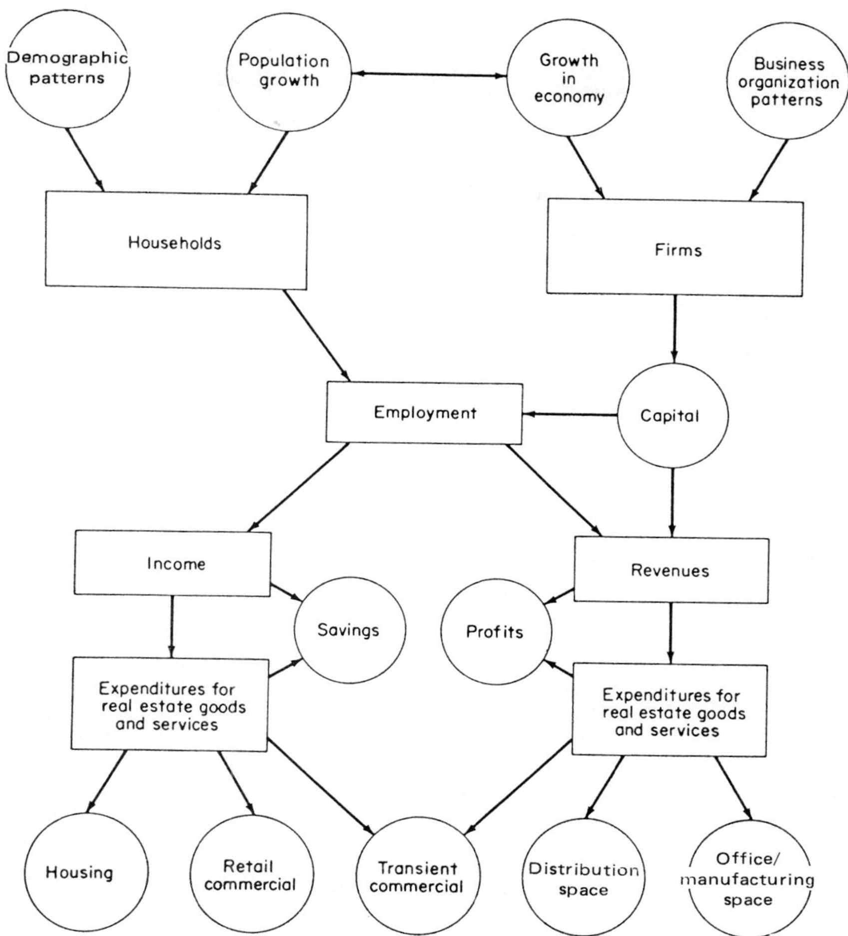

Figure 4-4. National demand patterns for real estate goods and services in the private sector.

rental units. The amount of rental payments depends on the cost of land and construction, financing, and annual costs of operating the apartment building. Higher land and construction costs require higher rents, thereby reducing the number of households that can afford the apartment units. Higher financing and operating costs have the same effect.

Retail Commercial. Americans historically have spent approximately 30 to 35 percent of their consumption expenditures on retail goods and services. These expenditures, in turn, create a demand for shopping centers and other facilities in which retail goods are sold or services provided. The amount of commercial space created is a function of the levels of expenditures and the number of households served by the facilities.

Transient Commercial. An increasing percentage of disposable income is spent on lodging, entertainment, travel, and recreational activities. These expenditures create a demand for hotels, restaurants, theaters, and recreational facilities, such as bowling alleys, tennis clubs, and golf courses. The demand for these facilities is a function of the level of household expenditures and the costs of reaching the facility. Changes in travel costs may affect the distance traveled, expanding or contracting the geographic market of the transient commercial facility. For example, the advent of jet aircraft reduced air travel costs, thereby opening up new resort development potential in Hawaii, Mexico, the Caribbean, and Europe—areas previously deemed too distant for most people.

Business Expenditures for Real Estate Goods and Services

Business firms generally spend a portion of their revenues for real estate goods and services. These expenditures may take the form of direct charges against current income or capital expenditures in anticipation of future income. As with households, expectations as to future prospects for income play a large role in determining the amount and nature of these expenditures. A firm expecting future growth in earnings may purchase or rent real estate goods and services beyond current needs. Types of business expenditures fall into three broad categories: (1) office and manufacturing space, (2) wholesale commercial activities, and (3) transient commercial activities.

Office and Manufacturing Space. The largest expenditure made by businesses for real estate goods and services is for office or manufacturing space in which to carry on their activities. The amount of office space needed is largely a function of the number of current employees, plus anticipations regarding the future; the type of activity in which the employer is engaged; and the operating "image" that the firm wishes to create. Demand for manufacturing space is a function of these factors, plus the space required for storing materials utilized in manufacture and the finished product.

Generally, increases in the level of employment will increase the amount of building space required. The amount of space is also affected by changes in technology. For example, computers have reduced the amount of space required for clerical personnel but increased the need for machine storage and operating areas. The cost per square foot of office space also has an impact on space requirements; firms are likely to be more generous in the amount of working space allotted to each employee in a lower-cost office building or during a period of substantial rent concessions.

Distribution Space. Business firms also depend upon wholesalers to supply them with goods required in the manufacturing process and to distribute the final product. The activities of wholesalers, in turn, create a demand for warehousing facilities. The level of demand for these facilities is a function of the markets served, transportation costs, and the level of inventories required to meet production levels and customer requirements. Again, technology may affect the amount of space required. The development of the forklift truck, for example, greatly expanded the use of single-floor, clear-span warehousing space, thus reducing the need for multifloor operations.

Transient Commercial. Businesses create a demand for hotels, restaurants, and other transient commercial activities. Business firms spend money for hotels to lodge personnel on business trips; in addition, companies and professional trade associations hold conventions and conferences in hotels. Restaurant expenditures come both from local business (e.g., the business lunch) and from out-of-town business travelers. Firms may also spend money on golf and tennis clubs, theater tickets, and other entertainment and recreational activities.

Public Sector Expenditures for Real Estate Goods and Services

The public sector also spends money for real estate goods and services. Housing authorities build and/or purchase public housing in many cities and rural areas. Health organizations build hospitals and outpatient centers. All levels of government build or lease office and other space for their employees. Public sector employees spend money for hotels, restaurants, and other transient commercial activities.

National Supply Patterns

The national patterns affecting real estate demand are often tempered by factors affecting the supply of land, construction labor and materials, and investment capital. In some cases, such as a change in legislation affecting land use or depreciation, the effect may be long-term in nature. In other cases, such as a national strike or embargo on a particular material, the effects can be immediate. Real estate is also particularly vulnerable to changing supply factors because it has been used by the federal government to facilitate changes in the overall economy and social fabric of the nation.

Land

In the United States, there is not now, nor has there ever been, a physical shortage of land for real estate activities. As land was required for farms, forests were cleared and pastures plowed. In the 1920s and early 1930s, drainage and irrigation programs opened up new land, leaving less productive lands to revert to pasture or forestry. The supply of forestry lands was further expanded by major reforestation programs begun in the early 1900s. As these shifts in uses occurred, the amount of land in other uses, including urban, expanded rapidly. By 1981, about one-third of U.S. land was in forests, one-fourth in meadows and pasture, and two-fifths in agriculture and urban uses.[29] Studies of selected urban areas indicate that around two-fifths of the developed area of a typical city is devoted to residential uses.[30]

The federal government can affect national land use patterns through such measures as maintenance of open space areas, changes in taxation policies, and even public ownership of land. All of these measures would tend to restrict or at least modify the supply of land for development purposes. The net result would be higher prices for land that is available for development. This, in turn, would no doubt lead to greater intensity of development on this land and/or the recycling of land that has already been developed.

Labor

A second factor affecting national supply patterns is the cost and availability of construction labor. Historically, the construction industry has had quite special labor characteristics. It has been subject to wide cyclic

[29]Raleigh Barlowe, *Land Resource Economics,* Prentice-Hall, Englewood Cliffs, N.J., 1986, p. 37.

[30]Ibid., pp. 41–42.

swings as a result of over- and underbuilding. In many areas, weather determines the seasons during which construction can occur on a full-intensity basis. The combination of cyclic and seasonal fluctuations has created a highly unstable employment pattern, with periods of high unemployment. The small-scale, fragmented, competitive nature of the construction industry contributes further to a relatively unstable employment picture.

To counteract these conditions, the trade union movement in the construction industry has adopted policies to protect its members. These policies tend to limit the supply and increase the cost of construction labor.

Materials

There are three basic sources of materials for construction: wood, concrete, and steel. The supply of wood and related products is a function of the production of trees and their use for paper, synthetics, and other uses. The supply of concrete and related products is relatively localized and largely inexhaustible, provided facilities are available for extraction and processing. The supply of steel is related to the availability of iron ore and coal; both resources are relatively abundant.

There are certain trade-offs among these basic materials. For example, if the supply of steel is particularly short or if prices rise too sharply, architects may shift to concrete as a substitute product. Generally speaking, these trade-offs are made from the higher-priced material to the lower-priced one. Local prices for a given material may also vary significantly, resulting in additional cost differentials.

Building materials are particularly subject to technological innovation. In many cases, innovation has increased the efficiency of building construction, thereby lowering costs. For example, gypsum wallboard lowered the cost of wall installation. Aluminum panels proved to be cheaper than steel or masonry curtain walls. In other instances, technological innovation may lead to lower maintenance costs, as did the fluorescent light and stain-resistant carpeting. In still other situations, improved technology has led to greater intensity of use on a site—for instance, the development of structural steel for skyscrapers and the introduction of the elevator.

Capital

The supply of capital for real estate development is a function of the total supply of capital in the nation and funds from foreign investors.

The supply of the nation's capital is, in turn, a function of the net savings of individuals, business firms, and governments. These savings are channeled into real estate in the form of either equity investment (ownership) or a debt instrument secured by the real property (mortgage). Equity investments are generally made directly by the individuals or institutions involved. Investments in debt instruments are generally made through financial intermediaries, such as insurance companies, savings and loan associations, or commercial banks.

Funds for real estate must compete with other uses of funds. Funds invested by the individual in equity positions in real estate must compete with other forms of investments: the stock market, bonds, and savings certificates. Public corporations investing in real estate must weigh the desirability of real estate investment against other uses of corporate funds. Financial institutions and pension funds must compare real estate with similar investments in stocks, bonds, commercial bank loans, or other debt instruments. As Figure 4.5 indicates, real estate has done a good job of effectively competing for capital with stocks and bonds.

With the exception of REITs, public syndications and other securitized issues, the real estate equity market is relatively informal and highly fragmented. The market for real estate debt instruments is more formalized: yields on mortgages compete directly with the yields on other forms of investment. The risk factor is usually low, since real estate debt is generally secured by real property assets. However, this is

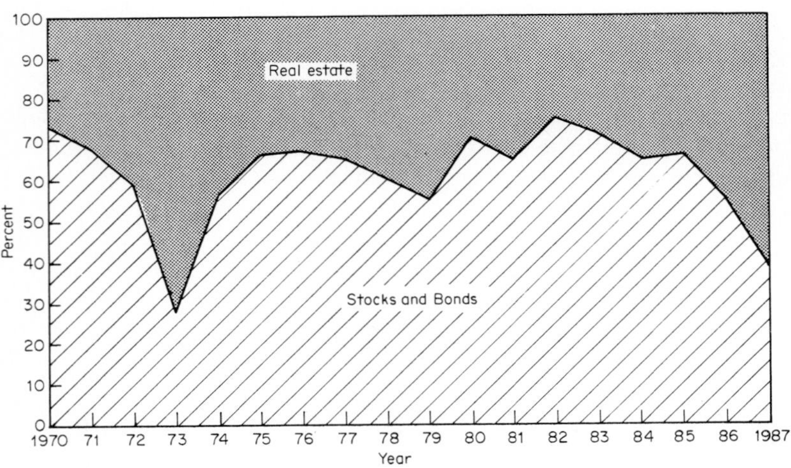

Figure 4-5. Stocks, bonds, and real estate investment as a percentage of annual net capital flows in real dollars. *(Securities and Exchange Commission, McMahan Real Estate Advisors, Inc.)*

offset somewhat by the relatively long-term nature of real estate investments, slow capital turnover, and the fixity of yields. The last two factors may retard the flow of funds into the real estate capital market, particularly when overall yields are relatively low.

The supply of real estate capital is also affected by government fiscal and monetary policy. The federal government has traditionally sought to make real estate, particularly housing, a more attractive investment by the use of accelerated depreciation and other tax write-offs. The Tax Reform Act of 1986, however, took away most of the benefits of real estate investment, and as a result a certain proportion of capital that might have entered the real estate market under the old tax laws may be invested elsewhere.

Monetary policy is also an area in which the government has a major impact on the supply of real estate capital. This impact may come indirectly, through changes in overall monetary policy that alter the flow of funds into the real estate market, or it may come directly, through the control of the cost and availability of funds for residential lending institutions. Housing is especially vulnerable to monetary policy because of interest-rate sensitivity. As a result, housing construction generally tends to be a leading indicator of economic expansion or contraction.

Real Estate and the Business Cycle

Historically, real estate construction has tended to move in a *countercyclical* pattern to the general business economy. This was primarily caused by the traditional dependence of real estate on large amounts of institutional mortgage financing. During periods of business expansion, demand increased for capital for other purposes (e.g., plant and equipment, working capital, consumer credit), driving up interest rates and making real estate less attractive to investors. As noted in Chapter 3, if short-term interest rates rose high enough, savings were withdrawn and invested directly in Treasury bills and other short-term instruments. When this occurred, a "credit crunch" was created where virtually no funds were available for real estate.[31]

During recessions, however, the opposite occurred. Reduced demand for funds by business led to a decline in short-term interest rates, and funds flowed back into savings accounts at thrifts and other financial institutions. Individuals, perhaps fearful of losing their jobs, reduced

[31]This occurred in 1966, 1970, 1973, 1974, and 1979.

spending and increased savings. Capital became available for real estate activity once again, with mortgage interest rates generally moving lower. Periods of real estate expansion, therefore, generally began in the midst of a recession.

The deregulation of financial institutions has made disintermediation and the credit crunch largely a thing of the past. Savings and loans, the traditional providers of funds to the housing market, can now offer the same rates as other financial institutions that formerly depleted their capital base during times of rising interest rates. As a result, real estate can now compete on its own merits as an investment, without the artificial constraints on capital availability imposed by a regulated marketplace.

Another factor altering real estate's traditional countercyclical relationship with the business cycle has been the policy of construction lenders to make loans without permanent take-out commitments. This allowed real estate projects to proceed almost regardless of the long-term financial market. As noted in Chapter 3, deregulation also allowed for the evolution of national construction lenders (usually money center banks) who actively competed with each other and with local and regional banks for construction projects. The deregulation of the thrifts, allowing for 10 percent investment in commercial real estate, was also a factor.

Finally, the emergence of new equity investors such as pension funds, syndications, and foreign investors reduced the real estate industry's reliance on interest-sensitive mortgage financing. This shift can clearly be seen by comparing the real (inflation adjusted) capital fueling the two most recent real estate construction booms: 1971–75 and 1983–87. The amount of real capital in the most recent period was $736.1 billion as compared with $625.3 billion in 1971–75, a 17.7 percent increase.[32] Equity capital increased 90.5 percent between the two periods, providing one out of three total capital dollars, versus one out of five dollars in the 1971–75 period.

Both of the boom periods resulted in substantial overbuilding and resultant disequilibrium in the real estate marketplace. Because of the availability of less disciplined construction financing and more equity money, the overbuilding of the 1983–87 period was more severe than the earlier period. The overbuilding of the 1971–75 period occurred during a major recession and, as such, was partially demand driven. The disequilibrium of 1983–87, however, occurred during a significant

[32]Investment properties only; excludes single-family and user-owned properties. Mortgage data exclude construction financing.

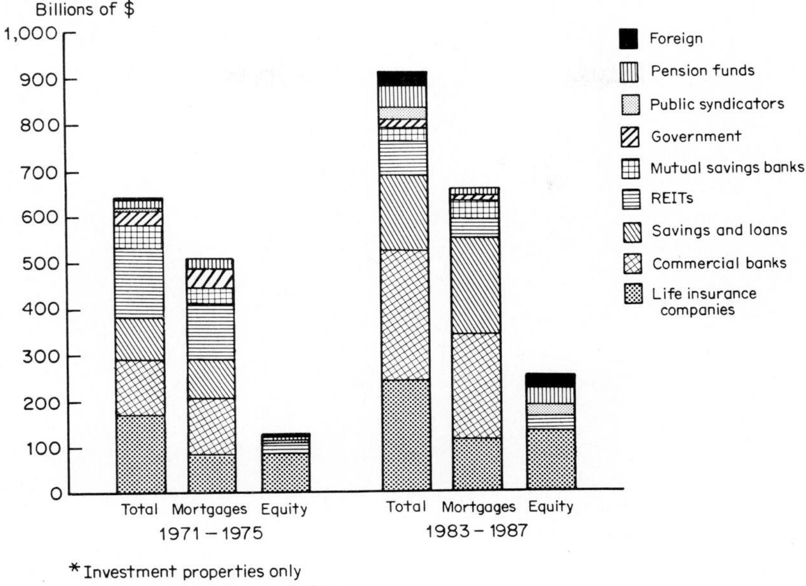

Figure 4-6. Sources of capital for two real estate boom periods.

expansion in office employment and therefore was mostly supply driven, fueled in large measure by a surplus of capital available to real estate.

In light of the excesses of the 1983–87 period, some might question whether the real estate industry has really benefited from its move from a sequestered, countercyclical capital market to a more independently driven economic force. Developers and investors now have to deal with a less predictable real estate capital market, with a greater probability of extreme disequilibrium. Consumers of real estate, on the other hand, are true beneficiaries, with greater product selection and lower overall occupancy costs.

5 The Economics of Real Estate at the Local Level

I will [tell] the story as I go along of small cities no less than of great. Most of those which were great once are small today, and those which in my own lifetime have grown to greatness were small enough in the old days.
HERODOTUS

Although national demand and supply patterns are important, regional and local patterns are what most critically affect the success of a particular real estate project. The strongest of national demand patterns won't be of much use to an overbuilt project or one caught in a slowly growing regional area. Conversely, a project in a rapidly growing area with reasonably balanced supply forces can be successful during a period of national real estate inactivity.

Demand for real estate at the local level comes from the expenditures of households for housing and retail services, from businesses for commercial space, and from both groups for lodging and entertainment facilities. Expenditure levels are a function of the number of households and businesses, their relative affluence, and their expectations of the future. The timing of expenditures depends on various supply factors, among them the availability of land, labor, materials, financing, and entrepreneurial talent. These factors, in turn, are directly related to the economic growth of the area.

Local Demand Patterns

What makes one area grow and another stagnate? Certainly, long-term shifts in population have an impact, positive or negative. But it's something of a "chicken and egg" situation—people wouldn't move to an urban area unless there were economic activity, and there would be no economic activity without people to produce and consumer goods.

Historical Growth of Cities

The origins of city life are not completely clear. Some have suggested that primitive peoples concentrated in certain locations to defend themselves against outside attack. Others believe the concentration of population stemmed from the desire to participate collectively in religious rites. Still others have viewed early human concentrations as political centers, where surplus agricultural production was collected by the local chieftain.[1] In any event, individuals began to group together in relatively central locations to carry out those functions which could best be done in close proximity to others.

Settlements soon found they had goods they wished to exchange with other groups. The place of exchange was a convenient, central location—perhaps at the convergence of two trails or along a riverbank. In this manner, the exchange of commodities, or *trade,* became a major force in preindustrial revolution cities. There was little specialization in the early cities: most performed similar functions on a relatively uniform basis. Most goods were produced locally, and prices were established by haggling. Since there was not much specialization and since most of the population lived in the surrounding economic rural area, there was little pressure to organize land uses into specialized functions.[2]

The coming of the industrial age had a dramatic impact on cities. As cities began to produce greater economic surpluses, they found it more

[1]Brian Goodall, *The Economics of Urban Areas,* Pergamon, Oxford, England, 1972, p. 24.

[2]Ibid.

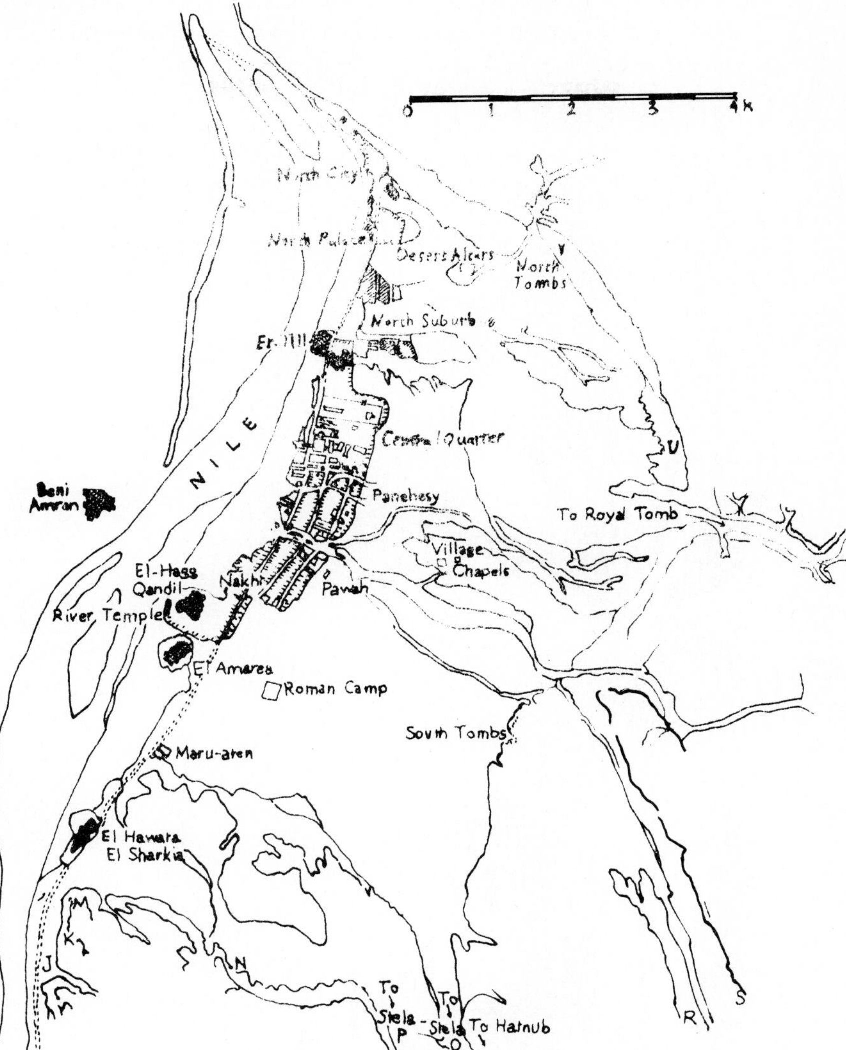

Figure 5-1. Map of Tell el 'Amarna, 1372–1350 B.C. *(From Arnold Whittick,* Encyclopedia of Urban Planning. *Copyright 1974 by McGraw-Hill. Used with permission of McGraw-Hill Book Company)*

efficient to specialize in one part of the production process, particularly if they had a natural resource (e.g., iron, coal, water power) which provided a competitive advantage over other cities. Greater production became possible via specialization. To attract the labor needed to operate these larger units, entrepreneurs had to offer higher wages than the surrounding areas. As people surged into the cities, local tradespeople found increased demand for their wares, and they too expanded their operations.

Concurrently, a revolution was taking place on the farm. Improved

"When Alexander the Great stopped here, we thought the town would take off. But it didn't."

production techniques made it possible for fewer people to produce the same amount of agricultural products. This further accelerated the move to the cities and provided seemingly unlimited labor for expanding urban industries. The cities, in turn, required agricultural production from the rural areas to survive, and therefore the demand for agricultural products increased. This reciprocity between urban and rural areas wasn't totally equal, however, and this led to a decline in agriculture's relative share, as well as a continued influx of rural migrants into the cities, long after the demand for rural labor in the cities had begun to decline.

As with many of the early trading cities, sites for industrial cities were often selected on the basis of access to good transportation facilities. As cities specialized, however, new and better means of transportation had to be developed to carry raw materials and finished and semifinished products between various points in the production process.

As these new transportation systems evolved, they often led to major shifts in the location and growth of cities. Many cities developed at points where routes crossed or goods were transported. Cities that lacked access to the new transportation system used political and economic pressure to be included, for they recognized that exclusion would ultimately bring economic stagnation.

It became necessary, as industrialized cities grew more specialized in economic functions, to separate various areas of the city for particular types of land use. Generally, areas nearest transportation facilities—particularly those fronting on oceans, lakes, and rivers—were set aside for industry. As railroads were developed, lines often were built along this industrial corridor on the waterfront. Consequently, much of the most desirable land in America became a tangle of industrial and transportation uses, preventing residential and recreational development on the waterfront. In nonwaterfront cities, industrial uses generally concentrated around natural resources or near transportation facilities, with the wealthy commanding the higher elevations and the less affluent occupying the valleys and plains. Commercial areas generally developed around existing trading centers or along heavily traveled routes.

Analyzing Economic Growth

Export Base Theory. One factor in the growth of industrial-age cities was that they *exported* more than they *imported* from other cities and/or the surrounding countryside. Observing this phenomenon, some economists developed the *export base* theory, which holds that *export industries* (generally manufacturing and those exploiting natural resources) which produce goods sold outside the region usually *support* a certain number of local service industries. That is, one manufacturing job will support, say, three jobs in retailing, finance, education, and the like. The ratio of the export sector to the total level of local economic activity is often referred to as the *multiplier effect,* or the degree to which total expenditures rise faster than payrolls in the export sector.[3]

Not everyone agrees with the export base theory. Some believe that local service industries are the basic economic strength of an area and that export industries merely provide an interim shot in the arm which must be replaced if the export industry disappears. Others point out that the theory is flawed because clearly the world economy grows without exports; therefore there is no reason to believe a regional economy must have exports in order to grow.[4]

The actual situation is probably somewhere between these extreme positions. The growth of national service industries has lessened the relative importance of manufacturing in the overall national economy. Improved communication and transportation systems have reduced the need to be physically near raw materials. But perhaps the most important reason is the increased emphasis of both management and labor on the quality of life. Areas that have climatic advantages and/or well-developed local services such as housing, education, and cultural arts are often in a more competitive position to attract industry.

Input-Output Analysis. Another way to measure regional growth patterns is by input-output analysis, which involves developing a matrix consisting of regional industries and an export category. After a number of iterations, a final matrix is developed which shows how one additional or *marginal* dollar spent in a particular industry affects sales in each of the other industries in the matrix. Input-output tables may be useful in projecting how growth in one industry will affect the rest of the region, but often the data used is inaccurate or old, reducing the value of the results.

Shift-Share Analysis. Shift-share analysis provides a method for analyzing a region's growth by looking at two measures of its industry in relation to the national economy. For each regional industry, a ratio is developed that compares the percentage of the region's jobs in that industry to the percentage of the nation's jobs in that industry. A regional economy will tend to be healthier if this ratio is greater than 1 for those

[3]Wilbur R. Thompson, *A Preface to Urban Economics*, Johns Hopkins, Baltimore, 1965, pp. 14, 27, 28.

[4]Charles Wurtzebach and Mike Miles, *Modern Real Estate*, John Wiley & Sons, New York, p. 41.

industries that are also growing on a nationwide basis. This means that the regional industry has more than its share of the total nationwide employment in a growing industry.

The second measure used in shift-share analysis is the ratio of regional growth in a given industry to nationwide growth in the industry. The region will be competitive if this ratio is greater than 1, that is, if regional growth rates are greater than national rates.

Population Migration Patterns

As areas expand and develop, shifts in population occur between various areas and, to some extent, within the area. These shifts in population, in turn, accelerate or retard the impact of economic growth. Certainly, the growth of areas such as California and Florida has been influenced by heavy in-migration. Similarly, it is exceedingly difficult to undertake economic development in areas of net out-migration.

Regional Migration. Several major long-term regional migration patterns have evolved during the last hundred years. The first is the continuing long-term shift of the population to the West. The Pacific and Mountain regions have generally had more people moving in than moving out. This trend continued through the 1970s and still holds true. Of the four fastest-growing states during the first half of the 1980s, three were in the West or Mountain regions: Alaska (29.7 percent), Arizona (17.2 percent), and Nevada (16.9 percent).[5] The movement to the West is also indicated by the steady westward march of the center of the nation's population. In 1790, the center was just outside Baltimore; by 1980 it had moved to a point about 30 miles southwest of St. Louis.

Another major long-term trend is the growth of the South Atlantic states. This area, which had consistently lost population after the Civil War, began to turn around following World War II. In the 1960s, this region emerged as a major growth center, with net migration of over 2.5 million. It is important to note that this is a "net" figure—although the total in-migration was much higher, it was offset by considerable out-migration, primarily of blacks.

During the 1970s the South Atlantic states experienced even greater growth, with net migration amounting to 3.4 million people. This included in-migration of blacks, reversing the trend of the previous de-

[5] *American Demographics*, April 1987, p. 14.

cade. More than 73 percent of this growth occurred in Florida, which grew by 2.5 million. The South Atlantic states continued their strong growth pattern into the 1980s. Net migration for the area in the first half of the decade was 2.1 million. Florida, once again, was responsible for the majority (68 percent) of the region's growth.

In any type of migratory pattern, some regions have to be losers. Following World War II, the East South Central continued the out-migration pattern that dated back to the end of the Civil War. During the 1970s, however, this pattern reversed, and the region experienced a net gain of half a million people. But the net population declined slightly by (40,000) again as people began moving out of the region during the first half of the 1980s.

Though less extreme, the West North Central region also has exhibited a long-term out-migration pattern which has lasted into the 1980s. The region has had long-term out-migration, but it was substantially reduced during the 1960s, largely because of the growth of Texas, and the flow of migrants out of the region was reversed during the 1970s for the same reason. During that decade the region experienced a net in-flow of nearly 2 million people, 1.5 million in Texas alone. The 1960s also marked the first decade since World War II when more people left the East North Central region than came in. This pattern continued through the 1970s and into the 1980s. The Middle Atlantic states barely

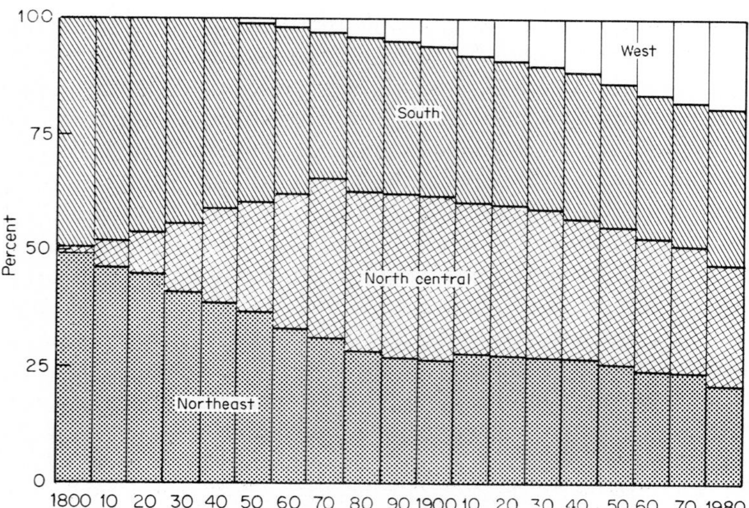

Figure 5-2. Percentage distribution of U.S. population by regions, 1800–1980. *(U.S. Bureau of the Census)*

held their own during the 1960s. They experienced a huge net loss during the 1970s of more than 2.6 million people and continued to lose population (but at a slower rate) into the 1980s.

One of the surprises of the 1960s was the 300,000 net increase in the population of the New England states, reflecting primarily the growth in the electronics industry. This trend reversed itself in the 1970s, however, when the area experienced a slight net loss of population. The trend was reversed again in the 1980s; during the first 5 years of the decade New England realized a small population gain of 28,000.

Another long-term trend appears to be the movement of Americans out of inland areas to areas near water. With the exception of the Mountain region, all of the regions exhibiting net in-migration during the 1960s were located on an ocean. By 1970 over one-half of the nation's population lived within 50 miles of the Atlantic or Pacific Ocean, the Gulf of Mexico, and the Great Lakes.[6] Strong migration into coastal states, particularly Florida and California, continued throughout the 1970s and into the 1980s.

The South and West have been the beneficiaries of 90 percent of the nation's growth since 1970. The population of the South increased 20 percent during the 1970s and another 8.6 percent between 1980 and 1985, while the West grew 23.9 percent between 1970 and 1980, and 10.8 percent during the first half of the 1980s. While the South and West together realized a net gain in population of 32 million between 1970 and 1985, the Midwest and Northeast regions added just 3.4 million people.[7]

Rural-Urban Migration. Another major long-term migration pattern in the United States is the shift from rural areas to cities. This trend is one of the major reasons behind the unprecedented growth of metropolitan areas, even in regions with declining in-migration. It helps to explain, for example, the growth of Minneapolis-St. Paul during the 1970s at a time when regional population in the North Central region experienced an overall decline.

Perhaps more than any other country, America has experienced expanding economic opportunity in the city and declining requirements for labor on the farm. United States farmers are generally regarded as among the most productive in the world, with 2.2 percent of the pop-

[6] *Report on National Growth 1972,* Executive Office of the President, Domestic Council Committee on National Growth, 1972, p. 12.

[7] U.S. Bureau of the Census, *Current Population Reports,* ser. P-25, no. 957, 1984, and unpublished data.

ulation producing food not only for domestic needs but for export to other nations as well.[8]

The migration of Americans from farms to cities was a slow but continuous process. In 1790, only 5.1 percent of the population lived in communities of more than 2500, and only half of the people lived in cities of more than 10,000. By the outbreak of the Civil War, one out of five Americans lived in urban places;[9] by the turn of the century, the number was two out of five. It wasn't until 1920 that the population living in urban places exceeded the population living in rural areas.[10] By 1980, three out of every four Americans lived in urban places.[11]

The migration to urban areas quite naturally resulted in an increase in the number of large cities. Before 1840, only New York, Philadelphia, Boston, and Baltimore had a population of 100,000 or more. In 1840, New Orleans became the next city to surpass 100,000. By 1860, the Midwest began to emerge: the population of Chicago, Cincinnati, St. Louis, and Pittsburgh reached 100,000. Ten years later, San Francisco became the first major urbanized area in California. By the turn of the century, there were thirty-seven major urbanized areas in the United States with populations of 100,000 or more. By 1920, this number had doubled to seventy; it doubled again during the 1950s. In 1970, there were 180 major urbanized areas in the nation.[12] During the next decade that figure doubled once more; by 1980, there were 366 major urban areas in the country.[13]

The magnitude of urbanized areas is also increasing. Only four urban areas exceeded 1 million in population in 1900; by 1970 there were twenty-five; by 1985, forty-three. Certain urban areas are also amalgamating into a type of large urban region known as a megalopolis. Some of these emerging regions have descriptive nicknames: "Bos-Wash" (the metropolitan region between Boston and Washington) and "Los-San" (Los Angeles-San Diego). In 1970, 49.1 percent of the pop-

[8]U.S. Bureau of the Census, *Current Population Reports,* ser. P-25, no. 957, 1984, and unpublished data.

[9]U.S. Department of Commerce, *Statistical Abstract of the United States,* Table 1093, p. 619, 1987.

[10]An urban place is an area with more than 2500 people. *Report on National Growth 1972,* op. cit., pp. 14–15.

[11]U.S. Bureau of the Census, 1980 Census of Population, *Characteristics of the Population,* 1983, Table 5, pp. 1–37.

[12]Jerome P. Pickard, *Dimensions of Metropolitanism,* Urban Land Institute, Research Monograph 14, 1967, pp. 18.

[13]1980 Census of Population, *Characteristics of the Population,* op. cit., Table 4, pp. 1–36.

ulation of the coterminous United States lived in urban regions.[14] By 1980, three out of four Americans lived in urban places, while only one in thirty-seven still lived on a farm.[15]

Urban-Suburban Migration. Even in metropolitan areas with declining economic activity, the movement of the population from central city to suburbs has boosted demand for real estate in certain portions of the those areas. This phenomenon accounts for real estate activity in metropolitan areas with a declining central city, such as St. Louis, Detroit and Cleveland.

At the turn of the twentieth century, approximately 38 percent of Americans lived in the suburbs, and central cities were growing at a faster rate. This continued until the 1920s, when the suburbs began growing at a faster rate. By 1950, 40 percent of metropolitan residents lived in the suburbs. During the 1960s, the suburbs became dominant; by 1970, 54 percent of the population of metropolitan areas was in the suburbs. Between 1950 and 1970, three out of every four new residents of metropolitan areas located in the suburbs. By 1974, the central cities were experiencing an absolute loss of population. Suburban growth rates have declined during the 1980s, but between 1980 and 1984 annual suburban growth rates were still double those of the central city (1.3 versus 0.6 percent).

Most of those who moved to the suburbs over time were white, middle-class people who could afford the new housing being developed. The poor and minorities were thus concentrated in the central cities. By 1979, 12.9 percent of central city families had incomes below the poverty line, versus 7.2 percent of those in the suburban fringe.[16]

In the 1970s and 1980s, middle-class households, primarily white, began moving to poor, primarily black neighborhoods which contained housing stock that was ripe for rehabilitation. This gentrification movement did not necessarily increase the level of urban integration, however, for in many cases, once the neighborhood was revitalized, sharp price increases forced the original residents to move elsewhere.

Interaction of Population Migration Patterns. These three national population migration patterns (regional, rural-urban, urban-suburban) generally interact. Since population growth usually influences real es-

[14]Pickard, op. cit., p. 23.

[15]Raleigh Barlowe, *Land Resource Economics,* 1987, op. cit., p. 60.

[16]1980 Census of Population, *Characteristics of the Population,* op. cit., Table 108, pp. 1–79.

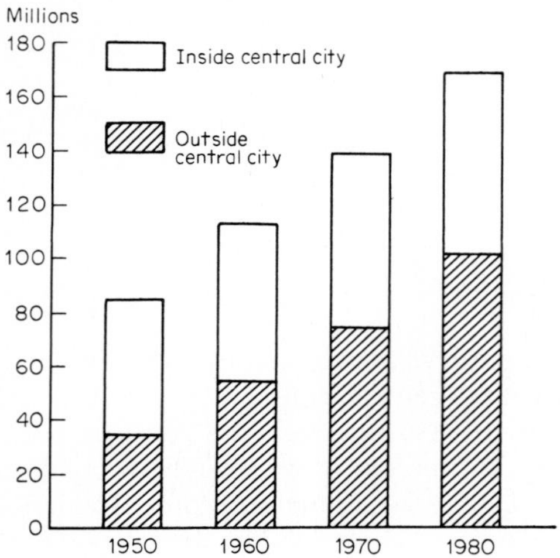

Figure 5-3. U.S. metropolitan population, 1950–1980. Data based on metropolitan area definition at the time of each census. *(U.S. Bureau of the Census)*

tate development activity, areas that experience population growth pressures from all three trends can be expected to present more relative development opportunities than those that are experiencing only one or two pressures. We can generalize about the ways in which these trends interact by exploring three hypothetical situations.

- *Situation A.* All three basic population migration patterns are occurring in a positive manner: the region is growing, the rural population is migrating to the dominant urban areas within the region (rather than to another region), and people and economic activity are shifting from the central city to the suburbs. An example of this situation would be Los Angeles during the 1950s, Houston in the 1970s, or Atlanta in the early 1980s.
- *Situation B.* The urban area is located in a region that is experiencing net out-migration, but the urban area is capturing a large share of the people within the region moving out of rural areas. An example of this would be the twin cities of Minneapolis-St. Paul.
- *Situation C.* Both urban and rural populations are leaving the region, and the central city is deteriorating. The only strong demand forces are in suburban areas, because of the exodus from the central city. Detroit is an example of this phenomenon.

Local Supply Factors

Local real estate markets are influenced by local supply factors as well as demand patterns. Demand patterns can vary greatly among local areas at any given time. They can also differ from national supply patterns, although such variations do not last indefinitely.

Land

One of the major factors affecting local real estate activity is the relative availability of land for development. Although there is no land shortage on a national level, within a local area—Manhattan Island, for example—land may be one of the dearest commodities in the local economy.

Many factors constrain the supply of land. Natural barriers like oceans, rivers, lakes, and mountains often limit the direction in which a city can expand. Sometimes the barriers are artificial: parks, railroad yards, airports, highways, and blighted neighborhoods. Land ownership patterns may prevent the assemblage of sufficiently large parcels for development. In many areas, the unavailability of utilities like water, electricity, and waste disposal facilities may limit development. Finally, the amount of land available for some specific use may be limited by governmental planning, zoning, building codes, environmental controls, and tax policy.

If the demand for land strengthens over a continuing period of time, it often becomes economically feasible to overcome some of these supply constraints. Rivers are bridged, lakes and swamps filled, mountains graded, railroad yards crossed or moved, new utility bond issues passed, zoning changed, or taxes modified. Pressures may also mount to increase the intensity of use of existing land. For example, residential zoning may be increased from single-family to multifamily or changed to commercial. Zoning and building codes may be modified to allow more intensive types of construction.

Existing Building Inventories

Another factor affecting local real estate development activity is the volume and quality of existing inventories of residential, commercial, and industrial buildings. Volume is important in the short run because extensive inventories created by overbuilding, such as occurred in many markets in the 1980s, can postpone new development activity. The quality of existing inventories can affect long-term development activity if there are substantial differences between older inventories and new

Figure 5-4. Overcoming land constraints: Copley Place, a mixed-use development in Boston's Back Bay. The project is built on a platform over a freeway interchange. *(Photo by Bill Horsman)*

construction. For instance, a portion of the demand for new housing following World War II resulted from significant improvements in design, since much of the existing inventory had been built in the 1920s and 1930s. The same is true of office and hotel construction in the central business districts of many cities, in which much of the existing inventory was functionally obsolete.

Labor

The supply of local labor is generally a function of national labor trends. Most local areas have large enough labor pools to handle normal development activity. In areas of rapid growth, however, short-term shortages in supply may develop. They are generally corrected by the migration of labor from other areas and/or the expansion of the local labor supply through training programs. The cost of labor may also vary among local areas, depending on the presence and strength of local unions. Lower hourly costs, however, may be offset by a lack of worker skills.

Materials

The supply of materials varies from one local area to another, depending on the availability of basic ingredients. For instance, areas in the Pacific Northwest are more apt to use wood in construction; areas with a good supply of clay will rely on brick construction. Sand and gravel for concrete are available in most areas and generally aren't supply problems; nor is steel, in most areas.

Capital

Local capital sources may vary considerably, and they often affect the level of real estate development activity in a particular area. Commercial banks often take an aggressive role in providing construction financing and access to long-term financing from other areas. This role is particularly important in small and medium-sized communities, where long-term institutional lenders may not be active on a direct basis. Savings and loan associations and mutual savings banks have been critically important in certain areas in providing needed funds for housing. Noteworthy are the savings and loans of California and Florida, which have channeled funds from other capital markets—particularly the Northeast and the Midwest—into housing in these rapidly growing areas. Mortgage bankers may be important in some communities, particularly in "packaging" the financing of highly specialized or particularly complicated real estate projects.

Entrepreneurship

In most local areas, entrepreneurs provide the creative force behind real estate development. The role of these individuals cannot be minimized. John Portman played a major role in the revitalization of downtown Atlanta. Trammell Crow helped make Dallas one of the major merchandising cities of the nation. Gerald Hines helped to establish Houston as a major corporate headquarters city. Nor can we overlook the earlier impact of the Tishmans and the Uris Brothers on the skyline of Manhattan or the more recent activities of Donald Trump in New York and Willard Rouse in Philadelphia. These entrepreneurs, and many more like them, creatively marshaled the components of development into building projects that have changed the shape of their communities.

Theories of Land Use Development Patterns

Four major theories have been proposed to explain how land develops within an urban area. Each of these theories is based upon empirical observation of the development of cities over a period of time, and each shares basic assumptions: a system of private land ownership, a commercial industrial economic base, a heterogeneous population, and economic competition for sites.[17]

Concentric Theory (1925)

This theory, based on studies of the development of Chicago by Ernest W. Burgess, concludes that land uses tend to develop in concentric circles out from a central point. Five zones of land use are identified: (1) a central business district (CBD), which is the center of activity from which all other zones radiate; (2) a transition zone of mixed commercial and industrial uses, many of which service the CBD; (3) a low-income housing zone containing the older housing inventory; (4) a middle-income zone consisting of many of the early suburbs; and (5) a commuting zone consisting of the newest suburban development.

This theory suffers from several discrepancies. First, it assumes that the CBD is the desired employment destination of most area residents. While this may have been true of the development of older cities, it has not been true of automobile-age cities, in which more than one center of activity exists. The theory also assumes that higher-income residents care more about the spaciousness of the suburbs than about accessibility to the CBD. In actuality, these two factors are often evaluated simultaneously, along with other factors such as neighborhood and schools and overall housing costs.

Axial Theory (1932)

This theory, propounded by F. M. Babcock, modifies the concentric theory to consider accessibility to the CBD. Accessibility is weighed in

[17]Goodall, op. cit., pp. 109–113.

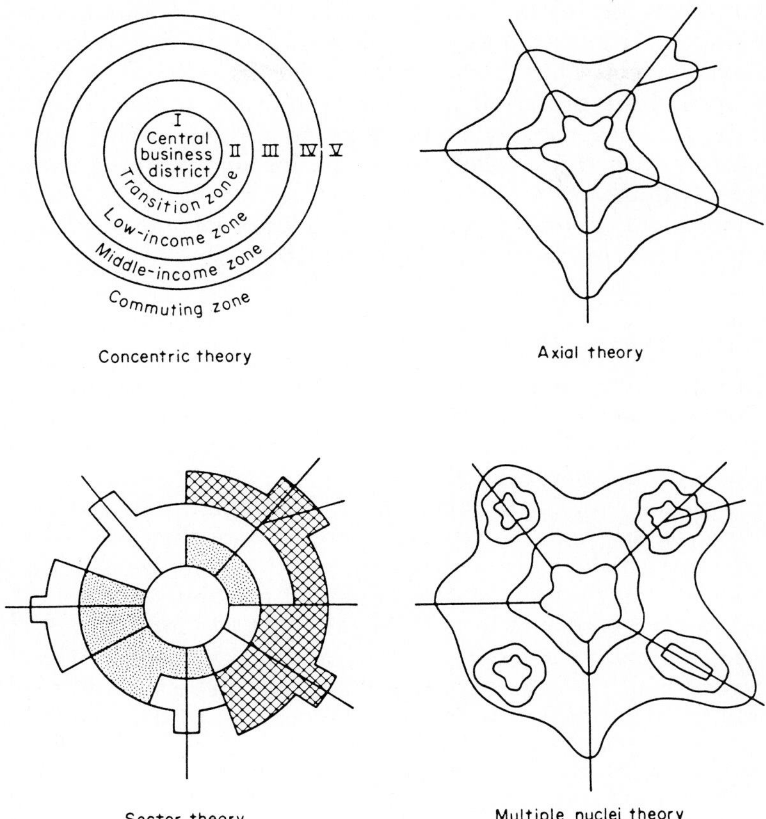

Figure 5-5. Theories of land use development patterns.

time-cost considerations in terms of a given transportation system. According to this theory, land uses tend to develop along the various axes to the CBD in terms of their time-cost relationships. A site farther from the CBD but adjacent to one of the axes would be more valuable than one that is closer but not near the transportation corridor. Except for its consideration of improved accessibility, this theory suffers from the same basic weakness as the concentric ring theory.

Sector Theory (1939)

First proposed by Homer Hoyt in 1939, this theory modifies the axial theory to consider attractiveness of one transportation corridor over another. A transportation corridor that is established early or is more accessible would tend to attract more development than one that develops later or is less efficient. Thus, higher-income housing tends to develop in a sector around the preferred transportation artery rather than in concentric rings, as proposed by earlier theories. Although this theory was originally developed to explain residential housing preferences, it relates more to commerce and industry, where accessibility to suppliers or customers is highly critical. It also applies to lower-income residents who depend on low-cost transportation to the CBD.

Multiple Nuclei Theory (1945)

In depending on the assumption that the CBD is the focal point of virtually all economic activity, the previous three theories are weak. While this may have been true of the development of earlier cities, it by no means explains the development of cities after the advent of the automobile. Recognizing this, C. D. Harris and E. L. Ullman proposed the multiple nuclei theory, which holds that there is more than one focal point of economic activity in any urban area and that land use patterns will evolve in relation to the type of centers and proximity of land to these centers. Such centers may include the original CBD, industrial districts, cultural centers, strip shopping areas, and major shopping centers. Residential land uses then arrange themselves in relation to the various commercial, industrial, and cultural centers. Of all the theories, the multiple nuclei theory comes closest to reflecting land use development patterns as they exist in most American cities.

6
The Economics of the Individual Parcel

Every man has by nature the right to possess property as his own. POPE LEO XIII

Within the urban framework of each metropolitan area, a series of economic, social, and political forces operates that influences the use and, ultimately, the value of each individual parcel of land. These forces are translated into value through the sale or lease of raw land or the development and sale or lease of improvements on the land. Generally, real estate values exist when the income stream generated by the sale or leasing of the property exceeds the costs involved in developing the stream. In some cases, such as a park, the surplus generated may be expressed in terms of the satisfaction of public needs rather than in terms of monetary return.

The Concept of Highest and Best Use

The relative ability of a parcel of land to generate a surplus of returns and/or satisfactions over its costs of utilization is called its *use capacity.* Assuming the same quality and type of improvement, the use capacity of an individual parcel depends upon its accessibility to markets vis-à-vis other parcels which have the same physical and legal characteristics. Generally, the closer the parcel is to the markets for its particular use, the higher its use capacity. The higher its use capacity, the higher the real estate value that ultimately can be created.

The ability of a given parcel to achieve its use capacity will vary over time, depending on market demand, environmental conditions, legal restraints, and the competition of other parcels. It is therefore necessary to evaluate the *highest and best use* of a parcel at any given time. Land is generally thought to be at its highest and best use when it is employed for purposes which have the highest comparative advantage or least comparative disadvantage in relation to possible alternative uses. In some cases, the highest and best use of a parcel at any given moment may be considerably different from or less than its use capacity. For example, a large, relatively flat tract of land may be ideally suited for industry, but limited industrial demand may dictate residential development as the highest and best use. A property's highest and best use may change over time as a result of changes in demand, technology, social values, or the quality of the land itself.

In general, commercial and industrial uses generate the highest economic returns and can outbid other uses for a particular parcel of land. Residential uses are generally next, followed by agricultural and forestry uses. Of course, there are exceptions to this hierarchy of land use priorities. For example, residential uses sometimes can outbid commercial or industrial uses, particularly in rapidly growing areas.

Not all property is utilized at its highest and best use. Because leases generally tie up a property for some time, it may be difficult to develop a property for its highest and best use immediately. For instance, in many downtown areas, long-term leases on parking lots or small commercial structures may thwart major commercial use of the property, even if commercial demand is strong. At the other extreme, properties may be overimproved in terms of their current highest and best use. An example is the older industrial and commercial area in which major structures are no longer supported by market demand, but demolition costs are too great to tear them down.

The Importance of Location

There is an old saw in real estate that the three most important factors in determining a good site are: (1) location, (2) location, and (3) location. While other factors are involved, it's amazing how often the basic truth of this homily is forgotten. A well-located project can often survive economically, even if its development is poorly planned or its management inept. However, a project that is not well located may fail even with the best of planning and management.

We noted in the Introduction that two basic characteristics of land are immobility and nonsubstitutibility. Each parcel of land is unique and has only one location. Location, therefore, is an important element in determining land value. Certain parcels have an *intrinsic locational value* as a result of a good siting, particular soils or mineral deposits, or a favorable exposure to the sun. Generally, however, the *relative locational value* of a parcel is what determines value. Relative locational value is the combination of the *spatial proximity* of a parcel to other parcels and the *linkage* between them. Spatial features may be desirable or undesirable in nature. Proximity to desirable uses generally increases a parcel's value; proximity to undesirable uses or features generally decreases value.

Several types of spatial proximity influence relative locational value. *Proximity to physical features* is often important. In beachfront recreational areas, land on or near the water commands higher values than more distant land. Proximity to lakes, rivers, mountains, or deserts may increase value; proximity to flood plains, earthquake fault zones, or fog pockets may reduce them.

Proximity to markets is also important. A residential development must be within a certain commuting distance to employment opportunities. Shopping centers must be within a certain proximity to sufficient resident buying power to support retail operations. Office and industrial facilities must be close to labor resources and support facilities. Hotels must be near other uses that generate guest-room demand. Without proximity to markets, other locational factors become largely irrelevant.

A third factor is *proximity to public services,* such as water, sewers, electricity, telephone, and other utilities. In recent years, the availability of water and sewers has become particularly critical to residential development. In some areas, proximity to these services actually determines land values, a situation which has accelerated as public agencies have learned to provide or withhold these services to effectively control and direct economic growth. As concern for more efficient use of energy grows, proximity to sources of power may also become important in determining the value of a site.

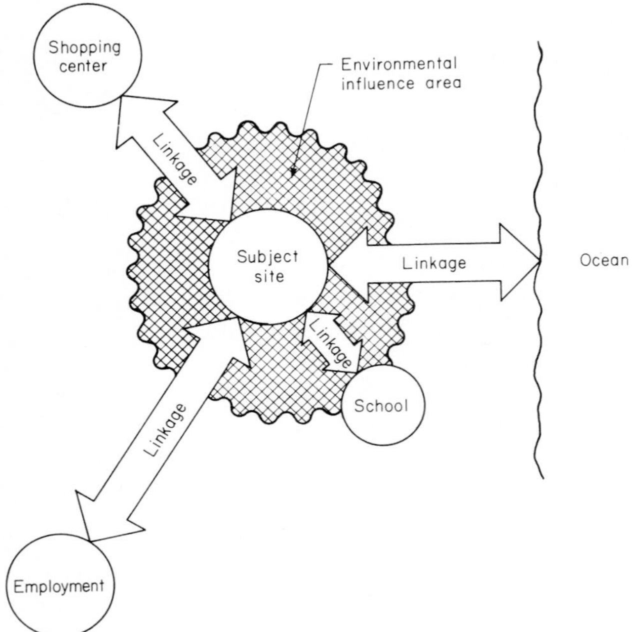

Figure 6-1. Relative locational factors, residential site.

Spatial proximity in itself will not create value unless there is effective and reliable *linkage* between the subject parcel and other parcels. Linkage is the ability to move goods and people between two points. In turn, linkage requires a *transportation system* and *accessibility* to the parcel. The transportation system may be as mundane as a sidewalk or path or as sophisticated as a rapid transit system. The most common type of system today is the private vehicle, street, and highway system. The transportation system is useless to a particular site, however, unless its users have accessibility to the system from the parcel. For example, a frontage parcel located between interchanges on a new limited-access highway may be less valuable than one located off the highway but near the interchange.

Increasingly, linkage is being measured in time rather than physical availability. Proximity to a freeway is of little value if traffic congestion is so great at the peak hour that it actually takes more time to reach site A than competitive site B, which can be reached by surface streets or rapid transit. Commuters may willingly increase their commuting costs by driving out of their way to reach freeways and arterials that will reduce their overall commute time.

(a)

(b)

Figure 6-2. Various forms of linkage. (*a*) Pedestrian skywalk in downtown Cincinnati, Ohio. *(Paul L. Wertheimer)* (*b*) Bicycle trail on Amelia Island Plantation, Nassau County, Florida. *(Sea Pines Company)* (*c*) A maze of freeways surround downtown Dallas, Texas. *(Brookhollow Corporation)* (*d*) Bay Area Rapid Transit (BART) car in Walnut Creek, California. *(Bay Area Rapid Transit)*

(c)

(d)

Figure 6-2. *(Continued)*

There is also evidence that users are willing to make site decisions on the basis of planned accessibility as well as existing transportation systems. Construction in advance of freeways or rapid transit systems is a good example. The major consideration appears to be the certitude that the facility will be developed.

The cost of a single movement along a given linkage is expressed in terms of the disutility, or *cost of friction,* in moving goods or people between two points. Ratcliff identifies four major components of the cost of friction:[1]

- *Transportation costs.* The direct costs of transportation can be measured in fares paid or in the operation costs of vehicles.
- *Travel time.* This factor is a function of the transportation facilities which are available, street system surfacing, traffic controls, and congestion. The time-cost depends on the value placed on the time of the person who is traveling or on the disruption of schedules, loss of business, or spoilage caused by delays.
- *Personal aggravation.* The discomfort of travel, the annoyances of delay and congestion, and the sense of danger are disutilities which increase friction.
- *Parking facilities.* For most automobile trips, terminal facilities are as essential to the free use of the motor vehicle as are the streets. Parking rates may also be a consideration.

The economic importance of a given linkage is the product of these costs of friction for each individual trip times the *frequency* of the trips undertaken. A linkage having relatively high costs of friction but requiring infrequent trips may be more attractive than one involving lower-cost, but more frequent, trips. As an example, the higher costs of large bulk shipments by rail may prove more attractive than lower-cost, but more frequently needed, shipments by truck between the same two points.

In making a site purchase or use decision, there are trade-offs between the cost of linkage and the value of the parcel. For example, in buying a home, an individual may trade off the lower housing costs in a neighborhood farther from his or her job against the added commuting costs. A shopping center may locate beyond an established residential area to obtain lower-value land (and therefore lower operating costs). An industrial firm may build a new facility on lower-value land in a distant suburb, trading off increased employee commute costs.

[1]Richard U. Ratcliff, *Real Estate Analysis,* McGraw-Hill, New York, 1961, p. 69.

Another location factor is the *environment influence area* within which the site is located. Spatial proximity and good linkages are of little value if the environment surrounding the site will dissuade potential users from coming into the area. A classic example is a potential shopping center site in a good market area, adjacent to a freeway and public services, but located in a physically deteriorating, crime-ridden neighborhood.

As with transportation systems, future expectations of change may be sufficient to motivate near-term investment decisions in environmentally depressed areas. If there is strong evidence that change will occur—urban renewal, upgrading of residential areas, and so forth—the negative aspects of present environmental conditions may be offset by future expectations.

A final locational factor primarily affecting commercial properties is the *exposure* of a given parcel of land to passing pedestrian or vehicular traffic. Value may be created in terms of direct exposure to potential customers, such as a motor hotel located along a heavily traveled highway or a retail shop on a busy street corner.

The Real Estate Market

If real estate were a highly organized, smoothly functioning market, the price of a property would accurately reflect its value. Theoretically, anyone wishing to know the value of a property would only have to look at price quotes in the morning paper, as is done for the stock or bond market. Unfortunately, the market for real estate is inefficient, and often there are serious short-term dislocations between price and value. It's essential, therefore, to understand how the real estate market functions and the pricing mechanism operates.

Characteristics of the Real Estate Market

In its most basic terms, the nation's real estate market is the sum of all buying, selling, renting, and investing transactions involving real property. Since real estate has a fixed location, real estate markets have tended to be local in nature, although this has been changing in recent years with the development of large syndications, REITs, national development corporations, and with the influx of foreign buyers into the marketplace.

Real estate transactions also tend to be relatively complicated legally and generally private in nature. Since the market lacks any centralized control, it is likely to be disorganized and fragmented. Consequently, the forces of supply and demand do not always function smoothly and often result in significant dislocations.

Real Estate Submarkets

No one single real estate market exists; rather, submarkets are generally organized around the type of real estate to be sold and the characteristics of the purchaser. Each submarket has its own set of buyers and sellers, its own legal framework to govern relationships, exclusive methods of financing, and specialized brokers and other individuals to handle the transaction.

Raw Land. This submarket deals with land that is several years away from development. It is generally located some distance from existing urban or recreational areas and is usually completely raw or being utilized for some type of agriculture. The seller is generally a farmer or other long-term landholder. The buyer is generally a speculator who plans to sell the property to a developer or another speculator. The speculator is usually an individual who is investing for long-term value appreciation. In recent years, the entry of large syndicators, public corporations, and other intermediaries has given the raw land market a somewhat institutional flavor. The major investor, however, is still usually an individual.

During the 1950s and 1960s, the long-term investment nature of land speculation was further enhanced by such tax benefits as prepaid interest, depreciation of agricultural resources, and capital gains treatment on sale. Most of these tax advantages have been eliminated by subsequent tax legislation so that the speculative land market is once more directed primarily at long-term appreciation.

Prices in this market tend to fluctuate widely, depending on events in the local economy, the national economy, and the amount of buying pressure. Most properties are sold on liberal terms, with the buyer making a small down payment and the seller financing the balance. Holding periods tend to range from 6 to 10 years.

User Properties. The second type of submarket is composed of individuals and institutions wishing to buy or rent properties for their own use. Individual home buyers make up the largest segment of this market, which is highly organized on a local level, with extensive advertising of available properties, established legal procedures, and a strong bro-

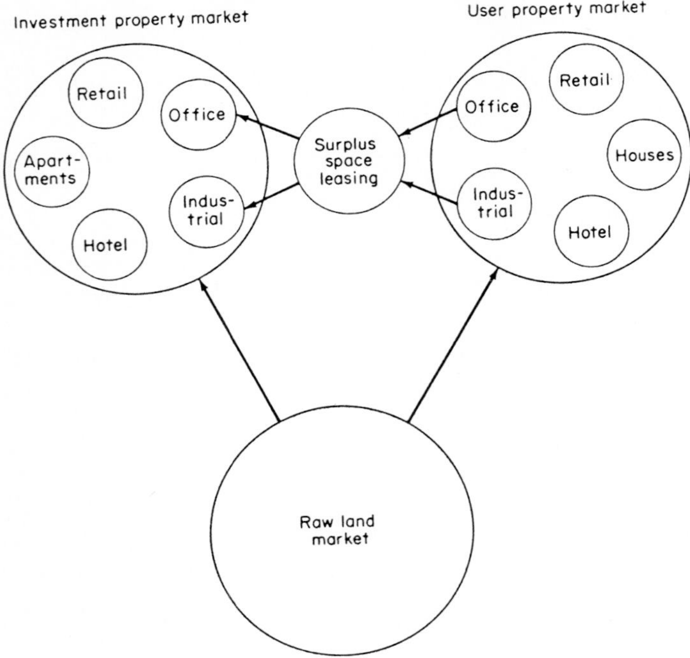

Figure 6-3. Real estate submarkets.

kerage network. Prices tend to move within fairly close ranges. Financing is largely institutionalized.

Business firms also seek out properties for their own use. This may involve purchasing land for development, entering into "build-to-suit" arrangements with developers, or purchasing or leasing existing improved properties. Although this market is generally less organized than the residential user market, it tends to be more sophisticated. Available properties are usually well advertised, but individual purchase and lease arrangements will vary significantly in terms of legal framework, financing terms, and rental or sales price. To provide for future expansion, user firms may also purchase or lease more space than they need and sublease the remaining space to other users. In this manner, they become both users and investors.

Investment Properties. A third submarket is for improved properties purchased for investment purposes. Sellers tend to be developers or other investors. Buyers are likely to be relatively sophisticated individual or institutional investors who are weighing real estate investments against other investment alternatives. The major interest of the buyer is usually the annual yield produced by the property and the possibility of appreciation. The market is relatively unorganized, with a variety of intermediaries in addition to brokers. Prices tend to fluctuate considerably, depending on the expectations of investors regarding the future in general and specific properties in particular. Legal procedures are highly flexible and often reflect the unique desires of buyer and/or seller. Financing tends to be institutionalized, and in some cases institutions are the major investors.

The Pricing Mechanism

The maximum price that buyers will pay and the minimum price that sellers will accept is determined by the pricing mechanism.

Floor and Ceiling Prices. Sellers of real property generally have a minimum, or floor price, below which they will not sell. It is usually highly subjective and varies among local areas, classes of properties, and individual sellers. The floor price may reflect the current level of income or satisfaction the seller is enjoying, the prices received by other sellers in the market, or, in the case of a user property, the cost of alternative facilities.[2] This floor price may change over time, particularly if the property has been up for sale for a long time.

Buyers also place an upper limit, or ceiling, on the price they will pay for a property. Home buyers generally relate this price to the amount of the down payment required and the annual or monthly debt service as related to disposable income. Most families will not pay more than 30 to 40 percent of disposable income for housing. Commercial and industrial users ordinarily fix the ceiling price that they are willing to pay on the basis of anticipated revenues and their operating costs. Investors generally set a maximum price on the basis of its impact on the annual yield generated. In essence, they are establishing a minimum yield that they wish to receive. This minimum yield will take into consideration their expectations about the future, the degree of risk inherent in obtaining the yield, and the yields obtainable in alternative investments. Tax considerations may also influence the investor's determination of minimum yield.[3]

Market Prices. A real estate transaction will occur as long as at least one buyer has a ceiling price higher than the floor price of the seller.

[2]Brian Goodall, *The Economics of Urban Areas,* Pergamon, Oxford, England, 1972, p. 54.

[3]Ibid., pp. 53, 54.

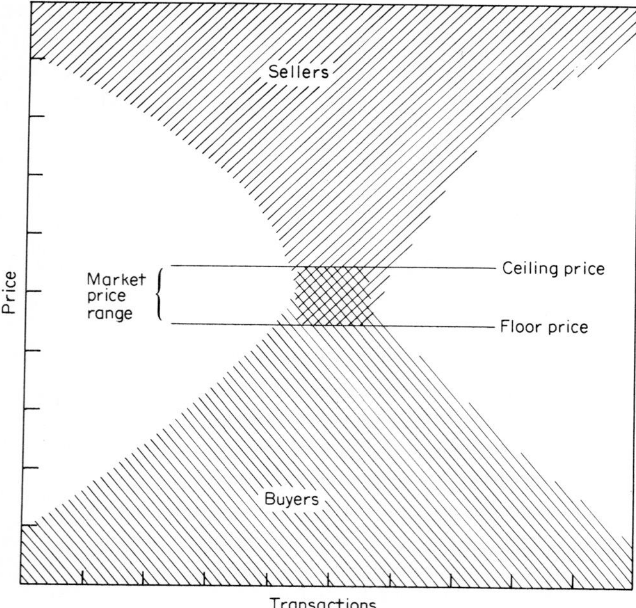

Figure 6-4. Floor and ceiling prices.

Market prices will range between the established floor and ceiling prices, depending on the number of buyers and sellers. If there are a large number of buyers in the marketplace at one time, market prices will tend to approximate the ceiling price level. If there are a large number of sellers, market prices will approximate the established floor price. If a disproportionate number of buyers or sellers exist for a sustained period of time, they will tend to bid up the price (more buyers) or depress the price (more sellers), and the floor or ceiling price level will change.

Movements in price will also affect supply. An increase in market price levels is likely to increase the rate at which properties are brought into the market. A decrease in market price levels may convince sellers to hold out for a better price, thereby reducing the supply of available properties. Changes in supply, in turn, ultimately affect the market price. An increase in supply will tend to depress market price levels; a reduction in supply, to drive prices upward.[4] As in most markets, the

[4]With increasing government regulation of land use, prices are often stated in terms of dollars per allowable unit of development (e.g., dollars per housing unit, dollars per FAR square foot).

pricing mechanism generally results in equalizing demand and supply over the long run.

The Purchase Transaction

The ownership of property in the United States rests on a foundation of constitutional and statutory laws and judicial interpretations which have been formulated and tested through the years. It's therefore almost always advisable that an attorney be involved in the purchase of real property for development or investment purposes. The attorney can advise the prospective buyer of his or her legal rights, as well as handle many of the legal questions involved and, in some cases, handle certain aspects of the purchase negotiations. Even with an attorney involved, however, it's still important for the prospective buyer to have a general understanding of the basic legal aspects of property acquisition.

Legal Description

Land is of little economic value unless certain legal rights can be ascribed to specific parcels. Distinguishing one parcel of land from another is accomplished through a *survey* which measures and delineates land and allows for a description in legal terms. In the early stages of America's development, legal descriptions took the form of *metes* and *bounds,* describing properties in terms of their relationship to landmarks and natural objects such as rocks, trees, and streams.

As the number of property owners increased, the rather cumbersome metes and bounds system gave way to the *rectangular system.* North-south *meridians* and east-west *base lines* were established at 6-mile intervals. The intersection of these lines created a *township* of 36 square miles; each square mile was called a *section.* Each section was then divided into 640 units referred to as *acres.*[5]

Land in urban areas is generally defined by the *platting* process, which subdivides the city or town as new development is proposed. A specific plan for development of the subdivision (called a tract map, subdivision map, or plat), which indicates streets and other public areas, is *recorded.* The remaining land is identified as *blocks,* and within each

[5]Recent advances in satellite technology may make it possible to establish ownership of land parcels more accurately and effectively than ever before.

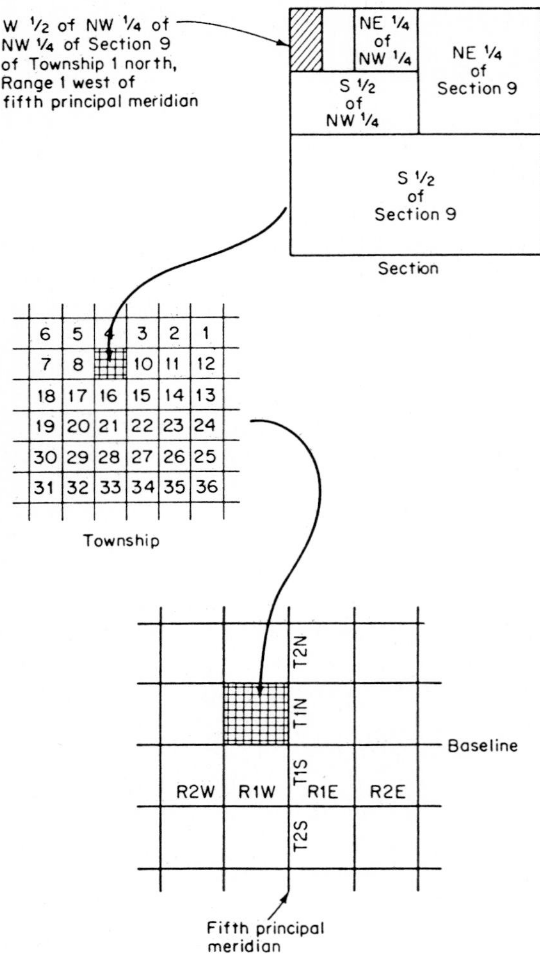

Figure 6-5. Rectangular survey system.

block are individual *lots*. The lots, in turn, may be further subdivided by means of *lot splits*.

Title

Once the land parcels have been identified, the ownership rights, or *title,* accompanying the parcel must be described. Real estate ownership rights involve not only the *surface rights* to the parcel but also the *air*

"LET'S DIVIDE THE EARTH UP INTO LITTLE SQUARES AND SELL THEM."

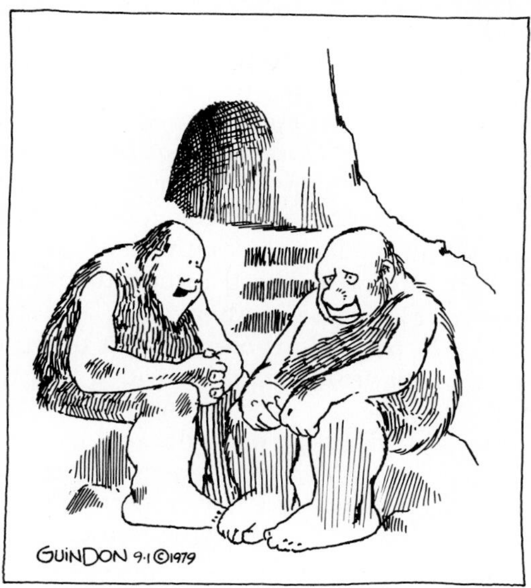

rights and *subsurface rights* (minerals, water, oil, and other natural resources). These ownership rights, or *estates,* can take many forms, the most common of which are freehold, or leasehold or easement. *Freehold estates* give the owner legal title to the land and exclusive right to its possession. Freehold rights may be of unlimited duration (*fee simple*) or for the life of a specified person (*life estate*). *Leasehold estates* convey the right to use and/or improve the land foı specified periods of time (the term). An *easement* conveys the right to use property, either exclusively or nonexclusively, for specific purposes without a conveyance of the underlying estate.

As James Graaskamp has pointed out, real estate rights include both space and time components:[6]

> Real estate can be defined generally as space delineated by man, relative to a fixed geography, intended to contain an activity for a specific period of time. To the three dimensions of space (length, width, and height), then, real estate has a fourth dimension—time for possession and benefit. This can be referred to as a *space-time*

[6]James A. Graaskamp, "Fundamentals of Real Estate Development," Development Component Series, Washington, D.C., the Urban Land Institute, 1981, p. 1.

characteristic. This space-time concept is illustrated by the terms apartment per month, motel rooms per night, square footage per year, and tennis courts per hour.

Title to private property is generally subject to public restrictions which are enforceable under the government's police powers. Activities that can be regulated under police power include the type of land uses (*planning and zoning*), the type and quality of new construction (*building codes*), and the quality of existing improvements (*fire and health codes*). To raise monies to pay for its services, the state has the *right of taxation* against private property. If property owners do not pay these taxes, they face the prospect of losing ownership rights. The state can also acquire private property for public purposes without the owner's consent, through the power of *eminent domain,* provided that the owner is justly compensated.

Certain private restrictions may also affect property ownership. Legal *covenants and restrictions* established earlier may affect subsequent owners. For example, a property may carry a covenant restricting its use to residential purposes only. Generally, the courts have upheld covenants and restrictions, provided they are not illegal.[7] A property may also be subject to an easement or *right-of-way* giving another property owner, public agency, or utility company the right to use part of the property for roads, utility lines or cables, or other special purposes. An *encroachment* exists when a building or other improvement extends across the property line or into a public right-of-way.

In earlier, simpler times, mere possession of property was sufficient evidence of ownership. As rights of ownership grew more complex, however, some more formal, legal method of protecting title was needed. Thus was born the *abstract of title,* in which the chronological history of the ownership of a parcel of property is indicated in a public place for all to see. By looking at this abstract, an attorney or title company can determine—by means of a *title search*—whether the title to the property is *clear* or *defective*. The title search also indicates all public and private restrictions on title that are of public record. The owner can purchase *title insurance,* which, although it doesn't guarantee title, does guarantee to pay damages arising from any title defects not indicated in the title report. Institutional buyers frequently require an American Land Title Association (ALTA) extended coverage policy which involves a survey of the property, insures that the ownership rights are true to the survey, and insures a purchase against certain other matters that may not be disclosed by the public record.

[7]The U.S. Supreme Court has held that covenants and restrictions based on racial or religious grounds are unconstitutional.

When property is sold, a *deed* transfers evidence of title to the new owner. If the previous owner had full rights to the property, a *general warranty deed* may be issued in which it is warranted that title to the property is "good and merchantable." Some sellers may only be willing to give a *special warranty deed* (*grant deed*) that warrants that the seller has not done anything to render the property unmarketable but contains no general warranty as to the actions of previous property owners. If the previous owner had less than full rights, a *quitclaim deed* will transfer what rights were possessed.

Transfer of Title

Once the decision has been made to purchase a piece of property, the prospective buyer makes an offer. It is usually in the form of a *deposit receipt* (also called a *binder* or *offer to buy*) which spells out the basic terms of the offer. The deposit receipt is ordinarily accompanied by a cash deposit, generally 10 percent of the anticipated down payment. If the terms are acceptable, the seller signs the deposit receipt and takes the deposit. If the terms are unacceptable, the seller may make a *counteroffer,* indicating the terms and conditions that would be satisfactory. In this manner the buyer and seller horse-trade until they reach a mutually acceptable deal or break off negotiations.

In recent years, institutional purchasers of real estate have utilized a nonbinding *letter of intent* rather than a deposit receipt or offer to buy. The letter of intent identifies the business aspects of the transaction such as price, terms, deposit, and closing conditions, as well as the information that will be required to perform the necessary *due diligence* prior to closing. Being nonbinding, the letter of intent does not usually require the involvement of an attorney, thereby saving costs and possibly avoiding a disagreement over legal matters before agreement can be reached on the business terms of the transaction. Depending upon the creditability of the buyer, deposits may not be required until the due diligence has been completed and the transaction approved by the buyer.

Once a deposit receipt or letter of intent has been accepted by both parties, attorneys for either the buyer or seller (usually the buyer) prepare a *purchase agreement* or *contract of sale.* This purchase agreement outlines in detail the terms of the sale and the actions required by both buyer and seller to complete the transaction. Generally, a contract of sale will include at least the following items:

- Parties to the transaction
- A legal description of the property
- Terms of the sale, including the total price, amount of deposit,

method of payment, and amount and type of any mortgage financing that may be involved

- A listing of any known encumbrances or title defects and the buyer's willingness to take title subject to these items
- A description (or copy) of the deed that will be utilized
- Any personal property or fixtures that are a part of the sale
- Any warranties or guarantees on the part of either buyer or seller
- Due diligence activities on the part of the buyer
- Assignment of responsibility for the costs of the transaction
- Method of establishing proration between buyer and seller of continuing expenses such as property taxes and assessments
- The time and place for the transfer of title

Additional items may be included by either the buyer or the seller, depending upon the terms of the deal, the state in which it is consummated, and the requirements of other parties such as lending institutions and public agencies. Often a variety of contingencies for consummating the transaction will be specified, including, for example, that the buyer can obtain the appropriate governmental approvals or the desired financing or that the results of soils tests or engineering reports be favorable.

Once a purchase agreement has been executed, the buyer begins due diligence activities. These will generally include:

- A review of the title report (usually ALTA) and underwriting of any exceptions
- A physical review of the property, including architectural design, structural engineering, mechanical and electrical engineering, and presence (if any) of asbestos or toxic waste
- A review of all leases and contracts to establish that they are as represented by the seller
- A letter from the local political jurisdiction confirming that the property conforms with local zoning and other land use controls

Many buyers undertake additional diligence including:

- Audit of books of account (if existing building)
- Interviews of tenants
- Market analysis

Figure 6-6. Not all closings are as well attended as was the December 1961 closing of the sale of the Empire State Building to a syndicate formed by Lawrence A. Wein. *(The Empire State Building Company)*

In performing its due diligence activities, the buyer is seeking to confirm that the property is as represented by the seller and that there are no significant problems with the property that would offset its value or prevent proceeding with the transaction. If relatively minor problems are encountered, the buyer and seller are usually able to adjust the transaction through changes in price or terms, and proceed. If major problems are uncovered, the buyer may decide to terminate the transaction. If deposits have been paid, they are generally returned at this time.

Once the due diligence has been completed and approved by the buyer, the final event in the purchase transaction is the actual transfer of title or *closing*. In some states the traditional closing requires the physical presence of all interested parties or their appointed representatives. Each of the parties produces the documents required by the contract of sale. These documents are reviewed by the other parties and, if acceptable, executed. Closing costs are calculated and agreed to between the parties. If all documents are in order, the seller signs the deed and gives it to the buyer, and the seller provides the necessary funds, thereby completing the transaction. A *closing statement*, indicating the allocation of closing costs between the parties, is prepared.

In many states the transfer of property is handled by an independent third party through an *escrow* arrangement. The third party, or *escrow holder*, has custody of the monies and documents, such as the deed, and also makes certain that all elements of the contract of sale are successfully completed. Generally, a set of *escrow instructions* is drawn up as part of the purchase agreement and agreed to by both parties. If circumstances change during the escrow period, these instructions can be amended, provided both parties agree. Once the escrow holder determines that all closing conditions have been satisfied, the monies and documents connected with the transaction are released to the various parties, accompanied by a closing statement.

If the buyer hasn't definitely decided to purchase the property, he or she may enter into an *option agreement* with the seller, which allows the buyer, for a consideration, to buy the property at a prearranged price within a specified period of time. Less binding is a *right of first refusal*. Here, the property owner agrees to give the holder of the right of first refusal a chance to buy the property before the owner accepts an offer to purchase from a third party. A difficulty with this approach is that it may complicate the sale of the property, as many buyers do not want to spend the time evaluating the property knowing that it may go to someone else.

PART 3

Analyzing Market Demand for the Project

7
Residential

But what on earth is half so dear—so longed for—as the hearth of home? EMILY BRONTE
A Little While

Once a property has been optioned or acquired, the focus shifts to formulation of a development program creating the greatest economic value consistent with aesthetic, environmental, and legal considerations. The first step is to determine market demand for each potential land use on the site. This chapter, the first of five dealing with market analysis, is concerned with demand for residential land uses.

As was noted in Chapter 4, overall residential market demand in a local area is determined by the interaction of household preferences and expenditures (demand) with the quality and availability of existing inventories (supply). Within overall demand patterns, the type of housing is a function of household characteristics (e.g., age, family size, incomes, life-style preferences), and density patterns (e.g., zoning, land values, transportation systems). On a more practical basis, these patterns are further influenced by mortgage costs and availability, developer capabilities, government tax policies, environmental pressures, and a myriad of other factors that vary from area to area and period to period.

In evaluating market demand for residential land uses, a particular site or housing concept must complement local housing demand characteristics in a particular area. Too much emphasis on national or regional housing patterns may create a noncompetitive project within a solid local market. Ignoring these patterns may make it hard for an otherwise sound project to "tough out" a weak housing market.

The Market for Primary Housing

A "primary home" is where people live most of the time. For most people, it is their only home; the growth in second homes is still limited to a small segment of the population. A primary home is also the largest investment most people make in a lifetime and therefore is generally treated very seriously. Furthermore, a person's home and neighborhood often directly reflect personality and self-image. For this reason, buying or selling a home is an emotional decision, fraught with ambiguities, irrationality, and indecision. Market analysis for primary housing must, therefore, effectively blend quantitative analysis and an understanding of consumer psychology.

Establishing the Market Area

Assuming that a land parcel has already been secured, the geographic market must be established for the subject site.[1] A market area has been defined as that geographic area "within which all dwelling units are linked together in a chain of substitution."[2] This means that all dwelling units of a particular type and price are mutually substitutible by a prospective buyer or renter. Obviously, it is difficult, if not impossible, to achieve this theoretical market area definition in practice. However, it is possible to fairly accurately define an area in which prospective buyers or renters would tend to shop for housing to satisfy their needs.[3]

Geographic market analysis initially establishes the places of employment from which buyers or renters might be attracted. This analysis requires an assumption of the maximum time that most people would de-

[1]Throughout most of the discussion of market analysis, it is assumed that the land has already been secured.

[2]The Institute for Urban Land Use and Housing Studies, Columbia University, New York, *Housing Market Analysis: A Study of Theory and Methods,* Housing and Home Finance Agency, Washington, D.C., 1953, chap. II.

[3]This discussion limits itself to primary housing for employed households. Demand for second homes is considered later in this chapter.

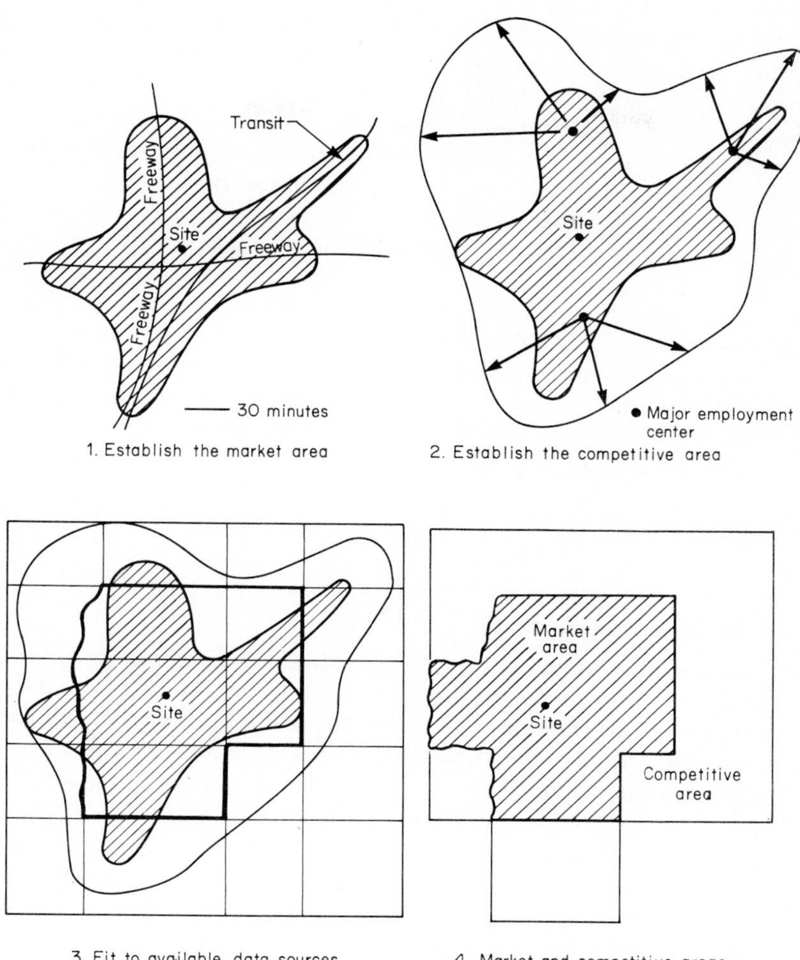

Figure 7-1. Delineating a residential market area.

vote to daily commutation. In auto-dominated cities, commutation usually involves the time it takes to drive to and from work. In areas with extensive public transportation, the process may be more complicated and require assumptions about the "modal split" between one form of transportation and another. Based on assumptions regarding commutation time, a map can be drawn indicating the geographic area which can be reached within this time from the subject site. This is the *market area.* Other geographic areas that will provide competition to the market areas must be considered. This is the *competitive area.*

Judgmental adjustments should then be made to reflect near-term changes that would affect the market area. For example, the opening of a new freeway or transit line could alter the configuration of a market area. Similarly, concern over excessive traffic congestion could restrict commutation time assumptions, thereby reducing market area size. Physical constraints, such as mountains, oceans, and lakes should also be considered.

Finally, the areas thus far defined must be adjusted to available data collection units, as defined by the U.S. Census Bureau and state employment agencies.[4] The resultant area and related data should now be reviewed judgmentally so as to avoid any specialized situations that would skew the data. For example, census data may vary from one census to another because of changes in tract boundaries or collection techniques. Generally, these specialized situations are explained in the published material or can be identified by the responsible public agency.

General Socioeconomic Data

Once a market area for the subject site has been established, pertinent economic data relative to the market area must be analyzed. These data generally fall into two categories: (1) general socioeconomic data which, properly interpreted, give the analyst a better profile of the market area and (2) specific data required for projecting local housing demand.

Employment. Employment-related data generally help establish the "profile" of the market area. Diversification of industry is important; a housing market dependent upon a single industry may experience severe economic disruptions (e.g., strikes, loss of contracts, material shortages) which can have a negative impact on housing demand. The type of industry is also important. Usually, finance, insurance, transportation, public administration, and service industries are more stable than manufacturing, mining, forestry, fishing, agriculture, construction, and wholesale and retail trade.[5] A housing market that depends on one of the less stable industries may be more susceptible to periods of unemployment, which can depress demand for housing. A final factor worth

[4]In the case of a discrepancy between census and employment area, the census tracts should be utilized.

[5]Based on unemployment rates by major industries.

reviewing is the overall growth in employment during the last 5 to 10 years. Generally, an area that is increasing in employment is also a growing housing market. This does not mean that employment growth is necessary to support housing demand. However, absence of growth may indicate a relatively weak housing market or intensive competition for what market may exist.

Age Distribution. Population age can also affect housing demand. In general, an area with a continually increasing population of older people will have less demand for new housing than one where new, younger households are being formed. On the other hand, an area with a disproportionately young population often will place heavy demands on educational facilities—often at the developer's expense. Age also determines the type of housing that will be required. An area with large numbers of elderly people, young singles, or young marrieds may be ripe for apartment or condominium development. An area with families mostly in the 25 to 45 age group is more apt to prefer single-family housing.

Mobility. Census data indicate the general population mobility and may help establish housing demand. An area of high mobility generally has a rapid turnover in housing, with relatively sophisticated buyers who are often willing to accept new ideas. Areas with less mobility may indicate relatively stable social patterns and more conservative housing preferences.[6]

Projecting Housing Demand

The second type of socioeconomic data relates to the specific problem of projecting housing demand for the market area.

Population Data. Data on population growth and characteristics are available from the decennial census and Current Population Reports published by the U.S. Bureau of the Census. Most local planning agencies also have interdecennial statistics, as well as projections of population growth by census tract. In recent years, the quality of these projections has improved markedly. It's still wise, however, to review projections carefully, particularly with regard to how current they are and their underlying assumptions, by spending a few minutes with staff

[6]In evaluating past population growth, the source of population growth for the market area makes a difference: the portion that was internally generated (births over deaths) as opposed to that which came from migration into the area. Such distinctions are important, because an area that is highly dependent upon migration for population growth may have its source cut off by changes in the overall regional economy.

personnel responsible for the projections. Projections made by chambers of commerce, public utilities, environmental groups, school boards, and others with a vested interest in population change should be subjected to especially careful scrutiny.

Nonhousehold Population. Once total population estimates have been developed, the next step is to identify the portion of the population not living in households. This includes institutional population, students in dormitories, and military personnel. Data regarding these groups are generally available from the census or the local planning agency. An area with a sizable nonhousehold population may indicate specialized housing opportunities that should be explored.

Households. By deducting the nonhousehold population, the population living in households can be determined. The next step is to establish the number of *households*. Data on households are available from the census, or they may be roughly established via building permit data maintained by local planning agencies. If the household population is divided by the number of households, the average size of households can be established. Trends in local household formation generally should mirror national trends. Aberrations may indicate local socioeconomic trends that may affect housing demand.

Housing Units. For the sake of analysis, it is assumed that future households and future *occupied housing units* are the same. There are, in fact, differences between these two numbers, but in most situations they are insignificant. Occupied housing units can then be translated

Table 7-1. Projected Housing Units, Market Area (in Thousands)

	Actual			Projected		
	1972	1982	1987	1990	1995	2000
Total population	36.7	65.5	85.3	95.0	105.0	110.0
Less: Nonhousehold population	1.1	1.8	2.3	2.9	3.1	3.3
Household population	35.6	63.7	83.0	92.0	101.0	107.0
Average household size	3.4	3.2	3.1	3.0	3.0	3.0
Households (occupied housing units)	10.5	19.9	26.8	31.0	34.0	36.0
Vacancy factor	6%	7%	7%	7%	7%	7%
Total housing units	11.1	21.4	28.8	33.0	36.0	38.0

into *total housing units* by adding a *vacancy factor*, reflecting the "slippage" between housing production and occupancy.

Changes in Housing Inventory. To determine the amount of new construction that will be required, reductions in the present housing inventory as a result of *demolitions* must be forecast. Demolitions can be the result of highway construction, urban renewal, or increases in housing density. Data on the rate and extent of past demolitions usually are available from the local planning agency. These data must be screened to remove any major demolitions skewing the statistics. Also, if the existing inventory is in a particularly deteriorated physical condition, it may be necessary to assume an increased rate of demolition.

By subtracting the housing inventory at the beginning of the period (adjusted for demolitions) from the housing inventory at the end of the period, the amount of new construction required in the future can be determined, as shown in Table 7.2.

Type of Unit. As indicated earlier, the type of housing unit demanded is a function of a variety of factors, including life-style preferences, incomes, family size, age, land prices, and zoning policy. Data regarding the popularity of particular unit types can generally be obtained from local planning agencies. When projecting housing preferences, however, it's important to consider any major changes occurring in the market area. For example, a rapid increase in land values may signal a more rapid increase in multifamily construction (see Table 7.3).

Unit Price or Rental. The approximate price-rental range for new housing can be established by analyzing income data for the market

Table 7-2. Changes in Housing Inventory, Market Area (in Thousands)

	Actual		Projected			Total
	1973–82	1983–87	1988–1990	1991–95	1996–2000	1973–2000
Inventory BOP	11.1	21.4	28.8	33.1	36.3	11.1
Less: Demolitions	0.4	0.6	0.8	0.9	1.0	3.7
Add: New construction	10.7	8.0	5.1	4.2	2.9	30.9
Inventory EOP	21.4	28.8	33.1	36.3	38.2	38.2
Average annual new construction	1.1	1.6	1.0	0.8	0.6	1.1

Table 7-3. Type of Housing Unit Required, Total Market Area (in Thousands)

	Actual		Projected			Total
	1973–82	1983–87	1988–1990	1991–95	1996–2000	1973–2000
Percentage distribution of new construction						
Single family	63.2%	57.5%	50.0%	40.0%	30.0%	53.3%
Multifamily	36.8%	42.5%	50.0%	60.0%	70.0%	46.7%
Total	100.0%	100.0%	100.0%	100.0%	100.0%	100.0%
New construction by type of unit						
Single family	6.7	4.6	2.6	1.7	0.9	16.4
Multifamily	3.9	3.4	2.6	2.5	2.0	14.4
Total	10.7	8.0	5.1	4.2	2.9	30.9
Average annual new construction by type of unit						
Single family	0.7	0.9	0.5	0.3	0.2	0.6
Multifamily	0.4	0.7	0.5	0.5	0.4	0.5
Total	1.1	1.6	1.0	0.8	0.6	1.1

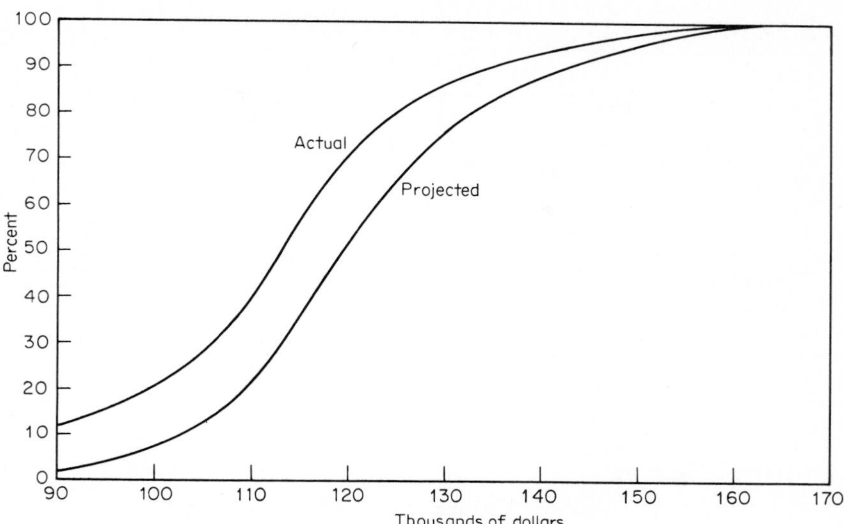

Figure 7-2. Percentage distribution of single-family units by sales price.

area. In some metropolitan areas, special studies have been undertaken which relate family or household income to housing price-rental ranges. If these studies are not available, the analyst must utilize national averages, adjusting for variances between national and local income patterns. The result should be an S-shaped curve which distributes housing units by price-rental range. Figure 7-2 indicates how such a curve might appear for a particular single-family housing market. The curve is then projected to reflect changes in income patterns during the target projection period. From the curve, it is possible to establish the number of incremental dwelling units that will be required in each price-rental range. The target range, or combination of ranges, which most closely approximates the quality of unit to be developed can then be selected. Table 7-4 illustrates these projections for the market area serving the subject site.

After completing the projection process, the analyst has a relatively good idea of the gross number of new units that will be required by type of unit and the approximate sales-rental range. It should be noted that this is, at best, an approximation. The market will, of course, vary considerably from one year to the next as a result of overbuilding or underbuilding, changes in mortgage rates, and changes in public policy.

Table 7-4. Projected Single-Family Demand by Price Range

	Actual, 1983–87		Projected, 1988–90	
	Units	(%)	Units	(%)
Over $150,000	143	3.1	128	5.0
$141,000–$150,000	175	3.8	205	8.0
$131,000–$140,000	317	6.9	256	10.0
$121,000–$130,000	653	14.2	639	25.0
$111,000–$120,000	1490	32.4	767	30.0
$101,000–$110,000	856	18.6	384	15.0
$91,000–$100,000	400	8.7	128	5.0
Under $90,000	566	12.3	51	2.0
Total	4600	100.0%	2557	100.0%

Competitive Survey

Another important element of market analysis is a survey of competitive projects affecting the market. This survey is undertaken in the field by competent staff or professionals and should focus on projects of the type and price-rental level anticipated on the subject site. Projects competing with the subject site are illustrated in Table 7-5. Factors that should be covered in the survey include the location of the project, floor plans and model types, unit mix (i.e., number of bedrooms and baths), size and price of units, price per square foot, planned number of units and units built to date, marketing strategy (e.g., advertising, models, signs), sales or rentals to date, absorption rate and vacancy rate, unit features (e.g., appliances, carpet, drapes, cable TV), project amenities (e.g., common areas, recreational facilities) or rental terms (e.g., length of lease, deposit), financing (e.g., mortgage terms, closing costs, concessions), and a judgmental evaluation of the overall competitiveness of the project.

If possible, it's also desirable to get some idea of the type of people buying or renting in each project. Such information can usually be gained through discussions with sales or rental representatives, although its validity should be questioned and cross-checked.

Market Capture

The final step in analyzing a primary housing market is to establish the extent of anticipated market capture on the subject site. This is largely a judgmental process, requiring the utmost care and objectivity. Advantages and disadvantages of the subject site have to be considered, particularly in relation to competitive projects. Allowance should be made for timing of the project and major changes in the market anticipated prior to initial marketing efforts. The sales abilities of the developer and the degree to which sales momentum can be established must also be considered.

In developing the market capture estimate, several indicators will prove valuable. The market capture figures obtained from competitive projects will, to some extent, indicate what can be expected at the subject site. The developer's past experience with similar projects also may be valuable. Once an estimate has been made, this percentage is applied to the total number of incremental units anticipated by type and price range, as shown in Table 7-6. The resultant number of units should then be translated into an absorption rate and compared to competitive projects and the developer's track record. If the projected absorption rate is significantly higher, the analyst should reweigh the factors that indicate better performance than the competition or previous projects.

Often, there is a tendency at this point to "sanctify" the numbers produced by the quantitative analysis, giving them more importance than they deserve. The purpose of quantitative market analysis is to provide a rough indication of market size and compatibility to a particular site. As such, quantitative analysis is a *supplement* to, not a *substitute* for, good judgment. Not only must good judgment be utilized in developing the quantitative assumptions; it must also predominantly determine final market feasibility. If there is a substantial difference between the numbers and what seems to make sense, question the numbers again and understand fully why the difference exists.

Also, it's important to remember that market analysis is just a *first step* in determining project feasibility. A positive market analysis says there's potential—nothing more. The critical problems of financing, planning, designing, building, and selling or renting a project to tap this potential still exist. Failure at any of these stages can render the quantitative market analysis meaningless.

Market Characteristics of Various Housing Types

The market analysis techniques that we have discussed thus far apply to all types of primary housing. However, unique characteristics associated with each housing type will determine the emphasis placed on certain data.

Single Family. The approach to analyzing the single-family housing market is generally as previously outlined. Since single-family housing is often produced in large quantities, emphasis should be placed on the

Table 7-5. Competitive Survey, December, 1987

Map	Project	Plan/ model	Unit type	Size	Unit price	Price/ sq ft	Planned	Built	Sales	Absorpt
1	Northglen	A	2bdr/1ba	1375	$135,700	$ 98.69	200	75	60	4.0
	Supreme Builders	B	2bdr/2ba	1450	141,800	97.79	300	125	115	7.7
	Opened: 4/87	C	3bdr/2ba	1600	160,000	100.00	300	100	87	5.8
							800	300	262	17.5
2	Meadowbrook	Blue	2bdr/2ba	1200	119,500	99.58	200	200	160	5.7
	Cosmic Dev. Co.	Red	2bdr;2ba	1250	123,500	98.80	350	350	241	8.6
	Opened: 3/86	Yellow	2bdr/2ba/den	1400	135,700	96.93	200	200	193	6.9
		Green	3bdr/2ba	1550	143,800	92.77	250	250	184	6.6
							1000	1000	778	27.8
3	Village Green	Baryview	2bdr/2ba	1450	156,000	107.59	60	60	12	1.3
	World Const.	Hillside	3bdr/2ba	1575	168,100	106.73	90	90	25	2.8
	Opened: 10/87	Parklane	3bdr/2ba/den	1750	182,300	104.17	40	40	9	1.0
4	Shadywoods	Aspen	2bdr/1.5ba	1250	135,700	108.56	190	190	46	5.1
	Beane Brothers	Spruce	2bdr/2ba	1325	137,700	103.92	200	120	27	2.3
	Opened: 7/87	Oak	3bdr/2ba	1500	151,900	101.27	300	180	36	3.0
							200	180	44	3.7
							700	480	107	8.9
Totals							2,690	1,970	1,193	

Table 7-5. *(Continued)*

Map	Project	Features: Unit	Features: Project	Financing	Competitive rating
1	Northglen	Cpt; dr; Dw; TV	Rec rom; pool	Conventional 10.5% 1pt; 10%down	Good
2	Meadow-brook	Cpt; dr; Dw; TV; A/C	Shopping Ctr; rec. room pool	Conventional 11.0% 1/2 pt; 10% down	Excellent
3	Village Green	Cpt; dr; Dw; TV; 3-car gar.	Re. room; pool; sauna	Conventional 11.0% 1pt; 20% down	Good
4	Shady Woods	Cpt; dr; Dw; TV	Rec. room; pool	Conventional 10.5% 2pts; 10% down	Good

Table 7-6. Projected Demand on Subject Site, 1988–1990

Single-family demand, total market area $111,000–$150,000	1867
Market capture by subject site	25.0%
Market demand on subject site	467
Average monthly absorption	13.0
Recommended program = 450–500 units	

overall *magnitude* of demand in the local market area. If demand is strong, a relatively well-planned project should prove successful, provided that it is competitively priced and well merchandised. Relatively weak demand situations require looking for "voids" in the market, generally involving smaller projects.

Condominiums. Condominiums constitute not a separate market but, rather, a different planning and legal approach to the traditional single-family market. Generally, people who buy condominiums as a primary home would otherwise have purchased a single-family home.[7] Market

[7]There is also a market for condominiums from apartment dwellers who wish to take advantage of the tax breaks associated with home ownership without having the burden of maintenance. This market is concentrated primarily in wealthy apartment neighborhoods.

analysis should focus on the reasons *why* people are buying condominiums in a particular market area, such as freedom from housing maintenance or more affordable pricing. Once these factors are determined, the project should be examined to determine the degree to which it meets the demand indicated. Condominium ownership is still not as well accepted in all parts of the country as is detached single-family housing. This may create special marketing problems in the sense that the resale market for condominiums may be limited. Buyers may be reluctant to purchase a unit which they may not be able to sell quickly. In this situation, extremely careful market analysis is necessary to ensure that the condominium concept will be accepted in the local marketplace.

Planned Unit Developments (PUDs). Like condominiums, PUDs represent a different approach to planning and zoning rather than a separate market. The market analysis approach should be the same as for single-family projects, noting any significant differences in unit layout or design which might affect market capture.

Apartments. The development of the condominium has helped to clarify the distinctions between home ownership and rental housing. No longer must a person desiring a low-maintenance living unit settle for an apartment. Some of the reasons for renting, therefore, become clearer. A person may rent an apartment because of a feeling of transience—an unwillingness to settle down, a desire to "try out" an area before making a commitment to home ownership, or an inability to come up with the necessary down payment or to qualify for the mortgage financing necessary for home ownership. Once the overall rental market for a particular market area has been determined, it's important to zero in on the specific segment most likely to be attracted to the subject site. Since apartments are generally rented for a short period of time, a fertile market is often found among the residents of existing projects. An evaluation of data provided by the competitive survey will indicate shortcomings of existing projects, which may represent possible "voids" in the local apartment market. If the proposed project overcomes these problems, present renters may prove to be a potential market.

An analysis of trends in the socioeconomic composition of the market area may also prove enlightening. An increase in the number of people in the 20 to 30 age group may indicate a market for apartments directed at single people and young married couples. Similarly, an increase in people over 55 may indicate a potential market among retired and semiretired individuals.

The approach to market analysis is similar for both garden and high-rise apartments. A note of caution, however, regarding high-rise apartments: unless there is an established local high-rise market, pioneering a project of this type may be fraught with risks. High-rise construction is substantially more expensive, leading to higher rents than garden apartments. High-rise projects also involve a different life-style than that preferred by most residents of single-family and garden apartments.

Cooperative Apartments. Cooperative apartments, or co-ops, are a cross between rental and home ownership. Concentrated primarily in New York City, co-ops are apartments in which individuals own "shares" in a corporation which owns the apartment building. The residents have proprietary leases to their apartments as long as they own the shares. Sales of the shares are subject to approval of the board of directors of the corporation.[8] The corporation assesses each shareholder on a pro rata basis for the costs of operating the building and servicing the mortgage. Unlike a condominium owner, the co-op shareholder is liable for the unpaid allocations of the other shareholders. As a result of this and other problems, co-op ownership may be unattractive to a potential market, particularly in areas where condominium ownership is possible.

Since co-ops are generally built in highly dense urban areas, the rental market is usually a better indication of the potential for co-op development than is the homeowner market. An extremely strong apartment market may indicate apartment residents who would like the tax and other advantages of home ownership but have no such opportunity because single-family housing is unavailable. Evaluation of socioeconomic patterns is also important because co-op owners will need sufficient wealth to make down payments and meet the financial standards established by the co-op board of directors and financial institutions active in co-op mortgage lending.

Manufactured Homes. Manufactured homes represent a segment of the primary housing market comprising those individuals who can't afford to purchase traditional site-built housing or who prefer the manufactured home community for life-style reasons. The approach to market analysis is similar to that of single-family housing except that emphasis is placed on individuals earning incomes *below* a certain level, as well as on those who have retired. This income level is a function of overall incomes in the market area and the price of single-family con-

[8] Approval of new shareholders is often a subtle method of racial, ethnic, religious, and occupational exclusion—perpetuating the continued use of the co-op in areas of social change.

struction. If this segment is relatively large, it may indicate a good market for manufactured home park development. It's also important to look at the magnitude and nature of existing manufactured home park developments. A competitive survey of these projects may indicate shortcomings that can be successfully overcome in a new park.

Retirement Housing. Market analysis of retirement housing projects is similar to single family, except that proximity to employment centers is not a major consideration and the analytical focus is on households over a certain age, usually 55. Within this segment, projects may vary from active retirement projects with large recreational facilities to congregate and life-care facilities which provide meals and selected levels of medical care. Considerable caution should be exercised in establishing the market capture rate for a retirement project as a large part of the market may prefer to continue to live in nonsegregated facilities.

The Market for Secondary Housing

The market for secondary housing is considerably different from the primary housing market. Since, by definition, a second-home owner already has a primary home, incomes must be relatively high to support the costs of two homes.[9] Since a second home is usually associated with leisure time activities, proximity to sources of employment is unimportant. Nearness to shopping, schools, and community services also becomes less critical.

With the second home, other factors take on greater significance. Most second-home developments are in areas which have some type of natural or artificial recreational features: lakes, rivers, seashore, ski facilities, golf courses, or tennis clubs. The quality of these facilities and their proximity often play a role in establishing a strong second-home market. Distance from the primary to the secondary home can also be important. Most second homes are built within 2 to 3 hours' driving time from a major urban area. The ability to rent the second home to others is also a factor. A good, consistent rental market means that the owner can defray many of the costs of carrying the second home. The potential rental income broadens the range of incomes of those who can afford secondary housing. In many cases second homes are sold on a timesharing basis, as discussed in Chapter 1. This is another way of ex-

[9] There are other costs as well: transportation, maintenance, and more costly financing.

Figure 7-3. Windward Harbor, a second-home community in Moultonboro, New Hampshire, attracts vacation homeowners with a combination of high-quality design and a variety of activities for the four seasons. *(Hare Enterprises, Inc.)*

panding the market for second homes by making them affordable to people in a broad range of income groups.

Other factors that help establish a strong second-home market include the quality of land use planning, the "snob appeal" of early purchasers, and the overall promotional image created by the developers.

Determining the Number of Visitors

Analyzing the market for second homes is much more difficult than for primary housing and generally less precise. Fortunately, since most second homes are located in recreational areas, it's possible to get some idea of the potential market by looking at the number and type of visitors to the area. Statistics are usually available through the operators of the recreational facility. If it is a governmental facility, such as a national forest, reservoir, or state beach, the statistics are usually reliable; if it is privately owned, it may be necessary to rely on statistics provided by auto clubs, airlines, local chambers of commerce, hotel operations, ski-lift operators, or other organizations. If no data are available, it may be necessary to take visitor counts on selected days and, based on discussions with people familiar with the local area, make extrapolations.

Establishing a Visitor "Profile"

The next step is to establish a profile of people currently visiting the recreational facilities. In some cases, such a profile may already have been prepared by a local business or governmental organization. If not, a consumer interview will be necessary. This interview is undertaken by competent professionals or staff personnel and should be held at the recreational facility or conducted by mail if lists of visitors are available.[10] Information that should be covered in the survey includes place of primary residence, method of arrival (e.g., auto, plane, train, bus), number of times the recreational area is visited each year and primary reason for visiting, length of stay, place of lodging during stay (e.g., hotel, motel, camping, friends), recreational facilities utilized, socioeconomic characteristics (e.g., age, family size, employment, income), and degree of interest in purchasing a second home.

From this survey, it's possible to get a preliminary feel for the market potential. The first test is income; if incomes aren't high enough to support a second home, there probably isn't much reason to go any further (except in the case of timeshare units). If incomes are sufficiently high, the next concern is the place of primary residence. If the visitors are widely scattered, merchandising costs are going to be exceedingly high; it's better if visitors are concentrated in one or a few urban areas. Another important factor is the timing and duration of stay. If the majority of respondents come sporadically or stay only a few days, they probably have little interest in buying a second home but may be interested in a timeshare arrangement. Where visitors stay is also important; campers and guests of residents are generally a poor market for second homes.

[10]One technique is to take down license plate numbers on selected days, obtain the name and address of the driver from the state licensing agency, and mail the questionnaire to the person's primary residence. Another is to obtain the guest lists of major lodging facilities in the area, agreeing to share the findings once the survey is complete. It may also be desirable to undertake competitive surveys in other comparable second-home market areas.

"You advertised a winter rental?"

Finally, a strong indication of interest in purchasing a second home at least means that the respondent is receptive to the idea. Negative responses would probably indicate that prohibitive marketing costs would be needed to create a market that didn't readily exist.

Projecting the Second-Home Market

If it appears from the visitor survey that there may be potential for second-home development, the next step is to forecast the size of this market by projecting the number of visitors and taking a percentage of these as potential second-home purchasers. If a second-home market is already in the area, building permit data may provide an indication of market size. If the area is relatively new, it may be necessary to rely on the visitor survey, particularly responses to the question, "Would you be interested in a second home?"

Competitive Survey

Once the size of the potential second-home market has been determined, a competitive survey should be undertaken. Data that should be collected include location of the project, proximity to major recreational facilities, planned number of units and unit mix, unit size and features, project amenities (emphasis on recreational facilities), sales terms, rental program, security systems, marketing strategy, sales to date, absorption rate, source of buyers and buyer characteristics, and a judgmental evaluation of the overall competitiveness of the project.

The reader will note that there are three major additions to the primary housing survey. The first is proximity of the project to the major recreational facility in the area. This must be analyzed in some detail because, as noted in Chapter 6, real estate values in second-home areas are often a direct function of proximity to the lake, river, beachfront, or ski lift. It's important, therefore, to establish in some detail how people get from each project to the recreational facility.

The second addition is the rental program. As noted earlier, a good rental program will broaden the potential market base and may be *the* feature in a successful sales program. Look for the average number of days annually that a unit is rented, the rental rate obtained, the percentage of rental that goes to the home owner, and how the rental program is organized and merchandised.

The third addition is concern for security. Since second-home owners are absentee owners, there is often a high incidence of theft and vandalism. It's important to discover how this is handled by the competition. Sometimes an independent check with the police department will provide additional information as to the effectiveness of the precautions taken.

Market Capture

It's much more difficult to establish a market capture estimate for a second-home market than for primary homes. Market area boundaries are somewhat fuzzy and the data are, at best, rough. It's usually more meaningful to compare projected absorption for the subject site with that of other projects in the market area and, if relevant, other market areas. The projected absorption rate can also be compared to the anticipated second-home market that was forecast earlier.

One additional comment is in order. Marketing generally will play a large role in the success of a second-home program, particularly if "voids" are discovered through the competitive survey which can be overcome in the proposed project. For example, if the competition is not offering a rental program, the establishment of such a program may allow a higher absorption rate than would otherwise be expected. Again, judgment and common sense must be utilized in the analytical process.

8
Retail Commercial

Buying and selling became not merely an incidental traffic in the conveyance of goods from producer to consumer: it became one of the principal preoccupations of all classes.

LEWIS MUMFORD

The Culture of Cities, 1938

In Chapter 4, demand for retail commercial facilities was shown to be a function of household size, age, income, and spending patterns. Other factors include the number and location of retail facilities in the trade area, the prices of goods and services, and the business acumen of the retailers. In the short term, demand may also be influenced by credit availability, economic expectations, advertising, and variations in merchandising policy.

The process of analyzing retail demand is more sophisticated and accurate than for any other land use. Good socioeconomic data are usually available, buyers like to talk about their shopping preferences, retailers generally keep detailed records regarding sales activity, associations like the International Council of Shopping Centers and the Urban Land Institute maintain industrywide data, and several well-tested theories of shopper preference patterns provide a good base for demand analysis.

Definition of Retail Terms

It's important to define a number of terms which play a significant role in retail demand analysis.

Types of Retail Goods and Services

Retailers offer a wide variety of goods and services, most of which can be classified by the way in which the consumer seeks them out:

- *Convenience goods.* Food, drugs, liquor, hardware and other items which are bought on a "convenience basis" (i.e., at the most convenient store, without comparison shopping). These goods vary little from store to store and are purchased relatively frequently.
- *Shopper goods.* Items which are purchased after some degree of deliberation or shopping around. Generally, they are differentiated through brand identification, retailer image, or shopping area ambience. Purchases are made less often, and the product usually lasts longer. Shopper goods include apparel, general merchandise, household furnishings, and specialty items like jewelry, cameras, and books.
- *Personal services.* Services provided on a relatively frequent basis, generally at the most convenient location. They include laundries, dry cleaners, barber and beauty shops, and shoe repair shops.
- *Specialized services.* Services provided on a less frequent basis. As with shopper goods, the purchaser often has to shop around before deciding on a particular service operation. Typical services include banks, insurance companies, real estate firms, and travel agencies.

It should be noted that these classifications are rather broad and often overlap.

Types of Potential Demand

According to Nelson, retail demand can be divided into three categories:[1]

- *Generative business.* This is business activity generated by a retail operation through its own efforts, historical reputation, advertising, or promotional gimmicks. A major department store is probably the

[1] Richard Lawrence Nelson, *The Selection of Retail Locations,* McGraw-Hill, New York, 1958, p. 53.

best example of an operation depending upon generative business. Usually, this type of business looks for a very accessible location to maximize its merchandising efforts.

- *Shared business.* This kind of business diverts customers who are attracted by the pulling power of a nearby generative business. This type of store, therefore, wants to be as close as possible to department stores or other generative operations, accounting for the "satellite" store designation.
- *Suscipient business.* This business activity is generated by people coming for a purpose other than shopping. Newsstands and tobacco stands in airports and train stations are examples. So are many downtown retail operations, which exist to serve office workers in the immediate area.

Generally, most stores receive their business from a combination of all three types of demand.

Types of Retail Facilities

Retailing generally tends to cluster in districts or shopping centers. Part of the reason is that clustering increases retailers' overall volume. Nelson attributes this phenomenon to the Theory of Cumulative Attraction: "A given number of stores dealing in the same merchandise will do more business if they are located adjacent or in proximity to each other than if they are widely scattered.[2] The various types of retail "clusters" are listed below; again, it should be noted that these are fairly broad classifications; a particular shopping area or center may combine elements of several categories.

Downtowns. For many years the focal point of retailing in most cities was "downtown." Historically, a wide variety of all types of retail uses evolved, largely on a nonplanned basis. With the rise of the suburban shopping center in the 1950s, downtowns declined, and downtown retailing fell by the wayside. But the rehabilitation of the central cities, discussed in Chapter 1, allowed downtown retailing to stage a comeback in the 1970s that continues today.

Suburban Shopping Districts. These are shopping areas which were developed on a nonplanned basis in older suburbs. Often these districts

[2]Ibid., p. 58.

emerged as strip commercial areas around a major arterial running from downtown to the suburbs. In other cases, they evolved around a major department store which had built an "uptown" branch. In still other situations, the districts represented the "downtowns" of small rural communities that had been swallowed up in the spread of suburbia.

Super-Regional Centers. Regional and super-regional shopping centers constitute the major form of retail activity in the United States today. Most cities have at least one major center. Super-regional centers, with at least three full-line department stores, are becoming even more prevalent than regional centers. Many of the regional centers have evolved into super-regionals over time by adding department stores.

Super-regional centers are anchored by at least three full-line department stores of not less than 100,000 square feet each and may contain a total area of more than 1,000,000 square feet. A 1987 survey of ninety-six super-regional centers indicated a median gross leasable area (GLA)[3] of 936,496 square feet.[4] These centers provide an extensive variety and depth of shopping goods, services, and recreational facilities.

Regional shopping centers. Regional centers provide a wide range of shopper and convenience goods as well as specialized and personal services and in some cases, recreational facilities. They are anchored by one or two full-line department stores of generally not less than 100,000 square feet of GLA each. In some cases the department stores may be independently owned although physically part of the center. The 1987 ULI survey of seventy-four regional centers indicated a median GLA of 511,976 square feet.[5]

Community Shopping Centers. These centers are generally smaller, offering convenience goods as well as a range of facilities for the sale of goods such as furniture and apparel. They are usually anchored by a junior department store, variety store, discount department store or off-price apparel store. Community centers offer more of a variety of

[3]The Urban Land Institute defines gross leasable area as "the total floor area designed for tenants' occupancy and exclusive use, including any basements, mezzanines, or upper floors, expressed in square feet and measured from the centerline of joint partitions and from outside wall faces." *The Dollars and Cents of Shopping Centers,* Urban Land Institute, Washington, D.C., 1987, p. 4.

[4]*The Dollars and Cents of Shopping Centers: 1987,* op. cit., p. 21. (Figure includes mall shops and department stores.)

[5]Ibid., p. 69.

Figure 8-1. With 5.2 million square feet of space for shopping and entertainment, Canada's West Edmonton Mall is the world's largest shopping center. *(West Edmonton Mall)*

services than neighborhood centers, but they don't have the drawing power of the regionals or super-regionals. The median GLA of 262 sample centers in ULI's 1987 study was 145,523 square feet.[6]

Neighborhood Centers. The smallest and most prolific shopping centers, they are directed at selling convenience goods and services. They are generally anchored by a supermarket or a large drug store. In a

[6]Ibid., p. 115.

1987 survey of 315 neighborhood centers conducted by ULI, median total GLA for these centers was 62,683 square feet.[7]

As supermarkets and drugstores have broadened merchandise lines, neighborhood centers have grown in size and merchandise coverage. Today's "super store" is often 2 to 3 times larger than the supermarket/drugstore of 5 to 10 years ago. As a result, some neighborhood centers closely resemble and often compete with community centers.

"Strip" Retail Centers. Strip retail centers are groups of six to twelve shops with parking in front. They are often anchored by "quick stop" markets such as 7-Eleven and Stop-n-Go. Many of these centers are springing up around the country in corner locations abandoned by gasoline stations during the past decade.

Freestanding Stores. Many stores not in shopping or strip centers are "freestanding." Such stores can range from a 2,000-square-foot delicatessen to a 500,000- or more square-foot discount or department store. In some cases, these were developed before the shopping center existed. In other cases, this is the preferred method of operation.[8]

Discount and Warehouse Stores. Discount and warehouse stores are usually freestanding, often 100,000 square feet or more. Initially, they featured appliances and other durable goods; however, in recent years they have added more nondurables. Store operation emphasizes substantial price reductions, with customer services at a minimum. Display areas are often utilized for storage.

Outlet and Off-Price Centers. Outlets and off-price centers are specialty merchandisers whose growth has been dramatic in the 1980s. An outlet center is a collection of factory outlet stores, usually with no anchor tenant. It is regional in scope and often has a strong base of tourists as customers.

The off-price center is a shopping mall containing shops selling higher-end, brand-name merchandise at deeply reduced prices. There is relatively little tourist business. The market area size is between that of a community center and a regional center. Off-price centers are similar in design to community centers. A variation is the "power" or "promotional" center, a large strip center with mostly national tenants who advertise heavily.

[7]Ibid., p. 163.

[8]Several clothing and shoe chains, for example, refuse to go into shopping centers as a matter of policy, preferring freestanding locations.

Fashion Center. The fashion center usually includes a small specialty store (e.g., a gourmet supermarket) in addition to shops carrying fashion merchandise. Fashion centers are most often developed in high-income areas, but they can draw from broad trade areas when high-income districts are scattered. Thus the fashion center could look like a neighborhood, community, or regional center.

Specialty and Festival Centers. In a number of cities, a relatively new retailing concept has emerged: the specialty center. These centers can range from 40,000 to over 300,000 square feet. While the shopping center industry has never agreed on a precise definition of specialty centers, they generally have two common characteristics:

1. They are developed around a special theme often through use of existing structures, such as an old chocolate factory (Ghirardelli Square in San Francisco) or a marketplace (Faneuil Hall, Boston). Recently, specialty centers have been developed from scratch with the theme created through architecture and planning. Examples include Ports-of-Call (San Pedro, California), Old Town (Dallas), and The Village Green at Heritage Village (Southbury, Connecticut).

2. There are no major retail anchors. The tenants are generally small (400 to 2000 square feet), primarily in the areas of apparel, household, and specialty goods. Restaurants and gourmet food outlets are often a major element of specialy centers. Entertainment facilities, such as theaters, may also be included. Generally, the emphasis is on merchandising depth (e.g., several tenants in each category) rather than on breadth.

Perhaps the most popular type of specialty center in recent years has been the "festival" center. This type of center was originated by the Rouse Company with its development of Faneuil Hall Marketplace in Boston. Such centers are developed with the idea of creating a particular experience, a place where people come for the entertainment value of shopping. These centers contain a large number of specialty restaurants and food vendors, the more unique the better.

Mixed-Use Developments. Retail activity is often a component in mixed-use developments. The retail component can range from convenience shops to an entire shopping center within the complex. Retail outlets in mixed-use developments are generally multileveled, and they are carefully integrated with the other components of the complex. Be

Figure 8-2. Faneuil Hall Marketplace, Boston, Massachusetts, one of the most prominent examples of the festival center. *(The Rouse Company)*

cause of its complexity, retail may be the most difficult land use to implement successfully in a mixed-use project.

Theories of Retail Location

Through the years, several theories have evolved to explain how consumers choose where they will shop. These theories provide the basis for projecting potential retail sales from a particular site and determining overall project feasibility. Although these theories are subject to criticism, it's important to understand them in general terms.

Reilly's Law

In 1929, William J. Reilly of the University of Texas studied shopping habits in various Texas towns and developed what he termed "The Law of Retail Gravitation." This law postulated that under normal conditions two cities draw retail trade from a smaller intermediate city or town in direct proportion to some power of the population of these two larger cities and in inverse proportion to some power of the distance of each of the cities from the smaller intermediate city.[9] Put simply, Reilly's Law says that people will shop in the biggest retail area that they can get to most easily.[10]

Since 1929, Reilly's Law has been modified to fit the needs of changing retail shopping patterns. Floor space of stores (or shopping centers) has been substituted for city population in the formula; driving time has been substituted for distance. Although this law has become widely used in retail analysis, it has some major weaknesses: (1) It was developed for rural trade areas where shoppers had few opportunities for comparison shopping, (2) the law doesn't consider variations in income, household size, or other factors affecting retail shopping patterns, (3) by concentrating on floor space and accessibility, the law overlooks price, store image, advertising, shopping ambience, and other factors which may be equally important in selecting a retail facility,[11] and (4) the law fails to take into consideration business that arrives by public transportation. Because of these shortcomings, several attempts have been made to improve on Reilly's Law.

"Vacuum" Technique

One variation is the "vacuum" technique, which attempts to establish the amount of unrealized retail potential within a trade area. The trade

[9]William J. Reilly, *Methods for the Study of Retail Relationships,* Bureau of Business Research, University of Texas, Austin, 1959 (original monograph published in 1929), p. 16.

[10]Mathematically this becomes

$$(Ba/Bb) = (Pa/Pb)^N(Db/Da)^n$$

where Ba = the business which City A draws from intermediate town T
Bb = the business which City B draws from intermediate town T
Pa = population of City A
Pb = population of City B
Da = distance of City A from intermediate town T
Db = distance of City B from intermediate town T
N = exponent of population
n = exponent of the inverted distance

Ibid., p. 48.

[11]A study by Albert Raeburn and George M. Jenkins, Jr., indicates that consumers often drive by stores located in large centers with easy access to shop in competing centers with less square footage. *Urban Land,* Urban Land Institute, Washington, D.C., vol. 24, no. 1, December 1965.

area is established around a site on the basis of driving times, adjusted for natural boundaries. The amount of retail business potential within the trade area is calculated through population, income, and expenditure data. The floor areas of existing stores in the trade area are measured and multiplied by national sales averages to arrive at the existing volume. Existing volume is subtracted from sales potential, and the remainder, or "vacuum," is the potential available to the new store or shopping center.

The vacuum approach was developed primarily for outlying shopping centers. Since people in these areas generally do a portion of their shopping downtown, in older centers, or by mail order, most of the studies tend to show a vacuum, when in fact none may exist. The approach also suffers from the same problems as Reilly's Law; it doesn't consider the type of retailing expenditures or the nature of the proposed retail operation.

Microanalysis Technique

This approach, developed by Real Estate Research Corporation, divides the trade area into a series of small units (e.g., blocks, neighborhoods). The potential business from each of these units is then calculated and distributed judgmentally among the various stores in the trade area. Any potential that cannot be distributed is assumed to be available to the proposed store or center.

The microanalysis approach has the advantage of dealing in units small enough to substantially reduce the chance of gross miscalculation. It also tends to produce a great deal of data about an area, some of which may be valuable in marketing the store or center. The major disadvantage is that it's considerably more expensive, requiring extensive interviewing to determine the flow of consumer purchases. This approach also has difficulty in dealing with rapidly growing areas, where new arrivals have shopping patterns which differ from those of established residents. It is still, however, a major improvement on both Reilly's Law and the vacuum technique.

Consumer Behavior Technique

In 1966, Claude and Nina Gruen published a technical bulletin which outlined a behavioral research approach to retail facility location.[12] This

[12] Claude Gruen and Nina J. Gruen, *Store Location and Customer Behavior,* Technical Bulletin 56, Urban Land Institute, Washington, D.C., 1966.

approach starts with the customers themselves. A customer profile is developed through extensive interviewing at the store's existing locations. The probability that the proposed store's customers will be similar to customers in the survey sample is established. A market area is delineated around the prospective store on the basis of information gathered in the interviews. The number of people in the market area possessing the profile characteristics is determined from census material. Projections of future profile residents in the market area are then made. Overlapping market areas are eliminated, and the probabilities indicated earlier are applied to the projections.

The resultant projections are broken down into cash and charge sale customers on the basis of the profile interviews and then multiplied by an annual average sale to arrive at projected total annual sales for the proposed store or center.

This approach has the advantage of considering characteristics of the potential consumer. While this may work relatively well for a highly specialized store, it may work less well for a multiline store or a shopping center. The approach relies very heavily on interviewing existing customers, without sufficient cross-checks to confirm the veracity of the profile or its applicability to the proposed market area. Also, the approach ignores the retailing operation which attempts to change its image over a period of time.[13]

Analyzing Retail Demand

While all of the above theories appear to contribute something to the analytical process, no single theory is sufficient. The rigorous analyst must utilize a combination of theories, continually cross-checking throughout the analytical process to reduce the reliance on any one particular assumption. With these precautions in mind, a workable analytic system can be evolved. The work may be performed by a professional consultant or the internal staff of the developer or major retail tenant.

Preliminary Development Scenario

The first step is to establish broadly the size and type of store or center to be developed. If the site is known, the maximum size is most likely a

[13] This applies to more retailers than one might think. Over the last two decades, Sears Roebuck, Broadway-Hale, J.C. Penney, Montgomery Ward, and others have spent millions of dollars trying to modify their image.

Table 8-1. Preliminary Development Scenario, 46-Acre Subject Site

Total land area	2000 sq ft (thousands)
Less: Streets, greenbelts, etc. (25%)	500
Usable land area	1500
Land for parking* (5 stalls/1000 sq ft GLA; 400 sq ft/stall; 2 levels)	1000
Land for building	500
Gross leasable area (two levels)**	1000

*If structured parking is not feasible, GLA would have to be scaled down and/or the amount of total land area expanded.

**Formula for determining GLA:

$$ULA = (GLA/L) + (GLA \times PR \times S)/L$$

Where ULA = usable land area
GLA = gross leasable area
L = number of building levels
PR = parking ratio (stalls/1000 sq ft GLA)
S = size of parking stall (sq ft)

function of physical design and zoning. A rough cut should be made of the maximum building area that can be built to determine if the project will be a single store or a neighborhood, community, or regional center. If the site is not known, determine judgmentally what type of center or store would be most logical.

Once the overall magnitude of the center or store is known, several scenarios of possible tenant mix should be established. If the center is regional, assumptions should be made regarding the number of department stores and their sizes. Possible satellite stores should be identified, as well as potential restaurants, offices, recreational facilities, and motor hotels. This exercise may appear premature, but it's actually very constructive at this juncture. It helps to refine the research program and make better use of available funds. It identifies immediate problems which might limit development of certain types of uses. If the program is under an extremely tight time schedule, it allows brokers to start looking for tenants while the research program is proceeding. As the research program unfolds, this scenario will be tested over and over again.

Establishing the Trade Area

The next step is to determine the potential trade area, based on how long it takes prospective shoppers to reach the subject site. In most cases, this will be determined by automobile driving time. If extensive public transportation is available, however, the trade area may be skewed along the transit service line(s). The maximum arrival time should be based on the type of center anticipated in the preliminary development scenario. The following is a rough rule of thumb:

Neighborhood centers	15 minutes
Community centers	30 minutes
Regional centers	45 minutes
Super-regional centers	60 minutes

The trade area should now be adjusted judgmentally to reflect natural barriers and possible changes that will affect commuting time to the subject site. The trade area is then adjusted to the nearest boundary line for appropriate data-gathering purposes (e.g., census, retail sales data).

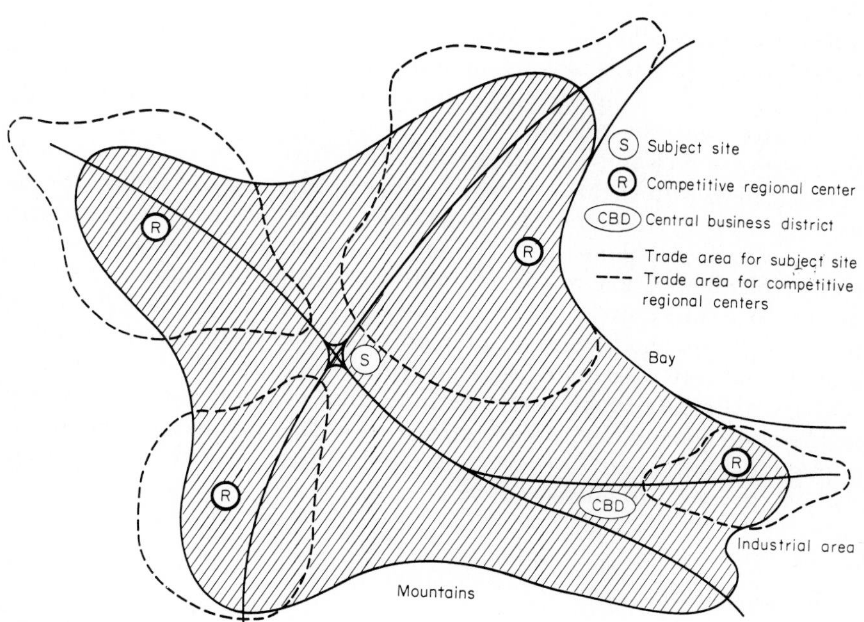

Figure 8-3. Establishing the retail trade area for a proposed regional center.

Retail Expenditures by Trade Area Residents

Once the trade area has been finalized, the next step is to estimate past, present, and future retail expenditures by residents of the trade area (see Table 8-2). The population and number of households in the trade area should be obtained from the local planning agency or census publications. Data on average household income should be taken from the census and updated to the current year, using state or national averages. The number of households should then be multiplied by the average income figures to arrive at the total household income for the trade area. Total household income is then translated into retail expenditures through a series of steps based on percentage expenditure patterns. If these data are not available for the trade area, it may be necessary to use national averages, based on the average household income for the trade area. Still another approach is to establish sales per capita for various retail categories and then multiply these numbers by trade area population data.

It's also desirable at this point to make a general analysis of other socioeconomic data to the extent that they are available. Important factors to explore include the rate of growth of the trade area compared to the region as a whole, existence of sufficient opportunities for new growth in the future (e.g., undeveloped land areas), the mix of household income and employment and how they compare with regional data, whether the trade area is dependent on one industry or, worse yet, on a single firm, and finally, the age composition of the trade area and how it compares with the region.

The purpose of this general analysis is to further refine the preliminary scenario with regard to possible development on the subject site. It helps to narrow subsequent research tasks and concentrate on what may turn out to be problems. In the case of single stores or specialized centers, it may be possible to considerably narrow the assumptions regarding the size and nature of the potential market. A high-fashion store, for instance, may wish to consider only families earning over $35,000 annually, a store catering to the elderly may be interested in people over 55, and maternity shops would be interested in the number of women in the childbearing age category. If the scenario involves a regional or super-regional center, however, it's doubtful that the trade area data can be narrowed to any significant degree.

Competitive Survey

Now it's time to move into the field and see what the potential competition is like. As with housing surveys, this fieldwork should be under-

Table 8-2. Retail Expenditures by Trade Area Residents

	Actual			Projected		
	1972	1982	1987	1990	1995	2000
Population	277,074	310,039	321,879	330,000	345,000	360,000
Population/household	3.08	2.70	2.67	2.65	2.65	2.65
Households	89,990	114,874	120,563	124,528	130,189	135,849
Average household income	$13,300	$ 31,963	$38,135	$42,000	$48,000	$55,000
Total household income*	$1196.9	$ 3671.7	$4597.7	$ 5230	$ 6249	$ 7472
Percentage disposable income	86.3%	85.7%	85.1%	85.0%	85.0%	85.0%
Total disposable income*	$1032.5	$3,144.9	$3914.4	$ 4446	$ 5312	$ 6351
Percentage consumption expenditures	88.8%	89.3%	90.4%	90.0%	90.0%	90.0%
Total consumption expenditures*	$ 917.2	$ 2807.4	$3537.9	$ 4001	$ 4781	$ 5716
Percentage retail expenditures	36.9%	32.6%	30.5%	30.0%	30.0%	30.0%
Total retail expenditures*	$ 338.4	$ 915.7	$1078.3	$ 1200	$ 1434	$ 1715

*In millions.

taken by experienced professionals or staff. Important data to cover in the survey include:

- Size of competitive center in Gross Leasable Area (GLA), with breakdown by major categories of retail goods and services.
- Estimated retail sales, sales per square foot, and market share, based on capture of trade area sales.
- Identification of major anchor tenants (e.g., department stores, junior department stores, drugstores, supermarkets). If the type of store for the proposed site is known, the research should be focused on similar competitive stores.
- Analysis of the marketing ability of the major tenants and other stores that would be directly competitive. This would include such factors as store appearance, marketing techniques, and price.
- An analysis of the number of parking stalls provided and the ease with which traffic moves through the center.
- Evaluation of the area surrounding the center, noting the type and quality of nonretail land uses.
- Qualitative evaluation of the center. This should consider shopping ambience, interstore locational relationships, overall maintenance, and other factors which go into making a good center.

The stores and centers covered in the survey should include all those in the trade area and those outside the trade area that can be reached within the same arrival time assumptions used to delineate the trade area. Table 8-3 illustrates a typical competitive survey.

At this point, it's possible to make another rough cut regarding feasibility. By multiplying the GLA by broad sales per square foot assumptions, the total sales of the competition can be ascertained. By comparing this number to the potential sales in the target area, it's possible to get a general idea as to whether the area is saturated with or underserviced by retail stores.

Retail Sales Data

Now it's necessary to develop retail sales data for the stores that service trade area residents (see Table 8-4). If the trade area is located in states where data are available from sales tax collection agencies, such as

Table 8-3. Competitive Survey, December, 1987

	Southgate		Bayside		Chandler Rd.		Westbrook	
	Outlets	Sq ft*	Outlets	Sq ft*	Outlets	Sq ft*	Outlets	Sq ft*
Shopper goods								
Apparel	16	60	28	107	6	19	22	74
General merchandise	2	265	4	526	2	110	3	460
Household furnishings	4	50	7	83	2	15	4	38
Specialty stores	27	62	41	118	11	23	34	62
Total	49	437	80	834	21	167	63	634
Convenience goods	11	54	18	86	8	48	13	66
Personal services	9	5	15	9	7	4	10	6
Specialized services	4	6	10	14	2	3	8	7
Total retail	73	502	123	943	38	222	94	713

*In thousands.

Table 8-3. Competitive Survey, December, 1987 (*Continued*)

	Southgate	Bayside	Chandler Rd.	Westbrook
Estimated retail sales (1987)*	$61,200	$168,800	$32,000	$111,900
Estimated sales/sq ft	$122	$179	$144	$157
Estimated market share**	6.8%	18.7%	3.5%	12.4%
Major anchors	J. C. Nickel Crown Variety	June Stores Rozenberger's Mainline Shoprite	Sherman's Fine Foods Eagle Drugs	Spear's Alamagamated Jerry's Drugs Food Mart
Merchandising level	Good	Excellent	Fair	Good
Retail parking				
No. stalls	2,900	5,000	1,130	4,000
Stalls/1000 sq ft GLA	5.8	5.3	5.1	5.6
Nonretail uses				
Office	10,000 sq ft	25,000 sq ft	12,000 sq ft	15,000 sq ft
Hotel/motel		100 rooms		
Restaurants	1	4	2	3
Other	Theater	Theater, bowling Day care Community center	Theater	Arcade
Overall center quality	Fair	Excellent	Poor	Good

*In thousands.
**As a percent of 1987 total retail sales.

Table 8-4. Retail Sales Data,Trade Area, 1985–87 (in Millions)

	1985 ($)	1986 ($)	1987 ($)	1987 (%)
Shopper goods				
Apparel	85.7	87.5	90.9	10.1
General merchandis	177.3	183.3	185.3	20.5
Household furnishings	82.9	85.7	89.3	9.9
Specialty stores	18.3	19.5	20.7	2.3
Total	364.2	376.0	386.2	42.8
Convenience goods	439.5	453.7	463.9	51.4
Personal services	19.8	18.6	20.3	2.3
Specialized services	31.4	31.9	31.7	3.5
Total	854.9	880.2	902.1	100.0

California, the problem is substantially reduced. Most of these agencies provide sales data according to retail category, provided that no individual store can be identified. Sales should be requested for at least the prior 3 years; 5 years' worth of data is preferable.

If the trade area is located in states that do not collect or divulge sales tax data, assumptions must be based on the competitive survey. This can be accomplished by multiplying the GLA in each retail category for each center by the average sales per square foot for the category (e.g., women's apparel, jewelry, home furnishings). The Urban Land Institute publishes these data according to region and size of the center in *The Dollars and Cents of Shopping Centers*. Be certain to use sound judgment when applying the data to a particular center. For example, it may be better to utilize the upper end of the range than the median if the center appears to be a particularly successful one; if the reverse is true, it may be better to utilize the lower end.

Consumer Survey

The most critical step in the analytical process is the consumer survey, which provides valuable insight into shopper attitudes—one of the most critical factors in successful retailing. The questionnaire design should be undertaken by professional or staff personnel with experience in questionnaire design and interviewing consumers. A mistake in design can alter the validity of the responses. The questionnaire should focus directly on the continually refined scenario of what type of store or center is anticipated and from what segment of the trade area residents will most likely be attracted to such a facility. Specific questions should be raised concerning stores or centers most frequently utilized for purchases similar to those that would be carried by the scenario store or center; attitudes toward these centers, good and bad; attitudes toward anchor stores anticipated in the scenario store or center, if known to respondent;[14] and classification data on respondent such as age, size of family, type of employment, and income. An example of data gathered by such a questionnaire is illustrated in Table 8-5.

Once the questionnaire has been designed, a sample of trade area residents should be drawn. Valid methods must be utilized in establishing the minimum sample size necessary for statistical accuracy within budget limitations. The sample itself is drawn, on a random basis, from all households in the trade area. Potential respondents are identified by name, address, and telephone number. Trained interviewers should conduct the interviews, which can take place either in person or by telephone. Generally, budget limitations make telephone interviewing more desirable, with no significant loss of accuracy. The questionnaire should be pretested on a cross-section of the sample and modified as necessary. The remaining interviews should be completed within a short time period to keep external conditions as comparable as possible.

Once the interviews are complete, the data can be coded for computer processing. The computer program should allow as much flexibility as possible in cross-analyzing various types of data, for example, analyzing purchases of particular retail goods by income level of the respondent. A flexible program is the key to getting as much as possible out of the consumer survey data.

The Retail Dollar Flow

When data-gathering is completed, the various phases of the analytic process can be tied together. The first objective is to determine the retail dollar flow. The socioeconomic analysis establishes the number of households in the trade area, their incomes, and actual and projected retail expenditure patterns. The consumer survey indicates approximately what percentage of these expenditures is made at stores located outside of the trade area. By deducting these "runaway sales," it is possible to determine the amount of retail expenditure by residents within the trade area. The retail sales analysis provides the total retail sales of the centers and other retail facilities located in the trade area. By deducting sales to residents from total sales, the amount of sales to nontrade area residents can be deduced. This is the retail dollar flow into and out of the trade area (see Table 8-6).

[14] Be certain that the anchor stores are disguised among other competitive stores so the answers to other questions are not skewed.

Table 8-5. Consumer Shopping Patterns, Trade Area Residents (N = 978)

	Regional centers (%)									
	Southgate	Bayside	Chandler Rd	Westbrook	Total	CBD (%)	Misc. strip areas (%)	Total trade area (%)	Out-side trade area (%)	Total (%)
1. Where do you most frequently purchase:										
Shopper goods										
Apparel	10.3	23.1	2.6	15.1	51.1	16.0	3.1	70.2	29.8	100.0
General merchandise	12.7	32.0	4.6	26.2	75.5	2.8	1.9	80.2	19.8	100.0
Home furnishings	11.3	22.8	2.9	10.0	47.0	11.3	16.0	74.3	25.7	100.0
Specialty items	13.0	31.4	4.1	15.6	64.1	11.6	5.4	81.1	18.9	100.0
Convenience goods	4.3	8.8	3.3	6.1	22.5	8.3	67.9	98.7	1.3	100.0
Personal services	1.2	2.5	0.9	1.2	5.8	32.8	59.3	97.9	2.1	100.0
Specialized services	3.1	7.6	1.5	3.8	16.0	53.4	15.3	84.7	15.3	100.0
Weighted average*	8.0	18.0	3.0	12.0	41.0	25.0	11.0	77.0	23.0	100.0
2. How would you rate these retail facilities in terms of:**										
Parking	4.8	6.5	4.3	4.2						
Quality of merchandise	6.1	8.3	5.4	6.4						
Variety of merchandise	5.7	7.8	4.8	6.1						
Sales personnel	5.5	7.3	3.7	6.1						
Appearance	4.3	6.9	2.6	5.6						
Shopping ambience	4.2	6.7	3.2	5.3						
Simple average	5.1	7.3	4.0	5.6						

Classification data

Income		Age		Occupation	
Under $20,000	6.7%	Under 18	19.2%	Professional, technical	23.2%
$20,000–$24,999	11.9	18–24	10.7	Managers	18.6
$25,000–$29,999	15.6	25–34	14.9	Sales	9.7
$30,000–$34,999	26.3	35–44	16.4	Clerical	12.3
$35,000–$39,999	23.6	45–54	14.7	Craftsmen	9.7
$40,000 and over	15.9	55–64	12.4	Operators	7.3
		65 and over	11.7	Other	19.2
Totals	100.0		100.0		100.0
Median	$32,800	38			

*Weighted by retail sales.
**Scale: 10 = excellent; 8 = good; 6 = fair; 4 = poor.

Table 8-6. Retail Dollar Flow, 1987 (in Millions)

		Reference/calculation
A. Retail expenditures by trade area residents	$1078.3	Table 8-2
B. Less: Expenditures outside trade area (23%)	$ 248.0	Table 8-5
C. Resident expenditures within trade area	$ 830.3	(A–B)
D. Add: Sales to non-trade-area residents	$ 71.8	(E–C)
E. Total retail sales within trade area	$ 902.1	Table 8-4

Projected Retail Demand in the Trade Area

Once it's understood how retail dollars flow in the trade area, the next step is to project a model of what will most likely happen in a "target year," 5 and even 10 years in the future. Future retail expenditures by trade area residents were developed earlier in connection with the analysis of socioeconomic data. Expenditures outside the trade area should be extrapolated from the percentage used in the retail dollar flow. The percentage should be modified up or down if changes are anticipated between the trade area and surrounding areas. As an example, a new freeway link to a strong retail center outside the trade area may increase runaway sales to trade area residents purchasing in other market areas.

The projected level of retail sales should now be cross-checked against other data such as sales per capita and annual percentage changes in anticipated sales volume in order to test the reasonableness of the projections (see Table 8-7).

Projected Demand on the Subject Site

Projected retail sales in the trade area are translated into demand on the subject site through the market capture estimation process outlined in Chapter 7, which is similar to that used in projecting primary housing demand. In arriving at an estimate of market capture, it's necessary to make certain assumptions about the competition based on the overall economic growth potential of the trade area. Consider the situation of a rapidly growing area with significant increases in trade area expendi-

Table 8-7. Projected Retail Demand in Trade Area (in Millions)

	1987	1990	1995	2000
Retail expenditures by trade area residents	$1078.3	$1200	$1434	$1715
Less: Expenditures outside trade area				
Percentage	23.0%	22.0%	21.0%	20.0%
Dollars	$ 248.0	$ 264	$ 301	$ 343
Resident expenditures within trade area	$ 830.3	$ 936	$1133	$1372
Add: Sales to non-trade-area residents				
Percentage	8.0%	8.5%	9.0%	10.0%
Dollars	$ 71.8	$ 87	$ 112	$ 152
Total retail sales within trade area	$902.1	$1023	$1245	$1524

tures. Stores or centers which are relatively built up (little room for expansion) and selling at a high rate per square foot can be expected to continue at present or slightly higher levels. Stores or centers with high rates per square foot and room for expansion can be expected to add additional space and achieve high rates in the new space relatively quickly. Those with lower sales rates per square foot can be expected to increase their rates and, in some cases, add additional space. Marginal stores or centers will probably continue in business, and some may even increase their sales rates.

Rough sales projections should be made for each type of existing facility for the target year. Generally, total future sales of existing stores or centers will be less than the retail sales potential for the trade area, reflecting incremental market potential.

In estimating how much of this potential can be captured by the subject site, it is always a good idea to assume that others will perceive the same market opportunity and that there will be other new stores or centers competing for incremental sales volume. For this reason it may be desirable to "buy position" by developing a smaller store or center earlier than demand indicates and expanding as the trade area grows or by accepting a lower level of sales per square foot for a certain period of time until market position can be established.

The situation is apt to be different in a trade area with less dynamic growth. Existing retailers with high sales rates can probably be expected to maintain their success. Marginal stores may go out of business. The growth that does occur will probably be absorbed by expansion of existing stores or centers and/or increases in sales per square foot. Unless there is a significant market void, newcomers must plan to compete toe to toe with existing merchants.

This intensive competition makes it more difficult to estimate market capture for the subject site (see Table 8-8). Demand comes primarily from four sources: (1) growth in retail expenditures, (2) reduction of sales rates at successful existing stores or centers, (3) diverting sales from marginal stores or centers, or (4) reduction of the amount of retail dollar flow leaving the trade area. Each situation should be examined carefully, zeroing in on the most likely possibility. Unless a significant market void exists (e.g., extremely high sales rate for existing facilities or high percentage of runaway business), a new center can expect extreme difficulty—sales success may occur only over an extended period of time and after substantial merchandising efforts.

In estimating market capture, the advantages and disadvantages of the subject site should be considered—such factors as location, accessibility, visibility, and proximity to other major uses. If the competitive surveys and consumer surveys indicate major weaknesses in existing facilities (e.g., lack of parking, lack of shopping ambience, poor marketing), consideration should be given to whether or not these conditions can be overcome in the design and operation of a store or center on the subject site.

It's also meaningful to look at the capture of market demand by an existing store or center that is roughly comparable in quality to the scenario store or center proposed for the subject site. For example, if the best existing facility can't capture more than 10 percent of the existing demand, it may be difficult for the proposed center to achieve these levels except in rapidly growing trade areas. It's best to compare the two situations carefully in terms of competitive strengths and weaknesses and of overall future growth of the trade area.

Once the capture rate has been established, the projected sales level on the subject site can be calculated. This sales estimate is then translated into square feet of GLA by assuming sales rates for each of the

Table 8-8. Projected Retail Demand on Subject Site

	1987	1990	1995	2000
Total retail sales within trade area*	$902.1	$1023	$1245	$1524
Capture by subject site		12.0%	15.0%	18.0%
Projected demandon subject site*		$ 123	$ 187	$ 274
Estimated sales/sq ft		$ 175	$ 220	$ 270
Square footage required**		702	849	1016
Recommended program**		700	850	1000

*In millions of dollars.
**In thousands of square feet.

projection years. These estimates should take into consideration the ability of seasoned retailers to increase sales rates as they improve marketing efficiency. By dividing the sales rate into the anticipated level of demand, the GLA range can be estimated. A recommended center size can now be established.

Recommended Center by Retail Line

The proposed center should be broken down by retail line, based on expenditure patterns established in the consumer survey as well as on the strengths and weaknesses of existing facilities (see Table 8-9). The amount of GLA indicated for each retail line should then be compared with the preliminary development scenario, as shown in Table 8-1. If the total amount of GLA indicated is reasonably close (i.e., 10 percent ±) the proposed store or center is probably a sound venture. If projected space is considerably greater than maximum site limitations, each assumption in the demand projections should be reanalyzed as to its validity. If the projections still hold, consideration should be given to expanding into nonretail uses on the periphery of the site. In all cases, the development scenario should be tested and retested, particularly in terms of "key" assumptions that may have a major effect on the overall success of the project.

Market Characteristics of Various Types of Retail Centers or Stores

The analytical process just outlined applies to most types of retail stores or centers. However, certain unique features associated with various retailing situations also should be considered.

Table 8-9. Recommended Center by Retail Line (GLA in Thousands)

Retail line	1990	1995	2000
Shopper goods			
Apparel	50	100	100
General merchandise	400	400	550
Household furnishings	50	100	100
Specialty stores	50	100	100
Total	550	700	850
Convenience goods	100	100	100
Personal services	10	10	10
Specialized services	40	40	40
Total	700	850	1000

Super-Regional and Regional Shopping Centers

The key elements in a successful regional or super-regional center include sufficient trade area demand, strength of the anchor department stores, variety and quality of the satellite stores, ease of accessibility and parking, overall shopping ambience created by the site plan and building design, and aggressiveness of the center's promotion. Weakness in any of these areas can lead to increased market penetration by competing centers.

In analyzing market potential for regional and super-regional centers, emphasis should be placed on the demand for shopper goods such as apparel, general merchandise, home furnishings, and specialty items. They represent the merchandise backbone of a successful super-regional or regional center. Care should also be taken to relate major anchor stores as closely as possible to the income levels and life-styles of households in the trade area.

Community Centers

The elements that make a successful community center are largely the same as those needed for a successful regional center but with less em-

Drawing by H. Martin; © 1976 The New Yorker Magazine, Inc.

phasis on anchor store strength and shopping ambience. Convenience of location and depth of trade area play a much bigger role; few customers will drive out of their way to find a community center.

The market demand analysis is generally similar to the process previously outlined except that it need not be as comprehensive in terms of trade area or data collected. Emphasis should be on possible market "voids" in particular merchandise areas and on the proximity of the subject site to the greatest concentration of population in the trade area. In some situations, it's desirable to look for some type of nonretail use (e.g., office building, motel, recreational facility) to help strengthen the center.

Neighborhood Centers

The important market factor in a successful neighborhood center is convenience, in terms of proximity to the customer's residence, accessibility, and parking. The strength and reputation of the supermarket tenant is also critical, particularly in the meat and produce departments.

Market analysis of neighborhood centers involves a relatively small trade area and a less involved analytical process. Emphasis should be on data which relate to food, drugs, and other convenience goods. Establishing consumer loyalty to existing supermarket chains may also be important, particularly in trade areas with considerable competition.

Strip Retail Centers

Market analysis for the strip retail center should also focus on convenience goods. Location is the single most critical feature of the successful strip retail center since the primary reason people shop at convenience stores is to save time. Adequate parking is also crucial to the success of such a center.

Discount or Warehouse Stores

Several major differences are involved in analyzing the market for discount or warehouse stores. Since most business is generative, the trade area can be significantly larger, perhaps as much as 45 minutes to an hour from the subject site. The competitive survey should focus on stores or centers doing a large business in household furnishings and general merchandise. The consumer interview should seek to establish the importance of merchandising in the trade area, as most discount or warehouse stores have little merchandising. The site for the discount operation does not have to be located in a premium area; in fact, many discount or warehouse operations utilize industrial facilities.

Off-Price and Outlet Centers

Market analysis for the off-price center should focus on potential demand from moderate-income households in the trade area. The size of the trade area is somewhere between that of the community center and the regional center, and the off-price center may compete with both, often in adjacent locations.. Competitive research should include analysis of community and regional centers in the trade area. Customer research should focus on local residents; off-price centers draw very little tourist trade.

The trade area for the outlet center is regional, with a strong customer base of tourists. Customer research should also focus on demand from low- to moderate-income households in the trade area. Analysis of the competition should cover regional centers in the trade area and specialty centers that draw heavily on the tourist trade.

Specialty Centers

Evaluating market demand for the specialty center is more complicated. If the proposed center is dependent upon tourist expenditures, the level of these expenditures must be established, as must a breakdown of where the money is spent. The proposed center must then be evaluated in terms of its potential appeal vis-à-vis other tourist attractions. Accessibility and proximity to tourist destination points may be important factors. Seasonal fluctuations in tourist expenditure patterns must also be considered.

If the proposed specialty center is directed primarily at a local market area, the analysis is generally similar to the procedures discussed earlier in this chapter, with two major exceptions. First, the retail trade area *must* be made up of higher-income families who can afford specialized merchandise. Second, the proposed specialty center should be located near a major regional center or within an established shopping area, to provide a "draw" for the specialized center. Specialty centers may also capture demand in certain merchandising categories from the regional centers or shopping areas.

9
Office and Industrial

The business of America is business.

CALVIN COOLIDGE

Office and industrial uses depend primarily on business firm expenditures. The vast majority of office and industrial space is utilized to house employees, machinery and equipment, and inventories used and produced by these firms. The amount of space required by a firm is a function of its existing operation and its anticipated future requirements.

In addition to space which business firms utilize directly, a sizable amount is required to "warehouse" products. In some cases, these facilities are owned or leased directly by the firm producing the product; alternatively, warehousing facilities are often used by wholesalers, jobbers, and distributors.

Office Land Uses

One major factor behind the postwar construction boom has been the building of new office space. New office development was undertaken not only in such traditional office centers as New York, Los Angeles, Chicago, Philadelphia, Boston, San Francisco, and Washington, D.C., but also in newer commercial centers like Atlanta, Dallas, Denver,

Houston, and Minneapolis-St. Paul. Even in smaller cities, office building development has expanded dramatically, although often in less intensive physical forms.

Office building development falls into two major categories: "custom construction" geared to the specific needs of the ultimate user (who is often the owner as well),[1] and buildings constructed on a speculative basis by individual developers. The public sector has also been instrumental in new office building development, either as tenant or, in many cases, as owner.[2]

The Demand for Office Space

Office building development occurs in most cities because of increases in demand and shifts within and among metropolitan areas. Demand has expanded through growth in office employment, as well as through changes in the nature of business activity.

Growth in Office Employment. If nothing else, the sheer expansion of America's postwar economy would have created demand for substantial amounts of new office space. While the labor force grew steadily in the postwar period, the percentage of office workers grew even faster. During this period, a surge in service industry growth also occurred, with many such firms requiring substantial amounts of office space. Between 1960 and 1970, office employment increased by 36 percent; between 1970 and 1980, it increased by 37 percent. By 1987, office workers accounted for more than two-fifths of the total labor force.[3]

In recent years, the growth of office workers has slowed. This is largely due to the completion of the entry of the baby boomers into the labor force and a leveling off in the participation rate of women. As a result of this slowing, the supply of office space caught up with demand in 1983 and has been leading demand ever since. In terms of the future, office employment is expected to grow only 1.7 percent for the period 1985–1995, compared to a 2.5 percent annual growth rate for the previous decade, 1975–1985, according to a study conducted by Dr. David Birch at MIT.[4]

[1]Also termed "build-to-suit."

[2]The increase in state and local government personnel in particular has required extensive amounts of new public office space.

[3]U. S. Bureau of Labor Statistics, *Employment and Earnings,* February 1987, p. 36.

[4]David L. Birch, "America's Office Needs: 1985–1995," Massachusetts Institute of Technology Center for Real Estate Development, 1986, p. 15.

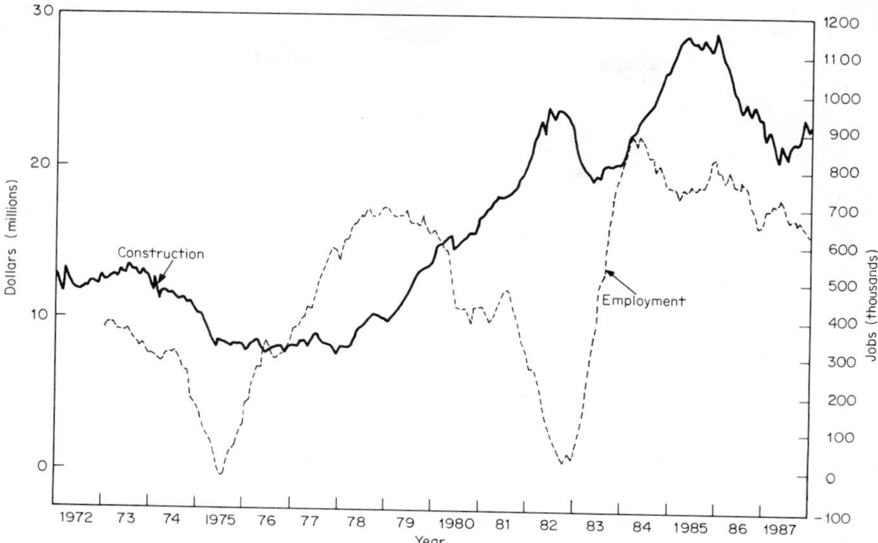

Figure 9-1. Office construction put-in-place (1982 dollars in millions) versus office employment: 1972–1987 *(Salomon Brothers Inc, U.S. Departments of Commerce and Labor, Coldwell Banker, Salomon Brothers)*

Changes in business Operations. While the number of office employees was increasing, changes were also occurring in the way businesses were utilizing office space. As firms grew in size and complexity, many tended to separate their office functions from manufacturing, particularly when they were geographically dispersed. The amount of office space per worker was also increasing. More space was required for the new office machines developed to assist in the flow of paperwork and for those who operated the equipment.[5] When firms moved to new quarters, they frequently introduced new functions such as computer rooms, libraries, executive dining rooms, and expanded conference and meeting rooms. Larger offices were also used to confer status on certain employees. For these and other reasons, total rented office space per employee expanded from 109 square feet in 1946 to 264 square feet in 1986.[6]

[5]This is sometimes offset by increased automation, which reduces the number of clerical employees required.

[6]Building Owners and Managers Association International, *1987 BOMA Experience Exchange Report,* Chicago, 1988, p. 25.

Shifts in Demand

In addition to heavier demand for office space, important shifts in demand within and among metropolitan areas have also occurred. While these shifts have not increased overall demand, they have often provided the impetus for substantial office building activity within some areas.

Upgrade Shifts. One of the major shifts in demand for office space after World War II was from older, often obsolete buildings to new office space. There was little office building development during the Depression and the war. When economic activity increased in the early 1950s, new office space started to come on the market.[7] This new space was often significantly superior in design and operation (e.g., high-speed elevators, air conditioning, fewer columns) to older space, and the "image" of new buildings was sometimes better. In some situations, management of older buildings had become unresponsive to changing tenant needs. For these and other reasons, tenants in older space began moving to newer facilities, forcing owners of older buildings to remodel their buildings and upgrade property management in order to remain competitive.

In most downtown areas, there is still potential for significant replacement shifts. Many tenants in older buildings have moved to newer buildings, or the older space has been upgraded. Nevertheless, the high vacancy rates caused by overbuilding in recent years continue to exert strong competitive pressures on the office marketplace in many downtown areas.

Much suburban space, built in the early 1950s, deteriorated or became functionally obsolete over the years, thereby becoming vulnerable to new competition. Efforts to upgrade the image of suburban office space were also made.[8] In the suburbs, the overbuilding problem has been even more severe than in downtown areas because of the availability of more land for expansion and lower construction costs. As a result, vacancy rates in the suburbs are higher than in downtown areas. Nevertheless, the demand for suburban office space in recent years has exceeded that of downtown by a great margin; in 1987, two-thirds of of-

[7]Fear of a major postwar recession caused a considerable delay in building new office space after the war.

[8]An example is the move from cheaply built two-story, wood frame office buildings to small and medium high-rise buildings and office parks.

Figure 9-2. High-rise office buildings dot the Chicago skyline. Many of the buildings in the center of the photo are a part of Illinois Center, developed by IC Industries. *(Tigerhill Studio/John T. Hill)*

fice space absorption occurred outside the central business districts of ten of the largest U.S. markets.[9]

Intraurban Shifts. Another major factor in recent office building development has been the shift in office-related activity within a metropolitan area. One of the best examples has been the move to the suburbs. In some areas, this trend is still strong, particularly where the downtown area has deteriorated rapidly or rents are substantially higher than in suburban areas.

In other cases, no-growth sentiment in the suburbs and changing lifestyle preferences have led to a revitalization of downtown office space and a move back to the central city. It is also common today for intraregional shifts to occur between suburbs, as one suburb or building project develops an advantage over another. There is also the shift totally out of the urbanized area into new towns and other types of outlying development.

[9]The Office Network, Houston, Texas, 1988.

Interurban Shifts. Less predictable is the shift in office demand from one metropolitan area to another. This type of shift reflects major changes in overall regional activity, often involving extensive regional promotional programs. In some cases, these shifts reflect consolidation of certain industries in a particular city, such as the move in the mid-1970s of several oil companies to Houston.[10] In other cases the shift may reflect "footloose" firms that can operate anywhere but choose a particular area for its life-style or climatic advantages.

Nodes of Office Building Activity

In most metropolitan areas, office building activity tends to cluster in "nodes" around centers of economic activity or, in some cases, transportation facilities.

Downtown (CBD). Office space has become the dominant land use for most downtowns. Generally, this space is occupied by financial institutions, large legal and accounting firms, governmental agencies, and headquarters of major corporations, most of which remained downtown during the flight to the suburbs. The degree to which a viable office market exists will depend greatly on the likelihood that these operations will remain in the downtown area. If they seem firmly committed, other investments are likely to remain or possibly be expanded.

Uptown. Many cities also have a strong uptown office node, generally located along a major arterial that provides access to the suburbs. Examples include Wilshire Boulevard in Los Angeles, Peachtree Street in Atlanta, Michigan Avenue in Chicago, and Colorado Boulevard in Denver. Demand in these areas has often come from intraurban shifts, generally out of the downtown. The shape of the node is usually linear, reflecting dominance of the arterial. Access tends to be by automobile, which often creates substantial congestion during peak hours.

Office Parks. In Chapter 1, the growth of office park developments was noted in many suburban areas. By 1986 there were roughly 6000

[10] In the 1970s, Houston's active promotion of oil and other companies was known in some circles as the "evacuation program," referring, of course, to the evacuation of New York City. With the decline of the oil industry in the 1980s, Houston discovered the problems of industry concentration and became an evacuation center in its own right.

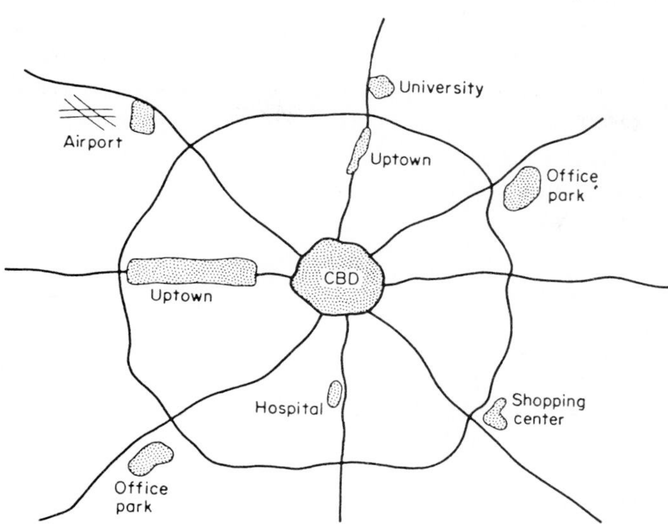

Figure 9-3. Typical nodes of office building development.

industrial and office parks located throughout the country.[11] Most parks today are devoted to light manufacturing, distribution, and service activities. Mixed-use office parks have grown in popularity, with a move away from parks that are classified as strictly industrial. Since the 1950s there has been a steady long-term trend of building more and more parks near interstate highways and, more recently, near airports.[12] Another trend in office park development has been a shift from complexes of one-story buildings to the high- or mid-rise business parks.

Shopping Centers. The growth of major regional shopping centers has produced nodes of activity to support office building development. Frequently, this type of space is oriented toward smaller users, many serving the residential households in the shopping center's trade area. Medical office development is often a frequent type of use in these nodes.

Special Nodes. Office building development also occurs around special activity nodes throughout a metropolitan area. Offices serving at-

[11]"Business Parks of the Nineties: More Attractive, More Flexible and Featuring More Amenities," *Site Selection Handbook 86,* Conway Data, Atlanta, p. 1266.

[12]Michael O'Connor, "New Survey Reveals Emerging Trends for Prepared Sites of the Future," *Site Selection Handbook/ 85,* Conway Data, Atlanta, 1985, p. 1148.

torneys and title companies often develop around major governmental buildings, particularly those containing public records or courts. Medical offices are built near major hospital complexes, allowing doctors easy access for their rounds and any emergencies that might develop. Universities often provide a focal point for R&D and other office building development. Firms utilizing frequent air service may rent space in office buildings near airports.

Analyzing Market Demand

Establishing demand for commercial office space is perhaps the most difficult and least accurate of all land uses. Statistics on office space occupancy are hard to come by and may be dated. The use of long-term leases reduces turnover; a firm may have a difficult time moving to new space, even if it wants to. The tendency toward wide swings in overbuilding or underbuilding can create market distortions. Finally, factors such as the "image" of a particular building, proximity to client firms, and quality of continuing property management are difficult to incorporate in the demand analysis.

Definition of Terms. Several terms utilized in office space analysis need to be identified:

- *Gross building area.* The total area of the office building or combination of buildings, expressed in square feet.
- *Net rentable area.* The amount of space in the building(s) available for rent to an office tenant. The exact definition may vary from one metropolitan area to another, but it generally excludes elements of the building (such as the elevator core and stairs) that penetrate through the floor to areas below, unless these elements are for the exclusive use of one tenant.[13] The ratio between gross and net area is called the *design efficiency* ratio.
- *Net rented area.* The amount of space in the building(s) under legal lease to tenants, whether the space is utilized or not.
- *Net occupied area.* The amount of space actually occupied by tenants.

[13] *1987 BOMA Experience Exchange Report,* Building Owners and Managers Association International, 1987, p. 482.

Establishing Demand in the Metropolitan Area. Office buildings have no market or trade area, as housing projects or shopping centers frequently do. In essence, office activities[14] can be conducted in virtually any section of the metropolitan area, depending upon the type of operation, availability of a good labor market, and desires of decision makers within an organization. In analyzing a market for office commercial development, therefore, it's helpful to understand overall demand in the metropolitan area.

The first step is to analyze the level of office demand, as shown in Table 9-1. Employment data are generally available from local planning agencies by category of employment. If not, other sources must be utilized.[15] Employment categories using large amounts of office space should be identified. Generally, these include finance, real estate, advertising, legal, insurance, and government services.[16]

Trends in historical data should also be evaluated. For example, a rapid buildup in governmental employees may indicate a market opportunity; conversely, a decline in financial employment may reflect a shift of activities to another metropolitan area. The overall trend in office employment categories should also be compared to growth in manufacturing employment. For example, an area with a rapid increase in manufacturing employment may indicate future demand for service business activities that utilize office space.[17]

The next step is to formulate the "space/employee ratio." Generally, data on the net rented area in the metropolitan area are available from local planning agencies or such private groups as the Building Owners and Managers Association.[18] By dividing the net rented area by the number of office employees, we arrive at the amount of office space per employee. These ratios are then projected into the future, considering any anticipated changes affecting the

[14]For the purpose of this discussion, office activities involve business activities physically disassociated from manufacturing or other industrial operations.

[15]For example, extrapolations of census or state employment agency statistics can be made. Private or university studies may also be helpful.

[16]*The Standard Land Use Coding Manual,* published by the U.S. Bureau of Public Roads and the Urban Renewal Administration in 1965, identifies twenty-two distinct types of activities under the category "offices."

[17]See the export-base theory of urban growth discussed in Chapter 5.

[18]It is to be hoped that data will be available for several years, for then discernible trends can be spotted. An increase in the ratio may indicate a reduction in employment, increased automation, a shift to lower-cost office space, a change in the employment mix toward higher-priced employees, or any number of possibilities.

Table 9-1. Projected Demand for Office Space, Metropolitan Area

	Actual			Projected		
	1972	1982	1987	1990	1995	2000
Total private employment*	243.6	290.3	343.9	385	435	475
Percentage office related	15.1%	17.3%	17.8%	18 %	19 %	20 %
Office-related employment*	36.7	50.3	61.3	69.3	82.7	95.0
Space and employee ratio	256.5	265.7	276.4	280.0	285.0	290.0
Net demand*	9,413.6	13,364.7	16,948.8	19,404.0	23,555.3	27,550.0
Average annual increase in net demand*		395.1	716.8	818.4	830.3	799.0
Average annual percentage increase		4.2%	5.4%	4.8%	4.3%	3.4%
Existing supply						
Completed	9,876.1	13,957.0	17,567.0			
Under construction	347.2	689.1	1,375.0			
Total	10,223.3	14,646.1	18,942.0			
Vacant space	809.8	1,281.4	1,993.2			
Vacancy rate	7.9%	8.7%	10.5%			
Incremental space at 10% vacancy				2,618	7,230	11,669
Incremental space per period				2,618	4,613	4,439

*Thousands.

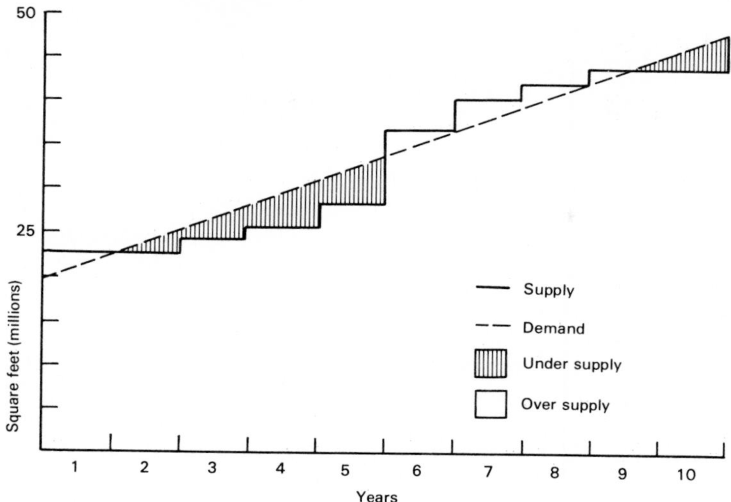

Figure 9-4. Office buildings: hypothetical demand/supply relationship.

market.[19] The projected number of office-related employees is then multiplied by the space/employee ratio to arrive at the net demand for office space.

Net demand is then matched with existing supply, including both completed buildings and those under construction. Incremental demand can now be projected, assuming a stabilized vacancy factor (10 percent in the example) in the future. If a period of extensive building is under way, it's wise to increase the vacancy allowance in the early years to reflect softer market conditions.

Projected levels of office space should then be compared with historical building activity. It's important, however, to recognize the impact of historical over- and underbuilding cycles on the data. Several tests of "reasonableness" can be used in comparing historical with projected data, including space per capita, absorption per year, and the experiences of similar cities. If the projections hold up, they are probably as accurate as expected, but remember that they provide extremely rough indications of metropolitan area demand.

Competitive Survey. Once overall demand trends in the metropolitan area are understood, the competition must be analyzed. This is illus-

[19]University studies, such as the recent study of office needs conducted by Dr. David Birch at MIT (cited earlier), can aid in developing projections.

trated in Table 9-2. The scope of the competitive survey will depend on the size and nature of the contemplated project. If it's a small or medium-sized office building directed at the general office market, a survey of the node in which the subject site is located will probably be sufficient. If the project is a large office building or one involving a specialized market, it may be necessary to survey other nodes as well. In general, the best policy is to first undertake a detailed survey of the node surrounding the subject site followed by a more generalized survey of other nodes, particularly those deemed most competitive.

As with any other survey, this should be undertaken by experienced professionals or staff. Information to be gathered includes the location of the office building, net rentable area completed and under construction, vacant space and rate (percentage), average rent per square foot, free rent concessions (if any), tenant finish allowance and items included (e.g., carpets, drapes, partitioning, telephone, and electrical outlets), expense stop,[20] parking provided (stalls per 1000 square feet) and monthly charge, and qualitative judgment regarding overall project competitiveness. It is also desirable to gather information about building amenities (e.g., conference facilities, restaurants, health clubs) and to acquire a list of major tenants and a profile of other tenants.

This information usually can be obtained from on-site inspections, discussions with leasing agents, a review of building plans, and discussions with tenants. In some situations, it may also be desirable to look for major leases which will come up for renewal within a 2- to 3-year period. These tenants may provide potential demand for the proposed project.

Projecting Nodal Demand. Information generated from the competitive survey explains the relative strength of major office nodes in a metropolitan area. The next step is to allocate future demand projections by each major node, as in Table 9-3. This is a purely judgmental decision and must take into consideration the current competitiveness of the node, new office space planned or under construction, economic trends in the metropolitan area, and problems such as traffic congestion, crime, and neighborhood deterioration. A good benchmark in projecting nodal demand is the node's current capture of metropolitan demand, which will change depending on the factors indicated above.

Estimating Market Capture. The final consideration in estimating market demand is the amount of incremental nodal demand that can be

[20]An expense stop is a provision in a lease that establishes the maximum level of operating expenses to be paid by the landlord; expenses beyond this level are reimbursed by the tenant.

Table 9-2. Competitive Survey, December, 1987

Map		Square footage (in thousands)					Average rent/square foot	Free rent (months)*	Average tenant finish/sq ft	Expense stop**	Parking			
		Completed	Under const.	Total	Vacant	Vacancy rate(%)					Stalls	Stalls/1000	Charge	Rating
	Central business district													
1	100 Main Street	900		900	103	11.4	$17.10	3	$15.00	$5.00	500	0.56	$50.00	Good
2	1 Washington Plaza	775		775	90	11.6	18.00	3	13.00	4.50	350	0.45	50.00	Very good
3	645 Third Avenue	1,600		1,600	160	10.0	16.50	3	15.00	5.00	750	0.47	45.00	Good
4	World Bank Plaza	1,300		1,300	90	6.9	15.25	0	12.00	4.00	675	0.52	50.00	Good
5	Cosmic Insurance Bldg.	1,100		1,100	60	5.5	16.00	0	10.00	5.00	600	0.55	55.00	Good
6	810 Fourth Avenue	870		870	15	1.7	14.50	0	12.00	4.50	425	0.49	60.00	Very good
7	State Bank Building		450	450	170	37.8	18.50	6	18.00	6.00	500	1.11	75.00	Excellent
8	730 Third Avenue		305	305	145	47.5	20.00	6	20.00	6.00	300	0.98	75.00	Excellent
	Other	2,430		2,430	265	10.9	13.50	NA	NA		3,000	1.23	45.00	Mixed
	Total CBD	8,975	755	9,730	833	8.6	15.73				7,100	0.73		
	Surburban nodes													
	Grand Boulevard	2450	100	2,550	310	12.2	12.50	3	12.00	4.00	9,300	3.65	20.00	Good
	Airport	1850	165	2,015	197	9.8	13.00	3	10.00	3.50	7,600	3.77	25.00	Good
	Technology Center	1375	240	1,615	345	21.4	14.50	9	15.00	4.75	6,500	4.02	15.00	Excellent
	University	540	35	575	65	11.3	11.00	6	12.00	4.25	2,000	3.48	20.00	Good
	Northgate Shopping Center	450	20	470	87	18.5	10.50	6	10.00	3.75	1,500	3.19	20.00	Fair
	Total suburban	6665	560	7,225	852	11.8	12.84				23,400	3.24	20.00	
	Nonnodal	1927	60	1,987	308	15.5	11.25	NA	NA				15.00	Mixed
	Total metro area	17,567	1375	18942	1993	10.5	14.15							

* Based on 5-year lease.
** Annual expense paid by landlord expressed in dollars per square foot per year.

Table 9-3. Allocation of Incremental Demand by Node*

			Incremental space						Total space	
	1987		1988–1990		1991–1995		1996–2000		2000	
	Sq ft	%	Sq ft	%	Sq ft	%	Sq ft	%	Sq ft	%
Existing nodes										
Central Business District**	9,730	51.4	785	30	1,845	40	1,775	40	14,136	46
Grand Boulevard	2,550	13.5	131	5	231	5	222	5	3,133	10
Airport	2,015	10.6	524	20	461	10	222	5	3,222	11
Technology Center	1,615	8.5	654	25	1,153	25	888	20	4,310	14
University	575	3.0	131	5	0	0	0	0	706	2
Northgate Shopping Ctr.	470	2.5	0	0	0	0	0	0	470	2
Total	16,955	89.5	2,225	85	3,690	80	3,107	70	25,977	85
New nodes		0.0	131	5	461	10	888	20	1,480	5
Nonnodal	1987	10.5	262	10	461	10	444	10	3,154	10
Total metro area	18,942	100.0	2,618	100	4,613	100	4,439	100	30,611	100

* Expressed in thousands of net rentable square feet.

** Subject site is in this node.

Table 9-4. Projected Demand on Subject Site

	1988–1990	1991–1995	Total
Projected incremental nodal demand (CBD)*	785	1845	2630
Estimated capture by subject site	10%	25%	21%
Projected demand on subject site*	79	461	540
Recommended program* (occupancy = 1990)	75–85	450–475	525–560

* Expressed in thousands of net rentable square feet.

captured by the subject site (see Table 9-4). Factors to be evaluated include location of the site within the node, other office buildings nearby, vehicular and public transportation access, views possible from the building, and address prestige. If a major anchor tenant is firm, the analysis should consider the image and operation of the anchor tenant. The capture estimate is then applied to incremental nodal demand to arrive at net rental space on the subject site.

Market Characteristics of Various Types of Office Projects

Single-Tenant Buildings. These are office buildings occupied primarily by a single tenant. Since the major user is identified early in the planning and development process, there are usually few marketing problems. The major analytical task is to determine future space needs of the dominant user by preparing a detailed analysis of future business activities to be conducted in the building. The business plans of operating subunits should be evaluated, as well as their relationship to other units and centralized facilities such as computer centers, libraries, and cafeterias.[21] Staffing levels necessary to implement the plans are assigned. Staffing levels are then translated into space requirements, utilizing space/employee ratios for various categories of employee (e.g., executive, technical, clerical). This process will indicate future space needs, including space for expansion to accommodate employee growth. Space not required immediately may be subleased on a short-term basis.

[21]This is usually a good time for management to rigorously evaluate operating functions, consolidating those deemed superfluous or overstaffed.

Figure 9-5. With its four high-rise towers and single-level Banking Pavilion, Toronto-Dominion Center is Canada's largest office complex. *(The Cadillac Fairview Corporation Limited)*

Multitenant Buildings. These are buildings usually developed by a nonuser, directed at securing a variety of tenants from the general office market. Although such a building may be "anchored" by one or more major tenants, it is not designed for their specific needs.[22] The market analysis procedures discussed in this chapter generally apply to this type of building, with emphasis on nodal demand, comparisons vis-à-vis competitive buildings, and opportunities for successful preleasing-

[22]In some cases, the building design is modified to fit the needs of an anchor tenant if the tenant has been secured early in the development process.

activities.[23] If the subject site is located in a specialized node (e.g., shopping center, airport, government offices), consideration should also be given to the down-side risk exposure if the catalyst creating the specialized node changes or diminishes in activity.

Office Parks. Since office parks create their own environment to a large extent, market analysis is more difficult than with an established node. If the park is located in or near a manufacturing district, consideration should be given to the percentage of manufacturing space that is office in nature and the degree to which it might be attracted to the office park. If the office park is part of a larger project, such as a new town, demand might be created by other land uses within the project. Footloose business operations may also be attracted because of the project's overall atmosphere. Evaluation of metropolitan area data and competitive surveys may also indicate demand for a specialized type of park (e.g., financial institutions, R&D firms).

Medical Offices. Medical and dental office projects are very specialized in terms of planning and design. The approach to market analysis is also different. The first step is to establish the number of doctors currently practicing within 20 to 30 minutes' driving time from the subject site. This can be accomplished through rosters published by medical associations or, in most cities, the yellow pages of the telephone book. A competitive survey should then be undertaken of existing office facilities in which these doctors are located. Information developed in this survey should cover the same items as in the office survey, with emphasis on proximity to major hospitals, specialized design to accommodate doctors' needs, the amount of parking provided, and special features such as pharmacies, medical libraries, and recreational facilities within the building.

If the competitive survey reveals that many doctors practice in their homes, nonmedical office buildings, or older, functionally obsolete medical buildings, there should be a relatively strong potential market for a new, functionally designed medical building. If, on the other hand, a series of modern medical facilities currently exists, the market will be difficult to penetrate unless specific lease or ownership deals can be prearranged.[24]

Demand can be established by projecting the number of doctors in each specialty using an average of approximately 1500 square feet per

[23]Lenders may require an office building to be 25 to 30 percent preleased before proceeding with construction; in a soft market, the percentage could be higher.

[24]Doctors like to participate in the ownership of a medical building, and a group of owning doctors can often assist considerably in leasing the rest of the building.

doctor. Capture estimates can then be applied to ascertain potential demand at the subject site. Generally, capture estimates shouldn't exceed 10 to 15 percent for any one specialty.[25] By cumulating demand from the various specialties, it's possible to get a rough indication of overall demand on the subject site. To this should be added sufficient space for a pharmacy, radiology laboratory, or other required facilities.

[25]Because specialists depend upon referrals from general practitioners, internists, and other specialists, they like to be the only ones within their discipline in a medical building, although this is not always possible.

Industrial Land Uses

Virtually every type of industrial activity requires land and buildings to fabricate, assemble, store, and transport its products.[26] When land was plentiful, industry utilized whatever land it wanted, as it wanted. As was noted in Chapter 2, however, a major thrust of planning and zoning in the United States has been regulation of industrial land use. Today, while most communities recognize the vital importance of industry to their economic base, they also realize that these activities have to be undertaken (1) in areas where they will be least harmful to other land uses and (2) under ground rules which assure conformity with minimum standards of health and safety. Some communities go even further, regulating the environmental and aesthetic quality of industrial land uses or banning them altogether.

Industry has also become more concerned about the way in which it utilizes land. The site selection process is considerably more sophisticated than it has been in the past. Firms are concerned about the type of community in which their employees live, as well as the quality of their industrial neighbors. To some extent, the interests of the firms and the communities in which they operate are more compatible now than at any time in the past.

Theories of Industrial Location

The theoretical framework of industrial site location goes back to the last century. In 1826, Johann Von Thunen related the intensity of land utilized for agricultural purposes to the distance (and, hence, transportation costs) from the city center.[27] A century later, Weber postulated that firms will seek that location which minimizes their labor, transportation, and raw material costs. The effect of the manufacturing process on transportation costs determines location to a large degree. If the product tended to lose weight through processing, the firm would be most likely to locate nearer sources of raw materials. If the product tended to add weight, the location would be nearer final consumption markets. Weber argued that firms will locate nearer a source of labor only if those costs savings are more than added transportation cost. He also noted that firms in certain industries tend to cluster ("agglom-

[26]Services are not included in our discussion, although some types of service firms occupy industrial-type space.

[27]J. H. Von Thunen, *Der Isolierte Staat in Beziehnug auf Landwirtschaft und Nationalokonomie,* Hamburg, 1826.

erate") in order to decrease production costs (e.g., automobiles, airplane manufacturers, motion picture production), and decentralize ("deglomerate") when external forces (e.g., high land costs, plant obsolescence) increase production costs.[28]

In 1939, August Losch, writing in *Economics of Location,*[29] showed that firms could penetrate their market through low prices only by locating at the lowest cost site. That is, plants located closest to the consumer would have the lowest transportation costs and would therefore be able to capture the largest share of the market.

In 1948, Edgar Hoover broadened the least-cost concept to include transfer costs, such as the cost of maintaining large inventories, loss of business as a result of slow deliveries, and increased cost of distribution as a result of slow deliveries, and increased cost of distribution as a result of distance. He also noted that the type of transportation was often as important as the distance involved; railroads may be better for longer distances, trucks for shorter ones. In essence, industrial site selection is a process of balancing various combinations of production and transfer cost.[30]

All these theories emphasized least cost as the basic determinant in locational decisions. In 1956, Melvin Greenhut challenged this reasoning, maintaining that profit maximization, not cost minimization, was critical. According to Greenhut, some firms will locate in a rapidly growing market area, even if it isn't the least-cost location. Other factors that may be as important as transfer and processing costs include competitiveness of the industry, size of the market area, proximity and direct contact with customers, location of competitors, and elasticity in product demand. Greenhut also introduced the idea that personal management preferences have an influence.[31]

Locational Orientation of Industrial Firms

Building on this theoretical base, William Kinnard and Stephen Messner identified and classified five major categories of firms by dom-

[28]Alfred Weber, *Theory of the Location of Industries,* C. J. Friedrick (trans.), University of Chicago Press, Chicago, 1929.

[29]August Losch, *The Economics of Location,* Yale University Press, New Haven, Conn., 1939.

[30]Edgar M. Hoover, *Location of Economic Activity,* McGraw-Hill, New York, 1948.

[31]Melvin L. Greenhut, *Plant Location in Theory and Practice,* University of North Carolina Press, Chapel Hill, 1956.

inant factors in the site location decision-making process:[32]

- *Market-oriented.* These firms are most oriented toward the market for their final product. This group includes consumer-oriented industries, which tend to follow concentrations of population, and firms that produce for other industries, which tend to follow the industry on which they are dependent.
- *Resource-oriented.* These firms are oriented primarily toward resources required for production. This may include a specific natural resource utilized directly in the production process (e.g., iron ore, cement, bauxite) or specific types of fuel required by the production process (e.g., hydroelectric power, natural gas, coal).
- *Transportation-oriented.* In some cases, transportation cost is the major consideration in a site selection decision. In these cases, firms generally tend to locate near the type of transportation that best serves their needs.
- *Labor-oriented.* Some firms are primarily concerned with the availability and cost of labor. Generally, labor-intensive industries tend to concentrate in areas where labor is plentiful, at relatively low cost. The degree of unionization of the labor force may also be a consideration. For some firms, however, the concern is not cost of labor, but its skill. In the case of highly technical industries, for example, proximity to universities and technical schools may be important.[33]
- *Footloose.* Some firms are not oriented toward any of these factors and generally locate in areas on the basis of life-style and image.

By understanding the basic orientation of a firm's locational decision, it's possible to establish its most probable location within a metropolitan area, the type of industrial land that will be required, the site services that will be needed, and the maximum price it can pay.

The Site Selection Process Today

Today, site selection for most firms is a highly sophisticated process which may take several years and involve outside consultants in addition

[32]William N. Kinnard, Jr., and Stephen D. Messner, *Industrial Real Estate,* Society of Industrial Realtors of the National Association of Real Estate Boards, Washington, D.C., 1971, pp. 53–55.

[33]The growth of the electronics industry in Boston, San Francisco, and Los Angeles was directly related to the presence of local universities with advanced technology programs.

to top executives. The process involves screening regions, metropolitan areas, and specific sites against criteria important to the firm.

Selecting the Region. In discussing regional locational decisions, it is necessary to distinguish between relocation and expansion. A firm relocating its activities to another region is probably responding to dwindling markets, higher labor and transportation costs, unionization, or other negative pressures in the region from which it is emigrating. Therefore, such a firm will be seeking a region where these problems are reduced or nonexistent. This type of regional relocation can become so prevalent within an industry that an individual firm may be forced to relocate to remain competitive.[34]

In the case of regional expansion, the decision has more to do with serving markets. As a geographic market expands, a firm producing in another region is increasingly tempted to open branch operations in the new market area. Often, this is accomplished when distribution branches evolve into manufacturing operations. In considering regional expansion, a firm must weigh costs of new plant and equipment against advantages of greater market penetration, lower transportation and distribution costs, and possibly lower production costs. In many cases, regional expansion decisions are a vital component of long-term corporate planning.

Selecting the Metropolitan Area. The next step is to select a metropolitan area within the region.[35] This decision involves an evaluation of market potential, operating costs, and certain external factors that affect the overall business and living environment. Market potential is important because it often costs less to service a major market immediately surrounding the production facility. The metropolitan area market therefore provides a nucleus for growth, in terms of potential purchasing power as well as the market's capacity to establish market trends for the region. Important factors in evaluating market potential include population, income, and expenditure patterns in the metropolitan area; strength and nature (i.e., local, regional, or national) of competition; and channels of distribution

[34]This explains, in part, the movement of the textile industry from New England to the Southeast and then overseas.

[35]Within geographic regions, extensive competition usually exists between metropolitan areas for industrial firms: Boston and Hartford in the Northeast; Atlanta and Orlando in the Southeast; Portland and Seattle in the Northwest; Dallas and Houston in the Southwest; Denver and Salt Lake City in the Rockies; and Los Angeles and San Francisco in the West.

The firm must also evaluate operating costs in each metropolitan area under consideration. These factors include availability, cost and skills level of the labor pool; availability and cost of land; cost of building materials; total tax loads, including property, sales, excise, income, and inventory taxes; and transportation and utility costs.

Most of these factors can be readily quantified. Less easily discerned are the more subtle external factors that may often affect selection of one metropolitan area over another, including the attitude of the metropolitan area toward industrial growth, the degree of unionization and attitudes of union leadership, availability of residential housing resources and community services (e.g., police, fire, schools, libraries, recreational facilities), cultural and entertainment facilities, overall "image" of the metropolitan area, tax abatement, and provision of free public services.

In many cases, final selection of a metropolitan area may involve a trade-off between market potential, operating costs, and external factors. The emphasis in the trade-off usually will depend upon the orientation of the firm. Market-oriented firms will tend to place greater emphasis on the stronger market area; transportation-, labor-, and resource-oriented firms will lean toward those areas with lower operating costs; nonoriented firms will focus on areas with more desirable images and life-styles.

Selecting the Site. Finally, a specific site must be selected. This is generally a fairly precise analytical process, involving extensive field investigation. Factors influencing this decision include parcel size (including land for expansion); cost of land and building development; accessibility to transportation; availability of utilities (e.g., electricity, gas, water, telephone); zoning and development covenants; type of firms in the surrounding area; proximity to residential neighborhoods, community facilities (e.g., vocational training schools, recreational facilities). and service facilities (e.g., hotels, restaurants, recreational facilities); local taxes (to the extent that they vary among sites within the metropolitan area); and any other site factors that might influence operating costs.

Each of these factors is assigned relative weights, either explicitly or implicitly, and the sites are compared. Again, the final site selection may involve a trade-off between various factors, depending upon their relative importance. Consideration is also given to community and developer concessions at this point, such as tax abatement, subsidized infrastructure, lower-cost financing, or expansion land banking.

Analyzing Market Demand

From the developer's point of view, the problem with projecting future demand for industrial land is that the focus of market analysis must be narrowed to those industries most likely attracted to an industrial park on the subject site. This requires some assumptions about the attractiveness of the subject site for industrial users. The location and nature of the site and the availability of transportation facilities will provide some clues. A site located in an established industrial area may be well suited to firms servicing existing operations in the area. A site with rail access may be more appropriate for distributive operations. A site with good physical features and neighborhood amenities may lend itself to a research and development park.

Once the general character of the park has been established, the next step is to select those target industries that will most likely be attracted to such a project (see Table 9-5). These industries should be selected by reviewing firms currently active in the metropolitan area and, more spe-

Table 9-5. Target Industries for a Potential Industrial Park

		Employment		
SIC no.	Target industries	1972	1982	1987
251	Household furniture	364	941	2130
252	Office furniture	37	105	232
254	Office and store fixtures	53	151	301
271	Newspaper publishing	434	1104	2269
272	Periodical publishing	94	209	417
275	Commercial printing	389	1046	2061
357	Computer and office equipment	196	836	1459
362	Electrical industrial apparatus	241	651	1251
363	Household appliances	209	546	1182
364	Electrical lighting and wiring	184	581	1204
365	Radio and TV manufacturing	143	395	867
366	Communications equipment	512	1496	2570
367	Electronic components	315	1081	2057
381	Scientific and research equipment	102	209	394
382	Laboratory appratus and optical measuring and controlling equipment	377	976	2130
384	Medical and dental instruments	65	244	533
386	Photographic equipment	94	325	652
387	Watches, clocks, etc.	37	93	185
394	Toys and athletic equipment	131	349	718
506	Electrical goods distribution	65	174	371
507	Plumbing and heating equipment distribution	41	105	232
Totals		4083	11617	23215
Total manufacturing employment		22434	57226	99837
Percent in target industries		18.2%	20.3%	23.3%

cifically, which have located in parks of comparable quality to the subject site. The industries should be categorized by a three-digit Standard Industrial Classification (SIC) code.[36]

With an understanding of the appropriate type of park and the target industries that might be attracted, the next step is to survey the competition, as shown in Table 9-6. The scope of the competitive survey will depend on the size and nature of the industrial project envisioned. A small project of 10 acres or less probably won't involve more than surveying the industrial projects in a 2- to 3-mile radius; as the proposed project becomes larger, however, the scope must be enlarged. If the proposed development is to be directed at national or regional firms or is highly specialized in nature, it's probably wise to survey major projects of a similar type throughout the metropolitan area. It's relatively certain that industrial firms looking for a site will not limit their evaluation to any one location.

The data to be developed in the survey are similar to what a firm would insist on in a site selection analysis: location, developer, project start date, total planned acreage and acreage sold to date, total and average annual absorption, average price per acre, accessibility to transportation (e.g., water, rail, highways, air), utility availability, site coverage standards, parking, development alternatives (e.g., land sale, build-to-suit, building lease), and a judgmental evaluation of the overall competitiveness of the project. It is also desirable to have data regarding development controls, project amenities (e.g., recreational center, conference facilities, landscaping), major firms that have already located in the project, and a profile of other firms. It may also be desirable to talk to executives of major firms in each project to get their views on the project and, more importantly, to discover any shortcomings that might be avoided in the proposed project.

The amount of nonindustrial park land used by or available to firms in targeted industries should also be tabulated. This usually can be accomplished through discussions with the local planning agency. Care should be taken that the acreage indicated relates primarily to those firms identified as being in one of the target industries.

The next step is to project the future land absorption that can be anticipated by target industry activities, as seen in Table 9-7. Employment in target industries should be forecast as a percentage of total employment or relevant employment categories such as manufacturing and wholesale and retail trade. The relationship between employment in the target industries and utilized land is then projected, based on past rela-

[36]The use of two-digit SIC data can lead to distortions as a result of the widely varying characteristics of firms within the classification.

Table 9-6. Competitive Survey, December, 1987

	Total planned acreage	Sold/ used	Va- cant	Total acreage absorbed	Average annual asorpt.	Average price per acre	Trans- portation	Utilities*	Cover- age (%)	Park- ing (sq ft)	Terms	Rating
1 South Central District J&P Developers, 1973	1500	920	280	1200	85	$ 55,000	Highway; RR	W/e/g	40	1/1000	Sale; BTS**	Good
2 Lake Industrial Park Diamond Corporation, 1985	250	140	25	165	66	$150,000	Highway	W/e/g	25	1/500	Sale only	Excel- lent
3 Wiley Road Park John Brown Co., 1983	200	120	20	140	35	$130,000	Highway	W/e	25	1/400	Sale; BTS; lease	Fair
4 Park 12, Fox, Morgan & Co., 1984	180	100	10	110	40	$130,000	Highway	W/e	25	1/500	Sale; BTS; lease	Good
5 Meadowland Park, Southern Atlantic RR, 1977	1000	600	130	730	73	$ 90,000	Highway; RR	W/e/g	40	1/800	Sale; BTS	Very good
Total	3130	1880	465	2345								
Other industrial land	2650	1607	462	2069								
Total	5780	3487	927	4414								

*W = water; e = electricity; g = gas.
**Build to suit.

Table 9-7. Target Industry Land Absorption, Metro Area

	Actual			Projected		
	1972	1982	1987	1990	1995	2000
Total manufacturing employment	22,434	57,226	99,837	135,000	195,000	240,000
Percentage in target industries	18.2%	20.3%	23.3%	25%	25%	25%
Target industry employment	4083	11,617	23,215	33,750	48,750	60,000
Employees/acre	15.3	17.6	19.8	20	20	20
Land utilized	267	660	1172	1688	2438	3000
Percent land held as vacant**	15.6%	18.3%	21.9%	23%	25%	25%
Total land absorbed*	316	808	1501	2192	3250	4000
Absorption for period*		492	693	690	1058	750
Average annual percentage absorption		15.6%	17.2%	15%	10%	5%

* Acres
** Includes land held for expansion.

tionships as well as future needs. In most metropolitan areas, the number of employees per acre is increasing as a result of increasing land costs and a shift to a higher proportion of office operations. The employee/acre ratio is then applied to employment projections to arrive at the number of acres required. An adjustment should be made for vacant land that is sold but not utilized for building purposes.[37] The resultant figure represents industrial land that will be absorbed by target firms during the projection period. This figure should then be translated into incremental acreage that will be required for each segment of the projection period.

The final step in the analytic process is to estimate the percentage of incremental demand that can be captured by the subject site. Capture estimates should be based on comparisons of the subject site with competitive projects. Consideration should be given to differences in proximity to markets, access to transportation facilities, property tax variations, zoning and development controls, land price, building rentals, and design quality. If some of the more competitive projects are run-

[37]Many firms purchase sizable amounts of additional land for future expansion.

Table 9-8. Demand on Subject Site (in Acres)

	1988–1990	1991–1995	1996–2000	Total
Absorption for period	690	1058	750	2498
Capture by subject site	15%	25%	20%	20.7%
Subject site absorption	103	265	150	518
Average annual absorption	34.5	52.9	30.0	39.8
Recommended program	90–110	250–275	125–175	465–560

ning out of land, the capture estimate for the subject site can be somewhat higher.

The market capture estimates should be applied to incremental demand estimates to arrive at overall projected demand for the subject site. These demand projections should then be translated into recommended absorption ranges, as shown in Table 9-8, and evaluated for reasonability. One test is to look at the absorption rates of the more successful industrial projects in the metropolitan area. If the absorption rates appear reasonable, they should then be translated into building scenarios, allowing for adequate streets, parking, and building setbacks. These scenarios should be adjusted to consider the size and mix of industrial firms.

Market Characteristics of Various Types of Industrial Projects

Projects Directed at Manufacturing Firms. Projects directed at manufacturing firms must offer a well-balanced blend of market proximity, labor resources, and housing availability; accessibility to transportation facilities; and a reasonably good overall environment. Development standards are important but not critical. The analytic process outlined previously applies to most projects of this type, but since manufacturing is such a broad classification, care should be taken to concentrate on target SIC categories that have particular promise.

Projects Directed at R&D Firms. Research parks are considerably different. Much greater emphasis should be placed on the overall quality of the subject site (e.g., natural beauty, views, topography). Proximity to high-quality residential neighborhoods, universities, and cultural and recreational facilities is also important. Development controls must be high, with guarantees that they will be maintained. Utility capability, particularly electricity, may be important if the firms are engaged in prototype experimentation. Proximity to air freight facilities may also be important.

Projects Directed at Distribution Firms. Distribution firms are primarily interested in proximity to their markets and transportation facilities. A combination of rail and highway facilities is usually desirable. Air freight is an increasingly important factor. Utility capacity is usually not critical, nor is proximity to residential neighborhoods. Inventory taxes may be an important consideration, if they differ significantly between areas in which competing projects are located. Development controls should be flexible, particularly in terms of interior road design, loading areas, and buildings.

Hybrid Projects. In recent years, a new type of building has been developed in California's Silicon Valley and other centers of high technology. This is the "hybrid" building containing manufacturing, R&D, office, and warehousing activities, all within the same building. Firms interested in this type of facility generally desire to have the space and layout of the building as flexible as possible in order that they may adjust the allocation and location of space to suit changes in their overall operation.

10 Transient Commercial

There is nothing which has yet been contrived by man by which so much happiness is produced as by a good tavern or inn.

SAMUEL JOHNSON

Transient commercial land uses consist of hotels, motels, motor hotels, resort hotels, and other development related to the commercial lodging industry. Most facilities provide travelers with a room to sleep in and a restaurant or a bar for convenient dining and entertaining. Some facilities also provide areas where travelers can assemble for meetings, speeches, and banquets, as well as retail stores where they can purchase various items.

Transient commercial facilities may also serve as focal points for local activities. Throughout history, the local inn has been a gathering spot for eating, drinking, talking, debating political issues, and even holding courts of law. Today, the successful hotel, motel, motor hotel, or resort hotel is among the most sophisticated land uses, effectively blending real estate fundamentals with sound business management and merchandising pizzazz.

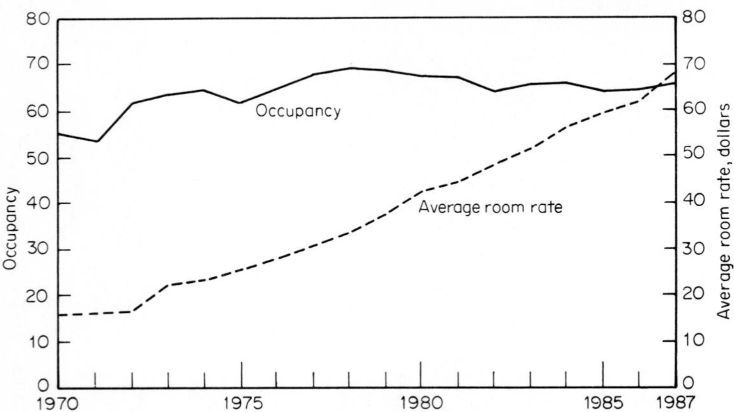

Figure 10-1. Transient hotel occupancy, 1970–1987. *(Laventhol & Horwath,* Lodging Industry Statistics*)*

Characteristics of Transient Commercial Facilities

Transient commercial facilities have several features that set them apart from other types of real estate:

- Management plays a much more critical role. Transient commercial facilities are basically services, and the quality of service is largely a function of management. A facility in a good location with poor management will have a difficult time surviving; an excellent management may overcome a deficient site location.
- Successful room rental is the key to operating success. While income from restaurants, bars, and other services is important, the maximization of room revenue is essential in developing and maintaining a successful operation. This is because the gross margins on room operations are so much greater than food and beverage.
- Maximization of room revenue requires a skillful balancing act between pricing policy and occupancy. Often, it's better to break even on room rentals than have them stand empty. Nothing is as unprofitable as a vacant hotel room.

Occupancy levels are highly vulnerable to changes in seasons, business cycles, life-styles, and the supply of hotel rooms. They must be projected and monitored carefully.

"Why can't you buy some hotels and make me your queen?"

Sources of Lodging Demand

The demand for lodging at transient commercial facilities arises from expenditures of both individuals and groups. Individuals may be traveling for pleasure or business; group business usually consists of conventions or tours.

Pleasure Travelers.[1] Pleasure travelers require lodging facilities both en route to their destination and once they arrive. During the journey, they are primarily interested in lodging that is easily accessible to the highway, rail station, or airport. Rooms should be clean, with a minimum of frills, and do not have to be very large. The most important features are the bed and the shower. A swimming pool is desirable, particularly for children. An on-premises restaurant may be a good idea, depending upon the proximity of other eating facilities. In virtually all situations, price is extremely important.

[1]Pleasure travelers are often referred to as *free, independent travelers,* or "FIT."

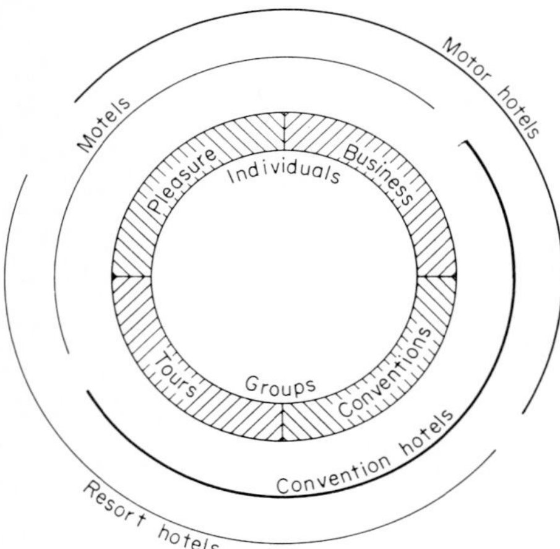

Figure 10-2. Sources of lodging demand.

Once pleasure travelers arrive at their destination, the nature of demand may change.[2] Proximity to some type of natural (e.g., ocean, lake, mountains) or artificial (e.g., golf course, Disneyland) attraction is of utmost importance. Because the stay tends to be considerably longer, much time will be spent in the room, making its size and amenities more important. An on-premises restaurant and bar are essential, as is good room service. Recreational facilities such as swimming pools, golf courses, tennis courts, and horseback riding are imperative, particularly if there is no natural attraction. Price is less significant, and it may often be tied into a package deal with transportation.

Business Travelers. Many people travel to accomplish a specific business purpose[3] and will generally stay 2 to 3 days. Since the hotel will probably be utilized as a base of operations, it's necessary to be near business contacts. The business traveler will probably want a little larger room with good telephone service and desk area. An on-premises restaurant is highly desirable, preferably with a bar or lounge. If sales presentations are necessary, an adjoining display area is required. In some cases, separate meeting rooms are desirable. Price is generally a factor, particularly to the business traveler on a commission or "per diem" expense account.

[2]Quite obviously some travelers proceed directly to their destination with no stops en route.

[3]"Business" is used here in the broad sense and includes employees of governmental agencies, labor unions, school and universities, and other nonprofit associations.

Conventioneers. The conventioneer's average length of stay is 2 to 4 days. Proximity to the conference or convention is essential. In some cases, conventioneers are accompanied by their spouses. The room itself should be the same as for the business traveler, unless entertaining is planned. An on-premises restaurant and bar, preferably with room service, are essential. A swimming pool and other recreational facilities are desirable. Price is not nearly as important as for pleasure or business travelers, and it may often be negotiated as part of an overall conference or convention package.

Tours. Tour groups are either created by members of existing organizations or specially formed to take a pleasure trip. Tours are arranged primarily by travel agents, although airlines, railroads, and bus companies may organize tours as part of a travel package. The individual or firm selecting facilities for tour groups is usually interested in getting the best bargain possible, because the tour organizer's profit is made on the spread between actual cost and the price charged for the package. Tour groups are usually given price breaks because they represent a guaranteed source of demand, especially during the off-season. Tour groups may also be given less desirable rooms, which otherwise might not be occupied.

Multiple Demand. Most transient commercial facilities spread their business over several types of travelers. A motel geared to pleasure travelers can also cater to business travelers, particularly traveling salespeople. Major hotels may cater to both business travelers and conventioneers, although they may not be the convention headquarters. A convention hotel may attempt to attract general business travelers when convention business drops off. In recent years, resort hotels have begun soliciting convention and conference business in off-peak seasons. This type of overlap among sources of demand can be healthy, particularly if it tends to stabilize occupancy throughout the year. Market analysis for a proposed transient commercial facility should first determine the primary source of demand. Common-sense reasoning, by and large, will do the trick. If the site is near a major natural or artificial attraction, a resort hotel will be the most likely prospect. If the site is near a highway or airport, pleasure and business travelers will predominate. If the site is near other hotels or convention facilities, convention business may provide the major source of demand. The business traveler will generally give the greatest demand impetus to a site in an industrial or office area.

Next, ascertain whether there are supplemental sources of demand that can be accommodated in the same facility without reducing demand from the primary source. Sometimes people from more than one demand source can be accommodated simultaneously (e.g., both business and pleasure travelers). A more realistic approach is to anticipate use of the facility by different groups during certain periods of the year. A convention facility, for example, could be redirected to serve pleasure travelers and tour groups in the summer. A resort hotel in a ski area could develop a conference business in the spring and fall. A motel servicing pleasure travelers in the summer could appeal to the business traveler during the rest of the year by adding a bar or restaurant. In all cases, the basic strategy is to maximize occupancy throughout the year by attracting new, complementary sources of business without destroying primary demand.

Projecting Market Area Demand

Once an operating scenario of the primary and supplemental sources of demand has been formulated, the overall market area should be established. The following involves a potential hotel site where the primary source of demand is expected to be convention business.

Conventions. Understanding how conventions are planned and organized is the first step in analyzing demand from conventioneers. Associations plan conventions; individuals attend them. Associations may range from 100 or so members of the local 4-H Club to the roughly 11,000 members who attended a recent meeting of the American Psychiatric Association.[4] Most of these associations have at least one meeting annually, generally planned 3 to 5 years in advance.[5] Most associations like to spread their convention business around; therefore, a city which has recently housed a convention is unlikely to be considered again until its "time has come."

Several factors determine which cities are to be considered. An early element in the selection process is the membership attitude toward a particular city. If they've already attended a conference there, they will be significantly biased by the earlier experience. Another factor is the attractiveness of after-hours activities; cities like New York, San Francisco, Miami, Las Vegas, and Los Angeles have built their conven-

[4] *1987 Directory of Conventions,* Bill Communications, New York, 1987.

[5] Associations are usually classified according to geographic coverage: international, national, regional, state, and district.

Figure 10-3 The Marriott Marquis Hotel in Times Square, New York City, designed by John Portman. *(New York Marriott Marquis Hotel)*

tion business around these activities.[6] This can be especially important if a large number of conventioneers are traveling with their spouses.

Perhaps the most important factor, however, is the quality of exhibition and meeting facilities. Exhibitors usually are tough business people who know exactly what exhibit facilities they need. If these facilities aren't available, their absence can wield a heavy hand in blackballing a proposed convention city. Therefore, most major cities have recently developed modern exhibit facilities, often at public expense.

[6]Sometimes the after-hours activities can go too far. More than one association has complained about the effect of 24-hour Las Vegas on meeting attendance.

The next most important factor is the public rooms for the various events that will comprise the convention. This usually involves a large auditorium for general sessions and several smaller rooms for individual workshops. A large banquet facility is also essential, preferably one which is separate from the auditorium and meeting rooms. Ideally, these rooms will be contained within a single hotel and the hotel will also include the exhibit facility.

The number and quality of available rooms can also be a deciding factor. Most cities maintain reasonably accurate inventories of available rooms at various quality levels.[7] The proximity of the rooms to each other also matters. The ideal situation is a cluster of hotels within walking distance of one another, as in Chicago, Miami, New York, Honolulu, and San Francisco. If no such proximity exists, at least adequate ground transportation between the various hotels and the exhibit and meeting facility should be available.

The final consideration is the headquarters hotel. As the command center of the entire convention, this hotel must have certain basic facilities. For small and medium-sized conventions, the headquarters hotel probably will provide all the facilities: exhibit, auditorium, meeting rooms, banquet facilities, and guest rooms. For larger conventions, the exhibit and auditorium activities can be separate but should be in close proximity. The headquarters hotel must also provide sufficiently large rooms and suites to handle the entertaining that inevitably accompanies a convention. In addition, a large block of rooms must be made available for delegates. Needless to say, the management of a headquarters hotel must be totally committed to satisfying the requirements of a convention in a speedy and cooperative manner.

Once the nature of convention demand is understood, market area demand can be projected, as illustrated in Table 10-1. The first step is to establish the number and type of conventions that will be coming to the market area by season. Since convention arrangements are made several years in advance, this is less difficult than it might seem. The local convention and visitors bureau in most cities maintains this type of information. A publication called *The Directory of Conventions* also publishes data on most major cities.[8]

A target year should be selected for projection purposes—say 3 to 5 years. Convention attendance for that year should be broken down according to the size of the convention, i.e., district, state and regional, and national. The number of attendees should then be converted into

[7]Most hotels have a policy on what percentage of their guest rooms will be made available for convention purposes.

[8]Published annually by *Successful Meetings* magazine, New York.

Table 10-1. Projected Convention Demand, Market Area, 1990

	Winter	Spring	Summer	Fall	Total
Convention attendees					
National	9,000	30,000	15,000	45,000	99,000
State and regional	15,000	25,000	20,000	40,000	100,000
District	40,000	100,000	80,000	120,000	340,000
Total	64,000	155,000	115,000	205,000	539,000
Persons/room					
National	1.50	1.50	1.50	1.50	1.50
State and regional	1.25	1.25	1.25	1.25	1.25
District	1.00	1.00	1.00	1.00	1.00
Average	1.10	1.11	1.08	1.13	1.11
Rooms required					
National	6,000	20,000	10,000	30,000	66,000
State and regional	12,000	20,000	16,000	32,000	80,000
District	40,000	100,000	80,000	120,000	340,000
Total	58,000	140,000	106,000	182,000	486,000
Duration of stay					
National	4.0	4.5	4.0	4.5	4.4
State and regional	2.5	3.0	2.5	3.0	2.8
District	1.0	1.5	1.0	1.5	1.3
Average	1.6	2.1	1.5	2.3	2.0
Room nights required					
National	24,000	90,000	40,000	135,000	289,000
State and regional	30,000	60,000	40,000	96,000	226,000
District	40,000	150,000	80,000	180,000	450,000
Total	94,000	300,000	160,000	411,000	965,000

guest room demand. This is accomplished by dividing the number of attendees by a factor representing the average number of persons per room for each season. The resultant number is the rooms that will be required to handle the projected convention business. The number of rooms is then multiplied by a factor representing the average duration of stay for each convention attendee; thus the number of room nights that will be required for each season is found.

In some cases, data for this analysis have been developed by local convention bureaus on the basis of questionnaire sampling. If these data are unavailable or only partially available, rough rules of thumb must be relied on, such as:

	Average persons per room	Average duration of stay, days
National	1.50	4.45
State and regional	1.25	2.73
District	1.00	1.25

These factors will vary to some extent, depending on the type of association, the stage of the economic cycle, and the geographic area where the convention is held. Religious and fraternal associations generally have more convention guests and therefore double up more frequently. In periods of recession, the convention guest factor and average duration of stay will decline, and the average number of persons per room will increase. If the convention is held in a vacation area or in a city with broad appeal (e.g., San Francisco, New York, Las Vegas, Honolulu), all factors generally will be higher.

Business Travelers. Once the primary source of demand has been established, the focus should shift to possible supplemental areas. In the case of a convention-oriented hotel, business travelers are often a good supplemental source. If the subject site is located in a well-defined business or industrial area, demand projections can be established through the interview process. By contacting each major firm in the business or industrial area, the interviewer can obtain the number of persons calling on these firms daily or weekly.[9] Some firms may even maintain records of the home base of the calling business people, which will help establish what percentage comes from out of town. This same interview

[9]The purchasing agent often is a good source. Visitor logs maintained in the lobby are another.

process should also establish the local firms' requirements for banquet and meeting room facilities.

If the subject site is not located in a well-defined business or industrial area, it may be necessary to use broad estimates of employment growth and annual business travel. Another indicator is the volume of overnight traffic at the local airport. If the site is near a major freeway, it also may help to analyze the volume of vehicular traffic on the artery, particularly in the nonpeak hours. Anticipated demand from business travelers should be translated into room night demand by season, employing the appropriate estimates of number of persons per room (generally 1.0) and duration of stay (generally 1 to 1½ days).

Pleasure Travelers. A second supplemental source might be pleasure travelers, particularly in the summer season, when convention and business traveler demand may be slack. Room demand generated by pleasure travelers tends to vary with the location of the city, the amenities available for vacation purposes, and the time of year. In resort areas, data on vacationing visitors are generally maintained by local tourist promotion organizations. In more urbanized areas, the data may be more difficult to secure and often may require considerable refinement. In all cases, it is necessary to translate the number of total visitors into guest room demand. This is accomplished by the same procedure as for conventioneers and business travelers, bearing in mind that the average number of persons is usually greater (1.5 to 2.5) and the duration of stay longer (3 to 8 days).

The demand indicated from each source should now be synthesized into a total demand projection for the target year by season and compared to present and prior periods, as shown in Table 10-2. Any overlapping among sources should be eliminated at this point. Also, if any of the projections is contingent upon another event (e.g., construction of a convention center or airport), an alternative set of projections should be available, indicating what will happen if the event does not occur.

Competitive Survey

A competitive survey of all existing and planned facilities in the market area is the next step in the analytic process. Table 10-3 shows a typical survey. Information to be developed from the survey includes:

- Name and location of facility
- Number of guest rooms
- Restaurant, bar, and nightclub facilities
- Banquet seating available

Table 10-2. Synthesizing Room Night Demand, Market Area

			1990				
	1982	1987	Winter	Spring	Summer	Fall	Total
Business travelers	786,000	1,043,000	275,000	250,000	415,000	300,000	1,240,000
Conventioneers	575,000	763,000	94,000	300,000	160,000	411,000	965,000
Pleasure travelers	255,000	319,000	75,000	50,000	185,000	50,000	360,000
Total	1,616,000	2,125,000	444,000	600,000	760,000	761,000	2,565,000

Table 10-3. Competitive Survey, Market Area, December, 1987

Map	Operation	Guest rooms	Restaurant*	Public space banquet**	Meeting**	Exhibit*	Retail**	Average room Rate	Average room Occupancy(%)	Market share(%)***	Features	Rating
Major first class hotel and motor hotel operations												
1	Ritzdorf	800	600	20,000	18,000	10,000	15,000	$75.00	72.0	23.6	TV; concierge; pool; health club; jogging track	Excellent
2	Royal Tower	500	450	10,000	10,000		10,000	72.00	68.0	13.9	TV; pool	Good
3	Amble Inn	300	200	4,000	2,000		5,000	70.00	62.0	7.6	TV; airport shuttle	Fair
4	Southern Pride	350	300	5,000	4,000		5,000	74.00	65.0	9.3	TV; pool; health club;	Fair
5	Rainmont	750	500	15,000	10,000	5,000	10,000	78.00	71.0	21.8	TV; 2 phones; conceirge; pool; health club	Excellent
6	Majestic Inn	500	400	10,000	5,000		8,000	82.00	67.0	13.7	TV; pool; sauna	Good
	Total	3,200	2,450	64,000	49,000	15,000	53,000	$75.80	68.7	90.1		
Other operations		350										
Total operations		3,550										

* Seats.
** Square footage.
*** Weighted by number of occupied rooms.

- Meeting room facilities
- Exhibit facilities
- Retail facilities
- Average room rate
- Average occupancy[10]
- Market share
- Features (e.g., television, bar, pool, golf course, tennis courts)
- Overall rating

This information can be developed largely by observation and discussions with facility managers. Several hotel guides[11] are also published that contain data on facilities (although these data should be verified in the field).

Demand on the Subject Site

Market capture estimates should be based on the competitiveness of the subject site as compared with other facilities of a similar type and quality, as identified in the competitive survey (see Table 10-4). Capture estimates should be applied to incremental demand, taking into consideration existing supply. In developing capture estimates, the location of the subject site vis-à-vis the competition should be considered. Proximity to demand generators should be especially noted: a convention hotel should be near exhibit facilities, a motel or motor hotel near a major highway or airport, a resort hotel near major recreational facilities. Any significant "voids" in existing facilities that may be filled by the proposed facility should also be considered. Finally, the quality of the proposed management of the facility should be considered in terms of merchandising, reservation system, food and beverage operation, convention-handling abilities, and so forth. If an operator is not known at the time of the market analysis, the characteristics of a hypothetical operator should be assumed on the basis of operators not now serving the market area.

[10] One rough indication of occupancy is the number of room boxes containing two keys, particularly late in the evening.

[11] Examples are the *Hotel and Motel Red Book, AAA Guide,* and, in Europe, the *Michelin Guide*.

Table 10-4. Incremental Room Night Demand, Subject Site, 1990

	Winter	Spring	Summer	Fall	Total
Market area demand					
Business travelers	275,000	250,000	415,000	300,000	1,240,000
Conventioneers	94,000	300,000	160,000	411,000	965,000
Pleasure travelers	75,000	50,000	185,000	50,000	360,000
Total	444,000	600,000	760,000	761,000	2,565,000
Existing supply	319,500	326,600	326,600	323,050	1,295,750
Incremental demand	124,500	273,400	433,400	437,950	1,269,250
Market capture by subject site	10.0%	15.0%	10.0%	20.0%	14.5%
Projected room night demand on subject site	12,450	41,010	43,340	87,590	184,390

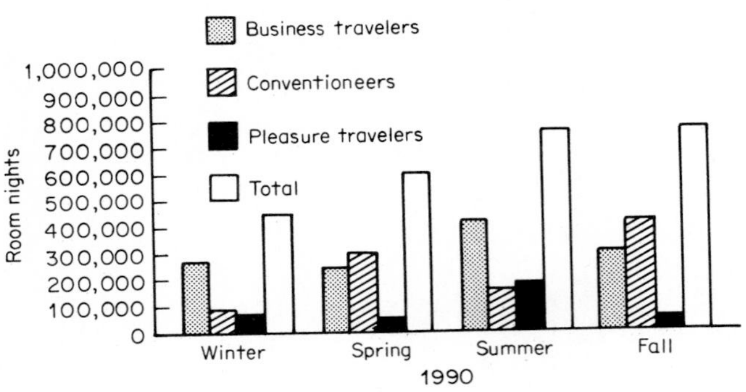

Figure 10-4 Projected room night demand, 1990.

Number of Rooms

Projected room night demand for the subject site should now be translated into the number of rooms to be built. This is often difficult, particularly in areas with great seasonal variation. The problem is to provide enough rooms to handle peak demand, but not so many as to create high vacancy at other times of the year. The objective is to maximize the total annual number of occupied room nights.

This is accomplished by determining the number of effective room nights, as illustrated in Table 10-5. The number of unoccupied room nights reflects the costs of building excess room capacity which is not supported by projected demand. The reverse situation—not building enough rooms to satisfy demand pressures—can also be costly and must be calculated. This is accomplished by subtracting the available room nights from demand projections. If the number is positive, there is unrealized demand. Negative numbers reflect unoccupied guest rooms. Note that each situation will be one or the other: unoccupied room nights or unrealized demand. They cannot occur simultaneously within the same scenario in any one season. By summing the effective room nights for each season, it is possible to determine which scenario optimizes demand and supply in order to obtain the highest number of total annual room nights.

Another forecasting method is to determine the "fair share" of room demand for each market segment that the proposed project would receive, based on the number of rooms as a percentage of total market inventory. The fair share can then be adjusted up or down, depending upon the project's competitive market advantage (disadvantage) for each market segment. This fair share approach also provides a comparable check on the more detailed room night analysis outlined above.

Table 10-5. Optimum Number of Guest Rooms, Subject Site, 1990

	Winter	Spring	Summer	Fall	Total	
Projected room night demand	12,450	41,010	43,340	87,590	184,390	
Available room nights under various scenarios						
400 rooms	36,000	36,800	36,800	36,400	146,000	
500	45,000	46,000	46,000	45,500	182,500	
600	54,000	55,200	55,200	54,600	219,000	
700	63,000	64,400	64,400	63,700	255,500	
800	72,000	73,600	73,600	72,800	292,000	
Effective room nights under various scenarios						
400 rooms	(23,550)	4,210	6,540	51,190	38,390	
500	(32,550)	(4,990)	(2,660)	42,090	1,890	Optimum
600	(41,550)	(14,190)	(11,860)	32,990	(34,610)	
700	(50,550)	(23,390)	(21,060)	23,890	(71,110)	
800	(59,550)	(32,590)	(30,260)	(14,790)	(107,610)	
Recommended program = 450–550 rooms						

Public Space

Once the number of rooms has been established, it's possible to estimate the amount and type of public space (e.g., restaurants, bars, theaters, retail) that should be developed. The first step is to determine what percentage of expenditures by room guests can be captured. By estimating the daily meal, bar, and retail expenditures for the type of guests who are anticipated and multiplying the expenditures by the number of room nights projected, one has a rough idea of total expenditure. Capture estimates should then be made for each type of expenditure, based on the location of the subject site vis-à-vis other restaurants, bars, and retail facilities. In the case of convention guests, projections of the amount of banquet activity that can be anticipated should be made.

Demand generated by people who are not guests of the facility should also be considered. If the facility is in an area of great activity (e.g., downtown, shopping center, or industrial park), demand from nonguests may exceed that from guests. A restaurant in a motor hotel, particularly if it is located on a major traffic artery, may also appeal to passing travelers. Restaurants in resort hotels may attract vacationers other than those staying in the hotel.

Total expenditures for each activity should then be projected by season and translated into physical facilities by dividing them by appropriate sales per unit averages. Restaurant sales should be divided by average dollars per plate per meal.[12] This number, in turn, should be divided by the average table turnover anticipated. Banquet demand is calculated in a similar manner but without an allowance for table turnover. The resultant figure will be the average number of tables required to service demand. Bar sales should be calculated as a percentage of food sales[13] or, if there is no food operation, on an average expenditure-per-stool basis. Retail space should be calculated on the basis of sales per square foot for the type of retail operations anticipated.[14]

[12] In some situations, such as areas with little weekend business, it's advisable to calculate on a day-by-day basis.

[13] Bar sales generally run about 25 percent of food sales.

[14] A rough method is to add approximately 25 to 30 percent to the sales-per-square-foot figures published in *The Dollars and Cents of Shopping Centers, 1987,* Urban Land Institute, Washington, D.C., 1987.

Market Characteristics of Various Types of Transient Commercial Facilities

Motels. A motel is a facility without a restaurant or other hotel-type services. Generally, most overnight guests arrive by car and drive directly to their rooms upon checking in. Pleasure travelers and limited expense account business make up the major source of demand for this type of facility. Proximity to major highways, preferably with direct visibility, is extremely critical.

Motor Hotels. Motor hotels are motels with certain types of hotel-type services and facilities. Generally, an on-site restaurant, bar, and small banquet rooms are included in the operation, although room service usually is not available. Pleasure and business travelers and some conference business constitute the major source of demand. Proximity to major highways or airports is essential. Proximity to business and industrial areas is also important in terms of business traveler demand.

In recent years a type of motor hotel has emerged in which all or a major portion of the rooms are suites, sometimes containing a kitchen. This type of facility often appeals to business or pleasure travelers who plan an extensive stay in one location. For such travelers, other features may prove important, such as photocopying and secretarial services, on-site grocery stores, etc.

Hotels. Hotels provide a full range of services, including rooms, restaurant and bar, and room service, plus retail services such as a barber shop and a beauty salon. Most hotels are located in major nodes of activity such as downtowns, airports, and major uptown centers. The majority of hotels have some type of banquet and meeting facilities. Hotels with extensive facilities of this type, as well as exhibit facilities, are considered convention hotels. The market analysis should emphasize the business traveler and conventioneer—the primary sources of demand for this type of facility. Since the hotel's public space facilities must cater to a market other than hotel guests, proximity to outside sources of activity is important.

Resort Hotels. Resort hotels are directed primarily to the pleasure traveler, although they may cater to group business in the off-peak season. These facilities generally provide all the services of a hotel, as well as extensive recreational facilities. Proximity to a major natural or artificial amenity and favorable weather critically affect the success of a resort hotel operation.

11
Multiuse Projects

They all laughed at Rockefeller Center. Now they're fighting to get in.

GEORGE AND IRA GERSHWIN
"They All Laughed," from Shall* We Dance *(1937)*

Thus far, we have discussed projects[1] involving primarily one land use. However, real estate projects have grown larger over the years and often involve more than one land use. Multiuse development is not a new concept. From ancient Greece to medieval Europe, commercial and residential land uses were closely connected. This intermingling of a variety of land uses—shops, bakeries, and offices alongside or on the ground floor of residential apartment buildings—is still a part of the charm of European cities.

The early development of cities in this country was also characterized by a broad mix of land uses in a concentrated area. Without access to good transportation, it was necessary for townsfolk to shop, live, and work close to home. But this changed with the advent of the automobile. People no longer had to be tied to an area of just a few blocks, making the wide separation of land uses feasible. Zoning laws also were used as a way of creating a more orderly environment out of what some considered the "sloppy" look of the turn-of-the-century city. As a result, the idea of multiple land uses existing side by side gradually lost favor as a way of structuring communities. Since the early 1970s, however, the concept of mixed use has once again been growing in popularity, and today there are several hundred such projects in the United States.

The Case for Multiuse Development

There are several reasons for the renewed enthusiasm for multiuse development. In urban areas, increasing land values have forced developers to utilize their properties as intensely as possible. In suburban areas, public agencies may be more receptive to projects involving multiple uses because planning controls can be more effective. Financial institutions like large multiuse projects because they can commit sizable amounts of funds over a measured period of time. Many developers believe that, with a large multiuse project, they can achieve greater efficiencies of management scale and use of infrastructure such as parking.

But the most important reason is that the public likes multiuse projects and seeks them out—whether as a shopper, office tenant, resident, or hotel guest. The superior physical environment of a large multiuse project, particularly dramatic interior space, is simply more enjoyable and exciting than the hodgepodge urban and suburban growth that occurs when a series of individual owners develop small parcels of land. In addition, with increasing congestion in the suburbs as well as the central cities, the idea of being able to satisfy multiple needs—housing, shopping and working—in a single location is once more an appealing public policy objective.

From the developer's point of view, multiuse development creates market synergy, resulting in a greater income stream than would be the case with a series of single-use projects. In an office-hotel-shopping center complex, office building tenants shop in the shopping center and eat in the hotel restaurant, and they may put up out-of-town visitors at the hotel. Hotel guests may shop in the shopping center or call upon tenants of the office building. Heavy parking infrastructure costs can be spread over several uses, often on a sharing basis which may reduce the number of spaces required. On a larger scale, the industrial base of a new town provides the jobs to attract residents for the housing and shoppers for the shopping center. In essence, the multiuse project captures demand that would otherwise go to another area or project.

The techniques used to analyze market demand for multiuse projects are similar to those discussed in Chapters 7 through 10 for individual land uses. However, some additional considerations should be noted:

- The "cornerstone" land use must be established early in the analytic process. In every multiuse project, one major land use is absolutely critical to the overall success of the project. If the nature of this use is not obvious from a judgmental point of view, it can be identified through a sensitivity analysis of each of the individual land uses. By removing each land use in turn from the analytic projections, the one which will most affect project success can be established.
- The synergy among land uses must be established. It's essential to know how much demand comes from other uses within the project and how much from outside sources.
- The timing of market demand for each land use is critical, particularly if one land use is dependent upon successful implementation of another. In a new town, for example, it's a "chicken and egg" problem to create a sufficient industrial base to supply jobs for residents; and yet firms will locate in the project only if certain housing resources are available.

Multiuse development encompasses a variety of types of projects involving more than one use of the land. Such projects can range from a multiuse building (such as the Museum of Modern Art building in Manhattan, with a residential tower atop the museum) to retail-residential-office complexes to completely planned new towns. The key types of projects that fall under the umbrella of multiuse development include *multiuse buildings, mixed-use developments,* and *new towns.*

Figure 11-1. Canal Place, a large MXD riverfront development in New Orleans. The complex includes a 650,000-square-foot office tower, a 260,000-square-foot shopping center, a 500-room hotel, and a 1500-car garage. *(Canal Place)*

Multiuse Buildings

Multiuse buildings combine multiple uses in a single structure. Since buildings are designed and built as a single unit and changes are difficult, if not impossible, to make once the building is completed, a problem with this type of development is choosing the right mix of land uses and locations within the building. For example, a highly successful office building may be canceled out by an unsuccessful apartment development within the same building.

The prospective demand for potential land uses in a multiuse building should be analyzed by means of the techniques discussed in the preceding chapters. It's important to be sure that there is strong demand for *all* uses.[1] If demand for one use is significantly greater than for the others, it may be best to design the entire building for the strongest use. It's also important to be certain that the development of all uses is synergistic; office demand should benefit from apartment or hotel proximity, and vice versa. Such an arrangement will probably dictate certain types of tenants, residents, and room guests. It's essential to know whether these users are present in the marketplace and can be attracted to the building.

Mixed-Use Development (MXD)

Over the past decade, the concept of mixed-use development has become increasingly popular. The Urban Land Institute has defined the mixed-use development as a subset of multiuse development that is characterized by three distinct features.[2]

- The project has at least three significant revenue-producing uses (retail, office, hotel, or residential).
- There is significant physical and functional integration of the components of the project.
- Development is carried out according to a coherent plan.

[1]Ground floor retail is usually related more to the demand characteristics of the surrounding neighborhood than to the uses on the upper floors. Few retailers could survive exclusively on the retail expenditures of the tenants and residents of the building in which they are located.

[2]Urban Land Institute, *Mixed-Use Development Handbook,* Washington, D.C., 1987, p. 3.

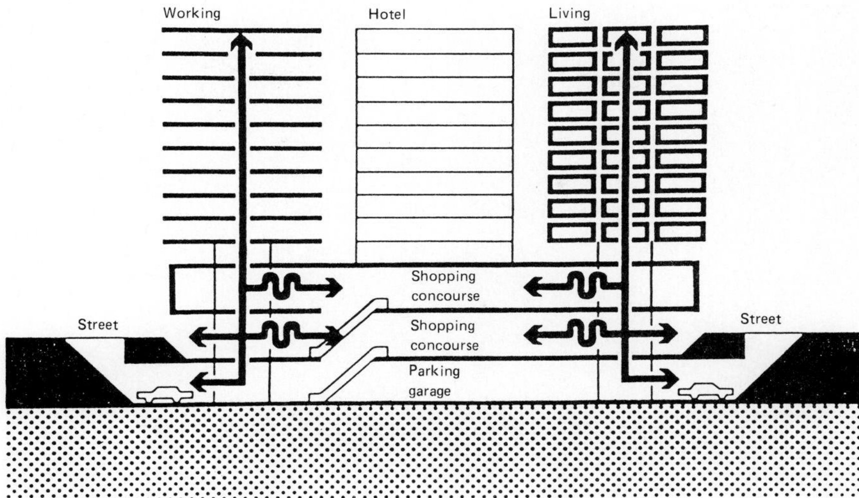

Figure 11-2. The planned integration of numerous uses that defines MXDs is illustrated in this early conceptual scheme for Westmount Square in Montreal. *(Reprinted from* Mixed-Use Development Handbook, *by permission of ULI—the Urban Land Institute)*

By its very nature, the mixed-use development is a large-scale project, usually at least 500,000 square feet, generally located in separate but connected buildings. This scale is necessary not only to effectively accommodate the various uses but also to create market synergy and attract the public to the project.

The MXD has evolved over the years; each generation of projects has taken on a flavor that is different from its earlier counterparts. Projects of the 1960s were more likely to emphasize residential uses. In the 1970s, MXDs (such as Embarcadero Center in San Francisco) often combined hotel, office, and retail uses. In addition, many of the 1970s projects were built "inward"; that is, they were totally self-contained, often including large atria. The Galleria in Houston, Chicago's Water Tower Place, and Renaissance Center in Detroit are examples of the inward-looking MXD.

Traditionally, most MXDs were built in the central business district. But as the concept caught on, more and more suburban projects have been developed. Several of these have been located in office parks (Forrestal Village in northern New Jersey) and shopping centers (South Coast Plaza in southern California). Some have become the focal points of new suburban downtowns (Las Colinas near Dallas and Tysons II in suburban Washington).

Projects have also been shrinking in size; from more than 2 million

Figure 11-3. Vertical mall in Chicago's Water Tower Place, a seventy-four-story, L-shaped MXD built in the 1970s. The complex includes a hotel, luxury condominiums, office space, and eight levels of retail shops. *(ULI—the Urban Land Institute)*

square feet of floor space before 1970, the average area of mixed-use developments in the 1980s has been less than 1 million square feet. Residential uses are once again becoming popular, particularly in the central city, where more and more people are rediscovering the benefits of living close to work. Retail has become more "festive" in nature, with inviting walkways, unique shops, and merchandising promotions. Hotels are emerging as a favored use to establish an identity for the MXD, unifying the various uses. Cultural and entertainment facilities have also been found to be effective in establishing a positive project image.

There has also been more concern that the mixed-use development blends in well with the surrounding environment, prompted in part by strong criticism of the "fortress" look of projects such as Renaissance Center. Several communities, such as Denver, Dallas, Baltimore, and Louisville, have pioneered the development of mixed-use districts where several blocks are combined into a special district to promote the physical and economic development of an MXD project. MXDs are also being tied in more closely with transportation systems. As an example, Bethesda, Maryland focused mixed-use development at a suburban transit station.

In establishing potential market demand for an MXD, the initial analysis is similar to that discussed in Chapters 7 through 10. Each land use is evaluated in terms of its potential demand as though it were a standalone project and not a part of an MXD development. The cornerstone use should receive the greatest amount of attention, but all major uses need to be analyzed in detail.

Office

Office is the most common land use in MXD projects. A survey by the Urban Land Institute in 1985 indicated that over 98 percent of MXDs contained some office space.[3] The median office space in the survey was 420,000 square feet.

[3]Ibid., p. 55.

Figure 11-4. Retail uses form the largest component of St. Louis Centre, a mixed-use development incorporating hotel, office, retail, and parking in the heart of downtown St. Louis. *(St. Louis Centre)*

Over 90 percent of the MXD developers surveyed indicated that they had approached the office market on a speculative basis without a specific tenant in mind. This means that the office market analysis is extremely important in establishing the viability of the project. The potential type of tenant for the project must be thought through carefully. As an example, large tenants desiring corporate identification may not be attracted to an MXD project where individual building identity is difficult and entrances difficult to locate. Smaller tenants, particularly professional organizations, on the other hand, may be attracted to the dramatic exposure of the space and the overall vitality provided by retail, hotel, and other uses. Market capture estimates become more difficult to formulate under these conditions.

Retail

Retail is an integral part of virtually all (98 percent) of MXD development, but it is not as frequently the cornerstone use that office buildings are. In the ULI survey, the median size of retail space was 87,000 square feet. The type of retail space varies considerably; 52 percent of MXDs in the survey included at least one restaurant; 46 percent had a fast food outlet; and 21 percent a department store.[4] In recent years, retail has been increasingly considered as a cornerstone use. This is partly the result of public policy pressures to encourage a return of retailing to the CBD (Horton Plaza, San Diego) or expansion of existing suburban shopping centers (South Coast Plaza, Tysons II). Not that developers need extensive prodding, for retail provides excitement and entertainment and helps to increase overall levels of activity for the MXD.

In evaluating market demand, the first step is to determine if major retail is possible in the project, perhaps even as a cornerstone use. The analysis is similar to the research program discussed in Chapter 8. Particular care should be taken in establishing market capture rates to distinguish the unique features (positive and negative) of the MXD project. It is not enough to assume that capture rates exhibited by suburban regional centers can be directly applied to an MXD project, particularly if it is located in the CBD.

If a major retail facility is not feasible, the retail component will consist primarily of convenience and service facilities, serving the needs of the MXD and the surrounding area. In essence, retail becomes a support to the other uses rather than a stand-alone use in its own right. The

[4]Ibid., p. 66.

size and character of this type of retail should await the market analysis of other uses in order to determine the amount of synergistic demand that can be anticipated.

Transient Commercial

Hotel uses are the third most common use in MXD projects (69 percent of projects in the ULI survey). The average number of guest rooms reported by survey respondents ranged from 260 in suburban MXDs to 400 in the CBD; the median was 360 rooms. Luxury hotels were the most common type of facility, followed by commercial and convention hotels.[5]

Hotel uses are increasingly being viewed as a cornerstone use, partly because of soft office markets but also because of some characteristics inherent in hotels that add to the overall success of the project. The 24-hour, 7-day operation of hotels infuses a vitality into an MXD project that few other uses can match. The identification of a major hotel chain can also help to promote the MXD, as well as serving as a focal point for entertainment and recreation. Hotels can also be attractive financially. From the developer's perspective they are generally more profitable than other uses; for the city, a hotel may generate as much as 5 times the tax revenue of an office building of comparable size.

In preparing the market analysis for potential hotel uses, the source of demand is very critical, particularly in terms of the other land uses. If conventions are the primary source of demand, retail may be a more compatible use than office space. Luxury and commercial hotels generally complement office and residential uses. The source of demand may also dictate the type of hotel operator that is required, which may be a factor in establishing the overall image of the MXD.

Residential

Forty-two percent of MXDs contain residential uses, according to the ULI survey, considerably less than those with office, retail, or hotel. The median number of residential units reported was 180; 42 percent of the projects had rental units and 64 percent had for-sale units. Residential uses were more likely to be found in suburban projects than in central city MXDs.[6]

[5]Ibid., p. 58.

[6]Ibid., p. 62.

Figure 11-5. Model of 900 North Michigan, a sixty-six-story multiuse complex of hotel, retail, office, and luxury residential space in downtown Chicago. *(Urban Investment and Development Co.)*

Residential uses are less common in MXD projects for a variety of reasons. With the exception of New York and a few other cities, demand for high-rise residential is often not strong. Even if demand is in evidence, the high cost of land may make residential development infeasible. In an attempt to overcome these market hurdles and encourage "downtown living," many local municipalities, including San Francisco and Washington, D.C., require developers to include housing in MXD and other commercial projects. In many cases a stated portion of this housing must be dedicated to low- and moderate-income households, further reducing the financial contribution that the residential portion can generate for the project. On the positive side, residential uses, like hotels, bring round-the-clock activity to the MXD.

In terms of market analysis, it is important to establish the acceptance of high-rise residential living in the market area before proceeding with the project; this is not a use that should be pioneered. Special attention should be given to the respective shares of the local market devoted to rental versus owner-occupied housing. A rental project would have a different impact on the community than would ownership housing, particularly in terms of the age, incomes, and interests of residents of the project. The market analysis should consider the possibility of selling and/or leasing units to corporations as well as individuals. An interview program with local firms may be helpful in this regard.

Other Uses

Other uses that have been included in MXD projects include convention centers (Franklin Plaza, Philadelphia), trade marts (Peachtree Center, Atlanta), sports arenas (Poydras Plaza, New Orleans), performing arts centers (Williams Center, Tulsa), marinas (Marina City, Chicago), ice rinks (Houston Galleria), and health clubs (Plaza of the Americas, Dallas). The major issue in introducing uses of this type is weighing the degree to which they will increase overall demand for the other uses against the cost and possible congestion associated with their introduction. The attraction of large numbers of people, for example, may also increase security and maintenance costs.

Market Synergy

Once the stand-alone demand for each of the potential uses has been established, including the approximate size of each use, the effects of possible synergy between uses can be estimated. This is accomplished primarily on a judgmental basis, based on the market data compiled in the stand-alone market research. There are several types of synergistic demand. The first is direct demand created by proximity to other uses. The retail component of the project is likely to benefit the most from this form of synergy, experiencing a significant increase in demand because of proximity to office, hotel, cultural, recreational, or other uses. This impact may translate into higher sales per square foot during normal retail hours (e.g., from office workers who shop during lunch) or in the ability to lengthen the retail day (to accommodate hotel guests, residents, cultural, or recreational attendees). The synergy created by an MXD may also allow for a broader mix of retail uses, including some that would not succeed on a stand-alone basis.

Hotels within MXDs may realize increased revenues from the demand generated by out-of-town visitors to office buildings or residential units in the project. If a convention facility is a part of the MXD, the

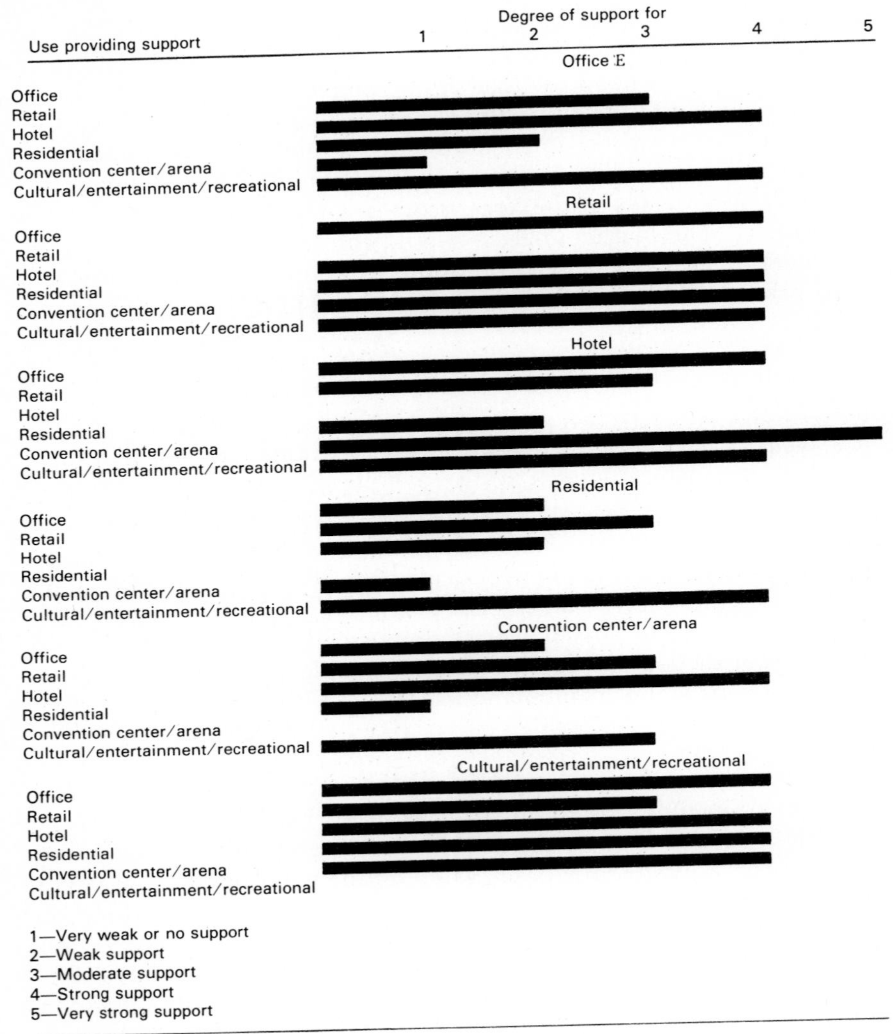

Figure 11-6. General framework for estimating on-site support and synergy in an MXD. *(Reprinted from* Mixed-Use Development Handbook, *by permission of ULI—the Urban Land Institute)*

hotel may stand to add significant additional revenue, perhaps enough to justify more rooms or additional public space.

The MXD hotel may also benefit from the retail component of the project, provided it is relatively large and diverse, as shoppers may spend the night in the hotel or make use of its restaurants or other facilities.

Less direct is the impact of synergy on office and residential demand. It is doubtful that additional office demand can be generated through proximity to other uses, but it may be an important factor in obtaining higher rents or fewer tenant concessions. The proximity of the office to other desirable uses may also prove helpful in reducing the lease-up period and minimizing tenant turnover.

Residential uses in MXDs may also benefit from the effects of synergy, although this impact is generally overestimated. Several early MXD projects included residential and office uses on the assumption that people wanted to live and work in the same complex. Follow-up studies indicated, however, that this was not the case—very few residents worked in offices located in the MXD. Perhaps a more important factor in determining residential demand is the overall environment created by the MXD, including the convenience afforded by proximity to retail, hotel, cultural, and recreational uses.

Consideration should also be given to demand created by virtue of the sheer scale of an MXD project. This is particularly true of projects located in remote areas or in transitioning neighborhoods. As this is the most difficult type of synergistic demand to identify, great care should be taken to be certain it is not overestimated in planning the project.

Once synergistic demand has been established, it is generally helpful to use a computer model to test the sensitivity of the project's success to synergistic demand. If a large amount of demand is based on projected synergy created by the mix of uses within the MXD, the developer must proceed very cautiously. Synergistic demand should be the added "extra" that helps the project succeed, not the foundation of the project itself. Computer modeling can also assist in the planning and design phase, weighing the costs and benefits of the incremental demand produced by synergy among project uses. It may be that the revenues generated by incremental demand are more than offset by additional infrastructure (e.g., parking) costs or negative impact on other uses (e.g., traffic congestion; additional security requirements).

New Towns

Chapter 1 discussed the fact that several new towns have been developed in the United States, which were modeled in part on similar developments in England, France, and other countries. Four basic types of new towns have been evolved:

- *"Pioneer" new town.* The most ambitious type of new town is the completely independent community of more than 250,000 people, located a considerable distance from existing urban centers. This type of new town has been utilized in situations involving the exploitation of natural resources in remote areas.[7] The extensive infrastructural costs (e.g., roads, sewers, schools) and the marketing problems of a remote area, however, have deterred most private developers.
- *Expanded communities.* This type of new town involves the expansion of an existing smaller community. Although this type avoids many of the problems and costs of infrastructure, the problem of dealing politically with the existing community arises, which may substantially reduce the developer's leverage and flexibility in getting the new town off the ground. The question of the "image" of the existing community and its effect on marketing the new town also comes into play.
- *New town intown.* As described in Chapter 1, this is basically a totally planned city within an existing urban area, designed to make a major economic and environmental impact on the surrounding and, usually, deteriorated neighborhood. It is hoped that the scale of the new town will be sufficient to offset existing environmental problems. The economics of high land cost are usually offset through urban renewal or the sale of surplus governmental property.[8] This type of new town has not been very successful to date.
- *Satellite new town.* This type of new town is created within the framework of an existing metropolitan region—close enough to draw upon the employment and cultural base of the urban center, yet removed enough to create a new environmental setting. Virtually all the new towns in the United States have been satellite new towns. Proximity to existing metropolitan areas also allows for a tie-in to existing public infrastructures, as well as improving chances of obtaining more favorable private financing.

Analyzing the market for a satellite new town largely involves determining how much of the activity in the metropolitan area can reasonably be captured by the new town. This activity will come not only from growth of the metropolitan area but also from shifts in housing and em-

[7]The federal government utilized this approach in developing Oak Ridge, Tennessee; Los Alamos, New Mexico; and other "atomic" cities.

[8]It's interesting, though, that Cedar-Riverside, Minnesota, one of the earliest of the new towns intown, was assembled largely through private channels.

ployment preferences from the central city and existing suburbs.[9] The degree to which the new town will achieve a successful capture rate will depend upon the location of the new town, the effectiveness of its planning, the quality and price of the housing and employment facilities offered, and the degree to which these factors are missing in the suburbs and central city of the existing metropolitan area. If a great contrast between the current living and working environment and that being created by the new town exists, the marketing program is much more apt to be successful.

A vital ingredient in analyzing the market for a new town is the relationship between housing and employment. The key is the proximity of the new town to existing suburbs and the strengths of suburban employment. If an extensive employment base exists in the suburbs, and the new town is within reasonable commuting time (20 to 30 minutes), the pressure to develop an independent employment base in the early years is less intense. Although individual and commercial tenants should be sought out, the emphasis is primarily on housing. The housing market is analyzed in largely the same fashion as discussed in Chapter 7. The market area will, of course, need to be drawn a little larger; but it should focus on a reasonable commuting time to and from employment resources in the nearest suburbs. Capture estimates should consider the planning and environmental advantages of the new town as well as ways to substantially improve the housing product over what is currently available in the competitive suburbs.

If the new town is not within reasonable commuting distance of a strong suburban employment base, the emphasis must then shift to developing that employment base. Firms can be attracted either from the central city of the metropolitan area or from other metropolitan areas. The central city, if it is rapidly deteriorating, may represent a good source of candidate firms. If the metropolitan area is growing rapidly, new firms entering the market may prove a more fruitful target. An analysis should be made of industrial and office development trends in the metropolitan area, generally along the lines discussed in Chapter 9. If this analysis indicates that an employment base can be created, this objective should be emphasized initially, even to the point of giving away the land to firms willing to locate in the project.

From the basic employment-population analyses, a projection model of household and business expenditures can be developed. Household

[9]There are some indications that new towns tend to pull more people from the older suburbs than from the inner cities. The new town, in essence, becomes a new "suburb" to employment opportunities in the existing suburbs.

Figure 11-7. Downtown Columbia, Maryland, one of the nation's largest satellite new towns, developed by James W. Rouse. *(The Rouse Company)*

expenditure patterns should be translated into demand for retail commercial facilities, as outlined in Chapter 8. The combined expenditures of households and business firms should be translated into demand for transient commercial facilities, as discussed in Chapter 10. It may be desirable to develop shopping and hotel facilities earlier than demand warrants, in order to provide facilities for housing and office and industrial uses.

The demand projections from the various land uses can now be translated into an overall "model" of market demand for the proposed new town. As with other multiuse projects, it's important to identify the amount of synergy created among the uses and the sensitivity of each of the major uses to the project's success. As with all market analyses, however, these numbers are, at best, rough estimates of how the private marketplace may react and should be continually subjected to the tried and tested "screens" of common sense and good judgment.

PART 4

Financing the Project

12 Mortgage Financing

Bankers are just like anybody else, except richer.
OGDEN NASH

Once sufficient market demand for one or more land uses on a particular site has been established, a preliminary analysis of the financial feasibility of a project should be made. As we noted in Chapter 4, the supply of capital available for real estate development is a function of the net savings of individuals, business firms, and governments. A portion of these savings is channeled into real estate in the form of (1) debt financing secured by the property, with loans generally made by financial institutions or sellers, and (2) equity investments made directly by individuals or institutions, through ownership of property. This chapter deals with debt financing.

The tradition of lending money on real estate is an old and proven one which rests on certain foundations:

- Real estate projects generally require sizable amounts of money, often beyond the resources of the individual or firm undertaking the investment.
- Land is a relatively "durable" form of investment which has represented "security" throughout history.

- Improvements placed on the land also are relatively long-term in nature, adding to the security of the real estate package.
- The economic return from developed real estate usually flows on a sustained, fairly predictable basis, thus providing a consistent source of repayment for monies advanced toward its development.
- Financial institutions require outlets for accumulated capital that provide safety for the funds lent and yet offer a source of continual repayment of capital and interest.
- Over time, a tested, legal framework has evolved to facilitate real estate financing in an orderly, reliable manner.

For these and other reasons, debt financing secured by real estate has become one of the major investment sources for individuals, firms, and financial institutions.

Legal Instruments

Real estate finance makes use of a variety of legal instruments for debt financing, all of which contribute greatly to its scope and stability.

Mortgages

Real estate debt financing most commonly involves the use of mortgages. A mortgage is the placement of a lien or an encumbrance on a property to secure repayment of a debt. If the debt is repaid by the borrower (*mortgagor*), the lien is released; if it is not repaid, the lender (*mortgagee*) can take steps to have the property sold to satisfy the debt.

The debt is generally evidenced by a negotiable *promissory note,* which contains the amount of the debt, rate of interest, schedule of payments of interest and principal, and date when the loan is due. The note may be an integral part of the mortgage or a separate document which is related to the mortgage security by reference.

The promissory note is secured by the mortgage, which normally contains a description of the property; the terms of the promissory note (directly or by reference); the obligations of the mortgagor to maintain the property, pay taxes and other assessments, and insure the property in favor of the mortgagee; a *defeasance clause,* which voids the mortgage upon payment of the debt; and a *default clause,* which defines the rights of the mortgagee in case the mortgagor fails to meet the terms of the agreement.[1]

A mortgage involves an interest in real property, and the nature of the interest varies significantly between jurisdictions. Two basic legal theories have evolved in the United States. Some older states, mostly east of the Mississippi, still adhere to the *title theory,* in which title transfers to the mortgagee (creditor) until the debt is repaid. With title, the mortgagee normally has the right of possession and can dispossess the mortgagor (debtor) at any time. The mortgagor retains physical possession of the property but only at the sufferance of the mortgagee. The mortgagor can regain title through the defeasance clause, upon meeting the obligations of the mortgage.

Recognizing that this approach unduly penalizes the mortgagor, most states now utilize the *lien theory,* in which title and the right of possession remain with the mortgagor. The mortgagee has a lien on the property, as security for the loan, which is extinguished when the loan is repaid.

Under both the title and lien theories, if the mortgagor meets all the terms of the note and the mortgage, the mortgage becomes void through the defeasance clause. If the mortgagor defaults on any of the terms of the mortgage, the mortgagee can begin *foreclosure* proceedings to satisfy the debt. Although these proceedings vary from state to state,[2] the mortgagor is usually allowed a period of time in which to satisfy (or reinstate) the obligations of the mortgage. If the obligations are not satisfied within this period, the property is sold at public auction to satisfy the debt. The mortgagee is usually allowed to enter a bid at this sale, up to the amount of the debt. In some states, if the proceeds of the public sale are less than the amount of the debt, the mortgagee can pursue a *deficiency judgment* against the mortgagor for the balance due. It is not uncommon after the public sale for there to be a period in which the mortgagor can repay the debt and regain title to the property.

An alternative form of security instrument used in some states is a *deed of trust,* which conveys legal title to a third party, or *trustee,* who holds it as security for repayment of the debt. As long as the mortgagor (*trustor*) is meeting the terms of the promissory note and the deed of trust (or *trust deed*), the trustee's title lies dormant. However, upon default, the trustee may sell the property, usually at public auction similar

[1]These are the basic elements. Mortgages may contain other terms and conditions, depending upon the state in which the property is located and the agreement between the parties.

[2]Since 1911, there have been many attempts to adopt a universal mortgage law which would cover all states.

to a defaulted mortgage, and pay the proceeds to the mortgagee (*beneficiary*). Any surplus reverts to the mortgagor.

A mortgage can be placed on either the landlord's or the tenant's interest in a property under lease, but the mortgage typically will be subject to the lease. This means that foreclosure of the mortgage will not affect the tenant's leasehold estate when the mortgage is on the landlord's interest and will not affect the landlord when the mortgage is on the tenant's interest. Conversely, mortgaged property can be leased, but the lease is subject to the mortgage, i.e., foreclosure of the mortgage will terminate the lease unless the mortgagee and the lessee have entered into an *attornment and recognition agreement* providing that foreclosure will not terminate the lease. In most cases, the mortgagor can sell his or her property and the mortgage can be *assigned* to the new owner.[3] The mortgagee also can assign his or her rights under the mortgage to another mortgagee.

Sometimes the property owner wishes to raise more capital than is possible through the first mortgage. *Junior mortgages,* which are subordinate to the first mortgage, can then be issued. The designation of "second," "third," or even "fourth" mortgage or trust deed indicates the seniority of the instrument as determined by the date of recording. Since junior mortgages carry more risk, they usually are written for shorter periods of time than a first mortgage and yield a higher rate of interest.

There are also variations in the terms of repayment of the note or other debt instrument. A *straight-term mortgage* requires no principal payments during the term of the mortgage (it is also called an *interest-only or "flat" mortgage*). A *fully amortized mortgage* calls for constant periodic payments (usually monthly, quarterly, or annually) of principal and interest, so that the principal is fully amortized over the term of the mortgage. Interest constitutes the major portion of the payments in the early years, and principal dominates the later stages. A *partially amortized mortgage* requires periodic payments of principal at selected points during the term of a mortgage, with the balance due at the end of the term. This balance is referred to as a *balloon payment*. Mortgages can be structured in any combination of these repayment schedules.

Inflationary pressures in the 1970s led to the adoption of mortgages in which the interest rate and/or payment schedule may vary over the life of the mortgage. In some cases, the interest rate is tied to a predetermined index (e.g., treasury bonds or a thrift industry cost of funds

[3]Many mortgages require approval of the mortgagee in the event of assignment. Failure to obtain approval may be an event of default, leading to the entire debt being due and payable.

Drawing by Sauers; © 1981 The New Yorker Magazine, Inc.

index) which reflects changes in the cost of capital; this is called a *variable rate mortgage*. At other times, a portion of the interest payable is tied to the economic performance of the property (e.g., a percentage of sales, hotel receipts, gross rentals); then it is termed a *contingent interest mortgage*. The *adjustable rate mortgage (ARM)* is a variation of the variable rate mortgage, with a cap on the interest that can be charged to the borrower. The *graduated payment mortgage* allows for smaller payments in the early years of the mortgage when borrowers' incomes are lower and is attractive to first time home buyers. *Shared appreciation mortgages* allow for lower interest rates in exchange for a future sharing of equity by the lender and are similar to contingent interest mortgages. *Growing equity mortgages* offer variable payment schedules, with increasing payments going to reduce principal. Interest rates on *renegotiable or rollover mortgages* are fixed for a specified period of time (usually 1 to 3 years), then adjusted based on prevailing market rates.

Two new mortgages attempt to give homeowners greater flexibility in changing financial markets. The *convertible ARM* allows the borrower to convert from a variable to a fixed-rate payment schedule when rates are more favorable. The *reduction-option mortgage* allows the borrower to reduce the interest rate (on a one time basis) between the second and fifth year of the mortgage, provided rates drop at lease 2 percentage points in a single year.

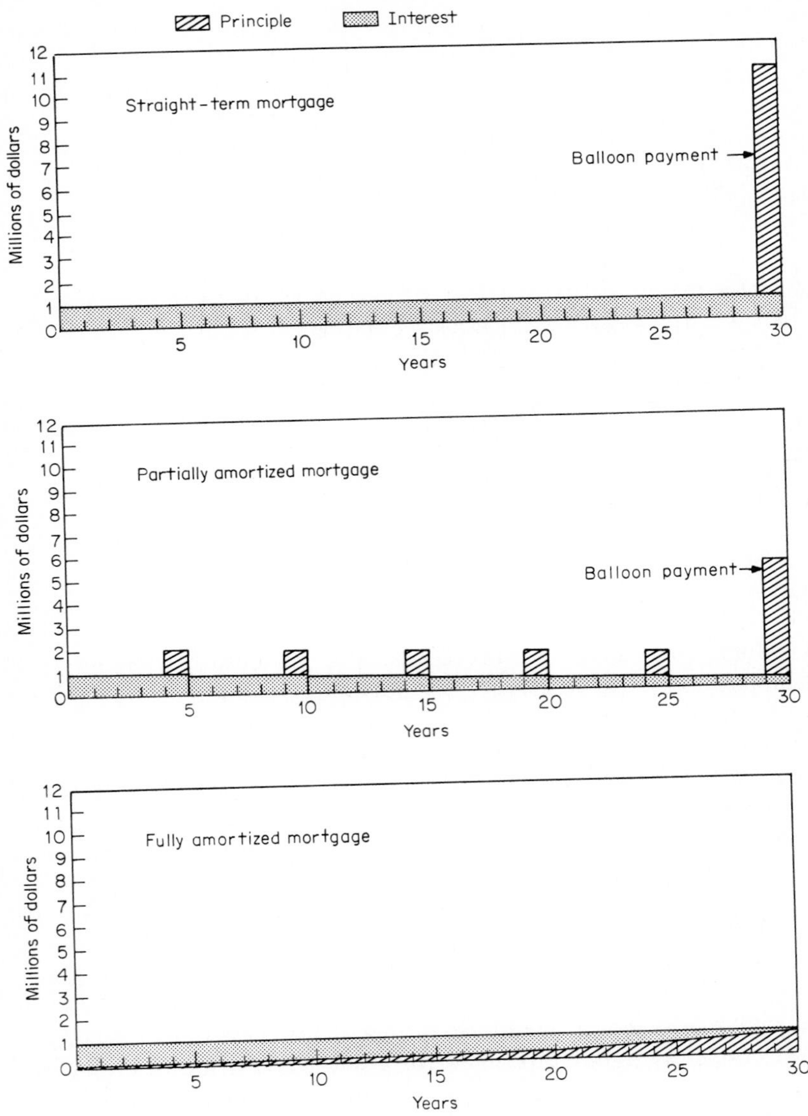

Figure 12-1. Methods of amortizing a mortgage ($10 million loan at 10 percent for 30 years).

In the commercial lending field, the fear of inflation was also a determining factor in the development of *quasi-equity* or *hybrid mortgages* which provide the lender with a measure of equity participation. In the case of a *participating mortgage,* the mortgagee does not have an equity interest in the property but has the contractual right to participate in cash flow beyond a certain point and, in some cases, in sales or refinancing proceeds beyond a certain value. The *convertible mortgage* gives the mortgagee an option which can be utilized at a future date (generally 5 to 10 years) to convert to full or partial ownership of the property. In some instances, the features of both of these instruments are combined in the *participating-convertible mortgage.* These instruments are also used by equity investors in situations where the property owner does not wish to sell or wishes to defer sale for tax or other reasons.

Another type of instrument, the *all-inclusive* or *wraparound mortgage,* places a new junior loan on a property without removing existing loans. The new loan generally exceeds the remaining balance on the existing loans, thereby releasing new funds and/or facilitating the sale of the property. The wraparound mortgage usually is written for a longer term than the existing mortgage and has a higher overall interest rate. The new mortgagee then makes payment to the old lender who holds the existing mortgage. This is sometimes referred to as a *blanket* or *extended first mortgage.*

Sometimes the seller of a property takes back the mortgage directly, not involving a financial institution. This *purchase money mortgage* is often used to facilitate the sale of raw land or improved properties where institutional financing isn't available. Purchase money mortgages frequently contain a *subordination clause* making the instrument a junior lien behind a construction or permanent loan utilized to finance the building of structures on the property.

The purchase money mortgage isn't the only method of financing property between buyer and seller without a financial institution. Investors in some states use the *installment land contract,* in which title to the property remains with the seller (*vendor*) until the buyer (*vendee*) has made a predetermined number of periodic payments or until the last installment has been paid. The vendee usually has the right to use the property while making payments. Both the vendee and the vendor have the right to sell or borrow on their interest in the property, subject to the terms of the contract. This form of financing is used in the sale of subdivision lots and for improved properties that are difficult to sell or during periods of market inactivity.

Ground Lease

A long-term *ground lease* is a form of real estate financing in which the developer obtains use of the land in return for periodic rent payments over an extended period of time (in essence the developer "borrows" from the landlord the value of the land). Although the period of the ground lease varies, generally it is long enough to let the developer recover the cost of improvements, plus a return on investment. At the end of the ground lease, the land and improvements revert to the owner of the land. This is known as a *reversionary right*. A ground lease is normally used in connection with a leasehold mortgage obtained to finance the construction of improvements. The ground lease will be senior to the leasehold mortgage financing and requires that the mortgage be based on the value of the ground lessee's *leasehold interest*. If the ground lessor is willing to subordinate its' fee interest to a first mortgage, the amount of the mortgage can usually be increased because the mortgagee has prior claim to both land and improvements. Ground leases usually have *escalation clauses* providing for periodic rental increases based on increases in the Consumer Price Index or some other price movement standard.

Mortgages can be placed on a lessee's leasehold interests in property and are called *leasehold mortgages*. Complex financing arrangements may involve both leasehold and fee mortgages on the same property.

Leaseback Financing

Over the years, various combinations of debt and lease instruments have come into use. In a *sale-leaseback*, a property owner sells the property and leases it back over a period of years. The property owner secures funds for development of the project in the form of sales proceeds; the lending institution (lessor) receives what amounts to an annuity of rental payments in an amount sufficient to amortize its investment and provide the desired return, plus reversionary interests in the land and improvements.

In a *land sale-leaseback with a leasehold mortgage* (or leveraged lease transaction), the land and improvements are separated; the land is sold and a mortgage is obtained on the improvement. If the land is subordinated, the proceeds may be sufficient to create 100 percent financing.

Sources of Financing

Debt financing of real estate can be obtained through several sources, both institutional and individual.

Life Insurance Companies

Life insurance companies are the oldest, most diversified real estate lending institutions. During most of the nineteenth century, mortgages

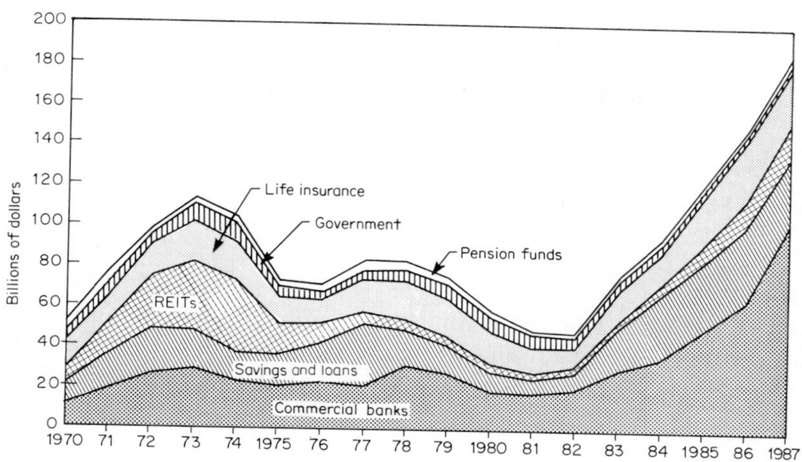

Figure 12-2. Annual real estate mortgage capital flows, 1970–1987, in real (inflation-adjusted) dollars. Investment properties only; does not include construction financing.

represented the major source of investment for life insurance companies, accounting for as much as 60 percent of total assets in 1860. As corporate and government bonds grew in favor, dependence on real estate as an investment source diminished to approximately 30 percent by the turn of the century. During the 1920s, the percentage increased to 40 percent but then fell to less than 20 percent during the Depression.[4] After World War II, investment in mortgages by life insurance companies picked up, rising to nearly one-third of total assets by the mid-70s but falling back to a level of 20.6 percent by the end of 1987.[5] By mid-1988, they held 7.2 percent of all mortgages outstanding.[6]

The percentage of its assets that an insurance company invests in real estate depends upon a variety of factors. Since insurance companies can invest in other assets, such as bonds and common stocks, real estate must compete with these instruments in terms of yield, risk, and liquidity. Generally, funds flow away from mortgages and into other debt instruments in times of increasing interest rates. Funds also flow out in periods of recession, when yields on real estate decline and foreclosures mount. Investment in real estate often is determined by the quality of real estate projects available and the overall credit of tenants.

The amount of money lent on an individual project generally is in-

[4] Henry E. Hoagland and Leo Stone, *Real Estate Finance*, Irwin, Homewood, Ill., 1973, p. 241.

[5] *Federal Reserve Bulletin*, November 1988, p. A27.

[6] *Federal Reserve Bulletin*, November 1988, p. A39.

fluenced by legislation in the states where life insurance companies are domiciled and in which they operate. Improved commercial and industrial properties and apartment buildings constitute the major portion of life insurance lending, with single-family residential loans representing a decreasing percentage of mortgage portfolios since the mid-1960s. Most life insurance companies today do not make residential loans directly; rather, they participate in the secondary mortgage markets. Most commercial loans are placed through third parties and for relatively short periods of time—generally 3 to 10 years.

Insurance companies are in a somewhat vulnerable position during periods of inflation, when yields on existing mortgage portfolios remain fixed at a time of rising money market interest rates. To offset this problem, many companies participate in the project's equity, whether through direct ownership, a percentage of the income stream, or both.

Savings and Loan Associations

The first savings and loan association, started in Pennsylvania in 1831, was patterned largely on "building societies" in England. These early institutions were frequently small, local groups of citizens who banded together to encourage home ownership through forced savings. People saved for their own homes, and if they moved or did not build homes, their savings were heavily penalized upon withdrawal. As savings and loan institutions grew, the virtues of thrift were extolled to encourage saving for future needs. The institution's early role was as much to safeguard the depositor's savings as it was to help it grow. Savings and loans now compete for savings by offering many types of interest-bearing accounts.

At the end of 1987, savings and loans held 24.4 percent of all outstanding mortgages in the United States. Of their total mortgage portfolio, 73.7 percent was in one- to four-family residential properties, 12.2 percent in multifamily properties, and 14.1 percent in commercial properties.[7] In addition, savings and loans have become active participants in the secondary mortgage markets, holding 15.8 percent of their assets in mortgage-backed securities by the end of 1987.[8]

Even with the deregulation of savings institutions in the late 1970s and early 1980s, savings and loans have continued to invest the bulk of their assets in mortgages; therefore, their portfolios (and earnings) are

[7]U.S. League of Savings Institutions, *Savings Institutions Sourcebook,* 1988, Table 14, p. 29.

[8]*Federal Reserve Bulletin,* June 1988, p. A26.

quite susceptible to changes in competing money market interest rates. These institutions essentially "borrow short and lend long." In periods of rising interest rates, the rate paid on savings accounts must increase in order for the institutions to remain competitive, and this requires increases in the interest rate charged on new loans. As interest rates on home mortgages increase, the demand for loans dries up, and savings and loans find it hard to maintain a "spread," with the increasing expense of higher interest rates on all savings, while only getting the benefit of high mortgage rates on a fraction of their portfolio. The variable rate mortgage has helped to protect savings and loans against the adverse effects of rising interest rates on their portfolios, but it has not solved the problem of weak loan demand in times of high interest rates.

The amount that a savings and loan can lend on an individual property also is set by law and regulations. Federally chartered associations can lend up to 100 percent of appraised value, but where the loan-to-value ratio is greater than 90 percent, the mortgagor must provide insurance for the portion of the loan that exceeds 80 percent of the value. State associations vary, but they often follow the guidelines set for federally chartered institutions.

Savings Banks

The first savings bank in the nation was the Philadelphia Savings Fund Society, which began operations in 1816. It was a mutual savings bank, that is, owned by its members, the savers and borrowers of the institution.[9] Savings banks were organized for much the same purpose as savings and loans; and until the Depression they were more significant in the national mortgage market. Because of losses through foreclosure during this period, however, savings banks started taking a much more conservative attitude toward mortgage lending. This posture kept the institutions from emulating many of the progressive steps of the savings and loans in the 1930s and 1940s. As a result, savings and loans became the dominant type of residential lending institution. Mutual savings banks have been limited geographically, primarily to the Northeast—especially to Massachusetts and New York.

Until 1979, savings banks were exclusively state chartered. In 1979 federal savings banks were introduced. Savings banks now operate under the same regulations as savings and loan associations. In 1987, savings banks had invested 53.4 percent of their funds in mortgages, a somewhat lower percentage than savings and loans (55.5 percent) be-

[9]Savings banks can also operate under a form of permanent stock ownership.

cause savings banks, until deregulation, had broader investment authority.[10]

Commercial Banks

In the early years of the United States, both state and national commercial banks were active in real estate. But an amendment to the National Banking Act of 1863 prohibited national banks from lending on real estate. With the Federal Reserve Act of 1913, national banks entered the real estate lending field again. The Act allowed them to lend on farms, on the basis of 50 percent of value. From this point on, legislation expanded the scope of real estate lending by national commercial banks; deregulation of the banking system in the late 1970s further relaxed the lending rules. Today, national banks generally lend up to 90 percent of appraised value, with an amortization of up to 30 years. In practice, loan-to-value ratios are more apt to be in the 70 to 80 percent range.

The proportion of real estate loans in a bank's portfolio varies with legislative standards, economic conditions, and bank policy. Legal loan limits for state banks vary considerably, depending on state law. Nationally chartered banks currently can lend up to 70 percent of time and savings deposits or 100 percent of capital stock and surplus, whichever is greater. The volume of real estate loans varies within these limits, depending on the tightness of money and alternative loan opportunities.

In addition to long-term mortgage financing, commercial banks are the largest providers of *interim financing* during the development phase. Construction loans up to 2 years on residential property and 5 years on commercial and industrial properties are exempted from the 70 percent limitation regulating national bank real estate lending. These loans usually require a firm commitment by a reputable long-term lending institution (e.g., life insurance company, savings and loan) to *take out* the loan upon completion of construction or maturity, whichever comes first. Commercial banks also are involved indirectly in other forms of real estate lending—through home improvement loans, equipment loans, and commercial lines of credit to other financial institutions, REITS, mortgage bankers, and developers.

REITs

As noted in Chapter 3, real estate investment trusts were created by Congress in 1960 as a possible solution to the liquidity problem facing

[10]U.S. League of Savings Institutions, *Savings Institutions Sourcebook,* 1988, Table 52, p. 46 and Table 14, p. 29.

the real estate industry. In the early 1960s a large number of REITs were brought to market, but the break in the stock market in 1962 brought down REITs shares along with other stocks. The REIT market was relatively dormant until 1968 when a new type of REIT, directed at investment in short-term mortgages, was introduced. The new vehicle was an instant success, and the REIT market prospered again.

The early 1970s were exceptional years for the REITs; by the end of 1974 REIT assets peaked at just over $20 billion,[11] most of which was invested in construction and development loans. As interest rates tightened in 1973, their ability to maintain a profitable spread diminished and many loans went sour. The stock of most REITs plummeted below book value and many declared bankruptcy. This period seemed to cast a spell over the whole industry and most of the stocks traded below book value for many years.

In 1983 and 1984, REITs were increasingly used as the core investment vehicle for securitized issues introduced by Wall Street. The Tax Reform Act of 1986 also made REITs, along with other income-oriented investment vehicles, more attractive. By the end of 1986, REIT assets reached a new peak of nearly $24 billion; by the end of 1987 assets had grown to more than $34 billion.[12] While much of this was equity capital, REITs still continue to underwrite and invest in mortgages and other debt instruments.

Pension Funds

In the 1950s, several major U.S. corporations, most notably General Motors, began developing private retirement systems for their employees as a supplement to Social Security. Labor unions and government organizations also began to set up employee benefit trusts (called EBT accounts) for future pension or profit-sharing needs. These accounts accumulate cash on a tax-exempt basis for future payment to retiring employees. The overriding investment objectives of most EBT managers have been to (1) protect the capital accumulated and (2) maintain sufficient liquidity to meet future payment requirements.

Virtually all of the funds that flowed into these plans in the early years were invested in fixed-income securities, primarily bonds. In the mid-1960s, thinking and policies changed to permit investment in stocks and other equity securities. A shift in capital began, with equities ultimately becoming the major asset of most retirement plans.

[11]National Association of Real Estate Investment Trusts, Inc.

[12]Ibid.

Pension funds have been modest investors in direct mortgages over the years, with most of this investment coming from public and union plans. In the mid-1970s, however, pension funds began investing in the secondary mortgage market in increasing amounts and today are the major source of investment capital for this market.

Individuals

Individuals also lend on real estate, generally through purchase money or junior mortgages. Although a large number of individual mortgages is recorded each year, the average loan amount is small, and it is usually for a short term. Most individual mortgages are connected with the sale of real property; however, some individuals invest in junior mortgages either directly or, in some states, through so-called "thrift" institutions.

Federal Government

The federal government finances real estate both through direct loans and grants and as guarantor and/or insurer of mortgages held by private institutions. HUD provides urban grants through the Community Development Block Grant program and the Rental Rehabilitation Program. Two federal programs also make loans for rehabilitation of rental property and for housing the elderly and disabled. The FHA provides mortgage insurance for a variety of housing projects. Mortgages for qualified veterans are guaranteed by the Veterans Administration at the federal and, in some cases, state level. The federal government has not participated extensively in the permanent mortgage market for investment properties. Its much larger role has been the creation and sponsorship of the secondary mortgage market.

The Secondary Mortgage Markets

One of the reasons investor interest in mortgages has traditionally been limited to insurance companies, thrifts, banks, and other financial institutions has been the difficult and cumbersome process of underwriting, known as *origination,* and processing payments, called *servicing*. Institutions required large, experienced staffs to locate and underwrite individual mortgages and develop diversified portfolios. Mortgages were seldom sold, as they were considered highly illiquid by the investment community.

This situation changed in the 1970s with the emergence of the secondary (post-origination) market directed at those who were interested in investing but who did not have the facilities (or interest) in loan origination and servicing.

The federal government took the lead in developing the secondary mortgage market, largely to achieve public policy objectives. The government wanted to keep interest rates low in order to encourage expanded levels of home ownership. If a broader, more efficient mortgage market could be established, perhaps more capital would be attracted, allowing greater numbers of mortgages at generally lower rates. There was also a desire to eliminate geographical capital imbalances, shifting funds from capital surplus areas such as the Northeast and Midwest to the high-growth areas of the West and South. At the same time, in the private sector, because of inflation many mortgage originators, particularly the thrifts, had large portions of their portfolios earning yields substantially under current market rates. As their investment spreads weakened, they needed to sell off mortgages to provide badly needed liquidity, but there was no market for their primary asset, the single-family mortgage.

The single-family mortgage was a particularly appropriate instrument for this new market. The historically low default experience suggested relatively low levels of risk. The development of standardized underwriting standards as a result of the activities of FHA, GNMA, and other private and government insurance programs provided a relatively homogeneous asset underlying the securities.

As previously discussed, pension funds were receptive to a vehicle which provided higher returns than bonds with equivalent levels of liquidity. Wall Street firms, most notably Salomon Brothers, saw the opportunity of creating a new market by matching the investment needs of the pension funds with the liquidity pressures of the thrifts, all the while furthering public policy goals.

"Pass Through" Securities

Real estate assets were first securitized when the Government National Mortgage Association (GNMA, usually referred to as "Ginnie Mae") developed a pass-through securities program for residential mortgages. This was followed by mortgage-backed securities programs introduced in the late 1970s and early 1980s by the Federal National Mortgage Association (FNMA, or "Fannie Mae") and by the Federal Home Loan

Mortgage Corporation (FHLMC or "Freddie Mac"), a public corporation owned by the thrift members of the Federal Home Loan Bank Board.

Investors who participate in the secondary mortgage market purchase an ownership interest in a pool of mortgages by means of a pass-through certificate. Regular monthly payments of principal and interest are "passed through" to the certificate holder along with any prepayment of the mortgages in the pool.

The growth of mortgage-backed securities has been truly phenomenal. These instruments, virtually untried in 1970, accounted for $92 billion of mortgage debt in 1979 and more than $718 billion of such debt by the end of 1987—almost one-fourth (24.4 percent) of outstanding mortgages.[13]

GNMA, which primarily backs FHA single-family residential mortgages, has been the largest source of growth in the secondary market. FHLMC is the largest issuer of mortgage-backed securities involving conventional loans; FNMA is the second largest. Private financial institutions provide another source of mortgage pools, primarily involving mortgages that don't conform to the standards (usually loan limits) set by FNMA, GNMA, and FHLMC.

Collateralized Mortgage Obligation (CMO)

In 1983 another securitized mortgage instrument, the collateralized mortgage obligation, was created in response to investors' need to reinvest the return of principal that they received as a result of unanticipated prepayment. The CMO is a debt instrument that combines features of mortgage pass-through securities and corporate bonds. The main difference between the CMO and the pass-through security lies in how interest and principal are paid out. Investors can buy various classes of CMOs (including "zero coupons"), which reflect short-, medium-, or long-term maturities. Interest and principal are paid according to class, with the faster-paying classes (shorter-term maturities) being retired first.

The CMO, along with other mortgage-backed securities, opened up the real estate market to investors who otherwise would have turned to

[13]*Federal Reserve Bulletin*, November 1988, p. A39.

other investments that had more certain repayment characteristics. Since 1983, more than $100 billion of CMOs have been issued.

Real Estate Mortgage Investment Conduit

The latest innovation in the secondary mortgage market is a variation of the CMO, the real estate mortgage investment conduit (REMIC). Its creation was authorized as part of the 1986 Tax Reform Act in order to overcome some of the problems of the traditional CMO.

The major problem was the tax treatment of the CMO; REMICs can qualify for the more advantageous sale-of-asset treatment for tax purposes. In addition, issuers of REMICs have much more flexibility to create a variety of mortgage instruments specifically tailored to individual investors. REMICs also qualify as mortgage assets for the special bad debt reserve tax deduction for thrifts and as acceptable investment assets for REITs. If certain procedures are followed, REMICs may also be exempt from foreign withholding tax.

Commercial Mortgages

For more than a decade, securitization of mortgages was confined to the residential market. In 1984, commercial real estate debt was first transformed into mortgage-backed securities; nearly $1.2 billion of commercial properties was securitized in that year. In 1985, more than $6 billion of new commercial issues came to market; in 1986, $6.3 billion; and in 1987, $9 billion.[14]

The securitization of commercial mortgages is still in its very early growth stages. Commercial mortgages present special problems for securitization. Unlike residential mortgages, they are not well standardized, and establishing a credit rating is often difficult [however, credit rating services, such as Standard and Poor's, have been working to come up with a rating which evaluates the general risk from real estate markets as well as that of the specific building(s) being considered]. Despite such problems, the secondary market for commercial mortgages is expected to grow rapidly. Savings and loan associations are a major target;

[14]Ibid., p. 6, and *Real Estate Market Review*, January 1988, Solomon Brothers Inc.

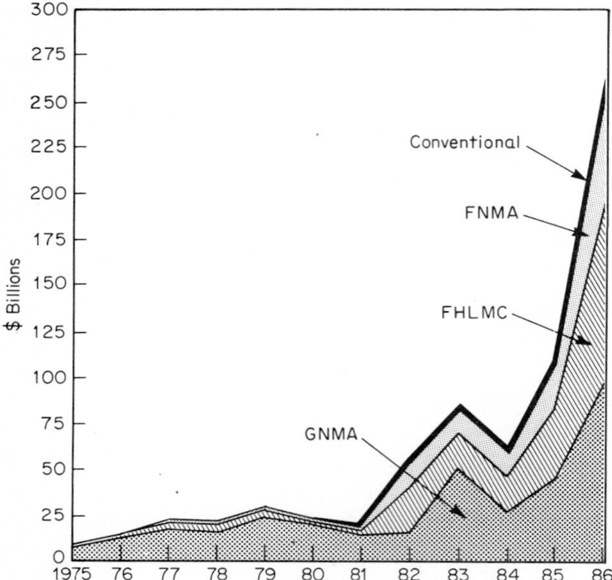

Figure 12-3. Flow of securitized single-family mortgages, 1975–1986. *(Sources: Salomon Brothers Inc, U.S. Department of Housing and Urban Development, Board of Governors of the Federal Reserve, GNMA, FNMA, FHLMC, Securities Data Corporation)*

commercial mortgage pools may provide an alternative to riskier direct investment in commercial real estate loans.

Credit Enhancement

A variety of techniques are utilized by underwriters to enhance the credit appeal of secondary market offerings. In the case of single-family housing, private mortgage insurance is the major enhancement device. Before the establishment of the FHA in 1934, private firms handled all mortgage insurance. During the Depression, however, most of these firms went bankrupt, and private mortgage insurance didn't really surface again until 1957, when the Mortgage Guaranty Insurance Corporation (MGIC) was formed in Wisconsin.

Today, MGIC and other private mortgage companies[15] generally in-

[15]At the end of 1987, there were 13 private mortgage insurance firms in the nation, insuring roughly one in every five new one- to four-family residential loans underwritten. Source: Mortgage Insurance Companies of America.

sure the top 20 to 25 percent of a mortgage loan, up to 95 percent of appraised value. Lending institutions thus can make higher-ratio loans with private mortgage insurance. Private mortgage insurance companies are limited to insuring one- to four-family residential properties. In recent years, the concept of mortgage insurance has broadened, and financial guarantee companies insure other types of real estate, including multifamily, commercial, and industrial properties, as well as leaseholds.

Other financing devices may be utilized to enhance credit in real estate transactions. Letters of credit are used to guarantee lease or mortgage obligations. Zero-coupon bonds can reduce debt service charges until lease revenue reaches acceptable levels or to give inflationary protection in the case of a long term, flat lease.

The Mortgage Lending Process

The Decision to Lend

The first step in the mortgage lending process is the decision by the financial institution to invest funds in real estate. Such a decision generally depends on the current state of the institution's investment portfolio, money market conditions, and expectations for the future, in terms of inflation and deflation, interest rates, economic growth, etc.

If an institution feels it has too high a proportion of mortgages in terms of its desired liquidity, it may decide not to lend until it has reduced its existing portfolio and/or expanded its capital base. However, in some cases an institution with a high proportion of mortgages may enter the market to improve the quality or average yield of its existing mortgage portfolio or to replace maturing loans. The current status of the money market also critically affects the lending decision. If interest rates are high, institutions may want to secure as many good-quality high-interest-rate mortgages as possible. However, this objective often is thwarted by a reduction in the supply of money, brought on by expanded demand for nonmortgage loans, changes in government monetary policy, or, most likely, a combination of these forces. When interest rates are lower, reflecting an expanded supply of money, institutions are under pressure to "get the money out" as rapidly as possible. It is during these periods that marginal loans frequently are made which often come back to haunt the institution.

Management's future expectations also influence the degree to which institutions actively enter the mortgage market. If rising interest rates are expected, lending may be postponed until greater yields can be obtained (although the growing acceptance of the variable rate mortgage has mitigated this problem). If falling rates are anticipated, management may attempt to "lock in" as many high-yield mortgages as possible. Expectations about the overall economy also have an effect. If a recession or depression is expected, the institution may shift from mortgages to more liquid investments, including mortgage-backed securities. If a sustained inflationary period is anticipated, management may seek out participation loans that partly offset fixed yields. These events and expectations are tightly interwoven and always changing. An institution may be out of the market one month and back in it the next. Also, most institutions set aside a portion of their portfolio to take advantage of "opportunity situations" that may arise and to finance developers with whom they have had long and successful relationships.

Evaluation of the Individual Loan

In evaluating a loan on an investment property, the institution considers two basic factors: risk and yield.

Risk. The value of the project itself is one way of measuring risk. This is generally established through an appraisal of the property, utilizing the techniques discussed in the Appendix. Most institutions are limited by law or internal policy to lending only a certain percentage of this value.

Another element of risk is the magnitude and reliability of the income stream generated by the project and the degree to which this stream "covers" the interest and principal payments on the loan. In speculative situations where no user is in evidence, most institutions look for a coverage of 1½ to 2 times the annual debt service. If the user is known in advance, this coverage ratio may be reduced, depending upon the credit strength of the user. Coverage ratios also may vary by geographical area and product type.

A final element of risk evaluation, particularly in new projects, is the financial strength and the proven ability of the developer to complete the proposed project on time and within budgeted costs. Yield is a function of the annual interest rate and fees and the term of the loan. The interest rate generally is conditioned by the current state of the money market and the internal costs of the institution's funds. In many cases, the interest rate is supplemented by *points*[16] which are paid directly from or charged as a discount from the loan proceeds. The term of the loan also influences the yield; longer loans generally require a higher

[16]These generally are expressed as a percentage of the total loan (1 point = 1 percent; ½ points = ½ percent, etc.).

yield, particularly when the interest rate is fixed rather than variable. Both interest rates and yield are closely tied to the degree of risk associated with the loan. Generally, the greater the risk, the greater the yield that will be required.

The Loan Package

Most institutions require submission of a loan "package" so that they can assess the risks and yield from an individual loan properly. Although the exact composition of this package varies with the nature of the project and the institution involved, it generally includes:

- Formal application for loan
- Description of the project
- Market study indicating demand for the proposed uses
- Preliminary plans
- Preliminary specifications
- Preliminary cost estimate
- Projected income and expenses
- Identification of any precommitted tenants with related credit information
- Information regarding the developer, architect, engineer, general contractor, and leasing agent and their experience with similar projects
- Financial statements on the borrower

Lenders may also require other material, such as copies of precommitted leases, title reports, appraisals, and—in the case of construction financing—evidence of a permanent loan commitment. Sometimes, information is submitted to a lender without a formal application in order to elicit informal reaction to the project prior to the final loan application.

In evaluating an individual loan, lenders look not only at the information contained in the loan package but also at the quality of the presentation itself—and the degree to which it reflects the developer's experience and track record.

The Role of the Mortgage Banker

After World War II, the United States experienced strong demand for housing. Simultaneously, there was a surplus of funds in government bonds and other securities. Life insurance companies and mutual savings banks wanted to invest their funds in mortgages as rapidly as possible, and therefore they selected knowledgeable real estate people in major cities to represent them as *correspondents* who would analyze, originate, and service loans originating in their local area. At first, these firms were largely mortgage brokerage operations; gradually, many began utilizing their own funds to finance projects on a short-term basis prior to permanent financing. Funds for this purpose were usually borrowed from local banks through a "warehousing" line of credit. Ultimately, some of the larger mortgage bankers began to make long-term loans of their own.

Traditionally, the mortgage banker played an important role in real estate financing, giving distant institutions valuable insight into a local market area without their having to develop large, internal staffs. On the basis of continuing relationships with one or more financial institutions, the mortgage banker could direct a loan application to the institution which was most likely to lend on that project, thus saving the loan applicant much time and aggravation. Mortgage bankers also provide other services, such as loan administration and servicing (i.e., collecting mortgage payments), property management, insurance, and, in some cases, real estate brokerage. With the growth of a large and complex secondary mortgage market in recent years, the role of the mortgage banker has expanded and become more formalized, dominated by large mortgage banking firms operating on a national scale.

Financing Characteristics of Various Types of Projects

This discussion pertains primarily to new construction, although the principles are basically the same for existing projects.

Primary Homes

Commercial banks and savings and loans generally provide construction lending on for-sale housing projects. Funds may be advanced with or without long-term permanent loan commitments on the individual dwelling units. Key factors considered in making the loan include the overall demand for housing in the market area, the price and quality of the units proposed, the margin of profit between total price and total costs (e.g., land, building, selling, interest), the builder's track record, and the builder's financial situation. Construction loans are generally for a period of 1 to 3 years, at rates based on the cost of short-term money to the lending institution. These loans usually are 1½ percent to 2 percent over the prime rate, plus a fee of 1 to 2 percent of the commitment amount.

The construction loan is repaid by funds from long-term loans and down payments on each unit. A savings and loan or savings bank usually makes the loan to the individual home buyer, which generally reflects 70 to 95 percent of the unit's sales price. The loans are based on the creditworthiness of the prospective home owner, and they take into consideration the amount of down payment, the personal income of the borrower, the income's relationship to the debt service required, and the general character and attitude toward debt repayment of the borrower. If the loans are to be insured by the FHA, Veterans Administration, or private mortgage insurance companies, there may be additional requirements. The interest rate and term of home loans vary with the region of the country, the current state of the money market, and the type of loan involved.

Second Homes

Lending practices on second homes are much more stringent than on primary homes. A major consideration is the borrower's ability to support payments on two mortgages simultaneously. The magnitude and nature of the applicant's income is therefore important. Since loans on second homes are felt to be more risky, they generally are at lower loan-to-value ratios, for shorter terms, and at higher interest rates.

Apartments

The same institutions that lend on for-sale housing projects frequently undertake construction lending on apartment projects. The major difference is that a precommitted, permanent loan is usually required. Savings and loans, savings banks, and insurance companies generally provide these permanent loans. In making a loan, factors include the overall demand and rental rates for apartments in the market area; the quality of the project and projected rental levels; the degree of debt service coverage provided by the projected income stream; the developer's track record in construction, rent-up, and management; and the developer's financial strength. FHA-insured loan requirements are more precisely defined, and they include strict design requirements. Most apartment loans are for 75 percent of the total market value, as determined by appraisal. Loan terms range from 15 to 25 years, depending on the type of project and its overall economics. Interest rates are generally higher than the prevailing rate on home mortgages.

Shopping Centers

Commercial banks usually make construction loans for shopping center development, and they almost always require some type of precommitted, permanent financing. Insurance companies, thrifts, REITs, or pension funds usually provide permanent financing. The key factor in shopping center financing is securing long-term leases from creditworthy retailers for a sizable portion of the gross leasable area. Most lenders like to see their loan fully or almost fully amortized by the base rentals of these anchor tenants. Other factors include the projected retail demand for the center, the projected rentals from the nonanchor tenants, and the proven ability of the developer to perform. Shopping

Figure 12-4. Horton Plaza, a modern urban shopping center widely recognized for its striking combination of architectural styles and its contribution to the revitalization of downtown San Diego. *(Horton Plaza)*

center permanent loans most often are for 15 to 25 years, at rates 2 or 3 percentage points above the prevailing rate for equivalent maturity U.S. Government securities.

Office Buildings

Loans for office and industrial buildings resemble shopping center loans. A precommitted, permanent loan almost always is required by an insurance company, commercial bank, thrift, REIT, or pension fund. Preleasing a portion of space (generally 30 to 40 percent) by one or more creditworthy tenants also is a general requirement. In some cases, the loan amount is staged in increments as the building is successively leased. The anchor tenant requirement may be waived or reduced if the building is in an exceptional location in a strong office market and the developer has 10 to 20 percent equity at risk. Office building loans generally are for 75 percent of appraised value, with fixed-rate loan terms ranging from 5 to 10 years and variable rates from 20 to 30 years.

Industrial Buildings

Loans on industrial buildings may or may not require leasing precommitments, depending on the size of the building and the strength of industrial space demand. In strong growth areas, speculative buildings sometimes are erected on the basis of the developer's financial strength, and they are leased on a short-term basis at relatively high rental rates. Loans to finance this type of development generally are for 5 to 10 years. Longer-term loans require long-term leases from users with strong credit. This type of loan generally is considered the least risky, and rates usually are the lowest of all real estate mortgages, often at loan-to-value ratios approaching 100 percent. In essence, both the lender and the investor are buying an income stream; the real estate is somewhat incidental.

Hotels and Motels

Loans on hotels, motels, and other transient commercial facilities generally require a precommitted operating lease or management agreement by an established, financially sound operating company. As with shopping centers, operating leases on hotels and motels usually call for a base rental which is sufficient to amortize the loan. Additional rent is provided by percentage clauses, depending on the success of the operation. In addition to the strength of the operator, lenders—usually insurance companies—look at the overall occupancy rate experience of similar facilities in the market area, the mix of revenue between guest rooms and public areas, cost per room, and the break-even occupancy level of the proposed operation. Being somewhat riskier, hotel loans generally are for shorter terms and at higher rates than other commercial mortgages.

Multiuse Projects

Multiuse projects require the greatest amounts of financing in real estate, often several hundred million dollars. With large amounts of capital required, and the fact that the development period of the project may be as great as 10 to 15 years, the financing may come from several sources. The developer must also have strong financial resources as the front-end costs may run into the millions before permanent financing can be secured. In order to share the risk the developer may enter into joint venture arrangements with financial institutions, other developers, or tenants.

Life insurance companies provide the bulk of permanent financing on multiuse projects, with banks providing construction financing. Public financing (through UDAG grants, state and local programs, land write-downs, infrastructure subsidies, and/or tax abatement) often contributes to multiuse projects, especially where adaptive use or rehabilitation of existing buildings is involved.

In the lender's analysis of financial feasibility, the project generally is viewed as a single one whose revenue comes from a variety of sources. Each element of the income stream is tested as if it were a single-use project. Leasing precommitments from anchor tenants generally are required for office and retail areas. Some consideration is given to the synergistic impact of this type of project on income, but such symbiosis must not determine the project's success or failure; the project must stand on the strength of its individual components.

New towns generally require several sources of financing. Infrastructure financing is provided by government agencies or insurance companies. Long-term commercial financing is supplied by an insurance company (often the same one providing infrastructure financing), a REIT, or a pension fund. Long-term for-sale or rental housing financing is provided by savings and loans or mutual savings banks. One or more commercial banks usually provide construction financing for virtually all elements of the project.

Fixture and Equipment Financing

In some cases, additional debt monies can be obtained by independently financing various building components. Items often financed in this manner include elevators, air conditioning, partitioning, restaurant equipment, and guest room furnishings. Frequently, a manufacturer provides financing to facilitate the sale of the product. Sometimes a leasing company or other equipment financing firm provides the financing. Usually, the loan is collateralized by the equipment only; lien rights, if any, are ordinarily subordinate to the first mortgage.

It should be noted that this brief discussion of the debt financing of various types of real estate projects is meant to give the reader a broad overview of those factors that various types of institutions consider important when they make loans on different types of projects. As mentioned earlier, this situation is very dynamic, and it is subject to major shifts as a result of changes in economic trends, the money market, government policy, and the investment objectives of individual institutions.

13
Equity Investment

Buying real estate is not only the best way, the quickest way, and the safest way, but the only way to become wealthy. MARSHALL FIELD

Real estate may not provide the only path to wealth, but it certainly offers one of the best-known, most proven ways. The historical attraction of individuals, corporations, and financial institutions to real estate as an investment has been noted throughout this book. Scores of other books exist on how to utilize real estate to achieve and maintain wealth. While this book's purpose is not to analyze the accumulation of large fortunes, the reader should understand how equity investments in real estate are made, their attractions and risks, and how to evaluate them.

Forms of Equity Investment

Equity investment in real estate can be made through a variety of legal forms, each having intrinsic advantages and disadvantages. The selection of the proper vehicle to hold real estate is largely a function of the investment objectives of the person or firm involved and the resources available for investment purposes.

"Think it over very carefully. After all, it's the biggest single investment you'll ever make."

Proprietorship

Sole proprietorship or direct ownership of the equity fee is the simplest form of equity ownership. The sole proprietor completely controls the development, management, and disposition of the property but bears the entire equity financing burden of the project, as well as unlimited liability. Continuity of management upon the death of the sole proprietor can also be a problem.

More than one person can own property directly, either through *joint tenancy* or *tenancy-in-common*. Under joint tenancy, each participant is personally liable for all expenses associated with the property. When one of the joint tenants dies, the property automatically goes to the surviving joint tenants. While this solves the problem of transfer at death, it considerably restricts the marketability of the joint tenant share. Under tenancy-in-common, each participant is personally liable only for his or her proportionate share of expenses. Upon death, the rights of a tenant-in-common can be willed to others. To some extent, this improves the marketability of these rights.

Partnerships

Often, it is desirable to have more than one investor in order to spread liability and financial risk. This can be accomplished by setting up a partnership to own, develop, and manage real property. In most states, a partnership is a separate entity which is capable of transacting necessary business activity in the partners' interests.[1] In terms of taxes, a partnership is a conduit which allows income and expense to flow directly to the individual partners.

A *general partnership* gives each partner full personal liability for all the debts of the partnership. Upon a partner's death, the partnership is terminated and the property is liquidated. The deceased partner's share is received by his or her estate. The *limited partnership,* more common in real estate investment, establishes at least one general partner and one or more limited partners. The general partner is responsible for managing the activities of the partnership and has general liability beyond that established for the limited partner. The limited partner is a "passive" investor with little voice in managing or controlling the partnership. Generally, the liability of a limited partner does not extend beyond the amount of that individual's investment. Income and expenses flow directly to the limited partner, based upon a predetermined percentage.

Limited partnerships hold many advantages for the real estate investor. They represent a flexible form of ownership, offering the limited partner limited liability, uninvolvement in management, and direct "pass-through" of income and expense for tax purposes. They provide the general partner with a source of financing without undue restrictions on management so long as the partner lives up to the terms of the partnership agreement. The limited partnership's major disadvantage is that traditionally there has not been an organized market in partnership interests.

In 1981 a new type of partnership, the *master limited partnership* (MLP), was created. The MLP is not a separately defined entity for tax or legal purposes. Rather, it is simply a large partnership that is publicly registered and whose shares are freely traded. The MLP has all the benefits of the limited partnership, and in addition it solves the problem of illiquidity, the one major drawback of the traditional limited partnership.[2]

[1]Most states have adopted the Uniform Partnership Act.

[2]Recent Congressional tax legislation has severely reduced the tax benefits of one level of taxation as applied to non-real estate investments. Industry concern over the possible extension of this legislation to real estate has substantially reduced the number of new MLFs being formed.

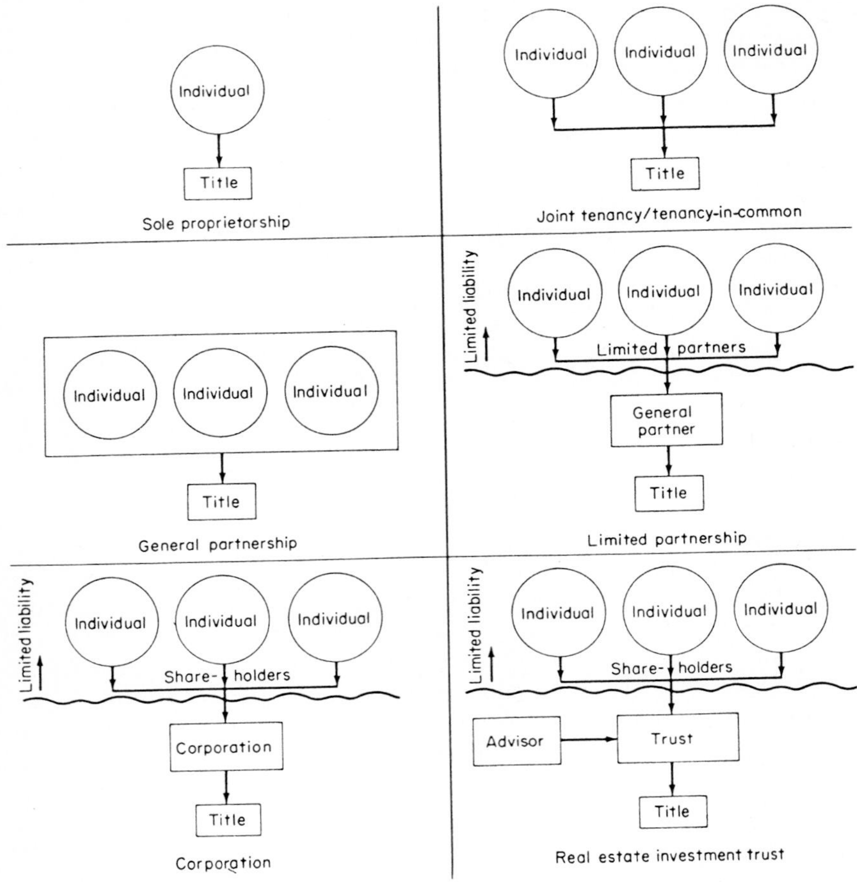

Figure 13-1. Forms of equity investment.

Corporations

The corporate form of ownership also resolves the transferability of interest problem. A corporation is an artificial entity,[3] created under state enabling powers.[4] A corporation may acquire, develop, and dispose of real property, as well as engage in any other legitimate business activity.

[3]IRS regulations establish six basic "tests" by which an entity (even an entity which has a different legal form, such as a partnership) is deemed to be a corporation for tax purposes: (1) centralized management, (2) free transferability of interests, (3) limited liability, and (4) continuity of existence. If the entity has two or more of these characteristics, it will be taxed as a corporation.

[4]In most states, this involves the articles of incorporation and corporate bylaws.

The corporation has a continuity of life, regardless of changes in its stockholders' status. As in a limited partnership, the stockholders' personal liability is limited to the amount of their investments, although under certain circumstances courts will "pierce the corporate veil" and impose liability on shareholders. The organization and maintenance of corporations is a complex legal area in which careful coordination with an attorney is essential. The stockholders' interests are evidenced by units of ownership (shares) that can be transferred to other investors, depending upon the legal nature of the stock[5] and market conditions.

The major disadvantage of corporate ownership of real estate is the impact of taxation. A corporation is taxed independently of its owners as a separate legal entity, currently at a maximum federal tax rate of 34 percent. The rate of state taxation varies according to the state of incorporation and operation; generally it ranges from 4 to 10 percent. When the corporation distributes income to its stockholders in the form of dividends, the income is taxed again, this time as ordinary income to the individual. On the other hand, if a corporation loses money, the shareholder cannot deduct these losses against his or her other income.[6] Furthermore, the corporation is subject to additional taxes if earnings are accumulated or if the corporation begins to assume the proportions of a personal holding company.

In certain cases, the taxation problem can be resolved through corporations organized under Subchapter S of the Internal Revenue Code. Owners of a "Sub S" corporation can choose to have the corporation's income and expenses passed through to them as individuals, much the same as in a partnership. However, these corporations are subject to several restrictions: for example, there can be no more than 35 shareholders, and losses from operations must not be greater than the stockholders' total investment, including stockholder loans to the corporation. Numerous other regulations govern establishing and maintaining a Subchapter S corporation.

REITs

As discussed in Chapter 3, REITs provide a vehicle with the transferability and personal liability advantages of a corporation as well as "pass-

[5]Common stock may bear a *legend* that specifies various restrictions on its transferability, or various permits or registrations may be required under federal and state securities laws.

[6]The corporation, however, can carry losses forward or backward to apply against profits in other years.

through" tax advantages. As long as the REIT meets various IRS tests, cash flows directly to the individual investor as a tax-free "return of capital." Transferability has been enhanced by the public market that has been established in REIT shares.

In order to qualify for tax-free status at the corporate level, REITs must meet certain qualifications. First, 95 percent of income of the REIT must be paid out annually to shareholders. Also, at least 75 percent of the REIT's income must come from real estate. Finally, there must be at least 100 shareholders, and the shares held by five or fewer shareholders cannot exceed 50 percent of total ownership.

Joint Ventures

A joint venture is an entity established between two or more parties to undertake a single project. It may involve individuals, partnerships, corporations, or REITs. Generally, the terms of the joint venture are outlined in an agreement stipulating the purpose of the joint venture, the interests of the parties, and the accounting of funds. Joint venture arrangements have been utilized extensively between developers and lending institutions. Such arrangements allow developers to raise substantial funds and financial institutions to realize a better than average return on their investment, minus the problems of project management. Legally, a joint venture is little different from a general partnership, but parties normally assume that a closer relationship exists with partners than with joint ventures.

Sources of Equity Capital

Financial Institutions

Life insurance companies are the major source of equity capital for real estate, both directly and as agents for pension funds, foreign investors, and others. Most of this investment is on an unleveraged basis involving all types of investment properties in markets throughout the nation. In some cases, insurance companies invest on a joint venture basis with developers, land owners, and major tenants. Pension funds and foreign investors, particularly the Japanese, are also sought out as joint venture partners.

Thrift institutions may undertake equity investing, usually as joint venture partners with single-family residential developers. Some of the larger savings and loans have helped to develop multifamily and commercial projects, often as merchant builders, with the objective of selling

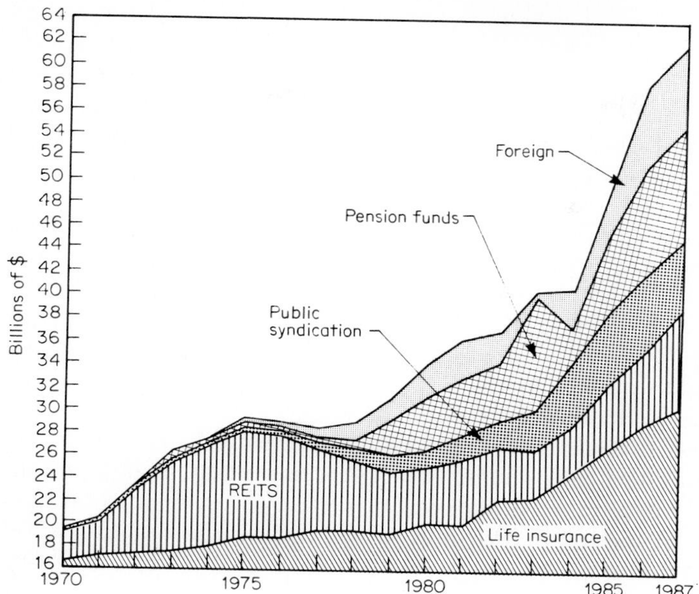

Figure 13-2. Annual real estate equity capital flows, 1970–1987, in real (inflation-adjusted) dollars. Investment properties only. (*McMahan Real Estate Advisers, Inc.*)

the assets upon completion of the projects in order to generate earnings. A few thrifts have entered the long-term equity investment arena as a method of hedging against inflation. Commercial banks generally do not invest in real estate equities, although they may represent other investors as agents.

Pension Funds

In the mid-1970s, rapidly spiraling inflation began eroding the value of financial assets, and pension fund managers became concerned with their ability to fund retirement liabilities. Fixed-income securities were particularly affected, but equities also did not offer the inflation protection that had been widely assumed.

Beginning with Prudential's open-end fund, PRISA,[7] in 1970, corporate retirement plans began moving into real estate equities. This investment was accelerated in the mid-1970s by pressures created by the Employment Retirement Income Security Act of 1974 (ERISA). While

[7]Prudential Realty Investment Separate Account.

ERISA did not specifically require investment in real estate, it did hold that a "prudent" investment policy should reflect more diversified holdings than the securities-dominated portfolios of most EBT accounts. This legislation, coupled with the dismal performance of the stock market in 1973–74, led many EBT managers to consider investment in real estate mortgages and equity. Several insurance companies and banks established *commingled funds* whereby EBT accounts could invest in real estate equities on a pooled basis. The earliest and largest type of these vehicles are *open-end funds* in which investors invest on the basis of the appraised value of the portfolio. Open-end funds have an infinite life and offer no cash income distributions. In contrast, *closed-end funds* have a limited life (usually 10 years) and distribute cash as it is earned. Pension funds also invest in real estate on a *separate account* basis by which they own and control the assets directly.

Pension fund investment in real estate accelerated in 1978 in response to inflationary fears, peaking in 1983 as inflation abated and investing in stocks proved attractive once more. However, the increasingly volatile stock market of late 1987 and renewed concerns about inflation caused many pension fund managers to consider once more adding real estate to their investment portfolios.

Syndications

As noted in Chapter 3, a major avenue for individual investment in real estate has been through syndications. A syndicate may be of any size and involve any of the forms of ownership previously discussed. The person who organizes the syndicate is called a *syndicator*. The syndicator may be a developer, real estate broker, investment broker, attorney, CPA, or other individual or firm involved in real estate. The syndicator may receive a fee, a percentage ownership of the project, or a combination of both.

Initially, most syndications were *specified asset* offerings in which the investor could review the assets which would be included in the investment package. In the last few years, most syndications have been *blind pools* which contain no assets at the time money is raised for the syndication. Investors participate primarily on the basis of the track record of the syndicator.

Syndication offerings are regulated by both state agencies and the Securities and Exchange Commission (SEC). Generally, smaller syndications are "private" and do not require SEC review. Larger syndications are usually "public," meaning they have met the disclosure requirements of the SEC and the "blue sky" laws of states in which the securities are marketed.

Public syndications gained momentum with the tax bill of 1981, which created a major windfall for real estate investors.[8] During the subsequent 5 years, public syndicators invested over $50 billion in equity real estate, largely multifamily and office projects acquired on a leveraged basis.

Passage of the 1986 Tax Reform Act created severe dislocations within the syndication industry among those individuals and firms involved in syndications solely as tax shelters. Since few syndication firms believed tax reform would pass, they did not take steps to diversify their businesses; with passage of the Act, the foundation of their businesses was virtually eliminated overnight.

As a result of tax reform, there has recently been some movement in the syndication community toward "economic" investment offerings in which cash yields rather than tax benefits are the focus of the investment. The difficulty with this approach is that aggregating large numbers of small investors is expensive, and these costs will no longer be offset by tax subsidy. Although syndicators have succeeded in reducing their fees to maintain a competitive stature, they have had difficulty in motivating distributors of their offerings, particularly during bull markets for stocks.

Recently, financial institutions have entered the syndication field through joint ventures with established syndicators, acquisition of syndication firms, and internal staff development. The expectation is that individual investors, somewhat disillusioned with the gyrations of the stock market, will once again seek equity real estate investments even if they do not involve tax shelter benefits.

Foreign Investors

As noted in Chapter 3, foreign investors have been an important source of equity capital for real estate. In the late 1970s, a relatively cheap dollar, coupled with a large, stable real estate market, made U.S. real estate highly attractive to foreign investors. The level of foreign investment declined in 1983 as the dollar strengthened and surpluses in the Middle East dried up, but it came back in 1986 as the dollar fell to new historical lows. The Japanese in particular became aggressive buyers of U.S. real estate.

The approach to U.S. real estate investment has varied by the origination of the foreign investor. In the United Kingdom and the

[8]Figures are not available for private syndications although it is believed that they exceeded the level of public syndication activity until the 1986 Tax Reform Act.

Netherlands, pension plans and other institutional investors have been investing on both a pooled and separate account basis for many years and are sophisticated investors in American real estate. They acquire most types of property in markets across the country and, on occasion, engage in the development process. Their major investment objective is generally cash flow and long-term appreciation.

Canadian and Australian investors are often large developers or construction firms who want to diversify their business operations. They also may be interested in acquiring non-real estate firms and liquidating their undervalued real estate holdings. Individual "safe harbor" investors from Europe, the Middle East, South America, and Asia are also investing in U.S. real estate as a means of diversifying their risk, although the motivation is more political than economic. Here, the primary investment objective is usually safety of principal.

Japanese investors span the full investment spectrum. Japanese financial institutions and wealthy individuals are primarily interested in long-term appreciation. Japanese syndicators look to profiting from real estate and currency yield spreads between the countries. Construction and development companies seek business opportunities in U.S. markets. Early Japanese investment was focused on "trophy" buildings in major U.S. markets, but now it includes smaller properties in a wider variety of locations, making the Japanese a major player in U.S. real estate equity markets.

REITs

As discussed in Chapter 12, REITs were originally conceived as equity investment vehicles but, through encouragement by Wall Street, were converted into conduits for mortgage investment. In recent years, however, REITs have returned to their original function as equity investment vehicles with a resurgence in popularity of equity REITs and their use in several securitized issues.

Individuals

In addition to investing in syndications and REITs, individuals may also invest in real estate directly. Many wealthy American families have major real estate investment programs. While some of these were originated for tax shelter purposes, most are directed at long-term equity appreciation.

Attractions of Real Estate as an Investment

In part, the attraction of real estate as an investment has come from certain emotional feelings about "the land." Emotional considerations aside, however, several very practical economic reasons explain why real estate has been sought out as an investment—reasons which were reinforced in the 1950s and 1960s by the rapid growth of urban areas, an expanded supply of mortgage capital, more liberal lending policies, and favorable federal income tax policies. The double-digit inflation of the mid-1970s further added to the appeal of real estate as a hedge against rising prices.

Appreciation in Real Values

As noted in Chapter 6, real estate is divided into three submarkets: raw land, user properties, and investment properties. All submarkets may appreciate or depreciate in value over time. The rapid growth of America's urban centers following World War II created unprecedented appreciation in real estate values. Market demand pressures on a limited supply of well-located land tend to increase the real value of land and buildings over time. The amount of appreciation depends upon the location of the property, its purchase price, the uses to which it can be put, and the overall demand for these uses in the local marketplace. To the extent that this appreciation exceeds the inflation rate, the property will experience increases in real (after inflation) value.

Inflation Hedge

One of the major attractions of real estate is its ability to provide a hedge against unanticipated inflation.[9] This is possible because new construction costs usually equal or exceed the general price index and rents on new buildings are tied to the cost of new construction through the yield pricing mechanism, provided local markets are in general equilibrium. If markets are tight, rent may exceed new construction costs; if they are soft, rents may be lower. But generally, rents on new buildings will be priced to return a yield consistent with new construction costs.

Returns for older buildings generally track on new buildings; owners are not going to lower rents in a market experiencing higher price lev-

[9] Investors can hedge against anticipated inflation in the bond market.

els. This does not mean that older buildings will generate the same rent as new buildings—although this does occur in certain markets—but rather, that there is a differential between older and newer buildings which is generally consistent over time.

Another reason real estate is such a good inflation hedge is that most commercial leases today are tied to a price index or "go to market" at selected intervals. This allows all or a portion of the rented space to adjust to changes in inflation at certain intervals. Fortunately for property owners, very few leases are indexed downward to provide for rental reductions if price levels fall, although market price adjustment may result in lower rents, particularly in soft markets.

A final factor is that increases in operating costs are generally borne by the tenant, with increases in revenue falling through to the bottom line. The combination of these factors gives real estate the ability to adjust—with some lag effect caused by lease rollovers—to changes in price levels. In essence, the inflation protection is built-in so that it is not necessary to liquidate the investment in order to protect yields from inflation.

Real estate's effectiveness as an inflation hedge has been documented in recent years by extensive analysis of real estate investment portfolios. In comparing portfolio returns during a generally inflationary period (1973–83), Hartzell, Hekman and Miles found that real estate experienced higher returns than other assets (e.g., Standard & Poor's, Treasury bonds and bills) with less variability. They also reported a high degree of correlation between real estate returns and changes in the general price level.[10]

Cash Yields

One of the three submarkets—investment properties—also provides a cash return in addition to real appreciation and inflation protection.[11] In fact, investment real estate is one of the few inflation hedges which also provides the investor with a monthly, quarterly, or annual cash return. The amount of the cash yield will generally range from 6 to 12 percent annually, depending upon the local market and the type of property.[12]

[10]David Hartzell, John Hekman, and Mike Miles, "Diversification Categories in Investment Real Estate," *AREUEA Journal,* vol. 14, no. 2, 1986, p. 230.

[11]Raw land and user properties may from time to time also provide cash returns if they enter the investment property market.

[12]Cash yields in Europe and Japan are substantially lower.

The cash yield, when added to (or subtracted from) the appreciation (depreciation) in the property, produces the *total return*. By deducting the inflation rate for the holding period, it is possible to determine the *real total return* for the investment. Zerbst and Cambon, in a wide-ranging survey of real estate returns, determined that pretax real returns from completed and leased investment properties ranged from 4.5 to 6.0 percent over most 5-year or longer holding periods. This level of real return was less than common stocks but higher than bonds.[13]

Lower Volatility

There is also some indication that returns from real estate investment properties have been less volatile than those from equity securities.[14] While the studies undertaken in this area are by no means conclusive, there is some logic to support this contention. Because most investment properties are leased to corporations, who pay rent before they pay stock dividends (and in some cases, bond coupons), lease payments are a nondiscretionary expense. A corporation simply has to pay its rent to stay in business.

Since it is possible to evaluate the credit of the tenant and since rent payments can be reliably projected over the life of the lease, it stands to reason that the income stream from a real estate property is less volatile than corporate earnings. Since income property generally sells on a capitalization of the income stream, changes in market value are also going to be less volatile.

Reduction of Systematic Risk

There are also data that suggest that real estate performs inversely with securities.[15] This means that when stocks are rising in value, real estate is declining; when stocks are down, real estate is up. The inclusion of real estate in a portfolio of stocks would therefore tend to offset movements in the stock market and lower systematic (nondiversifiable) risk.[16]

[13]Robert H. Zerbst and Barbara R. Cambon, "Real Estate: Historical Returns and Risks," *The Journal of Portfolio Management*, Spring, 1984, p. 20.

[14]Ibid., p. 17.

[15]Ibid., p. 19.

[16]The risk associated with a given asset portfolio can be divided into two components: *systematic risk* is the amount of variance in the expected return of an asset that is due to overall changes in the market; *nonsystematic risk* is the variance in expected return caused by the underlying risks of a particular asset.

With lower volatility, real estate would tend to dampen the overall volatility of the portfolio.

Leverage

For some, a major attraction is real estate's ability to utilize "other people's money" to finance real estate development or investment, thereby creating leverage. Put simply, leverage changes the rate of return on equity investment through borrowed funds. *Positive leverage* exists when the rate of return is higher through the use of borrowed funds than it would be without these funds. *Negative leverage* occurs when the return is lower. The degree of leverage is a function of the proportion and interest rate of borrowed funds utilized, and the overall earnings potential of the real estate project. Generally, the degree of leverage can be established by comparing the annual cost of amortizing the borrowed funds (*debt service*) with the annual income from the project. If the cost of borrowing is less than the income, leverage will be positive; if it is greater, negative leverage will result (see Table 13-1).[17]

Leverage is an advantage only if the economics of the project are sound. Small changes in the income stream can create negative leverage, and, if adverse conditions continue over an extended period of time, they can have an adverse effect on the investment. Fortunately for most investors, postwar America's inflationary pressures have prevented this. Income streams, often tied to cost-of-living indices, have tended to accelerate, creating an increasing spread over debt service charges established at a given point in time. Business recessions or the advent of a full-scale depression could create negative leverage situations for real estate investments with higher break-even occupancy.

Tax Advantages

Since World War II, real estate has enjoyed several tax advantages over other forms of investment. These advantages have tended to increase the yield of the projects themselves and, in some cases, to reduce taxes on other sources of income.[18]

[17]In the interest of simplicity, this discussion is concerned with a *pretax* situation. It should be noted that tax considerations may substantially alter the impact of leverage. An after-tax analysis over the entire life of the investment is therefore desirable in order to ascertain the true impact of leverage.

[18]Tax policy and practice change almost daily. This discussion is intended to give the reader an overview of tax considerations relative to real estate at the time this book was written. For answers to more specific questions, consult a CPA or tax attorney.

Table 13-1. Effect of Leverage on Simple Equity Return (%)*

Interest rate (%)	Annual constant	Loan/value ratio (%)							
		60%	65%	70%	75%	80%	85%	90%	
6.0	0.0720	14.2	15.2	16.5	18.4	21.2	25.9	35.2	
6.5	0.0759	13.6	14.5	15.6	17.2	19.6	23.7	31.7	
7.0	0.0799	13.0	13.7	14.7	16.0	18.0	21.4	28.1	
7.5	0.0839	12.4	13.0	13.8	14.8	16.4	19.1	24.5	Positive
8.0	0.0881	11.8	12.2	12.8	13.6	14.8	16.7	20.7	
8.5	0.0923	11.2	11.4	11.8	12.3	13.1	14.4	16.9	
9.0	0.0966	10.5	10.6	10.8	11.0	11.4	11.9	13.1	
9.5	0.1009	9.9	9.8	9.8	9.7	9.6	9.5	9.2	
10.0	0.1053	9.2	9.0	8.8	8.4	7.9	7.0	5.2	
10.5	0.1098	8.5	8.2	7.7	7.1	6.1	4.4	1.2	
11.0	0.1143	7.9	7.3	6.7	5.7	4.3	1.9	−2.9	Negative
11.5	0.1189	7.2	6.5	5.6	4.3	2.4	−0.7	−7.0	
12.0	0.1235	6.5	5.6	4.5	3.0	0.6	−3.3	−11.2	

*Assumptions:
a. $10 million project value.
b. $1 million annual net operating income without leverage.
c. 10% simple return without leverage ($1/$10 million).
d. 30-year amortization.

Depreciation. Today, the major tax advantage associated with real estate is depreciation, a tax allowance for reduction in the value of an asset over time. Annual depreciation charges increase expense, thereby reducing taxable income. However, since depreciation is essentially a bookkeeping entry, no cash is required to cover the expense item. Thus, monies which otherwise would have been paid in taxes are available for other purposes.[19] Annual depreciation can be utilized to offset other income to the extent that such depreciation exceeds the cash requirements for the project.

Prior to the Tax Reform Act of 1986, depreciation could be calculated either on a *straight-line* or an *accelerated* basis. Straight-line depreciation is simply the value of the depreciable assets, less salvage value, divided by the number of years of useful life. Accelerated depreciation involves larger amounts of depreciation in the early years of the project's useful life and lesser amounts in the later years. Straight-line depreciation for real property is the only method that is allowed under the current tax law. The Internal Revenue Service divides property into two categories for depreciation purposes: residential rental property must be depreciated over 27.5 years; nonresidential, over 31.5 years.

Under previous tax law, building components, such as walls, ceilings, electrical components, and air conditioning, could be assigned shorter useful lives for depreciation purposes, increasing the tax benefits of depreciation. Under current law, however, this tax benefit has been considerably reduced.

Capital Gains. Until the Tax Reform Act of 1986, sale of property or other investments held for more than 6 months received favorable tax treatment. Essentially, 60 percent of the gain could be deducted and tax was paid on the remaining 40 percent, cutting the effective tax rate on such sales by more than one-half. The 1986 Act, however, greatly reduced individual tax rates, and Congress consequently saw no need to extend preferential treatment for capital gains, which are now taxed as ordinary income.

Development Costs. In the past, many costs incurred during the development period of a project were deducted or amortized for income tax purposes. These included ground rent, property taxes, financing

[19]This sum can be calculated roughly by multiplying the amount of the annual depreciation by the taxpayer's marginal tax rate. The marginal rate is the incremental tax rate on the owner's new income added to an existing base.

fees, and interest on construction loans. Under current tax laws, virtually all development costs must be capitalized (corporations, however, are excepted from this new ruling). Operating losses during the rent-up period are generally deductible expenses.

Risks Inherent in Real Estate Investment

As with most investments, real estate has certain risks. These risks relate to individual properties and portfolios. Individual property risks often can be reduced, or at least better understood, through rigorous analysis and effective management. In certain cases, such as insurance, the risk can be shifted (for a price) to someone else. If several properties are involved, it may be possible to diversify risks to reduce the impact of a single adverse event on the portfolio.

Liquidity

Liquidity is one area in which real estate does not compare favorably with securities. The disposition of real property is a time-consuming process (3 to 6 months at a minimum) and requires almost as much effort and expertise as property acquisition. Furthermore, real estate should be disposed of on a well-planned basis, taking advantage of market conditions and desirable timing in terms of the life cycle of the property. Investors, therefore, should not count on real estate to provide liquidity but rather view it as a long-term asset, only to be sold in concert with a planned disposition strategy.

Loss of Principal

Capital invested in real estate can be lost through the physical destruction of the asset, changes in economic conditions, or the loss of legal ownership.

Physical Destruction. Real estate is a physical asset, fixed in location and subject to damage or destruction by a natural disaster. A real estate portfolio that is concentrated geographically intensifies this risk exposure. The classic case is the earthquake or tornado that destroys 30 to 40 percent of a real estate portfolio in a single stroke. While it is technically possible to protect the physical assets through insurance, this does not guarantee that the buildings can be re-leased after the disaster, which may be so intense that the overall economy of the area is adversely affected for many years.

Changes in Economic Conditions. The market value of a property may be adversely affected by long-term economic decline in a regional or local economy, such as has been experienced by the "rust belt" in the Midwest and, more recently, the "oil patch" states of the Southwest. Concentration of a real estate portfolio in geographic areas or industries affected by these changes may further aggravate the loss of value.

Concentration by investment vehicle may subject a portfolio to adverse pressure as a result of increases in inflation. Portfolios having a high proportion of fixed-rate mortgages, for example, were severely affected by the inflation of the 1970s and early 1980s. Property-type concentration can expose a portfolio to increased risk as a result of shifts in market preferences. Portfolios unduly concentrated in shopping centers in the late 1970s, for example, came under intense pressure as investor interest declined and market capitalization rates rose. This situation reversed in the 1980s as office buildings came under similar pressures as a result of overbuilding, and shopping centers once again returned to favor.

Property-type concentration can also lead to problems as a result of technological innovation. Portfolios of older office buildings have been hurt by advances in energy conservation resulting from innovative design and new technology, forcing owners to retrofit their buildings (if possible) or lose tenants, lower rents, or both.

In some cases the touted technology of one period may be the albatross of another. Buildings built between 1942 and 1974 were often insulated or fireproofed with the "wonder material" of the period: asbestos. Today, owners of these buildings are faced with monumental clean-up problems, the cost of which may not be recoverable through increases in rent. Failure to solve this problem could lead to a worse situation: a loss of tenants and the threat of lawsuits.

Geographically concentrated portfolios can be adversely affected by changes in land use regulations. Land values in many California coastal areas were seriously undermined by the passage of the Coastal Initiative. Similarly, changes in floor area ratios, parking requirements, and other land use controls can adversely affect a portfolio, if not immediately, at least by the time of disposition.

Changes in government fiscal policy also can affect a geographically concentrated portfolio. At the local level, a decision to increase property taxes or special assessments might inhibit the sale of the property in addition to reducing net operating income, particularly if increased expenses cannot be passed on to tenants.

Changes in federal fiscal policy can also have an impact, particularly if the portfolio is concentrated in tax shelter investments. When the time has come to dispose of the portfolio, buyers might not be willing to pay the same price for assets no longer carrying the same level of tax shelter benefits. Unfortunately, there is no simple way to underwrite economic change. There are few opportunities to shift the risk of such change; the developer and investor must rely on analytical skills and business judgment to manage the risk process as best as possible. To the extent that adverse economic change can be foreseen, of course, investments can be withheld, reduced, phased, or shared with others in order to minimize risk. But once a commitment has been made, it's much more difficult to reduce the inherent risk, particularly since real estate is a capital intensive, highly illiquid asset. The most realistic solution is to diversify investment portfolios in order to reduce the impact of a single event, carefully monitor economic change, and be prepared to modify or sell assets as quickly as possible.

Loss of Legal Ownership. Loss of legal ownership may occur if the equity owner cannot meet debt service obligations under the mortgage. In some states, this loss can exceed the amount of invested capital if the mortgagee can secure a deficiency judgment. This can also happen if the investor has personally guaranteed the mortgage.

While the risk of loss of legal ownership cannot be eliminated when a property is leveraged, it can be substantially reduced by limiting the amount of the mortgage and reducing the break-even level required to meet debt service. As an example, the amount of leverage could be based on the percentage of the property leased to major credit tenants on a long-term basis.

Loss of Yield

Investors also face a possible loss of yield as a result of revenues or costs being less or greater than anticipated. The major risk is in the development phase, when revenues and costs are pro forma in nature. There is also a yield exposure with operating properties, particularly when leases are turning, but it is much lower than with projects in the development phase.

It should be noted that prolonged earnings risks may ultimately turn into capital risks. If leveraged, continued cash outflows can eventually affect a project's ability to meet debt service payments, and foreclosure may result. Rates of return which do not match inflation may reduce the price at which a property can be sold.

Loss of Purchasing Power

During inflationary periods, there is a risk that, while the full amount of the original investment can be recovered, inflation will have eroded its purchasing power. However, this is probably less likely to happen with real estate, since the appreciation of real property has historically tended to meet or exceed inflation.

Risk Diversification

Experienced investors in securities know that diversification of risk is important in protecting their investments. The rationale for the diversification of securities portfolios and the means to achieve it have been well established in the academic and financial community for some time.[20] While the advantages of diversification of real estate risks are not as well understood or accepted, there are some important parallels to the securities industry, and some notable exceptions.

Geographical Diversification

Most observers agree that geographical diversification is important in protecting a real estate portfolio against the risks of natural disasters and economic and regulatory change. Geographical diversification is generally considered at the metropolitan area level, although some areas (Los Angeles, for example) are so large that it may be possible to hold multiple properties in the area and still remain diversified.

It is also essential to establish the "linkage" of metropolitan areas with similar economic characteristics. A portfolio of properties in Houston, Tulsa, Oklahoma City, and Denver, for example, involves metropolitan areas linked to energy production and would not be adequately diversified. Metropolitan areas subject to the same potential for natural disasters would also be considered closely linked for diversification purposes. Properties located in different metropolitan areas that are along the San Andreas fault would not constitute an adequately diversified portfolio.

Property Type

Recent research indicates that diversification by property type, *when combined with geographical diversification,* can be quite effective in re-

[20]Franco Modigliani and Merton H. Miller, "The Cost of Capital, Corporation Finance and the Theory of Investment," *American Economic Review,* June 1958; W. F. Sharpe, "Capital Asset Prices: A Theory of Market Equilibrium under Conditions of Risk," *Journal of Finance,* September 1964.

ducing risk.[21] Clearly, property type diversification within a single metropolitan area would not protect the portfolio against natural disasters, although it may provide some protection against economic change.

It should be noted that there is some disagreement as to the correct definition of property types. The National Council of Real Estate Investment Fiduciaries, for example, has recently split the FRC Industrial Property Index[22] and R&D components. Similar problems exist in defining other property types as well.

Tenant Industry

Another view is that the best form of economic diversification is across leaseholds, with no single industry dominating the tenant mix of a portfolio.[23] Utilizing this approach, existing areas of concentration would be eliminated as leases turn by accepting only tenants from other industries. New properties would not be added to the portfolio if they increased industry concentration; leasing programs for properties under development would focus on tenants in industries that diversified the existing portfolio.

While such an approach may be intuitively appealing, it may be difficult to implement, particularly for the developer or investor in a soft market where it is a relief to secure *any* tenants, regardless of industry. The approach also penalizes developers who have specialized in servicing the needs of a particular industry.

Lease Term

Still another approach stresses lease term diversification, attempting to avoid having a high percentage of the portfolio "turning" in any one year. Lease turn exposure is evaluated across an entire portfolio. This is accomplished on a continuing basis and provides an important input in the development or acquisition of additional properties for the portfolio. For example, a property with a high percentage of leases turning in 1990 should not be placed in a portfolio already having a high percentage of leases turning in the same year. Unfortunately, this approach is also difficult to implement because of the tendency of developers to

[21]Paul B. Firstenberg, Stephen A. Ross, and Randall C. Zisler, "Managing Real Estate Portfolios," *Goldman Sachs Real Estate Research Publications*, New York, November 16, 1987.

[22]The FRC Industrial Property Index is one of several indexes published by Frank Russell Company and the National Council of Real Estate Investment Fiduciaries.

[23]Firstenberg, et al., op. cit.

write leases that have similar maturities. This means that a property with staggered lease maturities should command a premium in the marketplace, particularly in metropolitan areas that tend to be consistently overbuilt.

Investment Vehicle

A final form of portfolio diversification is by investment vehicle. Utilizing this approach, a portion of the portfolio would be in equity ownership and a portion in mortgages or hybrid instruments. The objective would be to obtain a steady cash flow from mortgages to offset the variability of equity cash flow.

Diversification by investment vehicle is generally of more interest to investors than developers, most of whom have committed their careers to building equity portfolios and have little interest in holding mortgages or hybrid investments. In fact, developers could probably achieve the same objectives this approach stresses, with greater liquidity, by investing in the bond market.

Minimum Number of Properties to Achieve Diversification

What is the minimum number of properties required to achieve an acceptable level of portfolio diversification with respect to real estate? This was one of the questions addressed in a landmark court case, *Donovan vs. Mazzola,* brought by the U.S. Department of Labor in 1981 against Plumbers Union Local No. 38 in San Francisco.[24] In that case, the government's expert witnesses testified that the ownership of at least six properties was required to achieve a minimum acceptable level of portfolio diversification, assuming the properties in the portfolio were located in different geographical areas and involved different property types.

Since the Mazzola case, additional research on the diversification issue has been undertaken. In an analysis of a portfolio of 166 properties, Miles and McCue found that nonsystematic portfolio risk could be diversified relatively rapidly as portfolio size increased.[25] The study demonstrated, for example, that a portfolio consisting of four properties resulted in diversification of more than two-thirds of the portfolio's

[24]Empl. Ben. Cas. (BNA) 2115 (N.D. Cal. 1981).

[25]Mike Miles and Tom McCue, "Diversification in the Real Estate Portfolio," *The Journal of Financial Research,* vol. VII, no. 1, Spring 1984, p. 57.

Table 13-2. Reduction in Nonsystematic Risk through Diversification

No. properties	% reduced
1	.0
2	52.0
4	68.3
6	75.2
8	78.4
10	83.4
20	86.0
166	91.4

SOURCE: Mike Miles and Tom McCue, "Diversification in the Real Estate Portfolio," *The Journal of Financial Research,* vol. VII, no. 1, Spring 1984, p. 57.

nonsystematic risk; six properties, over three-fourths. Miles also found that adding properties to the portfolio beyond this point didn't proportionately reduce risk. With twenty properties in the portfolio, for example, nonsystematic risk reduction increased to 86 percent.

Diversification Summary

In summary, the research indicates that a diversified real estate investment portfolio should include four to six properties located in economically independent metropolitan areas. If possible, tenants should be diversified by industry and lease term. Diversification by property type may also be desirable, provided geographical diversification has already been achieved. Diversification by investment vehicle, while a desirable objective for some investors, may not be as critical to developers.

The Developer's Dilemma

Despite the advantages of diversification, the natural tendency of most developers is to concentrate their activities in one type of real property, located in one or a few metropolitan areas. There are several reasons for this. Intimate knowledge of a local area may be essential in locating good sites for development, securing necessary governmental approvals, and in successfully dealing with contractors and subcontractors. Experience in a particular property type often is important in understanding design trade-offs and in establishing credibility with key tenants.

In formulating and implementing a business strategy, therefore, the developer is faced with an interesting dilemma. As a creator of investment value, the developer benefits from concentration; as a holder of investments, from diversification.

Faced with this situation, one response on the part of the developer is to become a merchant builder, as outlined in Chapter 3, and pass on most of the responsibilities for diversification to investors acquiring properties upon completion of construction. The production portfolio (i.e., land and buildings under construction), however, is still subject to concentration risk, although the time frame is shorter and thus the risk is more manageable.

Another solution is to become a regional or national developer or to undertake the development of more than one property type. Clearly, as noted in Chapter 3, this has been a motivating factor on the part of many of the national firms that have evolved over the last decade.

Still another approach to portfolio diversification, one not widely utilized thus far, is to trade equity interests with developers and investors in other geographical areas or holding other types of real estate. In this way the risks inherent in concentration can be shared, while the production advantages of concentration are retained, without having to build a large regional or national organization, with all of the attendant overhead costs and management responsibilities that entails.

The Real Estate Risk-Yield Curve

The risk-yield curve for real estate generally corresponds to the steps of the development process (see Figure 13-4). Risks and yields are highest for those developers or investors willing to hold land and go through the approval process. The risks and yields begin falling as uncertainty is removed through the planning and design, financing, construction, and leasing stages. Once a project is completed and leased, the major market risk remaining for the investor is the uncertainty regarding lease terms and rental rates as leases turn over the holding period and the final sales price of the property.

In essence, the developer "rides the risk curve" by shouldering the development risks that most investors are not willing to assume. In so doing, the developer is adding value throughout the development process by orchestrating land, materials, labor, and services into a finished product—and is paid a development profit for this contribution.

The amount of development profit will depend upon the "spread" between the return that the developer receives and that of the investor. The degree of spread will vary between projects and markets depending upon the risk perceptions of the developer and investor, as well as

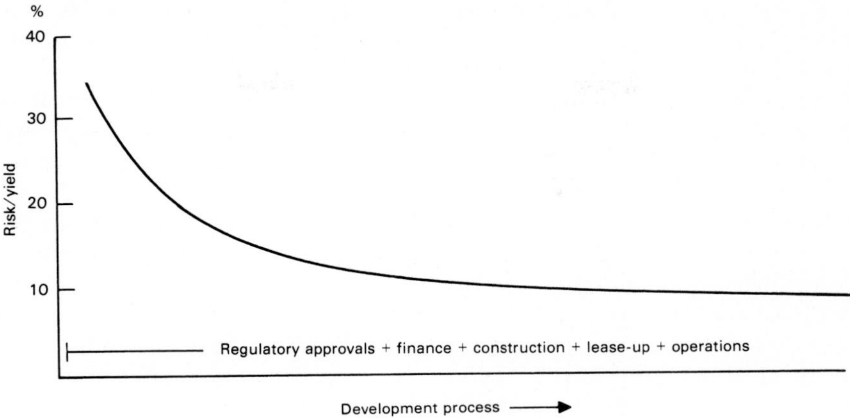

Figure 13-3. Real estate investment risk-yield curve.

general market conditions. As an example, in soft markets, investor yields generally rise to reflect increased market uncertainty and greater availability of investment alternatives. Developer yields, on the other hand, fall, primarily because of the cost of leasing concessions and the additional time required to lease the property. If the yield spread becomes too slim, the developer may begin buying properties, since there is little incentive to take on development risks at that point.

In a tight market, the spread widens and development profits increase. During these periods investors may decide to integrate back into the development process (move up the risk curve) in order to secure some of the profits that would otherwise go to the developer. Financial institutions, for example, may decide during such periods to become joint venture partners rather than lenders.

Investors may attempt to "market time" these yield changes over time, acquiring properties when yields are relatively high and holding them until yields move down and properties are sold. Studies of a $100 million hypothetical portfolio indicate that a 200 basis point[26] downward movement in capitalization rates (from 9.5 to 7.5 percent) can produce a 23.6 percent increase in real return over a 10-year period, all other factors being equal.[27] Investors may also attempt to arbitrage yields between different local markets or, as noted in Chapter 3, between different countries.

[26]Unpublished research, McMahan Real Estate Advisors, Inc., San Francisco, Calif., 1987.

[27]A basis point is one one-hundredth of a percent.

Swings in market conditions may also lead to investors preferring one type of real estate product over another. A good example is the strong preference for retail investments during the last few years, largely because office building markets were overbuilt and there was less certainty about their future income streams. This has led to higher prices in the retail segment of the market, with yields 100 to 150 basis points below office building projects.

Risks and yields may also vary depending upon the degree of "franchise" that a property enjoys. A well-located regional shopping center, downtown office building, or major hotel property may have lower yields because future income streams are more certain. A project in a community with strong growth controls may also enjoy a franchise as a result of anticipated lower levels of future competition. The less of a franchise that a project enjoys, the more it behaves like a "commodity"—nondifferentiated, easy to reproduce, interchangeable with other properties. The best example is the distribution warehouse, which varies little from site to site and market to market.

Certainly, no investment is risk-free; even insured deposits can lose purchasing power. The economic advantages of real estate, however, coupled with the general public's strong sense of the inevitability of increases in land values, may lead an investor to play down the risks involved in real estate investment. Too often the result is investments gone sour and capital dissipated. The real estate market appears to be particularly vulnerable to overly optimistic investment projections. Therefore, the prudent real estate developer or investor should weigh *all* the risks as carefully as possible before proceeding.

14
Measuring Real Estate Returns

Without development there is no profit,
without profit no development.
JOSEPH ALOIS SCHUMPETER

In evaluating the rewards of a proposed real estate investment, one of the key factors is a projection of the annual return that can be expected on the equity funds invested. Surprisingly, this is less simple than it sounds: return on investment (ROI) may vary considerably among projects, depending on the nature of the project, the impact of leverage, the type of legal entity, tax considerations, and the method and assumptions used to calculate ROI. Therefore it's important to understand how ROI is calculated by many real estate practitioners, how it *should* be calculated, and what it ultimately means in the overall evaluation of an investment opportunity.

Simple Return Analysis

The traditional method of calculating return on real estate investment is the simple return analysis. This approach, despite many fundamental shortcomings, is still utilized by a large portion of the real estate community. Figure 14-1 indicates conceptually how the simple return analysis operates. *Gross revenue* is estimated for a normal or *stabilized year* of operations. An allowance for *vacancy* is deducted to arrive at *effective gross revenue*. Annual *operating expense* is deducted to arrive at *net operating income* (NOI). NOI is divided by the total investment to arrive at the *free and clear return* (also called the *capitalization rate*). If the property is leveraged, the annual cost of debt service (principal and interest) is deducted from NOI to arrive at the amount of *spendable income*. Spendable income is then divided by the amount of equity investment to arrive at the *net spendable* or *cash-on-cash return*.

The following discussion applies this approach in step-by-step fashion to a 100,000-square-foot office building located in the suburbs of a ma-

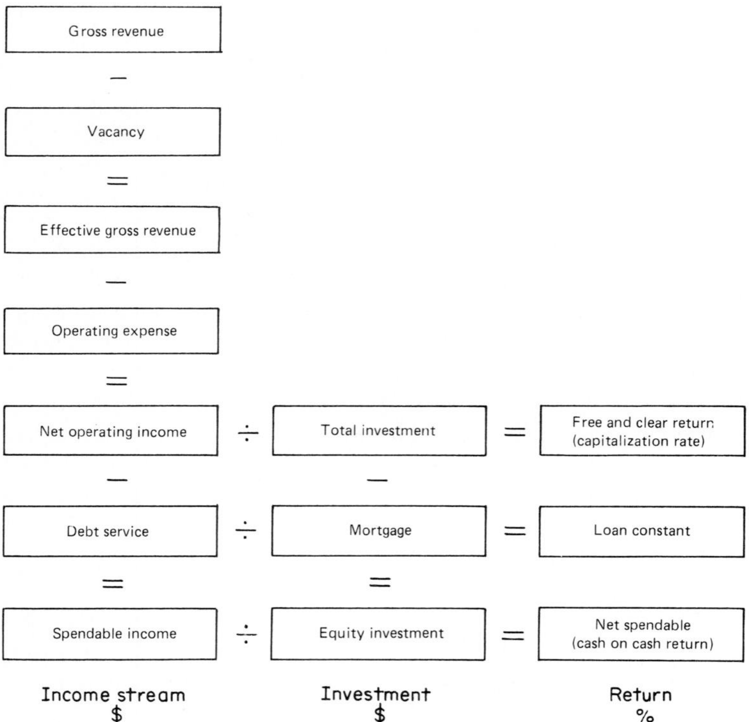

Figure 14-1. Simple return analysis: conceptual framework.

jor American city. The project requires 1 year to construct and a second year to reach stabilized operations. Both leveraged and unleveraged situations are considered; in the leveraged scenario, a $10 million loan is assumed with an interest rate of 12 percent for the construction loan and 10 percent for the permanent loan.

Total Investment

The first step in utilizing the simple return analysis is to estimate the amount of funds—both debt and equity—that will be required to develop the project. While many of these cost items must await definitive planning and design before they can be finalized, general estimates can help determine the financial feasibility of the project on a preliminary basis. Table 14-1 outlines the total investment for the example property, totaling approximately $11.5 million on an unleveraged basis and $13.6 million on a leveraged basis. All of the costs are for the first year except

Table 14-1. Total Investment

	Unleveraged	Leveraged
Land (217,800 sq ft @ $10)	$2,178,000	$2,178,000
Construction		
Site Development (217,800 sq ft @ $1)	217,800	217,800
Building		
Shell (100,000 sq ft @60)	6,000,000	6,000,000
Finish (92,000sq ft @17)*	1,564,000	1,564,000
Parking (350 stalls @ $1200)	420,000	420,000
Landscaping (25,000 sq ft @ $4)	100,000	100,000
Subtotal	8,301,800	8,301,800
Total land and construction (hard costs)	10,479,800	10,479,800
Interim		
Architecture & engineering (3%)	249,100	249,100
Developer overhead (3%)	256,500	256,500
Property taxes (1.5%)	78,600	78,600
Insurance ($.50/$100)	20,800	20,800
Leasing*	349,600	349,600
Construction interest (12%)**		1,800,000
Finance Fees (3%)		300,000
Permits	50,000	50,000
Legal	30,000	30,000
Misc.	25,000	25,000
Subtotal (soft costs)	1,059,600	3,159,600
Total	11,539,400	13,639,400

*Second-year cost.
**First- and second-year cost.

for tenant finish and leasing commissions, which occur in the second year, and construction interest, which occurs in both years.

Land. The cost of land should be expressed in terms of its current market value ($10 per square foot in the example). If the land is being purchased, this will not be difficult—the price is clearly established. However, if the land has been held for a considerable length of time, its current market value must be established through an appraisal, as discussed in the Appendix. Many developers and investors make the mistake of putting the land into the financial analysis on the basis of its original cost; this tends to understate the value of the land and to inaccurately increase ROI.[1]

Construction. *Site development* includes all costs needed to prepare the land for building construction, such as the demolition of existing structures, site preparation (e.g., grading and soil import or export), off-site improvements (e.g., sewer and street improvements), and on-site improvements (e.g., utilities, streets, and parking). They are calculated by extending a unit cost ($1.00 per square foot) by the amount of the total land area (217,800 square feet). *Building construction costs* are estimated by applying unit costs ($60 per square foot) to the gross building area (100,000 square feet). In the development of commercial and industrial buildings allowances should be made for the provision of minimum *tenant finish* (electrical outlets, lighting, air conditioning, partitioning, carpeting, painting, wall coverings, etc.). The level of finish will vary according to the type of project, local leasing customs, and the market strength of the project. Once these factors have been established, the cost of providing tenant finish is determined on a unit basis ($17 per square foot), multiplied by the amount of net rentable area (92,000 square feet).[2] Note that the net rentable area is less than the gross building area to allow for elevators, ducts, and other nonrentable space. The ratio between gross and net area is called the *design efficiency ratio*.

Parking is calculated on the basis of the number of stalls (350) multiplied by a unit cost per stall ($1200). *Landscaping* is determined by applying a unit cost ($4 per square foot) to the amount of land area net of building, streets, and parking (25,000 square feet). The total of all land and building costs ($10,479,800) is often referred to as the *hard costs* of a project.

[1]The illogic is apparent when an extreme case is considered: land that has been inherited and has no cost to the investor.

[2]These costs probably are underestimated more than any other. Often, there is a strong temptation to increase tenant allowances in order to close a deal, particularly in soft markets.

Interim Costs. In addition to land and building costs, a series of expenses will be incurred between the time the decision is made to proceed and stabilized operations are achieved. These are often referred to as *interim* or *soft costs.*

Architectural and engineering fees (A&E) are a percentage (3 percent) of the total construction costs calculated to date; *developer's overhead* is a percentage (3 percent) of all construction costs including the A&E fee. Most jurisdictions access *property taxes* as construction occurs; some also may increase the assessment on the land to reflect the increased value owing to development. Interim property taxes are calculated on the basis of the effective tax rate (i.e., legal tax rate times the assessed value as a percentage of market value) applied to the average value of land and construction in place at the time of assessment. In the example an effective tax rate of 1.5 percent is multiplied by 50 percent of the total land and construction (hard) costs. If the construction period had been 2 years, the effective rate would be applied against 25 percent of the total investment in the first year and 75 percent in the second year. *Insurance* costs are also generally calculated on the total cost of construction, expressed in terms of cost per $100 in value.

Leasing costs are incurred following the completion of construction and tenant occupancy of space leased (second year in the example). These costs are calculated as a percentage (5 percent) of the annual amount of effective rent (i.e., after any rental concessions) times the number of years in the lease. In the example, it is assumed that 60 percent of the space is leased for 3 years and 40 percent for 5 years. The calculation is:

Three-year leases	
92,000 sq ft × .6 × $20 × 3 × .05 =	$ 165,600
Five-year leases	
92,000 sq ft × .4 × $20 × 5 × .05 =	184,000
	$ 349,600

In the leveraged scenario, interim costs would also include one-time financing fees (points) on the construction (2 percent) and permanent (1 percent) loans. Interest is calculated on the basis of the average construction value in place each year of the construction period. During the first year this would be 50 percent ($5.0 million × 12 percent) and 100 percent during the second year ($10.0 million × 12 percent).

Other interim costs include *permits, legal fees,* and *miscellaneous costs,* such as escrow fees, title insurance, and appraisal. These are generally "lump sum" estimates.

Net Operating Income

The next step is to estimate the annual earnings that the proposed project will generate in a stabilized year of operations. These estimates should be based on information developed in the market analysis, adjusted to reflect near-term market demand and merchandising considerations (see Table 14-2).

Building revenue is based on the scheduled rent ($20 per square foot) times the net rentable area (92,000 square feet). *Parking revenue* is assumed at $25 per stall per month. A *vacancy factor* is then applied to account for the fact that the building will not be fully leased at all times. The vacancy factor will vary depending upon local market conditions, strength of tenants, and, of course, the risk perception of the developer or investor.

The rationale for a vacancy factor is based on the belief that there is a *natural vacancy rate* at which point real rental rates are not under pressure to change. Smith outlines five reasons for this:[3] (1) Time is required for landlords to search for tenants and tenants to search for rental space. (2) Time is required for landlords to make leasehold improvements. (3) New construction is "lumpy"; projects come on the

[3]Lawrence B. Smith, "Adjustment Mechanisms in Real Estate Markets," Salomon Brothers Bond Market Research – Real Estate, New York, June 1987.

Table14-2. Net Operating Income (NOI)

	Stabilized year	Lease-up year
Gross revenue		
Building (92000 sq ft @ $20)	$1,840,000	$1,840,000
Parking (350 stalls @ $25/mo)	105,000	105,000
Subtotal	1,945,000	1,945,000
Vacancy allowance (8%)	155,600	972,500
Effective gross revenue	1,789,400	972,500
Operating expense		
Property taxes (1.5%)	157,200	133,600
Insurance ($.50/$100)	41,600	35,400
Utilities (84,640 sq ft @ $1.40)	118,500	100,700
Repairs and maintenance (84,640 sq ft @ $1.60)	135,400	116,000
Property management (3.5%)	62,600	53,200
Subtotal	515,300	438,900
Net operating income (NOI)	1,274,100	533,600

market all at once, creating lease-up vacancies. (4) Returns may be maximized at less than full occupancy. (5) In soft markets, landlords may withhold space from the market to avoid having to enter into long-term leases at less than desired rents.

Vacancy allowances typically range from 5 to 15 percent; an 8 percent vacancy is assumed in the example. The vacancy factor is deducted from gross revenue to arrive at *effective gross revenue*.

Operating expenses are then considered, both fixed and variable. *Fixed operating expenses* are those that do not vary with occupancy, such as property taxes and insurance. These are calculated as a percentage of the total investment as outlined in the discussion of interim costs. *Variable operating expenses* vary to some degree with the occupancy of the building. Utilities and repairs and maintenance are calculated on the basis of unit costs times the amount of rented square footage (84,640 square feet). Property management is calculated as a percentage of effective gross revenue (3.5 percent). All or a portion of operating expenses may be reimbursed or paid directly by the tenants, depending upon the terms of the lease. In the case of industrial and hotel properties, expenses are typically paid directly by the tenant or operator. In the case of shopping centers, they are paid by the landlord but reimbursed by the tenants.[4] Apartment landlords generally absorb all operating expenses except utilities, provided they are separately metered.

Most office building leases contain a provision establishing a maximum level of operating expenses to be paid by the landlord after the first year of the lease. Expenses beyond this level are reimbursed by the tenant. This *expense stop* varies depending on market conditions; it will be greater in soft markets, when tenants can negotiate more favorable terms. In the simple return analysis example, no tenant reimbursement is assumed since the landlord absorbs all of the operating expense in the stabilized year of operations.

With the stabilized year calculated, it is now possible to determine NOI during the lease-up year. Vacancy is estimated to be 50 percent, with operating expenses 85 percent of the stabilized year, reflecting the "fixed" nature of most operating costs, even those considered variable.

Capital Structure

Certain assumptions about the capital structure of the project must now be made (see Table 14-3). Operating earnings during the leasing period

[4]Leases in which the tenant pays or reimburses for operating expenses are called *net leases*. In a *triple net lease* (net-net-net) the tenant is responsible for all operating costs.

Table 14-3. Capital Structure

	Developer	Investor**
Unleveraged		
Total investment	$11,539,400	15,000,000
Sources of capital		
Lease-up NOI	533,600	
Equity	11,005,800	15,000,000
Leveraged		
Total investment	13,639,400	15,000,000
Sources of capital		
Lease-up NOI	533,600	
Mortgage*	10,000,000	10,000,000
Equity	3,105,800	5,000,000

*30 years @ 10%; due in 10 years; 10.53 constant.
**Purchased @ 8.5% capitalization rate.

are considered in both the unleveraged and leveraged situation. The next step is to estimate how much can be borrowed against the property. This requires a rough appraisal, along the lines discussed in the Appendix. A percentage of this value should be taken to represent the potential loan that might be obtained ($10 million in the example). The percentage utilized will depend on the type of financial institution, the legal loan requirements under which the institution operates, the strength of the project, the credit strength of any known tenants, and the overall strength of the developer. Generally, this percentage will range between 60 and 100 percent of total investment (73.3 percent in the example).

The amount of loan anticipated should then be cross-checked in terms of other tests, such as the amount of loan per unit, loan per square foot, and most important, the coverage of annual debt service by net operating income, called the *coverage ratio* (1.2 in the example). It's wise to work with two or three possible loan alternatives: best possible, most likely, and worst possible. This gives a range of possibilities for analytical purposes. Any secondary financing should also be considered at this time. By deducting the amount of the anticipated loan(s) and leasing year NOI from the total investment, the amount of equity investment can be determined ($3.1 million in the example).

Table 14-3 also analyzes on a preliminary basis the capital structure that an investor would have if he or she were to purchase the building upon completion and lease-up. A capitalization rate of 8.5 percent is assumed in the example, divided into the net operating income for the first stabilized year of operations. The $10 million loan would then reflect approximately 67 percent of the purchase price, requiring the investor to come up with $5 million in equity funds.

Return Calculation

At this point, the simple return on investment can be calculated (see Table 14-4). If the project is unleveraged, the free and clear return can be determined by dividing NOI by the amount of total investment (11.6 percent in the example). If leveraged, the annual debt service (principal and interest) is deducted from project earnings to arrive at the annual spendable ($221,100). The amount of net spendable then is divided by the amount of equity capital required ($3.1 million), with the quotient (cash-on-cash return) expressed as a percentage (7.1 percent).

Another variation of the simple return is to divide the NOI or net spendable into the amount of total or equity investment to establish the number of years it will take to pay back the investment (*payback method*).

The return to a potential investor can also be calculated, based on the capital structure outlined in Table 14-3. Note that both the developer and investor experience negative leverage, for the reasons discussed in Chapter 13. Note also that the developer "rides the risk curve" with a risk spread of approximately 310 basis points on the unleveraged position. This "value enhancement" is worth approximately $4.0 million in potential development profit.

Table 14-4. Simple Return Calculation

	Developer	Investor	Developer profit
Unleveraged			
Net operating income (NOI)	$ 1,274,100	$ 1,274,100	
Equity investment	$11,005,800	$15,000,000	$3,994,200
Free and clear return (capitalization rate)	11.6%	8.5%	310 basis points
Leveraged			
Net operating income (NOI)	$ 1,274,100	$ 1,274,100	
Debt service	1,053,000	1,053,000	
Net spendable	221,100	221,100	
Equity investment	3,105,800	5,000,000	$1,894,200
Net spendable return (cash on cash)	7.1%	4.4%	270 basis points

Problems with the Simple Approach

While the simple approach is commonly utilized by real estate practitioners, it suffers from several major shortcomings. By utilizing an early year of operations, the approach doesn't consider the effects of varying flows in future years, including possible inflation and real appreciation. Since it does not consider free rent or other tenant concessions, the simple approach tends to overstate property values in soft markets. It also does not consider capital expenses as leases turn, such as leasing commissions and tenant improvements. Nor does it take into consideration the tax aspects of the project. Perhaps the most fundamental problem, however, is that it projects current returns infinitely into the future, ignoring the time value of money. For these reasons, the net spendable and other simple approaches may lead to the wrong decision and should be utilized only for preliminary tests of feasibility.

Discounted Cash Flow Analysis

Most of the problems associated with the simple return approach can be overcome by the use of *discounted cash flow analysis (DCF)*. The cash flow associated with a property includes the cost of proceeding with the project (investment), the annual cash flows during the holding period, and the proceeds from the sale of the project at the end of the holding period (usually 10 years). The cash flow from each year is then discounted to reflect the present worth of the annual flows. The discounted flows may be compared to a *predetermined minimum* investment standard (target rate, hurdle rate, etc.) in which a positive *net present value* (NPV) indicates an acceptable investment. More commonly, discounted flows are translated into an *internal rate of return* (IRR) which is then compared to a minimum percentage standard.

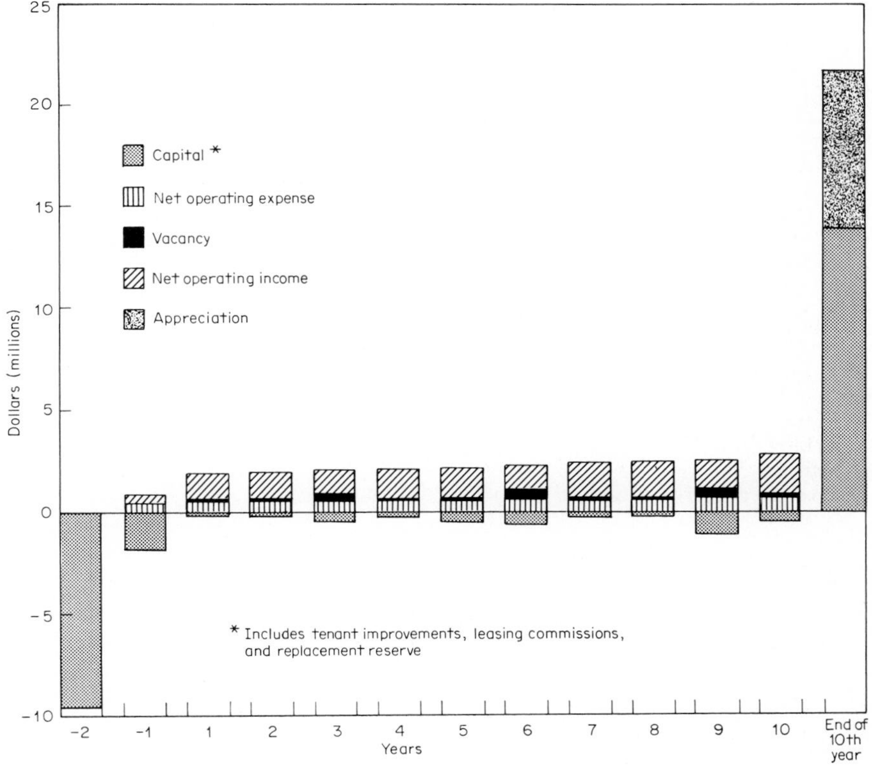

Figure 14-2. Investment cycle cash flow (unleveraged).

In order to demonstrate the discounted cash flow approach, the two-story, 100,000-square-foot suburban office building project utilized for the simple return analysis is broadened to incorporate the necessary additional assumptions. Table 14-5 summarizes these assumptions, which are linked directly to each of the following tables in order to facilitate changes in assumptions and, if desired, sensitivity analysis. Formulas are explained as they are introduced utilizing the substitutions outlined in Figure 14-3.[5] Years 1 and 2 are designated (− 2) and (− 1) so that the stabilized year becomes the first year (+ 1) of the 10-year holding period. The property is sold at the end of the tenth year, based on the eleventh year NOI. The analysis is on a pretax basis.[6]

[5]The formulas are designed for use with Lotus 1-2-3 or a similar spread sheet analytical program. Years are shown as subscripts.

[6]The impact of taxation on investment return will vary depending upon the investment vehicle utilized and the overall tax situation of individual investors. As noted in Chapter 13, most tax advantages of real estate were eliminated in the Tax Reform Act of 1986.

Table 14-5. DCF Assumptions

Space	
Land	217,800 sq ft
Building	
Gross	100,000 sq ft
Net	92,000 sq ft
Parking	350 stalls
Unit costs	
Land	$10.00 per sq ft
Site development	$1.00
Building	
Shell	$60.00 per sq ft
Finish	$17.00 per sq ft
Parking	$1,200 per stall
A&E fee	3.0%
Developer overhead fee	3.0%
Refurbish	
Stay	$4.00 per sq ft
Leave	$9.00 per sq ft
Operating expense	
Utilities	$1.40
Repairs and maint.	$1.60
Property management	3.5%
Replacement reserve	1.0%
Finance	
Construction	
Amount	$10,000,000
Term	2 years

Table 14-5. DCF Assumptions (*Continued*)

Finance (cont.)	
Construction (cont.)	
Rate	12.0%
Points	2.0%
Permanent	
Amount	$10,000,000
Term	15 years
Amortization	30 years
Rate	10.0%
Points	1.0%
Constant	10.53%
Balance @ 10 years	90.9%
Leasing (% rentable sq ft)	
Tenant mix	
Three	60.0%
Five	40.0%
Stay	
Three	60.0%
Five	75.0%
Leave	
Three	40.0%
Five	25.0%
Vacancy alowance	
Frictional vacancy	5 months
Free rent	
Leaving	3 months
Staying	1 month
Tenant default	1.0% building revenue
Rent	
Market building rent	$20.00 per sq ft
Market parking rent	$25.00 per stall
Leasing commission	5.0% building rent
Sale	
Stabilized cap rate	8.5% NOI_{I}
Disposition cap rate	8.5% NOI_{II}
Sales expense	3.5% sales price
Stabilized year	+1
Holding period	10 years
Inflation rate	5.0%
Convention	End of year

Space Analysis

The first step in the DCF analysis is to establish the amount of space that will be leased in each period (see Table 14-6), distinguishing between 3- and 5-year leases.

Figure 14-3. Abbreviations Used in Formulas

DCAP	Disposition capitalization rate
FL	Cost to refurbish leaving tenant space
FRTL	Free rent for leaving tenants
FRTS	Free rent for staying tenants
FS	Cost to refurbish staying tenant space
FV	Frictional vacancy
GR	Gross revenue
GRA	Gross building area
GRTL	Gross revenue from leaving tenants
GRTS	Gross revenue from staying tenants
LCOM	Leasing commission ($)
LCOMF	Leasing commission (%)
LTR	Tenant reimbursement by leaving tenants
MBR	Market building rent
MFL	Market refurbishment for leaving tenants (sq ft)
MFS	Market refurbishment for staying tenants (sq ft)
MPR	Market parking revenue
NOI	Net operating income
NRA	Net rentable area
PR	Parking revenue
RR	Replacement reserve (%)
S	Space occupied by tenants
SCAP	Stabilized capitalization rate
SE	Sales expense (%)
SL	Space occupied by leaving tenants
SP	Sales proceeds
SS	Space occupied by staying tenants
STR	Tenant reimbursement by staying tenants
T	Percentage of space leased

(Continued)

Figure 14-3. *(Continued)*

TD	Tenant default allowance
TL	Percentage of space occupied by leaving tenants
TOE	Total operating expense per square foot
TR	Tenant reimbursement
TS	Percentage of space occupied by staying tenant
TV	Termination value
Y	Lease term (years)

Note: Years are denoted by subscript numbers.

Three-year leases	Five-year leases
$NRA \times T_3 = S_3$	$NRA \times T_5 = S_5$
92,000 sq ft × .6 = 55,200 sq ft	92,000 sq ft × .4 = 36,800 sq ft

In the lease-up year, these formulas are factored by an occupancy rate of .5 (50 percent). For the years involving lease turns, the total amount of rentable space is multiplied by lease mix and the percentage of tenants staying (TS) or leaving (TL).

Three-year lease	Five-year lease
Tenants staying	
$NRA \times T_3 \times TS_3 = SS_3$	$NRA \times T_5 \times TS_5 = SS_5$
92,000 sq ft × .6 × .6 = 33,120 sq ft	92,000 sq ft × .4 × .75 = 27,600 sq ft

Three-year lease	Five-year lease
Tenants leaving	
$NRA \times T_3 \times TL_3 = SL_3$	$NRA \times T_5 \times TL_5 = SL_5$
92,000 sq ft × .6 × .4 = 22,080 sq ft	92,000 sq ft × .4 × .25 = 9,200 sq ft

If actual leases are in place at the time of the analysis, the terms of the leases should be substituted with appropriate staying and leaving assumptions.

Net Operating Income

The next step is to estimate NOI for each of the projected years, as outlined in Table 14-7.

Market Rent. As noted in the simple return analysis, market building rent (MBR) is forecast for the stabilized year at $20.00 per square foot. It is assumed that this rent level is the same in the leasing year. From the stabilized year forward, it is assumed that market rent increases at a 5 percent annual inflation rate.

$$\text{MBR} \times 1.05$$

Parking rent (MPR) was developed in a similar fashion.

$$\text{MPR} \times 1.05$$

Gross Revenue. The gross revenue (GR) of most mixed tenancy office buildings tends to move in a "stepped" fashion—steady flows for 2 or 3 years followed by increases (decreases) as leases turn.[7] In all years except the lease-up year and turning years, the formula is (for example, year 4):

Three-year lease	Five-year lease
$S_4\ 4 \times MBR_3 = GR_4$	$S_{5,4} \times MBR_1 = GR_4$
55,200 sq ft × $22.05 = $1,217,160	36,800 sq ft × $20.00 = $736,000

Note that the market rent is the base year of the lease, not the current year.

In turning years, the model should reflect the fact that building space will turn in a manner consistent with the original lease-up pattern in which the average lease begins at mid-year. This is accomplished in the case of staying tenants by assuming that one-half of the revenue in the

[7]Unless, of course, the leases are subject to an annual inflation adjustment.

Table 14-6. Space Analysis (square feet)

Activity	Construction	Leasing	Operations										Sale
Year	− 2	− 1	1	2	3	4	5	6	7	8	9	10	11
Three-year leases S(3)													
Nonturning years			55,200	55,200		55,200	55,200		55,200	55,200		55,200	55,200
Lease-up year		27,600											
Turning years													
Stay					33,120			33,120			33,120		
Leave					22,080			22,080			22,080		
Five-year leases S(5)													
Nonturning years			36,800	36,800	36,800	36,800		36,800	36,800	36,800	36,800		36,800
Lease-up year		18,400											
Turning years													
Stay							27,600					27,600	
Leave							9,200					9,200	
Total space leased		46,000	92,000	92,000	92,000	92,000	92,000	92,000	92,000	92,000	92,000	92,000	92,000

Table 14-7. Net Operating Income ($)

Activity	Construction	Leasing	Operations										Sale
Year	– 2	– 1	1	2	3	4	5	6	7	8	9	10	11
Market rent ($/ft²):													
Building (MBR)		20.00	20.00	21.00	22.05	23.15	24.31	25.53	26.80	28.14	29.55	31.03	32.58
Parking (MPR)		25.00	25.00	26.25	27.56	28.94	30.39	31.91	33.50	35.18	36.94	38.78	40.72
Gross revenue (GR):													
Building													
Three-year		552,000	1,104,000	1,104,000		1,217,160	1,217,160		1,409,256	1,409,256		1,631,160	1,631,160
Stay					696,348			787,925			912,125		
Leave					464,232			525,283			608,083		
Five-year		368,000	736,000	736,000	736,000	736,000		894,608	894,608	894,608	894,608		1,141,904
Stay							611,478					763,692	
Leave							203,826					254,564	
Total building revenue		920,000	1,840,000	1,840,000	1,896,580	1,953,160	2,032,464	2,207,816	2,303,864	2,303,864	2,414,816	2,649,416	2,773,064
Parking		52,500	105,000	110,250	115,752	121,548	127,638	134,022	140,700	147,756	155,148	162,876	171,024
Total gross revenue		972,500	1,945,000	1,950,250	2,012,332	2,074,708	2,160,102	2,341,838	2,444,564	2,451,620	2,569,964	2,812,292	2,944,088
Vacancy allowance (V):													
Frictional vacancy (FV)					203,022		93,263	235,064			272,077	119,043	
Free rent (FR)													
Leaving tenants					121,716		55,913	140,926			163,116	71,369	
Staying tenants					40,410		18,563	70,181			54,155	23,695	
Tenant default (TD)			18,400	18,400	18,966	19,532	20,325	22,078	23,039	23,039	24,148	26,494	
Total			18,400	18,400	384,114	19,532	188,064	468,249	23,039	23,039	513,496	240,601	235,527*

Effective gross revenue (EGR)	972,500	1,926,600	1,931,850	1,628,218	2,055,176	1,972,038	1,873,589	2,421,525	2,428,581	2,056,468	2,571,691	2,708,561
Operating expense:												
Property taxes	133,600	157,200	165,060	173,313	181,979	191,078	200,631	210,663	221,196	232,256	243,869	256,062
Insurance	35,400	41,600	43,680	45,864	48,157	50,565	53,093	55,748	58,535	61,462	64,535	67,762
Utilities	100,700	118,500	124,425	130,646	137,179	144,037	151,239	158,801	166,741	175,078	183,832	193,024
Repairs and maintenance	116,000	135,400	142,170	149,279	156,742	164,580	172,809	181,449	190,521	200,047	210,050	220,552
Property management	53,200	62,600	67,615	56,988	71,931	69,021	65,576	84,753	85,000	71,976	90,009	94,800
Total	438,900	515,300	542,950	556,089	595,988	619,281	643,348	691,415	721,995	740,820	792,295	832,200
Total operating expense/sq ft (TOE)		5.60	5.90	6.04	6.48	6.73	6.99	7.52	7.85	8.05	8.61	9.05
Tenant reimbursement (TR):												
Three-year												
Stay			16,560	7,286	24,288	38,088	15,732	29,256	47,472	17,554	30,912	24,288
Leave				4,858			10,488			11,702		
Five-year												
Stay			11,040	16,192	32,384	15,594	9,568	29,072	41,216	48,576	25,944	16,192
Leave						5,198					8,648	
Total			27,600	28,336	56,672	58,880	35,788	58,328	88,688	77,832	65,504	40,480
Net operating expense (NOE)	438,900	515,300	515,350	527,753	539,316	560,401	607,560	633,087	633,307	662,988	726,791	791,720
Net operating income (NOI)	533,600	1,411,300	1,416,500	1,100,465	1,515,860	1,411,637	1,266,029	1,788,439	1,795,275	1,393,479	1,844,899	1,916,841

*8 percent of total gross revenue; used to calculate terminal value only.

turning year will be at the base year market rate and one-half will be at the prevailing rate for the turning year.

As an example, the formula for space occupied by 3-year tenants, turning for the second time in the sixth year, is:

Staying tenants	Leaving tenants
$(SS_6 \times MBR_3 \times .5)$ $+ (SS_6 \times MBR_8 \times .5)$ $= GRTS_6$	$(SL_6 \times MBR_3 \times .5)$ $+ (SL_6 \times MBR_6 \times .5)$ $= GRTL_6$
(33,120 sq ft × \$22.05 × .5) + (33,120 sq ft × \$25.53 × .5) = \$787,925	(22,080 sq ft × \$22.05 × .5) + (22,080 sq ft × \$25.53 × .5) = \$525,283

Gross revenue for 5-year leases is determined in a similar fashion, utilizing the appropriate tenant mix and staying and leaving assumptions.

Parking revenue is a product of the number of stalls (PA) times the monthly charge per stall (MPR), converted into an annual number. For example, in the third year:

$$PA_3 \times MPR_3 \times 12 = PR_3$$

$$350 \times \$27.56 \times 12 = \$115{,}752$$

Vacancy Allowance. Unfortunately, most buildings do not operate at full occupancy throughout the holding period and some allowance must be made for future vacancy. Simple return analysis utilizes an annual allowance (8 percent in the example) applied against scheduled gross revenue. With DCF analysis, it's possible to break out the three components of vacancy and match them with the time period when they occur.

Frictional Vacancy (FV). This vacancy occurs when a tenant moves out of the space at the expiration of a lease and is replaced by another tenant. The allowance is stated in terms of months and includes the time to find a new tenant and build out the space. The factor is applied to the amount of market rent that would be paid on a new lease. As an example, 3-year leases turning in the sixth year with 5-months frictional vacancy (.417) would be calculated as follows:

$$SL_6 \times MBR_6 \times .417 = FV_6$$

$$22{,}080 \text{ sq ft} \times \$25.53 \times .417 = \$235{,}064$$

The same formula would also apply to 5-year leases.

Free Rent. In addition to frictional vacancy, it may also be necessary to make free rent concessions to new tenants (FRTL) and, if in a particularly soft market, staying tenants as well (FRTS). This is also calculated in terms of months and is applied against the market rent for the

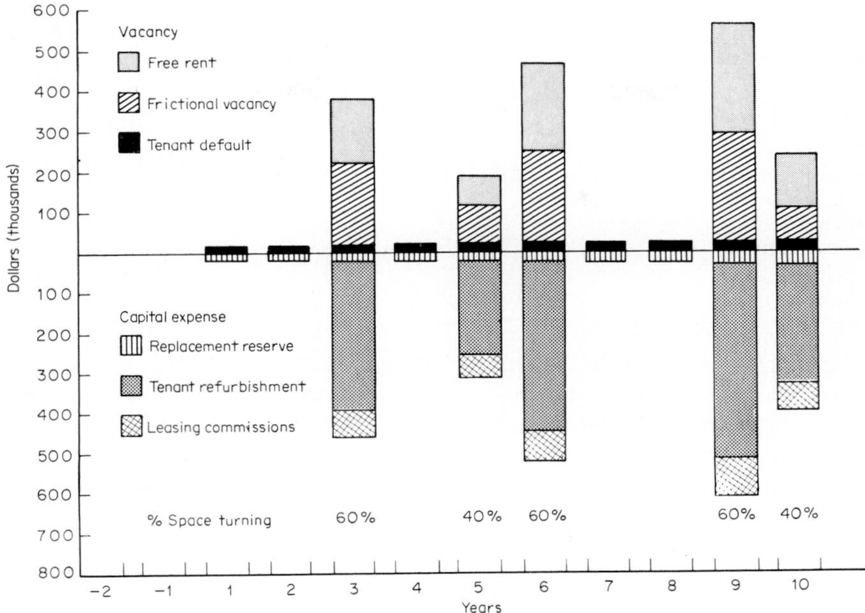

Figure 14-4. Impact of lease turnover (unleveraged).

new lease. The formula is similar to that used to determine frictional vacancy (year 6 example):

Leaving tenants (3 months free rent)	Staying tenants (1 month free rent)
$SL_6 \times MBR_6 \times .25 = FRTL_6$	$SS_6 \times MBR_6 \times .083 = FRTS_6$
22,080 sq ft × \$25.53 × .25 = \$140,926	33,120 sq ft × \$25.53 × .083 = \$70,181

The amount of rental concessions will vary, of course, with the overall softness or tightness of the market.

Tenant Default (TD). The final area of concern is the problem posed by tenants who default on leases as a result of bankruptcy, "kickout" clauses,[8] or other reasons to stop paying rent before the lease term expires. Since this phenomenon is not associated with a lease turn and furthermore is generally unpredictable, the only way to account for it is an annual percentage charge against gross building revenue which may vary depending upon the softness or tightness of local markets. This percentage will generally be approximately 1.0 percent. The formula is (sixth-year example):

[8]A clause found in retail leases which allows the tenant to get out of a lease if he or she doesn't reach certain volume levels or a competitor is allowed into the center.

$$GBR_6 \times .01 = TD_6$$

$$\$2,207,816 \times .01 = \$22,078$$

The total vacancy charge for the sixth year becomes:

Frictional vacancy	$235,064
Free rent:	
Leaving tenants	140,926
Staying tenants	70,181
Tenant default	22,078
Total	$468,249

Note that, in contrast to the simple analysis, parking vacancy is not included in calculating the allowance. This is because parking revenue is not always affected by building vacancy or, if it is, the magnitude is not sufficient to warrant separate treatment.

Total vacancy is then subtracted from scheduled gross revenue to arrive at effective gross revenue (EGR). Operating expenses must now be subtracted to arrive at NOI.

Operating Expenses. Operating expenses flow in a somewhat different fashion than revenue because expenses are subject to change each year and tenant reimbursement may vary, depending upon the terms of each lease. There also may be a lag effect caused by the billing of actual expenses in the year succeeding the one in which they were incurred.

Each operating expense is calculated in a manner similar to that discussed in the simple approach, distinguishing between fixed and variable costs. Operating expenses for the lease-up period are assumed to be 85 percent of the expenses in the stabilized year. Expenses after the stabilized year are adjusted by the inflation rate. A different inflation rate may be utilized for expenses than for revenue or, in some cases, between individual expense items, depending upon the characteristics and customs of the marketplace. Once a total for each year has been computed, it is divided by the amount of rentable square feet to arrive at the operating expense per square foot. This will be helpful in calculating tenant reimbursements.

Today, many property managers bill tenants on the basis of projected expenses, with an adjustment made when actual expenses are known. This permits a simplifying assumption that expenses are reimbursed in the year in which they are incurred, with no lag effect.

This leaves the problem of the amount of tenant reimbursement (TR) and the year in which it flows. In nonturning years, this amount is determined by subtracting the total operating expense per rentable square foot (TOE) in the base year from the current year expense. For example, for five-year leases in the fourth year:

$$(TOE_4 - TOE_1) \times S_5 = TR_4$$

$$(\$6.48 - \$5.60) \times 36{,}800 \text{ sq ft} = \$32{,}384$$

In turning years, the formula is factored by .5 to reflect the fact that reimbursements would only flow from the last 6 months of expiring leases. Also, the first 6 months of operating expenses for new leases would not be reimbursable as the base increases to the prevailing market rate. As an example, in the fifth year, tenant reimbursement from space occupied by 5-year tenants would be:

Staying tenants	Leaving tenants
$(TOE_5 - TOE_1) \times SS_5 \times .5 = STR_5$	$(TOE_5 - TOE_1) \times SL_5 \times .5 = LTR_5$
($6.73 − $5.60) × 27,600 sq ft × .5 = $15,594	($6.73 − $5.60) × 9,200 sq ft × .5 = $5,198

Net operating expense is calculated by deducting the amount of tenant reimbursement in each year from the total operating expense. Net operating income is then determined by deducting net operating expense from effective gross revenue in the appropriate year.

Cash Flow

Table 14-8 transforms net operating income into cash flow projections over the holding period by considering capital expenses and the proceeds from the sale of the asset at the end of the holding period. The level of total investment is based on Table 14-1, taking into consideration that tenant finish and leasing commissions occur in the second year of the development period.

Turning Costs. The first capital expense to consider is the cost of refurbishing the space as leases turn. For staying tenants, this generally involves, at a minimum, cleaning the carpet and drapes, and may include painting. For new tenants, it may be necessary to rebuild partitions as well.

The first step in calculating refurbishment costs is to estimate market costs per square foot of undertaking the required work, making a distinction between staying (MFS) and leaving (MFL) tenants. These estimates should then be inflated at the assumed inflation rate.

The amount of space turning is multiplied by the market refurbishment cost for the prevailing year. The example is for a 3-year lease with a ninth-year turn:

Table 14-8. Cash Flow ($)

Activity	Construction	Leasing	Operations										Sale
Year	−2	−1	1	2	3	4	5	6	7	8	9	10	11
Total investment*	9,625,800	1,913,600											
Net operating income (NOI)		533,600	1,411,300	1,416,500	1,100,465	1,515,860	1,411,637	1,266,029	1,788,439	1,795,275	1,393,479	1,844,899	1,916,841
Turning costs:													
Market refurbishment costs													
Stay (MFS)		4.00	4.00	4.20	4.41	4.63	4.86	5.11	5.36	5.63	5.91	6.21	
Leave (MFL)		9.00	9.00	9.45	9.92	10.42	10.94	11.49	12.06	12.66	13.30	13.96	
Tenant refurbishment costs:													
Stay (TRS)					146,059		134,136	169,243			195,739	171,396	
Leave (TRL)					219,034		100,648	253,699			293,664	128,432	
Total					365,093		234,784	422,942			489,403	299,828	
Leasing commissions (LCOM)					66,944		53,117	77,509			89,714	67,801	
Total					432,037		287,901	500,451			579,117	367,629	
Replacement reserve (RR)			19,450	19,503	20,123	20,747	21,601	23,418	24,446	24,516	25,700	28,123	
Sales proceeds (SP)												21,761,780	
Nominal cash flow	(9,625,800)	(1,380,000)	1,391,850	1,396,998	648,305	1,495,113	1,102,135	742,159	1,763,993	1,770,758	788,663	23,210,928	
Deflation factor	1.0000	1.0000	1.0000	1.0500	1.1025	1.1576	1.2155	1.2763	1.3401	1.4071	1.4775	1.5513	
Real cash flow	(9,625,800)	(1,380,000)	1,391,850	1,330,474	588,032	1,291,535	906,729	581,501	1,316,319	1,258,445	533,798	14,961,971	

*Tenant improvements and leasing commission are second-year costs.

Staying tenants	Leaving tenants
$SS_9 \times MFS_9 = FS_9$	$SL_9 \times MFL_9 = FL_9$
33,120 sq ft × \$5.91 = \$195,739	22,080 sq ft × \$13.30 = \$293,664

Leasing commissions (LCOM) are calculated on leaving space only. The custom in most markets is to apply the percentage commission (LCOMF) against the market building rent (MBR), multiplied by the lease term (Y), less any free rent concessions (FRTL). For example, space occupied by 3-year tenants, turning in the third year, would require leasing commissions as follows:

$$SL_3 \times MBR_3 \times Y) - FRTL_3 \times LCOMF = LCOM(22{,}080 \text{ sq ft} \times \$22.05 \times 3 \text{ years}) - \$121{,}716 \times .05 = \$66{,}944$$

In determining commissions on 5-year leases, 5 years would be substituted for 3 years in the above equation.

Total turning costs are the sum of tenant refurbishment costs and leasing commissions for each year.

Replacement Reserve. The replacement reserve is utilized to provide a reservoir of capital to handle the replacement of items too large to expense (e.g., elevators, roofs, HVAC systems, etc.).

There are many thoughts on how to handle replacement reserves. Perhaps the most rigorous approach is to calculate the anticipated life of each component and reserve sufficient annual funds to meet these obligations, assuming interest earned on the reserved funds. Clearly, once a property has been developed or acquired, this is the preferred approach.

In the early stages of the development process, however, it is sufficient to use a surrogate, such as a percentage of assets, or gross revenue. This discussion utilizes a factor of 1.0 percent of annual gross revenue.

Sale Proceeds. Having accounted for operating cash flows over the holding period, it is now necessary to establish a termination value for the asset. The most common approach is to utilize some capitalization of net operating income, reflecting the fact that this is the way in which investment properties are sold. While this approach mixes the simple return approach with discounted cash flow analysis, it seems to make sense in light of the universal use of the technique and the problems associated with a more sophisticated approach. Conceptually, the alternative would be to calculate the present value of the succeeding 10 years of holding, but, as the reader will quickly grasp, this is a circular process that would be unending.

In utilizing the capitalization approach, it is necessary to determine the year of NOI to capitalize and the appropriate capitalization rate. In most markets, properties are sold on a capitalization of the next year's pro forma earnings (eleventh year in the example), and this is the approach utilized. Using Table 14.7, a summarized sales pro forma for the eleventh year would be:

Gross revenue	$2,944,088
Vacancy allowance (8.0 percent)	235,527
Effective gross revenue	2,708,561
Net operating expense	791,720
Net operating income	1,916,841

Note that the vacancy allowance has been adjusted to reflect the simple return approach.

There is considerable controversy as to what capitalization rate to use. One body of thought maintains that the disposition capitalization rate (DCAP) should be lower than the stabilized capitalization rate (SCAP) in order to reflect the market appreciation of a mature property. Another school suggests raising the capitalization rate to reflect functional obsolescence.

Clearly, lowering the capitalization rate builds in a distortion of investment return and would not be appropriate. In utilizing a higher cap rate, however, the analyst is faced with the magnitude of the adjustment—to what extent would the market discount a property for technical obsolescence? In light of this dilemma, the preferable approach is to utilize the market capitalization rate prevailing in the stabilized year and assume that similar market conditions will prevail in the year of termination.[9] This approach, at least, neutralizes the impact of the sale cap rate assumption.

There is also the matter of sales costs such as sales commission, promotional brochure, advertising, seller's closing costs, etc. (SE). In our example these costs are assumed to total 3.5 percent of the sales price.

The formula to establish the amount of sales proceeds (SP) therefore becomes:

[9] Note that it is the "market" cap rate that is important, not the purchase price cap rate, which could vary considerably from market.

$$NOI_{11}/DCAP \times (1.00 - SE) = SP$$

$$\$1{,}916{,}841/.085 \times (1.00 - .035) = \$21{,}761{,}780$$

The various flows in Table 14-8 are then summed by year to arrive at nominal cash flow.

Real Cash Flow. Nominal cash flows are deflated at this point in order to eliminate any distortion brought about by the inflation assumption. This also allows comparison of results between time periods.

The reader might ask "Why use an inflation assumption at all?—Simply work with real numbers throughout." The problem is that this does not reflect the different ways in which inflation affects independent variables in the management of a real property. The most extreme example is the leveraged case in which debt service payments continue in fixed terms while rental income, adjusted for inflation, is reported in nominal terms.

But there are also varying impacts in the nonleveraged case. Rents may increase at a different rate than operating costs. Tenant refurbishment costs may increase (decrease) at a different rate than rents (and leasing commissions based on rents). Tenant reimbursement is based on a comparison with a base year in which costs could be substantially different (i.e., long-term lease). The solution, therefore, is to utilize an inflation assumption in developing the cash flow, but then to deflate the nominal cash flow to real terms.

Leveraged Analysis

Table 14-9 explores the impact of leveraging the example property. Interest and points on the construction loan are developed in the same manner as in the simple return analysis (Table 14-1). Debt service and loan payoffs on the permanent loan are calculated by use of an annual constant (10.53X) and loan balance factor (.909) taken from standard payment tables or through the use of a hand calculator, which are multiplied times the original amount of the mortgage. The cost of leveraging is then netted out in each year against the nonleveraged cash flow to arrive at the nominal leveraged cash flow. This is then deflated to produce the real leveraged cash flow.

Investor Analysis

Thus far we have been analyzing the position of the developer who retains ownership of the property throughout the holding period. Table

Table 14-9. Leveraged Analysis ($)

Activity	Construction	Leasing	Operations									
Year	−2	−1	1	2	3	4	5	6	7	8	9	10
Nonleveraged cash flow	($9,625,800)	($1,380,000)	$1,391,850	$1,396,998	$648,305	$1,495,113	$1,102,135	$742,159	$1,763,993	$1,770,758	$788,663	$23,210,928
Mortgage (MTG)	10,000,000											
Construction												
Points (PT)	200,000											
Interest (IC)	600,000	1,200,000										
Permanent												
Points (PT)	100,000											
Debt service			1,053,000	1,053,000	1,053,000	1,053,000	1,053,000	1,053,000	1,053,000	1,053,000	1,053,000	1,053,000
Payoff												9,090,000
Nominal leveraged cash flow	(525,800)	(2,580,000)	338,850	343,998	(404,695)	442,113	49,135	(310,841)	710,993	717,758	(264,337)	13,067,928
Deflation factor	1.0000	1.0000	1.0000	1.0500	1.1025	1.1576	1.2155	1.2763	1.3401	1.4071	1.4775	1.5513
Real leveraged cash flow	(525,800)	(2,580,000)	338,850	327,617	(367,070)	381,914	40,423	(243,552)	530,554	510,098	(178,914)	8,423,703

Table 14-10. Investor Analysis ($)

Activity	Construction	Leasing	Operations									
Year	−2	−1	1	2	3	4	5	6	7	8	9	10
Nonleveraged cash flow												
Nominal		(15,000,000)	1,391,850	1,396,998	648,305	1,495,113	1,102,135	742,159	1,763,993	1,770,758	788,663	23,210,928
Real		(15,000,000)	1,391,850	1,330,474	588,032	1,291,535	906,729	581,501	1,316,319	1,258,445	533,798	14,961,971
Leveraged cash flow												
Nominal		(5,000,000)	338,850	343,998	(404,695)	442,113	49,135	(310,841)	710,993	717,758	(264,337)	13,067,928
Real		(5,000,000)	338,850	327,617	(367,070)	381,914	40,423	(243,552)	530,554	510,098	(178,914)	8,423,703
Deflation factor		1.0000	1.0000	1.0500	1.1025	1.1576	1.2155	1.2763	1.3401	1.4071	1.4775	1.5513

14-10 looks at the situation of the investor who acquires the property at the end of the leasing year, based on a 8.5 percent capitalization rate of net operating income in the stabilized year of operations (year 1). All other assumptions through the holding period are the same as in the developer case.

Internal Rate of Return

A commonly used method of calculating DCF return is the *yield* or *internal rate of return* (IRR) method, in which flows from each year are compared to the equity investment in terms of an annual yield. Table 14-11 summarizes nominal and real IRRs to both the developer and the investor, on a leveraged and nonleveraged basis. Note that the risk spread between the developer and investor is more accurately reflected than with the simple approach. Also, when flows over time are considered, leverage is positive to both the developer and the investor, rather than negative as indicated in the simple return analysis.

Figure 14-5 illustrates graphically the IRR for both the developer and the investor. Note that a significant portion of the developer's return comes from the 2-year development period rather than the 10 years of operations. This helps to explain why developers often sell their projects upon completion rather than holding them as long-term investments, giving rise to the trend toward merchant building discussed in Chapter 3.

"Unbundling" Investment Returns

Table 14-12 "unbundles" the IRR calculation to determine the source of the return. This is accomplished by discounting the cash flow and eleventh-year sale proceeds by the IRR for the developer and investor. The percentage from each source is then established and multiplied by the total IRR. Note that the investor is more dependent upon appreciation than the developer.

Other unbundling variations are possible. As an example, the cash flow could be broken down by leases in place during the stabilized year versus those signed later. This gives some indication as to the risk inherent in lease turns. If the tenant mix is known, the cash flow could be unbundled by national versus local credits, providing some measure of default exposure. In mixed-use projects, the cash flow could be unbundled by major land use to see which land use is most critical in producing the investment return.

If debt is utilized, unbundling could establish how much of the return

Table 14-11. Internal Rate of Return (IRR)

	Developer	Investor	Risk spread
Nominal returns			
Nonleveraged	14.0%	11.0%	300 basis points
Leveraged	18.3%	12.4%	590
Real returns			
Nonleveraged	9.8%	6.4%	340
Leveraged	13.4%	7.6%	580

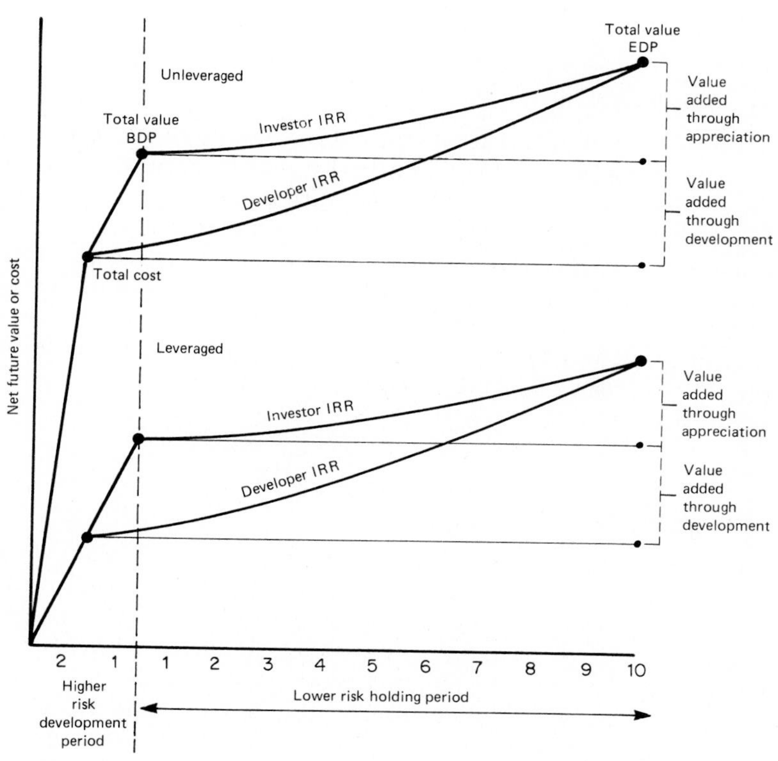

Figure 14-5. Developer and investor IRR.

Table 14-12. Unbundling of Real Return

	Developer			Investor		
	NPV @ 9.8%	%	IRR (%)	NPV @ 6.4%	%	IRR (%)
Cash flow	$5,898,821	73.2	7.2	$ 7,603,965	69.4	4.4
Appreciation	2,159,159	26.8	2.6	3,350,848	30.6	2.0
Total	8,057,979	100.0	9.8	10,954,813	100.0	6.4

is from leverage. For the taxable investor, unbundling could determine the portion of the return that is from tax subsidy as opposed to the intrinsic economics of the project.

Sensitivity Analysis

Another useful tool in analyzing proposed development projects and investments is sensitivity analysis. Sensitivity is calculated in terms of percentage change in IRR as compared with percentage change in the independent variable. Variables whose change produces a greater change in investment return are said to be sensitive; those producing less of a change are considered less sensitive. As an example, a 10 percent increase in market rent which produces a 15.0 percent increase in IRR is highly sensitive. A 10.0 percent increase in land cost which produces a 2.0 percent decrease in IRR is considerably less sensitive.

Probability Theorem

The degree of risk in a project can be considered through the use of probability theorem. An overall probability rate can be ascribed to the cash flow for each year to arrive at an adjusted cash flow. This flow is then discounted, in the manner previously outlined, to arrive at the *risk-adjusted rate of return*. The major concern with this approach is the manner in which the probabilities are established. Generally, it should only be utilized when the person(s) developing the probability rates has extensive experience in the type of project envisioned and familiarity with the probability theorem process.

Problems with IRR Analysis

There has been considerable discussion about the problems of utilizing IRR in discounted cash flow analysis.[10] One problem is that the IRR calculation assumes that profit not recovered as cash before maturity is reinvested and earns at the same rate as the IRR. Another problem is that alternating negative and positive flows after the investment year can result in multiple IRRs.

Several approaches have been suggested to resolve these problems. The *modified internal rate of return* discounts all negative cash flow back to the investment year and positive cash flows forward to the termination year.[11] The *adjusted rate of return* approach offsets negative and positive flows, discounting the net result.[12] The *financial management rate of return* discounts cash flows at a weighted average of the IRR consisting of a "safe" rate and a "reinvestment" rate.[13]

Unfortunately, each of these approaches has its own set of technical problems[14] which, when combined with the added complexity of the calculations, raise a serious question as to their usefulness. There is also some evidence that the impact of reinvestment assumptions has much less significance in reality than in theory.[15]

Rather than attempt to modify the IRR analysis, the most practical answer is to simply substitute the net present value approach in those situations where the reinvestment rates are unrealistic or where there are significant shifts in cash flow from positive to negative.

Application to Other Land Uses

This chapter has focused on analyzing investment returns from an office building. The same approach, with certain modifications, can be

[10]Paul E. Wendt and Alan R. Cerf, *Real Estate Investment Analysis and Taxation,* 2d ed., McGraw-Hill, New York, 1979, Chapter 3.

[11]James H. Lorie and Leonard J. Savage, "Three Problems in Rationing Capital," *Journal of Business*, October 1955.

[12]Donald J. Valachi, "More on the Arithmetic of Multiple and Imaginary Rates of Return," *Real Estate Appraiser and Analyst*, September-October 1980.

[13]Stephen D. Messner and M. Chapman Findlay II, "Real Estate Investment Analysis: IRR versus FMRR," *The Real Estate Appraiser,* vol. XXXXI, no. 4, July-August, 1976.

[14]Gaylon E. Greer and Michael D. Farrell, *Investment Analysis for Real Estate Decisions*, The Dryden Press, Chicago, 1983, Chapter 15.

[15]C. Conrad Doenges, "The Reinvestment Problem, Practical Perspective," *Financial Management,* Spring 1972.

utilized for other investment properties. Apartment buildings must be adjusted for the fact that operating costs are absorbed by the landlord; retail and industrial projects, for the fact that tenants generally pay all operating costs. Retail projects also should include revenue from percentage clauses, if such revenue is anticipated, and costs associated with common area maintenance (CAM). Hotel projects require the greatest adjustment, both in format and operation, to reflect the various sources of revenue and the characteristics of hotel operation.

In analyzing sale-oriented projects such as single-family housing, condos, second homes, and land development projects, it is best to utilize a model which allows for the complexity inherent in these types of projects. Here, the use of NPV is probably more useful than IRR and may prevent some of the problems discussed above.

A final note of caution: As with market analysis, sophisticated techniques in financial analysis are only as good as the accuracy of the numbers involved and the quality of the underlying assumptions. Too often, particularly when computers are involved, there is a tendency to view the output of the analysis as sacrosanct—possessed of some mystical quality in and of itself. It is critical for the developer or investor not to fall prey to this temptation. If the final result of the analysis doesn't make sense, go back over the inputs and assumptions again.

It should also be noted that the investment analysis is but one of the factors (albeit an important one) in the decision-making process. The results of the analysis must be weighed along with and against judgments as to economic conditions, market trends, political realities, and management skills and resources.

PART 5

Building, Marketing, and Managing the Project

15
Planning and Design

Sometimes, I think, the things we see
Are shades of the things to be;
That what we plan we build.

PHOEBE CARY

Although market analysis and successful financing are critical, real estate development is essentially a physical process—improving land and constructing buildings. However, before construction can take place, the building must be planned and designed so that it will efficiently accommodate the prospective uses, fit on the land parcel, and meet all legal requirements for the safety and welfare of the occupants and the community. This requires the talents of creative, trained professionals who, working as a team, will evaluate various alternatives and ultimately evolve a design solution that will be functional, economically sound, and aesthetically appropriate to its setting.

Unfortunately, in a preponderance of real estate projects, too little effort goes into the planning and design phase. Budgets are restricted; allocated time is too short; second-rate professionals are involved. At best, the result is a mediocre design which fails to realize the project's full potential; at worst, it is an unattractive and inefficient building which ultimately may threaten the economic success of the project. Therefore, the developer must thoroughly understand the planning and design process, evaluate and select the proper professional firms to undertake the effort, and orchestrate these firms so that they produce a satisfactory final project.

The Planning and Design Process

The physical process of planning and designing a real estate project can be divided into four major phases of activity: (1) land planning, (2) site planning, (3) preliminary design, and (4) contract documents for construction. It should be noted that these are rather broad categories, and the phases may overlap considerably. Also, the importance of any one phase may vary, depending on the size and nature of the project.

Land Planning

Land planning is the allocation of the subject site to various land uses.[1] A portion of the site will be set aside for residential, commercial, or industrial building development, based on the indicated market demand and preliminary tests of financial feasibility. Other portions of the site may be set aside for open space, active recreation such as parks and golf courses, and natural preserve areas such as forests, meadows, and mountain peaks. These land uses must be served by utility systems for water, power, and sewage and by a transportation system to link these uses to one another and to the outside world. The utility system may utilize sophisticated new technology for local sewage and water treatment or simply connect to established local systems. The transportation system may involve road (e.g., streets, highways, parking), rail, water, or pedestrian and bikeway systems or new technology such as people movers.

Several factors must be considered in the land-planning process. One is the carrying capacity of the site with respect to the natural ecosystem, which influences both the development of the site and the surrounding natural environment. As we noted in Chapter 2, the public is increasingly vigilant about protecting the natural environment. Important elements include geologic conditions, surface hydrology, soils, plants, wildlife, archeology, climate, sunlight, and the site's susceptibility to such natural calamities as earthquakes, floods, and hurricanes, as well as

[1] Land planning primarily applies to larger sites; smaller, single-use sites generally move directly into site planning.

other problems such as hazardous waste deposits, polluted ground water, and poor air quality.

From thorough analysis the land planner will find several factors of the site's relationship to natural features that may have an impact upon determining its suitability for development and how best to achieve the greatest economic benefit without environmental degradation. Generally, the land-planning process should emphasize providing the greatest exposure (views), accessibility to the positive natural features, and the protection of buildings on the site from the adverse consequences of negative factors such as landslides, tidal action, winter winds, and geologic failures. In urban environments, shadow and wind problems created by new buildings must be considered as well.

The topography of the site is also important: not only differences in elevation among various land formations to achieve views but also such factors as drainage, wind patterns, and gradient for vehicular and pedestrian movement must be considered. Natural features like cliff and rock outcroppings may be used to enhance the aesthetics of the site and reduce hazards to safety. Frequently there are topographical trade-offs. Steep terrain may provide excellent views but be more expensive and difficult to develop, thereby creating slide and erosion problems.[2] Flat land may reduce grading costs but increase sewage and storm drainage costs.

Soil conditions—the quality and nature of various soils found on the site—may affect the location of buildings, open space areas, and sewage and transportation systems. Soils also may influence water drainage patterns[3] as well as the location of underground utilities. If extensive grading is contemplated, the degree to which changes in soil patterns will affect the location and foundation requirements of building construction must be known.

Other factors also have to be considered: accessibility to major exogenous transportation systems, such as highways, rail lines, or waterways; the location and capacity of utility systems to handle water, electricity, waste disposal, and water runoff; proximity to institutional facilities, such as schools, parks, and government buildings; and proximity to private recreational facilities, such as golf courses, ski lifts, and marinas.

Many people participate in the land-planning process. The overall responsibility generally is in the hands of the land planner. There is no separate professional entity licensed to engage in land planning, nor

[2]Site development costs increase considerably when slopes exceed a 10 percent gradient. Very steep slopes in excess of 25 percent also reduce options in building layout.

[3]Gravel, sand, clay loam, or other porous soils generally provide the best drainage.

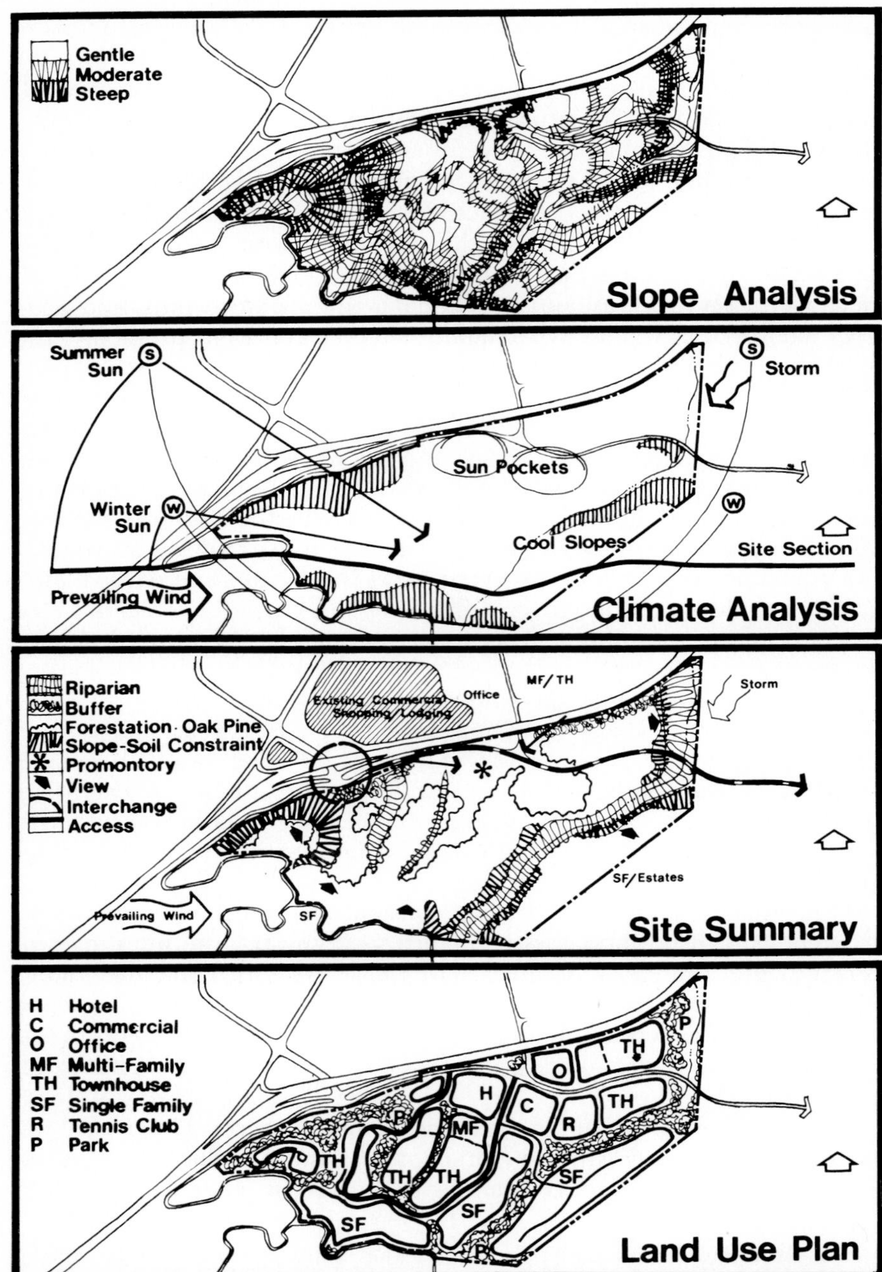

Figure 15-1. Evolution of land use plan.

does any one professional education concentrate on it as a specialized capability. Land planning requires a combination of skills, and the planner must be professionally equipped to deal with the land, the natural environment, socioeconomic data, physical planning, and design and construction, as well as be involved in such matters as zoning and marketing strategy and have the vision to recognize new opportunities.

The land planner may be an architect, a landscape architect, or a professional specializing exclusively in land planning. Several other disciplines may be involved in the team a land planner assembles. An ecologist may be involved to analyze the natural ecosystem of the site and the surrounding area in order to assess the impact of site development on this system. A geologist or soil engineer may be called in to analyze the nature and capacity of the soil, including any toxic waste problems from prior use of the site or adjoining areas. Traffic engineers help to develop the transportation system for the site. Civil engineers generally are responsible for laying out the utility systems, waste disposal, and flood control systems. Legal counsel may be required to interpret ordinances, variances, covenants, and other controls. With a thoroughly competent land planner leading a team of other professionals, the land-planning activity is a creative process which engages the developer and chosen specialists in market research, financial analysis, and project management. Ideas are proposed and tested against other alternatives until the best mix and fit is agreed upon.

The result is a land-development plan that indicates the location and magnitude of various land uses and a transportation and utility system to service these uses. If the site is large, the plan will identify the process for implementation by indicating the separate stages of a long-term development program which leads to a completed physical, social, and economic entity. The land use plan may be used to obtain public approval for zoning, for example, or commitments for public improvements. Usually, the plan is quite detailed in planning for the infrastructure and more generalized in dealing with building development. Specific areas are set aside for more detailed site planning as the development process proceeds.

Site Planning

Site planning is the detailed planning of a specific building site. This site may be part of a larger land plan, or—in more urban situations—involve a single parcel of land. If for a larger land plan, many parameters of building development will already have been established. When a single parcel of land is involved, it will usually be necessary to undertake special studies of foundation conditions, soil quality, utility availability, traffic circulation, zoning, and building code regulations before definitive site planning can proceed.

The major objective of site planning is to relate the specific building(s) to the characteristics of a given piece of property in the most aesthetic and economic manner possible. First, the specific indoor and outdoor space needs of the building(s) must be established so that a program of user relationships and requirements can be tabulated. This is to some degree influenced by the overall volume of the building(s). If the site planning is part of a broader land planning effort, the volume may have been established by the land plan and by public controls through ordinance, height limits, and so forth. Updated market studies may help to define site demand for each building use in terms of space and other features. If a single site is involved, market studies to establish the demand for one or more land uses on the site may be needed.

At this point, zoning must be considered, for it may not only limit the maximum volume of the building(s) on the site but also specify exactly what uses and densities are permitted. Zoning isn't market demand; however, it represents the desires of the community at one point in time and is a legal tool to enact public goals. Just because a site is zoned for a particular use doesn't necessarily mean that there's demand for that

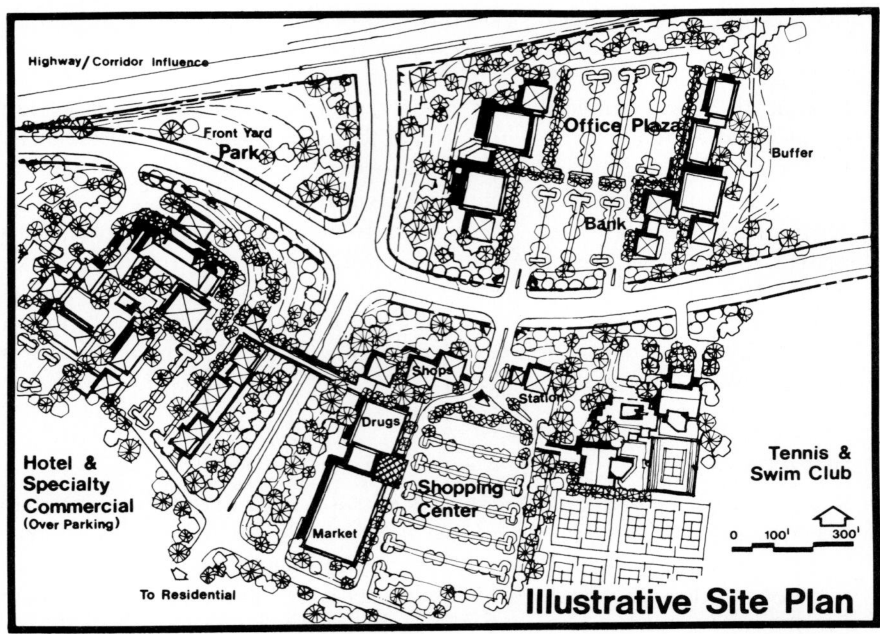

Figure 15-2. Illustrative site plan.

use. Therefore, zoning should be thought of as an opportunity or a constraint, not as a causative factor in successful development. The degree of constraint will depend upon the flexibility in securing variances. Some jurisdictions, particularly those which work extensively with PUD ordinances, basically "negotiate" with the developer to create a plan which is economically profitable and yet benefits the community.

The site planner may work with market demand estimates that are more refined than those used in land planning and also make more detailed analysis of zoning constraints to come up with a work program which indicates the building volumes that are economically and legally possible. This work program includes the necessary support facilities, such as parking, loading, and utility requirements. The next problem is how to physically fit the building volume and support facilities indicated in the work program to the subject site. There may be certain zoning constraints, such as building and floor area coverage ratios (FARs) setbacks, and open space maintenance areas that will affect the location of the building(s) on the site and the overall mass (e.g., high-rise versus low-rise, number of stories). Once these constraints have been established, the site planner has a legal "envelope" within which to design the building(s)[4] meeting the economic parameters established by the market research. Here, it's usually a good idea to make some preliminary assumptions about building design, materials, and construction techniques. It is at this point that the site planner who is not an architect would collaborate with one, so that they could compare various alternative approaches to construction in order to understand the various trade-offs involved.[5] Several alternative site plans and building forms would evolve in this search for the best solution.

The next step is to link the transportation and utility systems physically to the building envelope. In single-site projects, there may only be one choice: utility systems and vehicular access from a single street. However, larger projects may allow considerable flexibility in designing the transportation and utility support systems, and these factors should be weighed when establishing the location and magnitude of the building envelope.

The participants in the site-planning process are similar to those in the land-planning process, except that the planning and design of the building take on a more important role. An architect experienced in this phase of development may be the site planner and work closely with landscape architects and engineers. Both civil and structural engineer-

[4]This legal envelope shouldn't necessarily be accepted as final if there are legitimate reasons for variances.

[5]It also may be desirable to involve a contractor at this point.

ing become more important as the planning grows more definitive and detailed studies are required to estimate costs for and design major site work, utilities, and foundations. The traffic engineer is responsible for definitive parking and street design and may be required to make a detailed analysis of present and future traffic volumes and movement characteristics. The market analyst may continue to work with the site planner to react to ideas and problems during the site-planning process in order to maintain a continuous input of economic concerns.

The output of the site-planning process is a definitive site plan within which a building can be designed and built. It shows the location of all buildings, roads, and utilities and includes a specific building envelope, which has been established to meet legal and economic criteria. This preliminary evaluation has been made to ensure that the building(s) can be designed and built successfully within this envelope and the required transportation and utility support systems. Any piece of the development project can now proceed to preliminary design.

Preliminary Design

The purpose of the preliminary design phase is to design a building within the building envelope which was established in the site-planning phase.[6] Ideally, preliminary design will develop the building volume that was established in the work program in the most aesthetic and economical way possible. In reality, extensive trade-offs often occur between aesthetics and economics which must be resolved during the design process.[7] It may even be necessary to modify the work program and/or site plan to accommodate desirable building design objectives. In recent years, there has been a growing trend toward designing "smart" buildings with automated HVAC, lighting, communications and other systems, usually controlled from a central location.

At this point there should definitely be an architect taking major responsibility for the professional input to the project. The architect could possibly have been involved from the beginning or chosen at this stage because of particular experience with a certain building type or general

[6]The line between site planning and preliminary design is very fine. In most projects the phases proceed and interact simultaneously as the development proposal becomes more specific.

[7]Unfortunately, these trade-offs may be exaggerated by both developers ("good design always costs more") and architects ("cheap materials have to look cheap"). It's best to have an open mind and resolve honest trade-offs by means of a thorough analysis of the project and the objectives of the parties involved.

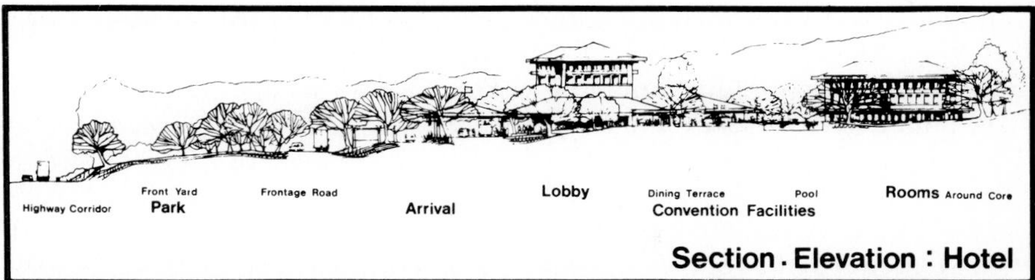

Figure 15-3. Preliminary design.

professional competence as a designer concerned for the objectives of the client. The architect's mechanical and electrical engineering consultants should also be involved at this point.

The architect's team starts by developing several schematic alternative building solutions in terms of space planning, structural systems, and mass within the allowable building envelope. These schematic designs will attempt to relate the various alternatives to the previously determined site plan and search for the appropriate aesthetic expression that fits the site and building type. It is at this stage that commitments determine what the place and the particular buildings will be like as a setting for effective use and quality environment. In an urban site, various design factors must be considered: view amenity, sun and wind conditions, building "mass" relationships to surrounding existing buildings and land uses, pedestrian movement patterns, and relationship to public transportation, as well as other factors relating the proposed building(s) to the immediate physical and social environment.

When one or more schematic designs appear desirable, the architect begins laying out building areas in an attempt to relate each alternative to very specific requirements of the work program. In most situations, the architect will find by testing the schematic designs against use relationships in the work program, the structural system, site-plan constraints, aesthetic expression, flexibility, and other objectives that all the requirements cannot be met. In this case, the architect may recommend modifications to the program. The developer must then weigh these proposed modifications in light of the advantages of the design alternative. If the proposed design will, in fact, improve the project economically (e.g., higher rental/sales levels, higher occupancy, lower maintenance costs), it may be a good idea to make modifications.

Ultimately, the architect narrows the choice of alternative schematic designs to one or more that conform to the requirements of the work program and meet legal, functional, and aesthetic objectives. The testing and retesting of those design alternatives will finally result in one or two design schemes which meet the work program criteria (modified, if necessary) and successfully function within the overall site and land plans.

A financial feasibility check and sensitivity analysis are wise at this point to determine whether any particular schemes are more desirable than others. The process is similar to that described in Chapter 14. Any assumptions that, if modified, could have a major impact on ROI should be looked at particularly carefully. For instance, one scheme may call for a building material that is in short supply at the time of construction—thereby raising construction costs beyond economic limits.

At this point the developer must select the scheme that best meets overall objectives. The architect then develops that design in greater detail so that all aspects of the building are investigated, including preliminary decisions on the structural and construction system, the mechanical system, materials, and equipment. All floor plans, elevations, and representative cross sections of the building are developed and shown in scaled drawings so that preliminary cost estimates can be made.

It may also be desirable during the preliminary design phase to retest some of the market demand assumptions. For example, a particular design alternative may suggest a more expensive product that will require higher sales or rental levels. Or an entirely new product concept may be introduced which wasn't contemplated when the original market research was undertaken. If additional market research is needed, the market information to be sought should be defined as narrowly as possible. It also may help to test-market specific design alternatives that are being considered.[8] At this point the developer must weigh the incremental attractiveness of the design modifications against the additional costs and time involved.

The key participant in the schematic and preliminary design process is the architect, who is supported by the original site planning team—particularly the structural and civil engineers and the landscape architect. Input from specialized consultants (e.g., interior designers, lighting specialists, acoustic experts, life safety consultants) may be required, depending upon the nature of the project and the specific problems involved. Advice from a contractor or other person currently involved in building the particular type of building proposed is also useful—especially when escalating construction costs can quickly invalidate an otherwise highly desirable design concept.

[8]This can be accomplished through consumer interviewing of potential users—or, more economically, through a consumer panel which reviews various design concepts and comments on their advantages and disadvantages.

The output of the preliminary design phase is one or more building designs that meet market, financial, and physical requirements. The designs should be illustrated graphically in two-dimensional (plan and elevation drawings) and three-dimensional (sketches) forms. A scale model of the project may help to visualize various design alternatives, and it may be useful in explaining the project to public agencies, community groups, prospective tenants, and others.

Once the preliminary design is completed, it's possible to "take off" preliminary construction cost estimates. To do this, the architect must prepare an outline specification. Estimates are made from this specification, taking into consideration the building space involved, the materials specified, and the construction techniques envisioned. The site-development costs which were formulated in the site-planning phase should be reexamined and modified, if necessary.

As Chapter 12 indicates, the preliminary design and cost estimates are an integral part of the loan package submitted for mortgage-financing purposes, and in some cases they may also help to secure zoning or variances in existing zoning. The developer should be responsive, at this point, to requests by lending institutions or government agencies for possible modifications in the preliminary design. To the greatest extent possible, any changes should be made before proceeding with contract documents.

Computer-Aided Design

For more than a decade, architects, engineers, and contractors have made use of computer-aided design (CAD) in the development process. These systems virtually eliminate the need for manual drafting, allowing for development of numerous design alternatives and modifications in a short time. The most sophisticated applications include generation of three-dimensional and color images of the building components. CAD has greatly increased the productivity and creative capability of building designers by allowing them to test various alternatives much more quickly and efficiently than before.

The Approval Process

As discussed in Chapter 2, the 1970s marked the beginning of an unpredictable and often unfavorable regulatory climate for real estate development. Developers found themselves dealing with a variety of regulatory agencies on several levels—federal, state, regional, city, and county—often with overlapping or contradictory requirements, many so vaguely drafted that they were subject to the interpretation (and whims) of the various agencies.

Today's developer must plan as carefully for securing project approval as for specific site and building design. In many projects, the approval process may require dealing with twenty-five or more regulatory agencies and, in the case of large developments, may cover a period of several years.

There are several key areas that are generally subject to development regulation by government agencies. Perhaps the most critical is the overall environmental sensitivity of the project—plant and animal life indigenous to the development area and the impact on traffic, water resources, and pollution. If the proposed site includes a large amount of environmentally sensitive property, it likely will be very expensive and time-consuming to secure all of the necessary permits and approvals to proceed with the project.

Before undertaking the project, the developer must understand the political climate of the area in which the development is to be built. In assessing the local political environment for development, the politics within the neighborhood of the project should not be overlooked. In addition to governmental agencies at all levels, neighborhood organizations may be a powerful force in delaying or halting a proposed project, if it has a perceived negative impact. The developer should include any influential neighborhood groups (both proponents and opponents) in the early planning stages of the development in order to prevent costly delays as the project proceeds. A host of other regulatory considerations must be incorporated in the planning process. The developer should plan in advance for the likelihood that the zoned density will be reduced (sometimes by more than half) in the course of the approval process. Water and sewer services must be provided for; as noted earlier, many states are restricting development on the basis of inadequate water supplies. If the project is to be developed in a wetlands area, the approval process is further complicated.

Because of the complex nature of the approval process, it is important that professional consultants be retained in order to secure the needed permits to proceed with development. The ability of these consultants to deal effectively with all of the governmental agencies involved in the permit process may make the difference between whether or not a project is approved. While consultant services can be expensive (more than $1 million for large developments), they can nevertheless save the developer time and money in the long run and, most importantly, increase the probability that the project will be approved.

Because of the major expense involved in the planning and approval process, it is necessary that the developer have adequate financing to cover the cost of undertaking the preparation of marketing, environmental, and other studies required by governmental agencies at all levels. Additional funds should be available to handle the unforeseen problems that inevitably arise throughout the planning and approval process.

Contract Documents

Once the developer has obtained satisfactory financial commitment and the necessary government approvals, it's possible to proceed with contract documents: detailed drawings and materials specifications from which construction cost estimates are finalized and contracts are let to construct the building. Therefore, the drawings must be exceedingly accurate and anticipate construction problems that will be raised in the field. The work is undertaken by an architect and several specialists working as a team to pull all the pieces together.

The first step is to determine the structural elements of the building, with the team coordinating their efforts closely with the structural engineer who conducts final tests on the stresses that the structure will impose. Columns, beams, and other structural components are sized and related to other elements of the building. Specifications are prepared, indicating the type, quantity, and tolerances of the structural materials to be utilized.

Once the structural elements have been determined, the nonstructural building elements must be finalized. These include walls, partitions, floors, roofs, stairs, windows, and so forth, although in some buildings they are part of the structural elements. Detailed drawings and specifications are then developed regarding the type of materials to be utilized and the construction techniques to be followed. At the same time, the mechanical and electrical systems are finalized, including elevators, escalators, plumbing, fire protection, heating, air conditioning, and waste disposal, as well as transformers, conduits, signal systems, and control panels. Plans detailing the location and design of each of these elements are prepared, as well as specifications indicating the type, capacity, and features of each system. All these elements will influence the architect's work as detailed decisions of the building interface with the mechanical and structural systems.

The next step is to design the interior, including ceilings, partitions, air conditioning zones, electrical and telephone outlets, carpeting, drapes, and other elements of interior finish. Some of these items are designed on a "minimum" basis, because tenants may wish to upgrade and otherwise modify their interiors according to their needs. The min-

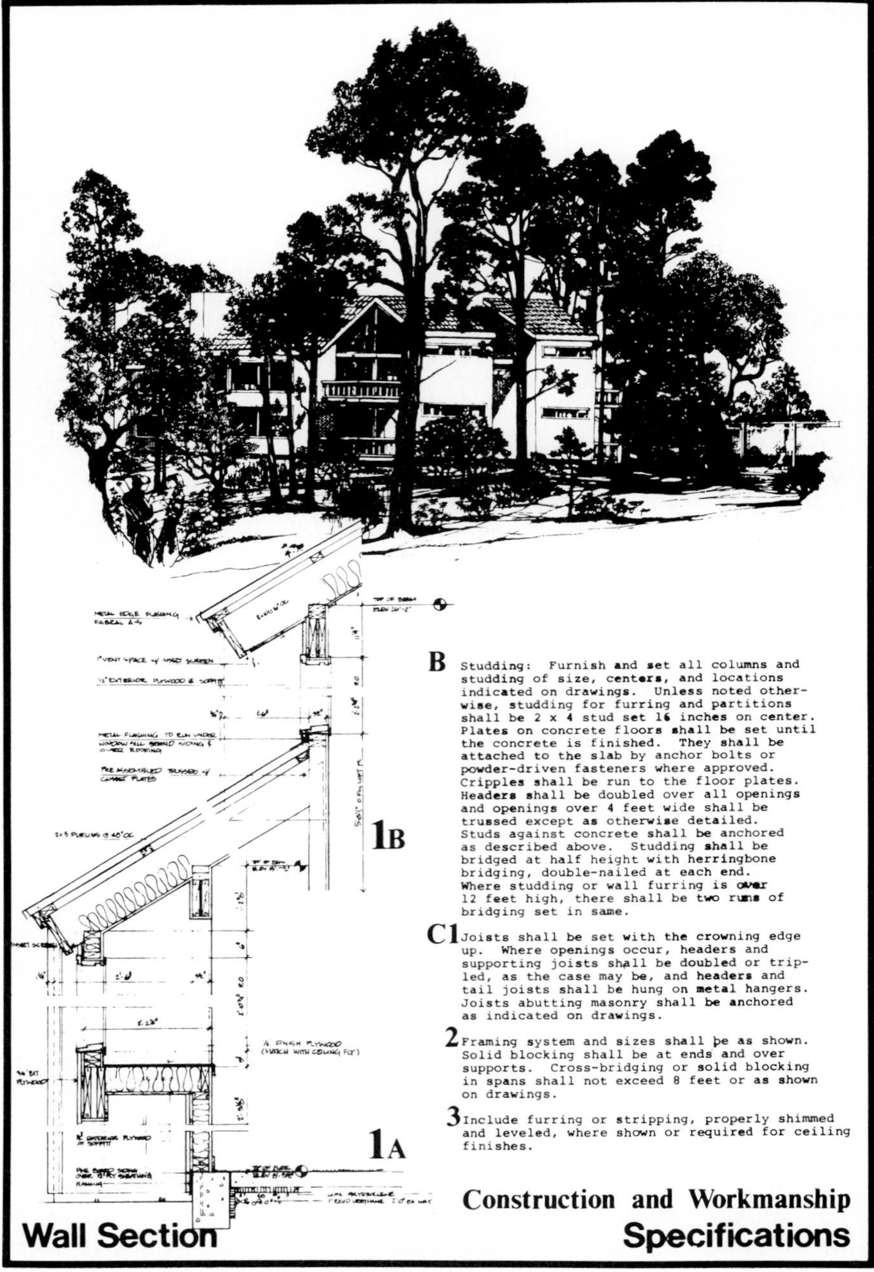

B Studding: Furnish and set all columns and studding of size, centers, and locations indicated on drawings. Unless noted otherwise, studding for furring and partitions shall be 2 x 4 stud set 16 inches on center. Plates on concrete floors shall be set until the concrete is finished. They shall be attached to the slab by anchor bolts or powder-driven fasteners where approved. Cripples shall be run to the floor plates. Headers shall be doubled over all openings and openings over 4 feet wide shall be trussed except as otherwise detailed. Studs against concrete shall be anchored as described above. Studding shall be bridged at half height with herringbone bridging, double-nailed at each end. Where studding or wall furring is over 12 feet high, there shall be two runs of bridging set in same.

C1 Joists shall be set with the crowning edge up. Where openings occur, headers and supporting joists shall be doubled or tripled, as the case may be, and headers and tail joists shall be hung on metal hangers. Joists abutting masonry shall be anchored as indicated on drawings.

2 Framing system and sizes shall be as shown. Solid blocking shall be at ends and over supports. Cross-bridging or solid blocking in spans shall not exceed 8 feet or as shown on drawings.

3 Include furring or stripping, properly shimmed and leveled, where shown or required for ceiling finishes.

Construction and Workmanship Specifications

Figure 15-4. Contract documents.

imum system therefore becomes the cost standard for preparation of the lease. Costs allocated for the minimum standard are then applied against the total cost of interior finish.

Finally, a full set of working drawings and specifications for all items of work are reproduced in contract document form. These documents are now available for final review by governmental agencies and the lending institution and for use by contractors to bid on the construction of the project. The drawings and specifications are also needed to obtain a building permit and are utilized in the field as the definitive description of all work to be performed. It should be noted, however, that no set of working drawings or specifications is absolutely final; changes and modifications will most likely be made in the field as unanticipated problems come up or as possible design improvements become apparent. These are generally handled by change orders or, if the changes are significant, by revisions to the drawings. This work is a major responsibility of the architect, who plays an important role in the final contract negotiations between owner and contractor and continues to represent the owner by administering the construction through periodic visits to the site, approving the work as it proceeds, and authorizing incremental payments to the contractor.

Planning and Design Aspects of Various Types of Projects

Residential

Single Family.[9] The first step in planning and designing single-family residential projects is to develop the best possible plan for the particular site. This process is essentially a "balancing act" between unit density, land development costs, site amenities, and unit sales price. It's necessary to generate a certain minimum level of density on the site in order to make the project economically feasible. Too low a density can result in insufficient revenue to cover land and site development costs. Too high a density, however, may destroy site amenities (e.g., trees) or create a claustrophobic feeling, either of which could reduce the sales price of the unit and/or projected absorption levels. The way to optimize the interaction of these forces is to prepare a series of land-planning alternatives and continually test their market and financial feasibility. If a particular alternative seems to create too much density, it should be

[9] This discussion applies to both detached and attached single-family development, as well as to horizontal condominiums (i.e., not high-rise).

reevaluated in light of the market research, particularly the survey of competitive developments in the market area. If it appears that the project still can remain competitive because of superior location or other factors, the high density perhaps can be maintained. If competition is stiff, or the subject site enjoys few locational advantages, it may be necessary to lower the density to maintain the anticipated price levels or lower the price unit levels to reflect higher density. Again, the major objective is to maximize overall ROI through the best optimization of these forces.

Density is not the only consideration in developing the single-family land plan. Arterial streets must be designed to allow through traffic with a minimum level of noise and danger. Local streets must be given good, safe access to arterials, but designed so that they don't become arterials themselves. Curvilinear street patterns, cul-de-sacs, and carefully designed intersections can accomplish this. The pedestrian movement system must also be considered—not only from street to unit but also from unit to schools, shopping, recreational areas, and public trans-

"Is the, er, curator of the house in?"

portation. Bikeways, horse trails, and cart paths also may affect the circulation element of the land plan.

Design of the utility system should proceed concurrently with transportation planning, since many of the utilities will use street right-of-ways and since linear costs often are the determining factor. Cluster design alternatives that reduce overall street and utility costs should be considered. The desirability of placing utilities underground must be determined at this point. In some communities, undergrounding is required by law; where it is not, the developer must determine the incremental cost and the degree to which this cost can be recovered through higher unit prices. Generally, unless undergrounding is significantly higher, the incremental cost can be recovered.[10]

As the street and utility patterns take shape, the land planner can begin to finalize other public facilities. If a school is planned within the project, it should be located and related to the vehicular and pedestrian transportation systems. Parks and other recreational areas should likewise be located so that they utilize natural features wherever possible. If neighborhood shopping areas are to be included in the project, they should be planned so as to provide the best commercial site possible, without reducing residential values within the project.[11] Basic landscaping, including street trees, is also considered at this point.

In evaluating various alternatives to land planning, the design of the individual unit must also be considered. Generally, three or four types of units will be offered, reflecting some combination of bedrooms and baths. The preliminary mix of these units should come from data supplied by the market research. For example, if the market area consists predominantly of families with children, the unit mix should have more three- and four-bedroom units. If elderly or young couples predominate, the mix would feature more two-bedroom units.

The exterior design of the units is largely a function of the architect's creativity and of the receptivity of the marketplace to this creativity. In some markets, consumer preference for traditional design is so strong that contemporary design solutions simply won't sell. In other markets, new design concepts can be introduced if they make sense in terms of the particular site involved. If the project is sufficiently large, a variety

[10]The competitive survey will provide some insight. If all competitive projects include underground utilities, the question is largely academic. If competitive projects have no undergrounding, it may prove to be a competitive advantage.

[11]Unless the residential project is quite large (e.g., over 1000 units), the commercial neighborhood will have to pull from other residential areas. The best location from which to accomplish this objective may conflict with residential development within the project.

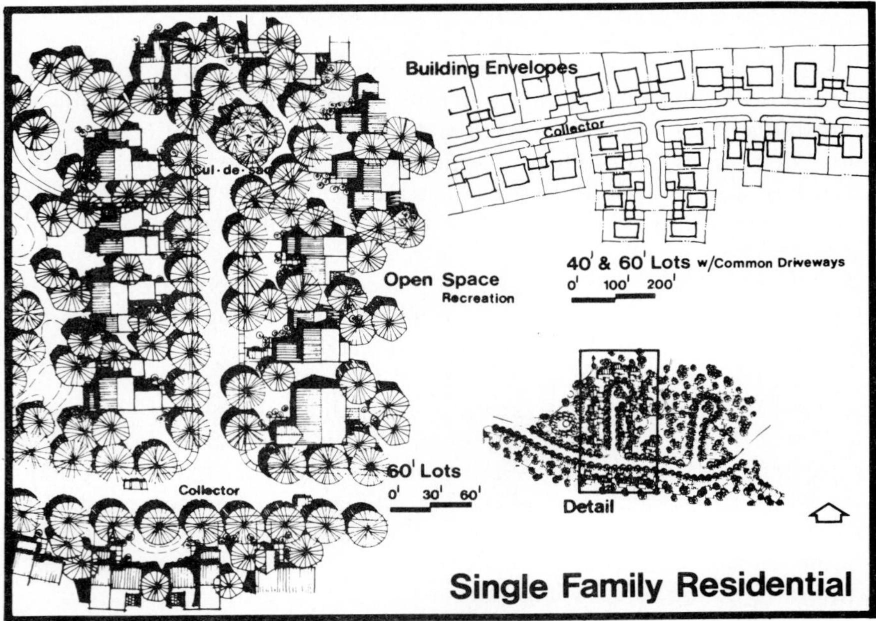

Figure 15-5. Single-family residential plan.

of exterior designs can be developed to reach a broader range of consumer preferences.

Within the units themselves are several important design considerations. The perception of space is important, particularly if the rooms are small. A feeling of spaciousness often can be created through such design features as cathedral ceilings, atriums, balconies, skylights, and window and door placement. Since the kitchen-dining-living areas often are utilized functionally as a single unit, particularly for entertaining, they must relate well to one another and to the rest of the unit. Other important functional design relationships include the entry-living room, bedroom-bathroom, garage-kitchen, and kitchen-waste disposal area. The designer must thoroughly think through these and other functional relationships, utilizing working models if necessary. Attention to such details as these in the design phase can often save construction costs later and also produce a product that is easier to merchandise.

Multifamily. The planning and design of multifamily projects is considerably different from single-family design. Individual unit design is very critical, since the designer usually works with smaller square footage. Again, the perception of space within the units is important. Maximizing favorable views and assuring privacy, including acoustic separation, are also major design considerations. Site planning must be carefully undertaken to minimize the "feeling" of higher density, with considerable attention given to pedestrian walkways, parking, and recreation areas.

High-rise apartments, as well as high-rise condominiums and cooperatives, require concentration on the individual unit design. The placement of columns and beams considerably constricts the layout of the units. Often, there is a trade-off between more merchandisable units and higher costs of structural construction, which must be thoroughly explored by both designer and engineer. The relationship between gross and net usable areas also is critical. Extensive design analysis is required to achieve the highest design efficiency ratio.

Second Homes. The planning and design of second homes involves most of the elements associated with primary homes. However, relating the units to specific natural and artificial recreational features, both in terms of access and view amenity, is emphasized more. There also are specialized aspects of unit design, such as security and fire protection systems, owner storage areas, waste removal, and antifreezing measures. Consideration should also be given to developing greater sleeping capacity through the use of loft areas, bunk beds, specially designed furniture, and so forth.

Retail Commercial

Regional Centers. The market research for a potential regional shopping center provides the initial work program for planning and design activities. The projected amount and type of GLA established by the market research is then refined and tested by preliminary leasing activities and discussions with lending institutions. The role of the planner and designer is to translate this evolving work program into a center that functions smoothly in terms of parking, pedestrian movement, merchandise handling, and other physical aspects of building and operating a regional shopping center. The planner and designer also must create an aesthetically pleasing environment for shoppers and merchants alike. It is to be hoped that the environment will be so outstanding that it will attract more shoppers than the market analysis indicates.

The first step in the planning process is to roughly allocate land area between buildings, parking, access roads, landscaped areas, buffer areas, and land held for further expansion. The amount of land held for buildings is determined by adjusting GLA to reflect common building areas, such as malls, corridors, rest rooms, elevators, loading areas, storage, and mechanical facilities. The *gross building area* is then divided by the number of floors to find the amount of land that will be required.[12] Generally, retail buildings should have as few floors as possible to encourage maximum pedestrian exposure. If more than one floor is involved, it should be designed to facilitate pedestrian movement to the more remote levels.

The amount of parking required will depend upon the size and nature of the GLA and local zoning requirements. The amount of land needed for parking often is related to the amount of land needed for building in terms of a *parking ratio* (e.g., 2:1, 3:1, 4:1), which is, at best, a very rough, preliminary planning tool. The *parking index* is more precise, measuring the number of parking spaces required per 1000 sq ft of GLA. Fairly reliable parking indices have been established for various types of stores, which should be applied to the recommended mix of uses proposed in the work program. Employee parking requirements should be determined at this time, as well as adjustments for shoppers arriving by public transportation. The total number of spaces should then be multiplied by the amount of space per parking stall to arrive at the amount of parking area that will be required.[13] The amount of land area needed to handle the parking area will depend upon whether multilevel parking structures are to be utilized. Most regional centers try to keep parking at grade as much as possible.[14]

The number of parking spaces should now be translated into traffic demand estimates, which are calculated at peak hours, and should consider the average *parking turnover* that can be anticipated—the number of times an individual space will be utilized during the peak hour period. Parking turnover generally is a function of the type of retail space in the center and of local shopping patterns. For instance, large regional centers in smaller communities generally can expect a lower turnover ratio than smaller centers in urban areas. Projected traffic demand at the peak hour will establish the number of lanes of access roads required. The amount of land required for these roads can then be calculated on the basis of minimum requirements for each lane, which are established by local building codes.

Land should also be allocated for other purposes. If the site is immediately adjacent to a residential area, a landscaped buffer to reduce noise and visual blight may be desirable. Other landscaped areas may

[12]The procedures for accomplishing this were outlined in Chapter 8.

[13]This space allocation should allow for internal vehicular circulation, turning, and storage. This generally is about 350 to 400 square feet per stall.

[14]This is changing, however, with rising land costs and greater consumer acceptance of multistory parking structures.

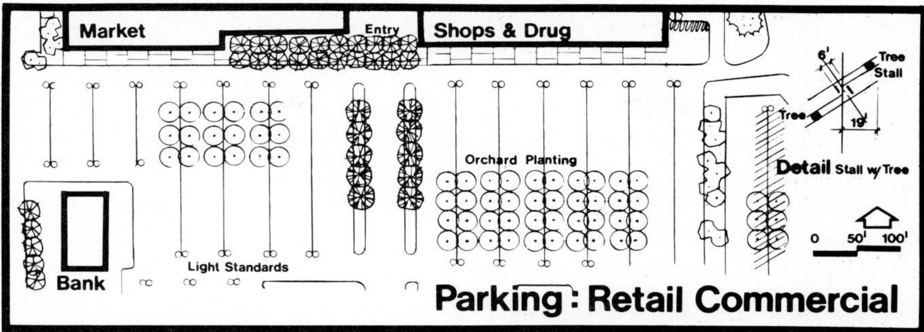

Figure 15-6. Retail commercial plan.

fulfill aesthetic purposes or provide playgrounds for children to use while their parents are shopping. If land is to be held for future expansion and/or other land uses, it should be set aside at this time.

This allocation process makes it possible to see how much land is required for the total center development. If there is sufficient land to meet the requirements of the work program, more definitive planning can proceed. If there is not sufficient land, building and parking structures must be reanalyzed. For example, a multistory building and/or parking may be physically necessary; the impact on construction costs and merchandising desirability must then be evaluated. If the impact is sufficiently negative, the amount of GLA to be developed may have to be scaled down, thus forcing (1) a decision as to which types of merchandising activities are to be reduced and (2) a revamping of the work program.

Once the allocation of land uses is complete, various locational alternatives for the uses must be analyzed. Generally, buildings should be located in that portion of the site where they will be as central to parking as possible, as well as most visible to passing vehicular traffic. The required parking area is then laid out around the buildings, with access roads planned to service the parking from the most convenient point of access. Traffic patterns on surrounding arterials should be evaluated to discover the impact of traffic generated by the center. If additional capacity must be developed off-site, who will pay for these improvements and how they can be phased into the overall program must be determined. Access roads for delivery vehicles must also be developed and linked to proposed loading facilities. Finally, landscaped areas and land held for future expansion should be located.

The building areas can now be refined, with emphasis on pedestrian movement between and within individual stores. The initial concern is where to locate the anchor tenants—usually department stores. The objective generally is to place the anchors at a comfortable walk's distance from each other, linked by a shopping promenade lined with satellite shops. In some centers, anchors may include retail operations other than department stores, such as large drug stores, variety stores, or discount houses, and perhaps nonretail uses such as hotels, office buildings, theaters, or major restaurants.

Once the anchor tenants have been located, satellite stores can be laid out along the connecting axes. Complementary satellite stores are usually clustered. Convenience stores, for example, should be clustered and given direct access to their own parking facilities.[15] The degree to which impulse buying influences the success of the store should also be considered. Gift shops should be located where pedestrian traffic is concentrated. A travel agency, like other sought-out operations, can be located in less well-trafficked areas. If specific tenants are known in advance, additional factors become important, such as price range of merchandising policy, local reputation, compatibility with other retailers, and parking requirements.

Now the plan can be finalized. Individual tenant areas are laid out in modular form to accommodate varying tenant space requirements. Pedestrian circulation elements, such as malls, plazas, rest rooms, drinking fountains, seating areas, and public assembly areas, are planned in detail. Parking and traffic circulation should be retested for accessibility to specific types of merchandising operations. Delivery and trash removal service should also be retested in terms of individual store requirements. Landscaping and buffer areas should be finalized, as should the possible interim treatment of areas held for future expansion. Specifications for building materials, landscaping, street furniture, and center signs should be developed. At this time, a policy regarding specifications for tenant signs should also be established.

Community Centers. The planning and design of community centers is similar to that of regional centers, except that the scale is much smaller. Since community centers generally involve sites with less land area, efficient parking and traffic circulation must be considered in order to develop as many parking stalls as possible. If more than two anchors are used (e.g., a variety store and a junior department store), they can function at both ends of the center, with "*in line*" satellite stores in between. If there is only one anchor, the designer must be careful to maintain satellite store exposure.

[15]Other examples of clustering include stores serving men (e.g., clothing, shoes, sporting goods), stores serving women and children (e.g., women's apparel, shoes, millinery, children's clothing, toys), and stores featuring hard goods (e.g., furniture, appliances, hardware, radios and televisions).

Neighborhood and Strip Centers. The planning and design of neighborhood and strip centers largely focuses on meeting the needs of the anchor tenants. Parking and traffic circulation probably will be the major concern, especially if the site is extremely tight. Providing exposure and parking for satellite stores may also pose a problem. Some centers resolve this by designing satellite stores as freestanding buildings ("pads"), thus allowing independent identification as well as providing direct access for customers who are not utilizing the anchor stores. If pads are utilized, it is also important to be certain they do not significantly block exposure of the in-line stores from the arterial.

Discount and Warehouse Stores. The major challenge in discount and warehouse store design is how to provide sufficient capacity for its activities. Since these operations usually carry more merchandise in the selling area than other types of stores and since turnover is much higher, capacity must be designed for the delivery, and storage and management of a wide variety of goods. Capacity matters in the store itself too, since shopper density often exceeds that of a department store. Parking and traffic-handling capacity are also important—particularly if the discount or warehouse store is located in an older industrial area.

Specialty Centers. The planning and design of a specialty center focuses on the degree of ambience created in the pedestrian circulation areas. Visitors to the center should be able to move through spaces which interest and involve them. These spaces should be small and relatively intimate, planned to create surprise and delight as shoppers discover them, and should allow for activities such as art exhibits, street musicians, and entertainers. If the center's theme is based on a historic building or group of buildings, they should be the focal point; shops and restaurants should be located along several pedestrian movement spines which are interlinked if possible. Parking should be on the extremities of or beneath the center, and vehicular traffic movement should be as unobtrusive as possible.

Office Commercial

Single-Tenant Buildings. A single-tenant building requires a highly customized design geared to the specific requirements of the dominant tenant. Future space needs, established during the market analysis phase, provide the basic work program. The location of specific activities within this program will depend upon the type of space required for the activity. For example, computer rooms can be placed in basements; conference rooms can utilize interior space; executive offices should be located at corners, if possible. The interface of a work activity with other activities also helps determine its location within the building. Since these activities often are dynamic and have continually changing space requirements, interior plans should be flexible. Space slated for future expansion also should be laid out as flexibly as possible in terms of both adaptability to other tenants and future use by the dominant tenant.

Multitenant Buildings. Flexibility is even more critical in designing multitenant buildings, where specific tenant requirements may not be known in advance. Generally, the most critical factor is the dimension between the window and corridor wall. This space must be sufficient to allow for the reception and offices of the small user (e.g., 500 to 1000 square feet) and yet not be so deep as to waste space for the larger user. The corridor itself must be carefully designed to provide access to as many tenants as possible with the least amount of space. The objective is to maximize design efficiency without sacrificing the space's marketability.

Flexibility is also important in providing lighting, telephone and electrical outlets, and air conditioning zones. The leasing agent and interior designer should be allowed to tailor the space to the requirements of specific tenants as much as possible, recognizing the possible trade-off with higher construction costs. Interior partitioning should be modular, which allows for modifications by the current tenant and by new tenants as leases expire.

Elevators also are a critical design element in a multitenant building. They must have sufficient capacity to handle peak loads without posing an undue construction or operating cost burden. Trade-offs between the number of elevators, their capacity, and the speed at which they operate are often necessary. Pedestrian movement elsewhere in the building—lobbies, garage access, connections to public transit, and so forth—must also be analyzed carefully. Retail space, if provided on the lower floors, must relate both to building tenants and to customers from the outside. Building security is an increasingly important consideration.

Material specification plays an important role in office building design. Most often, the trade-off is between higher costs of construction and lower maintenance costs. Various materials and products should be tested thoroughly before they are finally specified. Energy conservation and other considerations must be weighed in selecting the materials to be used. The day when a material could be selected exclusively on its aesthetic merits is over.

One of the major problem areas in office building operation is the

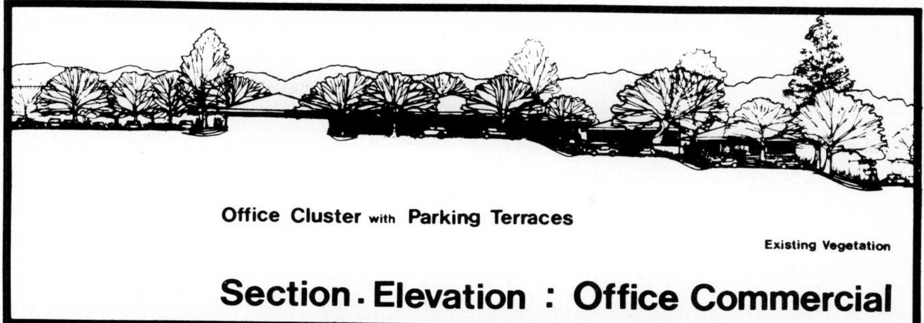

Figure 15-7. Office commercial section—elevation.

heating, ventilation, and air conditioning system (HVAC). Planning and design for this system should consider the various types of occupants and uses projected for the building. As an example, consideration should be given to off-hour HVAC operation, particularly in buildings directed at legal, accounting, engineering, and other professional tenants.

Office Parks. The planning and design of an office park combines elements of the office building, shopping center, and industrial park. Vehicular and pedestrian circulation should be carefully planned to accommodate peak loads. Access to servicing facilities must be provided. A certain degree of pedestrian ambience should be created through the use of malls, landscaping, and luncheon areas. Central facilities such as health clubs and day care centers must be planned to serve the entire park as efficiently as possible, as well as business generated from other areas. Land parcels should be platted flexibly to accommodate various user requirements. Finally, building standards, including signage, must be established to give the park an overall continuity once individual buildings have been completed.

Medical Buildings. Medical buildings are designed much like office buildings, but the efficient layout of doctors' offices is emphasized. Flexibility is not so important here, since office utilization is more standardized, with a doctor often using the same amount of space throughout his or her career. Plumbing and mechanical systems are a major cost factor in medical buildings and must be handled as efficiently as possible. If a pharmacy, radiology lab, or other doctor-service facility is provided, it should be in the most convenient location—generally on or near the building lobby. Parking requirements, particularly for the disabled, are greater for medical buildings and should be planned accordingly.

Industrial Land Uses

Of the important factors in planning and designing industrial parks, site flexibility is perhaps the most critical. Available parcels should be platted in modules of ½ to 1 acre so that they can be combined in various ways to accommodate users' needs without destroying the desirability of the remaining parcels. Streets should be designed to provide access to potential combinations of parcels and should be wide enough for large trucks to turn. If rail service is available, spurs to the various potential parcels should be provided, with a minimum loss of land. Utility lines should be readily available to all parcels, with sufficient capacity to handle peak requirements.

Because of the diverse uses and the building types and sizes generally prevalent in an industrial park, it is important to have basic standards for all potential users. These standards usually involve the type of industrial operation, site coverage, building height and setback, minimum on-site parking requirements, and location and size of loading docks and vehicle storage areas. In R&D and other high-quality parks, additional standards may be required relating to building materials, landscaping, sign control, and, in some cases, approval of building design Industrial park planning and design standards are generally enforced through legal covenants running with the ownership of the land.

Transient Commercial

Motels. A motel presents a relatively straightforward planning and design problem. The buildings should be designed to conform to the size and configuration of the site. It may be desirable to arrange the buildings around the swimming pool, if there is one, to give privacy and wind protection. As with apartment buildings, acoustic separation between the units is very important. Parking should be as close to the rooms as possible, with direct access to the motel office.

Motor Hotels. Motor hotels are planned and designed in much the same way as motels, except that public space, such as restaurants, banquet rooms, and conference rooms, takes on greater importance. These facilities should be convenient to the lobby and away from guest rooms so that the guests are not disturbed by noise. Additional parking should be provided for the public space facilities. If there is a restaurant, it

Figure 15-8. Hotel section—elevation.

should have its own identification through signs and, if possible, building design.

Hotels. Hotel planning and design is more complex, particularly if a large convention hotel is involved. The findings of the market research in terms of the primary source of demand should determine the mix of rooms; the use of connecting rooms can provide flexibility in the mix. The rooms should look spacious and be designed in the most efficient manner possible. In some cases, this can be done through balconies, high ceilings, and built-in furnishings. Baths should be "double-stacked" to reduce plumbing costs.[16] Walls should be insulated to prevent excessive noise transmission.

A key element in hotel design is efficient servicing of guest rooms. Within the rooms, this can be accomplished by using furnishings that resist dirt and dust and that allow carpets to be cleaned without having to move furniture. Outside the rooms, the goal is to minimize the number of steps taken by service personnel, which can be done by properly locating service elevators, linen closets, and trash and soiled linen chutes.

The planning of public rooms is also important. The lobby should be spacious, and services (e.g., registration, cashier, bell captain) should be close together and as near as possible to the elevators. Restaurants and retail shops should be accessible both from the lobby and the street. Conference and meeting rooms should be designed on a flexible module to accommodate various conference sizes. Room acoustics must be excellent and have a minimum of interroom noise. Banquet rooms

[16]Bathrooms in one unit are directly opposite facilities in an adjoining unit. Both utilize a single plumbing tree in the wall between the units.

should lead directly to the kitchen. The kitchen itself should be immediately accessible to service elevators to assure efficient room service.

Vehicular and pedestrian traffic must also be handled efficiently. Vehicular access should be directly off major arterials. There should be sufficient capacity for short-term parking and loading. If possible, taxis should have independent areas for queuing; charter buses should have their own waiting and loading areas. There should be enough parking for room guests to handle peak requirements. If extensive public space is involved, additional parking must be provided for nonguest vehicles. Pedestrian connections to other buildings, public transportation, or recreational areas may also be desirable.

Resort Hotels. The requirements for planning and designing resort hotels are similar to other types of hotels, depending on the size and nature of the operation. However, there are several additional considerations. As with second homes, the land planning must relate closely to the natural or artificial recreational facility. This also applies to the public space, unifying the guests' experiences. Since the stay is generally longer than in ordinary hotels, the guest rooms should be somewhat larger than rooms in urban hotels. Care must also be taken in planning the servicing of the rooms, especially if there are considerable distances between rooms and central service operations. If second homes are to be utilized as guest rooms under a coordinated hotel management, this should be considered when the units are planned and designed.

Multiuse Projects

Multiuse Buildings. In the design of multiuse buildings, the key element is location of the uses. Retail usually is on the ground floor in order to be exposed to pedestrian traffic. In general, residential uses should be on the upper floors, reflecting the rental value of good views and the lower costs of servicing (e.g., fewer elevators, less frequent cleaning and maintenance). In a hotel-office complex, it may be desirable to put the hotel uses on the lower floors to facilitate room service operations and proximity to public facilities, but this objective may be thwarted by the placement of structural columns.

Mixed-Use Projects. The planning and design of MXD projects is very complex and closely related to market and financial analysis, particularly as the effects of synergistic demand are analyzed. Many plans and computer iterations will be required as various trade-offs are considered in arriving at the final design. More than with any other type of project, communication must exist between developer and architect.

An important factor is the location of buildings within the project. For example, if the apartment market cares about views, it may be desirable to locate the apartment tower in that portion of the project that will afford the best views. If a hotel is involved, it should be located to the greatest extent possible in the portion of the project providing the greatest proximity to public services (e.g., convention center, taxis, passenger loading and unloading).

The pedestrian link between the various buildings is also extremely critical. Ideally, it should be an area of great activity, during both daylight and evening hours. Retail is an excellent link, particularly if restaurants, bars, theaters, and other focal points of night activity are included. If a hotel is one of the uses, the lobby also can be a linking element. The general feeling should be one of free flow among uses, with activities at as many points as possible along the way. Well-conceived vertical transportation is also important, particularly in mixed-use buildings, as well as emergency exiting systems.

Because of the great variations in electrical use by the individual components of the project, the base electrical system must provide for varying energy levels and tenant submetering, wherever possible. Fire protection systems become quite complex in MXDs and must be thought through well in advance.

Parking design becomes critical since a portion of parking resources will be based on the concept of "shared" parking between land uses. The peak parking demand for each use must be established and correlated with other uses. Major conflicts between uses in terms of parking demand may require modification in one or more of the uses in terms of size or location within the project.

Consideration must also be given to vehicular access to the project from adjacent streets and freeways to avoid traffic bottlenecks as much as possible. Providing adequate access to shipping and receiving areas is also critical, because of the intensity and possible overlapping of use by the various components of the project.

Public spaces must be planned carefully in order to create as much pedestrian excitement as possible but within a smoothly functioning movement system. Atria are often utilized in MXD projects to create drama, but they may produce other problems such as unbalanced HVAC circulation and increased security costs. Water and landscaping can also add drama to public areas but must be carefully thought through in terms of installation, maintenance, and effect on air quality (humidity).

Care must be taken that the public area of each use does not conflict with another use. As an example, residential lobbies require privacy and separate access from offices, retail, and other uses. Conference facilities in hotels should be near the hotel lobby and retail areas but separated sufficiently to allow meetings to proceed with a minimum of outside interference.

Consideration must also be given to the project's interface with surrounding land uses and the community at large. The days are probably past when an MXD project could turn its back on its neighborhoods (as many of the inwardly facing early projects were prone to do), but it is still possible for an MXD project to overwhelm a neighborhood if physical and psychological relationships are not carefully considered. Factors such as sunlight, wind, views, pedestrian entry points, public facilities, etc., must be thoroughly evaluated by the development team.

In terms of ongoing operations, the project design criteria should be attached to each lease, enabling the developer to control tenant material selection, image, and other elements of the design process. The objective is to achieve as much tenant individuality as possible, particularly in retail store fronts, within an overall framework of project design and image.

New Towns. The planning and design of new towns involves all the planning aspects that have been discussed thus far. The added ingredients are the flexibility afforded by starting from scratch with a large site and the exciting challenge of planning and designing a "total" community where people live, work, and play and where the process of town building will be continuous over several years. The major contribution of the planner of a new town is to set up a process which can respond to social and technological innovation but still have the conceptual strength that gives it direction as it grows. The phasing of the development plan also is critical, both in terms of costs and project marketability. A certain level of infrastructure must be developed during the first phase to provide a basis for various land uses and to demonstrate developer credibility. As each new land use is added to this infrastructure base, it should complement and support existing uses, as well as lay the groundwork for future uses. For example, the convenience goods phase of a new shopping center supports existing residential facilities and provides the base for expansion into shopper goods at a later date.

Conclusion

Regardless of the land uses involved, the planning and design phase efforts should be tested continually against the findings of the original market research and overall financial feasibility. It is this testing process that produces a sound plan and building design, so essential to a successful project.

16
Construction

Three things are to be looked to in a building: that it stand on the right spot; that it be securely founded; that it be successfully executed.
GOETHE

Once the contract documents have been completed, the construction process can begin. Construction essentially amounts to marshaling materials, labor, subcontractors, and equipment on a specific site to produce one or more buildings. The building(s) may be constructed of any combination of materials and involve one or more building techniques. The developer may undertake the construction as an owner, on a contract basis with a general contractor, or as a joint venture partner with a general contractor. A successful developer or investor doesn't need to engage in construction but does need to understand the overall process. Even the investor who purchases a completed building should understand the general mechanics of its erection so that it can be operated and maintained properly.

Types of Construction

Construction generally is classified by the type of material used for structural support: wood, masonry, concrete, steel, or various combinations of these materials.

"We got it! We got the pyramid contract!"

Wood

Wood frame, the most common type of construction, is used extensively for residential buildings in most parts of the country. Lumber creates a structural frame, which is then veneered with one or more materials, including wood, stucco, rock, masonry, and metal. Wood frame is superior in terms of availability, lower cost, and ease of construction. Buildings framed with wood can usually be built more rapidly than buildings using other structural materials. The major disadvantages of wood are susceptibility to fire, shrinkage, and limitation in height to two or three stories in most areas.

Several technological advances in wood frame construction have been made in recent years. Major components, like roof trusses, can be prefabricated in a factory and shipped directly to the site. The development of high-strength glues has led to the use of laminated woods for arches, beams, and other applications requiring heavy load-bearing qualities. Significant technological advances have been made with plywood, and this versatile material is widely used for both interior and exterior finishes. Reconstructed wood products or *particleboards,* formed from sawdust and planer shavings, have become increasingly popular as an alternative to plywood in construction. Because they make use of materials that otherwise would have gone to waste, particleboards are less expensive than plywood; they can also be stronger, more versatile, less likely to warp, and more weather resistant.

Masonry

The structural elements in this type of construction include building materials that are held together with mortar: brick, concrete block, hollow clay tile, stone, gypsum block, and glass block. Walls are often reinforced with steel to provide additional strength. Masonry is used primarily in residential construction, but it is also used in small commercial and industrial buildings. Concrete or steel frame high-rise buildings may also be faced with masonry.[1]

Masonry construction is usually more durable and fire retardant than wood frame construction, and maintenance costs may be lower. The major disadvantages are higher construction costs and, generally, longer construction periods. Technological advances in masonry construction have occurred primarily in the forming and reinforcing techniques utilized in concrete and clay block construction. A new spray-on method of bonding masonry units has also been developed, and it speeds up the construction process as well as provides a fire- and water-resistant wall. Prefabricated block panels are now being introduced to reduce costs and building time. Special saws for fabricating or modifying masonry products on site have been developed.

Concrete

Concrete construction is utilized extensively for residential, commercial, and industrial buildings where durability and low maintenance cost are desired. The most common method is *cast-in-place* construction, in which concrete is poured into wooden, steel, or plastic forms at the building site and allowed to set. Concrete mixtures may be prepared in a temporary facility on site or prepared in a batch plant and mixed in transit. Concrete batching is a highly scientific process; specialized chemicals accelerate or retard the hardening process. There has been

[1]Reinforced masonry bearing wall construction has been used for multistory buildings in Europe for some years, and it is gaining greater acceptance in the United States.

considerable technological advance in the pouring of concrete: towers, cranes, hoists, conveyors, and high-pressure concrete pumps are increasingly common. New types of pumps have been developed for pumping through small-diameter pipes, greatly extending this technique to smaller construction jobs. The *placing boom,* which resembles a hydraulic pump, can reduce the time spent pouring concrete by nearly two-thirds. Techniques have also been developed for protecting reinforced steel from corrosion in concrete bridge decks. A recent advance involving mixing fiber in concrete has eliminated the need for steel reinforcing bars in some cases.

Concrete may also be *precast* at another location and transported to the site where it is assembled. Precasting generally involves such structural elements as columns, T-beams, I-beams, walls, planks, and slabs—although precasting is being used increasingly for specialized, nonstructural applications. The precast slab can be sent to the factory, where workers can assemble and complete, for example, an entire bathroom, painted and finished down to door handles and hooks. On large building projects, more than one method may be employed; for example, precast walls and joists may be used when columns and/or slabs are in place.

The problems and costs involved in breaking down and reassembling forms, particularly in high-rise construction, have led to the use of a relatively old technique—*slip-form construction*—in which concrete is continually poured into a form that moves upward a small amount each day. The development of concrete pumps has advanced the slip-form technique. Another method employed in high-rise buildings is the *lift-slab* method, in which each floor is poured on top of previously poured floor slabs and, after hardening, lifted into position by powerful jacks. One- and two-story industrial and commercial buildings often are built with *tilt-up* wall panels, which are poured on the ground and then tilted into place.

Figure 16-1. Wood frame residential construction in Valencia, California. *(Larry Leach)*

In recent years, several efforts have been directed at increasing the load-bearing qualities of concrete without proportionately increasing the bulk. Many of these have involved *prestressing* techniques, in which the concrete is compressed, either before (*pretension*) or after (*post-tension*) pouring. Prestressing has contributed significantly to the use of concrete in structural element applications, where previously structural steel would have been used.

Steel

Steel frame construction is utilized in major high-rise buildings and in other structures where permanence and durability are required. Steel girders, beams, columns, joists, and floor decks are fabricated off site and welded or bolted together on site. Concrete is then poured into the steel decks to make a floor.[2] Flooring may also be installed by "dry" systems of reinforced concrete deck slabs which are welded to the steel frame. One major technological advance in steel construction has been the introduction of high-strength steel, which increases the length of the beam span, thereby creating greater flexibility in the placement of columns. High-strength *weathering steels* that are resistant to corrosion have recently been developed. New methods have perfected the continuous casting of steel into billets and slabs, speeding up the forming process. The handling of steel at the job site has also improved considerably, primarily because of high-capacity cranes. New bolting and welding techniques have simplified the erection of columns, beams, and girders. The *high-strength structural bolt* is a new type of fastener that is stronger, safer, and simpler to use, and it increases the speed of construction.

The use of steel in high-rise construction allows greater flexibility in designing building exteriors. Since walls do not provide major structural support, they function solely as exterior curtain walls; hence they can utilize glass, aluminum, lightweight steel, ceramics, and other lighter building materials.

Contract Construction

Many developers undertake all or a portion of the construction process with their own staffs. The vast majority of construction, however, is per-

[2]Pouring techniques involve composite action between the concrete, steel decking, and beams and girders. In essence, the molecular structure of concrete and steel are intertwined to provide greater strength.

Figure 16-2. Shortly after "topping out" a steel frame office building. *(Summa Corporation/Tooley & Company)*

formed by individuals and firms who are in the business of building for others for a fee. Generally, these activities are performed under the terms and conditions of a contract between the owner and the general contractor, translating the architect's working drawings into a definitive program to construct a building within a certain period of time and for a specified amount of money.

Parties to the Contract(s)

Owner. The building owner is the developer or other entity which will own the building at the time it is completed. Upon completion, the building may be utilized by the owner or sold or leased to another entity. In some cases, the owner uses an agent who is responsible for dealing with the contractor during the construction period. Architects and engineers also play an important role in supervising or coordinating the construction program.

General Contractor. The general contractor is an individual or firm responsible for producing one or more buildings which meet the specifications that were established in the contract documents. General contractors are licensed by state governments only after meeting certain minimum requirements regarding their knowledge and experience in the construction business.

Subcontractors. The general contractor may undertake all the functions required to complete the building or, more commonly, subcontract to firms specializing in one or more elements of building construction (e.g., site preparation, concrete, steel erection, wood framing, masonry, electrical, air conditioning, plumbing, carpentry, painting). Some general contractors subcontract all elements of construction and act solely as coordinators. The degree of subcontracting will depend on the proximity of the project to the general contractor's normal base of operations, the project's complexity or special technical requirements, the degree of involvement in other projects, the availability and costs of subcontractors, and the general contractor's overall operating policy.

Types of Contracts

Construction contracting has many variations, although most contracts fall into one or more of the following categories. A *lump-sum* or *fixed-price contract* requires the contractor to complete the building for a specified amount of money, which often is established as a result of competitive bidding. If the actual cost of construction is less, the contractor keeps the additional profit; if more, the contractor absorbs the loss. A *guaranteed-maximum-price contract* is similar to a lump-sum contract, except that the owner pays only for actual costs incurred within the maximum price guarantee; the contractor generally shares in any resultant savings. A *cost-plus-fixed-fee contract* reimburses the contractor for actual costs incurred and sets a predetermined fixed fee. This type of contracting often is desirable when time is important and/or the exact nature of the completed project is yet to be determined. *Construction management contracts* are utilized in large, complex projects where the owner trusts a contractor to take over all phases of project development, including such items as budgeting and cost control, review and approval of all subcontracting, analysis and approval of change orders, and preparation of financial reports in addition to the construction. The emphasis in the construction management approach is to reduce adversarial relationships by having the owner, architect, and contractor operating as a "team" to achieve project success.

Estimating

A critical element of all types of contracts (even cost-plus-fixed-fee) is that the contractor can properly estimate costs in advance. These estimates may be prepared by the project manager or by individuals who specialize in cost estimating. The first step is to break down the proposed project into its various components and establish which will be undertaken directly by the contractor's own crews and which will be subcontracted. The estimator develops the cost of direct work; the one or more subcontractors being considered for the project estimate the work to be subcontracted.

The technique of estimating is usually the same, whether it is done by the general contractor or the subcontractor. The physical quantity of each component (e.g, square feet, cubic feet, linear feet, hours) is established from the plans and specifications. These quantities are then extended by the cost per unit of the material or labor involved. Unit costs are developed based on experience with other, similar projects or from averages published by national services.[3] In all cases, the unit costs must be adjusted for projected material prices, changes in labor contracts, the geographic location of the project, and the time of year when the building will be under construction. Indirect costs, such as field offices, temporary utilities, insurance, taxes, and travel expenses, are then estimated and added to the direct costs. Depending upon the type of contract involved, a fee is added for the contractor's general overhead and profit (see Table 16-1). In large projects, the owner may retain an independent cost consultant to verify the cost estimates of the contractor.

[3]These include *Dodge Digest of Building Costs and Specifications,* McGraw-Hill, New York; R. S. Godfrey, *Building Construction Cost Data,* Robert Snow Means Company, Duxbury, Mass.; *Richardson Estimating and Engineering Standards,* Richardson Engineering Services, Downey, Calif.; and *ENR (Engineering News-Record),* McGraw-Hill, New York.

Table 16-1. Construction Cost Estimate for 100 Condominium Units

Acct. no.	Activity	Detail	Subtotal	Cum. total
200	Site improvements			
201	Site clearing	$ 80,061		
202	Sidewalk & paving	476,454		
203	Retaining walls	15,852		
204	Phone & TV cable	71,520		
205	Water	3,708		
206	Sewer	22,248		
207	Miscellaneous	3,500	$ 673,343	$ 673,343
300	Landscaping			
301	Planting	109,201		
302	Concrete	42,902		
303	Electrical	25,706		
304	Sprinklers	73,975		
305	Fencing	48,389		
306	Finish grading	14,090		
307	Miscellaneous	9,270	323,533	996,876
400	Building construction			
401	Concrete and steel	921,512		
402	Lumber	1,288,591		
403	Roofing and weather-proofing	236,528		
404	Insulation	45,757		
405	Fillwork	161,637		
406	Glass—doors & windows	65,300		
407	Rough hardware	32,655		
408	Fireplaces	45,310		
409	Heating & sheet metal	148,505		
410	Plumbing	436,804		
411	Electrical	169,863		
412	Stucco	83,319		
413	Painting	192,469		
414	Cabinets	161,854		
415	Marble tops	17,593		
416	Kitchen tops	13,619		
417	Resilient floors	30,452		
418	Tile	109,690		
419	Carpet	128,821		
420	Ornamental iron	5,988		
421	Mirrors and doors	68,617		
422	Shower doors	9,250		
423	Finish hardware	23,496		
424	Appliances	106,331		
425	Garage doors	58,772		
426	Cleanup	30,962		
427	Miscellaneous labor	38,934		
428	Temporary power	5,562		
429	Guard service	17,120		
430	Permits and fees	14,090	$4,669,421	$5,666,297
	Contingency (5%)		283,315	5,949,612
	Overhead (6%)		339,978	6,289,590
	Profit (4%)		226,652	6,516,242

Bonding

Owners will often require a general contractor to get a construction bond from a surety company. These bonds are based on the general contractor's experience, reputation, and financial strength. The type of bond obtained depends on the type of project, the method of contracting, and the degree of protection the owner desires. A *performance bond* guarantees the owner that the surety company will see the job through to completion, regardless of what happens to the general contractor. These bonds generally run 0.5 to 1.0 percent of total construction costs. When competitive bidding is involved, the performance bond usually is supplemented by a *bid bond,* which compensates the owner for the difference between the low bid and the next lowest bid if the low bidder fails to enter into a contract. *Subcontractor bonds* protect the general contractor against nonperformance by the various subcontractors. A *payment bond* ensures that suppliers will be paid in accordance with the terms of the purchase agreement.[4]

Selecting the Contractor

Several factors must be considered in selecting a contractor, regardless of whether the award is to be through competitive bidding, by negotiation, or through a joint venture arrangement.

Project Experience. Most important is the contractor's experience in the *type of project to be built on the subject site.* Contrary to what many contractors maintain, there are substantial differences in the construction of various types of real estate projects: an apartment house differs from an office building; a shopping center requires a different approach than a hotel. Each type of project has its own learning curves, and the experience must be gained beforehand. The prospective contractor should be asked for a list of similar projects, the original cost estimate, and the final, actual costs. A field inspection of each referenced project should be made, preferably with the architect of the proposed project. Discussions with the owners and architects of the referenced projects should be held. If the project is a rental one, the property manager and selected tenants should be interviewed. If the investigation yields consistently negative findings, the proposed contractor should be dropped from further consideration.

Local Experience. If possible, the contractor should have experience in building in the local area where the proposed project is to be located.

[4]James J. O'Brien and Robert G. Zilly, *Contractor's Management Handbook,* McGraw-Hill, New York, 1971, pp. 1-12, 1-13.

This is important because often there are significant differences in building codes, labor relations and practices, and material purchasing practices among local areas. A contractor who is not familiar with local practices may have trouble once the project is under way. If the proposed contractor has local experience, reference checks should be made with officials of the building department of the local government, major trade unions, architects of previous projects, and building supply houses or supplier representatives. Again, consistently negative findings should rule out the use of a proposed contractor.

Financial Strength. The contractor who meets the first two tests should then be asked for a financial statement. The statement should show consistent profitability (indicating good cost control), a good liquidity ratio (indicating sufficient cash to handle day-to-day operations), and no excessive short-term debt (which may create problems once the project has begun). Discussions also should be held with the contractor's bank and the proposed bonding company.

Subcontractor Relations. A general contractor is only as good as the subcontractors the firm uses. A list of major subcontractors to be employed on the proposed contract should be obtained. Major subcontractors should be questioned about their working relationships with the proposed general contractor. A pattern of long-term working relationships, based on mutual trust and respect, is most desirable. If such relationships do not exist, problems may occur once the job is under way.

Project Manager. The project manager for the proposed project, who should be interviewed in depth, ought to have at least 5 to 10 years' experience, preferably in projects similar to the one proposed, and should have a record of good management. Other projects which will be the project manager's responsibility during the construction period of the proposed project should be reviewed for possible overextension. If the proposed project is a large one, the general contractor should be required to guarantee that the project manager and his or her assistants will work exclusively on the proposed project. In some cases, a *construction manager* may be utilized; this manager would be involved not only in the actual building process but would be a part of the project team from its inception. The construction manager replaces the general contractor and plays the traditional role of the general contractor on the project team.

Price. Only if the contractor meets all the above tests should price be considered. If two contractors appear equally qualified, the deciding factor should be the difference in price. However, if there are two contractors who both meet the basic criteria but one of them seems more highly qualified and is more expensive, it's generally better to pay the higher price in order to get better quality and assurance of successful completion. Never take the lowest bid just because it *is* the lowest bid.

Elements of the Construction Process

It is important for the developer or other owner to understand the three major elements of the construction process, regardless of the experience or reputation of the contractor chosen.[5]

Materials

Materials generally constitute the major portion of the average construction contract, and their costs significantly affect the degree to which a project can be brought in within budget. Customarily, a construction project will use a wide variety of materials in one of three stages of fabrication. *Raw materials,* such as lumber for single-family buildings and sand and gravel for concrete construction, are often shipped directly to the job site. Increasingly, material used in construction is preassembled into *semifinished components* before being shipped. Examples are preassembled wood trusses, prestressed concrete wall units, and prefabricated steel or aluminum curtain wall panels. Finally, *finished materials* are delivered to the job site in completed form. Plumbing units, kitchen appliances, air conditioning condensers, elevators, and other items fall into this category.

The contractor faces several problems in trying to control the material element of the construction process successfully. The first problem is availability. Since shortages may occur in the construction industry, care must be taken to assure that a specified material will be available when it is required. It may be desirable to purchase it before it is needed and warehouse it until it is required on site. It also helps to anticipate the use of substitute materials in case the specified material is unavailable.

Once availability is assured, the next concern is price. Naturally, the contractor wants to purchase the material at the lowest possible price,

[5]For the purposes of this discussion, no distinction is made between subcontractual work and that undertaken directly by the general contractor.

consistent with the architect's minimum quality standards. Tighter specifications (often indicating a specific manufacturer) limit the contractor's purchasing flexibility. One alternative is to sacrifice quality by purchasing lesser-quality materials. The near-term cost savings may be offset, however, by higher costs of replacement if the material is rejected. Another possibility is to purchase in large quantities, thereby securing lower prices through quantity discounts. Unfortunately, cost savings may be eaten up through costs of warehousing and/or the write-off of unused surplus material. The best bet is generally to weigh each purchasing decision independently, considering price as only one factor.

The purchased material must be delivered to the site at the time when it is required. Often, this presents a scheduling problem. If the material is not on site when required, trades people may stand idle, thereby raising labor costs. If the material arrives too early, it may take up valuable storage space on the site or be at the mercy of weather or vandals. The contractor therefore must schedule the delivery date carefully. To be certain that the date will be met, the material supplier should be contacted regularly by telephone and visits.

The final problem is on-site storage of the material. If the project involves a "tight" construction site, storage space may be at a premium, requiring even more careful scheduling of delivery dates. It even may be necessary to lease additional land or warehouse space near the job site for material storage. If the material is affected by weather, it must be kept covered. Another problem is theft and vandalism. The material storage area must be adequately fenced; sometimes around-the-clock security guards will be required. An inventory control system should be utilized to check out materials to the various trades people, not only to determine which supplies remain but also to discourage internal pilferage.

Labor

The second major element of the construction process is labor. This includes skilled labor such as carpenters, plumbers, masons, sheet-metal workers, welders, concrete finishers, equipment operators, and as many as twenty other skilled trades. Unskilled labor is also required on site for site preparation, construction, and site cleanup. In addition, certain types of labor are needed to service the site, such as truck drivers, warehouse workers, and security officers. The type and amount of labor depend upon the size of the project, the stage of the construction process, and the work productivity of the labor employed.

The first problem facing the contractor is the availability of labor. In some areas of the country, construction is a sporadic activity, and skilled trades people are unavailable or in short supply. In other areas, where construction takes place on a continuing basis, the availability of labor for a particular project may be in especially short supply. The seasonal nature of construction and the overall business cycle also affect availability. If labor in a particular category is unavailable locally, the contractor must either import labor from other areas or—if the project is large enough—engage in on-site job training.

Whether to employ union or nonunion trades people must now be decided. The construction industry is heavily unionized, and in some areas there is no choice but to deal with the unions. If there is a choice, the question is largely one of how best to maximize productivity. It may be better to pay the higher costs of union labor to obtain greater experience and productivity, particularly if highly specialized trades are involved. The basic factor should be the cost per unit produced, not the labor rates that are charged.

If union labor is employed, the contractor must be thoroughly familiar with the labor contracts governing the trades people hired. These contracts are also subject to national labor legislation adopted under the National Labor Relations Act of 1935, the Labor-Management Relations Acts of 1947 and 1959, and the Civil Rights Act of 1964. These acts cover items such as trade jurisdiction, work rules, work hours, grievances, and equal opportunity in employment. In addition, most union locals have negotiated specific contracts with contracting employers regarding wage rates and other localized labor-management provisions. It's generally a good idea to request the contractor to provide a schedule of specific contract expirations or negotiations which might affect job progress and a contingency plan to avoid delays in completion of the project.

Next, the contractor must exercise great care to determine when certain skills will be required and to assure that they will be available and on site at the scheduled time. If crews are unavailable when a particular activity is required, project completion may be delayed. If crews are available too early, they may stand idle, increasing overall labor costs.

Once the project is under way, the contractor must be concerned with working conditions on the site. Areas must be set aside for cleanup, tool storage, rest rooms, and other facilities required for the workers. If union labor is used, these items are probably covered by the union contract. If not, the contractor should take the initiative to assure workers that these facilities will be available. Safety also is a major concern both to workers and management, particularly in light of federal legislation such as the 1970 Occupational Safety and Health Act (OSHA). Steps must be taken to avoid construction hazards, encourage safe work practices, and otherwise assure workers that they will be able to work in as safe an environment as possible.

Disputes between management and labor inevitably arise in every construction project. These may involve jurisdictional disputes, work practices, or events concerning individual workers. Again, if union labor is employed, these areas are probably covered by the union contract. If not, the contractor should establish procedures that will resolve differences as fairly and expeditiously as possible. If disagreements cannot be resolved, the contractor must be prepared to handle work slowdowns or strikes.

Equipment

The third major element of the construction process is the equipment that will be utilized on the job. With increasing labor costs and shortages of certain types of skilled trades, contractors have relied on more efficient equipment to offset rising production costs. Manufacturers have responded with more sophisticated, often highly specialized equipment, bearing higher and higher price tags.

The first problem is to determine what types of equipment to use on the project. In some cases, a certain piece of equipment will be required to perform a particular task, forcing the contractor to choose between competitive manufacturers. In other situations, the contractor must decide if it's desirable to use a particular type of equipment as a substitute for other costs, such as labor or project completion time. In either case, it's important to establish the exact task to be undertaken and the costs of various types of equipment that might be employed. If the equipment is insufficient for the task, the project may be delayed; if the equipment has excess capacity, the cost may be too great.

In determining the cost of equipment utilization, the key factor is not the price of the equipment but the production per unit for the task involved. This may be expressed in terms of yards of earth to be moved, board feet of lumber to be handled, or tons of steel to be erected. The equipment selected should handle the greatest volume of work at the lowest total cost. The best indicator of work capacity is prior experience on similar construction projects. If records haven't been maintained or if similar experience is unavailable, the dealer's or manufacturer's representatives should be contacted for on-site demonstrations of the work capability of their equipment.

The next step is to look at the total costs involved in utilizing the equipment. The original investment cost reflects the cost of purchasing or renting the equipment. Operating costs are operator wages, fuel,

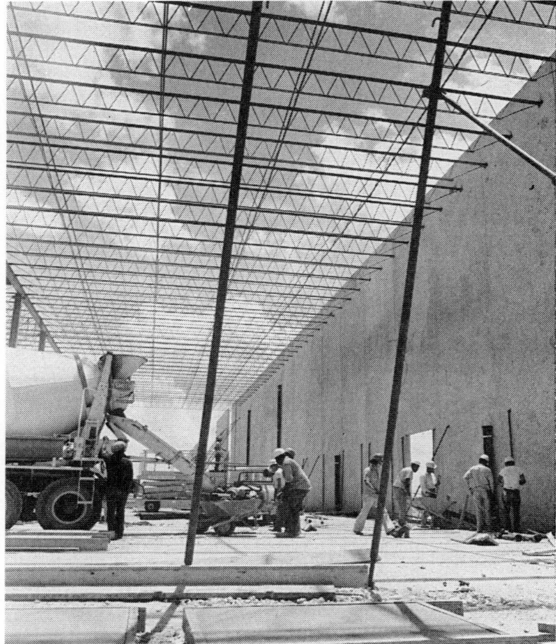

Figure 16-3. From transit truck to wheelbarrow to trowel; well-functioning equipment is vital to any construction job. *(Marjorie Maxfield)*

maintenance, parts, insurance, and the rate of depreciation. The source and availability of replacement parts may also be critical.

In evaluating investment costs, the contractor often weighs rental versus purchase. Renting may be desirable if the equipment is very expensive, highly specialized, or to be utilized only for a short period—e.g., a large crane used for lifting steel beams into place. Renting is also a means of testing equipment for subsequent purchase.[6] Renting is expensive, however, and purchasing may make more sense if the equipment is to be used for a large project or several projects. In considering purchase, the contractor must decide between new and used equipment. Although new equipment is more expensive, it may require less maintenance and have a longer economic life. Used equipment is considerably cheaper and often makes more sense, particularly for noncritical construction tasks or as a backup for new equipment. If used

[6]Some manufacturers have rental option plans, under which the contractor may apply a portion of rental payments against purchase at a future date.

equipment is purchased, it should be thoroughly inspected and, if possible, tested on site.

Once a piece of equipment has been rented or purchased, it must be operated properly on the job. It should not be tied up in downtime. Also, it must not be applied to tasks for which it has not been designed or which are beyond its capacity. The best way to avoid equipment abuse is to thoroughly understand its capabilities and assign its use exclusively to individuals who are experienced in its operation.

Proper maintenance also helps get the maximum service out of an individual piece of equipment. The day is long gone when a piece of equipment was repaired only when it broke down. Today, the contractor must be concerned with "preventive maintenance," i.e., the tune-up and adjusting necessary to keep equipment at peak operating efficiency. Minor problems must be corrected before they become major. A little downtime preventive maintenance is better than long periods of downtime because of equipment failure. Preventive maintenance requires continued inspection by persons operating the equipment and those responsible for its servicing.

Monitoring the Construction Program

Project Scheduling

A recurrent theme has been the importance of materials, labor, and equipment arriving at the site in the required quantities, at the right time, and in the proper sequence in the construction process. Any item that is out of sequence can cause delays or costly storage or downtime problems. In essence, the contractor orchestrates a complex fabrication and assembly process in which all components must be coordinated if the final product is to be on time, within budget, and to design specifications.

The key is preconstruction scheduling. A strategic plan of action must be developed which clearly indicates the objectives to be accomplished, the logical sequence of events required for their accomplishment, and the methods that will be used. This plan must then be put into a time frame, based on contract deadlines, resource availability, and construction season. Early postwar preconstruction scheduling was relatively crude—often no more than informal conversations between the contractor and suppliers, unions, and subcontractors. On large projects, contractors might have attempted to lay out the sequence of events, but they were often hampered by the need to handle great amounts of data.

With the development of the computer in the mid-1950s, several systems evolved to schedule increasingly larger and complicated construction projects more systematically. In 1956, E. I. du Pont de Nemours Company developed a logical network to explain the sequence of events on its construction projects. This provided the basis for the development of the critical path method (CPM) of scheduling construction activity. A few years later, the Navy, in an attempt to control the costs and delivery dates of the Polaris missile program, added other statistical techniques and formulated the program evaluation and review technique (PERT). In subsequent years, CPM and PERT have been so modified that both terms are used almost interchangeably to describe a logical-sequence system of project scheduling.

Two considerations determine the sequence of events: (1) which events *must* occur before another one can proceed (e.g., completion of walls before a roof can be added) and (2) which events *could* proceed, if desirable (e.g., fabricating various elements requiring the use of common equipment). The latter is particularly important in optimizing the overall efficiency of the project. Today, PERT and CPM software programs are available for personal computers, greatly expanding the use of these planning techniques to smaller projects.

Once a CPM plan has been finalized, work schedules can be prepared for various elements of the project. A labor utilization schedule can be prepared, indicating the days on which specific trades will be required and the number of workers who will be involved. Material purchasing schedules can be developed, indicating the type and quantities of materials which will be required on site and (utilizing delivery lead times) the days on which they should be ordered. Equipment scheduling documents can also be prepared, detailing the type of equipment that will be required on particular days and how long it will be utilized.

In recent years, the concept of *fast tracking* has become a popular, lower-cost alternative for building construction. Traditionally, developers have waited until all documents and drawings for a proposed building were completed before putting them out to bid. Under the fast tracking system, the bidding process is handled in phases, with preliminary construction—earthwork, foundations, steel and concrete placement—proceeding while architectural drawings are being finalized. This can result in a significant reduction of time and costs on a large project. If such a system is utilized, it can be incorporated into the PERT or CPM planning process.

Another concept that has been growing in popularity is design/build. Traditionally, the designing and building functions have been performed by two different firms. Under the design/build concept, one firm provides both functions. This can result in lower costs, since the design/build firm is responsible for keeping design costs in line with a total project budget which also includes the construction phase. It can also result in faster completion times because of the efficiencies of working with a single firm. Another advantage of the design/build concept is that a single firm is accountable for the project as a whole.

Value engineering is another concept that can be useful in cutting the costs of a project or getting the best quality for the money spent. The concept involves balancing the functional elements of a project with quality and cost to come up with the highest overall value. For example, a more-expensive HVAC system which operates more efficiently than a less-expensive system might be utilized in order to reduce overall system costs. A less-expensive curtain wall might replace the higher-price one originally specified, if it is determined that quality will not suffer as a result.

Sometimes value engineering is employed when a project budget must be reduced by a certain amount in order for the project to move forward. Building components are reviewed one by one to determine where less expensive components or building methods can be substituted to reduce costs without affecting quality. For example, the architect may have specified heavy and costly stonework where a lighter weight stone might work just as well and result in reduced costs for labor and materials. In other cases value engineering may simply involve finding the best-quality materials for a given budget. In this way the quality of the project is enhanced without incurring additional expense.

Construction Progress Monitoring

CPM also can provide an effective method of monitoring construction progress. In fact, since construction is a highly dynamic process, a CPM plan that is not continually updated will quickly lose its effectiveness. The monitoring should be undertaken by someone who understands both the construction process and CPM networking. This person should analyze data produced on the job (e.g., time reports, material purchases, equipment utilization) and compare the actual time expended with the time allocated in the CPM plan. Frequent discussions should be held with the project superintendent, supervisors, subcontractors, and others regarding construction progress. Field inspections should be undertaken to verify reports of progress.

If evidence exists that the actual time for a particular event will be greater than the time allocated, the CPM plan should be reexamined to determine the overall impact on project completion and the action necessary to bring the project back within budget. The costs of these actions must be weighed against the costs of exceeding the contract deadline (e.g., contract late penalties, loss of tenants, client displeasure). If changes are made, the entire network should be run again and a revised CPM plan adopted.

The development and refinement of the CPM technique has given contractors a common-sense method of planning and executing a successful building project. CPM, however, is no substitute for selecting the best contractor and maintaining close coordination with the progress (or lack of progress) that is being made. An owner who fails to do this can expect major problems in the quality of the building that is finally constructed and, possibly, significantly higher costs than anticipated.

The best method of maintaining close coordination is periodic meetings between the contractor, the architect, and the owner. At these meetings, the current status of construction can be reviewed and any modifications made to bring it more in conformance with the projected schedule. Changes in materials or construction techniques can be evaluated and firm action taken if a change appears desirable. Unique problems, which inevitably arise in a construction project, can be resolved. In all cases, the owner must be prepared to respond quickly and knowledgeably to decisions that the contractor and architect need to make to keep the construction program moving smoothly.

Unfortunately, today's increasingly complex and sophisticated building process may result in disputes and possible litigation between the parties. It is essential that a method of dispute resolution, usually arbitration, be established in the contract documents. The mechanics of the arbitration process should be as simple and efficient as possible, while retaining a concept of equity that will prove acceptable to the parties as being preferable to lengthy and costly litigation.

At the completion of construction, it's important to have a method established for "accepting" the building and making final payment to the contractor. The owner, or the owner's representative, should spend the time necessary to inspect for any defects in workmanship or material quality. Certain systems, such as elevators, air conditioning, heating, plumbing, and electricty should be in operation for a period of time before the building is finally accepted. It's generally wise to withhold final payment to the contractor until these steps have been satisfactorily completed.

17
Marketing

A salesman is got to dream, boy. It comes with the territory.
ARTHUR MILLER
Death of a Salesman

Many developers believe that marketing is appended to a project after construction has been completed. Nothing could be more untrue or potentially damaging to the ultimate success of a project. A sound marketing program is not an afterthought but rather an *organic extension* of the entire development program. If sound market research was undertaken initially, translated into a good physical plan by the planning and design process, and implemented by a quality construction program, the marketing program will follow logically and consistently.

While construction proceeds, the marketing program must be brought to a high level of activity. The original marketing strategy should be reevaluated and an experienced, highly motivated sales or leasing force developed. Advertising and other promotional devices should be used to create interest and to draw prospects to the project. In the case of residential and office projects, a sales compound may be effective in showing what the product will look like on completion. Ultimately, the prospect's interest must be translated into a closed transaction if the project is to attain sales or leasing projections.

Reevaluating the Marketing Strategy

Unfortunately, much time may have passed between the original market research and the formulation of the marketing program. Therefore, it's necessary to redefine the target market to determine what the competition has been up to in the intervening period and—possibly for the final time—objectively evaluate how strong the project really is.

Redefining the Target Market

As noted in Chapters 7 through 11, a real estate project should always be directed at a target market. This will vary with the location and nature of the market area, the degree and nature of competition, the advantages and disadvantages of the subject site, and the quality and responsiveness of the planning and design process. Before finalizing the marketing program, the developer should scrutinize the target market once again to determine how it can be reached most effectively.[1]

The characteristics and preferences of the target market should be described as simply and definitively as possible. For example, a residential sales project may be directed at a target market of "young couples, with one to two children, earning $35,000 to $50,000 annually, who are probably purchasing their first home." An office building in a prestige location might be directed at "small professional and business tenants related to the financial community."

There are two good reasons to define the target market so precisely. First, the developer is forced to ascertain that such a target market really exists and that the emerging project is relevant to this market. Second, the alternatives available in formulating the marketing program are narrowed considerably. The type of sales force, the promotional tools used, and the closing techniques should all be consistent with the needs and resources of the target market.

Reanalyzing the Competition

The next step is to look once more at the strengths and weaknesses of the competition. Major competitive projects that were identified in the original market research should be resurveyed, and particular attention paid to their current marketing program. The sales or leasing success of

[1]If much time has passed since the original research was undertaken (i.e., 1 year or more), it may be necessary to update the market analysis.

competitive projects should also be reexamined and correlated, wherever possible, with the marketing programs employed. A "shopping service"[2] may help ascertain the strength of marketing programs.

The original market research may have identified possible marketing "voids"—areas of opportunity not being serviced by existing projects. If the success of the proposed project depends heavily on relating to such a void, that void should be reexamined to make sure it still exists.

Objective Analysis of the Subject Project

The subject project must also be scrutinized closely to ensure that it is emerging as originally conceived. Locational advantages identified in the original market analysis should be reexamined to be certain that they have not been modified by (1) changes in transportation systems or (2) new projects intercepting potential areas of demand. Proposed planning and design advantages should also be reevaluated in light of possible changes in the competition and the degree to which they are actually materializing as construction proceeds.

This is an excellent time to be absolutely honest about any potential marketing problems the project may have. Too often, the developer rationalizes disadvantages such as poor location, negative neighborhoods, design flaws, or noncompetitive prices. It's far better to identify these disadvantages objectively and correct them if possible—or, if not, to develop a strategy to market around them. At this point, the developer has a current view of the target market for the project, the competition's strengths and weaknesses, and the suitability of the proposed project to the overall market situation. Within this market framework, a marketing program can be formulated to sell or lease the project. The first step is to decide how the sales force should be organized and motivated.

Developing the Sales or Leasing Force

The heart of the marketing program is a highly motivated, smoothly functioning sales or leasing force. Advertising and other promotional activities can interest people in the project, but interest is translated into an economic event only by means of a closed sale or lease. Successful closing requires contact with individual salespeople who properly interpret the needs of

[2]Researchers who survey projects by posing as potential purchasers or tenants.

the purchaser or tenant, relate these needs to specific aspects of the project, and convince the prospect to enter into a purchase or lease agreement.

Internal Sales Force versus Independent Broker

The debate over whether to use an internal sales force or independent brokers has continued for years and probably never will be satisfactorily resolved. A variety of factors enter into the decision to select one or the other option. A combination of internal salespeople and independent brokers, either concurrently or at different phases in the development of the project, may be desirable.

Internal sales personnel generally are most effective for large projects that require close coordination between planning, design, construction, and marketing—which in many cases can only be provided by individuals who are intimately acquainted with the day-to-day operations of the project team. A large project also requires continuity of top personnel in terms of dealing with the local business community and government officials as well as with prospective purchasers or tenants, who may make a final decision only after several encounters with the marketing staff of the project.

An internal sales staff may also be a sensible approach if the developer wants to maintain a continuing sales program in which several small projects will come on stream in serial fashion. This is particularly true if the developer is trying to establish an image for a type of development (e.g., congregate care facility, hybrid office building) requiring a learning curve on the part of the sales staff. The major problem with this approach is coordinating the staff's efforts between the completion of old projects and the initiation of new ones. There is also the potential problem that sales personnel from one project will not be compatible with another market area, regardless of the similarity of product.

The independent brokerage firm offers the advantages of familiarity with the local market area, the ability to move ahead immediately, fewer out-of-pocket costs prior to sale, and no continuing financial commitment once the project has been sold or leased. In leasing situations, the firm may also be able to refer potential tenants from other buildings or, in the case of a regional or national brokerage firm, from other metropolitan areas.[3] The independent broker may also provide other ser-

[3] This may also be an advantage in a sales situation where the brokerage firm is handling the sale of a home in the city a family is moving from.

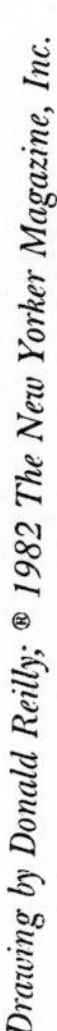

". . . and, of course, the fairways are—eee-yi!—right at your doorstep."

vices, such as market analysis, appraisal, mortgage banking, and property management.

Selecting an Independent Broker

There are several factors to consider when selecting an independent broker or brokerage firm. The broker's experience should be evaluated in relation to the target market for the proposed project. A shopping center broker may be a poor choice for a proposed office building; a residential sales broker may not fully understand apartment leasing, even though the market area is the same. The broker's experience also should be current; a good way of evaluating this is to interview developers who have recently used the proposed broker for similar projects.

The broker must believe in the proposed project. Prospective brokers should be thoroughly exposed to the planning and design of the project, construction to date, and the marketing advantages and disadvantages of the project vis-à-vis the competition. If the prospective broker can't enthusiastically endorse the project, it's better to seek out another than to accept a halfhearted commitment.

It's also important to be certain the broker is not involved in competitive projects which will create a conflict-of-interest situation. If a major conflict exists, it's probably wise to drop the broker at this point or to at least reach agreement that no competing projects will be undertaken during the period of the engagement. A more subtle, and potentially more damaging, problem may be that the broker represents too many clients already to ensure sufficient attention to a new one.

If the prospective broker meets the above tests, the next step is to identify the individual who will be assigned to the proposed project and ascertain the degree of commitment. If a large brokerage firm is involved, it's imperative to meet the broker who will be assigned to manage the sales effort. The individual should be experienced in the type of project proposed, have an in-depth knowledge of the market area, and believe in the marketing advantages of the subject project. The managing broker's personal image should be consistent with the project's image. The individual broker should provide information about the project to other brokers and sales personnel within the brokerage firm who might provide referrals for sales. Finally, the individual broker must be able to devote enough time to the subject project so that an effective sales or leasing effort results.

Listing Agreements

The relationship between the developer and the independent broker is spelled out in a *listing agreement,* which covers such matters as the properties involved, the services to be provided by the broker, the compensation to be received, and the duration of the relationship. The broker is, in essence, an agent of the developer or owner, and the listing agreement defines the nature of the agency relationship.

There are three basic types of agency. In the *open listing* the developer may employ many brokers and pays the commission to the broker who sells or leases the property. If the developer sells or leases the property directly, the broker does not receive a commission. In the *exclusive agency listing* the developer employs one broker exclusively, who receives the commission if the property is sold or leased by anyone other than the owner. Again, if the owner sells or leases the property, there is no commission. The third type of listing, and the most common in development projects, is the *exclusive right to sell contract,* in which the developer employs one broker exclusively, who receives the commission regardless of who sells or leases the property, even if it's the developer.

There are also certain combinations of these forms of agency, such as the *multiple listing,* in which properties listed with one broker are open to other brokers participating in the multiple-listing arrangement. The listing broker who sells or leases the property keeps the full commission.

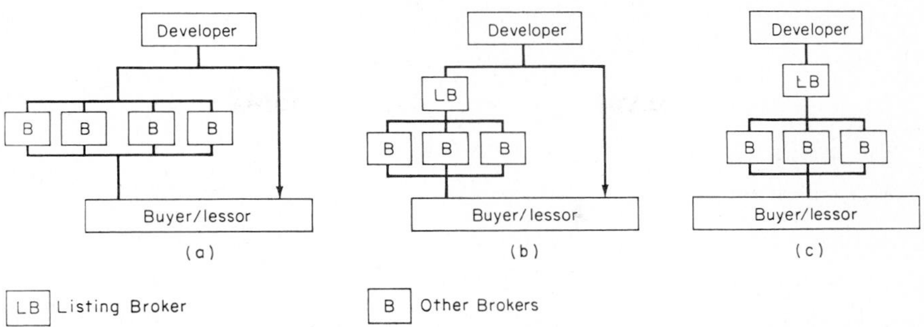

Figure 17-1. Types of listing agreements. (*a*) open listing; (*b*) exclusive agency listing; (*c*) exclusive right to sell contract.

If another broker sells the property, the commission is split on a predetermined basis. A *referral fee* is a flat fee paid by the listing broker to other brokers if they refer prospects who eventually purchase or lease the property.

Increasingly, brokers are representing buyers and tenants as well as developers and owners. Buyer or tenant brokers not only provide market knowledge to their clients but may participate in or handle the negotiations as well. The buyer or tenant broker's fees or commissions may be paid by the client or, more commonly, by the developer or owner. It's important that the buyer or tenant broker disclose early on in any contract with other parties the nature of his or her agreement and the principal(s) represented. In some states, this is mandated by law.

Commissions

Both an internal sales force and independent brokers are generally compensated on a commission basis. Three questions usually arise regarding commissions: (1) How much should they be? (2) What should they cover? (3) To whom should they be paid?

In theory, the amount of commission is established on an individual basis between the broker and the seller.[4] Sales commissions are generally computed as a percentage of the total sale price. Although they vary considerably throughout the country, average commission rates on most real estate sales for various property types are as follows:

[4]Antitrust law prevents brokers from publishing standard commission schedules. In practice, however, commissions tend to fall into predictable ranges.

Raw land	5–10 percent
Industrial building	2–4 percent
Single-family house	6 percent
Shopping center	2–4 percent
Apartment building	2–5 percent
Hotels	3 percent
Office building	2–3 percent

The commission rate also will vary with the dollar amount of the sale, usually decreasing as the size of the project increases.

Leasing commissions typically are based on a percentage of the total rental payments over the term of the lease. If the lease is for an extended term, the commission rate may scale down on annual intervals.[5] Representative examples are:

	Years						
	1	2	3	4	5	6–10	10 or over
Shopping center	6%	5%	4%	4%	3%	3%	3%
Office building	6	5	4	4	3	3	3
Industrial	5	4	3	2	1	1	1

These schedules should be viewed as guides to broker preferences. The actual commission paid is a matter of negotiation between the developer and the broker.[6] The developer should strive to establish a commission rate that provides the greatest motivation for the broker at the lowest total cost. This may not necessarily be the lowest commission rate. Often, it is better to pay a higher commission rate to achieve more rapid sales absorption.

Sales momentum is also a factor. Not only does faster sales absorption reduce holding costs but it also establishes the sales "tone" of the project. A project that is moving rapidly creates enthusiasm on the part of the sales staff and pressure on prospective purchasers or tenants to make a buy or lease decision. To achieve greater momentum,

[5]There is a growing trend away from declining commission rates and toward equal commission payments over the life of the lease.

[6]Leasing commissions may also be based on a fixed dollar payment per square foot of space leased.

it may be desirable to negotiate a commission schedule that pays higher commissions for early sales, scaling down as the project moves ahead.[7]

The second critical question is what the commission should cover. In some listing agreements, the broker is responsible for all advertising costs and possibly even the costs of maintaining the sales office. In other situations, the advertising and other sales costs are split between the broker and the developer on a percentage basis (in practice, the split is often 50-50). However, many developers prefer to pay all the sales costs and negotiate a smaller sales commission to the broker, thus assuring that sufficient advertising monies will be spent at the right time and giving the developer more control over the sales process.

The final question, to whom the commission should be paid or "split," is a topic of great concern to the brokerage community and one on which there is no firm consensus. Most brokers split the commission between the individual broker or salesperson and the brokerage firm. This split will vary, depending upon the strength of the brokerage firm and the individual broker's experience and sales ability. If more than one broker is involved in the sale, the formula may be more complicated—the sales manager gets a portion of each sale; the balance is split between brokers establishing initial contact and those closing the sales or lease transaction. Formulas also may be established to compensate outside brokers who bring a prospective purchaser or tenant to the project.

Project Promotion

The purpose of project promotion is threefold: (1) to identify the fact that the project exists, (2) to inform prospective purchasers or tenants about the project, and (3) to create a sufficiently good impression to bring prospects into the sales or lease compound or make them receptive to a field call. Advertising, public relations, and other promotional activities cannot close a sale or lease, but they can generate the traffic and positive perceptions from which closings are possible. Without the traffic, there never will be a close.

Advertising

Advertising in newspapers, magazines, and other periodicals, as well as on radio and TV, can be an important method of promoting real estate

[7]This approach may prove difficult if a sizable portion of the project is substantially less attractive: the good units or spaces move first, and there isn't sufficient commission to motivate the sales force to move the unattractive units or spaces.

projects. Its effectiveness depends on the type of project, the nature of the target market, the degree of competition, the creativity of the advertising, and the media chosen. The advertising program must be well planned, consistent with the overall marketing program, and targeted to a specific market.

The first step is to decide the extent and nature of the advertising. Generally, for advertising to be cost effective, the project should be relatively large. Smaller projects usually are better promoted through classified ads and signage.

Advertising is most effective when the target market can be reached through clearly defined media channels, for instance, doctors for a medical complex through medical journals or industrial park prospects through industry publications. As the target market broadens, advertising becomes more costly and less effective. Projects directed at widely dispersed target markets, such as single-family housing, must rely on general media channels, such as daily newspapers, general interest periodicals, and radio and television.

The strength of the project and the degree of competition also influence the type of advertising used. Projects located in relatively remote areas or in areas of strict sign control generally require more advertising than those located more favorably. Products in intensely competitive markets also require more advertising, if only to maintain position. The advertising policies of competing projects should be carefully examined, with particular attention paid to the correlation between strong advertising programs and sales or leasing success.

The developer also should decide on the exact role that advertising is to play. If it is primarily to identify the fact that the project exists, the campaign can be simpler and less frequent. If it is to indicate the advantages of the project over competitive projects, the advertising must be more descriptive and intensive.

The next step is to select the media channels for reaching the target market. Again, if the target market is relatively isolated, specific media channels can be readily ascertained. One way to narrow the field is to evaluate the geographic coverage of various media channels and concentrate on those that most closely correspond with the residence or place of business of prospective purchasers or tenants. Another way is to select media channels that appeal to the income levels or life-styles of sales or lease prospects.

The type of media should be considered. Radio and TV represent one-shot types of media: the message must be seen or heard on the spot or it is lost. For this reason, it is generally used as a "call to action," referring the listener or viewer to other media or a "hot line" telephone number. Newspapers and magazines are read at the convenience of the reader, thereby extending the life of the advertising message. Magazines also have a relatively high degree of "second readership"—that is, more than one person may see the same message.

The cost of various types of media also is important. Although TV and radio are expensive, they cover a broad market and the cost per person reached is often low. Newspapers and magazine advertising cost less but may have a higher cost per unit. A rough indication of media costs can be established by dividing the cost per message by the circulation or listening or viewing market of the media involved, expressed in cost per 1000. If the target market can be separated from the general market, target market numbers should be used in the calculation.[8]

Next, the timing of the advertising program should be established. Generally, advertising expenditures are greater in the early stages in order to establish project identity and generate sales momentum. This usually requires broader media coverage, larger ads, greater use of color, and more frequent insertions. If the project begins selling or leasing successfully, the number and frequency of advertising vehicles can be reduced. If sales are not proceeding, the advertising strategy should be reexamined and possibly revised.

Advertising copy is generally prepared by advertising agencies that specialize in real estate. The entire series of ads should be designed at one time so that the overall sequence can be examined. For example, ads run in the early phases of a project may concentrate on identifying the location and features of the project, and later ads may reinforce the image of the project. Ads keyed to special promotions should also be prepared in preliminary form, even if they are ultimately not used.

The advertising budget should now be established. Once the final budget is established, a contingency of 30 to 40 percent should be added to allow for an extended advertising program if sales or leases do not materialize as projected.

Pubic Relations

Public relations can also be effective in promoting a real estate project and creating a favorable sales or leasing image, particularly if it is closely coordinated with the advertising program. A specific strategy should be

[8]Most media maintain fairly detailed figures on their circulation or listening or viewing audience. It is generally wise to take target audience statistics provided by the media with a grain of salt, as they can be exaggerated in order to increase sales.

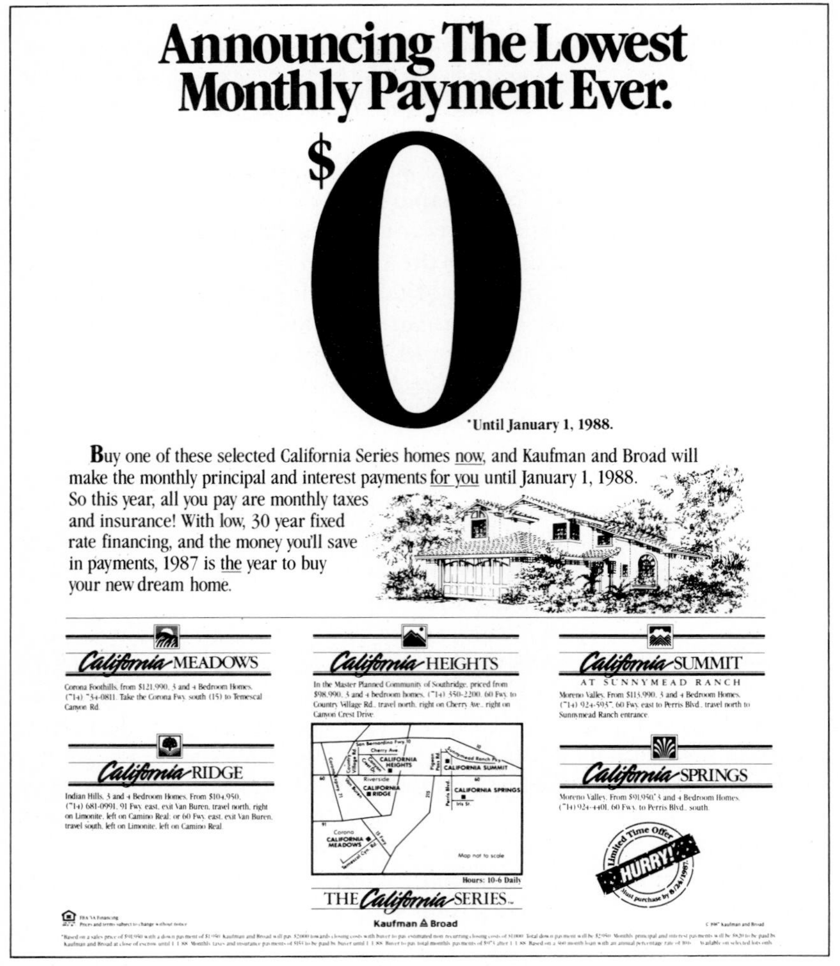

Figure 17-2. Newspaper advertisement designed to attract potential home buyers to a series of residential developments. The emphasis on reduced payments was aimed at the cost-conscious target market. *(Kaufman and Broad Home Corporation)*

adopted from the inception of the marketing program. This strategy should be established and executed by a firm specializing in real estate public relations, which has enough muscle to ensure that the scheduled news stories have a reasonable chance of appearing.

Public relations requires some form of event as a peg on which to hang a story.[9] There are only a few truly newsworthy events connected

[9]This excludes reciprocal PR, where a news story is run in return for display advertising.

with most real estate ventures: the announcement of the project, the opening of the project, ground breaking, topping off if the project is a high-rise building, major leases and high sales rates (residential). Therefore, each of these events should be viewed as an important opportunity to promote the project. Press releases should be prepared well in advance and keyed to release times that will assure maximum exposure. If possible, the event can be enhanced by promotional activities such as speeches, cocktail parties, celebrity appearances,[10] and anything else that will improve the newsworthiness of the release.

Small, specialized publications should not be overlooked. Often, what is not considered newsworthy to major periodicals will interest publications geared to a specialized market, which may coincide with the target market for the project. Display advertising also may be very important to these publications, which would increase the opportunities for reciprocal PR.

Public relations can take more subtle forms as well. Many developers, for example, sponsor cultural and athletic events in order to create goodwill in the community. One large developer recently built a child-care center in a California business park as a way of creating a positive link between the firm and the community.

A greater public relations effort is generally required for projects in large cities where there is more competition for buyers' or renters' attention. In smaller communities, large projects are developed less frequently and thus are more of an "event"; as a result, there is greater opportunity for free publicity.

The PR consultant must be prepared to handle events that might have a negative impact on the promotion program. Strikes, floods, fires, consumer complaints, and other events may damage the success of the project if they are not handled effectively. It's wise to anticipate possible negative events and ways to counteract them. It's better to be prepared to handle adverse publicity that doesn't materialize than to have to respond quickly under pressure.

Newsletters

Periodic newsletters can help promote large real estate projects, particularly those, such as new towns, that require extended absorption. The newsletter can be prepared by the developer or the PR consultant. It should cover newsworthy events associated with the project as well as

[10]Many developers now arrange to identify projects with a TV, movie, or sports personality, perhaps in exchange for a partial ownership position.

Kaufman and Broad Home Corporation

11601 Wilshire Boulevard
Los Angeles, California 90025-1748
(213) 312-5000

NEWS

Kaufman ▲ Broad

Contact:
Peg Hawthorne Kean
Public Relations
Representative

NEW PHASE OF CALIFORNIA MEADOWS HOMES FOR SALE

ANAHEIM, CALIF. -- 13 NOV. 87 -- Kaufman and Broad has released 13 new homes in its latest phase at its California Meadows community located in the foothills of Corona. Nearly 70% of the 345 single-family detached home community is sold with the new homes currently priced from $95,990 to $126,990.

"During the past two months, we have received a continuous flow of interested home buyers, averaging 105 families per week, and a sales average of approximately four houses each week," says Jeff Jameson, vice president of sales for Kaufman and Broad's Southeast Division. "With this most current release of new homes, we will be better able to meet buyer demand."

Kaufman and Broad's California Meadows community offers interested home shoppers five different floor plans.

The Timberland is a one-story, three-bedroom, two-bathroom home. Sloped ceilings add volume to the living room, kitchen and master bedroom suite. A brick, wood-burning fireplace sits in the living room and is visible from the entryway and dining area. A closet spanning almost one entire wall and a pot shelf above the closet appear in the master bedroom suite. The Timberland sells for $95,990.

The Woodland is also a single-level house with three bedrooms, two bathrooms and a private retreat area adjoining the master bedroom suite which can be converted into a fourth bedroom. A walk-in closet and double vanity sinks

- more -

Figure 17-3. A portion of a press release designed to boost ongoing sales in a single-family residential community. *(Kaufman and Broad Home Corporation)*

interviews with satisfied purchasers or tenants and tips on making better use of the facilities offered. It should also head off negative events before they hit the local press. The timing of the newsletter is important. It's best to anticipate anything newsworthy in the progress of the project and establish a schedule that keys every second or third issue to these events. Intervening newsletters can carry follow-up stories from the last news event and preparation stories for the next one.

Direct Mail

Direct mail can be effective in certain types of situations, particularly when the target market is clearly defined. The direct-mail piece should be designed with a specific purpose in mind (e.g., announcement of the project, special promotion, request for materials). The message should be hard-hitting and to the point; direct-mail pieces go into the waste-basket rather quickly. The message should conclude with a request for action on the reader's part, such as coming to visit the project, calling or writing for information, or allowing a salesperson to call. The mailing list should be screened to be certain it hits the target market and is current. The timing of a mailing should be carefully planned to increase the likelihood it will be read. The costs of direct mail are high, but a well planned and executed campaign can be very effective.

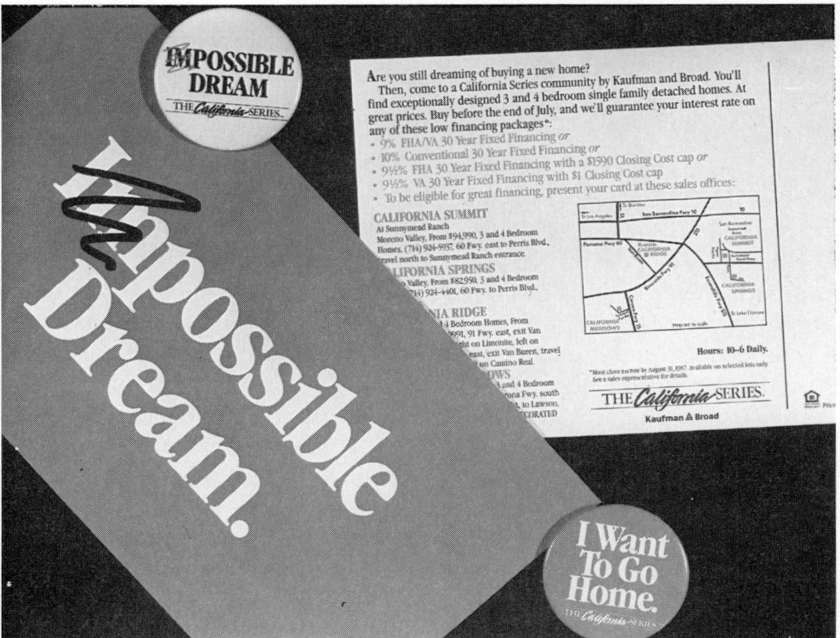

Figure 17-4. Promotional items tied to a direct-mail and newspaper marketing campaign. Postcards were sent to prospective home buyers responding to newspaper advertisements; campaign buttons were given out at the residential sales compound. *(Kaufman and Broad Home Corporation)*

Promotional Pieces

Several promotional pieces can be helpful in selling or leasing a project. A project brochure, explaining the advantages of the project, is necessary, and it should be designed and executed professionally and carefully aimed at the target market. Items subject to change, such as price schedules, should be printed separately. Reprints of ads and news articles also can be effective promotional tools, as can the project newsletter.

Slides, Video, and Films

Slides, video tapes, and films are increasingly used in marketing programs. The presentation may be mobile, allowing the salesperson to go to the potential buyer or tenant, or an integral part of a sales or leasing compound where every effort is made to give the prospect a "feeling" of the completed project. In some of the more elaborate leasing programs, the presentation may utilize a scale model for the filming so that the prospect can visualize how it would be to live, work, or shop in the completed project.

Signage

An effective signing program can be an important promotional tool for most real estate projects. There are three elements to a signing program: external, approach, and on-site signing.

A typical external signing device is a billboard. It can be used to announce the existence of the project and to establish a positive image. Billboards can also be effective where the market strategy is to pull office or industrial tenants from one area into another. For example, a new suburban office building may benefit from a billboard in the downtown financial district. Apartment and single-family projects also can benefit from external signing.

Approach signing has a twofold purpose: it advertises the project to potential purchasers or tenants driving by, and it gives prospects who already are aware of the project directions for finding it. Approach signing can be particularly effective in diverting the potential prospect from a competing project. Copy on the sign can be directed squarely at the advantages of the subject project over the competition, especially if it fulfills significant market voids. The best method of providing directions is by a simplified map or a short phrase (e.g., "first left after lake," "across from Central School").

The purpose of on-site signing is to announce arrival at the project and to provide directions for proceeding to the sales compound. The

pect and counter negative comments as they arise. This approach can also be taken with single-family projects, although the pressures of traffic flow can often diminish the effectiveness of the approach.

Within the models, it's generally best to let prospects move about freely, looking at whatever interests them. The salesperson or leasing agent should be near enough to point out features and answer questions, but far enough away to avoid pressuring the prospect. If there is more than one model, movement between the models should be clearly identified. Traffic should be moved through smaller models into larger ones, thereby creating a feeling of expansion.

After having viewed the models, the sales prospect should end up in the sales office for potential closing. Even if the prospect is being hosted by a salesperson or leasing agent, the model compound should be laid out so that the prospect must end up in the sales office. Here, the salesperson or leasing agent can decide whether to give the prospect brochures and other material or, if sufficient interest has been generated, sit down for serious discussion.

Promotional Aids

Promotional aids can be of considerable assistance to the sales force in successfully closing a sale or lease. Wall and free-standing graphics, such as photographs, ads, maps, renderings, site plans, unit plans, and developer profile as well as samples of material can be effective in establishing an overall sense of the project. A scale model of the project gives the purchaser or tenant a good perspective of the finished product and helps the developer identify sold or leased areas. Signs can be used to highlight specific features that make the project attractive.

The sales compound should also contain sales brochures, floor plans, direct-mail pieces, press releases, reprints of articles, and newsletters. Certain items, such as the sales brochure and floor plans, should be prominently displayed and have a sign which encourages the prospect to take copies home.

The Close

Everything in the marketing program is geared to one goal: the close of the purchase or lease agreement. No single event is more crucial to the success of the real estate project. Unfortunately, most developers don't spend enough time thinking through a sound closing strategy but leave it to the individual salesperson. Many salespeople have developed their closing techniques over the years and often resent the developer's or even the managing broker's involvement in the closing process. The task, therefore, is to develop a closing strategy that will complement the sales force's skills rather than infringe on their territory.

As all good salespeople know, a successful close will occur only after prospects have convinced themselves (both rationally and *emotionally*) that purchase or lease is the right decision. The mental checklist used to arrive at the decision varies with the general tightness of the market and the prospect's degree of sophistication. A person responsible for leasing space for a retail chain, for example, probably gives much more thought to the decision than a couple who are purchasing a home on a 2-day advance trip. In both cases, however, the ultimate decision must be a comfortable one, within the parameters of the marketplace and the amount of time available.

The prospect goes through a mental checklist something like this: "Do I need it? Do I like it? Is it the best available? Is the price right? (Is it a good value?) Should I act now?" The psychology of a successful close is to anticipate each of these questions and continually reinforce a positive decision on the part of the prospect. The question of need generally is established by the mere fact that the prospect is in the sales compound or leasing office or has allowed a field call. In some cases, the need to make a decision will be so intense that no additional pressure will be required. In other situations, a prospect may fall back on the question of need in order to avoid a final decision. Since some degree of need must have existed in the first place, a good salesperson can establish early in the sales conversation the nature of the need (e.g., forced move, expanded space, product upgrade), and, if the prospect appears to falter, adroitly reestablish the fact of the need. Referring to other individuals or firms often is a good method of handling this situation.

The question of liking is more difficult, since it involves individual tastes and preferences. Generally, a prospect must have a good visceral feeling toward a project before a successful close can be made. The problem facing the salesperson or leasing agent is how to identify the specific aspects of the project that the prospect likes best and subtly reinforce them at every possible point in the sales or leasing conversation (e.g., location, view, design, price, amenities), turning attention away from the less-attractive features.

Unless it's an extremely tight market, the prospect will compare the subject project with the competition. The salesperson has to sell against this competition, often without knowing how extensively the prospect has looked or what was found appealing. One way to resolve this problem is to ask the prospect early in the sales conversation which competing projects he or she has seen and then react accordingly. If the prospect has seen many competing projects, the salesperson can subtly sell against these projects by enumerating the more attractive features of the subject project; if the prospect hasn't seen the competition, the salesperson can restrict the conversation to the subject project exclusively.

In selling against the competition, the sales force must have in-depth information about these projects. A shopping service can document the advantages and disadvantages of the various projects, but sales personnel should also visit the competing projects and be completely familiar with their advantages and disadvantages. The sales force must be absolutely honest about the advantages of the subject project over the competition; most prospects will see through unfair or unrealistic comparisons, and this lack of forthrightness can negatively affect a close.

The prospect also will be weighing the price and terms of purchasing or leasing in the subject project versus other projects and in light of available resources. It's difficult to influence the latter, as resources are either available or not; and if they're not, it's probably better to avoid wasting valuable time. In terms of the competition, however, price policy is highly important. If the subject project is lower in price, this aspect should be emphasized as a major advantage (e.g., greatest value, major opportunities for appreciation). If it is more expensive, the salesperson should shift the emphasis to other features of the project.

If the price or rental rate is still an obstacle to closing, the salesperson should be flexible enough to make some adjustments. This is best accomplished by adding features within established price policy. For example, a salesperson in a single-family project might throw in more expensive carpeting or a washer-dryer; or an apartment prospect could get 2 months' free rent. With business prospects, the opportunities for price concessions are even broader, including higher tenant finish allowances, purchase of existing lease, rent moratoriums, more favorable lease terms, and so forth. Flexibility in pricing policy is important; however, pricing concessions should be considered closing tools—not to be employed unless absolutely necessary.

The final question on the prospect's mental checklist is whether to act immediately. In some cases, necessity will force immediate action. In other situations, the salesperson or leasing agent must encourage a decision, and a variety of ways are possible. If the project has developed sales or leasing momentum, fear of losing the unit or space to someone else can be exploited. Fear of external events, such as higher construction costs or higher interest rates, can also be effective in firming up a close. The secret is to make certain that a prospect is sold on the project and then move decisively to elicit action.

This action should always take the form of signing some type of agreement and accepting a monetary deposit from the prospect. If there is still some question on the prospect's part, the deposit can be used to keep the space or unit off the market for a brief period until a final decision can be made. If this approach is taken, the salesperson must follow up firmly and conscientiously; otherwise the prospect may have a change of heart.[16] There also should be some type of follow-up after the close—a telephone call or personal letter—thanking the purchaser or tenant for making the positive decision and extending a warm welcome to the project.

If the buyer or tenant is represented by a broker or agent, the exact nature of the agency relationship should be established early in the negotiation process, including the nature of his or her negotiating authority and the method and source of compensation. In some cases, however, the broker or agent will refuse to identify the principal,[17] and the developer or owner must rely on the professional reputation of the individual or firm involved.

Monitoring the Marketing Program

The developer must establish a system to monitor the marketing program, which should be as simple as possible, generated frequently, and in the shortest possible turnaround time. Such a system has several elements: the first is the overall status of the marketing program versus original projections. There are several key quantitative measures: the exposure of the project (i.e., traffic), the number of deposit receipts or lease deposits, the number of closings, the number of move-ins, and project market share.

Procedures should be established to generate these data at their sources, preferably on a weekly basis. The data should be compared to original projections, and if actual experience is significantly under projections, action should be taken to discover the reasons and remedy the problem.

The basic assumptions regarding the target market should be reevaluated continually. This can be accomplished by collecting data, again

[16]In some states, purchasers of residential units have a prescribed period (usually 48 to 72 hours) to rescind their transactions.

[17]This is often true with foreign investors and major corporate tenants who do not wish to disclose their activities to competitors prematurely.

preferably on a weekly basis, on the composition of the sales or leasing traffic. The sales or leasing log will furnish part of the data (e.g., geographic location of the purchaser, business affiliation). The sales force or leasing agents can also make notes after the prospect has left regarding age, family size, reasons for purchase, features found attractive, and other pertinent observations. If the traffic generated differs significantly from the target market, and sales or leases are not to projections, it may be necessary to reevaluate the marketing program.

It's also important to know how well the promotional program is operating. The cost of the program should be monitored and compared with original budget estimates. Prospects should be queried, through the log or verbally by sales or leasing personnel, as to how they found out about the project. If a considerable portion of traffic is being generated by a particular form of promotion, it may be desirable to allot more of the budget to this area.

The competition also should be monitored periodically. This can be

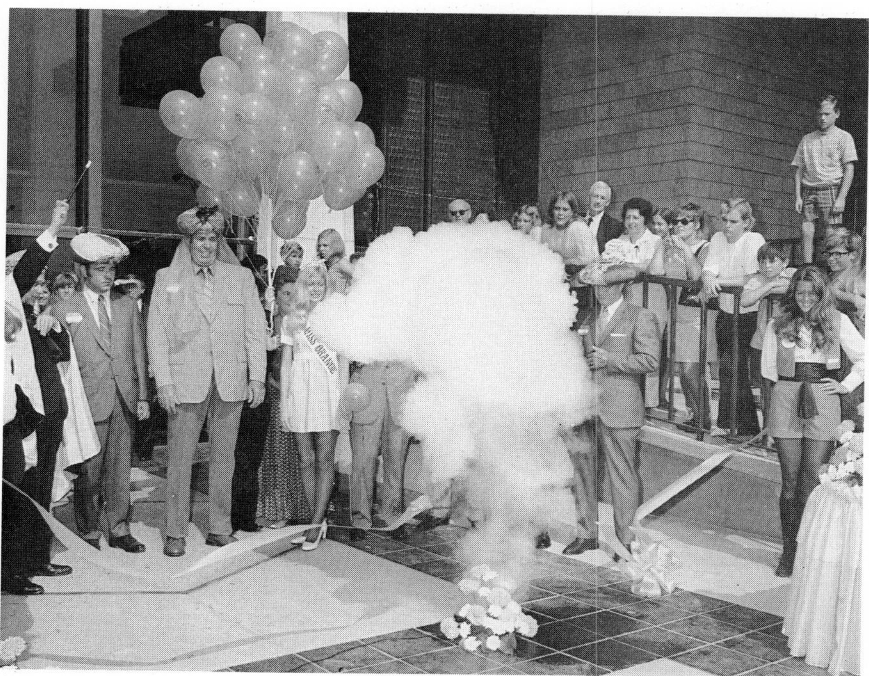

Figure 17-7. With a flourish of his "magic wand," a magician makes the ribbon disappear at grand opening ceremonies for the Mall of Orange in southern California. The novel event was in keeping with the mall's marketing campaign theme, "What the Future Holds in Stores for You." *(Newman Properties)*

accomplished by a shopping service or visits to the competing projects by the sales force. It's also advisable to maintain a continuing log of ads and other promotional devices used by the competition in order to detect changes in marketing policy or particularly successful promotional efforts.

A follow-up monitoring after move-in is also desirable. The purchaser or tenant can be interviewed a few weeks after occupancy to see if any problems have been discovered with the space or unit, as well as to discover which features have been found particularly attractive. Positive interviews also may be employed for promotional purposes if they are approved by the purchaser or tenant.

In monitoring the success of the marketing program, the impact of external forces must be realistically assessed. If the economy has moved into a recession or high interest rates are being used to slow inflation, the entire market for the project may be affected. If these changes appear to have long-term consequences, it may be necessary to revise the original absorption projections and/or modify the marketing strategy.

18
Property Management

I cleaned the windows and I swept the floor and I polished up the handle of the big front door.
GILBERT AND SULLIVAN
H.M.S. Pinafore

When construction has been completed, the project is ready for occupancy. In for-sale projects, such as single-family homes and industrial buildings, the developer's role is largely over; maintaining the facilities is primarily the responsibility of the new owners. In leased facilities such as apartments, shopping centers, and office buildings, however, the developer may retain ownership of the facilities, sell the project to investors, or enter into a limited partnership or other joint ownership vehicle. In all these situations, the developer and/or investor owners must have a systematic method of managing the property: keeping it in good repair, paying operating costs, answering tenant complaints, and securing new tenants as vacancies occur.

The Importance of Good Property Management

Many developers who are intensely involved in the planning, design, construction, and marketing aspects of real estate projects often prefer not to get involved in property management, although the same level of concern may make the difference between a successful and an unsuccessful project. There are several reasons for this. Property management requires extraordinary attention to detail that many developers or investors prefer to avoid. Developers often are "new deal" oriented—impatient with the problems of a completed project and anxious to begin a new one. Investors often are passive, preferring not to get involved in day-to-day operating decisions. Some aspects of property management (e.g., janitorial services, trash removal, repairs) involve functions which are beyond the personal interest or expertise of developers or investors. Finally, many leases contain escalation clauses which tend to lull developers or investors into believing that they are totally protected against cost increases.

For these and other reasons, many real estate people relegate property management to the back room. And yet probably no other area of real estate has a more pronounced and continuing effect on the success of a project. For one thing, a reduction in operating costs can often significantly affect ROI. For example, a 10 percent reduction in operating costs can improve cash flow by as much as 25 percent. Also, a properly serviced building will result in more lease renewals, thereby reducing turnover, vacancy, and leasing costs. A well-maintained building will result in prolonging the physical life of its components, thereby reducing repair costs and replacement frequency. A well-serviced and maintained building will command a greater price when the building is sold, all other factors being equal. Therefore, building owners should fully understand the important role of property management in a successful real estate investment and be certain that the property manager, whether a member of the internal staff or an outside contractor, is performing this vital function soundly and efficiently.

Who Should Provide Property Management?

The decision whether to develop an internal management capability or contract for services with an independent property management firm is fundamental. An internal staff generally makes sense if the project is large and near the developer's or investor's base of operations. The staff may include janitors, gardeners, and security and maintenance people, as well as secretaries, receptionists, bookkeepers, and other office personnel—all usually supervised by a building manager or superintendent, preferably situated in the building.

Independent property management firms should be used for smaller projects or those in distant geographic areas. Some firms specialize in certain types of property—residential, shopping centers, office buildings—and also may specialize according to the size of the projects or the level of rental income. The functions provided by these firms vary, but they generally include leasing, billing, paying expenses, contracting for or providing repairs and maintenance, and preparing operating statements. Since the deregulation of the telecommunications industry, some property managers also provide for shared tenant services such as telephone systems, word processing, and information systems. Compensation may be a fixed periodic amount, a markup on service contracts, or—most common—a percentage of effective gross revenue receipts, usually 3 to 5 percent. In most cases, the leasing and management functions are separated into fixed or percentage-of-gross fees for management and commissions for leasing activities.

An outside property management firm must be selected with great care. The building owner must decide the role that leasing will play. If the building is largely committed to long-term leases, the property management firm does not need a strong leasing capability. If leasing is slow, or high tenant turnover is anticipated, the firm's ability to secure new tenants becomes very important. The best way to determine the strong suits of various property management firms is to talk to building owners and tenants in properties managed by those firms. The individual who will be responsible for the subject building also should be interviewed in some depth.

Once a firm has been selected, a management contract, defining the responsibilities of the property manager and the method of compensation, should be executed. It should be for as short a term as possible or contain a 30-day cancellation clause; good property management firms are usually willing to have both their tenure and the method of payment based on actual performance.

The Lease

The foundation of an effective property management program is a soundly conceived, equitable lease between landlord and tenant. This legal document, and the atmosphere in which it is negotiated, establishes the original contact between the parties and the basic framework for their continuing relationship. It also provides the final statement of rights should there be a dispute. A well-drafted lease will, in most cases, encompass most of the rights and obligations of the parties. However, there is a wide range of judicial and statutory law which may limit permissible terms, aid in interpretation, or provide for given results where a lease fails to deal with an issue.

Determination of Rent

The amount of rent and the method of payment are important ingredients in any lease. There are several methods of calculating rent.

Gross Leases. Most apartment and office leases are gross leases, in which the landlord is responsible for all costs. The rent paid by the tenant may be a *flat rate* for the period of the lease, or it may *step up* or *step down* at a particular time during the lease term. In office leases, the gross lease has been modified to shift part of the costs to the tenant. As discussed in Chapter 14, an expense stop or base year is established with the tenant paying its proportionate share of increases in all or individually designated operating expenses. Generally, these costs are billed to the tenants monthly on an estimated basis and reconciled annually on a calendar year basis.

Net Leases. In a net lease, generally utilized with retail and industrial properties,[1] most of the operating costs are shifted to the tenant. The landlord may pay the operating costs and be reimbursed in full by the tenant or the tenant may be directly responsible to pay taxes, insurance, maintenance repairs, and improvements. Net leases most often are for relatively long periods of time; tenants usually command strong credit ratings. The amount of rent may be established as a percentage of the value of land and improvements.

Percentage Leases. Many shopping center and hotel leases contain percentage rent clauses which gear the amount of rent paid to the operating success of the commercial venture. These clauses may be based on a percentage of the gross receipts, gross margin, or net profits. With hotel leases, the rent may be based on the level of room occupancy. The amount of rent is fixed on the basis of operating results for a specific period, generally a quarter or a year. The landlord usually has the right to inspect the tenant's records and, if necessary, to audit operating results. Many leases provide for a *base rental* to be paid until such time as the percentage rent is greater. In essence, the base rental is absorbed into the percentage rent. The amount by which the percentage rent exceeds the base rental is known as *overage*.

Escalation Clauses. The double-digit inflation of the mid-1970s tended to decrease the yield on leases, leading many landlords to insist upon escalation clauses. An escalation clause adjusts the amount of rent

[1]Office building owners are increasingly using net leases as well.

paid by some indicator of change in monetary value. The most common indicators are the Wholesale Commodity Index and the Consumer Price Index, both maintained by the Department of Labor. Formulas for adjusting the rent on the basis of indicators are established in the lease; changes in the indicator are related to a base period, usually the first year of the lease. During the lower inflation and overbuilt period of the 1980s, tenants have been successful in negotiating fixed increases in rent equal to the current inflation rate as a hedge against future increases in inflation.

Reappraisal Clauses. If the rent has been calculated on the basis of a percentage of property value, a clause may be inserted to adjust the property value at periodic intervals through reappraisal. One approach is for the tenant and landlord each to appoint an appraiser to determine a new property value; if they can't agree, the appraisers appoint a third appraiser. Although the discussion may be acrimonious and the approach cumbersome, the clause protects the landlord, to some extent, against inflation.[2]

Duration of Lease Period

Types of Tenancy. The duration of a lease is influenced by the type of tenancy. Generally, there are three basic types of leasehold tenancies, classified in terms of their manner of termination: (l) tenancies for a fixed or definitive term, (2) tenancies for an indefinite term, subject to termination on notice (tenancy "from month to month" or "from year to year"), and (3) tenancies for an indefinite period, subject to termination without notice (tenancy at will or by sufferance).

If the tenant remains in the premises at the end of a fixed-term lease, a holdover situation is created. Holdover conditions generally are established in the lease or, if not, by statutory or common law. Generally, the landlord has the right to renew the lease or dispossess the tenant through specific means.[3] If a considerable amount of time passes in which the landlord does not take action, the lease may be assumed to be renewed.[4]

In the case of tenancies for an indefinite term which are subject to

[2]This approach is more common in Europe, particularly the United Kingdom.

[3]Most states provide an accelerated or "summary" procedure for removing tenants at the expiration of the term or in the event of its default.

[4]The tenant's position is considerably enhanced if the landlord has accepted rent from the tenant during the holdover period.

termination, notice should be given early enough to allow the tenant to leave the premises in an orderly manner. Sufficient time generally is considered to be the period of tenancy: 1 week in a week-to-week tenancy, 1 month in a month-to-month tenancy. But in the case of year-to-year tenancy, the period is usually 3 to 6 months. *Tenancies at will* are not common; generally, they arise when a lease does not conform to statutory law. A *tenancy by sufferance* occurs when the tenant's original rights to occupancy have expired, as in the case of the holdover tenancy.

Renewal Options. A fixed-term lease will expire at the end of the lease unless the parties have included a renewal clause. This clause generally gives the tenant the option to renew the lease, provided the tenant has not been in default during the lease term and gives the landlord written notice within a prescribed period of time prior to termination. To be binding, a renewal clause must provide a formula for determining rent under the renewed lease.

Option to Purchase. Leases may also contain an option for the tenant to purchase the building during or at the end of the lease period. If it is to be enforced, the option price and purchase terms must be clearly spelled out in the lease, or a specific method—such as appraisal—must be established to arrive at such terms. The tenant normally exercises the option by notifying the landlord in writing and placing the down payment in a purchase escrow.

Rights of First Refusal. The lease may also give the tenant the right to match a purchase or lease offer received from a third party. The offer must be a bona fide offer and indicate price and purchase or lease

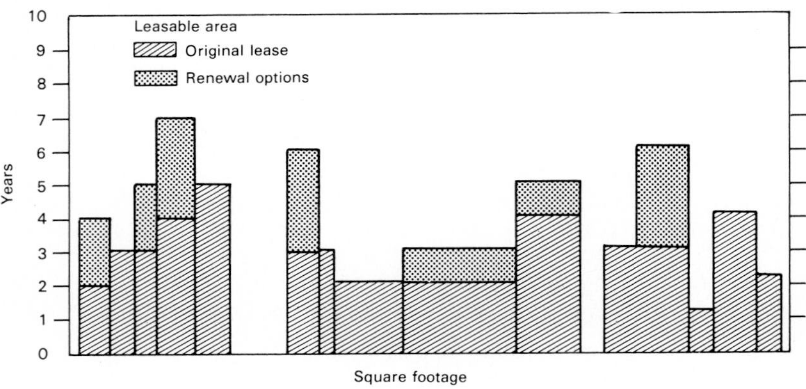

Figure 18-1. Office building lease profile. (*McMahan Real Estate Advisers, Inc.*)

terms. The tenant then has a period of time in which to match or refuse the offer. However, the landlord is not required to sell or lease to anyone.

Tenants' Rights and Obligations Possession. When a lease is executed, a tenant has the right of possession to the property unless other arrangements have been mutually agreed upon. If, for some reason, the landlord prevents the tenant from gaining access to the property, the tenant may have the right to withhold rent and, in some situations, collect damages. Once the tenant secures possession, the landlord cannot occupy the premises or give the right to anyone else.

Use of Property. Unless the lease otherwise specifies, the tenant has full use of the property, subject to the terms of the lease, applicable zoning ordinances, and general provisions regarding nuisance and unlawful acts. Lease terms regarding use generally restrict the tenant to activities in line with the purpose for which it has been rented (e.g., residential, retail business, office commercial).[5] The tenant, however, is usually prohibited from making major alterations to the property that will "injure or diminish the value of the landlord's interest." For example, a tenant could not alter a building structurally or cut down shade trees without securing the landlord's permission.

Covenant of Quiet Enjoyment. Most leases contain a provision that a tenant who pays rent and otherwise lives up to the terms of the lease will not have his or her possession disturbed by the landlord. The covenant normally also extends to claims by mortgagees and lien holders. If a tenant who meets the terms of the lease is evicted by the landlord, the tenant has a right to recover damages. If the tenant is evicted by a third party, however, the landlord is not responsible.

Repairs. The tenant is generally required to "keep the premises in good repair." Some leases require only that the tenant not damage the premises. Other leases specify that the tenant will make "all repairs not involving structural changes." In the most common arrangements, the landlord makes "ordinary repairs" and the tenant repairs flaws resulting from his or her neglect or misuse of the property (ordinary wear

[5]Over the years, use provisions in most leases have grown more restrictive.

and tear excluded). If the tenant fails to make the required repairs, the landlord usually has the right to enter the property, make the repairs, and bill the tenant for the costs involved. In some situations, the landlord may also have the right to terminate the lease if the tenant fails to make the necessary repairs.

Fixtures. Equipment, machinery, partitions, shelves, and other fixtures usually can be removed by the tenant at the end of the lease. This provision is particularly true in the case of fixtures installed for the purpose of conducting a trade or business. If the tenant fails to remove the fixtures after giving up possession, the fixtures usually are deemed the property of the landlord. This also is true if the removal of the fixtures would substantially reduce the value of the property. Occasionally, leases will provide that the tenant is obligated to remove certain fixtures if they are of little potential value to the next tenant.

Dangerous Conditions. Generally, a lease will place liability for dangerous or defective conditions on the party who is in possession and control of the property. This most frequently is the tenant, unless the landlord continues to control part of the property. If the condition existed prior to possession and is not brought to the tenant's attention, the landlord may continue to be responsible. However, if the condition is pointed out to the tenant and no corrective action is taken, the tenant may be liable with no recourse against the landlord. If the landlord is responsible for making repairs to the property and fails to do so, the landlord may become liable to the tenant and any others injured. If the landlord makes repairs, whether required to or not, in an improper or negligent manner, the landlord may become liable. If a public nuisance is created on the property, both tenant and landlord may be liable. This is increasingly true regarding toxic or hazardous substances where lawsuits may be filed against all parties involved, particularly those deemed to have "deep pockets."

Assignment. Some leases provide that a tenant can assign, or transfer, leasehold interests to a third party.[6] In such cases, the lease will usually require that the assignee assume the full rights and obligations of the lease for the unexpired term and be directly liable to the original landlord. The original tenant, or assignor, also continues to be liable for performance under the lease, unless the landlord has signed a release.

[6]Since assignment can materially change the credit worthiness of the lease, most landlords require written approval of the new assignee.

Subletting. Leases may also allow the tenant to sublet all or part of the property to another tenant. A sublease differs from an assignment in that the original tenant becomes the landlord with regard to the space subleased and the subtenant becomes the lessee. As the sublessor, the original tenant has the right to reenter the property prior to expiration of the original lease. The sublessee has no more rights than those that were granted the sublessor in the original lease. The sublessee pays rent directly to the sublessor, who, in turn, pays the lessor. If the sublessee defaults, the sublessor can exercise all rights open to a landlord to collect the unpaid rent and/or legal damages. If the sublessor defaults, the lessor can throw out both the sublessor and sublessee.

Security Deposit. It's customary in most leasing situations to require a security deposit; the amount generally is equivalent to 1 to 2 months' rent on short-term leases and as much as a year's rent on long-term leases. The deposit may be held by the landlord or placed in trust, with interest accruing to the tenant. If the tenant meets all the obligations under the lease, the deposit is returned at the expiration of the lease period. If default occurs, the landlord may use the deposit to cover any damages. In highly competitive leasing situations, tenants with strong credit may negotiate a waiver of the security deposit.

Sale of Property. If the leased property is sold, the tenant retains all rights existing under the lease. The tenant simply begins making payments to the new landlord and otherwise continues to possess and utilize the property.

Rental Income

Scheduled Rental Income

Chapter 17 discussed many aspects of marketing rental space. One of property management's continuing functions is to maintain an up-to-date gross rental schedule indicating the asking price for the units or space. This gross rental schedule should be based on the original rental projections, adjusted for changes in market conditions, increases owing to escalation clauses, and changes in marketing policy. As much as possible, variations in rent between units or space should reflect reasonable differences in value: unit or space configuration, location within building, space or unit amenities, view amenities, and the like.

Maintaining a gross rental schedule, even in buildings with long-term leases, provides a current view of the scheduled income that the building should produce. In buildings with tenant turnover, the gross rental schedule provides an up-to-date pricing list for marketing purposes. Lease terms should be examined continually to be certain the maximum amount of rent possible under the lease is billed.

Effective Rental Income

An effective rental schedule also should be maintained, with the gross rental schedule adjusted for any concessions that have been made. The effective rental schedule should explain the nature of the concession, who extended it, and its date of expiration. This schedule should be considered a confidential management document which is not for outside view. It should be updated as frequently as the gross rental schedule.

The effective rental schedule can help management assess leasing performance. The overall strategy should be to eliminate concessions gradually as the building nears 100 percent occupancy. The degree to which this is accomplished is indicated to some extent by the percentage spread between gross scheduled income and effective income for the space leased to date. If this gap is not narrowing, it may mean that leasing personnel are still extending concessions that may no longer be necessary. The nature of the concession should be continually reviewed in light of its effectiveness in leasing space.

Billing and Collection

The first step in collecting rents is to send the tenant a prompt, accurate billing. The billing should be based on the effective rental schedule, including all concessions, expense prorations, and escalation adjustments. Keeping these items absolutely current not only improves cash flow but also helps to maintain tenant relations. It can be exasperating to be billed for an expense that occurred several months earlier.

Most tenants will pay their bills promptly, making further action unnecessary. Some will not, however, and the manner in which a property management operation handles extended collections affects its success. A follow-up reminder should be sent if the bill is not paid within 5 days. If the bill is not paid within 10 days, a telephone call or personal visit should be made to the tenant, inquiring whether there are any problems with the payment. This personal touch, expensive as it may seem, will pay large dividends in terms of good tenant relations. If the tenant's reason for delay is valid, and the past record has been good, an extension to a firm date in the near future should be granted. If the manager has had little prior experience with the tenant's payment record, the manager must assess the tenant's overall credit worthiness and the probability of payment within the extension period.

If the firm extension date arrives and the rent still hasn't been paid, a final follow-up phone call should be made. If the check doesn't arrive within 24 hours after this phone call, future extensions should not be considered unless there are highly extenuating circumstances. At this point, unfortunately, informal persuasion has proved ineffective, and stronger action is required. A letter should be sent immediately, indicating the amount due and the legal steps that will be taken if the amount is not paid immediately.[7] If a security deposit is involved, reference should be made to the fact that the deposit will be debited for the amount owed and that a new deposit amount will be required.

If the letter does not bring immediate results, it's time to turn the account over to an attorney or collection agency. If the tenant has a record of collection problems in the past, it may be best to proceed with eviction. Recurring collection problems can only dissipate management time and resources, and, unless the market is extremely soft, it may be better to evict the problem tenant.

The collection procedure outlined above is based on three premises: (1) a punctual, accurate billing system, (2) an informal but firm procedure of handling delayed payments, and (3) immediate legal action if the informal procedures are not successful. Some property managers immediately move to threats of legal action; but these often prove hollow, destroying the credibility of the collection system. It's much better to work with the tenants if they have problems and only move to strong collection procedures after all else has failed. Once the move has been made, however, it should be swift and final.

Operating Expenses

Fixed Operating Expenses

As noted in Chapter 14, fixed operating expenses are those costs that do not vary significantly with occupancy: property taxes, insurance, basic utilities, maintenance, and office expenses.

Property Taxes. Property taxes generally are the largest item of operating expense and, unfortunately, the least controllable. However, the

[7] It's often wise to send a copy of this letter to legal counsel, with a notation to this effect.

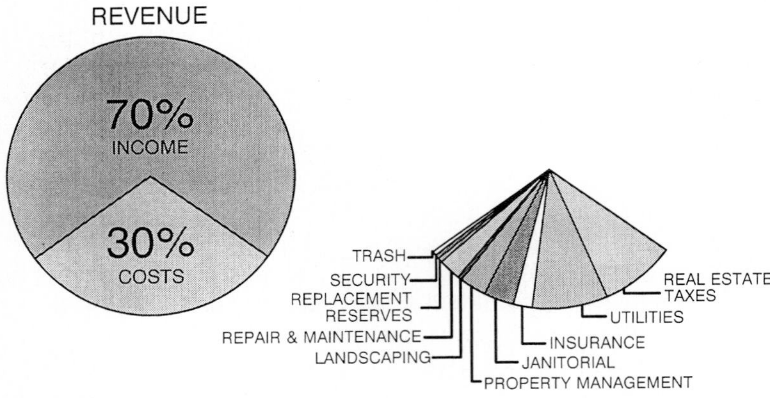

SOURCE: McMahan Real Estate Advisors, Inc.

Figure 18-2. Operating expense for hypothetical office building.

property manager can do a few, limited things to try to keep taxes as low as possible.

The manager should support lobbying efforts against property tax rate increases. Unless faced with a strong property lobby, local governmental jurisdictions will probably not seek other methods of raising public revenue.

Another possible action is to protest any assessment increases. Many property owners believe that assessments are established in a uniform, systematic manner. This is not always the case; often, significant differences exist between similar pieces of property. If the property owner has a strong case against an assessment increase, direct relief may be possible. Even if there is no strong case, sustained resistance by property owners will tend to keep the assessments lower and more in line with actual property values.

If all or a portion of property taxes are to be passed on to tenants, the amount should be billed concurrently with payment of taxes. This, at least, tends to reduce the cash drain created by the property tax payment. It's also desirable to notify tenants in advance of any anticipated increase in property taxes, and, if possible, secure their support in trying to head off the increase.

Insurance. Several types of insurance should be maintained on a building. *Property insurance,* commonly known as fire and casualty coverage, generally is required in an amount equal to 80 percent of the replacement cost of the building. Many owners now carry insurance at full replacement cost since reconstruction would occur under much more stringent building codes. An annual review of the amount of property insurance carried is wise in order to be certain that it is sufficient. It also may help to carry *loss of rental income insurance* to cover the period during which rental income abates because of destruction of the building. In areas where specific hazards exist (e.g., floods, tornadoes, earthquakes), insurance, provided that it is available and that the premiums aren't prohibitive, may be desirable.

Public liability insurance is also necessary for most buildings. The coverage should be reviewed periodically to be certain that major risks are covered and that the amount is commensurate with recent court rulings. It may also be wise to insure against liability claims from the failure of specific components in the building, such as *plate glass insurance* and *boiler and machinery insurance. Theft and vandalism insurance* is a good idea, particularly if the building is located in an area with a high incidence of crime. A collection agent, if used, should be *bonded.*

Insurance costs should be kept as low as possible. One way to do this is to remove or modify any hazards connected with the building that might affect insurance ratings. If costs are involved in making these modifications, they must be weighed against resultant premium reductions. Another way is to shop around for insurance coverage. Property managers often get locked into one insurance agent or company, unaware that they may be paying higher premiums than necessary or getting improper coverage. The insurance agent should be asked to submit the insurance program to several companies each time it comes up for renewal.[8] If the agent refuses, a new one should be considered.

Basic Utilities. Certain utility costs are incurred regardless of the occupancy level of the building. Lighting must be maintained; power must be available to operate elevators, air conditioning condensers and fans, and other service facilities; water is necessary for plumbing, irrigation, and maintenance of common areas; removal of refuse from common areas is also a basic requirement.

It is hard to control the costs of basic utilities, since they are usually provided by monopolistic enterprises whose rates are established by public regulatory agencies. In some cases, however, preferential rates

[8]This is a lot easier to accomplish if the program is handled by an independent agent.

based on usage are available and should be explored. Energy-saving lighting fixtures and improvements to the HVAC system should be investigated to determine if energy consumption can be reduced. With office and industrial buildings, consideration should also be given to shutting off basic utilities at certain times, such as the late evening and weekends. Care must be taken, however, that the overall level of service is not affected, as the cost of continued tenant dissatisfaction may more than offset any possible utility savings.

Common Area Maintenance (CAM). The common areas of the buildings should be kept in a presentable condition, regardless of occupancy. The lobby and corridors must be cleaned, landscaped and parking areas maintained, windows washed, and elevators and air conditioning serviced. Maintenance expenses for common areas can be controlled only by careful, continual analysis of the nature of the service and how it should be provided. A key question is whether to hire internal personnel to perform the service or to use outside contractors. This generally depends on the size of the project and the frequency of the maintenance service. For example, a project with extensive landscaping may require a full-time gardener; a large office building may call for a full-time janitor.

Office Expense. Certain fixed costs are associated with maintaining the office of the building. If the office is not on the premises, there may be a charge for rent. There are salaries for a building manager or superintendent, bookkeeper, secretary, receptionist, as well as such incidental expenses as office furniture, telephone, and office supplies. These costs should be analyzed and controlled on a case-by-case basis, depending on the size and image of the project, the ability to spread costs across several projects, and the strength of the rental market.

Legal and Accounting Expenses. Most buildings have some continuing legal and accounting expenses. Legal services may be required for lease preparation and review, rent collection, and litigation. Accountants are involved in preparing and reviewing operating statements, tax returns, and specialized analytical functions. The best way to control these services is to establish a minimum retainer amount to handle day-to-day items as they arise, providing more extensive services only on approval of the property manager.

Directly Variable Operating Expenses

These costs vary directly with the level of occupancy, and they increase as more space is rented. Examples include tenant utilities, cleaning of tenant areas, trash removal, and tenant maintenance.

Tenant Utilities. In buildings where utilities are paid for by the tenant, the specific utility should be submetered wherever possible; this reduces the possibility of misunderstandings between manager and tenant. If submetering is not possible, a method of cost allocation should be established in the lease, based on some rational standard (e.g., square footage, lighting and power outlets, air conditioning zones). If this was not provided for in the original lease, a memorandum of understanding should be prepared and circulated among the tenants.

In buildings where the landlord pays for tenant utilities, steps should be taken to minimize their use whenever possible. It may help, for example, to make the cleaning crews responsible for turning out all lights after they're finished. It may be possible to turn off heat and air conditioning at certain times when the tenant space isn't occupied. This, of course, has to be weighed against the start-up costs of heating or cooling the space when it is reoccupied.

Cleaning of Tenant Areas. The cost of cleaning tenant areas under a net lease should be based on an equitable proration, generally the square footage involved. With gross leases, cleaning costs can be controlled by scheduling the day and hour of cleaning to follow the period of most intensive tenant usage. In office buildings, for instance, this most often is in the evening, at midweek, and possibly on weekends. With retail facilities, it may be on Sunday or after evening shopping.

Whether to use an internal staff or to contract for outside janitorial services should be considered, depending on the size of the project, potential utilization of the staff on other projects, and the frequency of cleaning required. In either case, a detailed specification of duties to be performed and the frequency of performance is a must.

Trash Removal. Removal of tenant-generated trash should be undertaken periodically, preferably from a central trash collection area. Tenants should be informed when trash will be collected and where it should be placed for removal. Services for special situations, such as move-in, move-out, and parties, should be available.

Tenant Maintenance. Maintenance of tenant areas may involve a wide variety of services: plumbing, electricity, air conditioning, heating,

painting, and repairs. Again, it's important to determine which calls will be handled internally and which will be contracted for on the outside. Generally, it's best if the building superintendent makes this decision only after responding to the tenant call. Many maintenance items are minor and can be handled by the superintendent or internal maintenance personnel. Outside contractors are expensive and should be called only if their services are absolutely necessary. When using outside contractors, a single contractor in each trade should be responsible for all repairs. Thus, the contractor becomes familiar with the building, which reduces the service time and resultant costs.

Inversely Variable Operating Expenses

These costs usually decrease as the building is occupied. Examples include leasing commissions, advertising, promotion, and public relations.

Commissions. Chapter 17 discussed how to establish leasing commissions for investment properties. Most brokerage agreements also cover commissions for leasing activities after the building is in operation. These activities include securing new tenants for unoccupied space, subleasing by existing tenants, and lease renewals. Commissions for subleases and renewals generally are at a lower rate than new leases. In cases where a broker is serving as property manager, there may be no commissions—the building owner may be paying a single fee for both marketing and management.

Since commissions are paid only upon performance, there is little need to worry about controlling costs once the brokerage or property management contract has been negotiated. The funding of commissions, however, may be important in securing better broker performance and improving cash flow. Generally, in commercial leasing agreements, one-half of the commission is due when the lease is executed and the balance when the tenant takes occupancy and accepts the premises. Another method that is sometimes used is to prorate the brokerage commission over the term of the lease, paying only if the lessee makes rental payments satisfactorily. This is used in situations where the credit of the tenant is questionable and default a possibility. Another approach, less harsh on the broker, withholds a percentage of the commission (usually 20 to 50 percent), which is distributed each year as lease performance is realized. This approach works particularly well if the broker is also the property manager.

Advertising. The advertising budget for a building is generally higher during the leasing period and drops to a maintenance budget once a satisfactory level of occupancy has been achieved. In some situations, particularly those involving long-term leases, it may be possible to drop the advertising budget altogether. Another approach is to shift the emphasis of the advertising from leasing space to maintaining the image of the building. This may help to secure higher rents upon renewal and possibly a higher price, if the building is sold.

In the case of retail and transient commercial facilities, the building owner may help tenants carry the costs of their business advertising. This is particularly true with shopping centers, where as much as 20 to 30 percent of the center-related advertising may be paid for by the owner. Arrangements such as these generally are established in the lease or by operating memorandum. In some cases, the center owner may advertise independently in order to increase overall patronage.

Promotion. Special promotions may be used to supplement, or in some cases replace, advertising once a building project has been substantially leased. These promotions may range from pen sets and other mementos to art shows and musical entertainment. Some shopping centers have set aside space for meetings, exhibitions, dances, and other community events. Special promotions also may be employed in fixed-lease projects, such as apartments and office buildings, to maintain good tenant relations. Examples include free theater tickets, discounts on travel, and holiday parties.

Public Relations. A continuing budget for public relations may be advantageous, especially if the project is large and has an extended absorption period. Such a program should emphasize the overall image of the project, for instance through newspaper and magazine articles related to testimonials by satisfied tenants, descriptions of special promotions, and announcements of new building services or features. A newsletter can also be effective in this regard.

Figure 18-3. Many developers, such as The Irvine Company, financially assist merchant tenants with their advertising programs. *(The Irvine Company)*

Allowances for Capital Improvements

As discussed in Chapter 14, periodic allocations should be made from the revenue stream to a replacement reserve account to cover capital improvements that will be required as various parts of the building wear out. Examples include: exterior repainting every 3 to 5 years, new carpeting every 7 to 10 years, replacement of a boiler or air conditioning condenser every 12 to 15 years, replacement of elevators every 17 to 20 years. These costs are over and above normal maintenance and parts replacement and often require heavy outlays of capital.

In theory, capital improvements of this nature should be covered by charges to building depreciation. The problem is that depreciation has been so distorted by tax policy that it no longer applies to funding capital improvements. Furthermore, most building owners consider depreciation as an important ingredient in the cash flow from a building, often spending or reinvesting it as it is generated.

It's necessary, therefore, to set aside an amount each period as a reserve against future capital expenditures. The amount of this replacement reserve can be determined by estimating the physical life of various building components, establishing a cost of replacement (adjusted for anticipated inflation), and prorating the replacement cost over the physical life. These allowances should be funded in an interest-bearing account as they are generated, and they should not be used for other purposes.

Continuing maintenance is extremely important in order to avoid capital replacement earlier than necessary. Unfortunately, many property managers postpone maintenance and parts replacement so as to show better near-term operating profits. This can pose serious problems, especially if the problem is compounded by insufficient replacement reserves. Therefore, the owner must be certain that good maintenance practices are followed, even though they may depress current operating results.

Automation in Property Management

Automation has changed the role of the property manager over the last decade. As mentioned in Chapter 15, increasingly sophisticated "smart" building design now incorporates automation of many of the building systems formerly controlled manually, including the HVAC, lighting, communications, wiring networks, and fire and security systems. Such automation can result in smoother, more cost-effective functioning of the building and result in reduced operating costs. It also requires a higher level of sophistication and training on the part of the property manager.

Automation also has extended to the property management office. With the introduction of property management software that runs on personal computers, virtually any management firm can computerize and streamline office paperwork and increase the productivity of the property management function. Managers who formerly spent the greatest percentage of their time on the accounting function are now able to devote more time to managing their properties.

Computers, when properly used, can reduce the cost of property management. Generally accounting and budgeting are the first functions to be computerized, but many other functions are being handled more efficiently and economically by computers. Leases can be monitored to ensure timely updating of rents. Materials and vendors can be tracked to ensure use of the highest-quality materials at the most economical price. Preventive maintenance can be easily planned and monitored. Detailed space records can be input into the computer to ensure that tenants are being accurately billed for actual space they are utilizing. By using computers, property management firms can handle larger volumes of activity without incremental increases in personnel.

Tenant Relations

A key to successful property management is the ability to achieve the goals of the owner while maintaining good relations with the tenants. This is accomplished through good communications, both formal and informal. The property manager must be open and friendly, while maintaining a strong posture toward collection of rents and equal enforcement of rules and regulations.

This relationship between landlord and tenant begins during lease negotiations as the tenant reviews the physical premises. Upon occupancy, the manager should inspect the premises with the tenant to be sure that all tenant improvements have been provided as stated in the lease agreement. The tenant should be required to sign a formal acceptance of premises notice stating that all terms of the lease have been satisfied.

During the lease term, the manager should maintain contact on a regular basis, generally no less frequently than weekly for larger tenants and monthly for small users. Special billings, promotional or advertising programs, etc., are best discussed in person to gain the support and understanding of the tenant. Retail projects frequently have tenant committees for advertising and promotion and these meetings should be controlled by the property manager.

Lease renewal discussions are generally initiated between the tenant and property manager prior to the scheduled expiration date of the lease. The tenant's satisfaction with the service provided during the lease term can have a substantial impact on the decision to renew. Even if the owner directs negotiations through someone other than the property manager, the manager should participate in the negotiations.

The effective property manager understands the relationship between good tenant relations and net operating income. Consistency, frequency, and quality of service are critical to the successful management of a real estate project.

Monitoring the Property Management Program

The property manager should keep the building owner informed on a continuing basis. The cornerstone of this reporting system is a monthly operating statement showing revenue, vacancies, operating expenses, and capital allowance items. A brief report should accompany each statement, indicating any tenant changes, operating problems, or other events that might affect building profitability. Changes in the effective gross rental schedule should be forwarded as revised; substantial concessions should be explained in detail. The owner should also be informed of any major tenant relation problems, particularly if they might ultimately lead to litigation.

Many owners like to have the power of approval over major events, such as leases above a certain amount, capital expenditures in excess of a predetermined level, or substantive changes in the marketing program. These controls should be worked out in the property management agreement. However, while controls are important, they are no substitute for the integrity of a highly professional property manager. Such a manager can profoundly affect the continuing profitability of a successful building project.

Asset Management

As noted in Chapter 3, the increasing ownership of real estate assets by institutional and foreign investors has led to the development of real estate investment advisory firms which function as "asset managers." Generally the asset manager acts with most or all of the authority of the owner and directs the activities of the property manager. Stated differently, the property manager is one of the management tools the asset manager employs, the others being attorneys, accountants, appraisers, engineers, and real estate brokers.

The activities of the asset manager, therefore, are much broader than those of the property manager and typically include *strategic planning with the investor* to determine overall investment objectives, the ultimate size of the portfolio, proper levels of diversification, minimum return standards, and the timing of available funds; *establishment of investment criteria* for individual properties to be included in the portfolio, including, among other things, type of property (e.g., office, retail, industrial, hotel); acceptable geographical market areas; size of property; age of property; stage of development; minimum tenant credit standards; desirable lease terms; suitability of leverage; type of investment vehicles contemplated (e.g., all cash, convertible mortgage, participating mortgage, joint venture); specific exclusions (e.g., ground lease, flat leases, type of construction); and minimum annual return (e.g., capitalization rate; IRR); and *acquisition of assets meeting the investment criteria*. Activities of the asset manager in this area include locating the property; evaluating its appropriateness for the investor's portfolio; negotiating the purchase transaction; supervising due diligence activities; and overseeing the closing process, including the movement and temporary investment of funds.

Once a property has been added to the portfolio, the asset manager is responsible for its *operation over the holding period*. This typically includes:

- Selection and supervision of a property manager. In some cases, property management activities may be performed by the asset manager.
- Establishment of an annual operating plan and budget.
- Review and approval of all leases.
- Review and approval of all management contracts with outside services such as trash collection, security, and advertising.
- Review and procurement of required insurance.
- Maintaining relations with governmental agencies; ensuring compliance with applicable regulations.
- If the property is leveraged, maintaining relations with lenders; ensuring that mortgage payments are made and the lease is not in de-

fault. If desirable, recommending and implementing refinancing of the investment, which may be subject to investor approval.

- Supervising design and construction of tenant areas.
- Recommending and implementing design and construction related to remodeling, alterations, and additions to the building(s).
- Development and management of required accounting and reporting systems.
- Supervision of the management of cash generated by and invested in the property.
- Interfacing with investor attorneys regarding the operation of the property, including any possible litigation that might arise.
- Interfacing with investor accountants retained to determine the financial status of the property and reporting to applicable governmental agencies, including the preparation of annual income tax returns.
- Interfacing with investor appraisers to establish the overall operating performance of the property.

At some point in the holding period, the asset manager may *dispose of the property or recommend to the investor that the property be sold.* If this occurs, the asset manager may be responsible for any physical improvements prior to sale; supervising the preparation of promotional materials; interfacing with the brokerage community, if brokers are utilized; negotiations with prospective purchasers; and supervision of the closing process, including the management of funds and final reporting to the investor and any applicable governmental agencies.

With the separation of the production and ownership of real estate, the role of sound property management has become increasingly important. This has led to a broad effort on the part of professional associations, as well as universities and industry groups, to improve the training and quality of property managers. In many cases, developers have been in the forefront of this effort, recognizing that the investment potential of a property is not fixed at the time when construction is completed. Effective, ongoing property management is essential to maintaining and enhancing the value created by the development process.

Appendix

The Appraisal Process

Definition of Market Value

Unfortunately, there are no clear definitions of "value" as applied to real estate. Some economists believe that the value of a property is synonymous with market price, assuming that the price was reached under competitive conditions. Other economists feel that a property has an "intrinsic value" which may vary from the current meaning of value. While most appraisers believe that the value of a property is the price that a willing buyer would offer and a willing seller would accept, others qualify the motives of the buyer and the seller. This approach stresses that a property's value may vary, depending on whether it is to be sold quickly, held for speculation, or developed.

The major appraisal professional organization, the American Institute of Real Estate Appraisers, has defined market value as:

> The most probable price, as of a specified date, in cash, or in terms equivalent to cash, or in other precisely revealed terms, for which the specified property rights, should sell after reasonable exposure in a competitive market under all conditions requisite to fair sale, with the buyer and seller each acting prudently, knowledgeably, and for self-interest, and assuming that neither is under undue stress.[1]

The Institute goes further to stress that market value is the amount of cash paid to the seller, plus or minus adjustments for leaseholds, seller financing, or other benefits to the seller.

The purpose of this appendix is not to add further definitions of

[1]*The Appraisal of Real Estate*, 9th ed., American Insitiute of Real Estate Appraisers, Chicago, Ill., 1987, p.19d.

value but rather to inform the reader briefly about how professional appraisers estimate value, to point out certain problems and weaknesses with the traditional approach, and to discuss several techniques that offer promise in resolving these problems.

The Traditional Approach

It's important to understand at the outset that an appraisal is not an exact determination of value but an estimate, derived from a logical evaluation of observable facts, of the *probable value* of property. This logical evaluation traditionally involves at least seven major steps: (1) definition of the problem, (2) formulation of a plan to attack the problem, (3) collection and preliminary analysis of data, (4) highest and best use analysis, (5) an estimate of land value, independent of any improvements, (6) application of three separate and distinct approaches to estimating the value of both land and improvements, and (7) a reconciliation of the three approaches to arrive at a single estimate of value. Each of these steps is discussed below.

Definition of Problem

The first step in the traditional appraisal process is to define the problem. The subject property must be identified as to location, size, configuration, topography, and any other distinguishing characteristics. The "bundle of legal rights" to the property must also be specified. These rights might include fee simple ownership of both land and improvements, or the structures and land might be dealt with separately. Zoning and other development controls affecting the subject property should also be identified. Because both physical and economic factors change with time and affect the value of the property, the effective date of the appraisal should also be identified.

Since the appraisal establishes a "benchmark" of value for a particular decision, the appraiser must know and clearly understand the reason that the client wants the appraisal prepared. This objective will determine the definition of the value to be appraised—usually market value but possibly insurable, loan, rental, or merger value. These questions must be resolved at the beginning of the process, because the nature of the problem or the value to be estimated dictates the methodology to be used.

Formulation of Plan

Next, the appraiser develops a plan to attack the problem, outlining the procedures to be followed and the content of the report. The type of property and the purpose of the appraisal determine the data that will be required and, usually, the sources of those data.

Data Collection and Analysis

Data collection and analysis is a very important part of an appraisal. The output, or the appraised value of a property, can only be as good as the input. General data concerning the market area as well as economic levels and trends should be collected. Specific data concerning the subject property and comparative properties are also required. Only data which bear on the value of the property to be appraised should be considered.

Highest and Best Use Analysis

As noted in Chapter 6, a parcel of land is at its highest and best use when it is used for purposes which have the highest comparative advantage or least comparative disadvantage in relation to possible alternative uses. By undertaking a highest and best use analysis, the appraiser considers the various market forces that affect a property and identifies the use for which the market value estimate is to be based.

In identifying the highest and best use, the appraiser considers two situations: (1) the use of the land as though the parcel were vacant; and (2) the use of the property as improved. In some situations, the use under these scenarios is different, reflecting the fact that the property is under- or overimproved.

The highest and best use analysis of the land as vacant assists the appraiser in identifying comparable properties that have recently been sold in the marketplace. Properties that do not meet the use test are eliminated at this point. The analysis also will prove helpful in deriving a land value estimate for use in the cost approach to value. The analysis of the use of the property as improved also helps in establishing comparable properties, as well as determining whether the improvements should be retained, rehabilitated, or demolished.

Land Value Estimate

Once a parcel's highest and best use has been established, a separate valuation of the land parcel may prove useful, particularly if the cost approach to value is to be utilized. The land value can be established through a comparison to comparable land sales, a separation of value between land and improvements through income capitalization techniques, or, in the case of subdivision development, by subtracting the costs of development and discounting the net income over the absorption period.

Application of the Three Approaches to Value

In arriving at a final value estimate, the appraiser traditionally has considered three approaches to value: (1) the *sales comparison approach,* whereby the value is indicated by the recent selling prices of comparable properties, (2) the *income capitalization approach,* whereby the value is determined by capitalizing project income to arrive at an investment value, and (3) the *cost approach,* whereby the value is derived by estimating the cost to reproduce the building and then adjusting this estimate for appropriate depreciation and land value. This threefold approach to determining value is utilized in order to reflect the various ways in which properties compete with each other, as an internal check on the valuation process, and because market data often are not readily available.

The Sales Comparison Approach. The sales comparison approach to value compares the subject property with other similar properties that have been sold recently, as well as with current asking prices and offers. The first step is to collect data regarding sales of reasonably comparable properties. Such data should include the location and size of the property (both physically and in terms of its economic potential); legal restrictions such as zoning, deed restrictions, and easements; and any other pertinent information that would influence its market value.

The sales data then must be adjusted to be as comparable as possible to the subject property. This adjustment may be made judgmentally by evaluating all the factors which influence the value of the comparable sale and making a *lump sum* or *aggregate adjustment* reflecting the differences between the comparable sale and the subject property. For example, an appraiser might conclude that, on the basis of a comparable sale at $150,000, the subject property would have sold at $175,000. No distinction is made for the individual elements of difference between the two properties, although such distinction is inherent in the judgmental process.

A refinement of the lump sum approach is the *component approach,* in which each of the individual elements comprising value (e.g., location, quality of buildings, economic productivity, terms of sale) is broken down and evaluated independently. Positive or negative values are ascribed to each component to reflect differences between the comparable sales and the subject property. These values may be expressed in either dollar or percentage terms. An example of this approach utilizing dollar adjustment would be:

Comparable sale	Location	Terms of sale	Indicated value of subject property
$15,000,000	+$3,000,000	-$1,000,000	$17,000,000

This process can be repeated for each of the comparable sales collected.

Another approach to adjustment is the *index method,* also called *factor analysis* or the *grid system,* in which differences in value are expressed in terms of percentages instead of dollars, with the comparable property representing 100 percent. An example would be:

Comparable sale	Location	Terms of sale	Index of comparability	Indicated value of subject property
$15,000,000	120	93.33	113.33	$17,000,000

The comparable sales price is then adjusted by the index of comparability to arrive at the value of the subject property. Adjustments may also be made through use of percentages directly, without transforming them into an index. In some cases, the percentages are summed to arrive at an overall adjustment percentage. When this is done, it is important that the appraiser follows a consistent sequential pattern in arriving at the overall percentage adjustment. The sequence recommended by the American Institute of Real Estate Appraisers is:[2] (1) adjustment for property rights conveyed, (2) adjustment for financing terms, (3) adjustment for conditions of sale, (4) adjustment for market conditions, (5) adjustment for location, and (6) adjustment for physical characteristics. In this manner, the appraiser arrives at intermediate prices and applies subsequent adjustments to each previously adjusted price.

Once the comparable sales data have been adjusted to be as comparable as possible to the subject property, the timing of comparable sales is considered in order to determine the overall trend of value in the marketplace up to the time of the appraisal. In reaching a final determination of value, the most recent sales are usually assigned the greatest

[2]Ibid., p. 328.

value. If a significant amount of time has passed since sales have occurred, the appraiser may be forced to depend more on the income or cost approach.

The Income Capitalization Approach. This approach, primarily utilized with investment properties (e.g., apartments, office buildings, shopping centers), considers the income that the subject property can generate over its economic life and compares this income stream to other comparable properties in the marketplace, as well as other forms of investment. The future income stream is determined in a manner similar to that outlined in Chapter 14. Existing leases are evaluated or, if no leases exist, the most probable gross income that can be obtained, based on an evaluation of comparable properties, is evaluated. The first step is a rental survey to determine the market rent for the subject property, i.e., the rent that it could achieve if it were vacant and available for lease. It is critical to compare unit factors, such as rent per unit or rent per square foot, that are derived on the same basis. For example, a single-tenant office building might be leased on a gross area basis; most mid- and high-rise multitenant office buildings in suburban locations are leased on the basis of usable area. Rental rates that appear very different may in fact only be expressed relative to different measurable areas. Similarly, rental rates may vary because they cover different expenses. Again, an office lease might be gross, with the landlord paying all expenses (at least for the base year), or net, with the tenant paying all expenses.

Once all of the comparables have been expressed using a common unit of comparison, such as monthly gross rent per square foot of net rentable area, the rentals can be adjusted to provide an indication for the subject property. The process is essentially the same as that in the sales comparison approach. Adjustments are first made for any rental concessions, then for time, and next for location and physical characteristics. The result is an indication of market rent.

If the appraiser has been engaged to appraise the fee simple estate, the market rent per square foot will be multiplied by the appropriate area to reach an estimate for potential gross income (PGI) per year. If, however, the appraiser has been requested to value the leased fee estate, he or she will also have to reflect the contract rent payable under any existing leases. The value contribution of these leases is based on whether the contract rent less expenses is greater or less than the market rent less expenses. The margin between the net market and net contract rents affects value only for the duration of each lease. Therefore, the value of the contract is usually considered separately and after a conclusion has been reached for the value of the property as if leased at market rents. The one exception occurs if the contract(s) extends 10 years or more. The contract rent may then be used to develop potential gross income.

The potential gross income is converted to effective gross income (EGI) by deducting the vacancy and collection loss that can reasonably be expected over the life of the building. Any short-term vacancy higher or lower than the stabilized rate should be treated separately by discounting it over the expected period of duration.

The gross income generated is then reduced by the expenses that are consistent with the rent estimate. For example, if the market rent conclusion has been reached as a net rent per square foot, the only expenses will be vacancy and collection loss, management, and reserves. Additional expenses incurred if the lease is gross include property taxes, insurance, general operating expenses (e.g., utilities, air conditioning, trash removal, repairs and maintenance), property management costs, and miscellaneous expenses such as licenses, advertising, supplies, and telephone. Janitorial and security services may or may not be provided under a gross office lease. Also, it should be noted that market rent may be net, but existing leases may obligate the landlord to pay certain expenses. The pro rata share of these expenses attributable to the space occupied under the old leases is a property expense until the leases expire.

The projected expenses associated with the subject property are deducted from the gross income to arrive at net operating income. The appraiser then analyzes the income and expense projections to determine whether any of the projections are inconsistent with comparable properties in the area. If significant inconsistencies exist, the appraiser may stabilize income or adjust expenses to arrive at a more realistic level of net operating income.

Projected net operating income is then translated into a capital value through the capitalization process. The first step in this process is to determine the *capitalization rate,* or "cap rate," which reflects the relationship between the net income stream and the value of the property. The capitalization rate includes both (1) the *interest rate,* which is the rate of return on the investment and (2) the *recapture rate,* which is the rate of return of the investment.

Capitalization rates are determined by the *direct capitalization method* and the *yield approach.* In the direct capitalization method a single year's net operating income is divided by the capitalization rate to arrive at the value of the property. The capitalization rate is either an *overall capitalization rate* which includes land and improvements or a *split rate* which separates them for independent analysis.

The overall capitalization rate is established through a variety of techniques. The *market method,* also called the *comparative method,* is based on the ratio between the sales price of comparable properties and the income from these properties. For example, a property which sold for $20 million and had an annual net operating income of $2 million would have an overall capitalization rate of 10 percent ($2 million divided by $20 million).

It's important in comparing properties that operating expenses, financing terms, and market expectations are similar to the subject site. If this type of information is not available, it may be necessary to utilize a *gross income multiplier* approach in which the gross income of the property is compared with the sales price. Since the comparability of the properties is not known, this is generally a less desirable approach.

The *band of investment method,* also called the *synthetic rate method,* considers the debt financing on the subject property and the rate of equity return on the amount of equity funds required. This approach requires a current knowledge of both mortgage rates and the yield expected by equity investors. Such information can be gained by examining comparable projects in the market area or by broad rules of thumb based on current market conditions.

The equity capitalization rate represents the first year's pretax cash return anticipated by an investor. The capitalization rate for debt is the mortgage constant. Both debt and equity rates are multiplied by the percentage of the investment that they constitute in order to arrive at a weighted interest rate. For example, a property valued at $20 million with a mortgage of $18 million at 9 percent for 30 years would have the following overall capitalization rate:

Mortgage	$18,000,000	90%	.1009%	9.1%
Equity	2,000,000	10%	.0900%	.9
Totals	$20,000,000	100%		10.0%

Today, most appraisers use this approach as a check on capitalization rates derived from market comparables.

Another traditional method, now used primarily as a check on market derived data, is the *component rate method.* This approach attempts to identify the various elements affecting the investment, assigns a rate to each, and then sums the rates to arrive at an overall capitalization rate. Generally, a "safe rate of return" is established as a base, reflecting the rate of return on investments having the greatest liquidity and safety (e.g., long-term U.S. government bonds). To this base is added judgmental assessments of various rates, reflecting factors such as the degree of risk inherent in the land uses which generate the net income stream, the costs of managing the investment, and the nonliquidity of the investment. For example, a property might have the following component rates:

Safe rate	3.0%
Risk rate	2.0
Burden of management	1.0
Penalty for nonliquidity	0.5
Recapture of investment	3.5
Total rate	10.0%

The exact component will vary with each property being appraised. The risk rate generally will decrease as the quality of the income improves.

In addition to the overall capitalization rate, split rates are utilized, in which the land and buildings are capitalized at different rates (the rates of the land generally are lower, reflecting greater permanence and hence less risk). The rate is split to arrive at a separate value for land or buildings, through a technique known as the *residual approach,* used when the building value is known and the appraiser wishes to determine the value of the land (land residual) or when the land value is known and the building value is being sought (building residual). The two values are then summed to arrive at a total value for the subject property.

In recent years, the direct capitalization approach has been augmented and, in some cases, replaced by the yield capitalization approach. This method is similar to the discounted cash flow analysis discussed in Chapter 14, except that a current market value is solved for rather than a yield. The yield, or discount rate, is determined by the appraiser based on capital market considerations and the hurdle rates required by knowledgeable investors operating in the marketplace for similar types of property. In situations involving leverage, a separate yield rate may be used for mortgage and equity components.

Once the capitalization rate has been established, the market value of the subject property can be determined. If an overall rate is used, it is divided into the net income developed from market rent.[3] Any short-

[3]It may be divided into contract rent only if the contract is 10 years or longer, and the sales from which the overall rate was derived were similarly leased.

term positive or negative rental margins from existing leases are discounted over the remaining term of each lease, generally using the factor for the present worth of $1 per period. The present worth of the leases is then totaled and added to, or subtracted from, the value based on market rent.

If a yield rate is used, it is applied to a series of cash flows over a holding period. The property is assumed to sell at the end of this holding period, and the net sale proceeds are discounted back to the date of value and added to the present worth of the cash flows. Using this method, each lease is typically entered at the contract rate, rolling over to today's market rent increased by an inflation factor when the lease expires. Application of the yield rate to the cash flows generated by this revenue stream results directly in the leased fee value, without the need of valuing the fee simple estate as an interim step.

This valuation through the income approach is then compared to the valuation achieved through the market approach. If there are major divergences in the two approaches, the appraiser generally reviews the assumptions utilized in the income approach, since they are subject to greater distortion by the capitalization process. Unless the income stream is highly predictable and capitalization rates are well established in the marketplace, the appraiser usually will place greater emphasis on the valuation obtained through the market approach.

The Cost Approach. The third approach to value is the cost approach, in which the cost of reproducing the economic capacity of the building is estimated, less accrued depreciation to date, plus a separate value for the land. This approach generally is used as a check on valuations which have been estimated through the market or income approach or for special-purpose properties for which comparable market data are unavailable or the income approach is not applicable. The cost approach is also required by the Federal Home Loan Bank Board unless the appraiser can prove it's unnecessary.

The reproduction cost of the building is determined through one or more estimating techniques. One of the most common is simply to update the original construction costs by a *relative cost index* which compares current costs of reproduction with previous periods. This method is used primarily by assessors in appraising large numbers of properties. A more accurate, although time-consuming, method is to calculate the square foot area, cubic foot volume, number of rooms, or some other physical unit and multiply this by a current estimate of unit costs for the type of construction involved. This is known as the *comparison cost method* and is commonly required by construction lenders and the Federal Home Loan Bank Board.

The most accurate, and most time-consuming, method is the *unit-in-place method,* in which the appraiser actually performs a modified quantity takeoff, much the same as a building contractor. A quantity takeoff is based on detailed plans and specifications; the building is broken into its various components, and unit costs are developed for each component, based on local labor market conditions, material prices, overhead rates, and so forth. The appraiser does not use building specifications but breaks the building down into various structural elements (e.g., foundation, walls, floors, roof) and estimates the costs of materials, labor, and overhead for each element. Then the cost of architect's fees, contractor's profit, financing, property taxes and insurance during construction, and all other costs of project development are added.

Once the cost of reproducing the building has been determined through one or more of these techniques, the next step is to estimate the amount of accrued depreciation, or the loss of value that has occurred in the building since it was originally built. This loss is a function of physical deterioration, functional obsolescence, and economic obsolescence.

Physical deterioration is the reduced value of the structural elements of the building through decay, cracking, settling, or just wear and tear. The amount of depreciation resulting from physical deterioration is calculated by comparing the effective remaining physical life of the building with what it would be if it were new. For example, the depreciation charge for a building with 20 years' remaining physical life, which, if built new, would have a physical life of 50 years, would be 60 percent if a straight-line method were used. If the depreciation curve published in the *Marshall Valuation Service* were used, the depreciation would be only 34 percent. The depreciation is about one-half that using the straight-line method, because the curve reflects the fact that depreciation accrues slowly through a building's midlife and accelerates rapidly toward the end.

Functional obsolescence is reduced value owing to poor original design or to improvements in design which have made certain elements of the building obsolete. Examples include poorly placed columns, inadequate elevators, and lack of air conditioning. Depreciation charges for these are calculated on the basis of repairing or replacing the components of functional obsolescence, less the proportion of physical deterioration already charged. In the example above, if the cost of new elevators were $300,000, the depreciation charge would be $120,000

($300,000 less 60 percent). If the problem is incurable, the obsolescence is measured by capitalizing the rent loss.

Economic obsolescence occurs as a result of external forces, such as poor site location, deterioration in the neighborhood, or changes in tax or lending policies. A depreciation charge reflecting economic obsolescence can be calculated by comparing the rental value of the subject property with a similar type of improvement on a good site in a good location and adjusting for additional expenses associated with the "ideal" location. This lowered income stream is then capitalized to arrive at a depreciation charge that is caused by economic obsolescence. For example, if the subject site generates $10,000 less annually than it would in an ideal location but would cost an additional $4000 annually to be in the ideal location, the annual net loss is $6000. Capitalized at 10 percent, this would indicate a depreciation charge of $60,000. The charge can also be estimated by determining the present value of the rental loss at a predetermined discount rate.

The final step in the cost approach is to determine land value. This is usually based on a comparison of the land associated with the subject property with other similar property in the area, adjusting for differences such as size, location, or accessibility. A unit cost is developed for the adjusted value of the comparable properties and then multiplied by the square footage or acreage of the subject property. The value of the land estimated in this manner is then added to the cost of the improvements, less applicable charges for depreciation, to arrive at the total value derived through the cost approach. As noted previously, this step may have been taken earlier in the appraisal process.

Reconciliation of the Three Approaches

Traditional appraisal theory holds that it is wise to use all three approaches when valuing a property. However, these approaches usually result in different values. At this point, a more definitive value estimate will require a judgmental reconciliation of the three approaches. This entails some estimation as to which approach is most applicable and the relative strengths of the underlying assumptions. The greatest reliance is usually placed on the value estimated through the market approach. In investment properties, this value should correlate closely with the value obtained through the income approach. The value obtained through the cost approach generally should be employed only as a check on the other methods, unless the subject property is of a special-purpose nature or insufficient market data are available. The final value is then expressed in terms of a single-value estimate or, if there is considerable uncertainty, a range of values.

Problems with the Traditional Approach

The traditional approach to estimating value has several problems and limitations which concern the real estate appraisal profession. The criticism seems to occur on two levels: (1) attacks on the problems within each of the three approaches to value and (2) criticisms of the entire three-approach process.[4]

Most criticisms of the market approach relate to the adjustment process by which various properties are compared to the subject site. No one property is exactly like another, nor are the expectations of buyer and seller entirely similar in all transactions. In the traditional process, the appraiser attempts to make these adjustments quantitatively, either numerically or in percentage terms, based on professional judgment. Even the best appraisers, however, have difficulty in assigning quantitative values to these differences, particularly if the transactions are spread over an extended period of time. In addition, appraisers' professional abilities vary considerably, often leading to significant differences of opinion within the same procedural framework.

Problems also are inherent in the income approach to value. Since every piece of property is different and usually serves a different purpose, the future economic life is very hard to project, even in the most stable of economic conditions. Unless the property is leased on a net-net-net basis, the income stream is hard to forecast with any degree of reliability. Even among experienced appraisers there can be wide differences of opinion, resulting in greatly varying estimates of value.

Another problem with the income approach is the method of calculating the direct capitalization rate. Using the traditional approach, the cap rate is determined judgmentally, based on the appraiser's experience and exposure to the marketplace. Seldom, however, is there any attempt to determine how investors in the marketplace really evaluate investment decisions, despite the availability of survey techniques. The application of the direct capitalization rate to the future income stream

[4]An early critic of the traditional approach was Professor Richard U. Ratcliff of the University of Wisconsin. His and the thoughts of others were crystallized in the *1984 Real Estate Valuation Colloquium* edited by Professor William Kinnard of the University of Connecticut and published by the Lincoln Institute.

also poses a mechanical problem. The traditional process of dividing the capitalization rate into the income stream does not consider the future value of money or the anticipated sale of the project to another investor. These problems are largely overcome by using discounted cash flow analytical techniques and an increasing number of appraisers are adopting this approach rather than the direct capitalization method.

The cost approach has even more severe limitations. Traditionally, it has been assumed that the cost approach places an upper limit on market value. It was reasoned that a prudent person would not pay more for a building than what it would cost to buy the land and construct a similar building. But this reasoning ignores the synergistic combination of land and building that really creates market value and, in most situations, is greater than its replacement cost.

The inputs into the cost approach also pose problems. Cost estimation of a new structure is very difficult, as most contractors can readily attest. Manuals used to estimate costs are limited, labor requirements vary from area to area and from contractor to contractor, and the measurement of depreciation often is tenuous. It is virtually impossible to measure accrued depreciation independently by arbitrary or conventional methods.

In addition to criticism of each of the three approaches, there is also growing skepticism as to the validity of the three-approach process itself. Tradition has encouraged the use of all three approaches in almost every appraisal when, in fact, only one or at most two methods are appropriate. It would be much more meaningful to concentrate on the approach that is most relevant to the appraisal at hand.

The correlation process by which the results of the three approaches are reconciled into a single value also is under fire. With many properties, the three approaches may lead to quite different results, often for logical reasons. To arrive at a single value, the appraiser is forced to tamper with the inputs of one or more of the approaches. This negates the fundamental reasons for the three-approach process in the first place.

Future Directions

In light of these criticisms, many appraisers suggest that the income and cost methods be dropped altogether and that the market approach be the only determination of value. Others recommend that all three approaches be retained but that only the approach best suited for a particular situation be used. The concept of "investment value" has also emerged: the price that a specific investor would pay for a property, depending upon that individual's particular tax situation, available financing, and minimum acceptable rate of return.

The debate over appraisal theory has been sharpened by the availability of the computer and the emergence of several new mathematical techniques that may ultimately have a profound impact on the appraisal profession. New software programs enable appraisers to apply more sophisticated mathematical techniques to the analytic process, quickly and efficiently.

While a great deal of progress is being made, it's difficult to rapidly alter the traditions of the last 60 years. Many believe that the necessary changes in appraisal theory and practice will come slowly and only after much deliberation and debate.

The debate within the appraisal profession is being intensified, however, by governmental regulatory pressure, increased client involvement, and the emergence of new competitors. As a result of a series of scandals in the appraisal of single-family homes, the Federal Home Loan Bank Board has adopted very rigorous standards which are raising the complexity and cost of home appraisals. On a more far-reaching scale, legislation has been recently introduced in Congress to provide a regulatory agency to establish appraisal standards and police the appraisal profession.

Clients are also taking a greater interest in establishing appraisal standards. The Rouse Company pioneered the use of appraisals to value its investment portfolio and provide investors with a better indication of market value than possible through the exclusive use of accounting standards. More recently, investment advisory firms have developed model engagement letters in an effort to standardize appraisal assumptions and provide consistency in valuation methodology between various markets represented in the investment portfolio. Concerned about variations in investment performance reporting, the National Council of Real Estate Investment Fiduciaries has been working on industry-wide standards to guide the investment valuation process.

In addition to increasing regulation and client involvement, appraisers are now facing competition for the first time. Public accounting firms have established appraisal staffs in an effort to link auditing and appraisal activities into a single professional engagement. Credit rating agencies, such as Moody's and Standard & Poor's, are beginning to rate properties for securitized issues in a manner not dissimilar to the appraisal process.

It is hoped that, as a result of these events, the appraisal profession will ultimately evolve a sound policy which will strengthen the credibility of the appraisal process and provide investors and other concerned parties with accurate and meaningful indications of asset value.

Bibliography

Books

Adaptive Use: Development Economics, Process, and Profiles, Urban Land Institute, Washington, D.C., 1978.

Affordable Community: Adapting Today's Communities to Tomorrow's Needs, Urban Land Institute, Washington, D.C., 1982.

Affordable Housing: Twenty Examples from the Private Sector, Urban Land Institute, Washington, D.C., 1982.

Akerson, Charles B., *Capitalization Theory and Techniques: Study Guide,* American Institute of Real Estate Appraisers, Chicago, 1980.

America's Housing Needs: 1970 to 1980, Joint Center for Urban Studies of Massachusetts Institute of Technology and Harvard University, Cambridge, Mass., 1973.

The Appraisal of Real Estate, 9th ed., American Institute of Real Estate Appraisers, Chicago, 1987.

Approval Process: Recreation and Resort Development Experience, Urban Land Institute, Washington, D.C., 1983.

Arnold, Alvin, *Real Estate Investment after the Tax Return Act of 1986,* Warren, Gorham & Lamont, Boston, 1987.

Arnold, David E. et al./Laventhol & Horwath, *Hotel/Motel Development,* Urban Land Institute, 1984.

Atterberry, William, *Modern Real Estate Finance,* 3d ed., Grid, Columbus, 1984.

Barlowe, Raleigh, *Land Resource Economics,* 4th ed., Prentice-Hall,Englewood Cliffs, N.J., 1986.

Barrett, G. Vincent, and John P. Blair, *How to Conduct Real Estate Market and Feasibility Studies,* Van Nostrand Reinhold, New York, 1982.

Barstein, Fred (ed.), *Bowker's Real Estate Law Locator 1988,* Bowker, New York, 1988.

Blum, John M., et al., *The National Experience,* 6th ed., Harcourt Brace Jovanovich, New York, 1985.

Boyce, Bryl N., and William N. Kinnard, *Appraising Real Property,* Lexington Books, Lexington, Mass., 1984.

Bradbury, Katherine J., and Anthony Downs, *Urban Decline and the Future of American Cities,* Brookings Institute, Washington, D.C., 1981.

Clapp, James A., *The City: A Dictionary of Quotable Thoughts on Cities and Urban Life,* Center for Urban Policy Research, Rutgers University, New Brunswick, N.J., 1984.

Clurman, et al., *Condominiums to Cooperatives,* 2d ed., Wiley, New York, 1984.

The Community Builders Handbook, Urban Land Institute, Washington, 1968.

Cultural Facilities in Mixed-Use Development, Urban Land Institute, Washington, D.C., 1985.

DeGrove, John M., *Land Growth & Politics,* American Planning Association, Chicago, 1984.

Deatherage, George E., *Construction Company Organization and Management,* McGraw-Hill, New York, 1964.

De Chiara, Joseph, and John Hancock Callender, *Time-Saver Standards for Building Types,* 2d ed., McGraw-Hill, New York, 1980.

Demographic Changes and Their Effects on Real Estate Markets in the 80's, Urban Land Institute, Washington, D.C., 1982.

Developing with Recreational Amenities: Golf, Tennis, Skiing and Marinas, Urban Land Institute, Washington, D.C., 1986.

The Dictionary of Real Estate Appraisal, American Institute of Real Estate Appraisers, Chicago, 1984.

Dimensions of Parking, 2d ed., Urban Land Institute, Washington, D.C., 1983.

Downs, Anthony, *Neighborhoods and Urban Development,* Brookings Institution, Washington, D.C., 1981.

Downs, Anthony, *The Revolution in Real Estate Finance,* The Brookings Institution, Washington, D.C., 1985.

Downtown Development Handbook, Urban Land Institute, Washington, D.C., 1980.

Downtown Linkages, Urban Land Institute, Washington, D.C., 1985.

Downtown Office Growth and the Role of Public Transit, Urban Land Institute, Washington, D.C., 1982.

Downtown Retail Development: Conditions for Success and Project Profiles, Urban Land Institute, Washington, D.C., 1983.

Duncan, Delbert J., Stanley C. Hollander, and Ronald Savitt, *Modern Retailing Management: Basic Concepts and Practices,* Richard D. Irwin, Inc., Homewood, Ill., 1983.

Financing Real Estate in the 80's, American Bar Association, Chicago, 1981 (paperback).

Friedman, Jack P., et al., *Dictionary of Real Estate Terms,* 2d rev. ed., Barron's, New York, 1987.

Friedman, Milton R., *Contracts and Conveyances of Real Property,* 4th ed., Practising Law Institute, New York, 1984.

Gallion, Arthur B., and Simon Eisner, *The Urban Pattern: City Planning and Design,* 5th ed., Van Nostrand Reinhold, New York, 1986.

Goodall, Brian, *The Economics of Urban Areas,* Pergammon, Oxford, England, 1972.

Goodkin, Stanford R., *High Density Housing: Planning, Design, Marketing,* National Association of Home Builders, Washington, D.C., 1986.

Greenhut, Melvin L., *Plant Location in Theory and Practice,* University of North Carolina Press, Chapel Hill, 1956.

Gross, Jerome S., *Webster's New World Illustrated Encyclopedic Dictionary of Real Estate,* Prentice-Hall, Englewood Cliffs, N.J., 1987 (paperback).
Gruen, Victor, *The Heart of our Cities,* Simon and Schuster, New York, 1964.
——— and Larry Smith, *Shopping Towns USA: The Planning of Shopping Centers,* Reinhold, New York, 1960.
Haft, Robert J., and Peter M. Fass, *Real Estate Syndications Tax Handbook,* Clark Boardman, New York, 1986-87.
Hagman, Donald G. (ed.), *Land Use & Environment Law Review 1982,* Clark Boardman Company, Ltd., New York, 1982.
Harwood, Bruce, *Real Estate Principles,* 4th ed., Prentice-Hall, Englewood Cliffs, N.J., 1986.
Heilbrun, James, *Real Estate Taxes and Urban Housing,* Columbia, New York, 1966.
——— *Urban Economics and Public Policy,* St. Martin's Press, Boston, 1987.
Hines, Mary Alice, *Real Estate Investment,* Macmillan, New York, 1980.
Historical Statistics of the United States: Colonial Times to 1970, U.S. Bureau of the Census, Washington, D.C.
Hoover, Edgar M., *The Location of Economic Activity,* McGraw-Hill, New York, 1958 (paperback).
Hotel/Motel Development, Urban Land Institute, Washington, D.C., 1984.
Housing Supply and Affordability, Urban Land Institute, Washington, D.C., 1983.
1972 HUD Statistical Yearbook, U.S. Department of Housing and Urban Development, Washington, D.C., 1974.
Industrial Real Estate, 4th ed., Society of Industrial Realtors, Washington, D.C., 1984.
Infill Development Strategies, Urban Land Institute, Washington, D.C., 1982.
Institute for Urban Land Use and Housing Studies, Columbia University, New York, *Housing Market Analysis: A Study of Theory and Methods,* Housing and Home Finance Agency, Washington, D.C., 1953.
Irwin, Robert, *The McGraw-Hill Real Estate Handbook,* McGraw-Hill, New York, 1984.
Jacobs, Jane, *The Death and Life of Great American Cities,* Random House, New York, 1961.
——— *Cities and the Wealth of Nations: Principles of Economic Life,* Random House, New York, 1985.
Johnson, M. Bruce, *Resolving the Housing Crisis: Government Policy, Decontrol, and the Public Interest,* Ballinger, Cambridge, Mass., 1982.
Kratovil, Robert, and Raymond J. Weiner, *Real Estate Law,* 9th ed., Prentice-Hall, Englewood Cliffs, N.J., 1988.
Levy, Arnold S. and Robert F. Cushman (eds.), *The Handbook of Real Estate Development and Construction,* Dow Jones-Irwin, Homewood, Ill., 1987.
Livermore, Shaw, *Early American Land Companies: Their Influence on Corporate Development,* The Commonwealth Fund, New York, 1939.
Living with Environmental Law, Massachussetts Continuing Legal Education, Boston, 1984.

Lundberg, Donald E., *The Hotel and Restaurant Business,* Van Nostrand Reinhold, New York, 1984.

MacKaye, Benton, *The New Exploration: A Philosophy of Regional Planning,* rev. ed., University of Illinois Press, Urbana, 1962 (paperback).

Maisel, Sherman J., *Real Estate Finance,* Harcourt Brace Jovanovich, New York, 1987.

Making Infill Projects Work, Urban Land Institute, Washington, D.C., 1985.

Managing Development Through Public/Private Negotiations, Urban Land Institute, Washington, D.C., 1985.

Mayer, Harold M., *The Spatial Expression of Urban Growth,* Association of American Geographers, Commission on College Geography, Washington, D.C., 1969.

——— and Charles P. Hayes, *Land Uses in American Cities,* Park Pr. Co., Champaign, Ill., 1983.

McMahan, John, *The McGraw-Hill Real Estate Pocket Guide: Up-to-Date Terms and Tables for the Real Estate Professional,* McGraw-Hill, New York, 1979.

Messner, Stephen, and Bryl Boyce, *Analyzing Real Estate Opportunities: Market and Feasibility Studies,* Prentice-Hall, Englewood Cliffs, N.J., 1987.

Miller, Zane L., and Patricia M. Melvin, *The Urbanization of Modern America: A Brief History,* 2d ed., Harcourt Brace Jovanovich, New York, 1987.

Mixed-Use Development Handbook, Urban Land Institute, Washington, D.C., 1987.

Morgan, Howard E., *The Motel Industry in the United States: Small Business in Transition,* Bureau of Business and Public Research, University of Arizona, Tucson, 1964.

Mumford, Lewis, *The City in History,* Harcourt, Brace & World, 1961.

——— *The Culture of Cities,* Harcourt, Brace & World, New York, 1938.

National Directory of Real Estate Financing Sources, Prentice-Hall, Englewood Cliffs, N.J., 1984.

Nelson, Richard Lawrence, *The Selection of Retail Locations,* McGraw-Hill, New York, 1958.

Office Development Handbook, Urban Land Institute, Washington, D.C., 1982.

Paying for Growth: Using Development Fees to Finance Infrastructure, Urban Land Institute, Washington, D.C., 1986.

Planning and Design of Townhouses and Condominiums, Urban Land Institute, Washington, D.C., 1980.

Public Incentives and Financial Techniques, Urban Land Institute, Washington, D.C., 1985.

PUDs in Practice, Urban Land Institute, Washington, D.C., 1985.

Pyhrr, Stephen A., and James R. Cooper, *Real Estate Investment: Strategy, Analysis, Decisions,* Wiley, New York, 1982.

Rachlis, Eugene, and John E. Marqusee, *The Landlords,* Random House, New York, 1963.

Ratcliff, Richard U., *Real Estate Analysis,* McGraw-Hill, New York, 1961.

Readings in Highest and Best Use, American Institute of Real Estate Appraisers, Chicago, 1981 (paperback).

Real Estate Development and Construction Financing, Practising Law Institute, New York, 1986.

Real Estate Dictionary and Reference Guide, rev. ed., Career Publishing, Orange, Ca., 1987 (paperback).

Real Estate Index, 2 vols., National Association of Realtors, Chicago,1987.

Real Estate Valuing, Counseling, Forecasting: Selected Writings of John White, American Institute of Real Estate Appraisers, Chicago, 1984.

Regional Diversity, Growth in the United States 1960–1980, Auburn House Publishing Co., Boston, 1981.

Rehabilitating Historic Buildings, Real Estate Law and Practice Series, Practising Law Institute, New York, 1983.

Rental Housing, Urban Land Institute, Washington, D.C., 1984.

Research Parks and Other Ventures: The University/Real Estate Connection, Urban Land Institute, Washington, D.C., 1985.

Richardson, Harry W., *Regional Economics,* University of Illinois Press, Champaign, IL, 1979.

Robbins, Roy M., *Our Landed Heritage: The Public Domain 1776–1936,* University of Nebraska Press, Lincoln, 1942.

Rosen, Kenneth T., *Affordable Housing: New Policies for the Housing and Mortgage Markets,* Ballinger Publications, Cambridge, Mass., 1984.

Sakolski, A. M., *The Great American Land Bubble,* Harper, New York, 1932.

Samuelson, Paul A., and W. Nordhaus, *Economics,* 12th ed., McGraw-Hill, New York, 1985.

Scott, Randall W., et al., *Management & Control of Growth,* 3 vols., Urban Land Institute, Washington, D.C., 1975.

Seldin, Maury, and Richard H. Swesnik, *Real Estate Investment Strategy,* Wiley, New York, 1985.

Shared Parking, Urban Land Institute, Washington, D.C., 1983.

Shenkel, William M., *Marketing Real Estate,* 2d ed., Prentice-Hall, Englewood Cliffs, N.J., 1985.

——— *Real Estate Finance,* Business Publications, Plano, Tex., 1988.

——— *Modern Real Estate Principles,* 3d ed., Business Publications, Inc., Plano, Tex., 1984.

——— *Real Estate Finance,* Business Publications, Plano, Tex., 1988.

Shopping Center Development Handbook, 2d ed., Urban Land Institute, Washington, D.C., 1985.

Silverman, Robert A., et al., (eds.), *Corporate Real Estate Handbook: Strategies for Improving Bottom-Line Performance,* McGraw-Hill, New York, 1987.

Smart Buildings and Technology-Enhanced Real Estate, vols. I & II, Urban Land Institute, Washington, D.C., 1985.

Snyder, Thomas P., and Michael A. Stegman, *Paying for Growth: Using Development Fees to Finance Infrastructure,* Urban Land Institute, Washington, D.C., 1986.

Standard Industrial Classification Manual, 2d. ed., Executive Office of the President, Office of Management and Budget Division, Washington, D.C., 1987.

Stanger, Robert A., with Keith D. Allaire, *How to Evaluate Real Estate Partnerships,* Robert A. Stanger & Company, Shrewsbury, N.J., 1986.

Sussex, Margie, and John F. Stapleton, *The Complete Real Estate Math Book,* Prentice-Hall, Englewood Cliffs, N.J., 1988 (paperback).

Thomlinson, Ralph, *Urban Structure: The Social and Spatial Character of Cities,* Random House, New York, 1969.

Thompson, Wilbur R., *A Preface to Urban Economics,* Johns Hopkins, Baltimore, 1965.

Timesharing II, Urban Land Institute, Washington, D.C., 1982.

Urban Waterfront Development, Urban Land Institute, Washington, D.C., 1983.

Vernon, James D., *An Introduction to Risk Management in Property Development,* Development Component Series, Urban Land Institute, Washington, D.C., 1981.

Vested Rights: Balancing Public and Private Development Expectations, Urban Land Institute, Washington, D.C., 1982.

Von Thunen, J. H., *Der Isolierte Staat in Beziehnug auf Landwirtschaft und Nationalokonomie,* Hamburg, Germany, 1826.

Watson, Don A., *Construction Materials and Processes,* 3d ed., McGraw-Hill, New York, 1986.

Webber, Melvin M., et al., *Explorations into Urban Structure,* University of Pennsylvania Press, Philadelphia, 1964.

Weber, Alfred, *Theory of the Location of Industries,* C. J. Friedrick (trans.), University of Chicago Press, Chicago, 1972.

Weiss, Marc A., *The Rise of the Community Builders: The American Real Estate Industry and Urban Land Planning,* Columbia History of Urban Life Series, Columbia University Press, New York, 1987.

World Population Prospects: Estimates and Projections as Assessed in 1984, United Nations, New York, 1986.

Wurtzebach, Charles H., and Mike E. Miles, *Modern Real Estate,* 3d ed., Wiley, New York, 1987.

Zero Lot Line Housing, Urban Land Institute, Washington, D.C., 1981.

Periodicals

"Core" Publications

These are helpful in keeping up with the general real estate market and industry.

American Demographics, articles related to demographic trends in the United States, published monthly by American Demographics, Inc., Ithaca, New York.

BOMA Experience Exchange Report, an analysis of the operating results of selected office buildings, published annually by Building Owners and Managers Association International, Chicago.

The Dollars and Cents of Shopping Centers, an analysis of the operating results of selected shopping centers throughout the nation, published every 3 years by the Urban Land Institute, latest edition 1987.

Empire State Realtor, general interest articles discussing New York State real estate markets. Published 10 times per year by the State of New York.

Federal Reserve Bulletin, a news and statistical analysis of financial and economic trends and events, published monthly by the Federal Reserve System, Washington, D.C.

Journal of Property Management, articles related to property management, published bimonthly by the Institute of Real Estate Management of National Association of Realtors, Chicago. The Institute also publishes an annual income/expense supplement detailing operating costs of various types of property in selected cities.

Lodging Industry, a statistical analysis of the hotel and motel industry, published annually by Laventhol & Horwath, Philadelphia.

The Mortgage and Real Estate Executives Report, a general briefing newsletter on various aspects of real estate, published bimonthly by Warren, Gorham & Lamont, Boston.

National Real Estate Investor, articles on real estate with a focus on various metropolitan markets, published monthly by Communication Channels, Inc., Atlanta.

Real Estate Business, nontechnical trade journal, marketing oriented, covering articles of particular interest to residential brokers and sales associates, published quarterly by the Realtors National Marketing Institute, Chicago.

The Real Estate Center Journal, articles of general interest to real estate practitioners, based on research conducted by the Real Estate Center at Texas A & M University. Published quarterly by the Real Estate Center, Texas A & M University, College Station, Tex.

Real Estate Forum, general articles on the real estate industry, published monthly, with an extra edition in November, by Real Estate Forum, Inc., New York.

Real Estate Issues, articles of general interest to the real estate community, published semiannually by the American Society of Real Estate Counselors of the National Association of Realtors, Chicago.

Real Estate News, news magazine covering topics of general interest to real estate practitioners, published biweekly by the National Association of Realtors, Chicago.

Real Estate Review, articles on all aspects of real estate, published quarterly by The Real Estate Institute of New York University and Warren, Gorham & Lamont, Boston.

Real Estate Today, general articles on real estate topics, published monthly except February, July, and December by the National Association of Realtors, Chicago.

Shopping Centers Today, a monthly news magazine featuring articles on shopping center development and operation, published by the International Council of Shopping Centers, New York.

Shopping Center World, articles related to shopping center development and operation, published monthly by Communication Channels, Inc., Atlanta.

Survey of Current Business, a summary of general economic conditions, published monthly by the U.S. Department of Commerce.

Trends in the Hotel/Motel Business, a statistical analysis of the hotel and motel industry, published annually by Harris, Kerr, Forster & Company, Atlanta.

U.S. Housing Markets, a review of trends and conditions in major housing markets throughout the nation, published quarterly by Lomas & Nettleton, Detroit.

The U.S. Resort Lodging Industry 1987, 3d Annual Report, Laventhol & Horwath, Philadelphia, 1987.

Urban Land, articles on all aspects of urban land use, published monthly for members by the Urban Land Institute, Washington, D.C.

Specialized Publications

These are more specialized publications directed at various subsectors of the real estate industry.

Area Development, articles relating to site and facilities planning, published monthly by Halcyon Business Publications, Great Neck, New York.

Benefits Quarterly, articles related to employee benefit plans, published quarterly by the International Society of Certified Employee Benefit Specialists, Brookfield, Wis.

Building Construction Cost Data, a summary of current construction costs, published annually by Robert Snow Means Company, Duxbury, Mass.

Building Design and Construction, articles about the design of commercial, institutional, and industrial buildings, published monthly by Building Design and Construction, Des Plaines, Ill.

Building Operating Management, articles related to the building management function, published monthly by Trade Press Publishing Company, Milwaukee, Wis.

Buildings, articles related to facilities construction and management, published monthly by Stamats Communications, Inc., Cedar Rapids, Iowa.

Business Facilities, articles related to facilities construction and management, published monthly by Business Facilities Publishing Company, Red Bank, N.J.

Canadian Appraiser, articles about the professional practice of real estate appraisal, published quarterly by the Appraisal Institute of Canada, Winnepeg.

Construction Digest, articles related to public works and engineered construction, published semimonthly by Construction Digest, Indianapolis, Ind.

Construction Review, a statistical analysis of construction data, published monthly by Domestic and International Business Administration, U.S. Department of Commerce.

Corporate Design & Realty, articles about facility design, planning, and real asset management, published 10 times a year by Cahners Publishing Company, Newton, Mass.

Design Cost and Data, articles related to the management of building design, published bimonthly by Allan Thompson Publishers, Glendora, Calif.

Development, articles related to the industrial and office park industry, published quarterly by the National Association of Industrial and Office Parks, Arlington, Va.

Directory of Conventions, a listing of various types of conventions by location and date, published annually by the research staff of *Successful Meetings Magazine,* Bill Communications, New York.

Dodge Building Cost and Specification Digest, a summary of current construction costs, published annually by McGraw-Hill, New York.

Financial Management, general articles covering business, economic, and management issues, published quarterly by The College of Business at Florida State University, Tallahassee, Fla.

Golf Facilities in the United States, published annually by the National Golf Foundation, Chicago.

Hotel and Motel Management, articles of interest to hotel and motel managers, published 17 times a year by Harcourt Brace Jovanovich, New York.

Industrial Development and Site Selection Handbook, a monthly news magazine featuring articles on industrial development and site selection in the U.S., published by Conway Data, Atlanta.

Institutional Investor, articles related to pension fund and other institutional investment activities, published monthly by Institutional Investor, Inc.; New York.

Investment Decisions, articles related to investment and financial management, published 8 times a year by W.R. Nelson and Company, Rye, N.Y.

Journal of the American Institute of Planners, articles related to regional, city, and land planning, published bimonthly by American Institute of Planners, Washington, D.C.

Journal of Real Estate Research, academic articles related to investigations of micro-applications of real estate research, including the areas of valuation, investment, finance, market analysis, development, marketing, and management. Published semiannually by the American Real Estate Society, Sacramento, Calif.

The Journal of Real Estate Taxation, articles concerning tax considerations in real estate investment, published quarterly by Warren, Gorham & Lamont, Boston.

Life Insurance Fact Book, an analysis of factors affecting the life insurance industry including their real estate portfolios, published every other year, with annual updates, by the American Council of Life Insurance, Washington, D.C.

Monthly Retail Trade, a statistical analysis of retail sales in selected SMSAs, published monthly by the United States Bureau of the Census.

Mortgage Banking, articles about the mortgage investment markets. Published monthly by the Mortgage Bankers Association of America, Washington, D.C.

National Mall Monitor, articles related to the development and operations of shopping centers, published monthly by National Mall Monitor, Clearwater, Fla.

The OAG Travel Planner Hotel and Motel Redbook, a listing of various hotels and motels, and information on airport services, car and rail directions, city center maps, and other travel resources. Three editions (Pacific Asia, Europe, and North America) published quarterly by Official Airline Guides, Oakbrook, Ill.

Pension World, articles directed to plan sponsors and investment managers, published monthly by Communication Channels, Inc., Atlanta.

Pensions and Investment Age, newspaper covering issues of interest to corporate and institutional investors, published every other Monday by Crain Communications, Inc., New York.

Plants, Sites & Parks, articles on industrial and suburban office development, published bimonthly by Plants, Sites and Parks, Inc., Coral Springs, Florida.

Population Estimates and Projections, estimates of current population at the national level, published monthly by the United States Bureau of the Census.

Professional Builder, articles about housing and light construction, published monthly except for March and June, when two issues are published, by Cahners Publishing, Newton, Mass.

Real Estate Law Journal, articles on aspects of real estate law, published quarterly by Warren, Gorham & Lamont, Boston.

Realty Trust Review, a news analysis of securities of real estate investment trusts, published semi-monthly by Audit Investment Research, New York.

REIT Industry Statistics, a statistical analysis of the REIT industry, published quarterly by the National Association of Real Estate Investment Trusts, Washington, D.C.

Richardson Estimating and Engineering Standards, a summary of current construction costs, published annually by Richardson Engineering Services, Downey, Calif.

Savings Institutions Sourcebook, a statistical analysis of the savings institutions business, published annually by U.S. League of Savings Institutions, Chicago.

The Stanger Register, articles and information on real estate investment strategy, investment opportunities, and financial planning, published monthly by Robert A. Stanger & Company, Shrewsbury, N.J.

Largely Professional

AIA Journal, articles related to architecture and urban design, published monthly by American Institute of Architects, Washington, D.C.

The American Economic Review, academic articles related to national economic issues, published quarterly by the American Economic Association, Nashville, Tenn.

American Real Estate and Urban Economics Journal, articles on urban land economics, published quarterly by American Real Estate and Urban Economics Association, Hartford, Conn.

The Appraisal Journal, articles related to property appraisal, published quarterly by American Institute of Real Estate Appraisers, Chicago.

Appraisal Review Journal, articles related to property appraisal, published three times a year by the National Association of Review Appraisers, St. Paul, Minn.

Commercial Investment and Real Estate Journal, professional journal for those in the field of commercial real estate, published quarterly by the Commercial-Investment Real Estate Council of the Realtors National Marketing Institute of the National Association of Realtors, Chicago.

The Cornell Hotel and Restaurant Administration Quarterly, articles related to hotel planning and operation, published quarterly by the Cornell School of Hotel Administration, Cornell University, Ithaca, N.Y.

Hotel and Restaurant Administration Quarterly, professional publication for hotel and restaurant administrators, published quarterly by the Cornell School of Hotel Administration, Ithaca, N.Y.

Journal of the American Planning Association, a quarterly review of issues related to planning, building design, and public policy, published by the American Planning Association, Washington, D.C.

The Journal of Portfolio Management, academic and professional articles related to investment portfolio management, published quarterly by Institutional Investor, New York.

Journal of Regional Science, academic articles on regional economics, including land use, location theory, and housing markets. Published quarterly by Regional Science Research Institute, Peace Dale, R.I.

Land Economics, articles about urban land economics, published quarterly by the University of Wisconsin, Madison.

Planning, a monthly magazine featuring planning issues, published for members by the American Planning Association, Chicago.

Property Tax Journal, studies in property taxation and assessment administration, published quarterly by the International Association of Assessing Officers, Chicago.

The Real Estate Appraiser, articles related to property appraisal, published bimonthly by the Society of Real Estate Appraisers, Chicago.

Real Estate Finance Journal, articles for academicians and practitioners of real estate finance, published quarterly by Warren, Gorham & Lamont, Boston.

Index

Page references in *italic* indicate illustrations.

About the Author

John McMahan is founder and president of McMahan Real Estate Advisors, Inc., a real estate investment advisory firm based in San Francisco. During his nearly 30 years in the industry, he has acquired or developed several hundred million dollars of real estate assets. Mr. McMahan personally directed some of the earliest research for pension funds interested in real estate and was selected in 1981 to be an expert witness for the Department of Labor in the landmark Mazzola case.

A strong supporter of real estate education, Mr. McMahan is a member of the faculty of the Stanford Graduate School of Business and serves on the real estate advisory boards of the University of California at Los Angeles and the University of Southern California. He also speaks and writes extensively on issues of interest to the real estate community. Mr. McMahan is a graduate of the University of Southern California and the Harvard Business School.

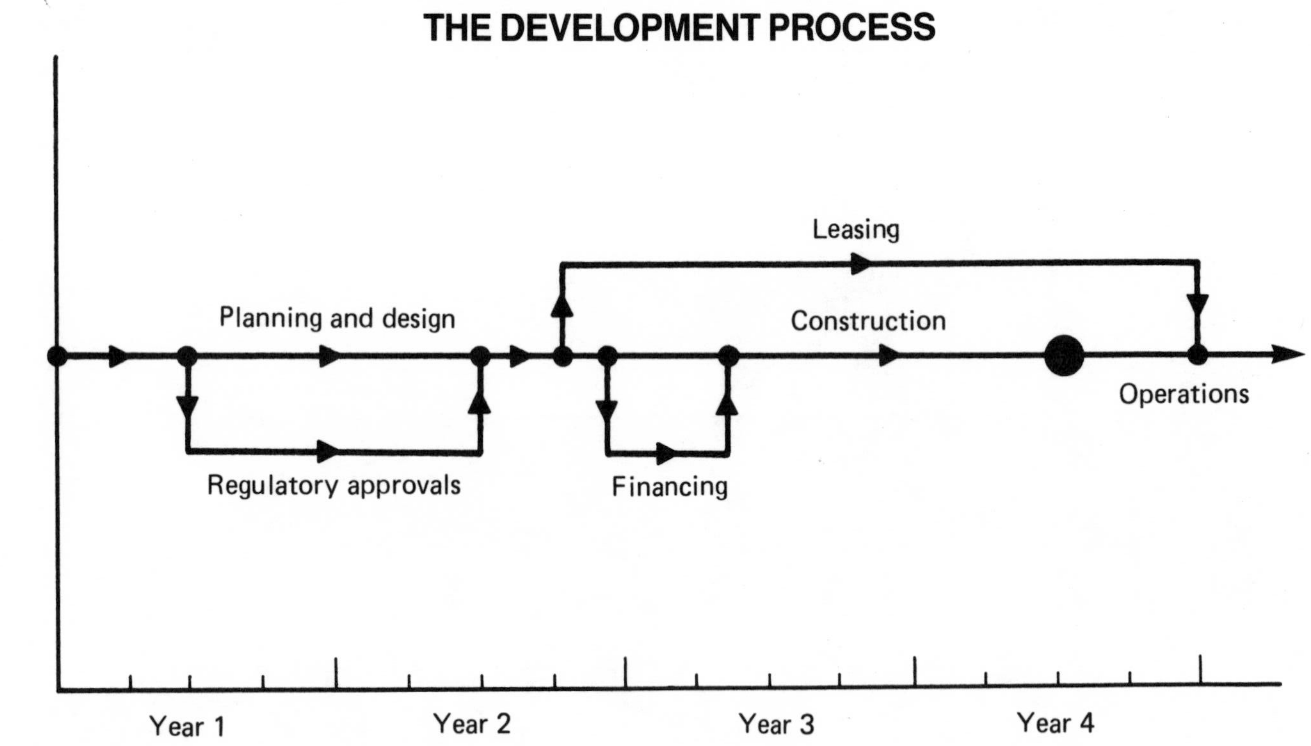
THE DEVELOPMENT PROCESS
Leasing
Planning and design
Construction
Operations
Regulatory approvals
Financing
Year 1
Year 2
Year 3
Year 4